The Classics of Interest Group Behavior

ROBERT M. ALEXANDER
Ohio Northern University

THOMSON
WADSWORTH

Australia • Brazil • Canada • Mexico • Singapore • Spain
United Kingdom • United States

To the Alexander girls—Shelleigh, Olivia, Anabel, and Amelia
and
to my family—Bob, Phyllis, and Caroline Alexander

The Classics of Interest Group Behavior
Robert M. Alexander

Executive Editor: David Tatom
Editorial Assistant: Cheryl Lee
Senior Marketing Manager: Janise Fry
Marketing Assistant: Teresa Jessen
Marketing Communications Manager:
  Nathaniel Michelson
Project Manager, Editorial Production:
  Paul Wells
Creative Director: Rob Hugel

Art Director: Maria Epes
Print Buyer: Judy Inouye
Permissions Editor: Stephanie Lee
Production Service: G&S Book Services
Copy Editors: Carrie Andrews and Jill Meyers
Cover Designer: Brian Salisbury
Compositor: International Typesetting
  and Composition
Printer: Transcontinental Printing/Louiseville

Printed in Canada
1 2 3 4 5 6 7 09 08 07 06 05

Library of Congress Control Number:
2005929382

ISBN 0-534-64384-1

Thomson Higher Education
10 Davis Drive
Belmont, CA 94002-3098
USA

For more information about our products,
contact us at:
Thomson Learning Academic Resource
Center
1-800-423-0563

For permission to use material from this text
or product, submit a request online at
http://www.thomsonrights.com.

Any additional questions about permissions
can be submitted by e-mail to
thomsonrights@thomson.com.

Contents

Preface

This text is intended to provide you with a better understanding of the role interest groups play in the American political system. It is further intended to provide my colleagues with an accessible source for what most scholars of group politics recognize as "classics." Distinguishing a classic is an awesome responsibility. Nevertheless, I have attempted to incorporate those readings that produced significant shifts in the study of organized interests—in what we study, how we study, and why we study groups. Many courses examining groups also investigate other elements of the political system (such as political parties, public policy, and political participation); consequently, time may be limited in many courses. This anthology should serve as an excellent primer for the study of interest groups and as a valuable companion to many of the standard texts that are currently used in interest-group seminars.

The catalyst for this project can be traced to my interest groups seminar during my second year of graduate school. I had the privilege of taking the class from Anthony Nownes. Many of the readings chosen for this book first appeared on the reading list for that seminar. Upon entering the professoriate, I sought to pass my knowledge of interest groups on to budding minds. Like many spirited professors, I found myself assigning many of these articles to my students. And then it happened—student complaints of unreadable pages; the reserve room refusing to maintain two chapters from the same book; the time spent making photocopies and running them down to the reserve room. My worthy intention of sharing essential readings with students soon turned into a nightmare.

Early in my graduate school career, I was made aware of the stable of classics anthologies that exist in a number of fields, and so I turned my attention to finding such a book for interest groups. To my surprise, such a book did not exist. Thus, the idea was born. Not only would I be able to accommodate students and the reserve room and make my life easier, I would also be able to provide a genuine service to my colleagues teaching courses on the role of interest groups in American politics.

The introduction to Arthur Bentley's *The Process of Government* notes that Bentley is more often cited than read. I have designed this text so that students will indeed read the classics and examine for themselves the articles upon which generations of scholarship has been based. The readings not only provide a firm grounding but should serve as launching pads for discussion.

There are many people who deserve my gratitude for their help throughout the years. My colleagues have been supportive throughout this process—from my Falcon colleagues, David Jackson, Jeff Peake, and Marc Simon, to my Bobcat colleagues, Yvonne Beal, John Bambacus, Scott Johnson, and Steve Hartlaub, to my current Polar Bear colleagues, Pat Badertscher, Andy Ludanyi, Mike Loughlin, JoAnn Scott, Bob Cupp, Ray Schuck, John Lomax, David Smith, and Ellen Wilson. David Saffell was particularly helpful while this project was still in the thought stages. All have been helpful and encouraging. My graduate mentors, Bill Lyons and Tony Nownes, were particularly helpful during those formative years. I could always count on Professor Nownes for a good pep talk.

I have had the good fortune to have several student assistants who have made my life much easier over the past couple years. The help from Adam Watkins, Sara Barnes, and Adam DeVore has been sincerely appreciated. Through a strange course of events, I taught courses on interest groups at three different universities in three successive years. The vigor exhibited by those students in each of those classes reinforced the worthiness of this project. My students have always worked to inspire me!

Without David Tatom's belief in this project, you would not be reading this right now. Thankfully, David saw the need for this text. Many of the folks at Wadsworth were quick to answer my questions and were quite patient with me throughout this process. Their help has been sincerely appreciated. I believe this book is much better due to the suggestions from the following reviewers: Jolly Emrey, California State University Los Angeles; Fred A. Meyer, Ball State University; Thomas T. Holyoke, The George Washington University.

Most of all, I want to thank my family: William and Annabelle Cheeks, Doc and Carolyn Alexander, Bill and Carol Watson, my many loving aunts, uncles, and cousins, and especially my beautiful sister, Caroline, and the most perfect parents in the world—Bob and Phyllis Alexander. Without my family, I would be nothing. They have always been my biggest supporters and continue to serve as a source of entertainment, laughter, and inspiration. You are the best! My warmest gratitude is reserved for the four great women who support, encourage, and motivate me toward all I can be. My wife, Shelleigh, and my children, Olivia, Anabel, and Amelia, are constant reminders of what is important in life. They are *my* "classics"!

1

Introduction

> The latent causes of faction are thus sown in the nature of man; and we see them everywhere brought into different degrees of activity, according to the different circumstances of civil society.
>
> JAMES MADISON
> THE FEDERALIST PAPERS

We have been called a nation of joiners. For James Madison, we cannot escape our desire to join together with other like-minded individuals. Aristotle noted that we are by nature political and social animals. Part of the impulse to engage others may manifest itself in our tendency to join with other people and form groups. Many scholars believe that groups are the *primary* unit of all social analysis. Some contend that individuals only exist as members of groups. As the logic goes, I am not Robert Alexander. Instead, I am an Alexander; I am a male; I am among the highly educated; I am a professor; I am a political scientist; I am a member of the American Political Science Association—and so on. My identity cannot be understood apart from the groups to which I belong. In short, groups define who we are.

While individualism has always been an important component of American political culture, group behavior has also been at the forefront of American democracy. Like individualism, the role of groups in American politics has been ridiculed, chastised, and simultaneously exulted. Americans have mixed emotions when it comes to the presence of groups in the political system.

From Madison's warnings about the dangers of faction to Jonathan Rauch's musings about *demosclerosis,* policy makers, scholars, and citizens alike have been concerned about the power of organized interests. Anthony Nownes dubs our ambivalence the "paradox of organized interests." He states that citizens are discouraged by the amount of power they believe special interests exert upon public policy. Yet we love the groups that represent *our* interests. This paradox underscores the conventional wisdom that groups play an important part in the political process. Groups clearly have a pivotal role in American politics. This book provides a first stop for those interested in learning about the formation, maintenance, activity, and power of interest groups.

Most textbooks examining interest groups discuss, mention, or at the very least cite the readings contained in this text. However, the richness offered by these original works is often lost when they are discussed secondhand. The excerpts and articles contained here represent key points in the study of interest group behavior. The authors of these works have changed the way we think about interest-group scholarship and often set new courses of study among scholars. These readings asked new questions and found new answers to age-old issues like representation and influence. By examining classic readings of group behavior, you can begin to gain a greater understanding of how organized interests operate in the United States. You will find that a number of these scholars draw upon each other's work. As you read through this collection of articles, you too should be attentive to the connections among these readings.

THE BASICS

One would be hard-pressed to deny the ubiquity of groups in the United States. Groups (both "political" and "nonpolitical") abound in contemporary society. When asked to describe an interest group, students often tend to focus on such groups as Greenpeace, the National Rifle Association (NRA), or the United Auto Workers (UAW). Most students recognize that various corporations, think tanks, churches, universities, and trade associations also can be thought of as interest groups. Table 1.1 provides some common examples and types of groups that operate in American politics. These groups represent a wide variety of interests.

It is estimated that there are over 200,000 groups in the United States. These groups are not only active in Washington, D.C., but also in state capitals throughout the country. As I write this, a google of the term "special interest" nets nearly 14 million hits. "Interest group" produces nearly 6 million hits. The sheer number of groups is apparent: cumulatively, these groups claim to represent virtually all Americans. And when 12 percent of the population belong to one group (the American Association of Retired Persons), one quickly recognizes some merit to the claim of representation. Granted, the AARP is the

Table 1.1 Interest Groups: Types and Examples

Type of Group	Example
Single-issue	National Rifle Association
Trade Association	Beer Wholesalers Association
Labor Union	United Auto Workers
Intergovernmental	National Governors Association
Professional Association	American Bar Association
Civil Rights	National Association for the Advancement of Colored People
Religious	Christian Coalition
Agricultural	National Grange
Public Interest Group	Sierra Club
Corporation	Honeywell
Think Tank	Center for Responsive Politics
Charity	Salvation Army

largest group, with 33 million members, but there are many groups with large membership bases.

There are myriad groups who claim no membership, apart from representing institutions. These nonmembership groups "represent" large numbers of individuals as well. For instance, although you are not a member of a group representing your college, it is highly likely that your school has a hired lobbyist who works on the university's behalf, and subsequently on *your* behalf.

Not only do groups have large numbers of supporters, but they also engage in a great deal of monetary giving. Groups spent over $1 billion in soft-money contributions to political campaigns over the past four years. Finance, insurance, and real-estate sectors contributed the most money in both the 2000 and 2002 election cycles. These industries alone donated over $200 million to candidates during this time period. The communications and electronics industry came in second, with nearly $150 million in soft-money campaign contributions. With their sophisticated voter targeting and deep pockets, these interest groups are clearly a central fixture within the American political system. Although these groups are quite prominent, they represent a small portion of the types of groups that are active in American society.

Robert Putnam refocused a great deal of attention on the importance of informal (and oftentimes nonpolitical) groups in American society. Little League baseball teams, philanthropic organizations (such as the Kiwanis), and even local bridge clubs help inculcate important social bonds in American communities. Involvement with these less-political groups often leads to greater political participation among their members. In addition, the social connectedness fostered by these groups is essential for the proper functioning of American democracy.

WHAT IS AN INTEREST GROUP?

So what exactly do scholars mean by the term *interest group?* Most often, scholars analyzing interest groups do not study the groups that Putnam discusses. Instead, we devote much greater attention to more "political" groups. The remainder of this section examines how scholars conceptualize interest-group politics.

Scholars in political science, and those in interest-group scholarship in particular, have always had a difficult time conveying the meanings and expressing the nuances of our concepts. Of course, detailing abstract concepts with precision is a tricky task. Nevertheless, scholars of group politics do have a common vocabulary. While disagreement exists regarding proper uses of terms, a general sense of understanding exists. Frank Baumgartner and Beth Leech note that this disagreement reflects the diversity of scholarship in the field of interest group politics.

We have used terms such as *factions, pressure groups, associations, interest groups,* and *organized interests.* Each of these permutations reflects a desire to better define what we study. In most cases, scholars have increasingly widened the scope of what we study. As fundamental changes occur in the political system, scholars work to adjust their vocabulary to these changes. An "interest group" may be quite different depending on the scholar you speak to. Rather than try to settle this issue once and for all, I provide some of the most common definitions in order to express the diversity of scholarship. Obviously, how scholars choose to define a group affects what they study and how they choose to analyze their subject matter. You should keep in mind how broadly (or narrowly) each definition considers the activity of groups in American politics. Clearly, it is important to understand the basics of what one is examining.

A sampling of texts examining interest groups reveals the following definitions.

- *Interest group.* An interest group is "any group that is based on one or more shared attitudes and makes certain claims upon other groups or organizations in the society" (Truman, 33). Also: "An aggregation of citizens with shared interests and with common political aspirations or objectives, especially where public policy making is concerned" (Mahood, 156).

- *Political interest group* or *organized interest.* "A collection of individuals or a group of individuals linked together by professional circumstance, or by common political, economic, or social interests, that meets the following requirements: (1) its name does not appear on an election ballot; (2) it uses some portion of its collective resources to try and influence decisions made by the legislative, executive, or judicial branches of national, state, or local governments; and (3) it is organized externally to the institution of government that it seeks to influence" (Wright, 22–23).

- *Organized interest.* Any "organization that engages in political activity" (Schlozman and Tierney, 10).

Baumgartner and Leech provide the most thorough examination of interest-group scholarship in their important contemporary work, *Basic Interests.* They devote a great deal of time trying to make sense of the many different definitions scholars have bestowed upon interest groups. They ultimately denote ten different types of definitions scholars have used for interest groups. These include: "social or demographic categories of the population; membership organizations; any set of individuals with similar beliefs, identifications, or interests; social movements; lobbyists registered in legislatures; political action committees; participants in rule-making or legislative hearings; institutions including corporations and government agencies; coalitions of organizations and institutions; and prominent individuals acting as political entrepreneurs or lobbyists" (Baumgartner and Leech, 29). Obviously, scholars have no consensus as to what constitutes an interest group.

What can be gleaned from these varying definitions? First, you should recognize that defining a concept is a difficult task. Second, some scholars attempt to widen their focus in order to be much more inclusive about what can be considered as an interest group. This enables scholars to consider a wider range of social phenomena that otherwise might be neglected. Although groups may not be overtly political, they always have the potential to become more politically involved, given the right circumstances. Third, by more narrowly defining what constitutes an interest group, scholars can be more precise in their analysis and consequently better able to produce theories of group behavior. In any event, students and scholars alike should be aware of these problems of definition as they read interest group scholarship and seek to understand how groups function in the political system.

WHY STUDY INTEREST GROUPS?

Now that we some notion of what an interest group is, it is important to ask why we need to study groups. The beginning of this chapter noted the accepted power that most people believe groups have. This power, coupled with the increasing presence of groups in Washington, D.C., state capitals, and many cities, demonstrates that groups have worked to impart their influence at every level and in all facets of government. David Truman first noted that groups in the United States are so abundant in part because of the multiple points of access they have with government. Separation of powers, our federal system, and various checks and balances provide many doors to which groups can come knocking.

If one door closes, groups simply knock on another. Certainly, the most powerful groups are knocking on a number of doors simultaneously. Groups with fewer resources must be more strategic about which doors they knock on. Knowing whom to contact is an essential tool groups must understand. This comes down to the amount of information and/or specialization groups have at their disposal. The ability (or inability) of a group to find an amenable door to knock on reveals the inequalities found in the interest group system.

Truman further noted that as societal complexity increases, it is likely that society will witness more group involvement. The more issues in society, the more groups will arise to support or oppose these issues. Greater affluence also may contribute to an increase in the number of interest groups in America. Jack Walker intimates that the interest-group universe reflects the wealthy patrons of the time. Walker states that many groups receive financial support from outside sources (i.e., patrons). This support helps groups to conduct business as they wish. Similarly, Robert Salisbury suggests that greater affluence makes it easier for individuals to join groups. He further contends that a robust economy allows more opportunity for motivated entrepreneurs to offer incentives to potential members and thus form more groups.

As affluence may be related to group formation, it is also associated with group power. The 2004 presidential campaign heralded the rise of a new term among observers of American politics, "527 groups." The term results from the tax-exempt status of an organization. Campaign-finance loopholes allow these groups to raise unlimited amounts of soft money that can be used for issue advocacy and voter mobilization. However, money cannot be used to lobby expressly for the defeat or election of a particular candidate. Ultimately, these groups took on a much more significant role in the 2004 election cycle. Interest groups formed a number of these 527 groups to funnel money into the campaign. Table 1.2 reports the top contributors among 527 groups to the 2004 presidential campaign. We see that nearly $300 million was spent by just these twenty advocacy groups. Although the law states that 527s are not to campaign directly for or against a specific candidate, the money these groups pour into campaigns certainly seek to tip the scales in their candidates' favor.

Some of you probably went to a concert funded by the Joint Victory Campaign 2004. This was a coalition of advocacy groups that sponsored concerts featuring Pearl Jam, Bruce Springsteen, Dave Mathews, and Neil Young, among others. These concerts took place in battleground states and were designed to get out the vote among young voters for the Democratic Party. Interestingly, many of the young people who went to these concerts had no intention of voting, and a good number did not even support the Kerry campaign. They simply wanted to go to a good concert.

Table 1.3 provides a list and description of many active groups from the 2004 campaign. Many of these groups are among those same 527 groups listed in Table 1.2. Take a minute and examine how innocuous the names of these groups are. Most of these groups have names that make it difficult to discern what party, candidate, or cause they support. Although their names suggest cooperation, unity, and red-blooded Americanism, the aims of these groups vary drastically from one another.

Many of these groups did not spend a great deal of money but had considerable effects on the campaign. Although the Swift Boat Veterans for Truth only spent about $3 million, the publicity generated by their commercials and activities held the media's attention for several weeks of the campaign. Not coincidentally, the margin of support for President Bush over John Kerry (whose Vietnam record the group was targeting) widened considerably during this same time period. This was not the sole reason for Bush's victory, but the Kerry campaign would have been better served had they not had to defend themselves against the Swift Boat allegations.

Table 1.2 The Top 527 Contributors in the 2004 Presidential Campaign

Contributor	Total
Joint Victory Campaign 2004	$56,654,391
Service Employees International Union	$53,187,817
American Federation of State/County/Municipal Employees	$30,327,630
Soros Fund Management/George Soros	$23,881,000
Peter B Lewis/Progressive Corp	$22,395,000
Shangri-La Entertainment/Steve Bing	$13,802,381
Victory Campaign 2004	$13,625,000
Golden West Financial	$13,012,959
AFL-CIO	$11,424,853
Perry Homes	$8,085,199
Sustainable World Corp/Linda Pritzker	$7,205,000
Gateway Inc	$5,010,000
Ameriquest Capital	$5,000,000
AG Spanos Companies	$5,000,000
BP Capital	$4,600,000
Sierra Club	$4,383,099
August Capital/Andrew Rappaport	$4,143,400
Amway Corp	$4,020,000
Chartwell Partners/Jerry Perenchio	$4,000,000
Laborers Union	$3,466,622
Total	**$293,224,351**

SOURCE: http://www.opensecrets.org/527s/527contribs.asp?cycle=2004 (Accessed June 30, 2005)

NOTE: Changing campaign finance regulations brought so-called 527 groups (named after their nonprofit tax status) to the forefront of political campaigns in 2004. Recall that 527 groups are not allowed to spend any money advocating for the election or defeat of any specific candidate. Nevertheless, these 20 groups alone spent nearly $300 million dollars trying to influence elections in 2004!

Looking at monetary figures is always fun, but it is also instructive to study perceptions of group power. Table 1.4 helps us understand what those in-the-know think about the power of groups in Washington, D.C. Recently, *Fortune* magazine compiled a ranking of the most powerful interest groups in the nation's capital. You are probably familiar with a number of the groups listed in Table 1.4. This list was compiled through a survey of nearly 2,700 "Washington insiders." These insiders represent the very people that groups attempt to influence—members of Congress, congressional staffers, White House aides, lobbyists, and lobbying firms. Long ago, E. E. Schattschneider asserted that the interest-group system might have an upper-class bias. A quick glance at Table 1.4 reveals that strictly "business" interests make up six of the top ten most powerful groups in America. It would be difficult to argue that *any* of the groups listed in the top twenty represent the interests of the less fortunate in the United States.

Table 1.3 Major Players in the 2004 Campaigns

Organization	Description
Alliance for Economic Justice	Liberal coalition of more than 20 unions, representing more than 5 million workers
America Coming Together	One of the leading Democratic interest groups dedicated to defeating President Bush
America Votes	Coordinated the activities of more than 20 Democratic interest groups
American Civic Coalition	Republican-leaning group aiming to help "grassroots" activists to educate the American public
Americans for a Better Country	Pro-Republican group aims to counter the efforts of Democratic-leaning groups
Americans for Job Security	Conservative, pro-business organization established to offset labor's influence
Americans for Jobs, Health Care & Progressive Values	Democratic group formed to promote the discussion of jobs and health care
Americans for Responsible Government	Republican group focusing on taxes, families, and economic growth
Billionaires for Bush	Organized opposition to the Bush administration through the Internet and street theater
Bring Ohio Back	Left-leaning group that aims to "educate Ohioans about the failure of the Bush administration"
Center for American Progress	Democratic think tank formed to find progressive solutions to a host of problems
Citizens United	Republican-leaning organization that wanted to "restore government control to the citizens"
Club for Growth	Dedicated to electing Republican fiscal conservatives
Daschle Democrats	Raised money in '02 to counter ads critical of Sen. Tom Daschle, D-SD
Grassfire.org Alliance	Media component of grassfire.net, a conservative, Pro-Bush organization
Grassroots Democrats	Channeled unlimited soft money to Democratic state and local parties
Leadership Forum	Conducted issue advocacy in support of Republican House candidates
League of Conservation Voters	"Political voice of the national environmental movement"
Legislative Education Action Drive	Conservative group that supported private-school voucher programs
Main Street Individual Fund	New York–based group founded to help elect moderate Republican candidates
Media Fund	Coordinated large ad campaign in support of the Kerry campaign
MoveOn.org	Aired TV ads critical of President Bush in key battleground states
National Committee for a Responsible Senate	Created to conduct issue advocacy in support of GOP Senate candidates
New Democrat Network	Helped to elect centrist Democratic candidates
New House PAC	Dedicated to supporting Democratic House candidates

Table 1.3 Major Players in the 2004 Campaigns (*Continued*)

Organization	Description
Partnership for America's Families	Conducted voter-registration drive in support of Democratic candidates
People for a Better Florida	Republican-leaning group that seeks to impact issues such as medical malpractice reform
People of Color United	Conservative organization devoted to informing people of color about the presidential contenders
Progress for America	Conducted issue-advocacy efforts in support of GOP candidates
Progressive Donor Network	Democratic group focused on opposing President Bush's reelection
Service Employees International Union	Union with 1.6 million members is the largest affiliate in the AFL-CIO
Sierra Club	National environmental organization with more than 700,000 members
Swift Boat Veterans for Truth	Conservative group of Vietnam Veterans that questioned Sen. John Kerry's Vietnam service
Voices for Working Families	Worked on Democratic voter registration in 16 battleground states

SOURCE: http://www.opensecrets.org/527s/527grps.asp (Accessed June 30, 2005)

NOTE: Table 1.3 provides a sampling of prominent actors in the 2004 campaign. It further illustrates the wide variety of interest groups attempting to exert influence in American politics. Although the names of these groups might be appealing to all Americans, their causes differ considerably.

This chapter started with a quotation from James Madison. His observation forces us to take notice of interest groups as an expression of our desire to join with others for a particular cause. The readings found in these pages should illustrate that our inclination to join groups is not necessarily a bad thing. Despite half-hearted pleas by policy makers to limit the involvement of groups in public policy making, interest groups serve valuable functions. By definition, interest groups represent interests. A utopian vision of the world might have all interests in society represented equally. However, in the course of human history, such a circumstance has failed to arise. Nonetheless, in a republican form of government, it is essential that a wide range of interests (and subsequently choices) are expressed to government.

Interest groups are a primary means by which various opinions, desires, and preferences are articulated to policy makers. This vital function cannot be overlooked. Groups often represent citizens who feel marginalized. As Arthur Denzau and Michael Munger suggest, groups can provide a means to represent the "unorganized" in American society. And while great inequity exists in American society, it cannot all be placed at the feet of organized interests. Scholars have criticized the interest-group system along multiple fronts. Some have charged that too many groups have too much power. Others assert that too few groups have too much power. In all likelihood, the truth probably lies somewhere in between.

Table 1.4 *Fortune* Magazine's Most Powerful Groups in American Politics

Rank

1	National Rifle Association
2	American Association of Retired Persons
3	National Federation of Independent Business
4	American Israel Public Affairs Committee
5	Association of Trial Lawyers of America
6	American Federation of Labor-Congress of Industrial Organizations
7	Chamber of Commerce of the United States of America
8	National Beer Wholesalers Association
9	National Association of Realtors
10	National Association of Manufacturers
11	National Association of Home Builders of the United States
12	American Medical Association
13	American Hospital Association
14	National Education Association of the United States
15	American Farm Bureau Federation
16	Motion Picture Association of America
17	National Association of Broadcasters
18	National Right to Life Committee
19	Health Insurance Association of America
20	National Restaurant Association

SOURCE: Adapted from the table entitled "The Power 25: Top Lobbying Groups," in Jeffrey H. Birnbaum and Russell Newell, "Fat & Happy in D.C.," *Fortune*, May 28, 2001, 94.

NOTE: This list identifies who Washington insiders perceive are the most powerful lobbying groups in the nation's capital. These insiders include members of Congress, White House aides, congressional staffers, and lobbyists.

PLAN OF THE BOOK

The remainder of this book relies upon eminent scholarship to detail important issues relative to interest groups in the United States. These articles are drawn from a wide variety of sources. Although a majority of these articles were originally published in academic journals, a number appeared in seminal texts examining groups in America. The driving force behind this anthology is that too often these classic readings are cited, but not read. The following readings should challenge you to think more broadly about the study of interest groups. In addition, you will quickly recognize that these readings are not the distilled "textbook" versions of group behavior you typically read. Instead, they require an attentive, engaged, and critical mind.

The first section focuses upon group formation and pluralism. James Madison's "Federalist No. 10" and Alexis de Tocqueville's observations provide early glimpses into the importance of group politics in American democracy.

Madison intimates early signs of pluralism in that he sees that encouraging freedom will be the best remedy against too few groups wielding too much power. A reading from Tocqueville's *Democracy in America* implies that the key to a properly functioning democracy may be the presence of an active array of groups. The writings of Arthur Bentley, David Truman, and Robert Dahl are emblematic of pluralist scholarship. Those working from this perspective see group power as relatively benign. Moreover, pluralists maintain that groups provide valuable opportunities for citizens to voice their concerns and insure some degree of representation. However, E. E. Schattschneider and C. Wright Mills depict a political system in which powerful interest groups may leave most other groups behind in the policy-making process.

The second section examines how groups mobilize and maintain themselves in the political arena. Many of these articles deal with the tactics and strategies that groups employ to help them exert influence in the political system. Mancur Olson's observation that small, highly organized groups may possess more advantages than larger groups provided the catalyst for a great deal of research on group formation and maintenance. Peter Clark and James Wilson examine how selective incentives are often used as a means to produce collective action. Their typology of incentives has been particularly useful to scholars of group politics. Robert Salisbury extends Clark and Wilson's analysis and documents how groups overcome the problem of free riders by offering a variety of benefits. His recognition of the role of entrepreneurs motivated scholars to dig deeper into the role of how groups subsist. Jack Walker's influential work provides yet another lens through which to view group maintenance. His recognition of the role that government plays in stimulating and sustaining groups generated another path of scholarship. Likewise, Salisbury further documents the role of institutions as important interest groups. Finally, Kay Schlozman and John Tierney's influential study of Washington groups reveals a great deal about what groups do to maintain their organizations and influence public policy. Their research has served as a benchmark for subsequent scholars examining group activity in the United States.

The final section explores the influence of groups in the political process. Theodore Lowi raises the question of hyperpluralism and the concomitant pressure placed upon the political system. Jonathan Rauch describes the sickness caused by hyperpluralism—*demosclerosis*. Working from another front, Hugh Heclo delineates how relationships among groups and the government changed from cozy iron triangles to more complicated issue networks. William Browne further elaborates how groups have attempted to be more strategic through specialization. The resulting issue niches illustrate elements of both pluralism *and* elitism. Employing another vantage point, John Wright discusses the power of groups by empirically examining the relationship between campaign contributions and roll-call votes. This line of research finds yet another voice in the work of Arthur Denzau and Michael Munger. They note that groups target legislators who are likely to be in agreement with them. Often, these legislators represent districts with similar preferences. Hence, they conclude that the unorganized may be represented through organized interests.

Richard Hall and Frank Wayman further illustrate the symbiotic relationship between members of Congress and interest groups in the formulation of public policy. Perhaps members of Congress use interest groups (especially for information) to their benefit rather than groups using Congress as their plaything. The concluding chapter brings to light problems detailing group influence. John Heinz, Edward Laumann, Robert Nelson, and Robert Salisbury discuss the problems associated with ascribing power to groups in the political system.

GENERAL QUESTIONS TO CONSIDER

1. What is an interest group?
2. Why do scholars have a tough time describing groups?
3. Why is it important to study groups?
4. What can the study of interest groups tell us about American politics?
5. How and why are interest groups able to gain access to political decision makers?
6. What similarities exist among the most powerful groups in the United States? Are these similarities coincidental? Why? Why not?

SUGGESTED READINGS

An excellent review of interest group scholarship can be found in Frank Baumgartner and Beth Leech's *Basic Interests: The Importance of Groups in Politics and in Political Science.* Princeton, NJ: Princeton University Press, 1998.

Other Important Texts Examining Group Politics

General

Ainsworth, Scott H. *Analyzing Interest Groups: Group Influence on People and Policies.* New York: W. W. Norton, 2002.

Cigler, Allan J., and Burdett A. Loomis, eds. *Interest Group Politics.* 6th edition. Washington, DC: Congressional Quarterly Press, 2002.

Herrnson, Paul S., Ronald G. Shaiko, and Clyde Wilcox, eds. *The Interest Group Connection: Electioneering, Lobbying, and Policymaking in Washington.* 2nd ed. Washington, DC: Congressional Quarterly Press, 2005.

Putnam, Robert. *Bowling Alone: The Collapse and Revival of American Community.* New York: Simon and Schuster, 2000.

Tarrow, Sidney. *Power in Movement: Social Movements, Collective Action, and Politics.* New York: Cambridge University Press, 1994.

Interest Groups and the Presidency

Peterson, Mark. *Legislating Together: The White House and Capitol Hill from Eisenhower to Reagan.* Cambridge, MA: Harvard University Press, 1990.

Interest Groups and Congress

Wolpe, Bruce C., and Bertram J. Levine. *Lobbying Congress: How the System Works.* 2nd ed. Washington, DC: Congressional Quarterly Press, 1996.

Wright, John R. *Interest Groups and Congress: Lobbying, Contributions, and Influence.* Boston: Allyn and Bacon, 1996.

Interest Groups and the Judiciary

Caldeira, Gregory, and John Wright. "Organized Interests and Agenda-Setting in the U.S. Supreme Court." *American Political Science Review* 82 (1988): 1109–27.

Samuels, Suzanne. *First among Friends: Interest Groups, the U.S. Supreme Court, and the Right to Privacy.* Westport, CT: Praeger Press, 2004.

Interest Groups at the State Level

Gerber, Elisabeth. *The Populist Paradox: Interest Group Influence and the Promise of Direct Legislation.* Princeton, NJ: Princeton University Press, 1999.

Gray, Virginia, and David Lowery. *The Population Ecology of Interest Representation: Lobbying Communities in the American States.* Ann Arbor: University of Michigan Press, 1996.

Rosenthal, Alan. *The Third House: Lobbyists and Lobbying in the States.* 2nd ed. Washington, DC.: Congressional Quarterly Press, 2001.

Interest Groups and Public Opinion

Kollman, Ken. *Outside Lobbying: Public Opinion and Interest Group Strategies.* Princeton, NJ: Princeton University Press, 1998.

For Further Consideration

Students interested in reading about current research on interest-group scholarship should consult the *American Political Science Review, American Journal of Political Science, Journal of Politics, Political Research Quarterly,* and *American Politics Research.* These journals typically include the most up-to-date research analyzing the role and effect of groups in the United States. Students interested in the role of groups at the state level should consult *State Politics and Policy Quarterly* or *State and Local Government Review.*

WEBSITES

Most groups have their own space on the World Wide Web. A great deal can be learned about these groups through their websites. Here is a sampling of some websites:

American-Arab Anti-Discrimination Committee http://www.adc.org

American Association of Retired Persons http://www.aarp.org

American Cancer Society http://www.cancer.org

American Civil Liberties Union http://www.aclu.org

American Conservative Union http://www.conservative.org

American Federation of Labor-Congress of Industrial Organizations http://www.aflcio.org

American Israel Public Affairs Committee http://www.aipac.org

American Medical Association http://www.ama-assn.org

American Political Science Association http://www.apsanet.org

Association of Trial Lawyers of America http://www.atla.org

Boycott-RIAA http://www.boycott-riaa.com

Christian Coalition of America http://www.cc.org

Council of State Governments http://www.csg.org

National Association for the Advancement of Colored Persons http://www.naacp.org

National Association of Manufacturers http://www.nam.org

National Association of Realtors http://www.realtor.org

National Education Association http://www.nea.org

National Organization of Women http://www.now.org

National Rifle Association http://www.nra.org

Recording Industry Association of America http://www.riaa.org

Sierra Club http://www.sierraclub.org

Tobacco Institute http://www.tobaccoinstitute.com

REFERENCES

Baumgartner, Frank, and Beth Leech. *Basic Interests: The Importance of Groups in Politics and in Political Science.* Princeton, NJ: Princeton University Press, 1998.

Mahood, H. R. *Interest Groups in American National Politics: An Overview.* Upper Saddle River, NJ: Prentice Hall, 2000.

Schlozman, Kay, and John Tierney. *Organized Interests and American Democracy.* New York: Harper and Row, 1986.

Truman, David. *The Governmental Process: Political Interests and Public Opinion.* New York: Knopf, 1951.

Wright, John. Interest Groups and Congress: Lobbying, Contributions, and Influence. Boston: Allyn and Bacon, 1996.

PART I

❖❖

Group Formation
and Pluralism

The articles in this part are wide-ranging. They include broad pronounce-
ments regarding the role of interest groups in society and the functions
groups serve. The pull of pluralism has been felt by those studying interest groups
since the founding of the United States. Pluralists contend that a great deal of
competition exists among groups in the policy-making process. A multitude of
interests are proposed to be represented by various groups throughout the political process. The diversity of interests evidenced among these groups speaks to
the level of representation in our political system. Virtually any interest can (and
often is) represented through the actions of groups. Because of the freedoms we
enjoy, a large number of groups are able to gain access to government. Group
activity is fueled by rights guaranteed under the First Amendment. Free speech,
the right to assemble, and a free press enable all segments of society to be heard.
Pluralists contend that, most often, people's voices are channeled through interest groups. Hence, groups represent the interests of citizens. For pluralists, interest groups are central to the political system and serve the beneficial purpose of
representing diverse interests. However, as you will see in the following readings,
pluralists have come under attack from a variety of fronts.

As you engage the following readings, you should critically analyze how well
these readings fit what you know about American politics. The following

questions should serve as a guide to help you comprehend the material. More specific questions are included at the beginning of each chapter. Finally, each chapter outlines a project that you can undertake to further your understanding of the subject matter.

GENERAL QUESTIONS TO CONSIDER

1. How do these authors relate to one another?
2. How do these authors differ from one another?
3. What is the relevance of their analyses today?
4. In your opinion, which author(s) comes closest to describing the world of interest groups today?
5. In the wake of such events and issues as 9/11, the war on terror, stem-cell research, gay marriage, job outsourcing, the increasing federal deficit, and the increasing cost of political campaigns, how well do the readings hold up to scrutiny?

2

Federalist No. 10

JAMES MADISON

"**F**ederalist No. 10" provides the classic warning about the danger of interest groups. Madison states that such "factions" will naturally arise among like-minded citizens pursing common goals. Madison argues that the best way to counter the negative effects of groups is to allow them to freely pursue their goals. He concludes that a large federal republic will pit numerous interests against one another and will create a situation in which it would be difficult for any particular interest to gain influence in government at the expense of the rest of the citizenry. In a sense, this is the classic pluralist argument that is addressed by other scholars, such as David Truman and Robert Dahl. "Federalist No. 10" shows that the important role of groups in American politics was clearly on the mind of the father of the American constitution.

QUESTIONS TO CONSIDER

1. What does Madison suggest we do to counter the problems associated with interest groups?
2. Do you believe Madison's strategy to stem group power is helpful?
3. What do you believe Madison would say about contemporary group politics?
4. Has the danger of faction been averted as Madison hoped it would?

Among the numerous advantages promised by a well-constructed Union, none deserves to be more accurately developed than its tendency to break and control the violence of faction. The friend of popular governments never finds himself so much alarmed for their character and fate as when he contemplates their propensity to this dangerous vice. He will not fail, therefore, to set a due value on any plan which, without violating the principles to which he is attached, provides a proper cure for it. The instability, injustice, and confusion introduced into the public councils have, in truth, been the mortal diseases under which popular governments have everywhere perished, as they continue to be the favorite and fruitful topics from which the adversaries to liberty derive their most specious declamations. The valuable improvements made by the American constitutions on the popular models, both ancient and modern, cannot certainly be too much admired; but it would be an unwarrantable partiality to contend that they have as effectually obviated the danger on this side, as was wished and expected. Complaints are everywhere heard from our most considerate and virtuous citizens, equally the friends of public and private faith and of public and personal liberty, that our governments are too unstable, that the public good is disregarded in the conflicts of rival parties, and that measures are too often decided, not according to the rules of justice and the rights of the minor party, but by the superior force of an interested and overbearing majority. However anxiously we may wish that these complaints had no foundation, the evidence of known facts will not permit us to deny that they are in some degree true. It will be found, indeed, on a candid review of our situation, that some of the distresses under which we labor have

SOURCE: From James Madison, "Federalist No. 10," *The Federalist Papers* (1787).

been erroneously charged on the operation of our governments; but it will be found, at the same time, that other causes will not alone account for many of our heaviest misfortunes; and, particularly, for that prevailing and increasing distrust of public engagements and alarm for private rights which are echoed from one end of the continent to the other. These must be chiefly, if not wholly, effects of the unsteadiness and injustice with which a factious spirit has tainted our public administration.

By a faction I understand a number of citizens, whether amounting to a majority or minority of the whole, who are united and actuated by some common impulse of passion, or of interest, adverse to the rights of other citizens, or to the permanent and aggregate interests of the community.

There are two methods of curing the mischiefs of faction: the one, by removing its causes; the other, by controlling its effects.

There are again two methods of removing the causes of faction: the one, by destroying the liberty which is essential to its existence; the other, by giving to every citizen the same opinions, the same passions, and the same interests.

It could never be more truly said than of the first remedy that it was worse than the disease. Liberty is to faction what air is to fire, an aliment without which it instantly expires. But it could not be a less folly to abolish liberty, which is essential to political life, because it nourishes faction than it would be to wish the annihilation of air, which is essential to animal life, because it imparts to fire its destructive agency.

The second expedient is as impracticable as the first would be unwise. As long as the reason of man continues fallible, and he is at liberty to exercise it, different opinions will be formed. As long as the connection subsists between his reason and his self-love, his opinions and his passions will have a reciprocal influence on each other; and the former will be objects to which the latter will attach themselves. The diversity in the faculties of men, from which the rights of property originate, is not less an insuperable obstacle to a uniformity of interests. The protection of these faculties is the first object of government. From the protection of different and unequal faculties of acquiring property, the possession of different degrees and kinds of property immediately results; and from the influence of these on the sentiments and views of the respective proprietors ensues a division of the society into different interests and parties.

The latent causes of faction are thus sown in the nature of man; and we see them everywhere brought into different degrees of activity, according to the different circumstances of civil society. A zeal for different opinions concerning religion, concerning government, and many other points, as well of speculation as of practice; an attachment to different leaders ambitiously contending for preeminence and power; or to persons of other descriptions whose fortunes have been interesting to the human passions, have, in turn, divided mankind into parties, inflamed them with mutual animosity, and rendered them much more disposed to vex and oppress each other than to cooperate for their common good. So strong is this propensity of mankind to fall into mutual animosities that where no substantial occasion presents itself the most frivolous and fanciful distinctions have been sufficient to kindle their unfriendly passions and excite their most violent conflicts. But the most common and durable source of factions has been the various and unequal distribution of property. Those who hold and those who are without property have ever formed distinct interests in society. Those who are creditors, and those who are debtors, fall under a like discrimination. A landed interest, a manufacturing interest, a mercantile interest, a moneyed interest, with

many lesser interests, grow up of necessity in civilized nations, and divide them into different classes, actuated by different sentiments and views. The regulation of these various and interfering interests forms the principal task of modern legislation and involves the spirit of party and faction in the necessary and ordinary operations of government.

No man is allowed to be a judge in his own cause, because his interest would certainly bias his judgment, and, not improbably, corrupt his integrity. With equal, nay with greater reason, a body of men are unfit to be both judges and parties at the same time; yet what are many of the most important acts of legislation but so many judicial determinations, not indeed concerning the rights of single persons, but concerning the rights of large bodies of citizens? And what are the different classes of legislators but advocates and parties to the causes which they determine? Is a law proposed concerning private debts? It is a question to which the creditors are parties on one side and the debtors on the other. Justice, ought to hold the balance between them. Yet the parties are, and must be, themselves the judges; and the most numerous party, or in other words, the most powerful faction must be expected to prevail. Shall domestic manufacturers be encouraged, and in what degree, by restrictions on foreign manufacturers? are questions which would be differently decided by the landed and the manufacturing classes, and probably by neither with a sole regard to justice and the public good. The apportionment of taxes on the various descriptions of property is an act which seems to require the most exact impartiality; yet there is, perhaps, no legislative act in which greater opportunity and temptation are given to a predominant party to trample on the rules of justice. Every shilling with which they overburden the inferior number is a shilling saved to their own pockets.

It is in vain to say that enlightened statesmen will be able to adjust these clashing interests and render them all subservient to the public good. Enlightened statesmen will not always be at the helm. Nor, in many cases, can such an adjustment be made at all without taking into view indirect and remote considerations, which will rarely prevail over the immediate interest which one party may find in disregarding the rights of another or the good of the whole.

The inference to which we are brought is that the *causes* of faction cannot be removed and that relief is only to be sought in the means of controlling its *effects*.

If a faction consists of less than a majority, relief is supplied by the republican principle, which enables the majority to defeat its sinister views by regular vote. It may clog the administration, it may convulse the society; but it will be unable to execute and mask its violence under the forms of the Constitution. When a majority is included in a faction, the form of popular government, on the other hand, enables it to sacrifice to its ruling passion or interest both the public good and the rights of other citizens. To secure the public good and private rights against the danger of such a faction, and at the same time to preserve the spirit and the form of popular government, is then the great object to which our inquiries are directed. Let me add that it is the great desideratum by which alone this form of government can be rescued from the opprobrium under which it has so long labored and be recommended to the esteem and adoption of mankind.

By what means is this object attainable? Evidently by one of two only. Either the existence of the same passion or interest in a majority at the same time must be prevented, or the majority, having such coexistent passion or interest, must be rendered, by their number and local situation, unable to concert and carry into effect schemes of oppression. If the

impulse and the opportunity be suffered to coincide, we well know that neither moral nor religious motives can be relied on as an adequate control. They are not found to be such on the injustice and violence of individuals, and lose their efficacy in proportion to the number combined together, that is, in proportion as their efficacy becomes needful.

From this view of the subject it may be concluded that a pure democracy, by which I mean a society consisting of a small number of citizens, who assemble and administer the government in person, can admit of no cure for the mischiefs of faction. A common passion or interest will, in almost every case, be felt by a majority of the whole; a communication and concert results from the form of government itself; and there is nothing to check the inducements to sacrifice the weaker party or an obnoxious individual. Hence it is that such democracies have ever been spectacles of turbulence and contention; have ever been found incompatible with personal security or the rights of property; and have in general been as short in their lives as they have been violent in their deaths. Theoretic politicians, who have patronized this species of government, have erroneously supposed that by reducing mankind to a perfect equality in their political rights, they would at the same time be perfectly equalized and assimilated in their possessions, their opinions, and their passions.

A republic, by which I mean a government in which the scheme of representation takes place, opens a different prospect and promises the cure for which we are seeking. Let us examine the points in which it varies from pure democracy, and we shall comprehend both the nature of the cure and the efficacy which it must derive from the Union.

The two great points of difference between a democracy and a republic are: first, the delegation of the government, in the latter, to a small number of citizens elected by the rest; secondly, the greater number of citizens and greater sphere of country over which the latter may be extended.

The effect of the first difference is, on the one hand, to refine and enlarge the public views by passing them through the medium of a chosen body of citizens, whose wisdom may best discern the true interest of their country and whose patriotism and love of justice will be least likely to sacrifice it to temporary or partial considerations. Under such a regulation it may well happen that the public voice, pronounced by the representatives of the people, will be more consonant to the public good than if pronounced by the people themselves, convened for the purpose. On the other hand, the effect may be inverted. Men of factious tempers, of local prejudices, or of sinister designs, may, by intrigue, by corruption, or by other means, first obtain the suffrages, and then betray the interests of the people. The question resulting is, whether small or extensive republics are most favorable to the election of proper guardians of the public weal; and it is clearly decided in favor of the latter by two obvious considerations.

In the first place it is to be remarked that however small the republic may be the representatives must be raised to a certain number in order to guard against the cabals of a few; and that however large it may be they must be limited to a certain number in order to guard against the confusion of a multitude. Hence, the number of representatives in the two cases not being in proportion to that of the constituents, and being proportionally greatest in the small republic, it follows that if the proportion of fit characters be not less in the large than in the small republic, the former will present a greater option, and consequently a greater probability of a fit choice.

In the next place, as each representative will be chosen by a greater number of citizens in the large than in the small republic, it will be more difficult for

unworthy candidates to practise with success the vicious arts by which elections are too often carried; and the suffrages of the people being more free, will be more likely to center on men who possess the most attractive merit and the most diffusive and established characters.

It must be confessed that in this, as in most other cases, there is a mean, on both sides of which inconveniencies will be found to lie. By enlarging too much the number of electors, you render the representative too little acquainted with all their local circumstances and lesser interests; as by reducing it too much, you render him unduly attached to these, and too little fit to comprehend and pursue great and national objects. The federal Constitution forms a happy combination in this respect; the great and aggregate interests being referred to the national, the local and particular to the State legislatures.

The other point of difference is the greater number of citizens and extent of territory which may be brought within the compass of republican than of democratic government; and it is this circumstance principally which renders factious combinations less to be dreaded in the former than in the latter. The smaller the society, the fewer probably will be the distinct parties and interests composing it; the fewer the distinct parties and interests, the more frequently will a majority be found of the same party; and the smaller the number of individuals composing a majority, and the smaller the compass within which they are placed, the more easily will they concert and execute their plans of oppression. Extend the sphere and you take in a greater variety of parties and interests; you make it less probable that a majority of the whole will have a common motive to invade the rights of other citizens; or if such a common motive exists, it will be more difficult for all who feel it to discover their own strength and to act in unison with each other. Besides other impediments, it may be remarked that, where there is a consciousness of unjust or dishonorable purposes, communication is always checked by distrust in proportion to the number whose concurrence is necessary.

Hence, it clearly appears that the same advantage which a republic has over a democracy in controlling the effects of faction is enjoyed by a large over a small republic—is enjoyed by the Union over the States composing it. Does this advantage consist in the substitution of representatives whose enlightened views and virtuous sentiments render them superior to local prejudices and to schemes of injustice? It will not be denied that the representation of the Union will be most likely to possess these requisite endowments. Does it consist in the greater security afforded by a greater variety of parties, against the event of any one party being able to outnumber and oppress the rest? In an equal degree does the increased variety of parties comprised within the Union increase this security. Does it, in fine, consist in the greater obstacles opposed to the concert and accomplishment of the secret wishes of an unjust and interested majority? Here again the extent of the Union gives it the most palpable advantage.

The influence of factious leaders may kindle a flame within their particular States but will be unable to spread a general conflagration through the other States. A religious sect may degenerate into a political faction in a part of the Confederacy; but the variety of sects dispersed over the entire face of it must secure the national councils against any danger from that source. A rage for paper money, for an abolition of debts, for an equal division of property, or for any other improper or wicked project, will be less apt to pervade the whole body of the Union than a particular member of it, in the same proportion as such a malady is more likely to taint a particular county or district than an entire State.

In the extent and proper structure of the Union, therefore, we behold a republican remedy for the diseases most incident to republican government. And according to the degree of pleasure and pride we feel in being republicans ought to be our zeal in cherishing the spirit and supporting the character of federalists.

PUBLIUS

PROJECT

Order a pizza to split with one friend. In one week, order some pizzas with ten of your friends. In which case were you able to get more of the toppings you wanted? How is this related to Madison's arguments in "Federalist No. 10"?

3

Political Associations in the United States

ALEXIS DE TOCQUEVILLE

*D*emocracy in America is a sage work written by Alexis de Tocqueville during his travels through the United States in the 1830s. Tocqueville masterfully examines American political culture. He observes that social networks are strong in the United States and the role of groups in these networks is paramount. For Tocqueville, the American's involvement with "associations" is everywhere perceptible. The relationships formed through these associations allow individuals to experience such essential democratic values as cooperation, tolerance, liberty, and reciprocity. It is in part through these interactions that we are taught to be good citizens.

QUESTIONS TO CONSIDER

1. What *type* of group is Tocqueville talking about? What would we call these groups in contemporary society?
2. In what ways do groups help socialize citizens?
3. Do groups teach people about the values of democracy?
4. Do you believe groups today are as active as Tocqueville suggests they were nearly 200 years ago?

Daily use which the Anglo-Americans make of the right of association—Three kinds of political associations—How the Americans apply the representative system to associations—Dangers resulting to the state—Great Convention of 1831 relative to the tariff—Legislative character of this Convention—Why the unlimited exercise of the right of association is less dangerous in the United States than elsewhere—Why it may be looked upon as necessary—Utility of associations among a democratic people.

In no country in the world has the principle of association been more successfully used or applied to a greater multitude of objects than in America. Besides the permanent associations which are established by law under the names of townships, cities, and counties, a vast number of others are formed and maintained by the agency of private individuals.

The citizen of the United States is taught from infancy to rely upon his own exertions in order to resist the evils and the difficulties of life; he looks upon the social authority with an eye of mistrust and anxiety, and he claims its assistance only when he is unable to do without it. This habit may be traced even in the schools, where the children in their games are wont to submit to rules which they have themselves established, and to punish misdemeanors which they have themselves defined. The same spirit pervades every act of social life. If a stoppage occurs in a thoroughfare and the circulation of vehicles is hindered, the neighbors immediately form themselves into a deliberative body; and this extemporaneous assembly gives rise to an executive power which remedies the inconvenience before

SOURCE: From Alexis de Tocqueville, "Political Associations in the United States," *Democracy in America,* trans. Henry Reeve (New York: Knopf, 1973), 191–98. Copyright 1945 and renewed 1973 by Alfred A. Knopf, a division of Random House, Inc. Used by permission of Alfred A. Knopf, a division of Random House, Inc.

anybody has thought of recurring to a preexisting authority superior to that of the persons immediately concerned. If some public pleasure is concerned, an association is formed to give more splendor and regularity to the entertainment. Societies are formed to resist evils that are exclusively of a moral nature, as to diminish the vice of intemperance. In the United States associations are established to promote the public safety, commerce, industry, morality, and religion. There is no end which the human will despairs of attaining through the combined power of individuals united into a society.

I shall have occasion hereafter to show the effects of association in civil life; I confine myself for the present to the political world. When once the right of association is recognized, the citizens may use it in different ways.

An association consists simply in the public assent which a number of individuals give to certain doctrines and in the engagement which they contract to promote in a certain manner the spread of those doctrines. The right of associating in this fashion almost merges with freedom of the press, but societies thus formed possess more authority than the press. When an opinion is represented by a society, it necessarily assumes a more exact and explicit form. It numbers its partisans and engages them in its cause; they, on the other hand, become acquainted with one another, and their zeal is increased by their number. An association unites into one channel the efforts of divergent minds and urges them vigorously towards the one end which it clearly points out.

The second degree in the exercise of the right of association is the power of meeting. When an association is allowed to establish centers of action at certain important points in the country, its activity is increased and its influence extended. Men have the opportunity of seeing one another; means of execution are combined; and opinions are maintained with a warmth and energy that written language can never attain.

Lastly, in the exercise of the right of political association there is a third degree: the partisans of an opinion may unite in electoral bodies and choose delegates to represent them in a central assembly. This is, properly speaking, the application of the representative system to a party.

Thus, in the first instance, a society is formed between individuals professing the same opinion, and the tie that keeps it together is of a purely intellectual nature. In the second case, small assemblies are formed, which represent only a fraction of the party. Lastly, in the third case, they constitute, as it were, a separate nation in the midst of the nation, a government within the government. Their delegates, like the real delegates of the majority, represent the whole collective force of their party, and like them, also, have an appearance of nationality and all the moral power that results from it. It is true that they have not the right, like the others, of making the laws; but they have the power of attacking those which are in force and of drawing up beforehand those which ought to be enacted.

If, among a people who are imperfectly accustomed to the exercise of freedom, or are exposed to violent political passions, by the side of the majority which makes the laws is placed a minority which only deliberates and gets laws ready for adoption, I cannot but believe that public tranquillity would there incur very great risks. There is doubtless a wide difference between proving that one law is in itself better than another and proving that the former ought to be substituted for the latter. But the imagination of the multitude is very apt to overlook this difference, which is so apparent to the minds of thinking men. It sometimes happens that a nation is divided into two nearly equal parties,

each of which affects to represent the majority. If, near the directing power, another power is established which exercises almost as much moral authority as the former, we are not to believe that it will long be content to speak without acting; or that it will always be restrained by the abstract consideration that associations are meant to direct opinions, but not to enforce them, to suggest but not to make the laws.

The more I consider the independence of the press in its principal consequences, the more am I convinced that in the modern world it is the chief and, so to speak, the constitutive element of liberty. A nation that is determined to remain free is therefore right in demanding, at any price, the exercise of this independence. But the *unlimited* liberty of political association cannot be entirely assimilated to the liberty of the press. The one is at the same time less necessary and more dangerous than the other. A nation may confine it within certain limits without forfeiting any part of its self-directing power; and it may sometimes be obliged to do so in order to maintain its own authority.

In America the liberty of association for political purposes is unlimited. An example will show in the clearest light to what an extent this privilege is tolerated.

The question of a tariff or free trade has much agitated the minds of Americans. The tariff was not only a subject of debate as a matter of opinion, but it affected some great material interests of the states. The North attributed a portion of its prosperity, and the South nearly all its sufferings, to this system. For a long time the tariff was the sole source of the political animosities that agitated the Union.

In 1831, when the dispute was raging with the greatest violence, a private citizen of Massachusetts proposed, by means of the newspapers, to all the enemies of the tariff to send delegates to Philadelphia in order to consult together upon the best means of restoring freedom of trade. This proposal circulated in a few days, by the power of the press, from Maine to New Orleans. The opponents of the tariff adopted it with enthusiasm; meetings were held in all quarters, and delegates were appointed. The majority of these delegates were well known, and some of them had earned a considerable degree of celebrity. South Carolina alone, which afterwards took up arms in the same cause, sent sixty-three delegates. On the 1st of October 1831 this assembly, which, according to the American custom, had taken the name of a Convention, met at Philadelphia; it consisted of more than two hundred members. Its debates were public, and they at once assumed a legislative character; the extent of the powers of Congress, the theories of free trade, and the different provisions of the tariff were discussed. At the end of ten days the Convention broke up, having drawn up an address to the American people in which it declared (1) that Congress had not the right of making a tariff, and that the existing tariff was unconstitutional; (2) that the prohibition of free trade was prejudicial to the interests of any nation, and to those of the American people especially.

It must be acknowledged that the unrestrained liberty of political association has not hitherto produced in the United States the fatal results that might perhaps be expected from it elsewhere. The right of association was imported from England, and it has always existed in America; the exercise of this privilege is now incorporated with the manners and customs of the people. At the present time the liberty of association has become a necessary guarantee against the tyranny of the majority. In the United States as soon as a party has become dominant, all public authority passes into its hands; its private supporters occupy all the offices and have all the force of the administration at their disposal. As the most distinguished members of the opposite party cannot surmount the barrier that excludes them from power, they must establish themselves outside of it and oppose the whole moral authority of the minority to the physical power that domineers over it. Thus a dangerous expedient is used to obviate a still more formidable danger.

The omnipotence of the majority appears to me to be so full of peril to the American republics that the dangerous means used to bridle it seem to be more advantageous than prejudicial. And here I will express an opinion that may remind the reader of what I said when speaking of the freedom of townships. There are no countries in which associations are more needed to prevent the despotism of faction or the arbitrary power of a prince than those which are democratically constituted. In aristocratic nations the body of the nobles and the wealthy are in themselves natural associations which check the abuses of power. In countries where such associations do not exist, if private individuals cannot create an artificial and temporary substitute for them I can see no permanent protection against the most galling tyranny; and a great people may be oppressed with impunity by a small faction or by a single individual.

The meeting of a great political convention (for there are conventions of all kinds), which may frequently become a necessary measure, is always a serious occurrence, even in America, and one that judicious patriots cannot regard without alarm. This was very perceptible in the Convention of 1831, at which all the most distinguished members strove to moderate its language and to restrain its objects within certain limits. It is probable that this Convention exercised a great influence on the minds of the malcontents and prepared them for the open revolt against the commercial laws of the Union that took place in 1832.

It cannot be denied that the unrestrained liberty of association for political purposes is the privilege which a people is longest in learning how to exercise. If it does not throw the nation into anarchy, it perpetually augments the chances of that calamity. On one point, however, this perilous liberty offers a security against dangers of another kind; in countries where associations are free, secret societies are unknown. In America there are factions, but no conspiracies.

Different ways in which the right of association is understood in Europe and in the United States—Different use which is made of it.

The most natural privilege of man, next to the right of acting for himself, is that of combining his exertions with those of his fellow creatures and of acting in common with them. The right of association therefore appears to me almost as inalienable in its nature as the right of personal liberty. No legislator can attack it without impairing the foundations of society. Nevertheless, if the liberty of association is only a source of advantage and prosperity to some nations, it may be perverted or carried to excess by others, and from an element of life may be changed into a cause of destruction. A comparison of the different methods that associations pursue in those countries in which liberty is well understood and in those where liberty degenerates into license may be useful both to governments and to parties.

Most Europeans look upon association as a weapon which is to be hastily fashioned and immediately tried in the conflict. A society is formed for discussion, but the idea of impending action prevails in the minds of all those who constitute it. It is, in fact, an army; and the time given to speech serves to reckon up the strength and to animate the courage of the host, after which they march against the enemy. To the persons who compose it, resources which lie within the bounds of law may suggest themselves as means of success, but never as the only means.

Such, however, is not the manner in which the right of association is understood in the United States. In America the citizens who form the minority associate in order, first, to show their numerical strength and so to diminish the moral power of the majority; and, secondly, to stimulate competition and thus to discover those arguments that are most fitted to act upon the majority; for they always entertain hopes of drawing over the majority to their own side, and then controlling the supreme power in its name. Political associations in the United States are therefore peaceable in their intentions and strictly legal in the means which they employ; and they assert with perfect truth that they aim at success only by lawful expedients.

The difference that exists in this respect between Americans and Europeans depends on several causes. In Europe there are parties which differ so much from the majority that they can never hope to acquire its support, and yet they think they are strong enough in themselves to contend against it. When a party of this kind forms an association, its object is not to convince, but to fight. In America the individuals who hold opinions much opposed to those of the majority can do nothing against it, and all other parties hope to win it over to their own principles. The exercise of the right of association becomes dangerous, then, in proportion as great parties find themselves wholly unable to acquire the majority. In a country like the United States, in which the differences of opinion are mere differences of hue, the right of association may remain unrestrained without evil consequences. Our inexperience of liberty leads us to regard the liberty of association only as a right of attacking the government. The first notion that presents itself to a party, as well as to an individual, when it has acquired a consciousness of its own strength is that of violence; the notion of persuasion arises at a later period, and is derived from experience. The English, who are divided into parties which differ essentially from each other, rarely abuse the right of association because they have long been accustomed to exercise it. In France the passion for war is so intense that there is no undertaking so mad, or so injurious to the welfare of the state that a man does not consider himself honored in defending it at the risk of his life.

But perhaps the most powerful of the causes that tend to mitigate the violence of political associations in the United States is universal suffrage. In countries in which universal suffrage exists, the majority is never doubtful, because neither party can reasonably pretend to represent that portion of the community which has not voted. The associations know as well as the nation at large that they do not represent the majority. This results, indeed, from the very fact of their existence; for if they did represent the preponderating power, they would change the law instead of soliciting its reform. The consequence of this is that the moral influence of the government which they attack is much increased, and their own power is much enfeebled.

In Europe there are few associations which do not affect to represent the majority, or which do not believe that they represent it. This conviction or this pretension tends to augment their force amazingly and contributes no less to legalize their measures. Violence may seem to be excusable in defense of the cause of oppressed right. Thus it is, in the vast complication of human laws, that extreme liberty sometimes corrects the abuses of liberty, and that extreme democracy obviates the dangers of democracy. In Europe associations consider themselves, in some degree, as the legislative and executive council of the people, who are unable to speak for themselves; moved by this belief, they

act and they command. In America, where they represent in the eyes of all only a minority of the nation, they argue and petition.

The means that associations in Europe employ are in accordance with the end which they propose to obtain. As the principal aim of these bodies is to act and not to debate, to fight rather than to convince, they are naturally led to adopt an organization which is not civic and peaceable, but partakes of the habits and maxims of military life. They also centralize the direction of their forces as much as possible and entrust the power of the whole party to a small number of leaders.

The members of these associations respond to a watchword, like soldiers on duty; they profess the doctrine of passive obedience; say, rather, that in uniting together they at once abjure the exercise of their own judgment and free will; and the tyrannical control that these societies exercise is often far more insupportable than the authority possessed over society by the government which they attack. Their moral force is much diminished by these proceedings, and they lose the sacred character which always attaches to a struggle of the oppressed against their oppressors. He who in given cases consents to obey his fellows with servility and who submits his will and even his thoughts to their control, how can be pretend that he wishes to be free?

The Americans have also established a government in their associations, but it is invariably borrowed from the forms of the civil administration. The independence of each individual is recognized; as in society, all the members advance at the same time towards the same end, but they are not all obliged to follow the same track. No one abjures the exercise of his reason and free will, but everyone exerts that reason and will to promote a common undertaking.

PROJECT

Think about the number of associations (or groups) to which you belong. Are you more or less involved with group activity than you thought? Be sure to count the nonpolitical groups Tocqueville describes. In what ways has your involvement with these groups taught you democratic values?

4

Group Activities

ARTHUR BENTLEY

Arthur Bentley's *The Process of Government* represents a marriage of two fields of study—political science and psychology. This marriage enables Bentley to look at group behavior through a different lens. Although "Federalist No. 10" is often cited as a work relating to pluralism, Bentley is the first to consciously use the pluralist framework. He suggests that all behavior can be interpreted through the interplay of groups in society. For Bentley, we are all products of groups. Our opinions are the opinions of the groups to which we belong because group identity trumps individuality. Thus, Bentley suggests that all politics should be viewed by looking at group interactions rather than the actions of individuals. His analysis held great sway with scholars, affecting how they studied politics as well as what they studied.

QUESTIONS TO CONSIDER

1. How does Bentley define an interest group?
2. What does Bentley say about public opinion?
3. In what ways do groups influence individual behavior?
4. How does Bentley approach and discuss measurement?
5. Do you find what Bentley says about individuality disturbing?

It is impossible to attain scientific treatment of material that will not submit itself to measurement in some form. Measure conquers chaos. Even in biology notable advances by the use of statistical methods are being made. And what is of most importance, the material the biologist handles is of a kind that is susceptible of measurement and quantitative comparison all the way through. The occasional recrudescence of vitalism in biology is not irreconcilable with this statement. It simply indicates that from time to time some investigator directs his attention to phases of life, ever lessening in extent, which, he holds, are not measurable by present processes, and which, it pleases him to feel, will remain unmeasurable.

In the political world, the dictum, "the greatest good of the greatest number," stands for an effort to make measurements. Sometimes, of course, it is simply the rallying-cry of particular causes. If we take it, however, where it pretends to be a general rule of measurement, we shall find that it applies itself not to what actually happens in legislation, but merely to what a thinker in some particular atmosphere believes ought to be the law; and this, no matter what systematic content of "goods" is pumped into it. I hope to make it clear later that even such a generalized social theory as this is nothing but a reflection, or an index, or a label, of some particular set of demands made by some particular section of society. It is not a measure of social facts which we can use for scientific purposes, and it would not be thus useful even if logically it could be regarded as a standard of measurement, which, of course, it cannot be without further specification.

SOURCE: From Arthur Bentley, "Group Activities," *The Process of Government: A Study of Social Pressures* (New Brunswick, NJ: Transaction Publishers, 1995), 200–222. Reprinted with permission.

Statistics of social facts as we ordinarily get them are, of course, measurements. But even after they have been elaborately interpreted by the most expert statisticians, they must still undergo much further interpretation by the people who use them with reference to their immediate purposes of use. As they stand on the printed page, they are commonly regarded as "dead," and they receive much undeserved disparagement. But by this very token it is clear that they do not adequately state the social facts. People who are in close connection with all that rich life-activity indicated by the "feelings" and the "ideas" feel that the heart of the matter is lacking in them.

But, now, the idea and feeling elements, stated for themselves, are unmeasurable as they appear in studies of government. This is a fatal defect in them. Any pretense of measuring them, no matter with what elaborate algebra, will prove to be merely an attribution to them of powers inferred from their results. Usually they appear in social discussions with wholly fictitious values, in support of which not even a pretense of actual measurement is presented. The measurements of experimental psychology are not such measurements as we need. They are measurements of activity looked upon as within the physical individual. The social content is incidental to them and is not measured.

If a statement of social facts which lends itself better to measurement is offered, that characteristic entitles it to attention. Providing the statement does not otherwise distort the social facts, the capability of measurement will be decisive in its favor. The statement that takes us farthest along the road toward quantitative estimates will inevitably be the best statement.

In practical politics a large amount of rough measuring is done. There is measurement with the sword when one nation defeats another in war. South American revolutions, which answer to North American elections, also use the sword as their standard of measure. Under Walpole the different elements in politics sought equilibrium in great part by the agency of gold coin and gold-bearing offices. In an election at its best in the United States, the measurement goes by the counting of heads. In a legislative body, likewise, the counting of heads appears. A referendum vote is political measurement.

This measuring process appears in various degrees of differentiation. In a battle the social quantities, and the measuring of those quantities which is taking place on the spot, are fused together, so that one has to make an effort to consider them separately. But in a vote in the federal House of Representatives differentiation appears. Here a much more complicated measuring process is carried through, which appears finally in a simplified form in the announcement of the vote for and against the project by the tellers. The student of political life has some hint of the measurements in the figures of the vote; but it is necessary for him to measure the measure, to go far back and examine the quantities that have been in play to produce the given results. The best of these practical political measures are indeed exceedingly crude. The practical politician himself is estimating quantities all the time; indeed his success is in direct proportion to his ability to make good estimates. He may show a preternatural skill. But his skill is of little or no direct use for the scientific student. The practical politician will never under any circumstances consent to make a plain statement of his estimates; indeed it is rare that he knows how to tell, even if he should wish to.

The quantities are present in every bit of political life. There is no political process that is not a balancing of quantity against quantity. There is not a law that is passed that is not the expression of force and force in tension. There is not a court decision or an executive act that is not the result of the same process. Understanding any of these phenomena means measuring the elements that have gone into them.

If we can get our social life stated in terms of activity, and of nothing else, we have not indeed succeeded in measuring it, but we have at least reached a foundation upon which a coherent system of measurements can be built up. Our technique may be very poor at the start, and the amount of labor we must employ to get scanty results will be huge. But we shall cease to be blocked by the intervention of unmeasurable elements, which claim to be themselves the real causes of all that is happening, and which by their spook-like arbitrariness make impossible any progress toward dependable knowledge.

I have used the word activity or action thus far to designate the point of view from which an adequate statement of the phenomena must be sought. The activity is always the activity of men. I might have said "men" straightway at the beginning, instead of activity, but "men" has too many implications which it was necessary to keep from creeping in where they would give rise to misconception. Perhaps now, however, I can discuss the same subject in terms of men direct.

Human society is always a mass of men, and nothing else. These men are all of them thinking-feeling men, acting. Political phenomena are all phenomena of these masses. One never needs to go outside of them. One must take them as they come, that is in the masses in which they are found aggregated. In some cases and for some purposes this is easy to do. At the time of the Russo-Japanese war it was easy to take Japan in one mass and Russia in another and watch them react upon each other. It is easy to take one of our American states as apart from some other, say California as apart from New

York, though the interactions which would require our taking them in this way are very rare and usually negligible. It is easy to take the mass, "New York City," and separate it from the mass, "New York State outside the city." Similarly in some societies one can take a family group and hold it fairly distinct from surrounding family groups, for purposes of examination.

But in the complex modern state it is seldom that our problems involve masses as sharply separated as these. Take, for example, New York City and New York State. The state includes the city. In many political problems involving the two we must hold the New York City people as city residents, apart from those same people as state residents. We must keep them distinct in their two functions. We find them in two groups, which must be separated in our analysis. The same physical men are among the components of both, and perhaps they find themselves in one group pulling against themselves in another group. It is exceedingly hard, indeed almost impossible, to hold such groups apart in terms of logic—witness the hair-splitting of the lawbooks over state and federal citizenship. Fortunately, it is much simpler in terms of facts.

Still the difficulty of picturing the nation as made up of groups of men, each group cutting across many others, each individual man a component part of very many groups, is by no means inconsiderable. But the difficulty disappears as practice shows us how to concentrate attention on the essential features and to strip off incidental points which appear to have extravagant importance because of the prepossessions as to the nature of human individuality with which the task is approached. With increased facility in thus observing society we find we are coming to state more and more adequately the raw material of political life. If a law is in question, we find that our statement of it in terms of the groups of men it affects—the group or set of

groups directly insisting on it, those directly opposing it, and those more indirectly concerned in it—is much more complete than any statement in terms of self-interest, theories, or ideals. If it is a plank in a political platform, again we find we can state its actual value in the social process at the given time in terms of the groups of men for whose sake it is there: a group of politicians and a number of groups of voters holding the prominent places.

The whole social life in all its phases can be stated in such groups of active men, indeed must be stated in that way if a useful analysis is to be had. Sometimes the groups, although not territorially distinct, gain a marked separation, so that two opposing parties may face each other with well-closed ranks. Then again all is seemingly confusion, and the crossed lines of different groups seem too tangled to be followed.

What a man states to himself as his argument or reasoning or thinking about a national issue is, from the more exact point of view, just the conflict of the crossed groups to which he belongs. To say that a man belongs to two groups of men which are clashing with each other; to say that he reflects two seemingly irreconcilable aspects of the social life; to say that he is reasoning on a question of public policy, these all are but to state the same fact in three forms. How was it with a cattle-raiser during the campaign for the passage of a meat-inspection law by Congress in the spring of 1906? All cattle-raisers had interests both as producers and consumers (I will presently return to this use of the word interest and justify it). Some reflected their producers' interest so strongly that it quickly dominated; they arrayed themselves with the opposition to the bill. Others, a much smaller number, it is true, reflected their producer's interests on broader lines, or reflected primarily the consumers' interests of the country, and found themselves lined up with the group

"raw material of political life"

behind the President. It is not the set of reasonings put forth by men on either side, but the position that they assumed, which had its roots—for the mass— much deeper than the reasonings, that is the vital political fact. The reasonings help us in the analysis, but only as indicating where to look for the facts; and one token is that in most cases the reasonings, at least the elaborate reasonings, come long after the assumption of position on the question, and as supplementary to it, and explanatory of it.

When one hears a loud public outcry against "corporations," it is easy to prove logically the folly of the outcry, but such proof is irrelevant and immaterial for genuine study of what is happening in society. The outcry, just as it is heard, indicates certain very real group facts, and these facts are themselves the vital facts of the process. The people afflicted with "corporationphobia" are much better justified in sneering at their intellectually arrogant critics than are the latter in sneering at them.

It is possible to take a Supreme Court decision, in which nothing appears on the surface but finespun points of law, and cut through all the dialectic till we get down to the actual groups of men underlying the decisions and producing the decisions through the differentiated activity of the justices. In most cases this substantial basis of the decisions does not readily appear, because of the foundation of habitual activity on which the facts rest. But in exceptional cases, as when the court strikes out on a new line of precedent or gives a decision of a kind which, say, ten years earlier it would not possibly have rendered, the analysis can be made with comparative ease.

There is ample reason, then, for examining these great groups of acting men directly and accepting them as the fundamental facts of our investigation. They are just as real as they would be if they were territorially separated so that one man could never belong to two groups at the same time. They lose nothing in reality because one man may belong to two conflicting groups and may be tossed up and down for a long time before he settles for the final steps of the process with one group to the exclusion of the others. They are vastly more real than a man's reflection of them in his "ideas" which inadequately interpret or misinterpret to him his course; which, as speech activity, help to reconcile him with the groups he deserts, and which help to establish him firmly with the group he finally cleaves to. Indeed the only reality of the ideas is their reflection of the groups, only that and nothing more. The ideas can be stated in terms of the groups; the groups never in terms of the ideas.

Every classification of the elements of a population must involve an analysis of the population into groups. It is impossible— at least, for any pending scientific problem—to make a classification so comprehensive and thorough that we can put it forth as "the" classification of the population. The purpose of the classification must always be kept in mind. This is because of the limitless criss-cross of the groups. It would only be in a rigorous caste organization of society, or perhaps in a very severe slavery in which one race held another in subjection, that the groups would so consolidate in separate masses of men that a classification—as, say, into white masters and black slaves—would serve for all the leading purposes of investigation. In nearly all cases of government with which we have to deal, and, I think I can say in practically all cases in modern society—excepting certain extreme cases of war, and these are more apparent than real—the varying sets of interests will not so settle or consolidate themselves upon masses of men as to make any one classification adequate for all interests. To illustrate, even in the case of our American Civil War, with North arrayed against South, there was a great array of groupings on other than war lines which cut across the war frontier. These reasserted themselves as soon as union was achieved, and would have reasserted themselves, though with more effort and less manifest result, had dis-union been the outcome.

Perhaps I may be permitted to offer a geometrical picture of this mixture of the groups, under the assurance, how-ever, that no proof depends on it, and that it pretends to be nothing more than a crude attempt at illustration. If we take all the men of our society, say all the citi-zens of the United States, and look upon them as a spherical mass, we can pass an unlimited number of planes through the center of the sphere, each plane repre-senting some principle of classification, say, race, various economic interests, reli-gion, or language (though in practice we shall have to do mainly with much more specialized groupings than these). Now, if we take any one of these planes and ignore the others, we can group the whole mass of the sphere by means of an outline or diagram traced upon the circle which the plane makes by its intersection with the sphere, and by partition walls erected on this outline at right angles to the circle. Our principle of classification may include the whole population, or it may have to allow for a section of the population indifferent to it; but the latter case can equally well be allowed for in the diagram. Similarly, by means of some other plane together with partition walls perpendicular to it, we can group the whole population on a different basis of classification: that is to say, for a different purpose.

Assuming perhaps hundreds, perhaps thousands, of planes passed through the sphere, we get a great confusion of the groups. No one set of groups, that is, no set distinguished on the basis of any one plane, will be an adequate grouping of the whole mass.

In case the planes should revolve till a great proportion of them came to

coincide, we would possibly, though even then not certainly, be able to take a single grouping as roughly giving us "the" grouping of the mass. A very rig-orous caste system, as before said, will somewhat answer to this condition, or two nations in war time, where we ignore the "habit background" on which the war is fought and a lot of other factors which still exist, though little vociferous, despite the war.

In great modern nations we are indeed often told that such a mass group-ing, such an all-embracing classification, does actually exist in the form of the classes that enter into the class war of socialism. No socialist or other person has made an analysis, however, which can in any sense be said to prove that this hard grouping exists; nothing better is offered than emotional assumptions and class "ideas." Moreover the observed reactions in our societies are not such as would follow from such a grouping in which the criss-cross had disappeared, and sharply defined outlines were trace-able—the war in fact is not to the finish, the socialism that extends itself to large portions of the population is, wherever we know it, a socialism that ends in polit-ical compromises. And compromise—not in the merely logical sense, but in practical life—is the very process itself of the criss-cross groups in action.

A classification into farmers, artisans, merchants, etc., will answer some pur-poses in studying our population, but not others. A classification by race answers some purposes, but not many unless it is fortified, as it may or may not be, by the coincidence with it of the planes of many other group classifications. One would be hard put, for example, to jus-tify emphasis on a distinction between Germans and English in treating the local politics of a city like Chicago. And the same would be true of other races, Italians, Poles, or any that are present in no matter how large numbers, regarded as groups to be distinguished from one another by the race test alone, and acting as such in the political field. "Representation of the race on the ticket" and to some extent, also, a difference in attitude toward the liquor problem, would be about all that one could find in the way of lines of activity, and even that would probably be exaggerated out of all proper proportion by those who talked about it.

The great task in the study of any form of social life is the analysis of these groups. It is much more than classification, as that term is ordinarily used. When the groups are adequately stated, everything is stated. When I say everything I mean everything. The complete description will mean the complete science, in the study of social phenomena, as in any other field. There will be no more room for animistic "causes" here than there.

But it is not our task in this work to make an analysis of the groups that operate in the whole social life. We are to confine our attention to the process of politics, and the political groups are the only ones with which we shall be directly concerned. And indeed, our task even here concerns the method of analysis, not the exact statement of the groups that are operating at any particular time or place.

It would at first sight seem that the political process could not be studied till the process of the underlying groups had been studied, for political groups are built up out of, or, better said, upon, the other groups. Political groups are highly differentiated groups reflecting, or representing, other groups, which latter can easily, and I believe for most purposes properly, be regarded as more fundamental in society. The political process goes on, so to speak, well up toward the surface of society. The economic basis of political life must, of course, be fully recognized, though it does not necessarily follow that the economic basis in the usual limited use of the word is the exclusive, or even in every detail the dominant, basis of political activity.

Nevertheless, it is my conviction that political groups, highly differentiated as they are, can well be studied before the other groups; and that indeed one has better chance of success in studying the political groups first than in studying the other groups first. The very fact that they are so highly representative makes it easier to handle them. They are in closer connection with "ideas," "ideals," "emotions," "policies," "public opinion," etc., than are some of the other groups. I would better say, they work through a process of ideals, etc., more plainly than do the deeper-lying groups. And as the same psychic process, including all its elements, is involved in the facts which enter into the interpretation of all forms of social life, we have better prospects of successful work in a field in which we can get it, I will not say in most direct, but in most manifest, most palpable, most measurable form. If I may be pardoned a remark from my own experience, I will say that my interest in politics is not primary, but derived from my interest in the economic life; and that I hope from this point of approach ultimately to gain a better understanding of the economic life than I have succeeded in gaining hitherto.

We shall confine ourselves then to the groups that appear in politics, and as they appear in politics. Now the political groups can never safely be taken to be the same identical groups that we would analyze out in studies of other phases of the social life. The political action reflects, represents, the underlying groups: but the political groups will have different boundaries than the other groups; there will be splittings and consolidations; and even if as regards the persons belonging to them they are ever the same, even then they will have different ways of reaction, different activities; and since the activities *are* the groups, they cannot properly be called the same groups under exact discrimination. I do not mean at all that political parties, the Democratic,

Republican, Prohibition, Socialist, and so on, are the essential groups for a political study. These are certain of the political groups, but we have to strike much deeper than their level. We have to get hold of the lower-lying political groups which they reflect or represent, just as in turn these lower-lying political groups reflect other groups, which are not properly speaking political. The "properly speaking," here, has merely to do with the particular plane of discrimination, the standard or test on the basis of which the group analysis is made. We shall have to take all these political groups, and get them stated with their meaning, with their value, with their representative quality. We shall have to get hold of political institutions, legislatures, courts, executive officers, and get them stated as groups, and in terms of other groups. The presidency, for example, is an institution that includes a considerable number of men in and out of office—ignoring for the moment constitutional theory on one side, and a little crackle of arbitrariness at the pinnacle on the other—and we must state it in terms of party and in terms of the nation, or rather in terms of those portions of the nation stated not in party but in deeper political groupings, which it represents at any moment or in any period. We shall have to get all the ideas and policies and selfishnesses that enter into current talk or specialized political talk stated in the same way, as differentiated activity, as the reflection of lower-lying activity.

When we have done all this in a preliminary manner, when we have our raw material in hand, then we shall be ready to set up theories about the relations of the activities. And so we can pass to a new and more adequate statement and at last to an interpretation, if we have fortune and perseverance, that will stand firmly the test of application. I do not mean by this, of course, to be outlining the path of this book, but to be outlining the long road on which the book is, I hope, taking some steps.

The term "group" will be used throughout this work in a technical sense. It means a certain portion of the men of a society, taken, however, not as a physical mass cut off from other masses of men, but as a mass activity, which does not preclude the men who participate in it from participating likewise in many other group activities. It is always so many men with all their human quality. It is always so many men, acting, or tending toward action—that is, in various stages of action. Group and group activity are equivalent terms with just a little difference of emphasis, useful only for clearness of expression in different contexts.

It is now necessary to take another step in the analysis of the group. There is no group without its interest. An interest, as the term will be used in this work, is the equivalent of a group. We may speak also of an interest group or of a group interest, again merely for the sake of clearness in expression. The group and the interest are not separate. There exists only the one thing, that is, so many men bound together in or along the path of a certain activity. Sometimes we may be emphasizing the interest phase, sometimes the group phase, but if ever we push them too far apart we soon land in the barren wilderness. There may be a beyond-scientific question as to whether the interest is responsible for the existence of the group, or the group responsible for the existence of the interest. I do not know or care. What we actually find in this world, what we can observe and study, is interested men, nothing more and nothing less. That is our raw material and it is our business to keep our eyes fastened to it.

The word interest in social studies is often limited to the economic interest. There is no justification whatever for such a limitation. I am restoring it to its

[margin note: definition ↓ Mass activity]

broader meaning coextensive with all groups whatsoever that participate in the social process. I am at the same time giving it definite, specific content wherever it is used. I shall have nothing to say about "political interest" as such, but very much about the multiform interests that work through the political process.

I am dealing here with political groups and other groups that function in the specifically social process, and not extending the assertion that the words group and interest coincide, over all groups that on any plane can be analyzed out of masses of human beings. One might put the blonde women of the country in one class and the brunettes in another, and call each class a group. It may be that a process of selection of blondes and brunettes is going on, and it may perhaps be—I am taking an extreme case—that it will sometime be found necessary to classify some phase of that process as social and to study it along with other social phenomena. I am not expressing an opinion as to that, and I have no need of forming an opinion. Whether that attitude is taken or not will depend upon practical considerations upon which the investigator himself must pass. I would not say that such a "group" for other than social studies could properly be described as having a blonde or brunette interest in the meaning here given to interest. It would not be a social group, and probably the equivalent of the interest could be better specified without the use of that particular word. But that is neither here nor there. The essential point is that if ever blondes or brunettes appear in political life as such it will be through an interest which they assert, or—what comes in general to the same thing, when the analysis is fully made—which is asserted for them through some group or group leadership which represents them.

In the political world, if we take the interest alone as a psychological quality, what we get is an indefinite, untrustworthy will-o'-the-wisp, which may trick us into any false step whatsoever. Once set it up and we are its slaves, whatever swamp it may lead us to. If we try to take the group without the interest, we have simply nothing at all. We cannot take the first step to define it. The group is activity and the activity is only known to us through its particular type, its value in terms of other activities, its tendency where it is not in the stage which gives manifest results. The interest is just this valuation of the activity, not as distinct from it, but as the valued activity itself.

In using the term interest there are two serious dangers against which we must carefully guard ourselves. One is the danger of taking the interest at its own verbal expression of itself, that is to say, the danger of estimating it as it is estimated by the differentiated activity of speech and written language which reflects it. The other danger is at the far extreme from this. It is that we disregard the group's expressed valuation of itself and that we assign to it a meaning or value that is "objective" in the sense that we regard it as something natural or inevitable or clothed in oughtness. If we should substitute for the actual interest of the activity some "objective utility," to use the economist's term, we should be going far astray, for no such "objective utility" appears in politics at all, however otherwise it may be attributed to the men who compose the society. It is like the undiscovered and unsuspected gold under the mountain, a social nullity. A man who is wise enough may legitimately predict, if he is addicted to the habit of prediction, that a group activity will ultimately form along lines marked out by some objective condition which he thinks he detects. But the interests that we can take into account must lie a good deal closer to the actual existing masses of men than that.

If we cannot take words for our test, and if we cannot take "bed-rock truth," one may say we are left swinging hopelessly in between. Quite the contrary. The political groups are following definite courses. They may appear erratic, but hardly ever to anyone who is in close enough contact with them. The business of the student is to plot the courses. And when he does that—it is the course of only a single step, not of a whole career, that he can plot—he will find that he has all together, the group, the activity, and the interest.

The essential difference between interest as I am defining it and the psychological feeling or desire qualities should be already apparent. I am not introducing any suppositional factor which can be taken in hand, applied to the social activities and used in the pretense of explaining them. I am not taking any mental or other possession which the individual man is supposed to have before he enters society and using it to explain the society. I am not dealing with anything which can be scheduled to any desired extent as a set of abstract general interests, capable of branching out to correspond with the complexity of the activity of the social world. I am not using any interest that can be abstractly stated apart from the whole social background in which it is found at the moment of use.

The interest I put forward is a specific group interest in some definite course of conduct or activity. It is first, last, and all the time strictly empirical. There is no way to find it except by observation. There is no way to get hold of one group interest except in terms of others. A group of slaves for example, is not a group of physical beings who are "slaves by nature," but a social relationship, a specified activity and interest in society. From the interest as a thing by itself no conclusion can be drawn. No fine logic, no calculus of interests will take us a single step forward in the interpreting of society. When we succeed in isolating an interest group the only way to find out what it is going to do, indeed the only way to be sure

we have isolated an interest group, is to watch its progress. When we have made sure of one such interest, or group, we shall become more skilful and can make sure of another similar one with less painstaking. When we have compared many sets of groups we shall know better what to expect. But we shall always hold fast to the practical reality, and accept the interests that it offers us as the only interests we can use, studying them as impassively as we would the habits or the organic functions of birds, bees, or fishes.

Such interest groups are of no different material than the "individuals" of a society. They are activity; so are the individuals. It is solely a question of the standpoint from which we look at the activity to define it. The individual stated for himself, and invested with an extrasocial unity of his own, is a fiction. But every bit of the activity, which is all we actually know of him, can be stated either on the one side as individual, or on the other side as social group activity. The former statement is in the main of trifling importance in interpreting society; the latter statement is essential, first, last, and all the time. It is common to contrast conditions in India or elsewhere in which "the community is the political unit," with conditions in our own society in which "the individual is the political unit." But in reality such a contrast is highly superficial and limited, made for special purposes of interpretation within the process. From the point of view here taken all such contrasts fade into insignificance except as they are "raw material" when the special processes in connection with which they are made are being studied.

When we have a group fairly well defined in terms of its interests, we next find it necessary to consider the factors that enter into its relative power of dominating other groups and of carrying its tendencies to action through their full course with relatively little check or hindrance. As the interest is merely a manner of stating the value of the group activity, so these factors of dominance are likewise just phases of the statement of the group, not separate from it, nor capable of scientific use as separate things.

First of all, the number of men who belong to the group attracts attention. Number alone may secure dominance. Such is the case in the ordinary American election, assuming corruption and intimidation to be present in such small proportions that they do not affect the result. But numbers notoriously do not decide elections in the former slave states of the South. There is a concentration of interest on political lines which often, and indeed one may say usually, enables a minority to rule a majority. I cannot stop here to discuss the extent to which majorities are represented by minorities under such circumstances, but only to note the fact. Intensity is a word that will serve as well as any other to denote the concentration of interest which gives a group effectiveness in its activity in the face of the opposition of other groups.

This intensity, like interest, is only to be discovered by observation. There is no royal road for scientific workers to take to it. Catchwords like race, ability, education, moral vigor, may serve as tags to indicate its presence, but they are of little or no help to us, and indeed they are more apt to do us positive harm by making us think we have our solutions in advance, and by blinding us to the facts that we should study. Mere vociferation must not be confused with intensity. It is one form of intensity, but very often the intensity of the talk does not correctly reflect the true intensity of the group. This must be allowed for.

Besides number and intensity, there is a technique of group activities which must be taken into account. Blows, bribes, allurements of one kind and another, and arguments also, are characteristic, and to these must be added organization.

A group will differentiate under fitting circumstances a special set of activities for carrying on its work. We must learn how these specialized activities vary under different forms of group oppositions, how the technique changes and evolves. We shall find that the change in methods is produced by the appearance of new group interests, directed against the use of the method that is suppressed. If violence gives way to bribery, or bribery to some form of demagogy, or that perhaps to a method called reasoning, it will be possible, if we pursue the study carefully enough, to find the group interest that has worked the change. That group will have its own technique, no more scrupulous probably than the technique it suppresses, but vigorously exerted through the governing institutions of the society, or possibly outside those institutions.

Technique will of course vary with the intensity of interest, as for instance when assassination is adopted by revolutionists who can find no other method to make themselves felt against their opponents. Number also has intimate relations with both technique and intensity. In general it is to be said that there is no rule of thumb which will point out to us any particular lines of activity in which the most powerful groups can inevitably be found. We may sometimes find the greatest intensity over matters that still seem to us trifles, even after we think we have interpreted them in terms of underlying groups, and again we may find slight intensity where we think there ought to be the most determined effort. It is solely a matter for observation. And observation shows, here as before, that no group can be defined or understood save in terms of the other groups of the given time and place. One opposition appears and adjusts itself and another takes its place; and each opposition gets its meaning only in terms of the other oppositions and of the adjustments that have taken place between them.

I have been talking of groups as so much activity capable of definition, each group for itself. When we analyze a group in a fairly satisfactory way, we usually give it some kind of a name, and set it off with a certain individuality; the individuality it has is, however, nothing more than the definition of its activity.

At the same time I have said that no group can be stated, or defined, or valued—I have used various words in this respect—except in terms of other groups. No group has meaning except in its relations to other groups. No group can even be conceived of as a group—when we get right down close to facts—except as set off by itself, and, so to speak, made a group by the other groups.

I have also made preliminary mention of the way in which some groups represent others, and have indicated the importance of this representative relation for our further study.

I have not called these group activities forces nor said anything about forces involved in them. The word force can be used, no doubt, even in sociology, to indicate phenomena for study, but it is too apt to drag in some metaphysical suggestion, and in social studies it connotes almost inevitably the isolated, metaphysically posited, individual feelings and ideas, which hypothesis places at the bottom of social life as its causes. Moreover we have little need for it. If we say activity, we have said all.

Now, as the points I have just reiterated imply, the activities are all knit together in a system, and indeed only get their appearance of individuality by being abstracted from the system; they brace each other up, hold each other together, move forward by their interactions, and in general are in a state of continuous pressure upon one another.

If we take a little different angle of vision we shall be tempted to state each group activity, not directly in terms of such and such other group activities, but as resting in a great sea of social life, of which it is but a slight modulation. We shall get the conception of a "habit background" in which the group activity operates. . . .

Suppose, for example, we take a modern battle, and note that it is fought, not with complete abandon, but under definite limitations which forbid certain cruelties, such as the poisoning of springs, the butchery of the wounded, firing upon Red Cross parties, the use of explosive bullets, or the use of balloon explosives. Or suppose we take a political campaign, and note that in one country the contestants use methods which are not used in another. The Cuban liberals used methods against President Palma which are not resorted to in the United States; Tammany uses methods when it can in connection with the New York City police force which no political party uses in London, and which would be injurious to any party that tried to use them. There are "rules of the game" in existence, which form the background of the group activity. There is no savage tribe so low but that it has rules of the game, which are respected and enforced. I hardly need to add that a large part of this habitual activity is commonly discussed in terms of moral factors.

The habit background may usefully be taken into the reckoning as summing up a lot of conditions under which the groups operate, but reliance on it is apt to check investigation where investigation is needed, or even become the occasion for the introduction of much unnecessary mysticism. By appealing to the habit background we must not hope to get away from the present in our interpretations. Just as ideas and ideals are apt to give us a false whirl into the future with our investigations, so in somewhat the same way the habit background is apt to carry us back into the past and thus away from our raw material. We set up "tradition" as established, and then we are apt to think that by appealing to tradition, and by tracing the methods of tradition, we are explaining some social phenomenon that we have in mind. But indeed if tradition is anything at all, it is an affair of the present. If we ever handle it except as a thing of the present—that is, of the particular date under consideration—we trust to it as a false support. Long, in point of time, as may be the trains of activity which we must follow, we never grasp them except at some present moment. The flight of an arrow will serve for illustration. We may plot the curve the arrow follows, but we must study its flight at each moment in terms of the forces in play at that moment. No arrow "tradition" will serve any good purpose.

If we have a form of activity traced down from a remote past—of the kind, say, that is usually called a belief—we have got to value it in terms of other activity at each moment of its career which we study. The question is always what other activities does it represent "now"? What relations, including oppositions, does it have with other activities? What are the underlying interest groups? It is certainly true that we must accept a belief group of this kind as an interest group itself. A totem group, imposing a certain duty as to the eating or the not eating of the flesh of the totem animal, is an established interest; it reflects certain other interests, probably involving the food supply, certain diseases, demons in the air or forest, or all of them together. If those other interest groups change in any way, the effect on the totem activity will be corresponding, whether it is an effect which an outsider can observe or not. It has a different meaning, a different value; in other words, it *is* a different activity. We cannot carry the belief up into the present out of the past and be effecting anything in our work beyond a rough sketch of the surface appearance. Nothing but the "present" can enter into a scientific balance of the group

activities against one another to show their tension and cohesion and lines of development.

Another difficulty which may arise from a misuse of the conception of the habit background needs mention. It is easy to generalize the background so much that one thinks he finds in it a "social whole" which he can treat as an active factor in his interpretative work. We are often told that social interests or social welfare demands this thing or that thing; that this custom or that institution has survived because it furthers the welfare of society. I do not want to go beyond my proper range in discussing this difficulty, but for political phenomena I think I am justified in asserting positively that no such group as the "social whole" enters into the interpretation in any form whatever. Where we have a group that participates in the political process we have always another group facing it in the same plane (to revert to the illustration of the sphere). It is true that if we have two nations at war we can treat for the purposes of the war, though only to a certain limited extent, each nation as a separate group; but it is clear that under such circumstances neither nation is the "social whole"; it takes the two together to make the society whose processes we are at the time studying. On any political question which we could study as a matter concerning the United States, for example, alone, we should never be justified in treating the interests of the whole nation as decisive. There are always some parts of the nation to be found arrayed against other parts. It is only by passing from the existing, observed, actual interests to the "objective utilities" I have mentioned above that we can drag in the "social whole," and there we are out of the field of social science. Usually we shall find, on testing the "social whole," that it is merely the group tendency or demand represented by the man who talks of it, erected into the pretense of a universal demand of the society; and thereby, indeed, giving the lie to its own claims; for if it were such a comprehensive all-embracing interest of the society as a whole it would be an established condition, and not at all a subject of discussion by the man who calls it an interest of society as a whole; except again when it is idealistically "objective" but humanly impossible. It is easy to say that it is to society's interest that airy, light lodgings should be provided for all the citizens. But it is plain that what is meant is that from some particular group's point of view, this "ought to be to society's interest"; for it is very clear that the actual interests now existing do not include it either among all tenants or among all landlords. It is easy again to say that "murder is against the social interest," but even if we ignore riot-suppression, police work, judicial executions, wars, and so forth, this "social interest" that is appealed to is not actually the interest of all the people. For besides the continually recurring crimes of passion, and the murders by professional thieves, there is a vast amount of homicide in routine features of our commercial life, such as railroad operation, food manufacture, sweat-shop clothes-making, and so on. And such murders answer to existing interests. All assertions of this kind need very careful qualification in any uses; and indeed need to be abandoned entirely to get any approximately exact statement of the processes under way for scientific investigation.

It may seem overstraining the point to say that in any community of Australian savages in which the main totem rules work continuously without a breach, in any Indian village in which crime is unknown for years at a time, it is wrong to speak of an "interest of the whole." But here the "interest of the whole" would be simply a statement of the established social habit, and whatever change came about in it would be brought about by changing conditions, or in other words by changing group interests; indeed should we go under the surface we could no doubt find a powerful and very definite group interest sustaining the habit by effectively suppressing diverging tendencies.

In the case of the totem tribe we might envisage the community of men and women as in opposition to the demon community, which is a very real social factor, however much the schoolboy may laugh at it; but the demons themselves would prove to have their meaning in terms of groups of the population. In the case of the Indian village, it may be that a very simple community under very favorable conditions of life— I mean food supply, instruments of production, etc.—shows the disappearance of certain tendencies which we, from our own experience, think ought to be present. In that case we might say that the tendency or interest was not present simply because the condition at which it is normally taken by us to be directed was not present. On these questions we need not pass judgment here. I have let them come into the text merely to broaden the issue.

As for political questions under any society in which we are called upon to study them, we shall never find a group interest of the society as a whole. We shall always find that the political interests and activities of any given group— and there are no political phenomena except group phenomena—are directed against other activities of men, who appear in other groups, political or other. The phenomena of political life which we study will always divide the society in which they occur, along lines which are very real, though of varying degrees of definiteness. The society itself is nothing other than the complex of the groups that compose it.

PROJECT

Assess the accuracy of Bentley's claims by examining a friend's view on an issue of public policy. Explore how he or she arrived at a conclusion. To what extent did group identification influence your friend's opinion? Think of all the ways your friend's group identity may have affected his or her beliefs.

observable action

Bentley: everything can be understood as representing some interest

how does a group gain power?
1. #'s
2. intensity
3. techniques

3 keys to pluralism
1. effective representation is achieved through group politics
2. all interests are represented in the system
3. no single interest dominates so there is open competition

[Handwritten annotations:]

interest groups enable a realistic analysis of the political process

Bentley
groups were a concept with which to organize all observable behavior in political life.

Truman
group behavior was not the only thing that constitutes political phenomena but i.g. pressures were enormously important

5

❖

The Alleged Mischiefs
of Faction

DAVID TRUMAN

avid Truman is seen as *the* pluralist scholar of the twentieth century. In *The Governmental Process,* Truman attends to the more benign effects of interest groups. Although he cites the anger with which many citizens look upon interest groups in American society, his analysis suggests that groups perform valuable functions in American politics and ultimately work to represent the interests of a wide range of people in the political process. This sanguine conception of group power was the dominant paradigm among scholars for a generation. In his book, Truman articulates his "disturbance theory," in which groups form around societal disturbances until they reach a state of equilibrium. This equilibrium includes groups that are antithetical to one another in what they want to achieve relative to public policy. The resulting equilibrium allows numerous interests to gain a seat at the policy-making table. Much as Madison did, Truman asserts that the multitude of these interests prohibits any particular interest from wielding too much power. Because of the multiple points of access in the American political system (e.g., federal, state, executive, legislative, and judiciary), interests have many opportunities to be heard. In the end, groups are seen as central to American democracy.

QUESTIONS TO CONSIDER

1. What functions do you believe groups serve in American politics?
2. Are all interests afforded a voice in American democracy? What evidence do you have to support your answer?

3. Are groups vital to American democracy? Why? Why not?

4. Truman argues that groups form due to increasing societal complexity. Do you believe this is accurate? Why? Why not?

Most accounts of American legislative sessions—national, state, or local— are full of references to the maneuverings and iniquities of various organized groups. Newspaper stories report that a legislative proposal is being promoted by groups of business men or school teachers or farmers or consumers or labor unions or other aggregations of citizens. Cartoonists picture the legislature as completely under the control of sinister, portly, cigar-smoking individuals labeled "special interests," while a diminutive John Q. Public is pushed aside to sulk in futile anger and pathetic frustration. A member of the legislature rises in righteous anger on the floor of the house or in a press conference to declare that the bill under discussion is being forced through by the "interests," by the most unscrupulous high-pressure "lobby" he has seen in all his years of public life. An investigating committee denounces the activities of a group as deceptive, immoral, and destructive of our constitutional methods and ideals. A chief executive attacks a "lobby" or "pressure group" as the agency responsible for obstructing or emasculating a piece of legislation that he has recommended "in the public interest."

From time to time a conscientious and observant reporter collects a series of such incidents and publishes them, exposing in the best muckraking tradition the machinations of these subversive "interests," and, if he is fortunate, breaking into the best-seller lists. Or a fictionalized treatment of them may be presented as the theme of a popular novel.[1]

SOURCE: From David B. Truman, "The Alleged Mischiefs of Faction," *The Governmental Process: Political Interests and Public Opinion* (New York: Knopf, 1958), 3–13. Reprinted with permission from Elinor G. Truman and Edwin M. Truman.

Such events are familiar even to the casual student of day-to-day politics, if only because they make diverting reading and appear to give the citizen the "low-down" on his government. He tends, along with many of his more sophisticated fellow citizens, to take these things more or less for granted, possibly because they merely confirm his conviction that "as everybody knows, politics is a dirty business." Yet at the same time he is likely to regard the activities of organized groups in political life as somehow outside the proper and normal processes of government, as the lapses of his weak contemporaries whose moral fiber is insufficient to prevent their defaulting on the great traditions of the Founding Fathers.[2] These events appear to be a modern pathology.

GROUP PRESSURES AND THE FOUNDING FATHERS

Group pressures, whatever we may wish to call them, are not new in America.[3] One of the earliest pieces of testimony to this effect is essay number 10 of *The Federalist,* which contains James Madison's classic statement of the impact of divergent groups upon government and the reasons for their development. He was arguing the virtues of the proposed Union as a means to "break and control the violence of faction," having in mind, no doubt, the groups involved in such actions of the debtor or propertyless segment of the population as Shays's Rebellion. He defined faction in broader terms, however, as "a number of citizens, whether amounting to a majority or minority of the whole, who are united and actuated by some common impulse of passion, or of interest. . . ." His observations on the source and character of such group differences merit quotation at length:

> The latent causes of faction are . . . sown in the nature of man; and we see them everywhere brought into different degrees of activity, according to the different circumstances of civil society. A zeal for different opinions concerning religion, concerning government, and many other points, as well of speculation as of practice; an attachment to different leaders ambitiously contending for pre-eminence and power; or to persons of other descriptions whose fortunes have been interesting to the human passions, have, in turn, divided mankind into parties, inflamed them with mutual animosity, and rendered them much more disposed to vex and oppress each other than to co-operate for their common good. . . . But the most common and durable source of factions has been the various and unequal distribution of property. Those who hold and those who are without property have ever formed distinct interests in society. Those who are creditors, and those who are debtors, fall under a like discrimination. A landed interest, a manufacturing interest, a mercantile interest, a moneyed interest, with many lesser interests, grow up of necessity in civilized nations, and divide them into different classes, actuated by different sentiments and views. The regulation of these various and interfering interests forms the principal task of modern legislation, and involves the spirit of party and faction in the necessary and ordinary operations of the government.

It should be noted that this analysis is not just the brilliant generalization of an armchair philosopher or pamphleteer; it represents as well the distillation from Madison's years of acquaintance with contemporary politics as a member of the Virginia Assembly and of Congress. Using the words "party" and "faction" almost interchangeably, since the political party as we know it had not yet developed, he saw the struggles of such groups as the essence of the political process. One need not concur in all his judgments to agree that the process he described had strong similarities to that of our own day.

The entire effort of which *The Federalist* was a part was one of the most skillful and important examples of pressure group activity in American history. The State ratifying conventions were handled by the Federalists with a skill that might well be the envy of a modern lobbyist. It is easy to overlook the fact that "unless the Federalists had been shrewd in manipulation as they were sound in theory, their arguments could not have prevailed."[4]

Since we have not yet come to the point of defining our terms, it may be asserted that the instances cited carry with them none of the overtones of corruption and selfishness associated with modern political groups. Such characteristics are not the distinguishing feature of group politics, but early cases of the sort are not hard to find. As early as 1720 a nearly successful effort was made to control the New Jersey Assembly, allegedly in the business interests of an outside manipulator.[5] The funding of the State debt in the First Congress provided a colorful record of the pressures used in support of the proposal. Senator William Maclay of Pennsylvania, a bitter partisan and therefore a not altogether objective observer, made the following entry in his diary under the date, March 9, 1790:

> In the Senate chamber this morning Butler said he heard a man say he would give Vining (of Delaware) one thousand guineas for his vote, but added, "I question whether he would do so in fact." So do I, too, for

he might get it for a tenth part of that sum. I do not know that pecuniary influence has actually been used, but I am certain that every other kind of management has been practiced and every tool at work that could be thought of. Officers of Government, clergy, citizens, Cincinnati, and every person under the influence of the Treasury. . . .[6]

Jefferson, no less partisan though perhaps somewhat more objective, in February, 1793, made the following note after a conference that he had had with President Washington:

> I confirmed him in the fact of the great discontents to the South, that they were grounded on seeing that their judgments and interests were sacrificed to those of the Eastern States on every occasion, and their belief that it was the effect of a corrupt squadron of voters in Congress at the command of the Treasury, and they see if the votes of those members who had an interest distinct from and contrary to the general interest of their constituents had been withdrawn, as in decency and honesty they should have been, the laws would have been the reverse of what they are in all the great questions.[7]

As a careful student of American legislatures has put it: "No one can read the story of the assumption of the State debts and the location of the capital without wondering whether the legislative manipulators of our day have really gone much beyond our forefathers in point of questionable practices."[8]

In the lusty years of the Jackson administration Alexis de Tocqueville, perhaps the keenest foreign student ever to write on American institutions, noted as one of the most striking characteristics of the nation the penchant for promoting a bewildering array of projects through organized societies, among them those using political means. "In no country in the world," he observed, "has the principle of association been more successfully used or applied to a greater multitude of objects than in America."[9] De Tocqueville was impressed by the organization of such groups and by their tendency to operate sometimes upon and sometimes parallel to the formal institutions of government. Speaking of the similarity between the representatives of such groups and the members of legislatures, he stated: "It is true that they [delegates of these societies] have not the right, like the others, of making the laws; but they have the power of attacking those which are in force and of drawing up beforehand those which ought to be enacted."[10]

Since the modern political party was, in the Jackson period, just taking the form that we would recognize today, De Tocqueville does not always distinguish sharply between it and other types of political interest groups. In his discussion of "political associations," however, he gives an account of the antitariff convention held in Philadelphia in October of 1831, the form of which might well have come from the proceedings of a group meeting in an American city today:

> Its debates were public, and they at once assumed a legislative character; the extent of the powers of Congress, the theories of free trade, and the different provisions of the tariff were discussed. At the end of ten days the Convention broke up, having drawn up an address to the American people in which it declared: (1) that Congress had not the right of making a tariff, and that the existing tariff was unconstitutional; (2) that the prohibition of free trade was prejudicial to the interests of any nation, and to those of the American people especially.[11]

Additional evidence might be cited from many quarters to illustrate the long

partisan aggregate

history of group politics in this country. Organized pressures supporting or attacking the charter of the Bank of the United States in Jackson's administration, the peculations surrounding Pendleton's "Palace of Fortune" in the pre–Civil War period, the operations of the railroads and other interests in both national and state legislatures in the latter half of the last century, the political activities of farm groups such as the Grange in the same period— these and others indicate that at no time have the activities of organized political interests not been a part of American politics.[12] Whether they indicate pathology or not, they are certainly not new.

POLITICAL GROUPS ABROAD

The political activities of organized groups are not, moreover, a peculiarly American phenomenon. As Herring observes: "Small groups have always striven for their particular interests before governmental powers."[13] If we look at the government of Great Britain, for example, we find such groups operating very much as they do in the United States, though with significant differences stemming in part from variations in the institutional milieu.

Organized political groups in Britain cover fully as extensive a segment of the life of the society as do such groups in the United States.[14] Industrial and trade organizations number in the hundreds; agriculture and its related activities are covered by twenty or thirty; welfare societies are "at least as numerous, though they are not so well organized for joint action" as are the trade groups; the hundreds of professional organizations place a major emphasis upon political activity; citizens who pay large sums in taxes are represented by associations, as are their counterparts in America; the "persistent" pedestrians are organized as well as the automobile owners; and there are the trade unions with their several million members.

Depending on their circumstances, these groups may take an open and active part in party politics in the electioneering sense—in fact, in several cases a far more active part than any such groups in this country. Such activity is not confined to the obvious case of the labor unions. The National Farmers' Union makes no pretense of impartiality between parties. It aids Conservative candidates not only by endorsement, but also by financial support. The National Union of Ratepayers' and Property Owners' Associations is a subsidiary of the Conservative party. The National Union of Teachers, in order to assure adequate representation in Parliament, is willing to give financial support to at least one member of the House of Commons.

An expected *quid pro quo* is quite as likely as in the United States to be involved in such partisan support. Jennings reports a series of demands by the National Farmers' Union after the general election of 1935 that will not sound strange to American ears. Following the election, in which it had given the successful Conservatives its usual support, the Union submitted to the Prime Minister a comprehensive policy for agriculture. A committee interviewed him shortly thereafter, and the President of the Union, who was a Conservative member of the Parliament, visited the Minister of Agriculture. Apparently dissatisfied with the results of these efforts, the Union urged each county branch to set up an "active parliamentary committee" and to engage in "intensive local propaganda so that members of Parliament in agricultural constituencies should be fully informed of the problems which were facing the industry."[15]

Because no private member's bill can pass over the Government's opposition in the House of Commons and because the Government's control of financial matters is complete, the major effort of most groups is focused on the ministers.

Jennings says of measures involving financial policy: "Where log-rolling takes place the Chancellor of the Exchequer captains the team. The pork-barrel is kept locked up in 11 Downing Street, and those who want to take part in the distribution must stand on the door-step and prove their credentials."[16] The process is different in detail from that in the Congress of the United States, because of differences in institutional practice, but the basic resemblance is unmistakable.

Although most legislation thus has its origins in the executive departments, the "inspiration" is shared with the organized interests. The groups may play an even more open role in the criticism and amendment of a proposed measure. The Government, for all practical purposes, can force the enactment of virtually any bill it chooses to support, but in a system that is fundamentally dependent on free elections the Cabinet will inevitably give satisfaction to any clear expression of public opinion. Less open methods of opposition failing, therefore, a group will attempt to bring an aroused public opinion to its support.

The political devices available under the American and British constitutions are not identical, but in both countries the organized political group is a major element in the political process. Other examples could be given to demonstrate further that the political interest group is not a peculiarly American institution. One might note that in France organized groups of business men, workers, and farmers, to say nothing of the Catholic Church, have been a central element in the governing process both before and since World War II.[17] One might elaborate on the development of such groups in Sweden, where they have become not only a vehicle for political demands but also, to a remarkable degree, administrative agencies of the state. Their activities are visible in every country where freedom of association is an element in the constitutional fabric.[18]

THE PROBLEM

It should be apparent from this brief discussion that the political interest group is neither a fleeting, transitory newcomer to the political arena nor a localized phenomenon peculiar to one member of the family of nations. The persistence and the dispersion of such organizations indicate rather that we are dealing with a characteristic aspect of our society. That such groups are receiving an increasing measure of popular and technical attention suggests the hypothesis that they are appreciably more significant in the complex and interdependent society of our own day than they were in the simpler, less highly developed community for which our constitutional arrangements were originally designed.

Many people are quite willing to acknowledge the accuracy of these propositions about political groups, but they are worried nevertheless. They are still concerned over the meaning of what they see and read of the activities of such organizations. They observe, for example, that certain farm groups apparently can induce the Government to spend hundreds of millions of dollars to maintain the price of food and to take "surplus" agricultural produce off the market while many urban residents are encountering painful difficulty in stretching their food budgets to provide adequately for their families. They observe that various labor organizations seem to be able to prevent the introduction of cheaper methods into building codes, although the cost of new housing is already beyond the reach of many. Real estate and contractors' trade associations apparently have the power to obstruct various governmental projects for slum clearance and low cost housing. Veterans' organizations seem able to secure and protect increases in pensions and other benefits almost at will. A church apparently can prevent the appropriation of Federal funds to public schools unless such funds are also given to the schools it operates in competition with the public systems. The Government has declared that stable and friendly European governments cannot be maintained unless Americans buy more goods and services abroad. Yet American shipowners and seamen's unions can secure a statutory requirement that a large proportion of the goods purchased by European countries under the Marshall Plan must be carried in American ships. Other industries and trade associations can prevent the revision of tariff rates and customs regulations that restrict imports from abroad.

In all these situations the fairly observant citizen sees various groups slugging it out with one another in pursuit of advantages from the Government. Or he sees some of them co-operating with one another to their mutual benefit. He reads of "swarms" of lobbyists "putting pressure on" congressmen and administrators. He has the impression that any group can get what it wants in Washington by deluging officials with mail and telegrams. He may then begin to wonder whether a governmental system like this can survive, whether it can carry its responsibilities in the world and meet the challenges presented by a ruthless dictatorship. He wants to see these external threats effectively met. The sentimental nonsense of the commercial advertisements aside, he values free speech, free elections, representative government, and all that these imply. He fears and resents practices and privileges that seem to place these values in jeopardy.

A common reaction to revelations concerning the more lurid activities of political groups is one of righteous indignation. Such indignation is entirely natural. It is likely, however, to be more comforting than constructive. What we seek are correctives, protections, or controls that will strengthen the practices essential in what we call democracy and that will weaken or eliminate those that really threaten that system. Uncritical anger may do little to achieve that objective, largely because it is likely to be based

upon a picture of the governmental process that is a composite of myth and fiction as well as of fact. We shall not begin to achieve control until we have arrived at a conception of politics that adequately accounts for the operations of political groups. We need to know what regular patterns are shown by group politics before we can predict its consequences and prescribe for its lapses. We need to re-examine our notions of how representative government operates in the United States before we can be confident of our statements about the effects of group activities upon it. Just as we should not know how to protect a farm house from lightning unless we knew something of the behavior of electricity, so we cannot hope to protect a governmental system from the results of group organization unless we have an adequate understanding of the political process of which these groups are a part.

Our first step in the development of a workable conception of political groups will have to be away from formal government and politics as such. We shall examine the dynamics of social groups in general, regardless of whether they are or are not involved in politics. What do we mean by the term *group?* What are the social functions of groups? What relation do they have to the behavior of individuals? How do they come into existence? Assuming that the political groups in which we are primarily interested are not basically different from other social groups, what are their distinguishing features? What variations in origin and function can we observe among political groups?

We may then consider certain general features of the relations between political groups and government in the United States. What are the difficulties that confront an attempt to analyze the role of groups in the political process? What are the connections between the increased complexity of governmental operations in the United States and the recent increases in the number of organized groups? Why have particular types of political groups become increasingly numerous and active? Why and under what circumstances do organized groups become involved in the operation of government?

In this general discussion of groups and government we shall note that the character of a group's relationship to the governing process is in part a function of the group's internal structure and of political behavior within its ranks. We shall therefore examine in some detail the variations in group organization, the factors affecting group cohesion, and the nature and techniques of group leadership. In this part of the analysis we shall be concerned with two major questions: How do these factors affect the relations between groups and government? What restraints, if any, do they impose upon the political activity of groups?

Upon these foundations we can begin to develop a meaningful conception of the role of political groups in the governing process. We shall look first at their propaganda activities and generally at their relation to what we call public opinion. We shall then analyze the connections between interest groups and political parties and their relations with the more formalized institutions of government at the various levels of the federal system. It will be convenient to discuss the latter under the conventional headings of the legislature, the executive, and the judiciary, but we shall be careful to focus our analysis upon observable operating relationships among, as well as within, these branches in order that we may avoid the pitfalls of a too literal formalism. Throughout this part of the book the questions with which we shall be primarily concerned will be: What are the factors which determine the power of groups in the various phases of the governmental process? To what extent and under what circumstances is government action the product of

organized group activity? What features of the American system tend to maximize the influence of organized groups and what features, if any, operate to confine the activities of such groups within tolerable limits?

A conception of the political process broad enough to account for the development and functioning of political groups is essential to a reliable evaluation of the alleged mischiefs of faction. To work out such a basis of interpretation is the purpose of this book.

NOTES

1. For early and somewhat quaint treatments of this sort, see the novels of Winston Churchill: *Coniston* (1906) and *Mr. Crewe's Career* (1908).

2. A learned example of this position is presented by Robert Luce: *Legislative Assemblies* (Boston: Houghton Mifflin Company, 1924), p. 385, quoting the opinion of a New York judge that contracts for lobbying services should not be enforced by the courts: "It is against the genius and policy of our government that her legislative and executive officers shall be surrounded by swarms of hired retainers of the claimants upon public bounty or justice." (Rose and Hawley v. Truax, 21 Barb. 361, 1855.) As Luce indicates, this view was not limited to the courts of New York.

3. For comments on the concern of ancient historians and of various political philosophers with the role of interest groups, see Robert M. MacIver: "Interests," *Encyclopaedia of the Social Sciences.*

4. Samuel E. Morrison and Henry S. Commager: *The Growth of the American Republic* (New York: Oxford University Press, 1930), p. 163. See also Charles A. Beard: *An Economic Interpretation of the Constitution of the United States* (New York: The Macmillan Company, 1913), chaps. 6, 8, and 9.

5. Cited in Luce: *Legislative Assemblies,* p. 367.

6. Quoted ibid., p. 409.

7. Quoted ibid., p. 410.

8. Ibid., p. 367.

9. Alexis de Tocqueville: *Democracy in America* (ed. by Phillips Bradley, New York: Alfred A. Knopf, Inc., 1945), Vol. I, p. 191. See also Vol. II, p. 106 and *passim*.

10. Ibid., Vol. I, p. 193.

11. Ibid., Vol. I, p. 194.

12. See, for example, E. Pendleton Herring: *Group Representation Before Congress* (Baltimore: The Johns Hopkins Press, 1929), pp. 30–9; A. M. Schlesinger, Jr.: *The Age of Jackson* (Boston: Little, Brown & Company, 1945), *passim*; G. G. Van Deusen: *Thurlow Weed: Wizard of the Lobby* (Boston: Little, Brown & Company, 1947), chap. 14; P. S. Reinsch: *American Legislatures and Legislative Methods* (New York: The Century Company, 1907), chap. 8; Robert Luce: *Legislative Assemblies,* chaps. 17–19. An especially interesting set of examples, notable for the careful analysis of the social setting of the groups and covering the State of Pennsylvania from 1776 to 1860, will be found in Louis Hartz: *Economic Policy and Democratic Thought: Pennsylvania, 1776–1860* (Cambridge, Mass.: Harvard University Press, 1948).

13. Herring: *Group Representation Before Congress,* p. 241. Copyright 1929 by and used with the permission of The Brookings Institution.

14. This section is based on W. Ivor Jennings: *Parliament* (Cambridge: Cambridge University Press, 1939), chaps. 2 and 7.

15. Ibid., p. 214.

16. Ibid., p. 189.

17. On the role of such groups in the Third Republic see David Thomson: *Democracy in France: The Third Republic* (London: Oxford University Press, 1946), pp. 39–74 and *passim*.

18. J. A. Corry: *Elements of Democratic Government* (New York: Oxford University Press, 1947), chap. 8; Gunnar Heckscher: "Group Organization in Sweden," *Public Opinion Quarterly,* Vol. 3, no. 4 (Winter, 1939), pp. 130–5;

interesting data on manufacturers' associations during the 1930's in Germany, Italy, Japan, France, Great Britain, and the United States are given in Robert A. Brady: *Business as a System of Power* (New York: Columbia University Press, 1943), chaps. 1–6, although the broad thesis advanced in the book is of dubious validity.

PROJECT

Conduct a case study on any specific interest group. When did it form? Why did it form? How did it form? Did it form in response to a rival group? Did a rival group form in response to your group? To what degree does the group have influence in its policy domain?

6

The Nature
of the Problem

ROBERT DAHL

This introductory chapter from Dahl's *Who Governs?* spells out a number of issues relevant to representation. Dahl contends that the American creed suggests that Americans believe in democracy (i.e., majority rule, minority rights, the rule of law) and trust that leaders will act according to the creed. Thus, political and social elites, political parties, and interest groups work on behalf of the citizenry at large. Dahl suggests that answering the question of who governs is contingent upon the policy under examination. Interest groups play an integral mediating role regardless of the policy. However, the knowledge and subsequent saliency of the issue in the minds of voters dictates the level of control the citizenry, policy elites, or interest groups will have. The more salient the issue, the more control citizens will have. Ultimately, it is not the masses or political elites that govern; rather, each has a significant part to play. Dahl's examination of power structures in New Haven provides an important empirical examination of groups in the policy-making process. In the end, his work offers support for pluralists who assert that groups serve a valuable and nonthreatening function in American politics. The following selection lays the foundation for Dahl's analysis.

QUESTIONS TO CONSIDER

1. Dahl finds great support for American democracy among Americans. Do you believe this is true today? Why? Why not?
2. Do you think whether you believe you have input in the political process affects your support for democracy?

3. To what extent do you believe policy makers attempt to shape public opinion?
4. How informed are citizens about public policies?
5. How much do you believe policy is affected by ordinary citizens?

In a political system where nearly every adult may vote but where knowledge, wealth, social position, access to officials, and other resources are unequally distributed, who actually governs?

The question has been asked, I imagine, wherever popular government has developed and intelligent citizens have reached the stage of critical self-consciousness concerning their society. It must have been put many times in Athens even before it was posed by Plato and Aristotle.

The question is peculiarly relevant to the United States and to Americans. In the first place, Americans espouse democratic beliefs with a fervency and a unanimity that have been a regular source of astonishment to foreign observers from Tocqueville and Bryce to Myrdal and Brogan. Not long ago, two American political scientists reported that 96 per cent or more of several hundred registered voters interviewed in two widely separated American cities agreed that: "Democracy is the best form of government" and "Every citizen should have an equal chance to influence government policy," and subscribed to other propositions equally basic to the democratic credo.[1] What, if anything, do these beliefs actually mean in the face of extensive inequalities in the resources different citizens can use to influence one another?

These beliefs in democracy and equality first gained wide acceptance as a part of what Myrdal later called the "American Creed" during a period when the problem of inequality was (if we can disregard for the moment the question of slavery) much less important than it is today. Indeed, the problem uppermost in the minds of the men at the Constitutional Convention in Philadelphia in 1787 could probably have been stated quite the other way around. To men concerned with what was then a unique task of adapting republican institutions to a whole nation, the very *equality* in resources of power that American society and geography tended to generate seemed to endanger political stability and liberty. In a society of equals, what checks would there be against an impetuous, unenlightened, or unscrupulous majority? A half century later, this was also the way an amazing and gifted observer, Alexis de Tocqueville, posed the question in probably the most profound analysis of American democracy ever written. For Tocqueville, the United States was the most advanced representative of a new species of society emerging from centuries of development: "In running over the pages of [European] history, we shall scarcely find a single great event of the last seven hundred years that has not promoted equality of condition." So he wrote in the introduction to the first volume of his *Democracy in America*.

Whither, then, are we tending? [he went on to ask] No one can say, for terms of comparison already fail us. There is greater equality of condition in Christian countries at the present day than there has been at any previous time, in any part of the world, so that the magnitude of what already has been done prevents us from foreseeing what is yet to be accomplished.

SOURCE: From Robert A. Dahl, *Who Governs? Democracy and Power in an American City* (New Haven, CT: Yale University Press, 1961), 1–8. Copyright © 1961 by Yale University Press. Copyright © renewed 1989 by Robert A. Dahl. Reprinted with permission from Yale University Press.

In the United States he had looked upon the future, on

> one country in the world where the great social revolution that I am speaking of seems to have nearly reached its natural limits . . . Men are there seen on a greater equality in point of fortune and intellect, or, in other words, more equal in their strength, than in any other country of the world, or in any age of which history has preserved the remembrance.[2]

The America that Tocqueville saw, however, was the America of Andrew Jackson. It was an agrarian democracy, remarkably close to the ideal often articulated by Jefferson.

Commerce, finance, and industry erupted into this agrarian society in a gigantic explosion. By the time the century approached its last decade, and another distinguished foreign observer looked upon the United States, the America of Tocqueville had already passed away. In how many senses of the word, James Bryce asked in 1899, does equality exist in the United States?

> Clearly not as regards material conditions. Sixty years ago there were no great fortunes in America, few large fortunes, no poverty. Now there is some poverty (though only in a few places can it be called pauperism), many large fortunes, and a greater number of gigantic fortunes than in any other country of the world.

He found also an intellectual elite, among whose members the "level of exceptional attainment . . . rises faster than does the general level of the multitude, so that in this regard also it appears that equality has diminished and will diminish further."

It was true that in America there were no formal marks of rank in the European sense. However, this did not

> prevent the existence of grades and distinctions in society which, though they may find no tangible expression,

are sometimes as sharply drawn as in Europe . . . The nature of a man's occupation, his education, his manners and breeding, his income, his connections, all come into view in determining whether he is in this narrow sense of the word "a gentleman."

Yet, remarkably, the universal belief in equality that Tocqueville had found sixty years earlier still persisted. "It is in this," Bryce wrote, "that the real sense of equality comes out. In America men hold others to be at bottom exactly like themselves." A man may be enormously rich, or a great orator, or a great soldier or writer, "but it is not a reason for bowing down to him, or addressing him in deferential terms, or treating him as if he was porcelain and yourself only earthenware."[3]

Now it has always been held that if equality of power among citizens is possible at all—a point on which many political philosophers have had grave doubts—then surely considerable equality of social conditions is a necessary prerequisite. But if, even in America, with its universal creed of democracy and equality, there are great inequalities in the conditions of different citizens, must there not also be great inequalities in the capacities of different citizens to influence the decisions of their various governments? And if, because they are unequal in other conditions, citizens of a democracy are unequal in power to control their government, then who in fact does govern? How does a "democratic" system work amid inequality of resources? These are the questions I want to explore by examining one urban American community, New Haven, Connecticut.

I have said "explore" because it is obvious that one cannot do more by concentrating on one community. However, New Haven embodies most of the equalities and inequalities that lend this enterprise its significance. In the course of the book, I shall examine various aspects of these that may be related to differences in the extent to which citizens can and do influence local government. But it will not hurt to start putting a little paint on the canvas now.

One might argue whether the political system of New Haven is "democratic" or "truly democratic," but only because these terms are always debatable. In everyday language, New Haven is a democratic political community. Most of its adult residents are legally entitled to vote. A relatively high proportion do vote. Their votes are, by and large, honestly counted—though absentee votes, a small fraction of the total, are occasionally manipulated. Elections are free from violence and, for all practical purposes, free from fraud. Two political parties contest elections, offer rival slates of candidates, and thus present the voters with at least some outward show of choice.

Running counter to this legal equality of citizens in the voting booth, however, is an unequal distribution of the resources that can be used for influencing the choices of voters and, between elections, of officials. Take property, for example. In 1957, the fifty largest property owners, in number less than one-sixteenth of one per cent of the taxpayers, held nearly one-third of the total assessed value of all real property in the city. Most of the fifty largest property owners were, of course, corporations: public utilities like the United Illuminating Company, which had the largest assessment ($22 million) and the Southern New England Telephone Company ($12 million); big industries like Olin Mathieson ($21 million) which had bought up the Winchester Repeating Arms Company, the famous old New Haven firearms firm; family-held firms like Sargent and A. C. Gilbert; or department stores like the century-old firm of Malley's. Of the fifty largest property owners, sixteen were manufacturing firms, nine were retail and wholesale businesses, six were privately-owned public utilities, and five were banks. Yale University was one of the biggest property owners, though it ranked only tenth in assessed value ($3.6 million)

because much of its property was tax-free. A few individuals stood out boldly on the list, like John Day Jackson, the owner and publisher of New Haven's two newspapers.

Or consider family income. In 1949, the average (median) family income in New Haven was about $2,700 a year. One family out of forty had an income of $10,000 or more; over one family out of five had an income of less than $1,000. In the Thirtieth Ward, which had the highest average family income, one family out of four had an income of $7,000 or more; in the Fifth, the poorest, over half the families had incomes of less than $2,000 a year. (Technically, the First Ward was even poorer than the Fifth for half the families there had incomes of less than $700 a year, but three-quarters of the residents of the First were students at Yale.)

The average adult in New Haven had completed the ninth grade, but in the Tenth Ward half the adults had never gone beyond elementary school. About one out of six adults in the city had gone to college. The extremes were represented by the Thirty-first Ward, where nearly half had attended college, and the Twenty-seventh, where the proportion was only one out of thirty.[4]

Thus one is forced back once more to the initial question. Given the existence of inequalities like these, who actually governs in a democracy?

Since the question is not new, one may wonder whether we do not, after all, pretty well know the answer by now. Do we not at least know what answer must be given for the present-day political system of the United States? Unfortunately no. Students of politics have provided a number of conflicting explanations for the way in which democracies can be expected to operate in the midst of inequalities in political resources. Some answers are a good deal more optimistic than others. For example, it is sometimes said that political parties provide competition for public office and thereby guarantee a relatively high degree of *role of parties*

popular control. By appealing to the voters, parties organize the unorganized, give power to the powerless, present voters with alternative candidates and programs, and insure that during campaigns they have an opportunity to learn about the merits of these alternatives. Furthermore, after the election is over, the victorious party, which now represents the preferences of a majority of voters, takes over the task of governing. The voter, therefore, does not need to participate actively in government; it is enough for him to participate in elections by the simple act of voting. By his vote he registers a preference for the general direction in which government policy should move; he cannot and does not need to choose particular policies. One answer to the question, "Who governs?" is then that competing political parties govern, but they do so with the consent of voters secured by competitive elections.

However, no sooner had observers begun to discover the extraordinary importance of political parties in the operation of democratic political systems than others promptly reduced the political party to little more than a collection of "interest groups," or sets of individuals with some values, purposes, and demands in common. If the parties were the political molecules, the interest groups were the atoms. And everything could be explained simply by studying the atoms. Neither people nor parties but interest groups, it was said, are the true units of the political system. An individual, it was argued, is politically rather helpless, but a group unites the resources of individuals into an effective force. Thus some theorists would answer our question by replying that interest groups govern; most of the actions of government can be explained, they would say, simply as the result of struggles among groups of individuals with differing interests and varying resources of influence.

The first explanation was developed by English and American writers, the second almost entirely by Americans. A third theory, much more pessimistic than the other two, was almost exclusively European in origin, though it subsequently achieved a considerable vogue in the United States. This explanation, which has both a "Left" and a "Right" interpretation, asserts that beneath the façade of democratic politics a social and economic elite will usually be found actually running things. Robert and Helen Lynd used this explanation in their famous two books on "Middletown" (Muncie, Indiana), and many studies since then have also adopted it, most notably Floyd Hunter in his analysis of the "power structure" of Atlanta.[5] Because it fits nicely with the very factors that give rise to our question, the view that a social and economic elite controls government is highly persuasive. Concentration of power in the hands of an elite is a necessary consequence, in this view, of the enormous inequalities in the distribution of resources of influence—property, income, social status, knowledge, publicity, focal position, and all the rest.

One difficulty with all of these explanations was that they left very little room for the politician. He was usually regarded merely as an agent—of majority will, the political parties, interest groups, or the elite. He had no independent influence. But an older view that could be traced back to Machiavelli's famous work, *The Prince,* stressed the enormous political potential of the cunning, resourceful, masterful leader. In this view, majorities, parties, interest groups, elites, even political systems are all to some extent pliable; a leader who knows how to use his resources to the maximum is not so much the agent of others as others are his agents. Although a gifted political entrepreneur might not exist in every political system, wherever he appeared he would make himself felt.

Still another view commingled elements of all the rest. This explanation was set out by Tocqueville as a possible course of degeneration in all democratic orders, restated by the Spanish philosopher, Ortega y Gassett, in his highly influential book, *The Revolt of the Masses* (1930), and proposed by a number of European intellectuals, after the destruction of the German Republic by Nazism, as an explanation for the origins of modern dictatorships. Although it is a theory proposed mainly by Europeans about European conditions, it is so plausible an alternative that we cannot afford to ignore it. Essentially, this theory (which has many variants) argues that under certain conditions of development (chiefly industrialization and urbanization) older, stratified, class-based social structures are weakened or destroyed; and in their place arises a mass of individuals with no secure place in the social system, rootless, aimless, lacking strong social ties, ready and indeed eager to attach themselves to any political entrepreneur who will cater to their tastes and desires. Led by unscrupulous and exploitative leaders, these rootless masses have the capacity to destroy whatever stands in their way without the ability to replace it with a stable alternative. Consequently the greater their influence on politics, the more helpless they become; the more they destroy, the more they depend upon strong leaders to create some kind of social, economic, and political organization to replace the old.

 If we ask, "Who governs?" the answer is not the mass nor its leaders but both together; the leaders cater to mass tastes and in return use the strength provided by the loyalty and obedience of the masses to weaken and perhaps even to annihilate all opposition to their rule.

A superficial familiarity with New Haven (or for that matter with almost any modern American city) would permit one to argue persuasively that each of these theories really explains the inner workings of the city's political life. However, a careful consideration of the points at which the theories diverge suggests that the broad question, "Who governs?" might be profitably subdivided

into a number of more specific questions. These questions, listed below, have guided the study of New Haven recorded in this book:

Are inequalities in resources of influence "cumulative" or "noncumulative?" That is, are people who are better off in one resource also better off in others? In other words, does the way in which political resources are distributed encourage oligarchy or pluralism?

How are important political decisions actually made?

What kinds of people have the greatest influence on decisions? Are different kinds of decisions all made by the same people? From what strata of the community are the most influential people, the leaders, drawn?

Do leaders tend to cohere in their policies and form a sort of ruling group, or do they tend to divide, conflict, and bargain? Is the pattern of leadership, in short, oligarchical or pluralistic?

What is the relative importance of the most widely distributed political resource—the right to vote? Do leaders respond generally to the interests of the few citizens with the greatest wealth and highest status—or do they respond to the many with the largest number of votes? To what extent do various citizens *use* their political resources? Are there important differences that in turn result in differences in influence?

Are the patterns of influence durable, or changing? For example, was democracy stronger in New Haven when Tocqueville contemplated the American scene? And in more recent years, as New Haven has grappled with a gigantic program of urban reconstruction, what has happened to popular control and to patterns of leadership? In general, what are the sources of change and stability in the political system?

Finally, how important is the nearly universal adherence to the "American Creed" of democracy and equality? Is the operation of the political system affected in any way by what ordinary citizens believe or profess to believe about democracy? If so, how?

The answers to these questions which seem best to fit the facts of New Haven will gradually unfold in the chapters that follow. I warn the reader, however, that I shall not attempt to dispose of all these questions in any one place. Each chapter tells only a part of the story; thus I shall not deal directly with the last pair of questions until the final chapter. Since each chapter builds upon those that precede it, the analysis in the final chapters presupposes knowledge of all that has gone before.

NOTES

1. James W. Prothro and Charles M. Grigg, "Fundamental Principles of Democracy: Bases of Agreement and Disagreement," *Journal of Politics,* 22 (1960), 278–94.

2. Alexis de Tocqueville, *Democracy in America* (New York, Vintage Books, 1955), 1, 5, 6, 14, 55.

3. James Bryce, *The American Commonwealth* (London, Macmillan, 1889), 2, 602–03, 606–07.

4. Assessments are from the city records. The average ratio of assessed value to actual prices on property sold in 1957 was 49.2, according to the New Haven Taxpayers Research Council, "Assessment of Real Estate," *Council Comment,* No. 36 (Mar. 9, 1959). Data on incomes and education are from a special tabulation by wards of the data in *U.S. Census, Characteristics of the Population, 1950.* Income data are estimates by the Census Bureau from a 20% sample.

5. Robert S. Lynd and Helen M. Lynd, *Middletown* (New York, Harcourt Brace, 1929) and *Middletown in Transition* (New York, Harcourt Brace, 1937). Floyd Hunter, *Community Power Structure* (Chapel Hill, University of North Carolina Press, 1953) and *Top Leadership, U.S.A.* (Chapel Hill, University of North Carolina Press, 1959).

PROJECT

Dahl's study examined local power structures. You, too, can conduct a similar study of power structures in your hometown. Interview elected officials, appointed officials, and local party leaders, and ask them how they perceive policy is made in your community. You should ask them about citizen influence, group influence, and the extent to which they try to shape public opinion.

7

The Contagiousness
of Conflict

E. E. SCHATTSCHNEIDER

Schattschneider's *The Semisovereign People* provides interesting insights into the "lay of the land" among interest groups in the United States. Specifically, Schattschneider introduces us to the "scope of conflict." Policy making is in large part determined by who can get into the policy-making ring. Recall that Truman suggests that the multiple channels available to interest groups through our separated, federal system serve groups well. However, Schattschneider raises some doubt regarding these claims. He contends that powerful groups purposely attempt to avoid attention and thus fly under the public's radar screen. One way to avoid attention is to curtail conflict. Like a fight that attracts notice, groups in the public's spotlight are much less likely to get things accomplished because they are under the watchful eye of the public. Additionally, Schattschneider suggests that powerful groups seek to monopolize the policy-making arena by keeping groups who could create conflict out of the ring. In the end, policy is determined by those who are able to get into the fight. The ability of a group to control the scope of conflict enables it to control the policy that is made in that domain. In short, if you cannot get a place at the table, you simply cannot eat. Schattschneider contends that most groups do not have a place at the dinner table. He criticizes pluralism and concludes that "the flaw in the pluralist heaven is that the heavenly chorus sings with a strong upper-class accent."

QUESTIONS TO CONSIDER

1. What is the scope of conflict?

2. How does one conceptualize the scope of conflict?

3. Why is the scope of conflict important?

4. For which public policies do you find conflict socialized *throughout* the citizenry?

5. For which public policies do you find very little socialized conflict among the citizenry?

6. Is it possible to widen the scope of conflict for all public policy?

7. Would we be better served if the scope of conflict is expanded among all public policies?

On a hot afternoon in August, 1943, in the Harlem section of New York City, a Negro soldier and a white policeman got into a fight in the lobby of a hotel. News of the fight spread rapidly throughout the area. In a few minutes angry crowds gathered in front of the hotel, at the police station, and at the hospital to which the injured policeman was taken. Before order could be restored, about four hundred people were injured and millions of dollars' worth of property was destroyed.

This was not a race riot. Most of the shops looted and the property destroyed by the Negro mob belonged to Negroes. As a matter of fact neither the white policeman nor the Negro soldier had anything to do with the riot they had set off; they did not participate in it, did not control it, and knew nothing about it.

Fortunately for the survival of American civilization conflict rarely erupts as violently as it did in the 1943 Harlem riot, but all conflict has about it some elements that go into the making of a riot. Nothing attracts a crowd so quickly as a fight. Nothing is so conta-

SOURCE: From E. E. Schattschneider, "The Contagiousness of Conflict," *The Semisovereign People, Re-Issue: A Realist's View of Democracy in America*. Reprinted with permission of © 1975. Wadsworth, a division of Thomson Learning, Inc.

gious. Parliamentary debates, jury trials, town meetings, political campaigns, strikes, hearings, all have about them some of the exciting qualities of a fight; all produce dramatic spectacles that are almost irresistibly fascinating to people. At the root of all politics is the universal language of conflict.

The central political fact in a free society is the tremendous contagiousness of conflict.

Every fight consists of two parts: (1) the few individuals who are actively engaged at the center and (2) the audience that is irresistibly attracted to the scene. The spectators are as much a part of the over-all situation as are the overt combatants. The spectators are an integral part of the situation, for, as likely as not, the *audience* determines the outcome of the fight. The crowd is loaded with portentousness because it is apt to be a hundred times as large as the fighting minority, and the relations of the audience and the combatants are highly unstable. Like all other chain reactions, a fight is difficult to contain. To understand any conflict it is necessary therefore to keep constantly in mind the relations between the combatants and the audience because the audience is likely to do the kinds of things that determine the outcome of the fight. This is true because the audience is overwhelming; it is never really neutral; the excitement of the conflict communicates itself to the crowd. *This is the basic pattern of all politics.*

The first proposition is that the outcome of every conflict is determined by the *extent* to which the audience becomes involved in it. That is, the outcome of all conflict is determined by the *scope* of its contagion. The number of people involved in any conflict determines what happens; every change in the number of participants, every increase or reduction in the number of participants, affects the result. Simply stated, the first proposition is that the intervention of Cole into a conflict between Able and Bart inevitably changes the nature of the conflict. Cole may join Able and tip the balance of forces in his favor, or he may support Bart and turn the balance the other way, or he may disrupt the conflict or attempt to impose his own resolution on both Able and Bart. No matter what he does, however, Cole will alter the conflict by transforming a one-to-one contest into a two-to-one conflict or a triangular conflict. Thereafter every new intervention, by Donald, Ellen, Frank, James, Emily, will alter the equation merely by enlarging the scope of conflict because each addition changes the balance of the forces involved. Conversely, every abandonment of the conflict by any of the participants changes the ratio.

The moral of this is: If a fight starts, watch the crowd, because the crowd plays the decisive role.

At the nub of politics are first, the way in which the public participates in the spread of the conflict and, second, the processes by which the unstable relation of the public to the conflict is controlled.

The second proposition is a consequence of the first. The most important strategy of politics is concerned with the scope of conflict.

So great is the change in the nature of any conflict likely to be as a consequence

of the widening involvement of people in it that the original participants are apt to lose control of the conflict altogether. Thus, Able and Bart may find, as the Harlem policeman and soldier found, that the fight they started has got out of hand and has been taken over by the audience. Therefore the contagiousness of conflict, the elasticity of its scope and the fluidity of the involvement of people are the X factors in politics.

Implicit in the foregoing propositions is another: It is extremely unlikely that both sides will be reinforced equally as the scope of the conflict is doubled or quadrupled or multiplied by a hundred or a thousand. That is, the balance of the forces recruited will almost certainly not remain constant. This is true because it is improbable that the participants in the original conflict constitute a representative sample of the larger community; nor is it likely that the successive increments are representative. Imagine what might happen if there were a hundred times as many spectators on the fringes of the conflict who sympathized with Able rather than Bart. Able would have a strong motive for trying to spread the conflict while Bart would have an overwhelming interest in keeping it private. It follows that conflicts are frequently won or lost by the success that the contestants have in getting the audience involved in the fight or in excluding it, as the case may be.

Other propositions follow. It is one of the qualities of extremely small conflicts that the relative strengths of the contestants are likely to be known in advance. In this case the stronger side may impose its will on the weaker without an overt test of strength because people are apt not to fight if they are sure to lose. This is extremely important because the scope of conflict can be most easily restricted at the very beginning. On the other hand, the weaker side may have a great potential strength provided only that it can be aroused. The stronger contestant may hesitate to use his strength because he does not know whether or not he is going to be able to isolate his antagonist. Thus, the bystanders are a part of the calculus of all conflicts. And any attempt to forecast the outcome of a fight by estimating the strength of the original contestants is likely to be fatuous.

Every change in the scope of conflict has a bias; it is partisan in its nature. That is, it must be assumed that every change in the number of participants is about something, that the newcomers have sympathies or antipathies that make it possible to involve them. By definition, the intervening bystanders are not neutral. Thus, in political conflict every change in scope changes the equation.

The logical consequence of the foregoing analysis of conflict is that the balance of forces in any conflict is not a better fixed equation until *everyone* is involved. If one tenth of 1 percent of the public is involved in conflict, the latent force of the audience is 999 times as great as the active force, and the outcome of the conflict depends overwhelmingly on what the 99.9 percent do. Characteristically, the potentially involved are more numerous than those actually involved. This analysis has a bearing on the relations between the "interested" and the "uninterested" segments of the community and sheds light on interest theories of politics. It is hazardous to assume that the spectators are uninterested because a free society maximizes the contagion of conflict; it invites intervention and gives a high priority to the participation of the public in conflict.

The foregoing statement is wholly theoretical and analytical. Is there any connection between the theory outlined here and what actually happens in politics? Since theoretically control of the scope of conflict is absolutely crucial, is there any evidence that politicians, publicists, and men of affairs are actually aware of this factor? Do politicians in the real world try to reallocate power by managing the scope of conflict? These questions are important because they may shed light on the dynamics of politics, on what actually happens in the political process, and on what can or cannot be accomplished in the political system. In other words, the role of the scope of conflict in politics is so great that it makes necessary a new interpretation of the political system.

If it is true that the result of political contests is determined by the scope of public involvement in conflicts, much that has been written about politics becomes nonsense, and we are in for a revolution in our thinking about politics. The scope factor overthrows the familiar simplistic calculus based on the model of a tug of war of measurable forces. One is reminded of the ancient observation that the battle is not necessarily won by the strong nor the race by the swift. The scope factor opens up vistas of a new kind of political universe.

In view of the highly strategic character of politics we ought not to be surprised that the instruments of strategy are likely to be important in inverse proportion to the amount of public attention given to them.[1]

Madison understood something about the relation of scope to the outcome of conflict. His famous essay No. 10 in the *Federalist Papers* should be reread in the context of this discussion.

> The smaller the society, the fewer probably will be the distinct parties and interests composing it, the more frequently will a majority be found of the same party; and the smaller number of individuals composing a majority, and the smaller the compass within which they are placed, the more easily they will concert and execute their plans of oppression. Extend the sphere and you take in a greater variety of parties and interests; you make it less probable that a majority of the whole will

have a common motive to invade the rights of other citizens.

While Madison saw some of the elements of the situation, no one has followed up his lead to develop a general theory. The question of the scope of conflict is approached obliquely in the literature of political warfare. The debate is apt to deal with *procedural questions* which have an unavowed bearing on the question. The very fact that the subject is handled so gingerly is evidence of its explosive potential.

While there is no explicit formulation in the literature of American politics of the principle that the scope of a conflict determines its outcome, there is a vast amount of controversy that can be understood only in the light of this proposition. That is, throughout American history tremendous efforts have been made to control the scope of conflict, but the rationalizations of the efforts are interesting chiefly because they have been remarkably confusing. Is it possible to reinterpret American politics by exposing the unavowed factor in these discussions?

A look at political literature shows that there has indeed been a *long-standing struggle between the conflicting tendencies toward the privatization and socialization of conflict.* On the one hand, it is easy to identify a whole battery of ideas calculated to restrict the scope of conflict or even to keep it entirely out of the public domain. A long list of ideas concerning individualism, free private enterprise, localism, privacy, and economy in government seems to be designed to privatize conflict or to restrict its scope or to limit the use of public authority to enlarge the scope of conflict. A tremendous amount of conflict is controlled by keeping it so private that it is almost completely invisible. Reference to this strategy abounds in the literature of politics, but the rationalizations of the strategy make no allusion to the relation of these ideas

to the scope of conflict. The justifications are nearly always on other grounds.

On the other hand, it is equally easy to identify another battery of ideas contributing to the socialization of conflict. Universal ideas in the culture, ideas concerning equality, consistency, equal protection of the laws, justice, liberty, freedom of movement, freedom of speech and association, and civil rights tend to socialize conflict. These concepts tend to make conflict contagious; they invite outside intervention in conflict and form the basis of appeals to public authority for redress of private grievances. Here again the rationalizations are made on grounds which do not avow any specific interest in an expansion of the scope of conflict though the relation becomes evident as soon as we begin to think about it. Scope is the unlisted guest of honor at all of these occasions.

It may be said, therefore, that men of affairs do in fact make an effort to control the scope of conflict though they usually explain what they do on some other grounds. The way the question is handled suggests that the real issue may be too hot to handle otherwise. We are bound to suppose therefore that control of the scale of conflict has always been a prime instrument of political strategy, whatever the language of politics may have been.

A better understanding of circuitous references to the strategic role of the scope factor may be gained if we examine some of the procedural issues which have been most widely debated in American politics. Do these issues have a bearing on the practical meaning of the scope conflict?

The role of conflict in the political system depends, first, on the morale, self-confidence, and security of the individuals and groups who must challenge the dominant groups in the community in order to raise an opposition.

People are not likely to start a fight if they are certain that they are going to be

repression as false unanimity

severely penalized for their efforts. In this situation, repression may assume the guise of a false unanimity. A classic historical instance is the isolation of the Negro in some southern communities. Dollard says of the southern caste system that "it is a way of limiting conflict between the races. . . . Middle class Negroes are especially sensitive to their isolation and feel the lack of a forum in Southern towns where problems of the two races could be discussed."[2] The controversy about civil rights in connection with race relations refers not merely to the rights of southern Negroes to protest but also to the rights of "outsiders" to intervene.

The civil rights of severely repressed minorities and all measures for public or private intervention in disputes about the status of these minorities become meaningful when we relate them to the attempt to make conflict visible. Scope is the stake in these discussions.

Attempts to impose unanimity are made in one-party areas in the North as well as in the South. Vidich and Bensman describe the process by which the school board in a small town in upstate New York undertakes to control a political situation by limiting conflict. Commenting on the procedures of the board, the authors say that it attempts to deal with critics by making "greater efforts at concealment." These efforts "result in more strict adherence to the principle of unanimity of decision."[3]

In a similar situation, in a Michigan village, "the practice of holding secret meetings was defended Monday night by Chester McGonigal, president of the Board of Education at James Couzen's Agricultural School. Mr. McGonigal said that the Bath school board would continue to hold discussion meetings closed to the public and that only decisions reached would be announced."[4]

Perhaps the whole political strategy of American local government should be re-examined in the light of this discussion. The emphasis in municipal reform movements on nonpartisanship in local government may be producing an unforeseen loss of public interest in local government. There is a profound internal inconsistency in the idea of nonpartisan local self-government.

In modern times a major struggle over the socialization of conflict has taken place in the field of labor relations. When President Theodore Roosevelt intervened in the coal strike in 1902, his action was regarded by many conservative newspaper editors as an "outrageous interference" in a private dispute.[5] On the other hand, the very words "union," "collective bargaining," "union recognition," "strike," "industrial unionism," and "industry-wide bargaining" imply a tremendous socialization of a conflict which was once regarded as a purely private matter concerning only the employer and the individual workman.

The scope of the labor conflict is close to the essence of the controversy about collective bargaining: industrial and craft unionism, industrywide bargaining, sympathy strikes, union recognition and security, the closed shop, picketing, disclosure of information, political activity of unions, labor legislation, etc. All affect the scale of labor conflict. At every point the intervention of "outsiders," union organizers, federal and state agencies, courts, and police, has been disputed. The controversy has been to a very large degree about who can get into the fight and who is excluded.

Each side has had an adverse interest in the efforts of the other to extend the scale of its organization. Says Max Forester, "Lately, American employers have been showing a renewed interest in industry-wide negotiations as a means of restoring a modicum of industry's 'lost power' at the bargaining table."[6]

The attempt to control the scope of conflict has a bearing on federal-state-local relations, for one way to restrict the scope of conflict is to *localize* it, while one way to expand it is to nationalize it. One of the most remarkable developments in recent American politics is the extent to which the federal, state, and local governments have become involved in *doing the same kinds of things* in large areas of public policy, so that it is possible for contestants to move freely from one level of government to another in an attempt to find the level at which they might try most advantageously to get what they want. This development has opened up vast new areas for the politics of scope. It follows that debates about federalism, local self-government, centralization and decentralization are actually controversies about the scale of conflict.

In the case of a village of 1,000 within a state having a population of 3,500,000, a controversy lifted from the local to the state or the national level multiplies its scope by 3,500 or 180,000 times. Inevitably the outcome of a contest is controlled by the level at which the decision is made. What happens when the scope of conflict is multiplied by 180,000? (1) There is a great probability that the original contestants will lose control of the matter. (2) A host of new considerations and complications are introduced, and a multitude of new resources for a resolution of conflict becomes available; solutions inconceivable at a lower level may be worked out at a higher level.

The nationalization of politics inevitably breaks up old local power monopolies and old sectional power complexes; as a matter of fact, the new dimension produces so great a change in the scale of organization and the locus of power that it may take on a semirevolutionary character. The change of direction of party cleavages produced by the shift from sectional to national alignments has opened up a new political universe, a new order of possibilities and impossibilities.

Since 1920 the Negro population of the United States has increased by nearly five million, but nearly all of the increase has been in the northern states. There

are now six northern states with a Negro population larger than the Negro population of Arkansas. These migrations have nationalized race relations and produced a new ratio of forces in the conflict over segregation and discrimination. The appeal for help in the conflict is from the 13 percent in the South to the 87 percent outside the South.

Everywhere the trends toward the privatization and socialization of conflict have been disguised as tendencies toward the centralization or decentralization, localization or nationalization of politics.

The question of scope is intrinsic in all concepts of political organization. The controversy about the nature and role of political parties and pressure groups, the relative merits of sectional and national party alignments, national party discipline, the locus of power in party organizations, the competitiveness of the party system, the way in which parties develop issues, and all attempts to democratize the internal processes of the parties are related to the scope of the political system.

The attack on politics, politicians, and political parties and the praise of nonpartisanship are significant in terms of the control of the scale of conflict. One-party systems, as an aspect of sharply sectional party alignments, have been notoriously useful instruments for the limitation of conflict and depression of political participation. This tends to be equally true of measures designed to set up nonpartisan government or measures designed to take important public business out of politics altogether.

The system of free private business enterprise is not merely a system of private ownership of property; it depends even more for its survival on the privacy of information about business transactions. It is probably true that the business system could not survive a full public disclosure of its internal transactions, because publicity would lead to the discovery and development of so many

conflicts that large-scale public intervention would be inescapable.

why democracy is important

To a great extent, the whole discussion of the role of government in modern
society is at root a question of the scale
conflict. *Democratic government is the greatest
single instrument for the socialization of conflict
in the American community*. The controversy
about democracy might be interpreted in
these terms also. Government in a democracy is a great engine for expanding the
scale of conflict. Government is never far
away when conflict breaks out. On the
other hand, if the government lacks power
or resources, vast numbers of potential
conflicts cannot be developed because
the community is unable to do anything
about them. Therefore, government thrives
on conflict. The work of the government
has been aided and abetted by a host of
public and private agencies and organizations designed to exploit every rift in the
private world. Competitiveness is intensified by the legitimation of outside interference in private conflicts. It is necessary
only to mention political parties, pressure
groups, the courts, congressional investigations, governmental regulatory agencies,
freedom of speech and press, among others,
to show the range and variety of instruments available to the government for
breaking open private conflicts. How does
it happen that the government is the largest
publisher in the country? Why is everything about public affairs vastly more news-
worthy than business affairs are?

The scope of political conflict in
the United States has been affected by
the world crisis, which has fostered the
development of a powerful national
government operating on a global scale.
Industrialization, urbanization, and nationalization have all but destroyed the meaning of the word "local" and have opened
up great new areas of public interest and
produced a new order of conflicts and
alignments on an unprecedented scale.
The visibility of conflict has been affected
by the annihilation of space which has
brought into view a new world. Universal
suffrage, the most ambitious attempt to
socialize conflict in American history,
takes on a new meaning with the nationalization of politics and the development
of a national electorate.

The development of American political institutions reflects the scale of their
participation in conflict. The history of
the United States Senate illustrates the
way in which a public institution is affected
by its widening involvement in national
politics. In a series of decisions, the Senate
first established the principle that individual senators are not bound by the instruc-
tions of state legislatures. Next, the direct
popular election of senators has assimilated the Senate into the democratic
system. It is noteworthy that the direct
election of senators was followed shortly
by the abolition of "executive" sessions.
Today the Senate is a national institution;
its survival as a major political institution
has depended on its capacity to keep pace
with the expanding political universe.

The history of the Presidency illustrates the same tendency. The rise of
political parties and the extension of
the suffrage produced the plebiscitary
Presidency. The growth of presidential
party leadership and the development
of the Presidency as the political instrument of a national constituency have
magnified the office tremendously. The
Presidency has in turn become the principal instrument for the nationalization
of politics.

The universalization of the franchise,
the creation of a national electorate, and
the development of the plebiscitary
Presidency elected by a national constituency have facilitated the socialization
of conflict. Thus, modern government
has become the principal molder of the
conflict system.

On the other hand, even in the public
domain, extraordinary measures are taken
occasionally to protect the internal processes of public agencies from publicity.

Note the way in which the internal processes of the Supreme Court are handled, or the way diplomatic correspondence is shielded against public scrutiny, or the manner in which meetings of the President's cabinet are sealed off from the press, or the way in which the appearance of unanimity is used to check public intervention in the internal processes of the government at many critical points. Or note how Congress suppresses public information about its own internal expenditures. Everywhere privacy and publicity are potent implements of government.

The best point at which to manage conflict is before it starts. Once a conflict starts it is not easy to control because it is difficult to be exclusive about a fight. If one side is too hard-pressed, the impulse to redress the balance by inviting in outsiders is almost irresistible. Thus, the exclusion of the Negro from southern politics could be brought about only at the price of establishing a one-party system.

The expansion of the conflict may have consequences that are extremely distasteful to the original participants.[7] The tremendous growth of the Democratic Party after 1932 gave rise to a conflict between the old regular organizations and the newcomers. Why, for example, do the regular organizations prefer to take care of the new party workers in ad hoc organizations such as the Volunteers for Stevenson?

Other tensions within the Democratic party resulted from the increased political activity of labor unions, tensions between the old regular Democratic party organizations and the new political arm of the labor movement. On the other side, a factor in the lack of success of the Republican party in recent years seems to have been the reluctance of the old regular Republican party organizations to assimilate new party workers. At a time when tens of millions of Americans have developed a new interest in politics, the assimilation of newcomers into the old organizations has become a major problem, made difficult by the fact that every expansion of an association tends to reallocate power. Thus the very success of movements creates difficulties.

Is this not true of the labor movement also? Is it not likely that undemocratic procedures in labor unions are related to the attempt of old cadres to maintain control in the face of a great expansion of the membership? The growth of organizations is never an unmixed blessing to the individuals who first occupied the field. This seems to be true of all growing communities, rapidly expanding suburban communities for another example.

The dynamics of the expansion of the scope of conflict are something like this:

1. Competitiveness is the mechanism for the expansion of the scope of conflict. It is the *loser* who calls in outside help. (Jefferson, defeated within the Washington administration, went to the country for support.) The expansion of the electorate resulted from party competition for votes. As soon as it becomes likely that a new social group will get the vote, *both* parties favor the extension. *This is the expanding universe of politics.* On the other hand, any attempt to monopolize politics is almost by definition an attempt to limit the scope of conflict.

2. Visibility is a factor in the expanding of the scope of conflict. A democratic government lives by publicity. This proposition can be tested by examining the control of publicity in undemocratic regimes. Says Michael Lindsay about Communist China:

> It is probably hard for the ordinary citizen of a democratic country to envisage the problem of obtaining reliable information about a totalitarian country. In democratic countries, especially in the United States, policy formation takes place with a good deal of publicity. When one turns to a totalitarian country, such

as the Chinese People's Republic, the situation is completely different. All publications are controlled by the government and are avowedly propagandist. Criticism and discussion only appear when the government has decided to allow them. The process of policy formation is almost completely secret.[8]

3. The effectiveness of democratic government *as an instrument for the socialization of conflict depends on the amplitude of its powers and resources.* A powerful and resourceful government is able to respond to conflict situations by providing an arena for them, publicizing them, protecting the contestants against retaliation, and taking steps to rectify the situations complained of; it may create new agencies to hear new categories of complaints and take special action about them.

Every social institution is affected by the way in which its internal processes are publicized. For example, the survival of the family as a social institution depends to a great extent on its privacy. It is almost impossible to imagine what forces in society might be released if all conflict in the private domain were thrown open for public exploitation. Procedures for the control of the expansive power of conflict determine the shape of the political system.

There is nothing intrinsically good or bad about any given scope of conflict. Whether a large conflict is better than a small conflict depends on what the conflict is about and what people want to accomplish. A change of scope makes possible a new pattern of competition, a new balance of forces, and a new result, but it also *makes impossible a lot of other things.*

While the language of politics is often oblique and sometimes devious, it is not difficult to show that the opposing tendencies toward the privatization and socialization of conflict underlie all strategy.

The study of politics calls for a sense of proportion; in the present case it requires a sense of the relative proportions of the belligerents and the spectators. At the outset of every political conflict the relations of the belligerents and the audience are so unstable that it is impossible to calculate the strength of the antagonists because all quantities in the equation are indeterminate until *all* of the bystanders have been committed.

Political conflict is not like a football game, played on a measured field by a fixed number of players in the presence of an audience scrupulously excluded from the playing field. Politics is much more like the original primitive game of football in which everybody was free to join, a game in which the whole population of one town might play the entire population of another town, moving freely back and forth across the countryside.

Many conflicts are narrowly confined by a variety of devices, but the distinctive quality of political conflicts is that the relations between the players and the audience have not been well defined and there is usually nothing to keep the audience from getting into the game.

NOTES

1. "The indirect approach is as fundamental to the realm of politics as to that of sex." Liddell Hart, quoted by Al Newman in *The Reporter,* October 15, 1958, p. 45.

2. John Dollard, *Caste and Class in a Southern Town,* 3d ed., Doubleday and Company, Garden City, 1957, p. 72. See also pp. 208–211 for a discussion of bipartisan arrangements in the South to depress conflict. Dollard discusses the impact of the one-party system on voting participation. Often the argument is made that the Negro *would be contented if left alone by outsiders.*

3. Vidich and Bensman, *Small Town in Mass Society,* Princeton, 1958. Members of the board resort to "inchoately arrived-at unanimous decisions in which no vote, or only a

perfunctory one, is taken." They "attempt to minimize or avoid crises, and this leads to further demands for unanimity and conceal-ment." pp. 172–173.

"There is always the danger that, should an issue come into the open, conflicting par-ties will appeal to outside individuals or groups or to more important figures in the machine. Public sentiment could easily be mobilized around the issues." p. 127.

"In the ordinary conduct of business in this manner, issues and conflict never become visi-ble at the public level. Undisciplined appeals to outside groups which would threaten the monopoly of power of the controlling group do not occur." p. 128. See also p. 133.

4. Lansing (Michigan) *State Journal,* July 15, 1958. The statement was made in response to a challenge following an election contest.

5. See Frederick Lewis Allen, *The Great Pierpont Morgan,* Bantam Biography, New York, 1956, pp. 175–177.

6. *New York Herald Tribune,* February 1, 1959. See also statements by George Romney, president of American Motors Corporation, *Wall Street Journal,* January 21 and February 2, 1959.

7. A classical case is described by John F. Fairbank ("Formosa through China's Eyes," *New Republic,* October 13, 1958), in terms of Chinese military and diplomatic history. "Contenders for power in traditional China commonly found it essential to utilize the barbarians, for the latter were powerful fight-ers, though often naïve in politics and easily swayed by their feelings of pride and fear. There is a great body of lore and precedent on this subject in Chinese historical annals. Sometimes the Chinese were out-manipu-lated by the barbarians. The Sung Emperors, for example, made a mistake in getting Mongol help against the Jurchen invaders from Manchuria; the Mongols eventually conquered China. Similarly the Manchus stayed to conquer and rule the country."

8. *New York Times Magazine,* "The Chinese Puzzle: Mao's Foreign Policy," October 12, 1958.

PROJECT

In Table 1.4 you saw lists of the most powerful lobbying groups in the United States. It is highly likely that you are not a member of any of those groups. It is also likely you do not know much about what these groups do, how they go about getting what they want, and how they affect public policy. Select one of those groups and examine the level of conflict they have in their policy domain. Tie your findings to the writings of the pluralists or the writings of Schattschneider.

8

The Higher Circles

C. WRIGHT MILLS

The Power Elite is representative of a wide literature criticizing democratic institutions. Like Schattschneider, some scholars are not convinced that democracy is well served by a diverse and widespread interest group system. These scholars argue that most American policy has been controlled by a small group of individuals who are disconnected from the democratic process. Most troubling, they suggest that it would be empirically impossible to detail who these elite are and how they produce public policy. Additionally, Mills and others contend that through the pleasantries of modern society many people become inattentive to what is going on in government. Not only do we not know what is going on, we cease to care about it. Consequently, the iron triangles of powerful groups, policy makers, and bureaucrats dominate public policy in their policy domains. For Mills, democracy is a sham.

QUESTIONS TO CONSIDER

1. In what ways does Mills's analysis differ from that of the pluralists? How do you think the pluralists would respond to his analysis?
2. Do you think Mills would change his analysis if he were writing today?
3. How accurate do you believe Mills's assessments are?
4. Are there some policies that may be more or less likely to be dominated by elites (as Mills describes them)? Why is this so?

The power of ordinary men are circumscribed by the everyday worlds in which they live, yet even in these rounds of job, family, and neighborhood they often seem driven by forces they can neither understand nor govern. "Great changes" are beyond their control, but affect their conduct and outlook none the less. The very framework of modern society confines them to projects not their own, but from every side, such changes now press upon the men and women of the mass society, who accordingly feel that they are without purpose in an epoch in which they are without power.

But not all men are in this sense ordinary. As the means of information and of power are centralized, some men come to occupy positions in American society from which they can look down upon, so to speak, and by their decisions mightily affect, the everyday worlds of ordinary men and women. They are not made by their jobs; they set up and break down jobs for thousands of others; they are not confined by simple family responsibilities; they can escape. They may live in many hotels and houses, but they are bound by no one community. They need not merely "meet the demands of the day and hour"; in some part, they create these demands, and cause others to meet them. Whether or not they profess their power, their technical and political experience of it far transcends that of the underlying population. What Jacob Burckhardt said of "great men," most Americans might well say of their elite: "They are all that we are not."[1]

The power elite is composed of men whose positions enable them to transcend the ordinary environments of ordinary men and women; they are in positions to make decisions having major consequences. Whether they do or do not make such decisions is less important than the fact that they do occupy such pivotal positions: their failure to act, their failure to make decisions, is itself an act that is often of greater consequence than the decisions they do make. For they are in command of the major hierarchies and organizations of modern society. They rule the big corporations. They run the machinery of the state and claim its prerogatives. They direct the military establishment. They occupy the strategic command posts of the social structure, in which are now centered the effective means of the power and the wealth and the celebrity which they enjoy.

The power elite are not solitary rulers. Advisers and consultants, spokesmen and opinion-makers are often the captains of their higher thought and decision. Immediately below the elite are the professional politicians of the middle levels of power, in the Congress and in the pressure groups, as well as among the new and old upper classes of town and city and region. Mingling with them, in curious ways which we shall explore, are those professional celebrities who live by being continually displayed but are never, so long as they remain celebrities, displayed enough. If such celebrities are not at the head of any dominating hierarchy, they do often have the power to distract the attention of the public or afford sensations to the masses, or, more directly, to gain the ear of those who do occupy positions of direct power. More or less unattached, as critics of morality and technicians of power, as spokesmen of God and creators of mass sensibility, such celebrities and consultants are part of the immediate scene in which the drama of the elite is enacted. But that drama itself is centered in the command posts of the major institutional hierarchies.

SOURCE: From C. Wright Mills, "The Higher Circles," *The Power Elite* (Oxford: Oxford University Press, 2000), 3–29. Copyright 1956, 2000 by Oxford University Press, Inc. Used by permission of Oxford University Press, Inc.

1

The truth about the nature and the power of the elite is not some secret which men of affairs know but will not tell. Such men hold quite various theories about their own roles in the sequence of event and decision. Often they are uncertain about their roles, and even more often they allow their fears and their hopes to affect their assessment of their own power. No matter how great their actual power, they tend to be less acutely aware of it than of the resistances of others to its use. Moreover, most American men of affairs have learned well the rhetoric of public relations, in some cases even to the point of using it when they are alone, and thus coming to believe it. The personal awareness of the actors is only one of the several sources one must examine in order to understand the higher circles. Yet many who believe that there is no elite, or at any rate none of any consequence, rest their argument upon what men of affairs believe about themselves, or at least assert in public.

There is, however, another view: those who feel, even if vaguely, that a compact and powerful elite of great importance does now prevail in America often base that feeling upon the historical trend of our time. They have felt, for example, the domination of the military event, and from this they infer that generals and admirals, as well as other men of decision influenced by them, must be enormously powerful. They hear that the Congress has again abdicated to a handful of men decisions clearly related to the issue of war or peace. They know that the bomb was dropped over Japan in the name of the United States of America, although they were at no time consulted about the matter. They feel that they live in a time of big decisions; they know that they are not making any. Accordingly, as they consider the present as history, they infer that at its center, making decisions or

failing to make them, there must be an elite of power.

On the one hand, those who share this feeling about big historical events assume that there is an elite and that its power is great. On the other hand, those who listen carefully to the reports of men apparently involved in the great decisions often do not believe that there is an elite whose powers are of decisive consequence.

Both views must be taken into account, but neither is adequate. The way to understand the power of the American elite lies neither solely in recognizing the historic scale of events nor in accepting the personal awareness reported by men of apparent decision. Behind such men and behind the events of history, linking the two, are the major institutions of modern society. These hierarchies of state and corporation and army constitute the means of power; as such they are now of a consequence not before equaled in human history—and at their summits, there are now those command posts of modern society which offer us the sociological key to an understanding of the role of the higher circles in America.

Within American society, major national power now resides in the economic, the political, and the military domains. Other institutions seem off to the side of modern history, and, on occasion, duly subordinated to these. No family is as directly powerful in national affairs as any major corporation; no church is as directly powerful in the external biographies of young men in America today as the military establishment; no college is as powerful in the shaping of momentous events as the National Security Council. Religious, educational, and family institutions are not autonomous centers of national power; on the contrary, these decentralized areas are increasingly shaped by the big three, in which developments of decisive and immediate consequence now occur.

Families and churches and schools adapt to modern life; governments and armies and corporations shape it; and, as they do so, they turn these lesser institutions into means for their ends. Religious institutions provide chaplains to the armed forces where they are used as a means of increasing the effectiveness of its morale to kill. Schools select and train men for their jobs in corporations and their specialized tasks in the armed forces. The extended family has, of course, long been broken up by the industrial revolution, and now the son and the father are removed from the family, by compulsion if need be, whenever the army of the state sends out the call. And the symbols of all these lesser institutions are used to legitimate the power and the decisions of the big three.

The life-fate of the modern individual depends not only upon the family into which he was born or which he enters by marriage, but increasingly upon the corporation in which he spends the most alert hours of his best years; not only upon the school where he is educated as a child and adolescent, but also upon the state which touches him throughout his life; not only upon the church in which on occasion he hears the word of God, but also upon the army in which he is disciplined.

If the centralized state could not rely upon the inculcation of nationalist loyalties in public and private schools, its leaders would promptly seek to modify the decentralized educational system. If the bankruptcy rate among the top five hundred corporations were as high as the general divorce rate among the thirty-seven million married couples, there would be economic catastrophe on an international scale. If members of armies gave to them no more of their lives than do believers to the churches to which they belong, there would be a military crisis.

Within each of the big three, the typical institutional unit has become enlarged, has become administrative, and, in the power of its decisions, has become centralized. Behind these developments there is a fabulous technology, for as institutions, they have incorporated this technology and guide it, even as it shapes and paces their developments.

The economy—once a great scatter of small productive units in autonomous balance—has become dominated by two or three hundred giant corporations, administratively and politically interrelated, which together hold the keys to economic decisions.

The political order, once a decentralized set of several dozen states with a weak spinal cord, has become a centralized, executive establishment which has taken up into itself many powers previously scattered, and now enters into each and every cranny of the social structure.

The military order, once a slim establishment in a context of distrust fed by state militia, has become the largest and most expensive feature of government, and, although well versed in smiling public relations, now has all the grim and clumsy efficiency of a sprawling bureaucratic domain.

In each of these institutional areas, the means of power at the disposal of decision makers have increased enormously; their central executive powers have been enhanced; within each of them modern administrative routines have been elaborated and tightened up.

As each of these domains becomes enlarged and centralized, the consequences of its activities become greater, and its traffic with the others increases. The decisions of a handful of corporations bear upon military and political as well as upon economic developments around the world. The decisions of the military establishment rest upon and grievously affect political life as well as the very level of economic activity. The decisions made within the political domain determine economic activities and military programs. There is no longer, on the one hand, an economy, and, on the other hand, a political order containing a military establishment unimportant to politics and to money-making. There is a political economy linked, in a thousand ways, with military institutions and decisions. On each side of the world-split running through central Europe and around the Asiatic rimlands, there is an ever-increasing interlocking of economic, military, and political structures.[2] If there is government intervention in the corporate economy, so is there corporate intervention in the governmental process. In the structural sense, this triangle of power is the source of the interlocking directorate that is most important for the historical structure of the present.

The fact of the interlocking is clearly revealed at each of the points of crisis of modern capitalist society—slump, war, and boom. In each, men of decision are led to an awareness of the interdependence of the major institutional orders. In the nineteenth century, when the scale of all institutions was smaller, their liberal integration was achieved in the automatic economy, by an autonomous play of market forces, and in the automatic political domain, by the bargain and the vote. It was then assumed that out of the imbalance and friction that followed the limited decisions then possible a new equilibrium would in due course emerge. That can no longer be assumed, and it is not assumed by the men at the top of each of the three dominant hierarchies.

For given the scope of their consequences, decisions—and indecisions—in any one of these ramify into the others, and hence top decisions tend either to become co-ordinated or to lead to a commanding indecision. It has not always been like this. When numerous small entrepreneurs made up the economy, for example, many of them could fail and the consequences still remain local; political and military authorities did not intervene. But now, given political expectations and military commitments, can they afford to allow key units of the private corporate economy to break down in slump? Increasingly, they do intervene in economic affairs, and as they do so, the controlling decisions in each order are inspected by agents of the other two, and economic, military, and political structures are interlocked.

At the pinnacle of each of the three enlarged and centralized domains, there have arisen those higher circles which make up the economic, the political, and the military elites. At the top of the economy, among the corporate rich, there are the chief executives; at the top of the political order, the members of the political directorate; at the top of the military establishment, the elite of soldier-statesmen clustered in and around the Joint Chiefs of Staff and the upper echelon. As each of these domains has coincided with the others, as decisions tend to become total in their consequence, the leading men in each of the three domains of power—the warlords, the corporation chieftains, the political directorate—tend to come together, to form the power elite of America.

2

The higher circles in and around these command posts are often thought of in terms of what their members possess: they have a greater share than other people of the things and experiences that are most highly valued. From this point of view, the elite are simply those who have the most of what there is to have, which is generally held to include money, power, and prestige—as well as all the ways of life to which these lead.[3] But the elite are not simply those who have the most, for they could not "have the most" were it not for their positions in the great institutions. For such institutions are the necessary bases of power, of wealth, and of prestige, and at the same time, the chief means of exercising power, of acquiring and retaining wealth, and of cashing in the higher claims for prestige.

By the powerful we mean, of course, those who are able to realize their will, even if others resist it. No one, accordingly, can be truly powerful unless he has access to the command of major institutions, for it is over these institutional means of power that the truly powerful are, in the first instance, powerful. Higher politicians and key officials of government command such institutional power; so do admirals and generals, and so do the major owners and executives of the larger corporations. Not all power, it is true, is anchored in and exercised by means of such institutions, but only within and through them can power be more or less continuous and important.

Wealth also is acquired and held in and through institutions. The pyramid of wealth cannot be understood merely in terms of the very rich; for the great inheriting families, as we shall see, are now supplemented by the corporate institutions of modern society: every one of the very rich families has been and is closely connected—always legally and frequently managerially as well—with one of the multi-million dollar corporations.

The modern corporation is the prime source of wealth, but, in latter-day capitalism, the political apparatus also opens and closes many avenues to wealth. The amount as well as the source of income, the power over consumer's goods as well as over productive capital, are determined by position within the political economy. If our interest in the very rich goes beyond their lavish or their miserly consumption, we must

examine their relations to modern forms of corporate property as well as to the state; for such relations now determine the chances of men to secure big property and to receive high income.

Great prestige increasingly follows the major institutional units of the social structure. It is obvious that prestige depends, often quite decisively, upon access to the publicity machines that are now a central and normal feature of all the big institutions of modern America. Moreover, one feature of these hierarchies of corporation, state, and military establishment is that their top positions are increasingly interchangeable. One result of this is the accumulative nature of prestige. Claims for prestige, for example, may be initially based on military roles, then expressed in and augmented by an educational institution run by corporate executives, and cashed in, finally, in the political order, where, for General Eisenhower and those he represents, power and prestige finally meet at the very peak. Like wealth and power, prestige tends to be cumulative: the more of it you have, the more you can get. These values also tend to be translatable into one another: the wealthy find it easier than the poor to gain power; those with status find it easier than those without it to control opportunities for wealth.

If we took the one hundred most powerful men in America, the one hundred wealthiest, and the one hundred most celebrated away from the institutional positions they now occupy, away from their resources of men and women and money, away from the media of mass communication that are now focused upon them— then they would be powerless and poor and uncelebrated. For power is not of a man. Wealth does not center in the person of the wealthy. Celebrity is not inherent in any personality. To be celebrated, to be wealthy, to have power requires access to major institutions, for the institutional positions men occupy determine in large part their chances to have and to hold these valued experiences.

3

The people of the higher circles may also be conceived as members of a top social stratum, as a set of groups whose members know one another, see one another socially and at business, and so, in making decisions, take one another into account. The elite, according to this conception, feel themselves to be, and are felt by others to be, the inner circle of "the upper social classes."[4] They form a more or less compact social and psychological entity; they have become self-conscious members of a social class. People are either accepted into this class or they are not, and there is a qualitative split, rather than merely a numerical scale, separating them from those who are not elite. They are more or less aware of themselves as a social class and they behave toward one another differently from the way they do toward members of other classes. They accept one another, understand one another, marry one another, tend to work and to think if not together at least alike.

Now, we do not want by our definition to prejudge whether the elite of the command posts are conscious members of such a socially recognized class, or whether considerable proportions of the elite derive from such a clear and distinct class. These are matters to be investigated. Yet in order to be able to recognize what we intend to investigate, we must note something that all biographies and memoirs of the wealthy and the powerful and the eminent make clear: no matter what else they may be, the people of these higher circles are involved in a set of overlapping "crowds" and intricately connected "cliques." There is a kind of mutual attraction among those who "sit on the same terrace"—although this often

becomes clear to them, as well as to others, only at the point at which they feel the need to draw the line; only when, in their common defense, they come to understand what they have in common, and so close their ranks against outsiders.

The idea of such ruling stratum implies that most of its members have similar social origins, that throughout their lives they maintain a network of informal connections, and that to some degree there is an interchangeability of position between the various hierarchies of money and power and celebrity. We must, of course, note at once that if such an elite stratum does exist, its social visibility and its form, for very solid historical reasons, are quite different from those of the noble cousinhoods that once ruled various European nations.

That American society has never passed through a feudal epoch is of decisive importance to the nature of the American elite, as well as to American society as a historic whole. For it means that no nobility or aristocracy, established before the capitalist era, has stood in tense opposition to the higher bourgeoisie. It means that this bourgeoisie has monopolized not only wealth but prestige and power as well. It means that no set of noble families has commanded the top positions and monopolized the values that are generally held in high esteem; and certainly that no set has done so explicitly by inherited right. It means that no high church dignitaries or court nobilities, no entrenched landlords with honorific accouterments, no monopolists of high army posts have opposed the enriched bourgeoisie and in the name of birth and prerogative successfully resisted its self-making.

But this does *not* mean that there are no upper strata in the United States. That they emerged from a "middle class" that had no recognized aristocratic superiors does not mean they remained middle class when enormous increases in wealth made their own superiority possible.

Their origins and their newness may have made the upper strata less visible in America than elsewhere. But in America today there are in fact tiers and ranges of wealth and power of which people in the middle and lower ranks know very little and may not even dream. There are families who, in their well-being, are quite insulated from the economic jolts and lurches felt by the merely prosperous and those farther down the scale. There are also men of power who in quite small groups make decisions of enormous consequence for the underlying population.

The American elite entered modern history as a virtually unopposed bourgeoisie. No national bourgeoisie, before or since, has had such opportunities and advantages. Having no military neighbors, they easily occupied an isolated continent stocked with natural resources and immensely inviting to a willing labor force. A framework of power and an ideology for its justification were already at hand. Against mercantilist restriction, they inherited the principle of *laissez-faire;* against Southern planters, they imposed the principle of industrialism. The Revolutionary War put an end to colonial pretensions to nobility, as loyalists fled the country and many estates were broken up. The Jacksonian upheaval with its status revolution put an end to pretensions to monopoly of descent by the old New England families. The Civil War broke the power, and so in due course the prestige, of the ante-bellum South's claimants for the higher esteem. The tempo of the whole capitalist development made it impossible for an inherited nobility to develop and endure in America.

No fixed ruling class, anchored in agrarian life and coming to flower in military glory, could contain in America the historic thrust of commerce and industry, or subordinate to itself the capitalist elite—as capitalists were subordinated, for example, in Germany

and Japan. Nor could such a ruling class anywhere in the world contain that of the United States when industrialized violence came to decide history. Witness the fate of Germany and Japan in the two world wars of the twentieth century; and indeed the fate of Britain herself and her model ruling class, as New York became the inevitable economic, and Washington the inevitable political capital of the western capitalist world.

4

The elite who occupy the command posts may be seen as the possessors of power and wealth and celebrity; they may be seen as members of the upper stratum of a capitalistic society. They may also be defined in terms of psychological and moral criteria, as certain kinds of selected individuals. So defined, the elite, quite simply, are people of superior character and energy.

The humanist, for example, may conceive of the "elite" not as a social level or category, but as a scatter of those individuals who attempt to transcend themselves, and accordingly, are more noble, more efficient, made out of better stuff. It does not matter whether they are poor or rich, whether they hold high position or low, whether they are acclaimed or despised; they are elite because of the kind of individuals they are. The rest of the population is mass, which, according to this conception, sluggishly relaxes into uncomfortable mediocrity.[5]

This is the sort of socially unlocated conception which some American writers with conservative yearnings have recently sought to develop. But most moral and psychological conceptions of the elite are much less sophisticated, concerning themselves not with individuals but with the stratum as a whole. Such ideas, in fact, always arise in a society in which some people possess more than do others of what there is to possess. People with advantages are loath to believe that they just happen to be people with advantages. They come readily to define themselves as inherently worthy of what they possess; they come to believe themselves "naturally" elite; and, in fact, to imagine their possessions and their privileges as natural extensions of their own elite selves. In this sense, the idea of the elite as composed of men and women having a finer moral character is an ideology of the elite as a privileged ruling stratum, and this is true whether the ideology is elite-made or made up for it by others.

In eras of equalitarian rhetoric, the more intelligent or the more articulate among the lower and middle classes, as well as guilty members of the upper, may come to entertain ideas of a counter-elite. In western society, as a matter of fact, there is a long tradition and varied images of the poor, the exploited, and the oppressed as the truly virtuous, the wise, and the blessed. Stemming from Christian tradition, this moral idea of a counter-elite, composed of essentially higher types condemned to a lowly station, may be and has been used by the underlying population to justify harsh criticism of ruling elites and to celebrate utopian images of a new elite to come.

The moral conception of the elite, however, is not always merely an ideology of the overprivileged or a counter-ideology of the underprivileged. It is often a fact: having controlled experiences and select privileges, many individuals of the upper stratum do come in due course to approximate the types of character they claim to embody. Even when we give up—as we must—the idea that the elite man or woman is born with an elite character, we need not dismiss the idea that their experiences and trainings develop in them characters of a specific type.

Nowadays we must qualify the idea of elite as composed of higher types of individuals, for the men who are selected for and shaped by the top positions have many spokesmen and advisers and ghosts and make-up men who modify their self-conceptions and create their public images, as well as shape many of their decisions. There is, of course, considerable variation among the elite in this respect, but as a general rule in America today, it would be naïve to interpret any major elite group merely in terms of its ostensible personnel. The American elite often seems less a collection of persons than of corporate entities, which are in great part created and spoken for as standard types of "personality." Even the most apparently free-lance celebrity is usually a sort of synthetic production turned out each week by a disciplined staff which systematically ponders the effect of the easy ad-libbed gags the celebrity "spontaneously" echoes.

Yet, in so far as the elite flourishes as a social class or as a set of men at the command posts, it will select and form certain types of personality, and reject others. The kind of moral and psychological beings men become is in large part determined by the values they experience and the institutional roles they are allowed and expected to play. From the biographer's point of view, a man of the upper classes is formed by his relations with others like himself in a series of small intimate groupings through which he passes and to which throughout his lifetime he may return. So conceived, the elite is a set of higher circles whose members are selected, trained and certified and permitted intimate access to those who command the impersonal institutional hierarchies of modern society. If there is any one key to the *psychological* idea of the elite, it is that they combine in their persons an awareness of impersonal decision-making with intimate sensibilities shared with one another. To understand the elite as a social class we must examine a whole series of smaller face-to-face milieux, the most obvious of which, historically, has been the upper-class family, but the most important of which today are the proper secondary school and the metropolitan club.[6]

5

These several notions of the elite, when appropriately understood, are intricately bound up with one another, and we shall use them all in this examination of American success. We shall study each of several higher circles as offering candidates for the elite, and we shall do so in terms of the major institutions making up the total society of America; within and between each of these institutions, we shall trace the interrelations of wealth and power and prestige. But our main concern is with the power of those who now occupy the command posts, and with the role which they are enacting in the history of our epoch.

Such an elite may be conceived as omnipotent, and its powers thought of as a great hidden design. Thus, in vulgar Marxism, events and trends are explained by reference to "the will of the bourgeoisie"; in Nazism, by reference to "the conspiracy of the Jews"; by the petty right in America today, by reference to "the hidden force" of Communist spies. According to such notions of the omnipotent elite as historical cause, the elite is never an entirely visible agency. It is, in fact, a secular substitute for the will of God, being realized in a sort of providential design, except that usually non-elite men are thought capable of opposing it and eventually overcoming it.[7]

The opposite view—of the elite as impotent—is now quite popular among liberal-minded observers. Far from being omnipotent, the elites are thought to be so scattered as to lack any coherence as a historical force. Their invisibility is not the invisibility of secrecy but the invisibility of the multitude. Those who occupy the formal places of authority are so check-mated—by other elites exerting pressure, or by the public as an electorate, or by constitutional codes—that, although there may be upper classes, there is no ruling class; although there may be men of power, there is no power elite; although there may be a system of stratification, it has no effective top. In the extreme, this view of the elite, as weakened by compromise and disunited to the point of nullity, is a substitute for impersonal collective fate; for, in this view, the decisions of the visible men of the higher circles do not count in history.[8]

Internationally, the image of the omnipotent elite tends to prevail. All good events and pleasing happenings are quickly imputed by the opinion-makers to the leaders of their own nation; all bad events and unpleasant experiences are imputed to the enemy abroad. In both cases, the omnipotence of evil rulers or of virtuous leaders is assumed. Within the nation, the use of such rhetoric is rather more complicated: when men speak of the power of their own party or circle, they and their leaders are, of course, impotent; only "the people" are omnipotent. But, when they speak of the power of their opponent's party or circle, they impute to them omnipotence; "the people" are now powerlessly taken in.

More generally, American men of power tend, by convention, to deny that they are powerful. No American runs for office in order to rule or even govern, but only to serve; he does not become a bureaucrat or even an official, but a public servant. And nowadays, as I have already pointed out, such postures have become standard features of the public-relations programs of all men of power. So firm a part of the style of power-wielding have they become that conservative writers readily misinterpret them as indicating a trend toward an "amorphous power situation."

But the "power situation" of America today is less amorphous than is the perspective of those who see it as a romantic confusion. It is less a flat, momentary "situation" than a graded, durable structure. And if those who occupy its top grades are not omnipotent, neither are they impotent. It is the form and the height of the gradation of power that we must examine if we would understand the degree of power held and exercised by the elite.

If the power to decide such national issues as are decided were shared in an absolutely equal way, there would be no power elite; in fact, there would be no *gradation* of power, but only a radical homogeneity. At the opposite extreme as well, if the power to decide issues were absolutely monopolized by one small group, there would be no gradation of power; there would simply be this small group in command, and below it, the undifferentiated, dominated masses. American society today represents neither the one nor the other of these extremes, but a conception of them is none the less useful: it makes us realize more clearly the question of the structure of power in the United States and the position of the power elite within it.

Within each of the most powerful institutional orders of modern society there is a gradation of power. The owner of a roadside fruit stand does not have as much power in any area of social or economic or political decision as the head of a multi-million-dollar fruit corporation; no lieutenant on the line is as powerful as the Chief of Staff in the Pentagon; no deputy sheriff carries as much authority as the President of the United States. Accordingly, the problem of defining the power elite concerns the level at which we wish to draw the line. By lowering the line, we could define the elite out of existence; by raising it, we could make the elite a very small circle indeed. In a preliminary and minimum way, we draw the line crudely, in charcoal as it were:

By the power elite, we refer to those political, economic, and military circles which as an intricate set of overlapping cliques share decisions having at least national consequences. In so far as national events are decided, the power elite are those who decide them.

To say that there are obvious gradations of power and of opportunities to decide within modern society is not to say that the powerful are united, that they fully know what they do, or that they are consciously joined in conspiracy. Such issues are best faced if we concern ourselves, in the first instance, more with the structural position of the high and mighty, and with the consequences of their decisions, than with the extent of their awareness or the purity of their motives. To understand the power elite, we must attend to three major keys:

I. One, which we shall emphasize throughout our discussion of each of the higher circles, is the psychology of the several elites in their respective milieux. In so far as the power elite is composed of men of similar origin and education, in so far as their careers and their styles of life are similar, there are psychological and social bases for their unity, resting upon the fact that they are of similar social type and leading to the fact of their easy intermingling. This kind of unity reaches its frothier apex in the sharing of that prestige that is to be had in the world of the celebrity; it achieves a more solid culmination in the fact of the interchangeability of positions within and between the three dominant institutional orders.

II. Behind such psychological and social unity as we may find, are the structure and the mechanics of those institutional hierarchies over which the political directorate, the corporate rich, and the high military now preside. The greater the scale of these bureaucratic domains, the greater the scope of their respective elite's power. How each of the major hierarchies is shaped and and what relations it has with the other hierarchies determine in large part the relations of their rulers. If these hierarchies are scattered and disjointed, then their respective elites tend to be scattered and disjointed; if they have many interconnections and points of coinciding interest, then their elites tend to form a coherent kind of grouping.

The unity of the elite is not a simple reflection of the unity of institutions, but men and institutions are always related, and our conception of the power elite invites us to determine that relation. Today in America there are several important structural coincidences of interest between these institutional domains, including the development of a permanent war establishment by a privately incorporated economy inside a political vacuum.

III. The unity of the power elite, however, does not rest solely on psychological similarity and social intermingling, nor entirely on the structural coincidences of commanding positions and interests. At times it is the unity of a more explicit co-ordination. To say that these three higher circles are increasingly co-ordinated, that this is *one* basis of their unity, and that at times—as during the wars—such co-ordination is quite decisive, is not to say that the co-ordination is total or continuous, or even that it is very surefooted. Much less is it to say that willful co-ordination is the sole or the major basis of their unity, or that the power elite has emerged as the realization of a plan. But it is to say that as the institutional mechanics of our time have opened up avenues to men pursuing their several interests, many of them have come to see that these several interests could be realized more easily if they worked together, in informal as well as in more formal ways, and accordingly they have done so.

6

It is not my thesis that for all epochs of human history and in all nations, a creative minority, a ruling class, an omnipotent elite, shape all historical events. Such statements, upon careful examination, usually turn out to be mere tautologies,[9] and even when they are not, they are so entirely general as to be useless in the attempt to understand the history of the present. The minimum definition of the power elite as those who decide whatever is decided of major consequence, does not imply that the members of this elite are always and necessarily the history-makers; neither does it imply that they never are. We must not confuse the conception of the elite, which we wish to define, with one theory about their role: that they are the history-makers of our time. To define the elite, for example, as "those who rule America" is less to define a conception than to state one hypothesis about the role and power of that elite. No matter how we might define the elite, the extent of its members' power is subject to historical variation. If, in a dogmatic way, we try to include that variation in our generic definition, we foolishly limit the use of a needed conception. If we insist that the elite be defined as a strictly coordinated class that continually and absolutely rules, we are closing off from our view much to which the term more modestly defined might open to our observation. In short, our definition of the power elite cannot properly contain dogma concerning the degree and kind of power that ruling groups everywhere have. Much less should it permit us to smuggle into our discussion a theory of history.

During most of human history, historical change has not been visible to the people who were involved in it, or even to those enacting it. Ancient Egypt and Mesopotamia, for example, endured for some four hundred generations with but slight changes in their basic structure. That is six and a half times as long as the entire Christian era, which has only prevailed some sixty generations; it is about eighty times as long as the five generations of the United States' existence. But now the tempo of change is so rapid, and the means of observation so accessible, that the interplay of event and decision seems often to be quite historically visible, if we will only look carefully and from an adequate vantage point.

When knowledgeable journalists tell us that "events, not men, shape the big decisions," they are echoing the theory of history as Fortune, Chance, Fate, or the work of The Unseen Hand. For "events" is merely a modern word for these older ideas, all of which separate men from history-making, because all of them lead us to believe that history goes on behind men's backs. History is drift with no mastery; within it there is action but no deed; history is mere happening and the event intended by no one.[10]

The course of events in our time depends more on a series of human decisions than on any inevitable fate. The sociological meaning of "fate" is simply this: that, when the decisions are innumerable and each one is of small consequence, all of them add up in a way no man intended—to history as fate. But not all epochs are equally fateful. As the circle of those who decide is narrowed, as the means of decision are centralized and the consequences of decisions become enormous, then the course of great events often rests upon the decisions of determinable circles. This does not necessarily mean that the same circle of men follow through from one event to another in such a way that all of history is merely their plot. The power of the elite does not necessarily mean that history is not also shaped by a series of small decisions, none of which are thought out. It does not mean that a hundred small arrangements and compromises and adaptations may not be built into the going policy and the living event. The idea of the power elite implies nothing about the process of decision-making as such: it is an attempt to delimit the social areas within which that process, whatever its character, goes on. It is a conception of who is involved in the process.

The degree of foresight and control of those who are involved in decisions that count may also vary. The idea of the power elite does not mean that the estimations and calculated risks upon which decisions are made are not often wrong and that the consequences are sometimes, indeed often, not those intended. Often those who make decisions are trapped by their own inadequacies and blinded by their own errors.

Yet in our time the pivotal moment does arise, and at that moment, small circles do decide or fail to decide. In either case, they are an elite of power. The dropping of the A-bombs over Japan was such a moment; the decision on Korea was such a moment; the confusion about Quemoy and Matsu, as well as before Dienbienphu were such moments; the sequence of maneuvers which involved the United States in World War II was such a "moment." Is it not true that much of the history of our times is composed of such moments? And is not that what is meant when it is said that we live in a time of big decisions, of decisively centralized power?

Most of us do not try to make sense of our age by believing in a Greek-like, eternal recurrence, nor by a Christian belief in a salvation to come, nor by any steady march of human progress. Even though we do not reflect upon such matters, the chances are we believe with Burckhardt that we live in a mere succession of events; that sheer continuity is the only principle of history. History is merely one thing after another; history is meaningless in that it is not the realization of any determinate plot. It is true, of course, that our sense of continuity, our feeling for the history of our time, is affected by crisis. But we seldom look beyond the immediate crisis or the crisis felt to be just ahead. We believe neither in fate nor providence; and we assume, without talking about it, that "we"—as a nation—can decisively shape the future but that "we" as individuals somehow cannot do so.

Any meaning history has, "we" shall have to give to it by our actions. Yet the fact is that although we are all of us within history we do not all possess equal powers to make history. To pretend that we do is sociological nonsense and political irresponsibility. It is nonsense because any group or any individual is limited, first of all, by the technical and institutional means of power at its command; we do not all have equal access to the means of power that now exist, nor equal influence over their use. To pretend that "we" are all history-makers is politically irresponsible because it obfuscates any attempt to locate responsibility for the consequential decisions of men who do have access to the means of power.

From even the most superficial examination of the history of the western society we learn that the power of decision-makers is first of all limited by the level of technique, by the *means* of power and violence and organization that prevail in a given society. In this connection we also learn that there is a fairly straight line running upward through the history of the West; that the means of oppression and exploitation, of violence and destruction, as well as the means of production and reconstruction, have been progressively enlarged and increasingly centralized.

As the institutional means of power and the means of communications that tie them together have become steadily more efficient, those now in command of them have come into command of instruments of rule quite unsurpassed in the history of mankind. And we are not yet at the climax of their development.

We can no longer lean upon or take soft comfort from the historical ups and downs of ruling groups of previous epochs. In that sense, Hegel is correct: we learn from history that we cannot learn from it.

For every epoch and for every social structure, we must work out an answer to the question of the power of the elite. The ends of men are often merely hopes, but means are facts within some men's control. That is why all means of power tend to become ends to an elite that is in command of them. And that is why we may define the power elite in terms of the means of power—as those who occupy the command posts. The major questions about the American elite today—its composition, its unity, its power—must now be faced with due attention to the awesome means of power available to them. Caesar could do less with Rome than Napoleon with France; Napoleon less with France than Lenin with Russia; and Lenin less with Russia than Hitler with Germany. But what was Caesar's power at its peak compared with the power of the changing inner circle of Soviet Russia or of America's temporary administrations? The men of either circle can cause great cities to be wiped out in a single night, and in a few weeks turn continents into thermonuclear wastelands. That the facilities of power are enormously enlarged and decisively centralized means that the decisions of small groups are now more consequential.

But to know that the top posts of modern social structures now permit more commanding decisions is not to know that the elite who occupy these posts are the history-makers. We might grant that the enlarged and integrated economic, military, and political structures are shaped to permit command decisions, yet still feel that, as it were, "they run themselves," that those who are on top, in short, are determined in their decisions by "necessity," which presumably means by the instituted roles that they play and the situation of these institutions in the total structure of society.

Do the elite determine the roles that they enact? Or do the roles that institutions make available to them determine the power of the elite? The general answer—and no general answer is sufficient—is that in different kinds of structures and epochs elites are quite differently related to the roles that they play: nothing in the nature of the elite or in the nature of history dictates an answer. It is also true that if most men and women take whatever roles are permitted to them and enact them as they are expected to by virtue of their position, this is precisely what the elite need *not* do, and often do not do. They may call into question the structure, their position within it, or the way in which they are to enact that position.

Nobody called for or permitted Napoleon to chase *Parlement* home on the 18 *Brumaire,* and later to transform his consulate into an emperorship.[11] Nobody called for or permitted Adolf Hitler to proclaim himself "Leader and Chancellor" the day President Hindenburg died, to abolish and usurp roles by merging the presidency and the chancellorship. Nobody called for or permitted Franklin D. Roosevelt to make the series of decisions that led to the entrance of the United States into World War II. It was no "historical necessity," but a man named Truman who, with a few other men, decided to drop a bomb on Hiroshima. It was no historical necessity, but an argument within a small circle of men that defeated Admiral Radford's proposal to bomb troops before Dien Bien Phu. Far from being dependent upon the structure of institutions, modern elites may smash one structure and set up another in which they then enact quite different roles. In fact, such destruction and creation of institutional structures, with all their means of power, when

events seem to turn out well, is just what is involved in "great leadership," or, when they seem to turn out badly, great tyranny.

Some elite men *are,* of course, typically role-determined, but others are at times role-determining. They determine not only the role-they play but today the roles of millions of other men. The creation of pivotal roles and their pivotal enactment occurs most readily when social structures are undergoing epochal transitions. It is clear that the international development of the United States to one of the two "great powers"—along with the new means of annihilation and administrative and psychic domination— have made of the United States in the middle years of the twentieth century precisely such an epochal pivot.

There is nothing about history that tells us that a power elite cannot make it. To be sure, the will of such men is always limited, but never before have the limits been so broad, for never before have the means of power been so enormous. It is this that makes our situation so precarious, and makes even more important an understanding of the powers and the limitations of the American elite. The problem of the nature and the power of this elite is now the only realistic and serious way to raise again the problem of responsible government.

7

Those who have abandoned criticism for the new American celebration take readily to the view that the elite is impotent. If they were politically serious, they ought, on the basis of their view, to say to those presumably in charge of American policy:[12]

One day soon, you may believe that you have an opportunity to drop a bomb or a chance to exacerbate further your relations with allies or with the Russians who might also drop it. But don't be so foolish as to believe that you really have a choice. You have neither choice nor chance. The whole Complex Situation of which you are merely one balancing part is the result of Economic and Social Forces, and so will be the fateful outcome. So stand by quietly, like Tolstoy's general, and let events proceed. Even if you did act, the consequences would not be what you intended, even if you had an intention.

But—if events come out well, talk as though you had decided. For then men have had moral choices and the power to make them and are, of course, responsible.

If events come out badly, say that *you* didn't have the real choice, and are, of course, not accountable: *they,* the others, had the choice and they are responsible. You can get away with this even though you have at your command half the world's forces and God knows how many bombs and bombers. For you are, in fact, an impotent item in the historical fate of your times; and moral responsibility is an illusion, although it is of great use if handled in a really alert public relations manner.

The one implication that can be drawn from all such fatalisms is that if fortune or providence rules, then no elite of power can be justly considered a source of historical decisions, and the idea—much less the demand—of responsible leadership is an idle and an irresponsible notion. For clearly, an impotent elite, the plaything of history, cannot be held accountable. If the elite of our time do not have power, they cannot be held responsible; as men in a difficult position, they should engage our sympathies. The people of the United States are ruled by sovereign fortune; they, and with them their elite, are fatally overwhelmed by

consequences they cannot control. If that is so, we ought all to do what many have in fact already done: withdraw entirely from political reflection and action into a materially comfortable and entirely private life.

If, on the other hand, we believe that war and peace and slump and prosperity are, precisely now, no longer matters of "fortune" or "fate," but that, precisely now more than ever, they are controllable, then we must ask—controllable by whom? The answer must be. By whom else but those who now command the enormously enlarged and decisively centralized means of decision and power? We may then ask: Why don't they, then? And for the answer to that, we must understand the context and the character of the American elite today.

There is nothing in the idea of the elite as impotent which should deter us from asking just such questions, which are now the most important questions political men can ask. The American elite is neither omnipotent nor impotent. These are abstract absolutes used publicly by spokesmen, as excuses or as boasts, but in terms of which we may seek to clarify the political issues before us, which just now are above all the issues of responsible power.

There is nothing in "the nature of history" *in our epoch* that rules out the pivotal function of small groups of decision-makers. On the contrary, the structure of the present is such as to make this not only a reasonable, but a rather compelling, view.

There is nothing in "the psychology of man," or in the social manner by which men are shaped and selected for and by the command posts of modern society, that makes unreasonable the view that they do confront choices and that the choices they make—or their failure to confront them—are history-making in their consequences.

Accordingly, political men now have every reason to hold the American power elite accountable for a decisive range of the historical events that make up the history of the present.

It is as fashionable, just now, to suppose that there is no power elite, as it was fashionable in the 'thirties to suppose a set of ruling-class villains to be the source of all social injustice and public malaise. I should be as far from supposing that some simple and unilateral ruling class could be firmly located as the prime mover of American society, as I should be from supposing that all historical change in America today is merely impersonal drift.

The view that all is blind drift is largely a fatalist projection of one's own feeling of impotence and perhaps, if one has ever been active politically in a principled way, a salve of one's guilt.

The view that all of history is due to the conspiracy of an easily located set of villains, or of heroes, is also a hurried projection from the difficult effort to understand how shifts in the structure of society open opportunities to various elites and how various elites take advantage or fail to take advantage of them. To accept either view—of all history as conspiracy or of all history as drift—is to relax the effort to understand the facts of power and the ways of the powerful.

8

In my attempt to discern the shape of the power elite of our time, and thus to give a responsible meaning to the anonymous "They," which the underlying population opposes to the anonymous "We," I shall begin by briefly examining the higher elements which most people know best: the new and the old upper classes of local society and the metropolitan 400. I shall then outline the world of the celebrity, attempting to show that the prestige system of American society

has now for the first time become truly national in scope; and that the more trivial and glamorous aspects of this national system of status tend at once to distract attention from its more authoritarian features and to justify the power that it often conceals.

In examining the very rich and the chief executives, I shall indicate how neither "America's Sixty Families" nor "The Managerial Revolution" provides an adequate idea of the transformation of the upper classes as they are organized today in the privileged stratum of the corporate rich.

After describing the American statesman as a historical type, I shall attempt to show that what observers in the Progressive Era called "the invisible government" has now become quite visible; and that what is usually taken to be the central content of politics, the pressures and the campaigns and the congressional maneuvering, has, in considerable part, now been relegated to the middle levels of power.

In discussing the military ascendancy, I shall try to make clear how it has come about that admirals and generals have assumed positions of decisive political and economic relevance, and how, in doing so, they have found many points of coinciding interests with the corporate rich and the political directorate of the visible government.

After these and other trends are made as plain as I can make them, I shall return to the master problems of the power elite, as well as take up the complementary notion of the mass society.

What I am asserting is that in this particular epoch a conjunction of historical circumstances has led to the rise of an elite of power; that the men of the circles composing this elite, severally and collectively, now make such key decisions as are made; and that, given the enlargement and the centralization of the means of power now available, the decisions that they make and fail to make carry more consequences for more people than has ever been the case in the world history of mankind.

I am also asserting that there has developed on the middle levels of power, a semi-organized stalemate, and that on the bottom level there has come into being a mass-like society which has little resemblance to the image of a society in which voluntary associations and classic publics hold the keys to power. The top of the American system of power is much more unified and much more powerful, the bottom is much more fragmented, and in truth, impotent, than is generally supposed by those who are distracted by the middling units of power which neither express such will as exists at the bottom nor determine the decisions at the top.

NOTES

1. Jacob Burckhardt, *Force and Freedom* (New York: Pantheon Books, 1943), pp. 303 ff.

2. Cf. Hans Gerth and C. Wright Mills, *Character and Social Structure* (New York: Harcourt, Brace, 1953), pp. 457 ff.

3. The statistical idea of choosing some value and calling those who have the most of it an elite derives, in modern times, from the Italian economist, Pareto, who puts the central point in this way: "Let us assume that in every branch of human activity each individual is given an index which stands as a sign of his capacity, very much the way grades are given in the various subjects in examinations in school. The highest type of lawyer, for instance, will be given 10. The man who does not get a client will be given 1—reserving zero for the man who is an out-and-out idiot. To the man who has made his millions—honestly or dishonestly as the case may be—we will give 10. To the man who has earned his thousands we will give 6; to such as just manage to keep out of the poor-house, 1, keeping zero for those who get in . . . So let us make a class of people who have the highest indices in their branch of activity, and to that class give the name of *elite*." Vilfredo Pareto, *The Mind and Society* (New York: Harcourt, Brace, 1935), par. 2027 and 2031. Those who follow this approach end up not with one elite, but with a number corresponding to the number of values they select. Like many rather abstract ways of reasoning, this one is useful because it forces us to think in a clear-cut way. For a skillful use of this approach, see the work of Harold D. Lasswell, in particular, *Politics: Who Gets What, When, How* (New York: McGraw-Hill, 1936); and for a more systematic use, H. D. Lasswell and Abraham Kaplan, *Power and Society* (New Haven: Yale University Press, 1950).

4. The conception of the elite as members of a top social stratum, is, of course, in line with the prevailing common-sense view of stratification. Technically, it is closer to "status group" than to "class," and has been very well stated by Joseph A. Schumpeter, "Social Classes in an Ethically Homogeneous Environment," *Imperialism and Social Classes* (New York: Augustus M. Kelley, Inc., 1951), pp. 133 ff., especially pp. 137–47. Cf. also his *Capitalism, Socialism and Democracy,* 3rd ed. (New York: Harper, 1950), Part II. For the distinction between class and status groups, see *From Max Weber: Essays in Sociology* (trans. and ed. by Gerth and Mills; New York: Oxford University Press, 1946). For an analysis of Pareto's conception of the elite compared with Marx's conception of classes, as well as data on France, see Raymond Aron, "Social Structure and Ruling Class," *British Journal of Sociology,* vol. I, nos. 1 and 2 (1950).

5. The most popular essay in recent years which defines the elite and the mass in terms of a morally evaluated character-type is probably José Ortega y Gasset's, *The Revolt of the Masses,* 1932 (New York: New American Library, Mentor Edition, 1950), esp. pp. 91 ff.

6. "The American elite" is a confused and confusing set of images, and yet when we hear or when we use such words as Upper Class, Big Shot, Top Brass, The Millionaire Club, The High and The Mighty, we feel at least vaguely that we know what they mean, and often do. What we do not often do, however, is connect each of these images with the others; we make little effort to form a coherent picture in our minds of the elite

as a whole. Even when, very occasionally, we do try to do this, we usually come to believe that it is indeed no "whole"; that, like our images of it, there is no one elite, but many, and that they are not really connected with one another. What we must realize is that until we *do* try to see it as a whole, perhaps our impression that it may not be is a result merely of our lack of analytic rigor and sociological imagination.

The first conception defines the elite in terms of the sociology of institutional position and the social structure these institutions form; the second, in terms of the statistics of selected values; the third, in terms of membership in a clique-like set of people; and the fourth, in terms of the morality of certain personality types. Or, put into inelegant shorthand; what they head up, what they have, what they belong to, who they really are.

In this chapter ... I have taken as generic the first view—of the elite defined in terms of institutional position—and have located the other views within it. This straight-forward conception of the elite has one practical and two theoretical advantages. The practical advantage is that it seems the easiest and the most concrete "way into" the whole problem—if only because a good deal of information is more or less readily available for sociological reflection about such circles and institutions.

But the theoretical advantages are much more important. The institutional or structural definition, first of all, does not force us to prejudge by definition that we ought properly to leave open for investigation. The elite conceived morally, for example, as people having a certain type of character is not an ultimate definition, for apart from being rather morally arbitrary, it leads us immediately to ask *why* these people have this or that sort of character. Accordingly, we should leave open the type of characters which the members of the elite in fact turn out to have, rather than by definition select them in terms of one type or another. In a similar way, we do not want, by mere definition, to prejudge whether or not the elite are conscious members of a social class. The second theoretical advantage of defining the elite in terms of major institutions ... is the fact that it allows us to fit the other three conceptions of the elite into place in a systematic way: (1) The institutional positions men occupy throughout their lifetime determine their chances to get and to hold selected values. (2) The kind of psychological beings they become is in large part determined by the values they thus experience and the institutional roles they play. (3) Finally, whether or not they come to feel that they belong to a select social closes, and whether or not they act according to what they hold to be its interests—these are also matters in large part determined by their institutional position, and in turn, the select values they possess and the characters they acquire.

7. Those who charge that Communist agents have been or are in the government, as well as those frightened by them, never raise the question: "Well, suppose there are Communists in high places, how much power do they have?" They simply assume that men in high places, or in this case even those in positions from which they might influence such men, do decide important events. Those who think Communist agents lost China to the Soviet bloc, or influenced loyal Americans to lose it, simply assume that there is a set of men who decide such matters, actively or by neglect or by stupidity. Many others, who do not believe that Communist agents were so influential, still assume that loyal American decision-makers lost it all by themselves.

8. The idea of the impotent elite ... is mightily supported by the notion of an automatic economy in which the problem of power is solved for the economic elite by denying its existence. No one has enough power to make a real difference; events are the results of an anonymous balance. For the political elite too, the model of balance solves the problem of power. Parallel to the market-economy, there is the leaderless democracy in which no one is responsible for anything and everyone is responsible for everything; the will of men acts only through the impersonal workings of the electoral process.

9. As in the case, quite notably, of Gaetano Moses, *The Ruling Class* (New York: McGraw-Hill, 1939). For a sharp analysis of Mosca, see Fritz Morstein Marx, "The Bureaucratic State," *Review of Politics,* vol. I, 1939, pp. 457 ff. Cf. also Mills, "On Intellectual Craftsmanship," April 1952,

mimeographed, Columbia College, February 1955.

10. Cf. Karl Löwith, *Meaning in History* (Chicago: University of Chicago Press, 1949), pp. 125 ff. for concise and penetrating statements of several leading philosophies of history.

11. Some of these items are taken from Gerth and Mills, *Character and Social Structure,* pp. 405 ff. On role-determined and role-determining men, see also Sidney Hook's discussion, *The Hero in History* (New York: John Day, 1943).

12. I have taken the idea of the following kind of formulation from Joseph Wood Krutch's presentation of the morality of choice. See *The Measure of Man* (Indianapolis: Bobbs-Merrill, 1954), p. 52.

PROJECT

Read "The Theory of Balance," chapter 11 of *The Power Elite,* and see how Mills directly criticizes his pluralist contemporaries. In your estimation, which perspective makes more sense? Why?

PART II

Group Mobilization
and Structure

The preceding readings assume that groups form as a natural means to accomplish goals. Part II shows us that a great deal of debate exists as to how groups form and how, once formed, they are able to maintain themselves. The economist Mancur Olson suggests that in many ways it is irrational to join groups. In order to entice membership, groups must offer selective incentives that are made available only to those who join the organization. Olson's observation about the costs and benefits of group membership stimulated a new stream of interest-group research. Many of the articles in this section examine how groups are able to gain members. Additionally, these articles plot out the structure of interest groups in the United States. Different types of interest groups face different mobilization and maintenance issues. The final chapter of this part illustrates the various tactics groups use to maintain themselves and influence public policy.

GENERAL QUESTIONS TO CONSIDER

1. How are these articles related to one another?
2. How do these articles differ from one another?
3. How accurate are these analyses today?
4. What are the most significant problems interest groups face regarding mobilization and maintenance?

9

From the Logic
of Collective Action

MANCUR OLSON

*T*he *Logic of Collective Action* broke from much of the earlier scholarship on interest groups. Its publication in 1965 spurred a new set of research questions examining group behavior. This introduction sketches Mancur Olson's larger arguments from that work. Olson's most significant observations deal with the problems associated with free riders, the nonpolitical nature of many interest groups, the importance of selective incentives, and the potential power of small groups over groups with larger membership. Olson's use of rational choice as a means to analyze group behavior has had a tremendous effect on interest-group scholarship.

QUESTIONS TO CONSIDER

1. What is a free rider?
2. Why are free riders a problem?
3. Are free riders a problem for all groups? Why? Why not?
4. Why are large groups more likely to attract free riders?

It is often taken for granted, at least where economic objectives are involved, that groups of individuals with common interests usually attempt to further those common interests. Groups of individuals with common interests are expected to act on behalf of their common interests much as single individuals are often expected to act on behalf of their personal interests. This opinion about group behavior is frequently found not only in popular discussions but also in scholarly writings. Many economists of diverse methodological and ideological traditions have implicitly or explicitly accepted it. This view has, for example, been important in many theories of labor unions, in Marxian theories of class action, in concepts of "countervailing power," and in various discussions of economic institutions. It has, in addition, occupied a prominent place in political science, at least in the United States, where the study of pressure groups has been dominated by a celebrated "group theory" based on the idea that groups will act when necessary to further their common or group goals. Finally, it has played a significant role in many well-known sociological studies.

The view that groups act to serve their interests presumably is based upon the assumption that the individuals in groups act out of self-interest. If the individuals in a group altruistically disregarded their personal welfare, it would not be very likely that collectively they would seek some selfish common or group objective. Such altruism, is, however, considered exceptional, and self-interested behavior is usually thought to be the rule, at least when economic issues are at stake; no one is surprised

SOURCE: Reprinted by permission of the publisher from *The Logic of Collective Action: Public Goods and the Theory of Groups* by Mancur Olson Jr. (Cambridge, MA: Harvard University Press, 1971), 1–3. Copyright © 1965, 1971 by the President and Fellows of Harvard College.

when individual businessmen seek higher profits, when individual workers seek higher wages, or when individual consumers seek lower prices. The idea that groups tend to act in support of their group interests is supposed to follow logically from this widely accepted premise of rational, self-interested behavior. In other words, if the members of some group have a common interest or objective, and if they would all be better off if that objective were achieved, it has been thought to follow logically that the individuals in that group would, if they were rational and self-interested, act to achieve that objective.

But it is *not* in fact true that the idea that groups will act in their self-interest follows logically from the premise of rational and self-interested behavior. It does *not* follow, because all of the individuals in a group would gain if they achieved their group objective, that they would act to achieve that objective, even if they were all rational and self-interested. Indeed, unless the number of individuals in a group is quite small, or unless there is coercion or some other special device to make individuals act in their common interest, *rational, self-interested individuals will not act to achieve their common or group interests*. In other words, even if all of the individuals in a large group are rational and self-interested, and would gain if, as a group, they acted to achieve their common interest or objective, they will still not voluntarily act to achieve that common or group interest. The notion that groups of individuals will act to achieve their common or group interests, far from being a logical implication of the assumption that the individuals in a group will rationally further their individual interests, is in fact inconsistent with that assumption. . . .

If the members of a large group rationally seek to maximize their personal welfare, they will *not* act to advance their common or group objectives unless there is coercion to force them to do so, or unless some separate incentive, distinct from the achievement of the common or group interest, is offered to the members of the group individually on the condition that they help bear the costs or burdens involved in the achievement of the group objectives. Nor will such large groups form organizations to further their common goals in the absence of the coercion or the separate incentives just mentioned. These points hold true even when there is unanimous agreement in a group about the common good and the methods of achieving it.

The widespread view, common throughout the social sciences, that groups tend to further their interests, is accordingly unjustified, at least when it is based, as it usually is, on the (sometimes implicit) assumption that groups act in their self-interest because individuals do. There is paradoxically the logical possibility that groups composed of either altruistic individuals or irrational individuals may sometimes act in their common or group interests. But . . . this logical possibility is usually of no practical importance. Thus the customary view that groups of individuals with common interests tend to further those common interests appears to have little if any merit.

None of the statements made above fully applies to small groups, for the situation in small groups is much more complicated. In small groups there may very well be some voluntary action in support of the common purposes of the individuals in the group, but in most cases this action will cease before it reaches the optimal level for the members of the group as a whole. In the sharing of the costs of efforts to achieve a common goal in small groups, there is however a surprising tendency for the "exploitation" of the *great* by the *small*.

The proofs of all of the logical statements that have been made above are contained in Chapter I, which develops a logical or theoretical explanation of certain aspects of group and organizational behavior. Chapter II, examines the implication of this analysis for groups of different size, and illustrates the conclusion that in many cases small groups are more efficient and viable than large ones. Chapter III considers the implications of the argument for labor unions and draws the conclusion that some of compulsory membership is, in most circumstances, indispensable to union survival. The fourth chapter uses the approach developed in this study to examine Marx's theory of social classes and to analyze the theories of the state developed by some other economists. The fifth analyzes the "group theory" used by many political scientists in the light of the logic elaborated in this study, and argues that that theory as usually understood is logically inconsistent. The final chapter develops a new theory of pressure groups which is consistent with the logical relationships outlined in the first chapter and which suggests that the membership and power of large pressure-group organizations does not derive from their lobbying achievements, but is rather a by-product of their other activities.

Though I am an economist, and the tools of analysis used in this book are drawn from economic theory, the conclusions of the study are as relevant to the sociologist and the political scientist as they are to the economist. I have, therefore, avoided using the diagrammatic mathematical language of economics whenever feasible. Unfortunately, many noneconomists will find one or two brief parts of the first chapter expressed in an obscure and uncongenial way, but all of the rest of the book should be perfectly clear, whatever the reader's disciplinary background.

PROJECT

Take a look around your campus. What groups do you believe have the administration's attention? Do they represent broad interests or narrow interests? Does the size of the group appear to matter? Do the groups have problems with free riders? Why? Why not?

10

Incentive Systems: A Theory of Organizations

PETER CLARK AND JAMES Q. WILSON

Mancur Olson's analysis provides great insights from the field of economics. Peter Clark and James Wilson's utilization of psychology further advances our understanding of how groups attract members. They offer a compelling treatment that examines how groups overcome the collective-action problem. Numerous scholars have applied their analysis of incentive systems to that subject. Scholars use their typology of incentive structures to understand how different types of groups with different types of membership conquer the hurdles associated with group mobilization.

QUESTIONS TO CONSIDER

1. What are material incentives?
2. What are solidary incentives?
3. What are purposive incentives?
4. What type of group would be most able to offer material incentives? Least able?
5. What type of group would be most likely to offer solidary incentives? Least likely?
6. What type of group would be most likely to offer purposive incentives? Least likely?

7. How does a group's ability to offer incentives affect its ability to gain membership?

8. What type of incentive do you believe is most effective in securing membership? Why?

The internal activity of organizations affects their purposes and the tactics they employ to attain those purposes. Organizational purposes and tactics, in turn, have clear influences upon social, economic, and political processes. This paper will suggest that much of the internal and external activity of organizations may be explained by understanding their incentive systems.

All viable organizations must provide tangible or intangible incentives to individuals in exchange for contributions of individual activity to the organizations. Analysis of the several kinds of incentive systems can provide not only a way to classify much existing data about organizations, but also the rudiments of a predictive theory of organizational behavior. Moreover, the analysis may be applied to all formal organizations—political interest groups, corporations, trade unions, universities, and political parties, for example—as well as to administrative agencies, to which it has already been fruitfully applied.[1]

Classification of incentive systems makes it possible to distinguish analytically significant types of organizations. Analysis of incentive systems also provides at least partial explanations of such varied phenomena as differences in group purposes and tactics, organizational cohesion, proclivities to expand, the likelihood of group survival, styles of leadership, and long-term trends in the activities of clusters of organizations.

The basic hypothesis of this paper is that the incentive system may be regarded

as the principal variable affecting organizational behavior. A secondary hypothesis is that the incentive system is altered (largely by the organization's executive) in response to changes in the apparent motives of contributors, or potential contributors, to the organization. These motives may change both collectively and individually. Collectively, the number of contributors (or potential contributors) seeking certain values may come to outweigh the number seeking other values. The rewards of membership in the organization must then be altered to correspond to the motives of new members or a potential clientele that it is deemed desirable to attract and hold. Individually, members may gradually change their motives for a variety of reasons. Some of these changes may be due to environmental factors—for example, changes in the level of economic activity, the distribution of resources, or the pattern of moral attitudes. Other changes in motives may represent a significant alteration in the level of expectations. The motives for organizational membership may change as notions as to what is possible are modified. Finally, motives may change as the organization itself changes its character from a formative stage (in which substantive goals may be of crucial importance) to a later stage (in which the rewards of membership come to be independent of substantive goals). At first, members may derive satisfaction from coming together for the purpose of achieving a stated end; later, they may derive equal or greater satisfaction from simply maintaining an organization that provides them with office, prestige, power, sociability, income, or a sense of identity.

SOURCE: Reprinted from "Incentive Systems: A Theory of Organizations," by Peter B. Clark and James Q. Wilson, published in *Administrative Science Quarterly* 6, no. 3 (September 1961): 129–66 (including the table), by permission of *Administrative Science Quarterly*.

If these hypotheses are valid, the analysis of incentive systems makes it possible to relate environmental trends, personality factors, patterns of expectation, and organizational history to the behavior of organizations and perhaps to bridge the gap between the study of individual behavior and the study of organizational behavior. In this study, the fundamental unit will be the organization as such and its principal attribute will be its incentive system. In this way it is hoped that a theory of organizations can be developed without reducing organizations to personality, small-group behavior, communications patterns, or isolated decision-making units. The point of view of this paper is that the most important thing to know about an organization is that *it is* an organization and that it seeks to persist.

This paper is divided into five sections. In the first, the nature and principal types of incentive systems are discussed and related to the function of the executive and the role of the leader. In the second, three types of organizations are described and propositions offered regarding their characteristic behavior. In the third, changes in organization behavior are related to environmental changes. In the fourth, the relationships among organizations are discussed in terms of the competition for autonomy and resources. Finally, some important changes in personal motives in American life affecting organizational behavior are suggested.

INCENTIVE SYSTEMS

The basic premises of the paper may be expressed by quoting from Chester Barnard:

> The contributions of personal efforts which constitute the energies of organizations are yielded by individuals because of incentives. The egotistical motives of self-preservation and self-gratification are dominating forces; on the whole, organizations can exist only when consistent with the satisfaction of these motives, unless, alternatively, they can change these motives. The individual is always the basic strategic factor in organizations. Regardless of his history or his obligations he must be induced to cooperate, or there can be no cooperation.[3]

Additional premises include the following:

1. Incentives are by definition scarce. Unless a commodity, a status, or an activity is relatively rare, it provides no inducement to anyone. A business firm has only a finite amount of money which it may offer to contributors of effort in the form of salaries and wages; a university can create only so many full professorships before watering the currency of their prestige value; there can be only so many committee heads in a women's club before a committee chairmanship ceases to be desired.

Tangible and intangible resources are not distributed equally throughout the population and a given incentive may have more effect upon some people than others. A small increment in wealth can rarely induce a multimillionaire to contribute time and effort to an organization. Social status, prestige, and respect are similarly unequally distributed. Membership in a given organization may represent "upward mobility" to one person, while it may imply degradation to another of higher social status. Incentives have a diminishing marginal utility.

2. An organization's incentive output must not exceed its available incentive resources.[4] Continued, excessive payments of wages and salaries can drive a business firm to bankruptcy. Similarly, a social club whose members cease to provide each other with the incentives of sociability approaches disintegration. A net outflow of incentive resources will produce decreases in organizational size or levels of activity, or

both, and will ultimately produce either an alteration in the incentive system or organizational collapse.

3. It is the function of the executive to maintain his organization. He does this by attempting to obtain a net surplus of incentives and by distributing incentives to elicit contributions of activity.[5] It is important to distinguish the executive function from what will here be called the leadership function, which is that of creating, clarifying, and promulgating substantive goals.[6] While both functions are occasionally performed by the same individual, it will be shown later that the demands of the two functions may conflict. Distributing incentives in order to maintain the organization is by no means always the same task as setting substantive purposes for the organization to pursue.

The executive has a strong personal interest in maintaining his organization. Generally, the minimal expectation of group members is that the executive will not allow his group to decline or collapse. The executive's reputation, and in some cases his livelihood and material success, depends upon successful fulfillment of this minimal function. And as many writers have observed, both executives and other contributors come to believe that their organizations must persist if they are to achieve their substantive purposes. Whatever else he may be able to do with or for his group, the executive must perpetuate it.

4. It is possible to distinguish one incentive system from another. For the purposes of this paper, incentives will be placed in three broad categories: material, solidary, and purposive.

a. *Material incentives:* These are tangible rewards; that is, rewards that have a monetary value or can easily be translated into ones that have. These include money in the form of wages and salaries, the tangible benefits of a taxpayers' association to its members, the improvement in property values for a neighborhood redevelopment association or the increase in wages and other tangible "fringe" benefits obtained by a labor union.

b. *Solidary incentives:* Solidary rewards are basically intangible; that is, the reward has no monetary value and cannot easily be translated into one that has. These inducements vary widely. They derive in the main from the act of associating and include such rewards as socializing, congeniality, the sense of group membership and identification, the status resulting from membership, fun and conviviality, the maintenance of social distinctions, and so on. Their common characteristic is that they tend to be independent of the precise ends of the association. Groups held together in general by solidary incentives are relatively flexible about the stated goals of the group. The group may raise funds to fight a disease, support a hospital, meliorate the lot of the indigent, conduct a fashion show, listen to after-dinner speakers, maintain a club house, and the like. Of course, in practice no group is utterly indifferent to its ends; if it were, it could not sustain itself in competing for members with other groups. There are many ways to obtain solidary benefits, and some purpose must generally be offered to persuade people to obtain these benefits from one group rather than another. What is stressed here is only the analytic nature of the incentives and their logical separability from ends. The practical consequences of this kind of incentive system will be discussed later.

c. *Purposive incentives:* Purposive, like solidary, incentives are intangible, but they derive in the main from the stated ends of the association rather than from the simple act of associating.[7] These inducements are to be found in the suprapersonal goals of the organization: the demand for the enactment of certain laws or the adoption of certain practices (which do *not* benefit the members in any direct or tangible way), such as elimination of corruption or inefficiency from public service, beautification of the community, dissemination of information about politics or city life, and so forth. Unlike solidary incentives, purposive incentives are inseparable from the ends being sought. (It is true that some people will belong to *any* organization that seeks to reform or improve *any* aspect of community life; to them the very act of protest may be more important than the specific object of the protest, but in most cases, there is a reasonable relationship between end and incentive for most contributors.) The end system is deeply implicated in the incentive system of the association. The members are brought together to seek some change in the status quo, not simply to enjoy one another's presence. The latter may be rewarding, but it is insufficient in itself to maintain the group. These purposive inducements must be carefully distinguished from solidary ones. If organizational purposes constitute the primary incentive, then low prestige, unpleasant working conditions, and other material and solidary disadvantages will be outweighed—in the mind of the contributor—by the "good" ends which the organization may eventually achieve.[8]

A particular organization may appeal to many motives. No business firm, for instance, relies exclusively upon material benefits. Pleasant working conditions, camaraderie with fellow workers, a sense that the firm is producing good and valued products, and many other incentives are offered to satisfy the variety of motives that help to maintain participation in the enterprise. Furthermore, organizations vary in internal complexity, and in the

more complex hierarchical organizations quite different kinds of incentives may be used at different levels. In corporations, the incentives offered to the highest ranking executives are different in kind as well as in degree from those provided to members of the labor force. An incentive analysis is incomplete if it fails to take account of differing incentive systems within a given organization.[9]

Nonetheless, many organizations may be distinguished by the incentives upon which they *principally* rely. Patterns of expectations develop for example, that a business firm should pay money wages, a university should appeal to students by providing education of a certain character, a social club should provide amiable companions, or that a political or social protest organization should seek to attain purposes that some people at least regard as important. While a business probably will provide supplementary incentives besides money, few would work for it if no money at all were paid. Few would remain in the social club if meetings consisted entirely of discussions of foreign policy. They might not even remain if they were paid small amounts to do so.[10]

TYPES OF ORGANIZATIONS

On the basis of the foregoing premises, hypotheses can be presented about the internal and external behavior of three types of organizations, each of which relies primarily upon one of the three basic categories of incentives.

Utilitarian Organizations

Organizations which rely largely upon material incentives include many business firms, most "bread and butter" trade unions, most business and trade associations, taxpayers' groups, and the traditional political party machines. These will be called *utilitarian* organizations. They seek material rewards for their members (and perhaps for others as well). There is a fairly precise understanding of the possible benefits and a reasonably exact means of determining the extent to which the goal is attained. There is, to borrow a phrase, a "cost-accounting" system. The costs of supporting the organization can be measured against some rough standard: reduction of taxes, achievement of a higher wage rate, obtaining the redevelopment project with some enhancement of property values, payment of a high dividend, improvement in retail sales, and so forth.

In practice, of course, there is often considerable difficulty in determining individual benefits. If this were not the case, the executives of such organizations would have greater difficulty than they do in maintaining their own positions. As it is, they can point to threats that were averted, progress toward an unrealized goal, and indirect benefits that supposedly accrue to members. In great part bureaucracy thrives on uncertainty. But although uncertainty is never absent, it is less extensive in purely utilitarian organizations than in other types. Executives here are under greater pressure to "produce," even though they can avert some of the pressure by pointing to deferred or indirect pay-offs.

In such groups, the executive's first concern will be to obtain the material resources that will provide incentives. Business officials single-mindedly devoted to the pursuit of money incomes for their firms; labor union executives concerned with obtaining wage increases, pension plans, paid vacations; executives of most taxpayers' associations; and the "boss" of the political machine interested in obtaining patronage are all examples of the preoccupation with material incentives.

The fundamental conflicts within organizations that rely heavily upon material incentives will center around questions of the distribution of the incentives. How are the benefits to be distributed? Who is to receive how much

salary? Which business firms will benefit the most from the association's campaign to reduce taxes? Which ward bosses will receive the highest-paying patronage jobs? Internal strife arises in the form of rather sharply defined conflicts of material interest. Given these executive preoccupations, the organization will act vis-à-vis the outside world mostly when opportunities are perceived to increase the input of material resources or when the loss of such resources is believed to be threatened. Their actions contrast with the external and political activities of organizations that rely upon other incentives, as will be seen.

The utilitarian organization and its executive pay relatively little attention to the substantive goals implied by its activities. Suprapersonal purposes will rarely be discussed, except at the most publicized of ceremonial occasions, for such purposes have little bearing upon the day-to-day problems of operating or maintaining such groups.[11] Members are employed to do whatever the organization requests them to do within the limits of propriety; individuals become contributors expecting that the organization will satisfy their *material* motives. They will rarely question or reflect upon the value of the organization's activity,[12] nor will they expect the organization to take account of their personal views about desirable purposes.

In some cases, however, utilitarian organizations announce general purposes which purport to be different from the motives of the members. For example, a businessmen's association may describe its purpose as that of "improving the life of the city" or "promoting community planning." In most cases, such rhetoric is a socially acceptable cover for a desire to improve property values, reduce taxes, or stabilize markets. (In some cases, this rhetoric becomes the principal source of inducements for members and, thus, the organization ceases to be utilitarian and must instead be considered either solidary or purposive. This is most often true when the organization fails to meet the material motives of the members and thus must endeavor to alter its incentive system in order to survive.) The significant point here is that in utilitarian organizations *stated* purposes are not important incentives and have relatively little impact upon incentives. Achievements of concrete material results will be more important than any announced general or intangible goals, and members will be relatively indifferent to what kind of activity (making soap, selling shoes, trading commodities) produces the desired flow of rewards.

Such organizations will thus be highly flexible about their activities. Activities may change without disrupting member participation as long as material incentives continue to be available. Businesses may shift to production of totally different products; labor unions may alter their demands from wage increases to fringe benefits; and political machines are not only facile in shifting their allegiances on policy positions but in some cases are able to deliver organization workers and blocs of votes to the opposite party—provided the material reward is adequate.

Such organizations will also be tactically flexible to the extent that tactical shifts do not interfere with their income of incentive resources. This is a function of both the fact that the rewards are relatively unambiguous and the fact that ends tend to be divisible and can be expressed in terms of more or less. They have no rationale other than their material value. Within certain broad ranges, means are selected which are best suited to the attainment of the ends at minimal cost. Strategists can be rational in an economic sense, concerned only with goal attainment and efficiency (the ratio between benefits and costs).

Internal conflicts, which in other types of organizations limit flexibility, have a minimal effect in utilitarian groups. Conflicts of interest between members can often be successfully *bargained* out, for material benefits are readily divisible and the propriety of compromising dollar benefits is widely accepted.[13]

Solidary Organizations

Organizations which rely heavily upon solidary incentives include many, if not most, service-oriented voluntary associations, colleges and universities (which employ solidary incentives to attract students, and also faculty members to a great extent), social clubs, certain political reform groups, and many others.[14] In groups such as a women's luncheon club, the underlying incentives for continued participation appear to be sociability and "fun." In other organizations—among the trustees and directors of universities, hospitals, and welfare organizations, for example—the personal prestige which membership provides is often a strong incentive. Board members not only contribute prestige to such boards, but their own prestige is enhanced through association with other high-status community figures and with the institutions themselves.

As in utilitarian organizations, the executive's first concern will be to obtain incentive resources, but here his effort will manifest itself in quite different forms, for the resources are different and obtaining them poses different problems. He must obtain not dollars or other material income but additional organizational prestige, publicity, or good fellowship. These incentives imply continued executive efforts to recruit members of high status and frequent occasions for public speeches and awards to heighten members' sense of the organization's importance and to reward individuals for exceptional service. They also imply frequent rotation of officers in order to distribute widely the perquisites of prestige.[15]

Solidary groups will act externally mostly in situations in which they perceive opportunities to improve their public image. They will undertake—and indeed seek out—worthy projects of a sort which will be widely recognized as good works. Such activity results in enhanced incentives, for a good public image attracts prestigious people who, in turn, reinforce the incentive for others to contribute.

Organizations that rely heavily upon solidary incentives will devote more conscious attention to purposes than will the utilitarian type. This is because publicly acceptable purposes are crucial in producing the desired image. A welfare voluntary association, for example, is much more interested in stating its goals than is a manufacturing firm. Although there are many goals that could provide the desired solidary rewards for the members of the organization, these goals usually possess certain important general characteristics. First and foremost, they must be noncontroversial, since solidary benefits are weakened by any risk that the goal of the association might divide the membership or impair its prestige. The goal ideally will be related to some "cause" (the distribution of benefactions) but never to an "issue" (the conflict of ends), since such organizations seek to avoid conflict with other associations as well as to avoid it internally. Serving on a women's auxiliary to the hospital board, raising funds with a ball or fashion show for some unobjectionable cause, and promoting a symphony orchestra or an art institute are all typical solidary activities.

In addition, the goal ideally implies some principle which allows membership to be restricted. Women's welfare groups are particularly illustrative. They are ranked, at least within general categories and sometimes with marked precision, by the women themselves in terms of their prestige and social standing.[16] This ranking is often institutionalized by linking the groups to organizations or causes which are themselves stratified socially. University and hospital boards

of trustees will usually have women's auxiliaries, with the social standing of the women roughly equivalent to the wealth of the male trustees. Separate social rankings seem to exist for each major religion. This reflects both the church-connected basis of many of these associations (hospitals and charities usually have a religious affiliation) and what may be a tripartite status hierarchy in the United States.[17] The principle of exclusion is sometimes related to the purpose of the group: thus, only persons holding the doctoral degree may become professors, only Presbyterians may be on the Presbyterian hospital board, and so forth.

In some cases, however, the activity of the organization requires a broader membership base, at least from time to time. The Red Cross and the Community Chest are examples of solidary groups with unrestricted or open membership. This presents certain problems. By becoming a mass association with a large membership, the possibility of providing valued solidary rewards often declines. This is usually met by creating two levels of membership: one, composed, for example, of upper-middle-class women, forms the cadre of the association; the other, composed of lower-status women who serve as neighborhood canvassers to solicit funds and who perform seasonal tasks, comprises the floating membership.

Solidary organizations cannot alter their activities as freely as utilitarian groups,[18] partly because of their greater concern with purposes (although purposes are derivative, not primary, incentives). To the extent that contributors are *interested* in the goals implied by their activities, executives will be constrained to adjust organizational activities to suit contributors' interests and demands. If contributors disagree among themselves about them, stated purposes will be moderated to a lowest common denominator acceptable to all. In utilitarian groups, contributors' behavior may be altered to correspond to altered organizational activities, but in solidary groups, activities will often be altered to correspond to the wishes of present and prospective contributors. The price of organizational maintenance may be changes in goals. This necessity to adapt activities to the membership partly accounts for the vagueness and ambiguity of the publicly stated goals of most voluntary associations (including the two major American political parties). It also helps to account for rapid shifts in the interests and activities of voluntary associations and for the fact that ostensible purposes often change in the face of internal conflicts.

More significantly, perhaps, solidary incentives will affect organizational structure and personnel practices so that solidary organizations will be much less flexible tactically than utilitarian groups. First, external actions intended primarily to increase prestige, stature, or "public image" are by no means identical with actions intended to achieve goals. For example, an organizational preoccupation with publicity may prevent secret action because secret activity is deemed to provide negative benefits to members of most solidary groups. Yet secret activity at times may be the most effective means to employ if goal attainment were the primary objective.

Second, the frequent rotation of officers in such organizations reduces continuity of service and prevents the development of experienced elites. The need to recruit contributors of high status, or socially acceptable contributors, or those who are friendly, may well limit an organization's external impact. In another case, a hospital board of directors composed entirely of "society" people is not well-equipped to solve problems involving Negroes, nor is it well-equipped to influence Negroes, even though a problem involving Negroes may be the outstanding issue facing the

hospital. Finally, to paraphrase Chester Barnard, groups which rely upon solidary incentives must gladly tolerate foolish behavior, for the toleration—perhaps the adulation—of foolish behavior is the incentive that must be provided to maintain the contributions of its perpetrators.[19]

The means selected by solidary groups must be appropriate to the class and status of the members and to their style of life. Class and status distinctions define possible incentives to an important degree. Middle-class, college-educated young adults can be brought into politics, if at all, only on the basis of a political style that involves the use of house parties, block clubs, democratic processes, sophisticated public relations, contact with voters on the basis of issues, and a "clean" atmosphere. Political machine members, on the other hand, typically prefer "clubhouse" politics with women and outsiders excluded, contacts with voters on the basis of personal friendship and favors, a minimum of publicity, and allegiance to a single leader charged with the responsibility for getting jobs. Upper-class hospital auxiliaries find it appropriate to raise funds through charity balls at which socially prominent families are present; middle-class PTA groups consider it proper to raise money with cake sales, rummage sales, and so forth; lower-income church groups may prefer to raise funds with bingo games and lotteries. The goals may vary widely but the means must not impair the members' self-conceptions nor lower the standing of the organization in the eyes of the nonmember audience with a comparable style of life.

The basic internal tensions in this kind of group will occur over the distribution of personal prestige and organizational status and over the admittance of new members, who, while useful in pursuit of the organization's stated purposes, are nonetheless regarded as personally or socially unacceptable to the existing membership. Such tensions can be very severe, and will be generally more severe than the tensions which typically arise in organizations relying upon material rewards. Status differentials apparently call into play some of the more basic emotions. And, while such tensions are not unknown in utilitarian organizations, they can there be assuaged by material compensations. A corporate official who fails to be promoted to a vice presidency may nevertheless be given a raise. But in voluntary associations, alternative incentives are rarely available. A personal slight may easily develop into an organizational conflict.

Purposive Organizations

Some groups rely almost exclusively upon their stated purposes as incentives to attract and hold contributors. The intrinsic worth or dignity of the ends themselves are regarded by members as justifying effort. Such a group is sometimes called an ideological organization. Many reform and social-protest groups provide the best illustrations—especially in the early stages of their existence. The communist parties represent approximations of a pure type. In contrast, local chapters of the NAACP are often difficult to distinguish from solidary groups.

As in other types, the central incentive predicts the executive's basic preoccupations: to create and state organizational purposes in such a way as to maintain contributions of effort. Purposes become the basic instrument of unity; but at the same time they become the basic source of potential cleavage. Conflicts over purpose—in purpose-oriented groups— will produce the most heated internal disputes. External actions will be efforts to achieve stated goals or to appear to be doing so.

Incentives are typically derived from organization goals that imply change. Thus, purposive groups tend to be oriented toward issues rather than toward causes. The continual problem of purposive organizations is to select ends that divide the association from other groups in the community without at the same time dividing the association's members from one another. Where there is a clear and deep line of cleavage separating the group's members from other persons in the community it is easier to find such issues. Thus, the NAACP can find a relatively large number of ends which tend to unite most Negroes against most whites. Ends can also be chosen so that they cannot be opposed without exposing oneself to moral censure or clear public disapproval. Such, for example, are the ends of the Crime Commissions, which seek better police protection. Sometimes, as in political-reform groups, the ends unite the members against an opponent because the members are separated from the opponents by clear lines of class and status. Machine politicians of Italian descent can be opposed by upper-middle-class Anglo-Saxon Protestants with little danger, in the usual case, that the reformers will have mixed feelings about or disagree over the propriety of such reforms.

The important aspect of most purposive organizations, however, is that they usually experience great difficulty in denoting their ends with any degree of specificity. Usually, such associations have general ends ("honesty in government," "separation of church and state," "civic planning," "better schools") which cannot be reduced to concrete proposals without serious risk of alienating some significant part of the membership. As a result, purposive organizations are frequently immobilized in the course of a real issue.

A less common problem afflicts those few purposive organizations which can specify their concrete ends. The ability to do so is typically a function of an extremist ideology or a basic cleavage in society which results in the alienation of some articulate minority. In this case, flexibility as to goals is reduced by the moral or sacrosanct quality with which they become imbued. Purposes can be made specific at the outset because of the extreme or alienated position of the initial members (as, for example, with urban socialists, agrarian radicals, or religious cultists) who often join in reaction against some organizational alternative. Changes of stated purposes then either drive members out or cleave the group into fragments. The loss of members from communist or socialist parties with every shift in party line indicates that many members regard these shifts as changes in purposes and not merely as tactical maneuvers.[20]

Thus goals can be inflexible for one of two reasons. In the case of most purposive organizations (which are typically not central to the lives of their members), goals are general and irreducible. Attempts to make them more specific threaten to divide the group. In the case of other, less common purposive groups (in which the organization, for a variety of reasons *is* central to the lives of the members), goals tend to be specific but inflexible because of their sacrosanct quality.

Tactical flexibility may be developed if members can be made aware of the crucial distinction between purposes and tactics. Success in this task will depend partly upon the size of the group and its elite, upon training and inculcation, and upon disciplinary control (which may depend largely upon negative inducements—punishments). Selznick has explained the factors which made tactical flexibility possible in the Russian Communist Party.[21]

Considerable attention will also be devoted to producing among members a sense of accomplishment—often spurious—which is essential in maintaining the force of the incentives. Executives can seldom point to significant steps taken toward achieving some explicit

end, simply because in most cases the end cannot be made explicit. Thus, executives of purposive organizations frequently tend to stress the "service" functions of the association: disseminating information through newsletters and a speaker's bureau, conducting research, mounting public relations campaigns on behalf of some general theme in which the group is interested, and the like. Service activities become a substitute for goal seeking. Rhetoric about "moral victories" may often replace actual achievements. If tactical flexibility is not possible, moral victories will have to replace actual accomplishments.

Failure to attain goals is a frequent source of intraorganizational conflict. Members and leaders, seeking explanations for failure, often fall to accusing one another.[22] Further, the goals of purposive organizations, particularly at the most general level, tend to be endowed with a moral or ideal rationale. Failure to realize ideals (as opposed to the simply utilitarian ends of the business firm) or disputes over the choice of ideals aggravates intra-associational conflict and produces a sense of frustration. This process is moderated in great part by the fact that most purposive associations have ends which are not held to be vital by most members. In cases where they are seen as vital, conflict is intensified. Thus, the NAACP is more likely to have internal disorder than the Citizens of Greater Chicago (which seeks only better government through reform legislation).[23]

Purposive as well as utilitarian and solidary organizations include both membership organizations and contributor organizations. *Membership* associations depend on numerous small contributions for finances, the votes of rank-and-file members for selecting officers, and the mobilization of volunteer workers for group ends. These groups include the American Jewish Congress, the NAACP, the Independent Voters of Illinois, and others. Intra-associational conflict is proportionally higher among these groups than among those which are based on contributors. *Contributor* associations receive donations from interested but not participating individuals, from business firms, or from other organizations. The work of the group is concentrated heavily in the hands of a paid staff with relatively little lay participation. Officers are chosen by a self-perpetuating board of directors with no popular contests. Examples of contributor-based groups would include the Chicago Crime Commission, the Anti-Defamation League of B'nai B'rith, and the Urban League. Contributor-oriented organizations tend to display fewer signs of internal conflict but also to be less likely to set explicit goals. A staff with a budget is typically more cautious than a volunteer officer with no tangible stake.

ORGANIZATIONAL CHANGE

If the behavior of organizations is closely related to their incentive systems, the dynamics of organizational change may be predicted by knowing the circumstances under which incentive systems change. It is here hypothesized that executives modify incentive systems in response to changes in organizational environments and in response to resulting changes in contributors' motives. The basic proposition is that incentive systems are modified in such a way as to bring supplies of available incentives into balance with demands for incentives.

For example, the executives of a manufacturing firm whose sales are declining will attempt to find and distribute something in addition to money to maintain the activity of employees. They may attempt to substitute prestige for money and award impressive-sounding titles to key employees; they may improve working conditions; or they may attempt to appeal to the workers' loyalties to the

firm and its traditions. Or a one-product firm may seek to diversify its operations in order to protect its supply of incentives against environmental change.

Executives continually make slight shifts in incentives in order to meet from limited supplies the demands for incentives. The most frequent changes will be shifts from material to solidary inducements, and vice versa. Under most circumstances, executives will avoid heavy reliance upon purposes as incentives, for these generally produce less stable and less flexible organizations. It is difficult to maintain consistent efforts, for, to be effective, purposes must be popularized and made widely known to contributors. But this very popularization makes failures to achieve purposes more obvious to contributors, which in turn produces restlessness and dissatisfaction. (The failures of religious organizations to achieve their purposes may go undetected, for some purposes are to be achieved either in an afterlife or at a distant millennium.[24]

Political reform groups, initially created to achieve major reorganizations of local governments, provide illustrations of these dynamics. As contributors discover that reform is painfully slow or impossible, executives attempt to redirect their attention to lesser ends—poll watching or neighborhood conservation—and simultaneously try to increase the importance of friendships, sociability, and organizational status as incentives. But as attention to the original purposes dwindles, contributors who had been induced by the reform goals leave the groups. If the groups persist at all, they do so at lower levels of activity and prestige.[25]

Moreover, fewer people are willing to accept organizational purposes as a primary incentive than are willing to accept material or solidary inducements. (At least this appears to be the case in contemporary America.) Hence, it is difficult to hold large numbers of people in purposive groups, especially if the groups require large contributions of activity.

Finally, maintaining a purposive group—at any given level of activity—requires that the executive must direct the processes of obtaining and distributing incentives, but in purposive organizations, the executive himself must *provide* many of the incentives through constant efforts to clarify purposes and to exhort efforts to achieve them. It may be easier for him simply to obtain money or to generate solidary incentives.[26]

However, under three conditions, usually temporary, in which alternative incentives are not available, purposes will be principally relied upon.

1. Groups that produce or obtain few material or solidary incentives will be forced to rely mainly upon purposes; for example, voluntary associations composed of very poor or low-status members.

2. During their *formative stages*, most groups will rely heavily upon purposes as incentives. Newly formed groups have few resources. Embryonic political clubs or parties usually possess only hopes; beginning voluntary associations merely have goals; even infant corporations may lack capital. After they become well-established, however, most organizations turn away from principal reliance upon purposes, for they can generate alternative incentives that are more reliable and more economical. Thus, the decay of purpose and fervor in maturing organizations reveals more than mere "bureaucratization," as it is sometimes called; it is partly the result of conscious or unconscious shifts from purposes to more economical incentives.[27]

3. Organizations will rely upon purposes during crises. In terms of incentive analysis, a crisis is an interruption in the expected, normal flow of incentives (e.g., the effects of an economic depression or a sudden injury to organizational prestige) or a sudden demand for additional contributions of effort, or both. Crises, of course, may be caused by changes either internal or external to the organizations. When such crises occur, executives are compelled to resort to appeals to shared and perhaps lofty ends. Labor unions unable to obtain wage increases for their members (or unions in which workers are apathetic and nonparticipative because their material expectations are being met) may postulate new purposes of a political or public-serving sort to maintain activity. Business associations that cannot obtain the material benefits businessmen want from governments may turn to rhetorical protests which are in some way related to what members believe to be the associations' purposes.[28]

Earlier, the executive function was distinguished from the leadership function. When executives turn to purposes as incentives they are "leading"; this is what is meant by "leadership behavior." It may now be seen that to the extent that an executive relies upon purposes to maintain his organization, he must also fulfill the function of leadership.

The analysis suggests that leadership (the use of purposes as incentives) will occur most frequently in groups composed of poor or low-status members, in newly created organizations, and in organizations facing internal or external crises.[29] Leadership will arise less frequently in utilitarian organizations that possess adequate supplies of incentives. In such groups, executives and would-be leaders will conflict, for leaders' attempts to introduce or change purposes will merely disturb the incentive system. In solidary groups conflicts between executives and potential leaders may also arise, because being a leader is often an incentive.

These propositions help to explain fluctuations in leadership. At some times executives will devote attention to purposes; at other times they will concentrate upon obtaining and distributing material and solidary incentives. These fluctuations will be responses to changes in the supplies of available incentives and to the demands for them. It seems likely that when the active minorities or elites of organizations select new officers, they consciously or unconsciously select men with a greater or lesser concern for substantive purposes, according to how the elites see the organizations' maintenance needs.[30]

Nothing has yet been said about the internal "distribution of power" as a factor affecting organizational behavior. Incentive analysis concentrates attention upon the executive as the focal point of internal power efforts to affect organizational purposes and behavior. From the executive's point of view, the potential power of any contributor depends upon the effect that contributor's presence or absence may have upon the survival of the organization.[31] Major contributors need not overtly threaten to withdraw; prudent executives will anticipate their desires. (Such implicit or explicit threats will be called acts of power.)

If internal power is based upon a contributor's effect upon organizational survival, it is clear that power may be based upon a wide range of tangible and intangible resources and that the distribution of power will vary according to the type of incentive system upon which the organization relies. The most powerful man in the voluntary utilitarian association (e.g., taxpayers' association) will probably be the biggest contributor of money; but in the social club the most powerful person may be the most popular. In certain other solidary groups, the most powerful may be the most prestigious. The capacity of a trade union to withdraw all organized employees may produce more power vis-à-vis a business enterprise than the combined effect of many corporate officers and stockholders.

These points imply that an individual will have power over a wide range of different organizations *only* when that individual possesses a wide range of incentive resources. That is, the possessor

of material wealth will possess little power over solidary or purposive organizations unless he also possesses the resources for other incentives, e.g., prestige, amiability, lofty moral purposes, and others.

This treatment of power also sheds light upon some of the crisis conditions which can impel executives to act as leaders. A contributor's threat to withdraw may threaten a decline in incentive resources (on balance, a contributor may *produce* more incentives for the organization to distribute to others than he receives from it). The executive's response to this threat will partly depend upon his assessment of the contributor's importance to the continuity of the group. If he judges him unimportant, the executive may ignore his request and allow him to withdraw.

But the executive's response will also depend upon the kind of demand the contributor makes. All contributor demands—all power acts—are demands for changes in the distribution of incentives. The contributor may seek more material benefits, or solidary perquisites, or—most significantly in terms of leadership behavior—he may demand either an increase in the importance of purposes or a substantive change in purposes.

In the last case, a successful act of power will (by definition) stimulate increased leadership behavior. The executive may respond with leadership behavior, however, even if the power act is unsuccessful, for, although he may choose to ignore the demands, the crisis produced by the contributor's withdrawal will often impel increased exhortations about purposes in order to compensate for the lost resources. In sum, then, acts of power tend to stimulate leadership behavior.

As is evident, the method of incentive analysis is related in several important respects to certain theories of social stratification. Social stratification is perhaps the dominant single concept in contemporary American sociology and the central organizing variable for much social analysis. A theory of organization must, at some point, refer to this dimension of society. The relationship between incentives and power has been suggested. This mode of thought could be extended by noting the similarity between the three principal types of incentives (and also the three major types of organizations) and the three major dimensions of social stratification. Following Weber, society can be viewed in terms of the unequal distribution of wealth, prestige, and power, which are the basis for distinctions of class, status, and party.[32] They correspond roughly to the distinctions made here between material, solidary, and purposive incentives (and organizations). Elites of wealth, prestige, and power may be found organized in groups which reflect the social value which the members possess to inordinate degree. Much of the difficulty in analyses of "elites" or "power structures" in the past has come from a failure to face squarely the problem of demonstrating that the disproportionate possession of one value (for example, wealth) leads inevitably to the disproportionate possession of another (for example, power). Whether one value can be exchanged for another at a favorable rate in any given situation is a question about which little is known. The extent to which utilitarian, solidary, and purposive organizations tend (at least in America) to be empirically as well as analytically distinct suggests that wealth, prestige, and power—while related—tend to function separately and that, as a result, few organizations can easily combine the three values (or three incentive systems).

ORGANIZATIONAL COMPETITION

The importance of incentive systems also becomes evident in the relationships among organizations. Organizations that share certain attributes (issues, markets, members, resources) tend to compete with one another. This competition usually centers on conflicting claims for scarce incentives. Each organization seeks to assert and maintain its autonomy or distinctive competence in order that it may lay unchallenged claim to a stock of potential incentives. This competition ranges from business competition through union jurisdictional conflicts to the struggle between civic associations. Just as businesses compete for scarce potential incentives (contracts, orders, market shares, and so on), which can be converted into actual incentives, so solidary organizations compete for causes, recognition, stature, and so forth, which can be translated into sociability and prestige, and purposive organizations compete for issues which can be translated into associational goals.

The nature of this competition varies with the kind of organization involved. Competition over tangible stakes tends to be more impersonal; it is somewhat easier to maintain a pattern of relationships with other organizations when the object of the struggle (a contract, for example) is distinct from the person or group acquiring it. When the stakes are intangible, the competition is often more personal and more intensely felt. It is difficult to maintain genial relationships when the stakes are either endowed with a moral or sacrosanct quality (as with some purposes) or are an attribute of personality and reputation (as with prestige, status, honor, conviviality, and so forth).

Organizations seek to maintain themselves. Few disband willingly, as neither executives nor members are eager to end an activity that rewards them. To maintain themselves, these organizations must not allow other groups to capture the stock of potential incentives. In doing so, organizations modify their character continually. The most obvious modification is by altering the stated goals of the organization. Ends are modified when previous ends have been achieved, when those ends cease to be an abundant source of rewards, or when another organization captures previous ends. Thus, Jewish community-relations agencies, created to defend Jews against organized anti-Semitism, now seek to attain general civil rights goals on behalf of other minority groups (particularly Negroes). Some Jewish "defense" goals have been attained; those that remain cannot provide the large existing organizations with a sufficient supply of incentives; as a result, new ends must be selected.

This commonly observed aspect of organizational activity has been called the displacement of goals.[33] Ends originally stipulated for the group—which, indeed, formed the reason for creating the association—are displaced by other, and sometimes contradictory, ends which result from the need to maintain the organization, the bureaucratization of the organization, or changes in the environment of the organizations.[34] If the principal goal is attained, then (as in the case of the National Foundation for Infantile Paralysis) other ends are substituted to extend the life of the group. This is an *intended* displacement of goals. Equally important is the *unintended* displacement of goals. A civic association may exist to achieve some stated objective, but because of the nature of the issue, the inhibiting role of other factors, or the large resources required to wield influence, the association may only provide a legitimacy for more powerful actors who actually create the issue and determine the terms of its resolution. Urban renewal and neighborhood conservation in Chicago, for example, was formally the object of a neighborhood association of very active members. The impetus for and terms of the actual renewal project came from a group of large institutions (business and university). The neighborhood association, with only a few exceptions, functioned to gain consent for the program, give it

grass-roots legitimacy, and act as a lightning rod to attract and divert opposition. (To obtain this co-operation, of course, the more powerful group had to make some concessions to some of the substantive ends of the association.)[35] In large American cities, it may well be that this function is the most significant one performed by most civic associations.[36]

The proliferation of associations and the division of labor in society has meant that there is almost no way for an organization to preserve itself by simply seeking ends for which there are no other advocates. Thus, the maintenance of organizational autonomy is a critical problem. By *autonomy* we refer to the extent to which an organization possesses a distinctive area of competence, a clearly demarcated clientele or membership, and undisputed jurisdiction over a function, service, goal, issue, or cause. Organizations seek to make their environments stable and certain and to remove threats to their identities.[37] Autonomy gives an organization a reasonably stable claim to resources and thus places it in a more favorable position from which to compete for those resources. *Resources* include issues and causes as well as money, time, effort, and names. The intensity of the competition for these can be viewed as a function of the scarcity of resources and the autonomy of the association. Competition increases as resources become more scarce and as the autonomy or jurisdiction of two or more organizations becomes less clear.

Various organizations can be compared on the basis of the extent to which they compete. This comparison could be displayed in a fourfold table as shown below. In cell I, would be found groups which are clearly autonomous and for which resources are relatively abundant. Solidary groups drawing upon upper-class women and firmly identified with a specific cause (the auxiliary board of a hospital) are relatively noncompetitive because resources and autonomy are

Table 10.1 Relationships Among Organizations.

	High Resources	Low Resources
High autonomy	I	II
Low autonomy	III	IV

SOURCE: Reprinted from "Incentive Systems: A Theory of Organizations," by Peter B. Clark and James Q. Wilson, published in *Administrative Science Quarterly* 6, no. 3 (September 1961): 159, Table 1, by permission of *Administrative Science Quarterly.*

both fairly high. Business or utilitarian associations, formed to pursue a clearly stated material end and deriving support from large corporations with a stake in that goal, are also relatively noncompetitive. In cell II are Negro civic associations (for example, the NAACP and the Urban League), which operate on the scantiest resources. Budgets are generally very small and the funds available from the community meager (although conceivably not as meager as the budgets would suggest). But the functions of these two organizations are relatively clear and distinct. The scarcity of resources is partially offset by the small number of the groups and their relatively high autonomy. Each of the two major associations has a virtual monopoly over its special services—protest, legislative activity, and legal defense in one case; research, counseling, public relations, and community organization in the other. Thus, competition exists but it is not usually severe. These Negro groups can be compared to the Jewish community-relations associations in cell III. Here the resources are much more abundant—there are many affluent businesses and individuals on whom to draw for funds.[38] Such organizations, however, are also more numerous, and their individual autonomy is relatively low. The four major Jewish "defense" associations have overlapping jurisdictions, share essentially the same issues, and compete for resources from a clientele that is only roughly differentiated by class and national origin. The rivalries of these groups are notorious

and have been a theme of self-analysis.[39] In cell IV might be found embryonic organizations, lacking in both resources and autonomy. Such groups rarely survive without an "angel" (to provide a large stock of resources) or an unusual cause (to provide a degree of autonomy).

Maintaining a distinctive identity, character, or autonomy is not easy. Ends sought may divide the membership. But even more generally, the *kind* of association that is desired is often a matter of dispute. There develop tensions between those who derive primarily solidary rewards from the groups and those who derive purposive rewards. For example, the NAACP is divided on occasion not only by conflicts of purpose, but by the question of the nature of the association itself. For many middle-class Negroes, the NAACP is a social group which provides solidary benefits, and this is reflected in the concern many of these members have for avoiding unnecessary conflict, adopting a moderate tone, and bargaining with whites rather than protesting to them. Other members shun solidary rewards and are satisfied only with purposive rewards. This implies an opposite strategy.

The Negro leader who seeks to emphasize the solidary aspects of the association is in conflict (*a*) with members who seek purposive rewards but also (*b*) with whites for whom the very essence of the association is one of protest, radicalism, and aggressiveness. Leaders become trapped in tension-producing conflicts between their interests and the interests of others, as well as between their definition of the nature of the association and the definition imposed upon them by outsiders with whom they must deal and who sometimes refuse to recognize NAACP officers as moderate men and insist on dealing with them as if they were radicals.

Preserving the identity of the association is important for utilitarian groups also. They avoid including members whose presence might suggest that the group was bent on reform and who might thus deter the contributions of others. Thus, some associations exclude Negroes simply in order to prove that they are not idealistic reformers seeking controversial ends—i.e., that they are not purposive.[40]

Responses to problems of interorganizational competition are varied. Much of this competition remains chronic, but some modifications of structure and function occur under certain circumstances. Such changes include (*a*) the creation of new agencies, (*b*) the allocation of functions, and (*c*) mergers. New agencies are created by existing associations when these parent groups are threatened with a loss of their tax-exempt status or when issues are divisive of their memberships. Both purposive and utilitarian associations habitually create *ad hoc* or "front" agencies to seek goals felt to be generally within the competence of the parent group but contrary to the character of that group. Thus, a community-relations association whose maintenance requires it to proceed through bargaining and persuasion cannot engage in a militant protest campaign against public authorities. In this case, the staff of the agency will help to create an *ad hoc* group which will protest and in which the more militant members of the parent group can participate. Or new groups are created to settle jurisdictional disputes. When several Jewish agencies all offered services in the field of employment discrimination, the solution was to create a new agency, supported by the original groups, which provided the service for all on a common basis.

The allocation of functions is repeatedly attempted in order to clarify and render certain the autonomy of competing organizations. Allocating functions is typically easier when the competing agencies seek solidary rather than purposive incentives. Welfare services seem, in their nature, to be more divisible than civic issues. Jewish philanthropic agencies have found it easier to associate for the end of allocating functions (i.e., defining jurisdictions) and funds (i.e., bargaining over resources) in such collectivities as the Federation of Jewish Philanthropies than have Jewish reform groups which (at least in larger cities) resist incorporation into such bodies as the National Community Relations Advisory Council. Issues are more difficult to allocate than causes, and hence purposive associations experience more problems in defining their autonomy than solidary groups.[41]

Mergers are rare and usually the result of external forces which compel this outcome. When two hospitals in Chicago merged for economic reasons, the solidary associations which were clustered around each were required to merge as well. This created difficulties, because one solidary group was small, distinctly upper-class, and based on social-register families, while the other was larger, more heterogeneous, and drew from middle-class sources.[42] The special identity of each was jeopardized, and hence (particularly for the more exclusive one) the value of the solidary rewards was threatened.

Many organizations, of course, co-operate rather than compete. The conditions under which co-operation can occur are obviously of great importance. These conditions can be described in general, but they seem to vary in detail from society to society. The fact that logically comparable incentives some-times produce dissimilar activity suggests the importance of cultural differences in incentive systems.

Co-operation implies agreement by two or more organizations on a set of rules that will govern their behavior vis-à-vis one another in such a way that the autonomy of each is respected, an allo-cation of potential incentives is agreed upon, and the rewards of observing the rules are held to be greater than the rewards of breaking them. Clearly, certain kinds of organizations are more likely to co-operate than others. Co-operation is most likely among utilitarian organiza-tions and least likely among purposive groups. The same factors which facilitate co-operation within utilitarian organiza-tions promote such co-operation between these organizations. The stakes are imper-sonal and tangible, the incentives are divisible, the pay-offs are unambiguous, and announced organizational purposes are both of minor importance and of little moral significance. Further, co-operation is more likely when the orga-nizations involved are few in number and uncertainty can thereby be reduced. The consequences of the actions of each orga-nization can be assessed with some preci-sion, the number of decisions that must be made to evolve a co-operative for-mula are relatively few, and coalitions can easily be formed in order to punish those who violate the rules of co-operation.

The contrary of any of these condi-tions will generally make co-operation more difficult. In the case of many pur-posive organizations, the stakes are intan-gible and often personal, the incentives are indivisible, the pay-offs frequently ambiguous or uncertain, and organiza-tional purposes are of crucial impor-tance and often endowed with a moral rationale. Further, since purposive incen-tives are both intangible and infinite (the range of conceivable purposes, even within a given area, is as large as the range of conceivable ideas), it is difficult,

if not impossible, to "control the market" sufficiently to prevent new organizations from arising or schisms occurring in such a way that co-operative agreements can ever be stabilized. A high degree of uncertainty will always prevail.

Historical and cultural factors can alter these forces in significant ways. Some purposive organizations can co-operate in part, it seems, because their goals and autonomy have become tradi-tional to the extent that real challenges are unlikely. Although rivals are possible, the organization has a sense of security and self-confidence born of a long his-tory and a recognized competence. Secure purposive organizations are more likely to co-operate than insecure ones.[43] Co-operation between purposive groups will also be facilitated if members are made aware of the distinction between tactics and purposes. If such a distinction can be made convincing, then (as with some communist parties) members will agree to co-operation for purely tactical reasons. If it cannot be made plausible, co-operation is more difficult. Co-operation with another group is unlikely if it implies accepting the other group's purposes. After all, differences in purposes distin-guish the two groups and justify their sep-arate existence.

On the other hand, some factors can reduce the likelihood of co-operation between utilitarian groups. Similar market situations in Europe and America, for example, produce strikingly different competitive responses. There appears to be much more co-operation (carteliza-tion, market sharing, administered pric-ing, and so forth) in European business than in American. These differences can apparently be accounted for only on the basis of differences in motive and vary-ing assessments of the rewards of risk taking. When men place widely differ-ing values on risk, they will respond dif-ferently to co-operative arrangements to eliminate risk. There will be less co-operation among utilitarian organizations when the rewards of risk taking are felt to be high. As the next section implies, there may in America be a decline in the value placed on risk and uncertainty, and hence a shift in the nature of the incentive systems in utilitarian organizations.

MOTIVATIONAL CHANGE

Over time, changes in the economy in moral beliefs, and in other attitudes produce corresponding changes in personal motives. The distribution of motives throughout the society defines the potential contributors to various organizations. As motives change, so will organizations. Some organizations will grow or decline spontaneously as the particular incentives they offer become relatively more or less appealing; other organizations will make changes consciously. Incentive analysis permits some inferences about the dynamics of such long-term changes.[44]

The decline of political party machines illustrates one case. The monetary incentives that held machines together lost force as party workers became increasingly able to earn more money at jobs which were widely regarded as more respectable than party patronage positions and occasional corrupt rewards. Simultaneously, the sources of the machines' money were reduced by new laws controlling financial contributions, the rise of civil service, and the growing moral disapproval implemented by the spotlight of journalistic and academic publicity.[45] Machines found themselves increasingly composed of smaller numbers of less competent party workers. Some machines disappeared. The character of other party organizations changed. Some are being staffed by amateurs who are impelled by the enjoyment of politics or by the good purposes which they impute to, and seek to impose upon, the political parties they serve.[46]

Large business corporations provide a second illustration of such long-term shifts. It is widely recognized that the officials of the largest corporations are now salaried managers rather than owner proprietors. Moreover, the income tax structure drastically decreases the dollar value of salaries at the higher income levels, and businessmen have been severely criticized for placing material gains above other considerations. These changes, coupled with what appears to be a generally increasing interest in a social status not measured entirely by dollars, have importantly reduced the significance of material incentives in the largest corporations.[47]

The executives of many large firms have responded to these trends more flexibly than political bosses by placing increasing reliance upon a wide range of solidary incentives, and occasionally upon certain social purposes as incentives. Corporation officials are strongly motivated by personal prestige and by the prestige of the firm. The size of the firm, rather than its net profit, becomes the index of prestige. The corporate drive to expand produces not only more material incentives but more prestige. Corporations are also increasingly engaging in community civic affairs through contributions of money and considerable executive time. In the last few decades, the executives of some corporations have spoken more frequently about "business' community responsibilities" and about the generalized social purposes that business helps to achieve. These activities are not solely directed as public relations to consumers and governments. Some of them, it may be suggested, are intended for internal influence. The community-serving activities of corporations are intended in part as incentives supplementary and complementary to salary and wages. It seems reasonable to predict a continuation and expansion of this form of corporate activity.

The motivational trends considered here seem to be reducing the importance of material, and perhaps of purposive, inducements. At the same time, solidary incentives are apparently increasing in importance. This suggests gradual movement toward a society in which factors such as social status, sociability, and "fun" control the character of organizations, while organized efforts to achieve either substantive purposes or wealth for its own sake diminish.

NOTES

1. Chester Barnard, who first systematically developed the incentive analysis, defines a formal organization as a "system of consciously co-ordinated activities or forces of two or more persons" (*The Functions of the Executive* [Cambridge: Harvard University Press, 1938], p. 73). For Barnard's general analysis, upon which this paper is based, see especially his chapter xi, "The Economy of Incentives." Further theoretical development and illustrations are provided by Herbert A. Simon, *Administrative Behavior* (2nd ed.; New York, 1959), ch. vi; Edward C. Banfield, *Political Influence* (Glencoe, 1961) and *Government Project* (Glencoe, 1949), ch. xv; James Q. Wilson, *Negro Politics: The Search for Leadership* (Glencoe, 1960); and Peter B. Clark, "The Chicago Big Businessman as a Civic Leader" (unpublished Ph.D. dissertation, University of Chicago, 1959), ch. v.

    The authors would like to acknowledge the financial assistance of the Committee on Political Behavior of the Social Science Research Council which made possible research drawn upon for certain portions of this paper.

2. Cf. Philip Selznick, *TVA and the Grass Roots* (Berkeley and Los Angeles, 1949), p. 79: "All formal organizations are moulded by forces tangential to their rationally ordered structures and stated goals." The same point is the theme of David L. Sills, *The Volunteers* (Glencoe, 1957).

3. Barnard, *The Functions of the Executive,* p. 139. The desire to achieve an abstract social good may, of course, be subsumed under the "egotistical motive of self-gratification." The point is that the organization must satisfy some aspect of the *contributor's* motives— whatever those motives may be.

4. See Simon, *Administrative Behavior,* ch. iv. and p. 181. As Simon notes, the output of incentives may exceed the input, at least for a short period of time. There is no "law of the conservation of energy" at work in organizations in any strict sense. This is because the very existence of the organization itself is a source of incentives of a kind; dying organizations still hold some members out of a sense of duty or in hopes of an improvement in its fortunes. Some people will act out of even slim hopes for future rewards.

5. "Executive work is not that *of* the organization but the specialized work of *maintaining* the organization in operation" (Barnard, *The Functions of the Executive,* p. 215; italics in the original). "In all sorts of organizations the affording of adequate incentives becomes the most definitely emphasized task of their existence. It is probably in this aspect of executive work that failure is most pronounced, though the causes may be due either to inadequate understanding or to the breakdown of the effectiveness of the organization" (*ibid.,* p. 139). Executives will, of course, attempt to create conditions under which contributions of activity become habitual, where contributors rarely assess the benefits of the incentives they receive against the opportunity costs of incentives they forego by not joining alternative organizations. When such conditions are created, the organization need provide to contributors only a small net balance of satisfaction over dissatisfactions. It is not intended to suggest that all contributors to all organizations are constantly and consciously assessing the benefits (incentives) against the costs of their contributions, but conscious weighing occurs often enough that the problem of organizational maintenance represents the most salient fact of organizational life for the executive. It is important to note that many incentives are not consciously produced and distributed by anyone. The location of a factory in Florida may be an incentive to a sun-seeking worker, although the decision to locate the plant in Florida may not have been made with this inducement in mind.

(An executive, of course, may be plural. The actual executive of many voluntary associations is not the layman president but the professional executive secretary.)

6. Philip Selznick, *Leadership in Administration* (Evanston, 1957), develops a somewhat similar view of leadership. See pp. 25–28, and chs. iii, iv.

7. The notion of organizational purpose is a confusing one in almost all the literature on the subject. Barnard (*The Functions of the Executive,* pp. 86–89), Simon (*Administrative Behavior,* pp. 4, 63, 132, 246). and James G. March and Herbert A. Simon (*Organizations* [New York, 1958], p. 201) assume that all organizations have a purpose or goal. What they mean by purpose is never very clear. In one sense, of course, almost all human activity is purposive in that some goal can be found toward which the activity is at least presumptively directed. Depending on one's point of view, a shoe factory may have as its "purpose" making money for stockholders, distributing wages and salaries to employees, providing shoes for customers, or enhancing the power and prestige of its officers. When used in this paper the word *purposes* refers to explicitly stated substantive goals, which are suprapersonal (i.e., they will not benefit members directly and tangibly) and which have nonmembers as their objects. By contrast, when we refer to a business making money for its members (which some might call its "purpose"), we shall call that process the *activity* of the organization. *Activity* is used broadly to refer to whatever an organization does from the point of view of the observer; *purpose* is used narrowly to refer to goals of a suprapersonal, extraorganizational character stated by the organization itself. It will be noted that *purposes* are heavily future-oriented.

8. It is also important to distinguish between the incentive provided by loyalty to an organization (as a concrete entity) and the incentive provided by belief in the organization's purposes. The former (which is often consciously fostered) is here regarded as a solidary incentive. Loyalty to an organization's *purposes* is certainly analytically distinct from loyalty to the actual organization. In many cases it is also concretely distinguishable as when, for example, people choose to leave an organization which they believe is no longer fulfilling its ostensible purposes.

9. The question arises as to whether these distinctions are purely analytical or whether they correspond to concrete organizations. The differentiation of incentive systems is primarily analytical and its value will depend on the extent to which it is useful in specifying and explaining organizational behavior even if no one organization embodies a single incentive system. Therefore, an important aspect of incentive analysis will involve delineating the relationships between analytically distinct incentives within a single organization. . . . There are many examples of organizations, however, which rely primarily on a single incentive system—certain businesses, voluntary associations, and the like—and thus the analytical distinctions correspond to at least some concrete cases. This paper, then, is largely an exposition of an analytical framework applied to relatively simple concrete cases. The cases of organizations with mixed incentive systems—such as armies, churches, government agencies, newspapers, certain labor unions, and organizations undergoing internal conflict—will be treated elsewhere.

This paper views individuals in organizations from the point of view of the executive. The other side of the equation—the organization as seen by contributors—is only sketchily treated. For a discussion of differences among contributors, see Barnard, *The Function of the Executive,* pp. 74–77, and Simon, *Administrative Behavior,* ch. vi.

10. These points reinforce the common-sense observation that organizations are not always what they seem to be. A foreign policy discussion group may in fact fulfill the function of providing social interaction or entertainment. This may easily be detected if the latter ceases, but the foreign policy discussion is earnestly continued. Membership, it could be predicted, would fall.

11. Under conditions of high public exposure, of course, utilitarian organizations will undertake ritualistic expressions of purpose, for it is expected that organizations must justify themselves in terms of some goals other than mere perpetuation or expansion. No organization can admit that its "purpose" is merely the gratification of its contributors' private motives. However, in materially induced organizations such ceremonial expressions of purpose are intended

largely for external consumption and will have much less effect upon organizational behavior than in the other types of groups to be discussed.

12. In an article which implicitly employs an incentive analysis. Robert Heilbroner reaffirms this point. "The people who make [machine] politics their occupation do do not tend to thrive on ideas and ideals, and the Tammany clubs—indeed, machine clubs everywhere—tend to become pleasant fraternities where the boys' can sit around and play poker, gossip, get away from their wives, and relax" (De Sapio: The Smile on the Face of the Tiger, *Harpers,* 209 [1954], 30).

13. For the same reasons, co-operation among groups relying upon material incentives may be somewhat more likely than among the other two types of organizations. However, all groups which use the same incentives will compete for the same pool of scarce resources and all, of course, will struggle to grow in order to obtain and distribute both material and nonmaterial incentives.

14. The use of the term "solidary" here should not be confused with the use found in Max Weber, *The Theory of Social and Economic Organization,* trans. A. M. Henderson and Talcott Parsons (Glencoe, 1947), pp. 136–143. Weber refers to two kinds of "solidary social relationships"—pure, self-serving associations (*Zweckverein*) and absolute or ideological associations (*Gesinnungsverein*).

15. This probably accounts for the fact that in most universities academic offices such as departmental chairman and dean, where solidary considerations (prestige and honor) are uppermost, are rotated more frequently than are positions in the central administration such as registrar and admissions director, where material incentives (income) may be primary.

16. Joan Moore, "Stability and Instability in the Metropolitan Upper Class" (unpublished Ph.D. dissertation, University of Chicago, 1959), gives an analysis of the welfare associations found among Chicago upper-class women and a detailed discussion of two of them. Note also E. Digby Baltzell, *Philadelphia Gentlemen* (Glencoe, 1958).

17. See Will Herberg, *Protestant, Catholic, Jew* (rev. ed.; New York, 1960), esp. pp. 27–45.

18. Contrast Selznick (*Leadership in Administration,* p. 16), who says "a university has more such leeway [to develop in response to social forces] than most businesses, because its goals are less clearly defined and it can give more free play to internal forces and historical adaptation." It is here suggested that the stated purposes of universities tend to constrict their behavior more than the stated purposes of business firms constrain theirs. University goals may be less *clearly* defined than businesses', but they are certainly more widely known and they certainly establish constricting expectations on the part of their contributors. Few employees of a shoe firm would object if some of the firm's resources were allocated to education, but universities could not easily be converted to the production of shoes. It would seem that the flexibility of business activities (and stated purposes) is limited mainly by sunk capital and established markets, and relatively little by the expectations of the people who work for businesses.

19. Barnard, *The Functions of the Executive,* p. 221, n. 2.

20. Simon, *Administrative Behavior,* p. 118.

21. Selznick, *Leadership in Administration,* pp. 45 ff., and *The Organizational Weapon* (Glencoe, 1960), ch. i.

22. Cf. March and Simon, *Organizations,* p. 119.

23. Wilson, *Negro Politics,* chs. vi, ix.

24. See the description of the problems of a Negro religious sect in Essein Essein-Udom, *Black Nationalism* (Ph.D. dissertation, University of Chicago, 1960).

25. A description of this process in a Chicago reform group is presented in Clark, "The Chicago Big Businessman," ch. v.

26. These points suggest that organizational executives of exceptional energy to a large extent rely upon purposes to elicit activity. Conversely, when a group finds itself with an executive lacking energy, the group's apparent purposiveness may also decline.

27. Russia's postrevolutionary history may illustrate these dynamics. It is also useful to compare the relatively mature contemporary USSR with the young, highly purposive, and extremist Communist China. This process has also been described in the case of Negro political organizations. See

Wilson, *Negro Politics,* chs. ii, iii, iv; and Wilson, Two Negro Politicians: An Interpretation, *Midwest Journal of Political Science,* 4 (1960), 346–369.

28. The National Association of Manufacturers may provide an example. The increasingly "ideological" nature of the NAM's statements may be not only a cause but also a consequence of its political ineffectiveness. A staff member of a business association recently told an interviewer that "the NAM has a tremendous staff. It is a gigantic bureaucratic organization that is completely staff run. Their [staff members'] principal concern is to keep their members happy and to give to them what they want to hear. If they can say in seventeen ways that Walter Reuther is a Communist—so much the better." The extremist statements made by "losing" organizations may result much more from conscious efforts to maintain organizations than from psychological frustrations.

29. Selznick (*Leadership in Administration,* pp. 107 ff.) suggests that leadership is required when "critical" rather than "routine" organizational decisions are needed. It is here suggested that, broadly speaking, "critical" decisions are impelled by declines in incentive stocks or increases in needs for contributions.

30. Leadership, of course, may also arise by "accident," as when a man with great energy or strong personal proclivities toward substantive purposes is unknowingly selected to be the executive. Some men are more interested in achieving substantive purposes than they are in maintaining their organizations. Such tendencies toward leadership may be very useful at times, but the analysis suggests that they may also be injurious to organizational maintenance. Voluntary association staffs, therefore, devote much time to "training" their lay officers to understand the importance and tactics of organizational survival.

31. Cf. Barnard, *The Functions of the Executive,* p. 250, heading 3. The contributor's actual power also depends upon the executive's assessment of the likelihood that the contributor will in fact withdraw. Is the contributor bluffing? Is the issue crucial to him?

32. Max Weber, *Essays in Sociology,* trans. H. Gerth and C. Wright Mills (London, 1948), pp. 180 ff. The parallel between Weber's scheme and the present one is, of course, not exact. For example, purposive organizations are not analogous to "party" except in the very general sense that all purposive groups necessarily are concerned with altering the distribution of power in society in order to achieve their goals.

33. Cf. Philip Selznick, An Approach to the Theory of Bureaucracy, *American Sociological Review,* 8 (1943), 49; Robert Merton, *Social Theory and Social Structure* (Glencoe, 1949), pp. 220–221.

34. Cf. Sheldon L. Messinger, Organizational Transformation: A Study of a Declining Social Movement, *American Sociological Review,* 20 (1955), 3–10; David L. Sills, *The Volunteers* (Glencoe, 1959), pp. 62–77; and Herbert Garfinkel, *When Negroes March* (Glencoe, 1959), pp. 17, 170, 174.

35. This is brought out in Peter H. Rossi and Robert Dentler, *The Politics of Urban Renewal* (Glencoe, forthcoming).

36. Cf. Banfield, *Political Influence,* and Clark, "The Chicago Big Businessman."

37. Cf. Earl Latham, "The Group Basis of Politics: Notes Toward a Theory," in Heinz Eulau *et al., Reader in Political Behavior* (Glencoe, 1956), p. 236.

38. Fund raising in Jewish groups is treated in Norman Miller, "The Jewish Leadership of Lakeport," in A. Gouldner, *Studies in Leadership* (New York, 1950), pp. 195 ff.

39. See Robert MacIver, *Report on the Jewish Community Relations Agencies* (New York, 1951), together with the rejoinders issued by various affiliated associations.

40. Cf. Clark, "The Chicago Big Businessman," ch. v. Most utilitarian organizations consciously seek to exclude members who have expectations of purposive rewards.

41. Cf. Ray Johns, *The Co-operative Process among National Social Agencies* (New York, 1946). He notes (p. 199) that co-operation is also related to formal structure. Agencies with a "federated" structure are more likely to co-operate than similar agencies with a "unitary" structure.

42. Cf. Moore, "Stability and Instability in the Metropolitan Upper Class," chs. v, vi, vii.

43. See James Wilson, "Negro Civic Leaders," paper read before the annual meeting of the

American Political Science Association, September, 1960, New York City, on the consequences of growing security for co-operation between Negro and white organizations on race relations.

44. If an organization persists, it may be asked, is this because a favorable balance of incentives happens to be available to it, or is it because of the executive's skill in obtaining and distributing incentives? The only answer is that the theory calls attention to these difficult questions. The questions can probably be answered adequately only through careful gathering of data. Further, the test of organizational survival is probably too coarse a measure of executive skills. Subtle but significant differences among organizations may be ignored if one is preoccupied only with mere survival. We stress that we are concerned with the consequences of different methods of maintenance, not with maintenance simply.

45. And, of course, the machines also declined as the incentives machine workers could offer became progressively less valuable to *voters*. The incentives of personal services

and welfare no longer elicited contributions of votes for the machine as prosperity increased, governments provided bureaucratized welfare, and immigrants became more familiar with the society.

46. Cf. Heilbroner, "The Smile on the Face of the Tiger," on Tammany's decline and the influx of amateurs. See Francis Carney, *The Rise of the California Democratic Clubs* (New York, 1958), and James Q. Wilson, *Intellectuals as Politicians* (Glencoe, forthcoming) on the development of California political clubs induced partly by sociability. These trends suggest that local party organizations will provide less continuity of effort in the future, that traditional, routine local party chores will go unattended, and that unless substantial agreement develops about party purposes the parties will become increasingly fragmented.

47. Among the best analyses of what appear to be trends away from corporate "economic man" are Robert Gordon, *Business Leadership in the Large Corporation* (Washington, 1945), and Theodore Levitt, *The Twilight of the Profit Motive* (Washington, 1955).

PROJECT

Think about a group you belong to. What incentives were offered to you to join? Does Clark and Wilson's analysis conform to the experience you have had in the group?

11

An Exchange Theory
of Interest Groups

ROBERT SALISBURY

In this article, Robert Salisbury identifies the notion of interest-group entrepreneurs. These entrepreneurs shoulder the cost of attracting citizens to join
an interest group. Using Olson's rational-choice perspective, Salisbury finds that
entrepreneurs offer benefits to individuals in exchange for their membership in
the group. The entrepreneurs receive a return on their investment: the power to
lobby policy makers on behalf of the group.

Olson contributed greatly to our knowledge of group formation, but Salisbury
notes that Olson neglects to examine the stimulus for group organization. Salisbury
identifies the entrepreneur as this stimulus. Additionally, he theorizes that increasing affluence enables more individuals to take on the role of an entrepreneur. Thus,
we are likely to see more groups form during times of economic prosperity.

QUESTIONS TO CONSIDER

1. What is an interest-group entrepreneur?
2. What does an interest-group entrepreneur want to accomplish?
3. How do interest-group entrepreneurs entice people to join their groups?
4. How does Salisbury's analysis add to Olson's analysis?
5. What do Salisbury's observations about affluence say about interest-group
   representation?

In one of those apparently casual passages into which enormous significance may be read David B. Truman remarks that "the origins of interest groups and the circumstances surrounding their orientations toward the institutions of government [are] . . . among the factors most relevant to a description of group politics."[1] He goes on to suggest or imply some fragments of general theory concerning group formation which remain largely undeveloped, either by Truman or by other students of interest groups. Issues of major theoretical relevance are raised in these fragments, however, and we propose to examine them closely to see whether they, and the data concerning interest group formation, may lead to some fuller theoretical understanding of interest group phenomena.

We shall focus much of our attention on the development of American agricultural groups. In part, this focus is the product of convenience and ready accessibility of illustrative data.[2] In part, however, this sector of American group development is especially apt for the testing of extant theories of group formation. In addition to farm groups we shall refer to other types of groups sufficiently often to indicate the range of application of the argument. It should be noted at the outset that the argument presented here has many close links to an intellectual focus now attaining major stature in other social sciences; namely, exchange theory.[3] This paper represents an effort to contribute to that development by applying its terms to, and reinterpreting them in the light of, interest groups in politics.

Briefly, the argument is that interest group origins, growth, death, and associated lobbying activity may all be better explained if we regard them as exchange relationships between entrepreneurs/organizers, who invest capital in a set of benefits, which they offer to prospective members at a price—membership. We shall compare this approach to others in an attempt to explain the data of group origins and elaborate its terms to explore the implications of the argument for other facets of group activity.

One other prefatory note should be entered. Our concern here is with organized interest groups or, in Truman's term, formal associations. We wish to explain how such associations come into being, the conditions affecting their growth or decline, their internal structures of action and their role in the political process. We do not wish to develop an interest group theory of politics, a la Arthur F. Bentley. That is quite a different intellectual enterprise and one that is largely unrelated to the present analysis. This is an effort to develop a theory of interest groups, not an interest group theory of politics, and it is hoped that any disputation which might center on the latter issue may be avoided.[4]

THEORIES OF PROLIFERATION AND EQUILIBRIUM

One fragment of extant group formation theory we may call the proliferation hypothesis.[5] It argues, in effect, that as a consequence of various processes of social differentiation, especially those linked to technological change but including others as well, there is within a given population more and more specialization of function. Increasingly specialized sets of people are observed engaged in a growing range of particular economic activities or specific social roles and from this specialized differentiation of role and function comes greater and greater diversity of interests or values as each newly differentiated set of people desires a somewhat different set of social goals.

SOURCE: From Robert H. Salisbury, "An Exchange Theory of Interest Groups," *American Journal of Political Science* 47(1): 1–32. Reprinted with permission from Blackwell Publishing Ltd.

For example, it may be argued that American farmers became increasingly specialized in terms of the commodities raised in a particular area or by particular farmers and also in terms of that corollary of specialization—interdependence with other segments of the economy; banks, merchants, railroads, and the like.[6] Ever since the Civil War, it is quite clear farmers have grown more and more differentiated as technological innovations, such as mechanical combines and cotton pickers or refrigerated transport, combined with other factors, such as the increased use of less flexible, arid land, and changing demand patterns in both peace and war, to induce each farmer to concentrate his resources on the commodity he could produce to greatest advantage rather than try to supply himself with a wide range of necessary foods and fibers. In short, the full scale commercialization of agriculture, beginning largely with the Civil War, led to the differentiation of farmers into specialized groups with specialized interests, each increasingly different from the next. These interests had to do with such questions as prices and market shares for the farmers and also for those with whom the farmers dealt in the market place. The interdependence which accompanied the specialization process meant potential conflicts of interests or values both across the bargaining encounter and among the competing farmers themselves as each struggled to secure his own position.

The proliferation hypothesis now simply adds that as a "natural" social response among these conflicting specialized groups formal associations are created, or emerge, to represent the conflicting claims of each differentiated set of interested parties. The association articulates the interest, and by organizing its adherents provides more effective bargaining power vis-à-vis other groups. It may be, as Bentley put it, "mere technique" since the association is seen as a kind of automatic fruit of the process of social differentiation, but it has an independent effect upon the political processes in which the group may be concerned. Thus unorganized groups, i.e., people with differentiated but unarticulated values, are presumed to be weaker than organized groups. The questions of whether truly differentiated interests will actually languish for long in unorganized circumstances is a matter which remains unclear in the theoretical fragments we have to work with.[7] It does seem that, taken over time, such interests are expected to achieve organizational expression even though the specific process by which formal organizations are generated are nowhere examined and seem rather generally to be regarded as inevitable consequences of differentiation itself. In any case, for our purposes, the salient points concerning the proliferation hypothesis are three: (1) associations are products of differentiated sets of values or interests, (2) over time there will appear more and more different, diverse, specialized groups in the political arena as the processes of social fission continue, and (3) it is to the processes by which values are altered that one must look for an explanation of group formation.

A second proto-theory, so to speak, of group formation may be referred to as the homeostatic mechanism hypothesis.[8] This argument places much less emphasis on the processes of social differentiation and the generation of "new interests" thereby. Rather it assumes a certain differentiation and suggests the following sequence as typical of group origins. A putative equilibrium among social groups is disturbed as a consequence of such socially disruptive factors as technological innovation, war, transportation or communications changes, and such macro-social processes as major population movements, business cycle fluctuations, and industrialization. The disequilibrium will evolve a response from the disadvantaged sectors as they seek to restore a viable balance. A principal way of doing so is by organizing a formal association because, as Truman points out, this not only improves bargaining power but it also helps to stabilize and strengthen relationships within the group by increasing the mutually supportive interaction among members and thereby the range and salience of their shared values. Notice that the organization is seen as a more active agent in this approach than from the proliferation perspective. Its operations contribute directly, if only marginally, to the changing of member values and it is thus much less dependent on underlying social processes to show the interest direction the group should pursue.

Truman observes that "the formation of associations . . . tends to occur in waves"[9] because once a group organizes in order to reassert a satisfactory equilibrium it may inspire counterorganization among rival groups in a kind of dialectical process. Presumably there is an equilibrating tendency underlying this process, however, so that once a set of social group bargaining encounters has been organized on all sides there is an end to the group formation process and a stability to the associational activities. In this respect the homeostatic mechanism hypothesis differs from the proliferation hypothesis since the latter predicts the continuing development of new interest configurations and hence of new associations.

We may well have read distinctions into remarks which were intended for less intensive exegetical use, but the two theoretical sketches outlined above do occasionally appear in the literature. The two approaches differ in emphasis and in certain of their assumptions, but they are not mutually exclusive. The critical question is which hypothesis gives the better empirical return, or, if neither is adequate, is there a superior alternative? Attention to the formation of agricultural groups in the United States leads us to find congenial elements in both hypotheses, but there are disquieting

elements as well. Let us examine, albeit briefly, the relevant data.

By either of our hypotheses the growth of politically relevant farmer organizations would be expected in the post-civil war period. On the one hand, the spectacular rise of the Grange from 1867 until about 1875 is a sufficiently prominent datum that no theory of group formation would be likely to miss it. At the same time, it is clear that agricultural technology changed dramatically in the direction of mechanization during this period. The dislocations of war and the railroad-assisted post-bellum westward expansion contributed, as did the growth of corporate industrial power, to the transformation of the farmer's circumstances. In large measure, it appears that the proliferation hypothesis has somewhat the better case for the immediate postwar period in its stress upon the generation of new interest and value configurations as a consequence of social differentiation. Clearly, it was not simply a matter of older groups coming into a new situation, for, outside the South, there had never before been large groups of commercial farmers with such dependence on the market and so vulnerable to its vicissitudes.

But it is also clear that for nearly half a century farm groups did not proliferate into more and more organizations, each with its specialized concerns.[10] At least until after 1900 the overwhelming bulk of farm organizations which were formed were aggregated under the comprehensive embrace of few, though often loose, organizational structures.[11] Thus the Grange was followed by the Farmers Alliance in the 1880's, the Populist Party in the 1890's, and the Agricultural Wheel, the Farmers Union and finally the Farm Bureau in the first part of the twentieth century. Although each of these organizations was composed of a large number of local and state units, and in the case of the Farmers Alliance there were several distinct regional components which were partly or wholly autonomous, no real evidence can be found of a fission-like process. Rather a rapid series of local organizational successes was followed by official aggregation under a broad group banner and then, until this century, by the equally rapid demise of the organization, in its power if not, as usually happened, in its very existence.

This sequence of organizations may seem to disconfirm the proliferation hypothesis, but it does not readily fit the homeostatic mechanism theory either.[12] The rapid rise and fall of actual farm associations in a period, 1867–1900, which was one of consistent market disadvantage for most farm groups could hardly be construed as conducive to the reassertion of a viable equilibrium. It may be argued that whether they were successful or not the groups were certainly organized in order to reassert just such an equilibrium, and of this there can be little doubt. The rhetoric of farm protest groups has consistently stressed the postulate that a primeval state of grace had been violated by this industrial revolution and public policy should work toward the restoration of Eden. But rhetoric which evokes Arcadia may be distinguished from empirical social theory, and neither proliferation nor the homeostasis hypotheses seem adequate to explain the succession of organizational failures among people who, it has generally seemed, were in considerable distress and needed political and organizational help. Both our theories seem to assume that under such conditions organized groups will emerge and in some sense succeed. Yet the empirical landscape is cluttered with abandoned farm group vehicles, and effective theory must deal with the relics as well as the survivors.

Another set of data with which extant theories do not satisfactorily cope relates to organizational membership figures. The proliferation hypothesis implies not only that the number of organized groups will increase over time

but also that total membership will probably grow. This might follow for such social psychological reasons as that the more groups there are the more opportunities for a given person to participate actively in one and the more inducement therefore to join. It might also follow from the expectation that the greater the specialization the greater or more wide-reaching the self-consciousness of group involvement and hence the greater the likelihood of formal group membership.

Homeostasis theory, on the other hand, implies a cyclical pattern of membership. If groups are formally organized as a response to bargaining disadvantage, so their membership would be expected to rise in conditions of adversity and, probably, to decline or at least stabilize when adversity was overcome. So long as the organization's existence remained essential to the new equilibrium the membership might not fall off precipitately but it would still follow a kind of cycle over the course of the fluctuating fortunes of the group involved.

Group membership data are generally rather elusive and sometimes a bit suspect too. For some groups, especially those of a professional and technical occupational character, there appears to be a slightly uneven but generally rather steady growth in membership.[13] In some groups there is a rapid surge, often followed by a precipitate decline even to disappearance of the group altogether.[14] In two socio-economic sectors, however, agriculture and labor, the data are reasonably complete and follow similar curves; namely, they show a growth of membership in times of comparative prosperity and a decline during economic recession.[15] For example, in the first decade of the twentieth century, a decade of relatively favorable farm prices and income after thirty-odd years of almost unbroken decline, farm group membership increased five hundred per cent! The Grange, by then politically quiescent, more than doubled. The Farmers Union and the American Society of Equity were formed and each quickly attracted one hundred thousand members. Numerous commodity groups were organized at this time, and finally, still under relatively favorable economic conditions which extended until about 1919, the local and state farm bureaus were organized, to be federated in 1919 in the American Farm Bureau Federation.

Once the happy times for farm prices of World War I were over, prolonged farm depression set in and lasted until about 1926. During this period farm group membership generally declined. In the mid-western heartland of the Farm Bureau membership fell by almost one-fourth between 1920 and 1925. The Farmers Union lost forty percent of its strength between 1915 and 1933. Efforts to organize new farm groups out of the disequilibrium conditions of the early 20's uniformly failed. Decline in membership again was noticeable in the early Depression years of the 1930's, but this was followed by a spectacular recovery and growth between 1940 and 1950. In this decade, which was again one of greatly increased prosperity, the three main general farm organizations, the Grange, the Farmers Union, and the Farm Bureau went from a combined total of 866,224 family memberships to 2,108,849. Since 1950 a slow growth has continued despite the continuing decline in farm population.

Broadly, a similar pattern may be observed in the labor movement with substantial union growth during the prosperous periods of high employment, such as both World Wars, and decline in periods of recession. Additional variation is introduced by such factors as the passage of legislation like the Wagner Act, and changes in industrial technology, but the point remains. In these areas, at least, organized group membership varies directly with the relevant portion of the business cycle, going up with good times

and down with bad, and this is exactly the opposite of the expectations derived from the homeostasis hypothesis.

Although the proliferation hypothesis is vague with respect to expected patterns of group membership over time, it clearly does not lead to a cyclical pattern linked to the business cycle. This hypothesis fares much better, however, especially in the period of the last thirty-five years, regarding the number and variety of distinct organizations. More or less paralleling the enormous infusion of science into agriculture has been a very striking growth in the number of specialized commodity associations. Cotton and tobacco organizations like specialization in the production of these crops, are older, dating from around 1900. But wheat, corn, cranberries, turkey broilers, and several dozen other groups have been formed more recently as an undoubted consequence of the proliferation of farming interests.[16]

Yet as we consider the appearance of, say, the National Corn Growers Association in the mid-1950's one cannot seriously regard it as any kind of an organizational manifestation of the differentiated corn growers partly because corn growers had been differentiated for years and partly because they have not joined the group in appreciable numbers. The NCGA seemed much more a kind of letterhead organization which might, if its founder's dreams materialized, someday speak for a sizable portion of the corn growers but it had hardly yet begun to climb toward such eminence. It was still a small, struggling business enterprise, and the example suggests a very important modification required of the proliferation thesis—to establish some analytical distance between the technological and other social forces, on the one hand, and the emergence of organized interest groups, on the other.

Before we pursue this theme, however, let us again consider the implications of the cyclical pattern of group membership. There appears to be a fairly straightforward, one might almost say simpleminded, explanation for this pattern. It is simply that in times of prosperity potential group members are much more likely to have the dues money and be willing to spend it for membership,[17] while in hard times group membership may be one of the first luxuries to be sacrificed. Thus union membership regularly declines in the face of unemployment, and it is clear that for some portion of the members membership itself is a very marginal investment. At the same time, however, group leaders, faced with declining membership in hard times, may step up the tempo of agitation, both to hold on to their organizational membership and to alleviate the underlying group distress. Farm group leaders undoubtedly increased their public militance in the early 1930's,[18] as did unions, while their organized strength was shrinking. But leadership vigor cannot therefore be treated as an unambiguous indicator of group emergence or strengthening. Again, the point is that group strength, insofar as it implies or involves either weight of numbers or the formation of new groups, is generally greater in prosperity than in times of trouble, and thus a significantly revised theory of group origins is required.

ENTREPRENEURS/ ORGANIZERS

We find congenial a conceptualization of interest groups which regards them as benefit exchanges. Let us think of them in the following way. Entrepreneurs/ organizers invest capital to create a set of benefits which they offer to a market of potential customers at a price. If, and as long as, enough customers buy, i.e., join, to make a viable organization, the group is in business. If the benefits fail, or are inadequate to warrant the cost of membership, or the leaders get inadequate return, the group collapses. *All* interest

groups are conceptualized within this frame; it follows therefore that only "organized" groups, in the sense of entrepreneured exchange relationships, whether formally self-identified as organizations or not, are observable. The frame is inclusive and, it is argued, encompasses all cases without altering its basic terms.

It should immediately be noted that the conceptual scheme employed here is closely akin to an analytical frame which presently is of burgeoning interest to sociologists and represented especially in the work of Peter Blau and George Homans. At the same time, there are major identities of thought as well as language with economic theory where, after all, exchange behavior is the heart of an economists' world. Indeed, a partially parallel argument about interest groups has already been presented by economist Mancur Olson, Jr.

Many of the substantive hypotheses to be suggested here are rather direct transfers from simple economic models, and there is every reason to suppose that more elaborate and complex formulations can also be exchanged among disciplines as clarity increases respecting just how much alike our conceptual apparatuses are. The point should hastily be added, of course, that a significant residue of hypotheses in the present work is derived from distinctively political problems of types which other social scientists seldom if ever are compelled to face.

Let us now consider the core meaning of our crucial terms. These are four in number; entrepreneur/organizer, benefits, group member, and exchange. In several ways the notion of entrepreneur/ organizer is particularly central to the argument. The entrepreneur in any organizational situation is the initiator of the enterprise. Behaviorally, it is always true that he must make the first move if any exchange activity is to occur. Economics is not simply adopting a useful fiction when it singles out capital formation and investment as critical to economic development and entrepreneurs as the behavioral units involved in putting capital to work. In fact, that is what happens. Entrepreneurs use capital to generate goods or services, which, they hope, will be valued enough to be wanted; people desiring to satisfy wants work and save, and a growth spiral is set in motion. And unless the valued goods and services are offered no latent demand can be observed, only postulated. Capital formation processes must, to be sure, come before the entrepreneur can begin to work, but in terms of any specific organized economic exchange the entrepreneur is the starting point.

If we are to apply this analogy to the phenomena of interest groups, it will be necessary for us to identify specific entrepreneurs whose activities constitute the first visible signs of every particular organized group. It will also be necessary to identify some sort of capital which is invested to launch a group enterprise. If we can meet these tests, we will then also wish to inquire concerning such questions as the sources and processes of recruitment of interest group entrepreneurs.

It would be helpful to have a systematic array of group origins data to work from, but for the moment we must be content with illustrative cases to buttress the assertion that in no instance does an entrepreneurial theory of group formation fail to apply. Again the history of American farm groups demonstrates the point. The first big group to be organized was, of course, the Grange. It was initiated by Oliver Hudson Kelley who, by dint of considerable personal sacrifice and some generous friends, managed to survive until his organizational dream began to take hold.[19] Similarly Newton Gresham, having failed as a newspaper publisher, fed his family on credit and neighbors' largesse for more than a year until his Farmers Union began to attract enough dues-paying members to sustain him.[20] There is evidence of personal

investment, though less dramatic, on the part of leading organizers of more recent groups such as the Farmers Holiday Movement, the National Corn Growers Association and the National Farmers Organization.[21] And clearly a great many contemporary interest groups active in such fields as civil rights or foreign policy are headed by persons who have made heavy personal investments in their respective organizations.

Several of the early, large, farm groups were begun by publishers of small newspapers or periodicals serving primarily rural markets.[22] The new organization was partly conceived as a circulation building mechanism and members received an immediate tangible benefit in the form of a subscription. In addition, the publication gave publicity to the group and in various ways capitalized its formation. It should be noted that these publisher-organizers may have had quite diverse *reasons* for establishing their groups. Conceptually, however, the reasons are less significant than the behavioral patterns.

A considerable number of farm groups were subsidized by other, older, groups. In part, of course, the Farm Bureau was organized and long sustained by subsidies, some from federal and state governments and some by local businessmen.[23] The expectation that the Bureau would be a supportive group, economically and perhaps politically, no doubt underlay these subsidies, but similar expectations must usually inform the subsidizing of one group by another. The organizing of sub-units under subsidy from the parent organization may be thought of as a variation on the same theme, though the latter is so "normal" and "legitimate" an aspect of organizational growth that it occasions no comment from observers. Inter-group subsidy, however, is very often regarded with suspicion by observers who somehow expect someone to be corrupted in the process.

In any case, it is clear that both capital costs and specific entrepreneurs have often come from other, older, organizations. This seems to be particularly significant as a source of entrepreneurial recruitment, at least in the case of farm groups, but perhaps for others too. Not known as a form of subsidy but rather as a training ground and example of the possibility of establishing viable organizations of farmers, the early Grange provided the first real organizational experience for an enormous number of people. Many organizers of the Farmers Alliance had had experience in the Grange. In turn, Newton Gresham had been a zealot with the Alliance, allegedly organizing some fifteen hundred sub-alliances, before he attempted to establish the Farmers Union. Contemporaneously, other former Alliance and Grange organizers, such as Isaac McCracken of the Brothers of Freedom and Harvie Jordan of the Southern Cotton Growers' Association, were at work organizing their new enterprises. Saloutos is able already to refer to Jordan as a "professional farm organizer and lobbyist."[24]

What seems to have occurred is that once the Grange had set the example of a viable organization of farmers, a large number of people, especially those with direct experience in the prototype group, were attracted by the prospect of establishing farm groups of their own. One might follow as another collapsed. They might be differentiated by region or by crop or both. They might stress somewhat different combinations of material or political or rhetorical objectives. But in a broader sense they were all in the same line of business, and many of these businessmen came to constitute a rather specialized and self-sustaining subset of farm organizers. It seems warranted to suggest that a large portion of labor organizers have come from backgrounds closely associated with the union movement, or that both right and left wing group organizers

tend to have long careers in that kind of activity—as *organizers,* not necessarily as heads of any particular group.

One important point which is suggested by the foregoing discussion is as follows. If groups must be organized by organizers investing capital, and if very often these organizers and this capital are derived, either as a subsidy or a legacy, from older organizations, then the emergence of extensive organized group life in a political system will tend (a) to be a gradual process, partially dependent on the spread of the organizational experience to socialize and recruit organizers, and (b) will depend upon the accumulation of social capital sufficient to invest in the formation of durable organizations. To the extent that the capital required is material, group formation requires, and must largely wait upon, industrialization. This is in no sense a novel conclusion, of course, but the argument by which it is reached is quite different from most.

THE NATURE OF "BENEFITS"

We turn now to our second key concept. It should be understood at the outset that we do not attempt to assess "real" or "true" benefits. Rather we assume that people do or pursue those experiences and things which they value, for whatever reasons, and *in this sense only* may be regarded as rational. We assume that people mainly do or seek, subject to periodic evaluation and correction, whatever brings them a positive balance of benefits over costs. (It may be simpler to think only of positive and negative benefits since the latter is really what the notion of costs mean.) Notice that this is a conceptual assumption which is useful in thinking about certain kinds of behavior and of no necessary relevance either to normative theories of behavior or to motivational analysis.

How then shall we conceptualize benefits? A useful beginning point is the threefold distinction suggested by Clark and Wilson with reference to organizational incentives.[25] They distinguish among material, solidary and purposive incentives. By material incentives they mean the tangible rewards of goods or services or the means, such as a job, by which goods and services may be obtained. Material incentives—or, in our terms, benefits—are always extrinsic to the parties involved in the transaction and are typically instrumental toward more fundamental values such as deference or well-being. Solidary benefits, on the other hand, are intrinsic to the parties. They are experienced directly and within the self. Clark and Wilson suggest that solidary values "derive in the main from the acts of associating and include such rewards as socializing, congeniality, the sense of group membership and identification, the status resulting from membership, fun and conviviality, and so on."[26]

Purposive benefits or incentives consist of the realization of suprapersonal goals, goals of the organization or group. Although, of course, the benefits of such achievement may accrue to particular individuals they are not ordinarily divisible into units of value allocated to specific persons or charged against unit costs. Nor can purposive benefits always be confined to the parties seeking them. Thus "good government" or "peace" or "states rights" or "civil liberties" are all desired by individuals and benefit individuals, but the benefits cannot readily be cost analyzed and they accrue to all sorts of people who took no part in the efforts to secure them. Blau employs a related concept when he discusses "expressive" social actions, as distinguished from instrumental actions. Expressive actions are those where the action involved gives expression to the interests or values of a person or group rather than instrumentally pursuing interests or values. Presumably one cannot *express* material values; one must pursue them and achieve them. Similarly, one

can only enjoy solidary benefits by having them. But one can often derive benefits from expressing certain kinds of values. Opposition to war on poverty and affirmation of free speech or civil rights are contemporary examples of values many people wish to express and, what is of critical importance for our purposes, they are willing to join groups which provide mechanisms for the public expression of those values. Whether the expression is instrumentally relevant to the achievement of the values in question is, for the moment, not at issue. The point here is that important benefits are derived from the expression itself.

We prefer here to use the notion of expressive benefits rather than Clark and Wilson's term, "purposive." They were dealing only with intra-organizational incentives and consequently were untroubled by whatever complexities might appear regarding transactions between an organization's leaders and other groups. Clearly, however, some interest group leaders lobby for suprapersonal organizational goals—price supports, let us say, or a tax cut—which are purposive in Clark and Wilson's sense but also material in their explicit anticipated consequences. Material, solidary and expressive benefits would seem to constitute mutually exclusive categories at the conceptual level, though the difficulties of empirical specification and measurement can hardly be exaggerated.

Our argument is that the group entrepreneur invests his capital to create a set of benefits, composed of some combination or mix of the types mentioned, which he offers at a price to a market. The price is group membership, which may cost as little as a supportive signature or as much as the heavy dues attached to some trade association memberships. The market is whatever range of people the entrepreneur chooses to try to attract. This leads us to an examination of the implication of our three-fold typology of benefits for the entrepreneurial activities of group organizers. We then shall consider group members and potential members as sets of markets with demand patterns or preference schedules and see what implications this angle of vision may have.

What benefits are in fact offered by the entrepreneur/organizer to potential members of his group? It is clear that in a high proportion of cases the benefits initially offered are largely material. In the case of the early farm groups, for example, beginning with the Farmers Alliance and continuing through the Farmers Union and the Farm Bureau as well as a host of smaller groups, the initial exchange centered around some form of economic cooperation, for buying or selling or both. Cooperatives were sometimes promoted by stressing their ideological virtues, but in every case they were also expected to return direct economic benefits to those who joined. Obviously the same has been true of labor unions and also of most business trade associations.[27]

To observe the initial stress on material economic benefits in so many groups is to call attention to a closely related phenomenon which any theory of group formation and functioning must take into account. This is the phenomenon of organizational failure. No extant theory of interest groups seems to recognize the evident fact that a great many specific organized groups go out of business. Turnover is extremely high. Now if groups are organized through benefit exchange, it follows that they will dissolve whenever the benefits are inadequate to warrant continued support of the group. If the organizer fails to maintain the flow—if, for instance, the cooperative fails—the members will quit. So will they if they can no longer afford the cash dues. And this is precisely what happened to numerous farm groups and sub-groups during the latter nineteenth century. What were essentially small business operations failed;

often because of bad management, but in several cases because of the special adversity of recession, as in 1893.

Not every group is organized around material benefits, of course. The early local agricultural societies probably flourished on the basis of the solidary benefits derived from membership, and it has long been standard to attribute much of the success of the Grange to the high solidary benefits resulting from the semi-secret rituals and Grange Hall–centered fraternal activities of the group. From the point of view of an entrepreneur, however, solidary benefits are often difficult to sell unless the market has special characteristics. An organizer can build a clubhouse but he cannot easily guarantee it will be worthwhile to go there. The solidary benefits may develop but the entrepreneur is especially dependent on his customer to help him create his product. Furthermore, it is not clear that for most people sociability is valued highly enough to persuade them to join a new group to get it. They may do so if there are no other alternatives—if the market is genuine virgin territory regarding group association as the post bellum farming frontier largely was. Or people may join solidary benefit groups which provide a generous admixture of other types of benefits too. A typical mix is solidary benefits mixed with rather a specialized type of expressive benefits. For example, cell-based organizations, which certainly have structures conducive to providing solidary benefits, tend also to be linked to extremist ideologies, often fraught with conspiratorial theses. In the small group situation of the cell, "the enemy" can be denounced enthusiastically and thereby maximize both expressive and solidary benefits of membership. Nevertheless, we tend to regard those interest groups which stress solidary benefits as "fringe" groups, unlikely to have much impact on public decisions, perhaps precisely because so much of their membership satisfaction is provided within the group itself.

It is probably the case, however, that we do not concern ourselves with solidary groups, or, for that matter, with material exchange groups either, unless there is also some kind of politically relevant expressive content to the group's internal exchange. Thus we care about the Grange not because of its fraternal rituals but because of the political relevance of the values and interests expressed by its leaders through its various official mechanisms. Still, it is one thing for, say, a material benefits group to acquire an overlay of expressive benefits and quite another to organize a group around the exchange of expressive values to begin with. The latter is a frequent phenomenon but one of special characteristics.

For the entrepreneur it is comparatively easy to essay establishing an expressive group. It requires little capital to articulate a cause and go about promoting the nascent group as guardian of that cause. On the other hand, this type of group presents especially high risks too. The cause may be a popular one without there being any persuasive reason for people who believe in it to join the particular group whose organizer claims to be the *true* defender of the faith. Moreover, it is likely that expressive groups are especially vulnerable to slight changes in circumstances, including many over which the group has no control. For example, America First and the Committee to Defend America by Aiding the Allies were wiped out organizationally by Pearl Harbor.[28] More broadly, for most people the act of joining an expressive group—contributing dues to ACLU or signing a Viet Nam protest petition—is a marginal act. The benefits derived from value expression are seldom of great intrinsic worth. Consequently, even if civil liberties remain equally endangered, a slight change in the member's resources or social pressures

may lead to his failure to renew his membership.[29]

Two points of quite general political relevance follow from this line of analysis. On the one hand, expressive groups, being cheap to organize, will abound in a political system to whatever extent there may be entrepreneurs available to organize them, but they will tend to be highly transient. They will be easily established and as easily disappear. They will utilize communications media, especially the mail, more than face-to-face contacts; they may alter their expressed position to meet changing "market conditions." But above all they are unstable organizations. The corollary point is that expressive group organizers may be expected to infuse other types of benefits into the group in order to give it stability. They may attempt to enlarge the solidary benefits, for example, through the use of direct action protests. Whether a group moves from expressive toward solidary or the other way is an empirical question, but our analysis has suggested that a group originally stressing one type will tend to add the other in order to increase its stability as an organization.

We observed earlier that political scientists take notice of groups only if there is some politically relevant expressive content to the groups' activities. But, we have argued, strictly expressive groups are unstable and transient. At the same time, stable groups such as those based on viable economic benefit exchanges may not have any politically relevant values. Must our concern with groups be only sporadic, incorporating them only when they enter the political arena and ignoring them otherwise? It would appear that, in fact, this is what we have done and it has led us to assume a durability and politicization of interest groups far in excess of reality. The theoretical posture adopted here, which deals with organized groups as generic phenomena, not simply in their politically relevant aspect, leads to the conclusion that most group activity has little to do with efforts to affect public policy decisions but is concerned rather with the internal exchange of benefits by which the group is organized and sustained. But surely, one may argue, some significant fraction of the universe of groups is established *in order to affect* and with the consequence of affecting policy outcomes. To consider this question properly we must also consider the work of Mancur Olson, whose argument is in many ways parallel to this one.[30]

Olson is concerned with the question of why people maintain membership in interest groups. He demonstrates that in most familiar group situations it is not rational for any member to be part of an interest group in order to support a lobby, even though he genuinely desires the goals toward which the lobbying is directed. The argument hinges primarily on the distinction between what Olson calls *collective benefits*—those which accrue to people in a particular situation or category regardless of their organizational affiliations—and *selective benefits*—those which accrue only to members of the association. Thus the Farmers Union may lobby for price supports; i.e., collective benefits, but its members will receive the benefits of price supports whether they stay in the Union or not. Olson shows that therefore its members would not stay if they rationally balance the cost of membership against its benefits insofar as these benefits are collective. But cooperatives and cheap insurance may be available only to members. They are selective and may be entirely sufficient to induce continued membership.

Thus far Olson's argument differs little from the present one except that it is less clearly couched in exchange terms and thus does not explicitly examine the entrepreneur/organizer as a functionally distinct role from that of group member. Olson does not contend that all group members are rational, but only that to

the extent that they are they will not normally join organizations in order to seek collective benefits. Two main exceptions are noted: where the members are philanthropic and seek through group membership to obtain benefits for others; and where membership is coerced, as in union operating under a closed shop agreement. Yet the broadened conception of benefits we have employed, including the notion that costs, *e.g.,* of coercion, are the same as negative benefits, allows us to subsume these exceptions under the same headings as in the central argument. Moreover, as we noted earlier, we can assume that rationality in the sense of purposiveness or goal-orientation is characteristic of such a preponderance of behavior that any observed exceptions will not affect the main contentions.

There are two critical points in Olson's argument, both of them points of omission, with which we must take issue. Olson does not examine how groups are first organized but assumes a going system. As a consequence he does not adequately deal with group development through time.[31] If one looks at group formation, however, one finds that some organizations such as the Farmers Alliance were indeed organized around the exchange of selective benefits but that others, such as the Grange, were organized initially, at least in significant part, in order to alter public policy; *i.e.,* to secure collective benefits. Granted that many of the groups in the latter category may later have introduced selective benefits in order to hold the members, we must still account for the initial appearance. And Olson's argument does not hold for this situation. Is it relevant for farmers to join together in order to bring about policy change? Does organization improve their bargaining power? Political lore and science agree on the affirmative. How many farmers must join before this power is sufficient to secure any collective benefits through policy change? The answer is, within very broad limits, indeterminate. Accordingly, it may be entirely rational for any potential member to join until the benefit is achieved as long as his costs in joining are exceeded by his anticipated benefit from the collective good. Once the latter is a reality, however, the indeterminacy disappears and Olson's analysis comes into play; the member ought rationally to withdraw unless selective benefits are introduced. Thus a sizable array of organized groups *may* appear on the political scene to lobby for collective good but, lacking selective benefits, their mortality rate is likely to be high.

Olson's second omission is any explanation of the phenomenon of lobbying. We shall deal with this whole subject in greater detail below, but it should here be noted that Olson's argument accounts for the maintenance of groups without regard to their impact on public policy but does not explain why groups lobby or how lobbying is related, if it is, to the dynamics of intra-group relationships. Nevertheless, Olson has performed an important service in destroying the comfortable myth of an interest group behaving in a simple representational way, seeking public policy goals because these goals are desired by the group's members.[32]

GROUP MEMBERSHIP

We must now consider a very tricky but important component of our conceptual structure, the matter of consumer, or member, preferences. It seems fair to say that at bottom extant interest group theory assumes that group members have public policy-related interests, values, or preferences which (1) antedate the existence of the organized association, (2) are the rational basis for joining and remaining as members of the association, (3) are articulated and heightened by virtue of the associational interactions, and (4) are represented through the association to the policy-making arenas by virtue of lobbying activities. As we have seen, Olson undermines the logical plausibility of points 2 and 4 and, in a sense, renders point 3 beside the point for explaining interest group phenomena. But there are additional difficulties even in the first item. How do we know that a particular array of interests exists? Conventionally we have approached the issue in two very different ways. We may impute interests to categories of people—workers, farmers, etc.—on the basis of some theory about how individual values are derived and ordered, say Marxism or its variants. Thus we conclude that factory workers desire policies which raise wages, or give authority to unions, or the like. Alternatively, we may infer preferences from observed behavior. Thus some types of workers join unions more readily than others and are presumed therefore to place a different valuation on union membership. Most behaviorally derived preference schedules look far more diverse than do those imputed on the basis of more abstract theories about how values are formed. One might therefore suppose that empirical inquiry into preference schedules ought to be urged to test competing analytic strategies. But here one runs into the problem that inter-subjective comparisons of utility schedules are, in virtually all cases, impossible.[33] Without examining the large body of literature on this point, we may apply this conclusion to our situation in the following manner. Preferences and their orderings may be established for any set of people only on the basis of their behavior. Although he may make a reasonable estimate in advance, say on the basis of some kind of market research, the only way a producer really determines what consumer preference schedules are is by offering a good at a price, or at varying prices, and observing the differential demand schedules. Similarly, the only way empirically to determine the existence of an interest is to articulate a position (expressive benefits) or offer material or solidary incentives at one or more price levels and to observe the incidence and distribution of support—membership, votes, money, or whatever else is valued political currency. Price, a behaviorally derived result of exchange activity, resolves the dilemma posed by the non-comparability of inter-subjective preferences. And this means that interests of a group or class of people may be observed *only* by examining exchanges between political entrepreneurs and consumer/member/voters.

The analytic problem is thus, *a fortiori,* resolved by conceptualizing interests and interest groups in terms of exchanges of benefits between entrepreneurs/leaders and consumer/followers. This point does not, however, affect the relevance of individual preferences or of questions concerning how those preferences are formed or changed. Thus one may still argue that technological changes affecting the structure of economic activity may alter the preference schedules of many persons. These new schedules may constitute a promising potential market for political entrepreneurs, or, indeed, they may adversely affect a particular entrepreneur's market. Variables affecting market potential are relevant to an understanding of group formation and development. But, as we have stressed, they are never a sufficient explanation of interest activity and their aggregate structure cannot be more than guessed at in the absence of group organizing activities.[34]

THE EXCHANGE

It follows from what we have said that the "potential group" or market is a matter of great uncertainty from the point of view of the group organizer.

The latter, having invested his capital in an array of benefits, offers these benefits at a price—membership in the group—which he hopes will attract members and also maintain a viable organization. Entrepreneurs/organizers generally appear to select their markets on the basis of their own experiences and contacts or by emulating other, similar, organizational efforts, as when they purchase or borrow mailing lists of similarly inclined groups or publications. Farm organizers are closely affiliated with farmers, labor organizers with workers, rightists with rightists, and so on, and seldom do group entrepreneurs seem to cross over from one field to another. Thus, they have some expectation concerning the probable demand curves of the market they seek to reach, but they must be unsure whether the response will be sufficient to sustain the organization. And in order to sustain a group organization, it is necessary to maintain an adequate flow of benefits both to members *and* to the organizers themselves. In short, there must be a mutually satisfactory *exchange.*

Now what kinds of benefits are derived from these group organization exchanges by the entrepreneurs? The economists have no difficulty with this question, which they assert is answered by the notion of profits. If, in addition to profits, an entrepreneur derives other types of job satisfactions, profits remain the key requirement for continuation of the enterprise, and in abstract economic models of intrepreneurial activity the profit must approach some optimal return on the capital investment or the investment will be transferred to some other, more promising, enterprise.

It may be that many kinds of group organizing capital are not as easily transferred as straight money capital; a prosperous labor union probably will not subsidize other enterprises randomly nor will a farm organizer equally well defer his spending in order to organize in the urban ghetto. The *tendencies* would surely be for investment to go toward expressively supportive organizations, cognate markets and relatively familiar territories, geographical and functional. Yet we can cite numerous examples to show that even this capital is transferred from one enterprise to another within quite broad limits. Let us, therefore, consider what is implied by the notion of profit in respect to political entrepreneurs.

As a minimum we may assume that, so long as the entrepreneur desires to maintain the organization as a going enterprise, he must get a sufficient return in the form of membership support to enable him to continue to provide the benefits which attract members. Over some initial period of time the benefits may be more costly than membership will pay for, but, unless the enterprise is permanently subsidized, the returns must ultimately match the cost of providing the benefits. Where the benefits to members are material, of course, the membership must also provide material rewards in exchange. But even in solidary and expressive groups the entrepreneur must derive enough material return to pay the overhead costs *and* keep him sufficiently satisfied so as not to shift his energies to some other enterprise. Conceptually, the entrepreneur's reward may be viewed as profit. Thus: Entrepreneurs provide benefits to members whose membership must entail a return sufficient to pay the costs of the benefits received plus some profit to the entrepreneur.

What form does group organizer profit take empirically? A common form is that of the salaried executive. In some groups the organizer may be chosen president of the group he develops and paid a salary. In other cases he may occupy the position of executive secretary or its equivalent. In either situation he must maintain an adequate flow of benefits to members or lose his position, either because the enterprise goes bankrupt or

because he is dismissed somewhere short of organizational catastrophe. If the organizer does not desire or cannot obtain a paid position from his entrepreneurial activities, he may nevertheless persist in them if they have sufficient expressive value for him, and many expressive groups probably are developed in this fashion as avocational or philanthropic concerns substitute for entrepreneurial "profit motives." Even here, however, organizing is costly, and there must be subsidies drawn from other extra-group sources to sustain the activity or the group will shortly be bankrupt. The great difficulty experienced by many civil rights groups in keeping their leadership afloat illustrates the point.

I do not wish to argue that group organizers are classic "economic men" whose conscious motives are to secure the largest possible financial return. Indeed, although there surely are examples of such motivation among extant interest group entrepreneurs, taken as a whole their conscious intentions are undoubtedly very diverse. The point is rather that "profit" to the leadership is a necessary part of the exchange with the members and without it the leaders cannot continue.

One implication of the foregoing discussion is that any *election* of leaders by members, or of representatives by constituents, may be regarded in terms familiar to economic analysis of the firm.[35] Thus the minimum return required on investment is reelection to office, and office must provide sufficient resources to motivate and to maintain the flow of benefits to members/constituents. Dissatisfied members of a voluntary group may quit or switch to a rival group; dissatisfied constituents may be expected to switch to a rival candidate. But the logical and conceptual relationship is the same. It is an exchange which must satisfy both parties.

Now, let us go an additional step. It may be observed that large numbers of

organized interest groups do go bankrupt in some sense. They fail as enterprises. Their organizers/leaders must
find some other line. But large numbers
of groups survive over long periods of
time. Moreover, it is characteristic of
many relatively stable groups, especially
those involving primarily material benefits exchanges, to exhibit great stability
in their paid leadership personnel.
Further, it may be suggested that the
"profits" accruing to this leadership
from providing members with selective
benefits, available only to group members, very often exceed by a comfortable
margin the minimum requirements of
sustaining the enterprise. How may we
think about this "surplus"?

From the standpoint of the entrepreneurs, whose decision it is to dispose of
his "surplus profits," there may be a
number of options. He may, for example,
enlarge the benefits available to members
in order to restore the balance between
his costs and his profits. Or he may spend
his profits in various private, but personal,
activities—higher salary, extra-group
activities, or whatever. Perhaps he builds a
fancy new building as an organizational
headquarters. But, if his enterprise is
internally prosperous, he may spend some
of his "profits" in public activity. He may,
for example, lobby for legislation which
he thinks desirable and do so quite independent of any views his members have
on the question.[36] When he does so, he
cannot expect his members to agree with
him, but, as long as his organization sur-
vives and he with it, it does not really
matter. He takes his policy positions and
invests what he has in the way of profit in
promoting them not because his membership demands that he do so but only
because his membership makes it possible
for him to pursue his private desires by
providing him a profitable exchange.
Now it may be that his desires are not
incongruent with those of his members.
It may also be that he seeks legitimation
and support for his desires by asserting

that they conform to those of his members. But it may also be that those whom
he attempts to persuade to his views are
unimpressed by his claims of membership
support, and his success must then be
achieved by other bargaining tactics.
Applying this same conception to a legislator we often say that he has a considerable number of "free votes" on which
constituency demands are absent or conflicting or vague and which he casts
according to bargaining criteria which he
derives independent of constituency
pressure. Yet unless he satisfies the minimum constituency expectations of benefits he will not survive in office long
enough to spend his profits in his "free
votes."

It is not argued that "profit consumption" is the sole explanation of lobbying or influencing activity or that all
such activity is equally well explained
this way. It is contended, however, that a
significant portion of what we observe
to be lobbying activity by group leaders
may result not from a mandate derived
from membership demands but from the
personal choices and values of the group
leaders. This conception would fit and
make sense of a broad spectrum of data
which show group spokesmen taking
public policy positions at variance with
the apparent views of their members
and still suffering no reprisals. Indeed, as
Milbrath among others has pointed out,
a major focus of lobbying is not the
policy-makers at all but the group members themselves.[37] If lobbyists were
simply reflecting membership demands,
they would not spend so much time
"farming the membership."

Moreover, we may in this way more
easily make sense of the reported disregard of lobbyists, or at least extremely
uneven response to them, by policy
makers.[38] And, finally, we may thus square
the lack of logical necessity for lobbying
by group spokesmen, which Olson
shows, with the obvious fact of extensive
lobbying in the observable world.

There remains a significant portion of lobbying activity which may be regarded as instrumental to the benefit flow and exchange of the group and it would be wrong to ignore this portion. As we noted in criticizing Olson's argument, the problematic but presumably positive relationship between group strength and activity and the achievement of public decisions providing collective good makes it rational, within broad limits for individuals who value the good to join a group which proposes to lobby for it. Moreover, many collective goods are provided in discontinuous or, at least, recurrently renegotiable form so that simply because an act is passed providing a given level of farm subsidies for three years does not guarantee it will be renewed or, if renewed, maintained at the same level. Group lobbying may often, therefore, be instrumental in securing or maintaining the flow of collective benefits, and, while not all those affected by the benefits will join the group, or join for that reason, some may do so and press the entrepreneurs to act accordingly.

In addition, for some groups potential public policy decisions constitute a significant source of the selective benefits by which the group's internal exchange is sustained. This would be true, for example, of a significant portion of the licensing regulations applicable to professional groups who secure the legal authority to control entry to the profession, and, having such authority, make it attractive thereby for prospective practitioners to join the association. Or for a labor union, policy decisions involving picketing, antitrust applications to union activities, yellow-dog contracts, and the like directly affect the ability of the union leadership to provide selective benefits to its members through favorable contracts. Whenever this is the case, it is obvious that lobbying by the entrepreneur leaders requires no additional conceptual trappings for satisfactory explanation.

CONTINUITY OF GROUP LEADERSHIP

In the analysis we have presented the focus has been mainly on the initial organizer/entrepreneurs of the group. There are good reasons for this emphasis. It reminds us that existing organizations such as unions or major farm groups, which sometimes seem to be permanent features of the political landscape, have quite specific origins and originators. Moreover, it has been useful to examine those origins and the individuals who played the key entrepreneurial roles in establishing the groups. But one need not rely on state of nature assumptions in the analysis of contemporary groups. A large proportion of the extant roster of politically relevant groups are durable enterprises with origins which may or may not shed light on their present affairs. Implicit in our argument, however, is the view that all groups may be approached in the same terms. If the entrepreneur/organizer is easier to identify through examining group origins, his role is conceptually identical with that of the leader of a going group concern. It is, therefore, group leadership generally that we are discussing in a framework of benefit exchange. The entrepreneurial role is generically identical with that of leader; the leader is perforce an entrepreneur.

We will not repeat what has already been said of the entrepreneur in order to make clear its application to leadership generally. Nor is it possible here to do more than assert that the argument may be transferred *in toto* to the consideration of leadership generally, not simply group leadership. Suffice to say that although we begin with an attempt to develop an empirically valid and logically secure theory of interest groups we find ourselves with a formulation of truly generally proportions.

Let us here add only one additional point of substance derived from our general argument. We have already noted that among material benefit groups leadership tenure has generally been very secure. There are, of course, some notable exceptions, but most union or farm or business group leaders have had long careers, seldom challenged. On the other hand, what we have referred to as expressive groups are frequently characterized by bitter schisms. Does our formulation contribute to an explanation of this phenomenon? We indicated earlier that expressive groups are cheap to organize but fragile. If they are cheap to organize, they are also cheap to factionalize. A rival to the leadership needs only a membership list and a better line to support a factional fight. The fruits of victory may be great or small, depending on what the faction leaders value and how prosperous or prestigious the group is. What are the potential costs of attempting a factional fight? The ultimate cost is expulsion. But seldom is an expressive group the sole guardian of expression of a value. If one is kicked out of CORE or the John Birch Society one is not thereby denied the opportunity to express one's position but probably only of whatever solidary values the group conferred on its members.

On the other hand, consider a comparable situation in a union or a farm organization. In order to mount a serious effort to unhorse the leadership, factional leaders must, in effect, assemble enough capital, perhaps from anticipated profits, to promise enough increased benefits to attract support for themselves and away from their rivals. This is typically very difficult to do partly because the capital to organize a factional drive is hard to assemble, partly because the existing leadership faced with factional opposition may often reinvest more of their profit into membership benefits, and sometimes may simply coopt potential factional leaders into the existing leadership cadre. Moreover, uncompromising factional rivals may be met with exclusion from the group which in turn

may mean exclusion from a substantial array of material benefits available only to group members. For all these reasons then factional efforts in established material benefits groups are comparatively rare and often come to grief.[39] And this is true even though the profits available to material benefit group leaders are often substantial and hence might be expected to attract rival entrepreneurs. But the capital requirements to capture control of the UAW or set up a rival union in the same employment markets would surely not be much less difficult to manage than capturing control of, or establishing a rival to, General Motors. Finally, material benefit interest groups have been successful as have business firms in coopting potential factional leadership into an orderly hierarchy with sufficient profits derived from the group's exchange structure to sustain the full cadre.

CONCLUSION

In concluding a paper of this kind one is tempted simply to restate the core of the argument, recognizing that for the most part the usefulness of the kind of conceptual orientation presented here depends upon its plausibility and suggestiveness as a heuristic model. In the main it is neither true nor false but to be tested by its intellectual utility. Nevertheless, the utility of such a scheme must ultimately rest on whether one can imagine ways by which to derive reasonable empirical applications which are amenable to testing against data. One such application has been illustrated here in the discussion of farm group origins, and our conclusion was that an entrepreneurial exchange hypothesis both fits and explains the data better than alternative hypotheses. It has also been suggested that this formulation accounts for the high incidence of schism among ideological or expressive groups and the low incidence of severe faction-alism among material benefit groups. One must recognize, however, that in the latter explanation the data are largely impressionistic since they assume more knowledge than we have of the kind of benefits exchanged in the two categories of groups. In principle, however, such data could be obtained by inquiring of group members, and of people solicited to join who decline, what benefits they derive from membership and determining the points at which, under various conditions, marginal costs equate with marginal ben-efits or utility.

Another empirical test might be undertaken by examining closely and systematically the behavior of group leaders over time. It was argued that much lobbying activity by group leaders may be understood as a form of personal consumption of profit derived from their intragroup exchanges. If this is cor-rect, it would follow that when their membership declines or is threatened with decline such profit is reduced and the lobbying for policies that are non-instrumental to the group's exchange structure would also decline. If, that is, UAW membership declines, Walter Reuther should spend more time on contract bargaining and union-related instrumental lobbying and less time on policy issues of a more personally expres-sive character. Without gainsaying the dif-ficulties of making such observations, one may suppose that they are possible and would constitute an empirical test of the theory.

Finally, and whatever the empirical outcomes of the specific inquiries pro-posed or of others which might be imagined, we must assert the crucial importance of developing systematic empirical theory, of interest groups as of other politically relevant phenomena, to bring greater order and clarity to the extant array of literary theory. Nearly two decades ago David Truman demon-strated extraordinary imagination in

assembling a vast array of fragments into a richly suggestive fabric of com-mentary and insight. Ironically, his accomplishment was so complete that remarkably few political scientists have worked ahead with the tools he sought to fashion. By employing a more generic conceptual orientation to examine inter-est group phenomena, perhaps we may at least hope to revive the substantive investigation into their characteristic properties and more systematically relate them to other facets of the political system.

NOTES

1. *The Governmental Process,* New York: Knopf, 1951, p. 66.

2. Professor John P. Heinz and I are engaged in an extended study of U.S. farm policy for-mation and that inquiry stimulated much of the present analysis as well as providing much illustrative material for it.

3. The principal works thus far which attempt to develop reasonably general statements of exchange theory include Peter Blau, *Exchange and Power in Social Life,* New York: Wiley, 1964; George Homans, *Social Behavior: Its Elementary Forms*, New York: Harcourt, Brace and World, 1961; James A. Coleman, "Foundations for a Theory of Collective Decisions," *American Journal of Sociology,* Vol. LXX, May, 1966, pp. 615–628; Mancur Olson, Jr., *The Logic of Collective Action,* Cambridge: Harvard University Press, 1965.

4. It may be noted that, Truman aside, there is remarkably little recent literature which deals, empirically or theoretically, with inter-est groups as primary units for analysis, as dependent variables, rather than independent variables related to policy outcomes or processes. Among the exceptions may be cited Lester Milbrath, *The Washington Lobbyists,* Chicago: Rand McNally, 1963; Norman Luttbeg and Harmon Zeigler, "Attitude Consensus and Conflict in an Interest Group: An Assessment of Cohesion," *American Political Science Review,* Vol. LX, September, 1966, pp. 655–667; Frank Nall, "National Associations," in W. Lloyd Warner,

ed., *The Emergent American Society, Large-Scale Organizations,* New Haven: Yale University Press, 1967, pp. 276–314.

5. For elements of this argument, see Truman, *The Governmental Process,* especially pp. 52–62. See also, Robert MacIver, *The Web of Government,* New York: The Macmillan Company, 1947, pp. 52 ff. The formulation is familiar in the standard sociology and anthropology writings also, and Truman cites representative authorities.

6. The growth of specialized commercial agriculture is traced by a number of agricultural historians. See, for example, Everett E. Edwards, "American Agriculture—the First 300 Years," in *Farmers in a Changing World, The Yearbook of Agriculture, 1940*, U.S. Department of Agriculture, 76th Congress, 3rd Session, House Document No. 695, Washington, D.C., 1940, pp. 171–277; Fred A. Shannon, *The Farmers Last Frontier,* New York: Farrar and Rinehart, 1945.

7. The theoretical uncertainty in which Truman left his concept of the "potential group" is examined in Roy C. Macridis, "Interest Groups in Comparative Analysis," *Journal of Politics,* Vol. XXII, February, 1961, pp. 25–45; and in Mancur Olson, Jr., *The Logic of Collective Action,* pp. 128–130.

8. Again, cf., Truman, *The Governmental Process,* pp. 52 ff.

9. *Ibid.,* p. 59.

10. One must distinguish between the politically relevant groups of this period and the older, localized, agricultural improvement societies organized mainly for self-help and the promotion of fairs. See Carl C. Taylor, "Farmers Organizations," in *Encyclopedia of the Social Sciences,* New York, 1931–7, Vol. 6, pp. 129–131.

11. A particularly valuable discussion of farm group organizations in this period is Theodore Saloutos, *Farmer Movements in the South, 1865–1933*, Berkeley: University of California Press, 1960. For the early twentieth century see Theodore Saloutos and John D. Hicks, *Agricultural Discontent in the Middle West, 1900–1939*, Madison: University of Wisconsin Press, 1951.

12. See also Olson's observation that Truman "assumes *organized* (italics his) groups arise because there is dislocation or 'need' for them, and this is neither factually nor theoretically substantiated." *The Logic of Collective Action,* p. 123, n. 50.

13. In the ABA and AMA membership shows rather a rapid early growth, averaging more than ten per cent per year until up to one-fourth of the potential members were enrolled. Thereafter growth has averaged approximately three per cent per year. There are very few periods of absolute decline, however, with 1933–34 being much the worst. Membership in the NEA, an organization of more ambiguous professional status and with a less well-defined market, has fluctuated much more widely.

14. The Farmers Alliance is estimated to have gone from one million members in 1890 to near extinction by 1893. See Robert L. Tontz, "Membership of General Farmers' Organization, United States, 1874–1960," *Agricultural History,* Vol. 38, July, 1964, pp. 143–157.

15. See Tontz, *passim,* and sources cited therein. Tontz himself argues that membership does go up when farm conditions go down but with a three to five year lag. The data fit as well, however, to a direct and positive relationship between prices and membership.

16. In 1957 and 1958 some thirty-seven regional and national farm commodity organizations joined the National Conference of Commodity Organizations, an organization attempting to build program agreement among the disparate interests of commodity groups. NCCO had brief success in 1958 but shortly foundered.

17. Saloutos notes that "The farmers joined the Farmers Union for various reasons. The quest for higher cotton prices naturally was an important factor, but the fact that producers were benefitting from a rising market was equally significant. It was much easier for farmers to pay dues in 1903 when cotton commanded 13 cents a pound than in 1898 when it brought only 6 cents." *Farmer Movements in the South,* p. 187.

18. See, for example, John L. Shover, "Populism in the Nineteen-Thirties: The Battle for the AAA," *Agricultural History,* Vol. 39, No. 1, January, 1965, pp. 17–24.

19. See Saloutos, *Farmer Movements in the South,* p. 32. Generally, on the Grange, see Solon J. Buck, *The Granger Movement,* Cambridge: Harvard University Press, 1913.

20. Saloutos, *Farmer Movements in the South,* pp. 184–186.

21. The origins of the National Farmers Organization are described by Charles Walters in "History of the National Farmers Organizations," *Farm Tempo USA,* Vol. 3, November, 1966, pp. 16–20.

22. Milton George, editor of the *Western Rural,* founded the National Farmers Alliance and the paper advanced the early money and absorbed headquarters costs. Saloutos, *Farmer Movements in the South,* pp. 77–78. William Hirth did much the same later on in organizing the Missouri Farmers Association. See Ray Derr, *The Missouri Farmer in Action,* Columbia, Missouri: Missouri Farmer Press, 1953.

23. On the formation of the Farm Bureau see O. M. Kile, *The Farm Bureau Through Three Decades,* Baltimore: The Waverly Press, 1949; and Grand McConnell, *The Decline of Agrarian Democracy,* Berkeley: The University of California Press, 1953. See also the convenient summary in Olson, *The Logic of Collective Action,* pp. 148–153. The efforts of John L. Lewis and his associates in subsidizing union formation, especially through the Steel Workers Organizing Committee, in the mid-1930's provide other well-known examples.

24. *Farmer Movements in the South,* p. 156.

25. See Peter B. Clark and James Q. Wilson, "Incentive Systems: A Theory of Organizations," in *Administrative Science Quarterly,* Vol. 6 (September, 1961), pp. 129–166. Clark and Wilson are concerned more generally with organizations than with interest groups *per se,* but their analysis is generally relevant even when only implicitly so. Some of their hypotheses are similar to those suggested here, some are not. For example, they suggest that organizations will stress purposive incentives in the formative stages. We argue the contrary for farm groups and many others. See especially p. 151. See also the similar typology developed by Amatai Etzioni for discussion of ways by inducing compliance of members of organization with leaders. His typology includes utilitarian, coercive and normative incentives. *Comparative Analysis of Complex Organizations,* New York: The Free Press of Glencoe, 1961.

26. "Incentive Systems," pp. 134–135.

27. A recent careful history of the development of cotton textile trade associations describes the early importance of exchanging technical information about a rapidly changing technology as a motivating factor inducing cooperation. See Louis Galambos, *Competition and Cooperation: The Emergence of a National Trade Association,* Baltimore: The Johns Hopkins Press, 1966, pp. 11, ff. The list of additional examples among trade associations alone could be enlarged to almost any desired length, limited only by gaps in our information about the specific entrepreneur/organizer.

28. See Wayne S. Cole, *America First,* Madison: University of Wisconsin Press, 1953.

29. Unfortunately, there are large gaps in our knowledge about membership in most types of voluntary organizations. Most studies have concentrated on characteristics of members compared to non-members or in the grosser aspects of organizational involvement generally in the society. Important reviews of pertinent literature include J. M. Scott, "Membership and Participation in Voluntary Associations," *American Sociological Review,* Vol. 22, 1957, pp. 315–326; Charles R. Wright and Herbert Hyman, "Voluntary Association Memberships of American Adults," *American Sociological Review,* Vol. 23, 1958, pp. 284–294. Lacking a viable typology of groups, few have inquired into differential propensities to join or withdraw from different types of groups. For illuminating case studies, however, see Joseph Gusfield, *Symbolic Crusade,* Urbana: University of Illinois Press, 1963; Raymond E. Wolfinger, Barbara Kaye Wolfinger, Kenneth Prewitt, and Sheilah Rosenhack, "America's Radical Right: Politics and Ideology," in David Apter, ed., *Ideology and Discontent,* New York: The Free Press of Glencoe, 1964, pp. 262–293.

30. *The Logic of Collective Action.*

31. Indeed one might argue that in most interest group studies the two elements most often missing have been individual behavior associated with differentiated roles and changes over time. Concern with origins forces us to consider interest groups longitudinally and we are led to useful insights in the process.

32. I do not wish to imply that in stressing any differences with him I have adequately represented everything Olson says in his remarkably suggestive book. Many of the points he stresses are very much like the arguments here, and I am delighted to acknowledge my debt to him.

33. See, for example, R. Duncan Luce and Howard Raiffa, *Games and Decisions,* New York: John Wiley and Sons, 1957, pp. 33–34, and Chapter 14; Kenneth J. Arrow, *Social Choice and Individual Values,* 2nd ed., New York: John Wiley and Sons, 1963, especially pp. 109 ff.

34. The discussion here of potential markets, a familiar enough notion in economic analysis, would seem to incorporate the principal meaning of Truman's oft maligned concept of potential group. Truman imputed a political impact to potential groups, however, which is quite absent from any understanding one might have of potential markets. Again, the latter are truly fallow until cultivated by entrepreneurs.

35. I do not wish here to offer more than the mere suggestion that the conceptual orientation employed here has extremely general application to politically relevant phenomena and that, if pursued, it may yield enormous returns in terms which subsume many types of representative relationships under the headings of exchange theory.

36. Olson also notes that group leaders may employ "profits" to lobby for objectives other than those desired by the members. He suggests that these "profits" are often a consequence of some degree of monopoly power vis-à-vis the potential membership market and would be absent if there were perfect competition among groups. As we have said earlier, however, Olson does not clearly differentiate the role of the entrepreneur and so does not emphasize the personal choice he may exercise in lobbying as we have done. *The Logic of Collective Action,* pp. 133–134, n. 2.

37. *The Washington Lobbyists,* p. 205.

38. Cf., for example, Raymond A. Bauer, Ithiel de Sola Pool, and Lewis A. Dexter, *American Business and Public Policy,* New York: Atherton Press, 1963.

39. It may be observed that the argument here and throughout this paper has major implications for discussion more commonly framed in terms of oligarchy or, in Truman's terms, the active minority. What we are saying, in effect, is not that such formulations are wrong, but that by employing an exchange schema we can account for a much wider variety and range of data, including oligarchy data, within the same theoretical framework.

PROJECT

Select any membership interest group. Conduct research on the origins of the group. How was it formed? Can you trace its formation to an entrepreneur? If not, what can it be traced to? If so, do you believe affluence had a role to play?

12

The Origins and Maintenance of Interest Groups in America

JACK WALKER

Although many theories about interest groups existed by the early 1980s, little empirical evidence was available to scholars. Jack Walker's survey was an attempt to bring empiricism to the study of interest groups. The survey revealed a new wrinkle in group mobilization and maintenance. Walker found that group leaders were often successful in their pursuit of outside resources to help fund group activity. Groups in the survey reported receiving money from a variety of sources (or patrons). Funding for groups included individual donations, gifts from foundations, and grants from the government. The resources provided by patrons enable groups to pursue policies that both patrons and groups seek to influence or understand. Hence, a symbiotic relationship between groups and patrons emerges. Walker suggests that the U.S. government has significantly contributed to the growth of interest groups in America. This is in large part because the government seeks information from a wide array of groups.

QUESTIONS TO CONSIDER

1. What is a patron?
2. Why do patrons give money to groups?
3. Do different types of groups differ in who gives them money? Do these differences translate into policy success?
4. How do you feel about the government's role in contributing to interest groups?

It is not surprising that huge, concentrated industries such as the automobile manufacturers or the major aerospace contractors have successfully organized to advance their interests in Washington, but it is not obvious that the American political system would inevitably have spawned groups like the American Alliance for Health, Physical Education, Recreation and Dance; the National Council of Puerto Rican Volunteers; the International Center for Social Gerontology; or The Friends of the Earth. Yet all these groups exist, along with hundreds more that crowd the office buildings and congressional hearing rooms of Washington. Most previous investigations of interest groups have been designed to measure their influence, but have taken their existence for granted. In this article the process will be reversed. I begin by taking for granted that under certain circumstances, interest groups exert influence over legislators, bureaucrats, and the public and will concentrate my attention instead on the ways in which these groups are created and the means by which they remain in existence.

The central question being posed is: why does the current set of groups exist

SOURCE: From Jack L. Walker, "The Origins and Maintenance of Interest Groups in America," *American Political Science Review* 77 (1983): 390–406 (including tables and figure). Reprinted with permission from Cambridge University Press.

Thanks are due to the Earhart Foundation for a grant that originated this research, and to the National Science Foundation, the Guggenheim Foundation, and the Woodrow Wilson International Center for Scholars for grants that maintained it; to Smothers Shaw, Fran Featherston, Cynthia Robinson, Tom Gais, and Mark Peterson, graduate students who assisted in gathering, coding, and analyzing the data; to the Institute of Public Policy Studies at The University of Michigan, which paid certain costs and provided a challenging intellectual environment; to Jeffrey Berry, John Chamberlin, Stephen Elkin, Edward Gramlich, Hugh Heclo, John Jackson, John Kingdom, Nelson Polsby, Michael Reagan, Steven Reed, Michael Reich, Clarence Stone, Janet Weiss, Ernest Wilson, Mayer Zald, and William Zimmerman who provided constructive criticisms of earlier drafts of this article; to Tom Gais and Mark Peterson for stimulating questions about every paragraph of every draft; to Jackie Brendle who typed version after version of the questionnaire and addressed hundreds of letters and postcards; and to Judy Jackson who corrected my spelling and saved me from several grammatical errors while typing this manuscript.

rather than some other set one might imagine, which would represent other segments of society? How can recent increases in the number of groups be explained, and have these increases caused significant changes in the character of interest groups? How do these organizations—some of which have elaborate bureaucracies that rival many small business firms—find money to pay their bills? All organizations must devise a successful strategy for obtaining resources, but what are the implications for the political system of the kinds of strategies that have been devised by successful groups in the United States?

THEORIES OF GROUP FORMATION

David Truman (1951) began the post–World War II dialogue over group theory with the assertion that interest groups arise more or less spontaneously in response to feelings of common interest among individuals who are experiencing some form of deprivation or frustration. Economic or political changes disturb the lives of potential group members, prompting them to interact and become increasingly aware of their shared interests. If this awareness grows and their concerns become sufficiently intense, they may form an association to serve as their representative. However, this new organization may itself constitute a social disturbance that affects the interests of other potential groups, and these groups may be stimulated, in turn, to form associations that will represent them. A process of competitive mobilization begins, leading to waves of group formation until social equilibrium is reestablished and the system begins to function smoothly again, awaiting yet another disturbance that will set off another round of group formation.

Truman's central psychological assumption about group formation was challenged by Olson, who asserted that individuals cannot be expected to organize spontaneously once they become aware of a threat to their common interest. As long as individuals are likely to receive the collective goods that interest groups are working to obtain, regardless of whether or not they make a contribution toward the effort, it will be exceedingly difficult, as a practical matter, to spur many of them into action. Olson (1965) showed that the marginal costs of political participation differ greatly among social groups and explained why individual incentives for political action are generally so weak.

Olson's original insights stimulated a large body of theoretical work in the logic of collective action.[1] This body of literature, along with pioneering work by Edelman (1964), Gamson (1975), Lipsky (1970), Salisbury (1969), and Wilson (1973) have clearly demonstrated how difficult it is to organize groups whose members have nothing more in common than an idea or a cause. Associations which attempt to represent socially disadvantaged elements of the society and which depend entirely on their members for financial support in response to mainly purposive incentives typically will be short-lived.[2]

DESIGN FOR AN EMPIRICAL STUDY

The vigorous theoretical dialogue in this field concerning the personal trade-offs facing prospective group members and the larger social dilemma over the provision of public goods is an excellent point of departure for explaining how the current set of interest groups came into being. Empirical work in this field, however, has not been pursued with nearly as much imagination as the the-orists have displayed.[3] Much of the theoretical work draws upon a small number of well-known case studies. Most descriptive accounts deal either with the history of a single group, or more often, with small clusters of groups in a single policy area. There are almost no comprehensive descriptions of the world of interest groups in America at any historical period.[4] My aim in reporting a small number of facts about a large number of groups is to create a general framework for interpretation that will bring new life to existing case studies by showing just what they are a case of.

DATA

The basis for the descriptive framework I wish to build is a mail survey of a large sample of interest groups conducted during 1980 and 1981. The objects of this survey were all the voluntary associations in the United States which are open to membership and are concerned with some aspects of public policy at the national level.

This somewhat vague working definition was precise enough to exclude two very important components of the national representative structure: trade unions and business corporations. Almost every policy area is influenced by lobbyists for organized labor, and trade unions also provide financial support for many interest groups, such as the National Council of Senior Citizens or the Leadership Conference for Civil Rights.[5] In recent years many business firms also have begun to exert direct influence in Washington either by retaining local law firms to act as their representatives or by opening offices which are dedicated exclusively to government relations. These corporations usually maintain their memberships in trade associations, but operate independently as well. Any study of the exercise of influence would be incomplete

if it did not take into account the activities of such massive agencies as the
Teamsters Union, the United Auto
Workers, U.S. Steel, or American
Telephone and Telegraph. This study,
however, is not concerned with the
influence being exerted by all vested
interests in the political system, but only
with the origins and maintenance of
voluntary associations. Trade unions and
business corporations play vitally important roles in the political system, but
membership in either is not entirely voluntary, and their problems of organizational maintenance are entirely different
from the those experienced by the
interest groups analyzed in this study.

My working definition narrowed
the field even further by excluding hundreds of nonprofit corporations, public
interest law firms, university-based
research centers, independent commissions, semi-autonomous advisory committees for federal agencies, operating
foundations, newsletters, trade publications, consulting firms, and the lobbying
operations of state governments, munici-
palities, and other public bodies. It also
excluded many thousands of membership groups that are devoted to religious
worship, recreation, charitable causes, or
other nonpolitical activities as well as
many groups that are directly concerned
with public policy, but confine their
activities to individual states, regions, or
metropolitan areas. A comprehensive
study of representation in American
democracy would require a much more
inclusive working definition of interest
groups, but the data collected in this
study are more comprehensive than
almost any other conducted so far and
will demonstrate important and little
understood facts about a central component of the system of representation in
the United States.

Even after the field of study was limited, it was still difficult to draw a sample
of national interest groups because there

is no reliable, comprehensive list of such
groups in existence. After checking several sources against each other and evaluating their strengths and weaknesses, The
Congressional Quarterly's *Washington
Information Directory* (1980) was chosen as
the source of group names most likely to
provide a balanced picture of associations
concerned with national affairs. Ques-
tionnaires were delivered to 913 interest
groups mentioned in this directory, and
usable responses were received from 564
(64.8%).

A TYPOLOGY OF ASSOCIATIONS

The first step in this study was to create
a new typology that organized the data
into mutually exclusive categories that
reflect the fundamental social structure
of interest groups. All existing classification schemes present difficult problems
of measurement, and when most scholars have tried to write comprehensive
descriptions of the world of interest
groups, they have usually ignored the
more complex typologies.[6] Most textbook
authors simply subdivide groups into the
policy areas in which they operate or the
constituencies they claim to represent,
with chapters on such categories as business groups, civil rights groups, groups
representing the handicapped, and the
environmentalists (Ornstein & Elder,
1978; Wilson, 1973; Ziegler & Peak, 1972).
There is seldom any theoretical justification supplied for this kind of typology. It
is the common-sense usage of most journalists and politicians in Washington, and
most scholars have also adopted it, generally without reservations or qualifications.

In order to create an analytically
useful typology grounded in a general
theory of groups, I began by dividing my
sample into 1) those groups that require
members to possess certain professional

Table 12.1 Typology of Occupational Roles

	Percentage	N
Occupational		
profit sector	31.7	179
mixed sectors	11.9	67
nonprofit sector	36.6	201
Nonoccupational citizen groups	20.7	117

SOURCE: Jack L. Walker, "The Origins and Maintenance of Interest Groups in America," *American Political Science Review* 77 (1983): 393, Table 1. Reprinted with permission from Cambridge University Press.

or occupational credentials, and 2) those that are open to all citizens regardless of their qualifications. The basis for mutual interest around which most groups are formed is an occupational specialty, not some broad social cause or abstract idea about the public interest. Almost 80% of the respondents reported that membership in a certain profession or industry was either a requirement for entry into their group or was exceedingly important, leaving barely 20% of the groups open to citizens without special occupational qualifications. This large, unwieldy set of occupationally based associations had to be broken down into smaller, homogeneous groupings if this classification scheme was to have any analytic utility, but the subdivisions had to be based upon important structural features in the data, features that have important political implications.

Several writers have argued that the central cleavage in the American political system is the clash between social elements organized around the business community and those organized around government and not-for-profit institutions in the public sector. As E. E. Schattschneider (1960, p. 118) argued: "the relations of government and business largely determine the character of the regime . . . the struggle for power is largely a confrontation of two major power systems, government and business."[7] These writers imply that there

are two distinct realms within the world of groups: one comprises the commercial interests in society which are defending themselves against intrusions by government or searching for government assistance; the other is composed of both the providers and the recipients of public services who are seeking to increase public investment in activities ranging from education for the physically handicapped to the performance of grand opera, which they believe will languish if left to depend upon the market economy.

In order to find whether there was such a great divide between the public and private sectors, the occupationally based groups identified after the first division of the data were divided once more into 1) those whose membership worked predominantly either in private, profit-making enterprises, or if self-employed, were operating on a fee-for-service basis, and 2) a second set whose members worked predominantly in public sector, not-for-profit organizations.

These two passes at the data—first, the division into occupationally based groups and citizen groups, and second, the subdivision of the large occupational category into three smaller classes based on the background of the membership—produced a fourfold classification that will be referred to as the *typology of occupational roles*.[8] The results are presented in Table 12.1.

Efforts to code the data into these two mutually exclusive classes were generally successful. A distinct set of profit-sector groups emerged which was made up primarily of trade associations designed to represent single sectors of the economy, such as The Mortgage Bankers Association, the National Tank Truck Conference, the National Soybean Producers Association, or the Motorcycle Industry Council. Included along with the trade associations were groups of professionals who operate mostly on a fee-for-service basis or work mainly for profit-making business firms, such as The American College of Apothecaries, the American Dental Association, or the National Association of Life Underwriters.

The grouping of occupationally based public sector associations also was quite homogeneous. It included what might be called public sector trade associations—groups representing a certain type of government agency or non-profit organization, such as the Association of American Medical Colleges, the National Association of Counties, or the American Association of Homes for the Aged. It also included professional societies made up mainly of individuals working for nonprofit agencies, such as The National Association of State Alcohol and Drug Abuse Directors, the International Association of Fire Chiefs, or the National Association of Student Financial Aid Administrators.

Most groups fit clearly into either the public or the private sectors, but there are 67 groups in the sample—almost 15% of the total of occupationally based groups—whose members' backgrounds are so evenly distributed between the public and private sectors that they did not belong to either category. This mixed sector includes professional societies, such as the American Planning Association, the Society of America Foresters, or the National Society of Professional Engineers, and trade associations, such as the American Hospital Association or the National Association of Broadcasters. Thus the data themselves indicate a natural division into three categories: groups whose members come from the private sector, groups whose members come about equally from both the private and public sectors, and groups whose members are predominantly from the public sector.

As might be expected, the associations referred to as citizen groups in Table 12.1—those that have no occupational prerequisites for membership—made up the least homogeneous class. The category included, as it was meant to, almost all the public interest groups organized around ideas or causes, such as Citizens for Clean Air, Young Americans for Freedom, the Women's International League for Peace and Freedom, and Common Cause. Not all the groups in this category are entirely divorced from somewhat narrow social roles, however; some of the larger, general purpose veterans groups, such as AMVETS or the Veterans of Foreign Wars, were placed among the citizen groups, for example, because they do not require members to be veterans, and many apparently are not. Groups like the National Association of the Visually Handicapped or other general-purpose associations representing the mentally retarded, the aged, or other readily identifiable elements of the society also were designated as citizen groups because they regard themselves as general-purpose, public interest groups open to all persons, regardless of professional or organizational affiliations.

The citizen groups are often filled with professionals whose work has brought them into contact with the issues around which the group is organized. Environmental groups, for example, are naturally attractive to many people who work in the recreation industry, forestry, wildlife management, or some other relevant occupation. The data from the survey indicate, however, that most citizen groups have a mixed membership that does not come predominantly from either the public or the private sector.

Schattschneider was right in believing that a great political divide exists in American society between government and business, a divide that provides structure for the world of interest groups, but the lines are blurred and many groups are successful in straddling the boundary.

THE RECENT HISTORY OF GROUP FORMATION

The data in Table 12.1 provide a portrait of the group structure in 1980, but the past 20 years represents one of the most unsettled periods in American political history. Newspapers have been full of reports of the formation of new associations, and political leaders have complained loudly about unreasonable pressures from "single interest groups."[9] These reports imply not only that the number of groups is increasing, but that the number of citizen groups is growing more rapidly than all other types, creating a trend away from the predominantly occupational basis of the interest group system.

Despite all the reports in the press, however, there are no comprehensive historical data available that document recent historical trends in group formation. One is forced to rely upon scattered estimates by observers from different periods. Herring (1929, p. 19) estimated that there were "well over 500" lobbies at work in Washington. Fifty years later, in 1977, the reference book *Washington Representatives* (1981) estimated that there were approximately 1,300 Washington-based associations, and in 1980 this estimate was increased to 1,700. These estimates are not strictly comparable because different definitions of groups were being used, and all of them are probably low because of the difficulty of tracking down many of the smaller groups at work in the city which employ part-time staff members or rely heavily upon volunteers, but they lend plausibility to the claim that there are more groups in existence now than there were several decades ago.

There is no doubt that the number of citizen groups has grown rapidly during the past twenty years in several policy areas. Recently published histories of the women's movement describe in detail the sharp increase during the 1970s (Boles, 1970, Chapter 3; Carden, 1974; Freeman, 1975; Gelb & Palley, 1982, Chapters 2–3 and 8). The environmental movement experienced much the same kind of expansion at roughly the same time (Fox, 1981), and beginning in the late 1950s there was an unprecedented flowering of groups representing the elderly (Pratt, 1976). When J. L. Freeman (1969) wrote his classic study of the sub-government surrounding the Bureau of Indian Affairs in 1960, only about 16 interest groups were in operation with any concern for public policies toward American Indians. During the next 20 years the number grew steadily to a total of at least 48 operating in 1980.[10]

Evidence of recent growth in the interest group structure also exists in the data from my survey. All respondents were asked to report the founding dates for their associations, and these data were assembled cumulatively in Figure 12.1 for each of the categories in the typology of occupational roles. The data demonstrate that the first occupational groups were founded in the middle of the nineteenth century, and that it took almost another century to create the first half of these groups. The remainder of the occupational groups in my sample were founded since World War II. In contrast, the first half of the citizen groups did not come into existence until 1960; then, during the next 20 years, there was a period of explosive growth during which citizen groups multiplied at twice the rate of all types of occupationally based groups.

Both the historical evidence and the data from my survey provide powerful circumstantial evidence of recent growth

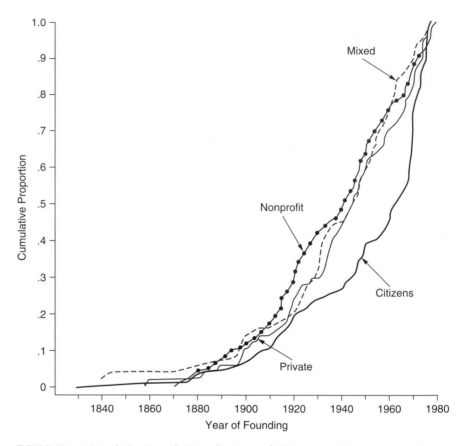

FIGURE 12.1 A Cumulative Count by Founding Date of All Groups in this Survey Sample Divided by Sector Types from the Typology of Occupational Roles.

SOURCE: Jack L. Walker, "The Origins and Maintenance of Interest Groups in America," *American Political Science Review* 77 (1983): 395, Figure 1. Reprinted with permission from Cambridge University Press.

in the interest groups structure, but neither constitutes conclusive proof that such growth has actually occurred. It is possible, although unlikely, that citizen groups in areas ignored by historians were declining in numbers during the 1960s and 1970s, thus canceling out the reported gains. The analysis of founding dates of the groups in my survey is suggestive, but it may be only a statistical artifact, because I have no data on the number of groups that were formed in earlier years but went out of existence before 1980, when the survey was conducted. If citizen groups have a higher mortality rate than occupational groups—

which is likely—an analysis of founding dates at any period would always indicate that more of the existing citizen groups were founded within the recent past than the longer-lived occupational groups. Without reliable estimates of both the birth and death rates of different types of groups it is not possible to reconstruct history conclusively with data from a cross-section survey. Furthermore, even if the number of citizen groups grew more rapidly during the past 20 years, this growth may have been part of a cycle that is rapidly coming to an end. Several observers in the late 1970s reported increases in the formation of associations representing business inter-ests, so the trend toward larger propor-tions of citizen groups may already have been reversed (Shabecoff, 1979; Wilson, 1981).

Despite these reservations about each source of data, all available evi-dence points in the same direction, namely that there are many more inter-est groups operating in Washington today than in the years before World War II, and that citizen groups make up a much larger proportion of the total than ever before. This transformation may not be as large or dramatic as the data sug-gest, or as some journalists and political leaders have implied, but there are good reasons to believe that far-reaching changes took place during the past two decades in the system of interest groups in the United States.[11]

RECENT HISTORY AND THE THEORY OF GROUP FORMATION

How can these recent changes in the interest group system be explained? The work of Olson largely undermined Truman's theory of the spontaneous generation of groups, and yet, despite the power of Olson's analysis, at first glance recent increases in the number of groups suggest that Truman has the data on his side. After reading about the many obsta-cles that must be overcome before groups can be formed, one would not expect to find that so many new ones have been created during the past 20 years, and especially citizen groups, the type most affected by the collective goods dilemma. These trends in group formation raise serious questions about the predictive utility of the line of theory founded by Olson.

An increase in the number of groups, by itself, would not disconfirm Olson's theory. Faced with these data, an observer who accepted Olson's analysis

might immediately suspect that the citi-zen groups were offering some new kind of desirable benefit in exchange for membership that was not available to nonmembers. If these selective benefits were desirable enough, groups might attract large numbers of members and become rich enough to employ a large and talented staff, even though many of their members might actually disagree with the group's goals. The twin groups of the National Retired Teachers Asso-ciation (NRTA) and the American Association of Retired Persons (AARP) are included in my study and classified as citizen groups, since they have no occu-pational prerequisites for membership.[12] In 1965 the combined membership of NRTA/AARP stood at approximately 750,000, and by 1979 it had grown to 13 million members, making it one of the largest voluntary associations in the world. The secret of this phenomenal growth, however, was not the attractive-ness of the policies being advocated by the group; rather, it was the special med-ical insurance policies available to older people only through membership, the tours and vacation trips conducted by the groups with the special needs of the eld-erly in mind, the commercial discounts and many useful personal services avail-able for retired persons through member-ship. In Olson's terms, these two groups grew because of their ability to provide selective material benefits for their mem-bers, not because of the devotion of their members to the common interests of the elderly.

The NRTA/AARP is an important voice in the national dialogue over policy toward the aged, but the data from my survey suggest that its reliance on selective benefits is also quite *unusual*. Only about 15% of the citizen groups in my sample even offer insurance as a benefit to their members, and of those who do, over one-third believe it to be an unimportant part of their benefit package. Even fewer citizen groups offer discounts on consumer goods, and only

30% of these groups sponsor trips for their members. Where benefits for members are concerned, citizen groups are hardly distinguishable from groups in the occupational categories. In fact, occupational groups built around relatively small communities of professionals or small groups of firms with common commercial interests can provide selective benefits in the form of friendships, professional contacts, and in-service training that most citizen groups can provide for only a small segment of their memberships, if at all. Publications are provided by groups of all types and universally thought of as among their most important benefits, but citizen groups have no unique advantages where publications are concerned. My data show that citizen groups receive a smaller proportion of their total revenue from publications and conference fees than any of the other types of groups. Citizen groups, on the average, also report that only about 1% of their total revenues are derived from insurance commissions or direct services to individuals.

If the availability of selective benefits will not explain recent changes in the group structure, an observer following Olson might suspect that group leaders had somehow managed to find ways to coerce new members to join against their self-interest. Olson demonstrated persuasively how legal forms of coercion contributed to the creation and maintenance of American trade unions. Without closed shops and mandatory payment of dues through payroll deduction, union membership would almost certainly plummet as many workers dropped out to become "free riders," fully expecting to receive the same benefits from their employers that were granted to union members (Olson, 1965, pp. 66–97).

Even though trade unions were not included in this study, interviews with group leaders have convinced me that a few of the groups in my sample are able to exercise subtle forms of coercion which

may have inflated their membership rolls during this period. For example, certain trade associations sponsor the creation of codes meant to govern the specifications of goods produced by their industry. Uniform sizes of components or safety standards established in these private codes are often accepted by government or private purchasing agents as minimum requirements and may sometimes be written directly into state or local statutes, thus taking on the force of law. Many small firms may feel compelled to join trade associations to protect themselves from arbitrary changes in such codes which might suddenly render their products unmarketable or require them to make large investments in new tools or equipment (Wines, 1981).

Similarly, many associations of professionals in both the public and private sectors have managed to gain significant influence over licensing procedures, and several serve as accrediting agencies for educational programs in their professional specialties. Until a decision by the Supreme Court in 1978 prevented the practice, many associations required any person wishing certification in the field to hold membership in the group—a direct form of coercion—but even now that this practice has been made illegal, many professionals apparently regard membership in their professional society as a hedge against decertification.[13]

These practices are consistent with Olson's theory, even though they affect a relatively small number of groups, but they will not serve as a satisfactory explanation for the maintenance of citizen groups since they are not able to employ either tactic in order to gain membership. These coercive practices have been employed for many years, and in fact, action by the government and the courts during the 1970s significantly reduced their usefulness as spurs to group formation and membership growth. Our conclusion must be that neither Truman's nor Olson's theories offer convincing explanations of the changing composition of the group structure in the United States. The political system is beset by a swarm of organizational bumblebees that are busily flying about in spite of the fact that political scientists cannot explain how they manage it.

TOWARD A NEW THEORY OF GROUP ORIGINS AND MAINTENANCE

The Origins of Groups

There was no single explanation for the increase in the number of groups operating at the national level in American politics. Long-term improvements in educational levels provided a large pool of potential recruits for citizen movements; the development of cheap, sophisticated methods of communication, such as the new direct mailing systems or the WATTS long-distance telephone lines, allowed leaders in Washington to reach members in all parts of the country; a period of social protest that began with the civil rights demonstrations of the early 1960s called many established practices into question, created concerns about the future stability of the American political system, and provided a powerful impetus for change. Once these mutually reinforcing factors led to the creation of massive new government programs in social welfare, education, health care, housing, and transportation, newly created government agencies and foundations began to foster voluntary associations among the service providers and consumers of the new programs. During this period the new regulatory legislation in civil rights, consumer protection, environmental preservation, pollution control, and occupational health and safety prompted business groups to organize in self-defense—as Truman would have predicted—to protect themselves against the authorities who were

charged with enforcing these broad new legislative mandates.

These complex changes in American politics and public policy during the past 30 years, and the fundamental transformations in the political environment they generated, go a long way toward explaining recent changes in the structure of interest groups. So many influences have been at work, however, that the fundamental character of the group formation process has been partially obscured. This study shows that during recent years, group leaders learned how to cope with the public goods dilemma not by inducing large numbers of new members to join their groups through the manipulation of selective benefits, but by locating important new sources of funds outside the immediate membership.

The first problem facing would-be interest group organizers is to bring their groups into being and to keep them going until revenues are large enough to meet operating expenses. Profit-sector groups that emerge from relatively small and closely knit occupational or industrial communities can often begin their activities on tiny budgets and can continue operations for several years without a professional staff. In the not-for-profit sector, groups often come about at the urging of federal officials who need to have regular contact with administrators of state or local agencies receiving aid from some new federal program. There is a need to share information, develop standard administrative practices, create model bills for adoption by cities or states, and of course, work to expand support for their programs in the Congress. Members of most public and private sector occupational groups are able to charge their travel costs to their firms or agencies and can easily agree to meet together periodically to exchange information and to work out common positions on outstanding questions of public policy.

Citizen groups face an entirely different set of initial circumstances. Their

Table 12.2 Percentage of Groups by Sectors that Received Financial Aid from any Outside Source in Order to Start Operations

Sector	Percent receiving aid	N
Profit	33.9	174
Mixed	56.1	66
Nonprofit	60.0	190
Citizens	89.0	115

SOURCE: Jack L. Walker, "The Origins and Maintenance of Interest Groups in America," *American Political Science Review* 77 (1983): 398, Table 2. Reprinted with permission from Cambridge University Press.

potential membership is extremely large and, in most cases, unknown to one another. There is no ready-made community waiting to be organized, no readily available sources of money, and often not even a clearly articulated common interest in creating an organization. Citizen groups must begin with a fairly large staff, or they will have little chance of reaching enough of their far-flung potential membership to create a stable organizational base.

Because of the organizational problems facing citizen groups, they must almost always gain financial assistance in order to launch their operations. All respondents in my survey were asked whether their group had received any form of financial assistance from an outside source at the beginning of its history, and as reported in Table 12.2. 89% of the citizen groups reported that they had, whereas only 34% of the occupationally based groups from the profit sector had received financial aid.

Not only were the nonprofit and citizen groups more likely to receive aid at the initial stages, but further analysis of the data shows that access to outside funding has increased in recent years. In Table 12.3, all groups in my sample which were founded before 1945 are contrasted with those founded after 1945. The end of World War II is a convenient point for dividing the data because it breaks the

sample almost exactly in half, and the postwar period also was marked by the increasing prominence of citizen groups and the growth both in the number of private foundations and activist administrative bureaus in the national government, two of the most important sources of patronage for political action.

Emerging from Table 12.3 is a picture of the evolution of funding sources that have produced the group structure of the 1980s. The entries report the percentage of groups founded in each period that reported receiving start-up funds from four different sources: individuals, foundations, other associations, and government agencies. Large gifts from individuals have been highly important sources of funds in all four sectors and have been steadily rising in importance, especially for the citizen groups, but the sharpest changes have occurred in the three other funding sources. First, the group structure in the mixed, nonprofit, and citizen sectors has been elaborating itself as associations have helped to spawn new ones in order to build larger networks of groups around volatile issues like civil rights or around constituencies like the elderly or the handicapped.

Second, both government agencies and private foundations have steadily become more important patrons of interest groups in the mixed, nonprofit, and citizen sectors. Both government

Table 12.3 Percentage of Groups Receiving Financial Aid at Time of Founding from Four Sources of Funds by Sector Type, 1840–1945 and 1946–1980

	TIME PERIODS	
Funding Sources	**1840–1945**	**1946–1980**
Profit sector groups		
Individual Gifts	19.1	19.8
Foundation Grants	1.1	2.3
Other Associations	6.7	3.5
Government Grants	3.4	5.8
N =	(89)	(86)
Mixed sectors groups		
Individual Gifts	25.0	28.1
Foundation Grants	3.1	15.6
Other Associations	12.5	25.0
Government Grants	6.3	12.5
N =	(32)	(32)
Nonprofit sector groups		
Individual Gifts	26.0	20.9
Foundation Grants	21.2	32.6
Other Associations	12.5	17.4
Government Grants	10.6	31.4
N =	(104)	(86)
Citizen groups		
Individual Gifts	65.7	68.4
Foundation Grants	17.1	39.2
Other Associations	5.7	22.8
Government Grants	8.6	10.1
N =	(35)	(79)
Total N =	(260)	(283)

SOURCE: Jack L. Walker, "The Origins and Maintenance of Interest Groups in America," *American Political Science Review* 77 (1983): 399, Table 3. Reprinted with permission from Cambridge University Press.

agencies and foundations are active in sponsoring groups built around professional specialties in areas like health care, education, welfare administration, mass transportation, scientific research, and other program areas that depend heavily on federal funds. Government agencies and foundations both made contributions to the founding of a few groups in the profit sector, but their efforts are clearly concentrated in the mixed, nonprofit, and citizen sectors. After 1945 the government supplanted foundations as a source of start-up money for groups in the nonprofit sector, while foundations shifted more of their attention toward the citizen groups.

It requires boldness to provide start-up funds to an untested political entrepreneur or to patronize a cause that might create controversy. My data demonstrate that among all the patrons

Table 12.4 Timing of Support from Three Types of Patrons of Political Action as a Percentage of All Groups Reporting

	Government	Foundations	Individuals
	%	%	%
Start-up funds: patron acting alone	12.8	15.7	41.7
Start-up funds: more than one patron	17.2	34.4	22.1
Maintenance support	70.0	49.9	36.2
N	(210)	(189)	(257)

SOURCE: Jack L. Walker, "The Origins and Maintenance of Interest Groups in America," *American Political Science Review* 77 (1983): 399, Table 4. Reprinted with permission from Cambridge University Press.

studied, private individuals are the most likely to provide backing for new organizational ventures, far outdistancing foundations and government agencies in their willingness to take risks. Table 12.4 shows that only 13% of the groups that received government support got it in the form of start-up money when the government agency was acting as the sole source of patronage. Another 17% of the groups that received government support received it as start-up funds when the government agency was acting in league with other patrons, but 70% of the groups reporting support from government received it solely for maintenance of their operations, only after they were successfully launched and had established a record of performance. Foundations are more likely than government agencies to sponsor new groups, but the data show that the most adventurous patrons are clearly private individuals. Of the groups who reported receiving support from individuals, 42% got it to help establish their operations when individuals were acting as their only patrons, and another 22% received start-up support when individuals were joined by other types of patrons. Patronage for political action from large institutions has increased in importance in recent years, but wealthy individuals are still a crucial source of the venture capital needed by aspiring political entrepreneurs.

The Maintenance of Groups

Once groups have been brought into being with the aid of a patron, in most cases the patron continues to support the group once it is a going concern. New groups sometimes are weaned from dependence on other associations as a source of continuing support, although there is a positive tau-b correlation of .21 between the receipt of start-up funds from other associations and the receipt of continuing support from them. Groups evidently find it even more difficult to become independent of reliance on grants from individuals, private foundations, and government agencies. The tau-b correlations between the receipt of start-up funds from a source and the continuing receipt of support for maintenance from the same source are .37 for government agencies, .43 for foundations, and .44 for individuals. These figures indicate that once groups come into being with support from a patron, they tend to maintain financial connections of some kind with these sponsors throughout their existence.

All groups in the survey were asked to describe their current budgets; the results are displayed, according to the typology of occupational roles, in Table 12.5. The patterns of support that were evident in the data on group origins appear once again in this table, which presents the financial situation as it was in 1980. Citizen groups received less than half

Table 12.5 Average Percentage of Revenue Obtained by Groups from Each Source in 1980 Budgetary Year by Sector Type

	SECTOR TYPE			
	Profit %	Mixed %	Nonprofit %	Citizens %
Routine contributions from members or associates				
Dues	76.8	47.7	45.7	36.3
Publications	5.3	14.2	8.8	8.8
Conferences	7.1	11.9	8.8	2.3
Subtotal	89.2	73.8	63.3	47.4
Nonrecurring contributions from nonmember institutions and persons				
Individual gifts	1.0	3.8	3.5	17.2
Foundations	0.2	3.2	4.2	12.8
Government	1.2	9.3	14.6	8.9
Other associations	0.5	2.3	1.9	4.0
Subtotal	2.9	18.6	24.2	42.9
Miscellaneous recurring and nonrecurring contributions				
Investment income, commissions, sales, fees	6.9	6.9	10.8	7.6
Loans	0.4	0.2	0.4	0.6
Other	0.7	0.7	1.4	1.5
Subtotal	8.0	7.8	12.6	9.7
Total	100.1	100.2	100.1	100.0
N	(154)	(54)	(169)	(90)

SOURCE: Jack L. Walker, "The Origins and Maintenance of Interest Groups in America," *American Political Science Review* 77 (1983): 400, Table 5. Reprinted with permission from Cambridge University Press.

of their support from member dues, the sale of publications, and conference fees in that year, whereas profit sector groups received 89.2% of their funds from these sources. The government was an important patron for groups of professionals in both the mixed and public sectors, and the combination of private individuals and private foundations together provided 30% of the funds available to citizen groups.

Table 12.5 provides much valuable information about the maintenance of interest groups, but it is slightly misleading in two ways. First, although dues are shown to be an important source of revenue for groups of all kinds, it must be remembered that they are not, in every case, voluntary contributions from individuals who have made a rational decision to join a group in the hope of advancing some ideological or personal goal. Many individuals in both the private and public sectors are allowed by their employers to charge the cost of their dues, publications, and travel to association meetings to their agency budgets. Without those subsidies, many of these individuals would not participate in group activities. The data reported in Table 12.5 on the support from dues for both private and public sector groups, therefore, include an unknown, but probably substantial, amount of indirect patronage from the budgets of government agencies or private corporations.

Besides providing indirect patronage to private sector groups by subsidizing the memberships of their employees, many large private corporations provide a second form of patronage to trade associations by making extraordinary contributions that are labelled as dues. Most trade associations employ sliding scale or "split" dues schedules under which a small number of large firms contribute much larger amounts than the rest of the members, much as Olson suggested they would in his discussion of "the exploitation of the great by the small" (Olson, 1965, pp. 3, 27–32, 34–36). McKean (1949, p. 489) reported that in the 1940s, 5% of the membership of the National Association of Manufacturers contributed approximately 50% of the funds needed for the group's maintenance. The average dues payment in 1981 from the 215,000 members of the U.S. Chamber of Commerce was approximately $265, based on a sliding scale that ranged from $100 to more than $75,000 for a handful of major corporations. Most of the Chamber's member firms are small—91% have fewer than 100 employees—yet the Chamber's Board of Directors is overwhelmingly dominated by the large national and multinational corporations that make the maximum dues payments (Richman, 1982). Arrangements of this kind apparently are typical in cases where a single firm (such as Ralston Purina in the feed manufacturing business) or a small number of large firms (as in the production of agricultural chemicals) account for most of the sales in the industry.

Many private sector groups receive patronage from large corporations through the unequal sharing of financial burdens by their membership, but it was not possible in this survey to obtain reliable estimates of the number of such groups or the patterns of dues support they employ. However, these systems of unequal contribution constitute a form of corporate patronage that closely resembles the subsidies from government and foundations that are extended to groups in the public sector. If accurate data could be assembled on all forms of financial assistance, it would surely show that many profit sector groups are heavily dependent upon patronage from private sources.

PATRONS AND PUBLIC POLICY

Financial support is usually provided to groups for a purpose, since patrons expect to receive benefits in return for their aid, but these benefits do not always involve public policy. In many instances patrons are mainly interested in enlisting the support of associations in reaching broad economic, scientific, or administrative goals. Beginning with efforts to improve agriculture at the turn of the century and continuing through the War on Poverty in the 1960s, most American social policies have been highly elaborate cooperative efforts involving many levels of government in the federal system, along with both private and public corporations. Federal agencies have an interest in encouraging coordination among the elements of these complex service delivery systems and in improving the diffusion of new ideas and techniques. Groups like the American Public Transit Association or the American Council on Education, both of which receive extensive patronage from federal agencies and foundations, serve as centers of professional development and informal channels for administrative coordination in an otherwise unwieldy governmental system.

Besides their administrative and professional functions, however, groups obviously also play an important political role, and most patrons are fully aware of this role when they agree to provide financial aid. There are many types of patrons, each with a distinctive interest in public affairs. One of the chief reasons that business firms join trade associations,

Table 12.6 Relationship between Receipt of Government Financial Aid and Support for Increased Government Intervention in Society

Receipt of government funds	DESIRED LEVEL OF GOVERNMENT INTERVENTION			
	More	Present Level	Less	
Yes	46.1	30.9	23.0	= 100%
No	21.4	16.6	62.0	= 100%
	N = 319		tau-b	= .32

SOURCE: Jack L. Walker, "The Origins and Maintenance of Interest Groups in America," *American Political Science Review* 77 (1983): 402, Table 6. Reprinted with permission from Cambridge University Press.

for example, is their desire to secure sympathetic public policies or to mount effective defenses against government regulation. Government agencies organize their constituents not only in order to improve coordination in the federal system, but also to lobby the Congress and the presidency on their behalf. The social movements and political upheavals of the 1960s prompted many individuals and foundations to act as patrons for a variety of challenging groups. Several of the country's largest foundations only began serious operations in the 1950s and were in search of a meaningful role in American life.[14] Foundation officials believed that the long-run stability of the representative policymaking system would be assured only if legitimate organizational channels could be provided for the frustration and anger being expressed in protests and outbreaks of political violence during this period.[15] Another important form of patronage came from already established interest groups, which assisted in the creation of new groups in their fields, especially if these new organizations promised to perform services or reach constituencies that had not yet been exploited by existing organizations. Public policy concerns may not always be the primary consideration when assistance is granted, but patrons are not likely to support groups for any purposes that do not share their general approach to social policy.

A graphic illustration of the close match between the interests of patrons and the general attitudes of the groups they patronize is provided by the data in Table 12.6. All respondents in the survey were asked whether, in general, they favored more, less, or the present level of government provision of social services. They were also asked whether the policy of their associations called for more, less, or the present level of regulation of business and industry. The responses to these two questions were combined to produce a three-point scale measuring the respondent's overall preference for governmental intervention in the society.[16]

Most groups take a practical view of general questions of this kind. They would favor increased services if it seemed to be in their interest to do so and would oppose any increases that seemed opposed to their interest. Many groups refused to answer these two questions on the grounds that they had no general attitude toward the role of government, but a majority of the respondents did answer at least one of the two questions. The resulting scale reflects their general predisposition toward the role of government in society.

The strong relationship in Table 12.6 speaks for itself. Groups receiving money from government agencies are much more likely than those not funded to believe that an expansion of governmental

Table 12.7 Rank-order Correlations for the Relationship between Receipt of Government Financial Aid and Support for Increased Government Intervention in Society, by Group Sector

	GROUP SECTORS			
Total sample	Profit	Mixed	Nonprofit	Citizen
tau-b = .32	.33	.28	.21	.21
N = (319)	(114)	(34)	(116)	(55)

SOURCE: Jack L. Walker, "The Origins and Maintenance of Interest Groups in America," *American Political Science Review* 77 (1983): 402, Table 7. Reprinted with permission from Cambridge University Press.

activity would be desirable. This relationship holds, furthermore, even within sector type, as illustrated by the positive correlations shown in Table 12.7. This pattern of correlations provides strong circumstantial evidence that government agencies are unlikely to sponsor groups that do not share their fundamental political sympathies. Government agencies make grants or issue contracts to improve the training of professionals, to increase citizens' understanding of public policies, or to encourage local bureaucracies to employ the most effective administrative practices, but while carrying out these more or less neutral programmatic and administrative tasks, the agencies are also furthering their own political objectives.

PATRONS OF POLITICAL ACTION AND THE THEORY OF GROUPS

Patrons of political action play a crucial role in the initiation and maintenance of interest groups.[17] This does not mean that Olson's emphasis upon the incentives facing likely interest group members is misplaced, or that Salisbury's ideas about the importance of entrepreneurial leadership are wrong. Our attention certainly should not shift entirely away from groups toward the motives and activities of patrons. This analysis points, however, to another important method,

beyond the provision of selective benefits and the use of coercion, which groups have employed to cope with Olson's dilemma of collective action.

Efforts to form new groups and associations have occurred in every decade of the past century, but Truman was surely correct in arguing that the propensity to form groups increases during periods of general social upheaval, as in the 1930s and 1960s, when challengers to the established order may ride upon great outbursts of protest and the political leadership is divided (Gamson, 1975; Goldstone, 1980; Jenkins & Perrow, 1977). No matter what propensities exist, however, large amounts of capital are needed to form most interest groups. The key to success in these efforts usually is the ability of group organizers to secure both start-up funds and reliable sources of continuing financial support from patrons of political action. Furthermore, now that a decade has passed since the turmoil of the 1960s it is clear that most of the groups founded in the wake of the civil rights and peace movements that were unable to secure adequate patronage have disappeared. The much-publicized effort during this period to organize college students, for example, failed in large part because no patron could ever be attracted who was willing to back the effort; or, as in the case of the National Student Association, one of the patrons that was secured proved to be so unpopular with the potential membership that its sponsorship seriously damaged the group's credibility. The NSA almost collapsed in 1967 after revelations that it had been receiving financial aid for years from the Central Intelligence Agency (Meyer, 1980).

The stormy history of the Students for a Democratic Society illustrates the importance of patronage in the maintenance of challenging groups. SDS began in 1959 as an effort to challenge the conservative political consensus prevailing on American college campuses during the Eisenhower years. The group began as an affiliate of the League for Industrial Democracy, a small socialist organization that had itself been supported for several decades mainly by private gifts. After a bitter controversy in the early 1960s in which the LID threatened to withdraw its support over supposed Communist infiltration, the SDS quickly grew from the dedicated band of 150 activists who gathered in Port Huron, Michigan, in 1962 to ratify its manifesto into a vigorous organization with over 20,000 dues-paying members in 1966. Besides its campus activities, SDS employed more than 300 full-time field workers engaged in grass-roots community organizing in several large industrial cities. Dues and private gifts were important sources of funds during this period, but the principal income of SDS was a series of grants from the United Auto Workers Union to conduct the SDS campaign of community organization and much of the group's publishing and issues research.

Factional infighting intensified in the late 1960s as the group became a kind of revolutionary vanguard rather than a broadly based student movement. Despite warnings from some of its leaders, SDS soon took itself beyond the political and ideological reach of the UAW, which finally terminated its grants. This withdrawal of patronage led almost immediately to a collapse of the group's staff and organizational center. Having drifted beyond the normative boundaries of the political system as defined by the values of its principal patrons, the SDS soon disintegrated into brawling factions of

extreme radicals, and finally into the terrorist fantasies of the Weathermen, whose activities eventually were financed primarily by robbing banks.[18]

Most groups formed during this period, however, did not force their way in from outside the system; they were brought into being at the bidding of the patrons themselves in a form of political mobilization from the top down. More than half of the 46 groups representing the elderly in my study were formed after 1965, the year of the great legislative breakthroughs of Medicare and the Older Americans Act. Many other groups in fields like education, mass transportation, and environmental protection also sprang up *after* the passage of dramatic new legislation that established the major outlines of public policy in their areas. In all of these cases, the formation of new groups was one of the *consequences* of major new legislation, not one of the *causes* of its passage. A pressure model of the policymaking process in which an essentially passive legislature responds to petitions from groups of citizens who have spontaneously organized because of common social or economic concerns must yield to a model in which influences for change come as much from inside the government as from beyond its institutional boundaries, and in which political entrepreneurs operating from bases in interest groups, from within the Congress, the presidency, or many private institutions, struggle to accommodate citizen discontent, appeal to emerging groups, and strive to generate support for their own conceptions of the public interest.[19]

Changes in the structure of the interest group system cannot be understood only through the study of shifts in public opinion or the clever tactics of innovative leaders. The success of efforts to create and maintain political interest groups also depends upon such legal and institutional factors as the provisions of the tax code governing the ability of business firms to claim deductions for the expenses of lobbying, subsidies in the form of reduced postal rates for not-for-profit groups heavily dependent upon direct mail solicitation, the availability of financial support from regulatory agencies for groups that wish to testify at administrative hearings, the rules concerning the registration of lobbyists and the financial disclosures they are required to make, legal restraints on the accessibility of foundations, and many other policies and actions by government or other patrons that either stimulate or inhibit the process of political mobilization. Since the number of interest groups and their rate of growth is so heavily influenced by the incentives, supports, and opportunities created through public policies and legal provisions, most governments choose to promote the mobilization of their allies, as the Johnson administration did through the War on Poverty, Model Cities, VISTA, the Older Americans Act, and many other programs of social reform; or to frustrate or demobilize its antagonists as the Reagan administration seems to be doing through budget cuts in the discretionary programs of the Great Society, raises in postal rates, and challenges to the not-for-profit status of several groups and publishing enterprises (Babcock, 1982; Mackenzie, 1981; Peterson, 1981; Seaberry, 1982; & Stanfield, 1981).

The energy that drives the process of group formation may come from below in the from of social movements arising out of widespread popular discontent, or from individual political entrepreneurs operating largely on their own. Initiative may also come from above in the form of efforts by trade unions, government agencies, private corporations, churches, and other large organizations in the public and private sectors sponsoring groups that they believe will further their interests. Wealthy individuals and private foundations often take the lead in promoting groups designed to mobilize large segments of the public in support of controversial causes. Without the influence of the patrons of political action, the flourishing system of interest groups in the United States would be much smaller and would include very few groups seeking to obtain broad collective or public goods. If all sources of patronage suddenly disappeared, the interest group system would immediately shrink until it included only a small set of highly unstable insurgent groups that would remain in existence only as long as they were able to command the loyalty of some aroused segment of the public, and another set of more stable associations that represented only small, tightly knit, commercial, occupational, ethnic, or religious communities, those groups able to draw successfully upon the resources of their members to meet their operating expenses.

The findings of this study lead to the principal conclusion that the number of interest groups in operation, the mixture of group types, and the level and direction of political mobilization in the United States at any point in the country's history will largely be determined by the composition and accessibility of the system's major patrons of political action. The American system of political patronage has grown dramatically and become more diversified during the past 30 years so that many new opportunities have arisen for aspiring political entrepreneurs of both liberal and conservative persuasions. As the patronage system has grown, so have the number and variety of interest groups. The key to the origins and maintenance of interest groups in the United States lies in the ability and willingness of the patrons of political action to expand the representative system by sponsoring groups that speak for newly emerging elements of society and promote new legislative agendas and social values.

NOTES

1. For a comprehensive critique and review of recent work, see Moe (1980).

2. The apparent contradiction, however, between the explanations of Truman and Olson may be illusory. See the argument developed in Moe (1981).

3. A useful annotated bibliography of the literature in this field is Smith and Freedman (1972).

4. An important exception that concerns both the United States and Canada in the 1960s is Presthus (1974).

5. The two best studies of unions in American politics are Greenstone (1969) and Wilson (1977).

6. Typologies abound in this field. For examples, see the work already cited by Wilson and Edelman, along with Lowi (1964) and Hayes (1981).

7. Also see Lindblom (1977) and Greenstone (1982), and for a thoughtful critique see Elkins (1982).

8. Those interested in further details concerning the construction of this typology should consult the methodological appendix included in an earlier version of the paper presented at the 1981 annual meeting of the American Political Science Association. Copies are available from the author.

9. There were hundreds of complaints about undue pressures upon government during the past two years. See Carter (1981) and the series of articles following the career of freshman Congressman Michael L. Snydar, first-term Representative from Oklahoma. See especially Roberts (1980).

10. See Freeman (1969) and Barbrook and Bolt (1980, pp. 150–159). The estimate of the total number of Indian groups was produced by a survey of groups listed in *The Encyclopedia of Associations* (Detroit: Gale Research, 1980).

11. This conclusion is shared by all recent observers. See Berry (1977), Broder (1980), Gunther (1976), Heclo (1978), Hrebenar and Scott (1982), McFarland (1976), Schlozman and Tierney (1982), and Wilson (1981).

12. This group began as an association of retired teachers and thus would have been categorized as an occupational group within the not-for-profit sector, but after its merger with the AARP, all occupational prerequisites were dropped so that it has clearly become a citizen group. For a description, see Pratt (1976), pp. 119–213.

13. The Supreme Court decision is: *National Society of Professional Engineers* v. *U.S.,* 435 U.S. 679, 98 S. Ct. 1355, 55 L. Ed. 2 637, 1978.

14. For a review of recent history see *Foundations, Private Giving and Public Policy* (1970), Goulden (1971), and Nielsen (1972).

15. The best study of early foundation thinking is Marris and Rein (1973).

16. The exact wording of the two questions was: "In general, do the policy positions of this association tend to call for: much more government provision of social services, some additional government provision of social services, present level of services, less government provision of social services? In general, do the policy positions of this association tend to call for: much more government regulation of business and industry, present level of regulation, less government regulation of business and industry, much less government regulation of business and industry?"

17. Sociologists have come to much the same conclusion concerning the rise and fall of social movements. See McCarthy and Zald (1978), Marx (1979), and Oberschall (1973).

18. For the history of the SDS see Newfield (1966), pp. 83–108; Adelson (1972), Barbrook and Bolt (1980), pp. 274–280; and for a similar account of the Student Nonviolent Coordinating Committee, see Carson (1981).

19. Much recent scholarship suggests that political leaders often play a largely autonomous role in policymaking. For illustrative commentary see Nordlinger (1981) and Walker (1977).

REFERENCES

Adelson, A. *SDS.* New York: Scribner's 1972.

Babcock, C. R. Policies of education grants becomes issue. *The Washington Post,* August 14, 1982, p. 5.

Barbrook, A., & Bolt, C. *Power and protest in American life.* New York: St. Martin's, 1980.

Berry, J. *Lobbying for the people.* Princeton, N.J.: Princeton University Press, 1977.

Boles, J. K. *The politics of the equal rights amendment.* New York: Longman, 1970.

Broder, D. S. *Changing of the guard: power and leadership in America.* New York: Simon and Schuster, 1980.

Carden, M. L. *The new feminist movement.* New York: Russell Sage Foundation, 1974.

Carter, J. E. Farewell address. *The Washington Post,* January 15, 1981, p. A4.

Clayborne, C. *In struggle: SNCC and the black awakening of the 1960's.* Cambridge, Mass.: Harvard University Press, 1981.

Commission on Foundations and Private Philanthropy. *Foundations, private giving and public policy.* Chicago: University of Chicago Press, 1970.

Edelman, M. *The symbolic uses of politics.* Urbana: University of Illinois Press, 1964.

Elkins, S. L. Markets and politics in liberal democracy. *Ethics,* 1982, *92,* 720–732.

Fox, S. *John Muir and his legacy: the American conservation movement.* Boston: Little, Brown, 1981.

Freeman, J. *The politics of women's liberation.* New York: David McKay, 1975.

Freeman, J. L. *The political process: executive bureau—legislative committee relations* (Rev. ed.), New York: Random House, 1969.

Gamson, W. *Power and discontent.* Homewood, Ill.: Dorsey Press, 1968.

Gamson, W. *The strategy of social protest.* Homewood, Ill.: Dorsey Press, 1975.

Gelb, J., & Palley, M. L. *Women and public policies.* Princeton, N.J.: Princeton University Press, 1982.

Goldstone, J. A. The weakness of organizations: A new look at Gamson's *The strategy of social protest. American Journal of Sociology,* 1980, *84,* 1017–1042.

Goulden, J. C. *The money givers.* New York: Random House, 1971.

Greenstone, J. *Labor in American national politics.* New York: Alfred A. Knopf, 1969.

Greenstone, J. D. (Ed.). *Public values and private power in American politics.* Chicago: University of Chicago Press, 1982.

Gunther, J. *Moralists and managers: public interest movements in America.* New York: Anchor Books, 1976.

Hayes, M. T. *Lobbyists and legislators.* New Brunswick, N.J.: Rutgers University Press, 1981.

Heclo, H. Issue networks and the executive establishment. In A. King (Ed.), *The new American political system.* Washington, D.C.: American Enterprise Institute, 1978.

Herring, E. *Group representation before Congress.* Washington, D.C.: Brookings Institution, 1929.

Hrebenar, R. J., & Scott, R. K. *Interest group politics in America.* Englewood Cliffs, N.J.: Prentice-Hall, 1982.

Jenkins, J. C., & Perrow, C. Insurgency of the powerless: farm worker movements: 1946–72. *American Sociological Review,* 1977, *42,* 248–268.

Lindblom, C. E. *Politics and markets.* New York: Basic Books, 1977.

Lipsky, M. *Protest in city politics.* Chicago: Rand McNally, 1970.

Lowi, T. J. American business, public policy: case studies and political theory. *World Politics,* 1964, *16,* 677–715.

Mackenzie, A. When auditors turn editors: the IRA and the nonprofit press. *Columbia Journalism Review,* 1981, *20,* 29–34.

Marris, P., & Rein, M. *Dilemmas of social reform* (2nd ed.). Chicago: Aldine, 1973.

Marx, G. T. External efforts to damage or facilitate social movements. In M. N. Zald & J. D. McCarthy (Eds.), *The dynamics of social movements.* Cambridge, Mass.: Winthrop, 1979.

McCarthy, J. D., & Zald, M. N. Resource mobilization and social movements: a partial theory. *American Journal of Sociology,* 1978, *82,* 1212–1241.

McFarland, A. *Public interest lobbies: decision making on energy.* Washington, D.C.: American Enterprise Institute, 1976.

McKean, D. D. *Party and pressure politics.* Boston: Houghton Mifflin, 1949, p. 489.

Meyer, C. *Facing reality.* New York: Harper & Row, 1980.

Moe, T. M. *The organization of interests.* Chicago: University of Chicago Press, 1980.

Moe, T. M. Toward a broader view of interest groups. *Journal of Politics,* 1981, *43,* 531–543.

Newfield, J. *A prophetic minority*. New York: Signet Books, 1966, pp. 83–108.

Nielsen, W. A. *The big foundations*. New York: Columbia University Press, 1972.

Nordlinger, E. A. *On the autonomy of the democratic state*. Cambridge, Mass.: Harvard University Press, 1981.

Oberschall, A. *Social conflict and social movements*. Englewood Cliffs, N.J.: Prentice-Hall, 1973.

Olson, M., Jr. *The logic of collective action*. Cambridge, Mass.: Harvard University Press, 1965.

Ornstein, N. J., & Elder, S. *Interest groups, lobbying and policymaking*. Washington, D.C.: Congressional Quarterly Press, 1978.

Peterson, B. Coalition pushes block grants to "defund" the left. *The Washington Post,* July 2, 1981, p. 6.

Pratt, H. *The gray lobby*. Chicago: University of Chicago Press, 1976.

Presthus, R. *Elites in the policy process*. New York: Cambridge University Press, 1974.

Richman, T. Can the U.S. chamber learn to think small? *Inc.,* 1982, *4,* 81–86.

Roberts, S. V. An angry young congressman criticizes special interest groups. *The New York Times,* January 10, 1980, p. 1.

Rossellini, L. How conservatives view the U.S. posts. *The New York Times,* June 21, 1982, p. 12.

Salisbury, R. H. An exchange theory of interest groups. *Midwest Journal of Political Science,* 1969, *8,* 1–32.

Schattschneider, E. E. *The semi-sovereign people*. New York: Holt, Rinehart and Winston, 1960.

Schlozman, K. L., & Tierney, J. T. More of the same: Washington pressure group activity in a decade of change.

Presented at the annual meeting of the American Political Science Association, Denver, September 3, 1982.

Seaberry, J. The mailed fist: nonprofit groups hit by postage jump. *The Washington Post,* January 7, 1982, pp. 1; 14.

Shabecoff, P. Big business on the offensive. *The New York Times Magazine,* December 9, 1979, pp. 134–146.

Smith, C. E., & Freedman, A. *Voluntary associations: perspectives on the literature*. Cambridge, Mass.: Harvard University Press, 1972.

Stanfield, R. "Defunding" the left. *National Journal,* August 1, 1981, pp. 1374–1378.

Truman, D. B. *The governmental process*. New York: Alfred A. Knopf, 1951.

Walker, J. L. Setting the agenda in the U.S. Senate: a theory of problem selection. *British Journal of Political Science,* 1977, *7,* 423–445.

Washington Information Directory, Washington, D.C.: Congressional Quarterly Press, 1980.

Washington Representatives; 1981, Washington, D.C.: Columbia Books, 1981.

Wilson, G. K. *Interest groups in the United States*. New York: Oxford University Press, 1981.

Wilson, G. K. *Unions in American national politics*. London: Macmillan, 1977.

Wilson, J. Q. *Political organizations*. New York: Basic Books, 1973.

Wines, M. Should groups that set standards be subjected to federal standards? *National Journal,* September 26, 1981, pp. 1717–1719.

Ziegler, H. L., & Peak, W. C. *Interest groups in American politics*. Englewood Cliffs, N.J.: Prentice-Hall, 1972.

PROJECT

A number of government agencies contract with groups to help them carry out the administration's agenda. Select any government agency. With whom does the agency conduct business? Do you believe these relationships help or hinder democracy? How do they fit within the pluralist-elitist framework?

13

The Three Modes of
Political Mobilization

JACK WALKER

At its publication in 1983, *Mobilizing Interest Groups in America* contained cutting-edge articles examining the formation of interest groups and how formation patterns ultimately affect political representation. The concluding chapter from that text squarely addresses these issues. In addition to categorizing various types of groups, Walker examines the different strategies that groups use to affect public policy. Implicit in his analysis is the tension between pluralist and elitist scholarship. On the one hand, Walker finds that a wide number of majoritarian interests are well represented in the political process. On the other hand, he notes that minority voices (or discontents) are likely underrepresented.

QUESTIONS TO CONSIDER

1. Do the unemployed lack representation as Walker suggests?
2. How is cooperation related to group success?
3. What are "insider" and "outsider" strategies?
4. Who is most likely to use insider strategies? Why do you think this is the case?
5. Who is most likely to use outsider strategies? Why do you think this is the case?

The American political system is one of the most permeable in the world, yet not all social groups are equally represented before government. One example of inactivity that is especially puzzling is the lack of political organization among the unemployed—a large group that obviously is suffering distress. Members of Congress often call for action to end unemployment, and several pieces of legislation meant to deal with the problem have been passed during recent sessions of Congress, yet no organization is operating in Washington claiming to directly represent those who are out of work. Trade union leaders attempt to speak for them but usually oppose measures like the graduated minimum wage, subsidized employment of teenagers, or any other proposal that might possibly impose costs upon their membership or diminish their control over entry into the skilled trades.

Recent studies of unemployment conducted by Schlozman and Verba, however, clearly show that the unemployed are suffering an extraordinary amount of personal distress, and that most of them believe that the government should take measures either to create new jobs or help them find work (Schlozman and Verba 1979). Almost all of those surveyed felt that the government was not doing enough to alleviate their distress. The unemployed are not as politically aware as employed workers; they are dispersed, typically uneducated, and not well equipped for political activity; but they believe that their government should intervene in the economy in their behalf, and that they have a right to such aid. These same surveys

SOURCE: From Jack L. Walker, "The Three Modes of Political Mobilization" in *Mobilizing Interest Groups in America: Patrons, Professions, and Social Movements* (Ann Arbor: University of Michigan Press, 1991), 185–96 (including tables and figure). Reprinted with permission from the University of Michigan Press.

also uncovered virtually no evidence of any organizational activity on behalf of the unemployed. Most of those who lost their jobs immediately dropped out of their unions, leaving themselves isolated and politically impotent.

There is no way to prove that the unemployed in America *ought* to be better organized for political advocacy than they are, but research has shown that their feelings, attitudes, and beliefs make them ripe for political action. Since so many new political organizations representing other distressed groups— such as African-Americans, Hispanics, native Americans, the handicapped, children, and the mentally ill—have been organized during the past 20 years, the question arises once again. Why is there no organization to directly represent the unemployed? To state the problem broadly, why within the same political system, do levels of organization differ for what would seem to be analogous social groups?

. . . Without entirely discounting the importance of the great differences in the capacity of citizens to understand questions of public policy or in the skill with which they utilize the political resources at their disposal, I have argued that the differential rates of political mobilization among social groups within any population are mainly a product of the structure of opportunities presented to each citizen by the legal, political, and organizational environment. Members of different social groups face entirely different sets of opportunities and obstacles to political activity. The actions of groups representing them depend not so much upon their constituents' level of education or their annual income, their values, or the intensity of their feelings, as upon the organizational, legal, financial, and institutional environment in which they find themselves. Political action is seldom a spontaneous outburst growing out of frustration, anxiety, or personal strain. In predicting whether the unemployed will organize for political action, it is useful to know whether they feel exploited or whether they believe that they have a right to relief from the government. However, it is much more important to understand the political scope allowed by the tax code to nonprofit agencies working in their behalf, whether foundations exist that will take an interest in their cause, how willing government agencies are to sponsor political advocacy in their favor, or, even more important, the likely political or financial sanctions that would be applied against any individual or organization that took up their cause.

To put my central point more precisely, the amount of political action engaged in as a result of individual distress in the American political system at any time is determined mainly by political and administrative policies toward political activity, the presence and accessibility of willing patrons of political action, and the patterns of conflict and social cleavage in the society. If groups do not materialize representing the unemployed, this does not automatically mean that people who are out of work are essentially satisfied with the prevailing distribution of goods or status. It also is not necessarily an indication that they are too cynical or alienated to take part in the democratic process. Although citizens are not likely to become involved in politics if they feel no distress at all or have no desires that could be fulfilled through public policy, institutional and organizational variables are more important as determinants of political mobilization than the attitudes, feelings of political efficacy, or the political beliefs of individual citizens. Political action is largely the result of the differential impact of the rules of the political game on citizens.

Although the particular rules, political cleavages, and institutional configurations confronting specific constituencies vary enormously from one to another, the preceding chapters have demonstrated the close connections among a group's constituency, political context, sources of financial support, and political strategy. These interrelationships suggest that there is a small number of general modes of mobilizing and representing political interests in the American system. If that is true—and I believe it is—then it is possible to predict whether a group such as the unemployed will be vigorously represented in American politics by determining whether it could possibly fit into one of these representative modes.

THREE CLASSIC MODES OF POLITICAL MOBILIZATION

There are essentially three main formulas for success in organizing political groups that have been used in our political system. These three schemes form the basis for the three central methods of political mobilization in America.

The first, and most familiar, organizational formula is to base an association upon a tightly knit commercial or occupational community in the profit sector whose members share a concern for protecting or advancing their economic interests. Such a group usually can be supported with membership dues and patronage in various forms from business firms operating in the area. The most familiar and numerous political organizations in American politics are classic economic interest groups of this type, such as the American Petroleum Institute, the National Association of Automobile Manufacturers, or the Mortgage Bankers Association. The second formula for organizational maintenance is also rooted in occupational communities and capitalizes upon the possibilities for strong institutional support, but entrepreneurs following this strategy operate in the nonprofit or governmental realm and often make strong appeals to the professional needs and obligations of their potential members. Groups of this kind,

Table 13.1 Composition and Revenue Sources of Three Policy Communities in 1980

	COMMUNITY		
	Farmers	**Handicapped**	**Women**
Group type[a]			
Profit	82	3	8
Mixed	10	3	8
Nonprofit	4	57	14
Citizen	4	37	70
Total	100	100	100
N	52	35	50
Revenue source[b]			
Dues	75	44	39
Government patron	7	11	9
Private patron	3	18	26
Other	15	27	26
Total	100	100	100
N	40	33	40

[a]Each entry is the percentage of interest groups in the policy community of each membership type.

[b]Each entry is the mean percentage of total revenues from a specific source.

such as the National Association of State Alcohol and Drug Abuse Directors or the Association of American Medical Colleges, often are instigated, supported, and encouraged by permanent agencies of government. These groups began appearing in Washington in the latter part of the nineteenth century and have increased in number in recent years, stimulated by the rapid growth of government since the late 1960s.

The third type of successful organizational formula taps the enthusiasm and energy of social movements. Groups such as the Wilderness Society, Common Cause, Citizens for Clean Air, and the Women's International League for Peace and Freedom are based on the commitment of individuals attracted by a cause, along with a package of financial contributions and other forms of patronage from foundations, wealthy individuals, churches, and other institutions that operate mostly in the nonprofit realm.

In order to illustrate how these three organizational formulas are used in the real world of interest groups as the basis for the mobilization of large segments of the population, three sets of interest groups operating at the national level in 1980 are examined in Table 13.1. First, there are the groups that claim to represent farmers, a classic economic policy community; second are groups representing the handicapped, a policy community dominated by public sector professionals who act as advocates for their disadvantaged clients, with support and encouragement from many institutional patrons, including the government; and third are groups making up the women's movement, a community of interest groups that emerged from one of the most important social movements of recent years.

The data in Table 13.1 show that each of the three policy communities was dominated by a different type of group. The table shows that most groups with an interest in agricultural issues in 1980, not surprisingly, had members who came from occupations in the profit sector. Most of the groups in this field actually were built around the cultivation of specific crops or were restricted to certain areas of the country. A small number of groups were built around public sector professions, such as feedgrain inspectors or agricultural educators and, in recent years, a few citizen groups were organized in this area, usually attempting to represent consumers or seeking to raise environmental issues. The citizen groups increased in number during the 1970s and interjected new issues and an unfamiliar source of conflict into this once settled, predictable policy community.

Presenting a sharp contrast to those in agriculture, most organizations that expressed an interest in the problems of the handicapped in 1980 were made up of public sector professionals working in nonprofit agencies engaged in delivering services to handicapped people. There were a few trade associations made up of firms that manufactured products or equipment used by the handicapped, and there were a number of citizen groups operating in this field, often begun by the parents of handicapped children or by social service professionals concerned in general about the social status of handicapped persons.

Among the groups engaged in 1980 in the debate over women's issues, citizen groups predominated. There were a small number of women's groups made up of professionals in the profit sector, but even these groups were principally concerned with the general status of women in society. Since there were few social service programs targeted specifically for women in 1980, there were not many social service specialties that could serve as the foundation for interest groups in the nonprofit area.

We can also see that the funding patterns for the groups in these three policy communities fit neatly with the types of groups that predominated in each area. Financial support for political activities in the agricultural area was available from large firms that manufacture farm implements, chemicals, and feeds, and in dues from the individual farmers who could expect to receive important individual benefits if their advocates were successful in the legislative process. Groups representing the handicapped had the most diversified sources of income. They received less than half of their support from membership dues but were much more likely than the farm groups to receive grants from private foundations, wealthy individuals, and government agencies. Women's groups were the least dependent on member dues, and the most likely to receive money from patrons outside the government.

Since many of the members of the occupationally based groups in the agricultural and handicapped areas were business firms or social agencies rather than individuals, Table 13.1 does not accurately portray the amount of patronage received from institutions. Even where a group is made up entirely of individuals, their participation often has been encouraged and subsidized by their employers, who believe that these activities add to the knowledge and professional standing of their employees.

These data illustrate the importance of financial support from institutions and other patrons of political action, but patrons cannot operate in the political realm with impunity. They must be careful not to put their own operations in jeopardy by supporting causes or taking actions that might invite some form of political retaliation. The extent to which patrons support political causes depends, to a large degree, on the amount of conflict existing in the area and on the likelihood that important political leaders would come to their defense if they came under attack for becoming involved in controversial questions of public policy. Patrons do not automatically withdraw

Table 13.2 Amount of Political Conflict within Three Policy Communities

Policy Community	N	Level of Reported Conflict[a]
Farmers	45	.31
Handicapped	26	−.69
Women	28	.31

SOURCE: 1980 Survey.

[a]Entries represent standard deviations from the sample mean.

once conflict begins, but they are likely to continue their activities only so long as they feel that they can muster the necessary political support to protect their interests.

This sensitivity to conflict is illustrated in Table 13.2, where we summarize the answers of groups in the three communities to questions about whether there were any organized opponents to their political activities in 1980. The entries in Table 13.2 show the number of standard deviations between the mean for the groups in the cells of the table and the mean for the entire sample of national interest groups in the 1980 survey. A positive number in the table indicates that groups report more organized conflict in the area than average, and a negative number means that less conflict is reported than average.

These data reveal an uneven pattern of conflict that helps to explain the types of patronage these groups depend on. Both the women's groups and the agricultural groups were more likely than average to report the existence of organized opponents working against their interests. Both areas stand in sharp contrast to the handicapped groups, which seldom reported the existence of any organized opposition. Many political leaders strenuously opposed the Equal Rights Amendment or called for an end to agricultural subsidies. Some also complained about the size and cost of the welfare state and called for a general reduction in government spending, but no prudent politician in 1980 would have openly attacked programs for the handicapped. In highly consensual policy areas dealing with the handicapped, the aged, children, or other obviously vulnerable groups, government agencies could risk providing financial aid for their constituents, but they were bound to be much more cautious in the conflictual atmosphere surrounding policies toward women or agriculture (Nelson 1984).

The varying configurations of conflict and the demands of organizational maintenance determine the relationships between government agencies and interest groups. Advocates for the handicapped were able to make strong financial and political alliances with normally cautious administrative agencies of government in 1980 because they were almost never directly confronted by interests intent on reducing benefits or terminating programs designed for their clients. The Department of Agriculture had a close, supportive relationship with most of the largest interest groups that represented its constituency, because those groups were closely allied with the committees and subcommittees in Congress that exercised control over the department's affairs. Women's groups, on the other hand, were not closely allied with any large bureau or agency because there were few programs in place (at the

Table 13.3 Degree of Conflict with Bureaucratic Agencies within Three Policy Communities

Index of Bureaucratic	POLICY COMMUNITY		
Cooperation	Farmers	Handicapped	Women
High	84	90	42
Low	16	10	58
N	52	35	50

SOURCE: 1980 Survey.

NOTE: Each entry is the percentage of interest groups placing high or low on the index of bureaucratic cooperation. This index is an additive combination of answers to three questions: "Does the Executive Director or any member of the permanent staff currently hold a position on an official government advisory committee or commission? [Yes or No]"; "How frequent is the interaction of this association's staff and officers with agencies of the national government? [Frequent, Infrequent, or No Interaction]"; "Is this association regularly consulted by government agencies when they are considering new legislation or changes in policy? [Yes or No]."

time) that delivered social services directly to women. Lacking close ties with government, most of the women's groups engaged in highly controversial efforts to change established social customs and public policies.

The situation facing the women's movement might have been entirely different if Richard Nixon had not vetoed the Comprehensive Child Development Act that was designed to create a national system of day care centers in 1972. Such a large national program, employing many social service professionals, would have been an important source of leadership and patronage for political action—important enough, perhaps, to have produced a different type of women's movement in the 1980s with much closer ties to government. It was organizational and strategic considerations of this kind, shaped by history and the development of public policy, that determined for each of the three policy communities the characteristic relationships with agencies of government that they experienced in 1980. These relationships are illustrated by the data presented in Table 13.3.

In order to produce an index of cooperation between government agencies and interest groups, answers to three questions concerning relations with

government agencies were combined. . . . A group receiving the very highest score on this index reported that a member of its staff served on an advisory committee for a government agency, that the group had a high level of interaction with government agencies, and that agencies consulted with the group prior to making policy decisions. Groups with the lowest possible score had no advisory committee memberships, little interaction, and were not consulted prior to policymaking. Scores were combined to produce two categories, high and low cooperation. Placement on this index, reported in Table 13.3, reveals that groups representing the handicapped, which were predominantly composed of public sector professionals and nonprofit social service agencies, reported the closest relationships with government agencies, followed closely by the groups representing farmers. Women's groups, not surprisingly, were clearly the least well connected on average, with only 42 percent reporting high scores on government interaction. In fact, almost one-third of the women's groups reported no contact of any kind with agencies of the federal government.

. . . Groups that experience little conflict and enjoy close, cooperative

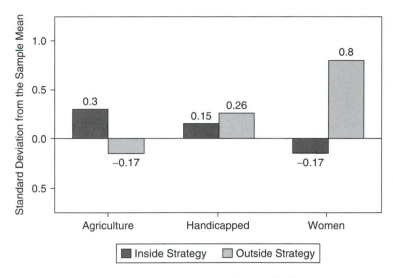

a. **Inside and outside strategy indices**

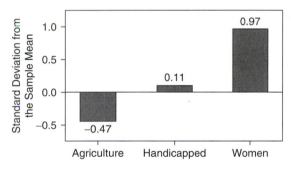

b. **Index of outside strategies minus index of inside strategy**

FIGURE 13.1 Balance between inside and outside strategies. (Data from 1980 Survey.)
SOURCE: Jack L. Walker, "The Three Modes of Political Mobilization," *Mobilizing Interest Groups in America* (Ann Arbor: University of Michigan Press, 1991), 193, Figure 10-1. Reprinted with permission from the University of Michigan Press.

relationships with government agencies are unlikely to spend much time trying to influence public opinion. Programs designed to serve them are usually in place, and their access to government policymakers is one of their most important sources of strength. These advantages lead them to work within the established legislative process to exploit their favored role in the system. The opposite might be expected of groups that are not readily accepted within the inner circles of government, whose financial support comes largely from sponsors that expect strenuous advocacy for controversial causes in exchange for their patronage. Such groups might be expected to adopt an outside strategy, one directed toward changing the fundamental political environment as a first step toward achieving their goals. The choice of political strategies by any interest group, in other words, reflects the financial, organizational, and political realities it faces.

In order to illustrate the sharp differences in the tactics employed by the groups representing farmers, the handicapped, and women in 1980, an index of inside strategies was created, based on the degree to which groups engaged in lobbying Congress, administrative agencies, and the judiciary. A contrasting index of outside strategies was also created, based upon whether groups made appeals to the public through the mass media, staged large informational conferences open to the public, provided speakers at conventions and other events, and engaged in protest demonstrations. The dramatic differences between these three policy communities is illustrated in Figure 13.1, where the use of inside and outside strategies and the balance between them are portrayed.

If groups emphasized a strategy more than the interest-group sample as a whole, their scores will be above the line in Figure 13.1, but if their emphasis on inside or outside strategies was less than the sample, their scores will fall below the line. The graph shows clearly that the agricultural groups were trying to exploit their connections to policymakers in 1980 by heavy reliance on lobbying with few efforts to mold public opinion, while the women's groups were mainly trying to expand the scope of the conflict through appeals to the public and acts of protest, rather than concentrating on conventional means of policy-making through the established procedures of the legislative or other institutional processes. The groups representing the handicapped enjoyed close relationships with policymakers but also engaged in efforts to educate the public about the special problems of their members, thus employing almost an even balance of tactics. Figure 13.1 summarizes these different strategic approaches by displaying a single index measuring a group's reliance on outside over inside strategies. The dominant political strategies in each of these communities of groups could hardly be more different.

SUMMARY AND CONCLUSION

Political mobilization is seldom spontaneous. Before any large element of the population can become a part of the American political process, organizations must be formed, advocates must be trained, and the material resources needed to gain the attention of national policymakers must be gathered. The key to successful political mobilization is seldom an upsurge of intense feelings of discontent within the disadvantaged group—many important political movements in America were long underway before there was any indication of widespread discontent among those in whose behalf the efforts were being made. The essential prerequisites for successful political mobilization are mainly organizational, and many are subject to manipulation through public policy.

The Reagan administration, for example, in its campaign to "defund the left," proposed a change in the rules covering government contractors that would prevent any group receiving federal funds from using the space or equipment paid for with these funds in any form of political advocacy. This would have required many organizations in Washington to rent separate facilities and equip them with separate telephones, furniture, and office machines if they wanted to make presentations to Congress or the bureaucracy on behalf of their members or clients. Even though this rule was not enacted in such an extreme form, it illustrates how dependent the modern advocacy system has become on the rules governing contracting and consulting with the federal government, on the tax laws that govern the political behavior of business firms and nonprofit corporations, and on a series of other rules and common practices that regulate the interactions among advocates, their patrons, elected policymakers and their staffs the court system, the federal bureaucracy, and the electoral system.

... Most citizen groups that emerged from social movements in the past have simply faded away once the intense enthusiasms of their followers began to cool, or when a string of policy defeats or compromises caused marginal supporters to lose hope. In the 1980s, however, many of the citizen groups born during the 1960s and 1970s were still in business, with help from their individual and institutional patrons, even though public interest in their causes had declined. These groups now promote concern for their issues and stand ready to exercise leadership whenever there is a new burst of public enthusiasm.

Political mobilization led by social service professionals, government agencies, and other patrons from the nonprofit sector has been successful mainly in areas of low controversy. It cannot be used whenever the level of controversy rises, because the policy professionals and bureaucrats who take the lead in this process cannot count on support from the political leadership to protect their agencies against hostile critics. If a single majority party with a clearly articulated ideology were firmly in control of the entire governmental system for a prolonged period—as was the Social Democratic Party of Sweden for more than four decades after the 1930s—bureaucratic leaders might enter more willingly into potentially explosive policy areas. In the decentralized American political system, however, where control of the presidency and each house of Congress often is not in the hands of the same political party, public officials must exercise caution. The Administration on Aging may work openly to organize the elderly—sometimes going as far as paying to transport their clients to state legislatures to lobby their elected representatives in favor of programs for the aged—but government agencies working in less consensual areas must be careful not to make themselves vulnerable to attacks from antagonists who do not approve of their

programs or missions (Pratt 1976; Hayes 1981; Chubb 1983; Nelson 1984).

Our analysis takes us full circle, returning to the problem of representation for the unemployed. One of the principal reasons there is no organization dedicated exclusively to advancing the welfare of the unemployed is that their cause is inherently controversial, and there are no readily accessible patrons prepared to subsidize political entrepreneurs who might wish to organize them. There are no agencies of the government or private foundations that feel politically capable of organizing bus loads of the unemployed for marches on their state capitals—much less Washington. Nor is there any professional community whose institutional roles and norms clearly and exclusively ally them with the needs of the unemployed. Marches on Washington by Coxey's Army of the unemployed in 1894 or the Bonus Army of unemployed veterans in 1932 were met with hostility, and eventually the marchers were dispersed by force. Without the appropriate political, organizational, and financial prerequisites, a group called the National Association of the Unemployed is unlikely ever to appear.

The reason why some of the most deprived elements of American society are either ignored or represented in the legislative process only by small, nonmember organizations is not that they are essentially satisfied with their status and have no interest in political activity; it is because there is no institutional foundation from which a successful effort at mobilization can be launched. Political mobilization of those at the bottom of the social order is exceedingly difficult because there are few patrons able or willing to risk the danger to their own political well-being that might arise from heavy political conflict over redistributive social programs. Elected officials, of course, are free to take the lead in promoting legislation designed to aid disadvantaged groups without prompting from any outside force, but they know that once conflict begins over their proposals, there will be few organizations in place that can mobilize expressions of support, supply information and ideas, or raise the financial resources needed to combat the program's critics. The uneven pattern of political mobilization resulting from these forces is reflected in our bewildering array of narrowly focused social welfare programs, each dealing with some purpose upon which consensus among the political leadership has been achieved. The American system provides veterans of World War II with a wide range of services, including a comprehensive system of socialized medicine in government-owned hospitals with government-paid physicians, while providing little assistance at all for black teenagers, almost half of whom are unemployed (Steiner 1971).

This book began by asking why certain groups were represented in Washington by political organizations while others were not, even though they seemed equally in need of representation. The explanation I have offered does not allow us to predict exactly which groups will be mobilized and which will not, but it does lead to the conclusion that only certain types of discontent are likely to gain expression. Political entrepreneurs are required to initiate the process of mobilization, but a successful set of political organizations representing a constituency will not come into being, no matter how clever or energetic the leaders of the movement may be, unless institutions can be identified that will serve as sponsors or patrons for their efforts. The behavior of potential patrons is largely determined by the degree of conflict or consensus revolving around the policies being proposed by the political movement. Some proposals and some groups are simply outside the prevailing consensus among elected representatives and the attentive public. It is doubtful that any political organization could be maintained over a long time providing exclusive representation for such groups. The array of political advocates existing at any moment in our political system does not accurately mirror the pattern of discontents felt by the citizenry; it is a much better reflection of both the prevailing consensus over the legitimate scope of public policy existing among those active in politics and the institutions in the society that are available as patrons of political action.

REFERENCES

Chubb, John E. 1983. *Interest Groups and the Bureaucracy*. Stanford, CA: Stanford University Press.

Hayes, Michael T. 1981. *Lobbyists and Legislators*. New Brunswick, NJ: Rutgers University Press.

Nelson, Barbara J. 1984. *Making an Issue of Child Abuse*. Chicago: University of Chicago Press.

Pratt, Henry J. 1976. *The Gray Lobby*. Chicago: University of Chicago Press.

Schlozman, Kay Lehman, and Sidney Verba. 1979. *Injury to Insult: Unemployment, Class, and Political Response*. Cambridge, MA: Harvard University Press.

Steiner, Gilbert Y. 1971. *The State of Welfare*. Washington, DC: Brookings Institution.

PROJECT

Because you are in college, you are a member of a specific group that is different from many others in society. Conduct research on what groups are looking out for your interests as a college student. Do you feel your interests as a college student are "represented"?

14

Interest Representation: The Dominance of Institutions

ROBERT SALISBURY

In spite of a number of advances in the study of group formation and maintenance, a great void in the structure of the interest-group system persisted into
the 1980s. This article by Robert Salisbury simultaneously addresses group formation and group structure. He notes that many groups are not groups at all
because they have no real membership and instead represent institutions. In
recognizing institutions, Salisbury identifies a significant and understudied element of group politics.

Churches, universities, corporations, and intergovernmental bodies constitute a large component of interest groups operating in the United States. These
interests represent the desires of the institution independent of the members of
the institution. Salisbury shows how institutions are not susceptible to the problems of membership identified by Olson. These observations have advanced our
knowledge of group politics in significant ways, leading scholars to conceptualize groups in much broader terms.

QUESTIONS TO CONSIDER

1. What is an institution?
2. How do institutions differ from groups? Why is this distinction important?
3. Why do institutions get involved in political action?

4. How are Salisbury's observations relevant to Mancur Olson's examination of interest groups?

5. How do institutions achieve representation in Washington?

6. In what ways do Salisbury's observations affect notions of representation?

It is common for academics to divide the American political world into two parts, governmental and nongovernmental. In turn, the actors occupying nongovernmental roles of significance sufficient to require textbook chapters treating them are individual citizens (also aggregated into "public opinion"), political parties, and interest groups. The latter two were once often closely tied together, in texts and in courses, with parties clearly the dominant concern (e.g., Key, 1964). In recent years interest groups have come to constitute a largely autonomous subject matter, but almost always they are placed into a conceptual framework that links them closely to parties. Functional arguments assign groups and parties to the articulation-aggregation portions of the functional space, and process formulations place both on the input side of policymaking. By treating parties and interest groups as two types of political organization, Wilson (1973) has perhaps best reflected the implicit conceptual assumption governing descriptive work and shaping the definitions of theoretical problems.

The American political universe, in fact, contains a considerably more diverse

SOURCE: From Robert Salisbury, "Interest Representation: The Dominance of Institutions," *American Political Science Review* 78 (1984): 64–76 (including the tables). Reprinted with permission from Cambridge University Press.

This article owes much to the stimulus of a collaborative research effort, sponsored by the American Bar Foundation, on the role of Washington representatives, in which John P. Heinz, Edward O. Laumann, Robert L. Nelson, and I are currently engaged. Michael Powell was associated with an earlier stage of this work and contributed to my thinking. My colleagues at Washington University—Robert Blackburn, John Kautsky, Michael MacKuen, and Kenneth Shepsle—read earlier drafts and as usual provided trenchant and constructive criticisms, as did the anonymous referees of the *Review*.

array of actors than these conventional headings suggest. In particular, notable omissions from textbook treatments and most research literature include individual corporations, state and local governments, universities, think tanks, and most other *institutions* of the private sector.[1] Likewise unnoticed are the multitudes of Washington representatives, freestanding and for hire, including lawyers, public relations firms, and diverse other counsellors. Ad hoc coalitions, issue networks and other "loosely coupled"cooperative structures of activity are occasionally acknowledged but are rarely described or given a place in academic characterizations of the essential features of the American system. Yet, attentive readers of what might be called the "inside press" of American politics, such as *Congressional Quarterly* and *National Journal,* are regularly informed about these kinds of activity and given to understand that they are often of critical importance to policy outcomes.

In this article I propose to argue that institutions have come to dominate the processes of interest representation in American national politics. Institutions present somewhat different theoretical problems from those we are accustomed to encountering in regard to membership-based interest groups. Moreover there are important empirical differences between a system driven by membership groups and one in which institutions occupy center stage. As the characterization of Washington representation undergoes reconstruction, two important strands of empirical theory come under scrutiny, interest group theory and theories of representation. It is thus an enormously ambitious undertaking, even presumptuous, that is attempted here. It is intended really as a beginning, however, or perhaps a midstream rechanneling, so as better to accommodate the observables of Washington politics.[2]

There are four essential concepts involved in the proposed reconstruction: interest, organized interest group, institution, and representative. I will seek where appropriate to incorporate the results of recent discussions of these ideas, and in the latter part of the article I will present some fragmentary data illustrating and amplifying the arguments. In general, I will not be concerned as much with defining the key terms with unchallengable clarity as with conveying rather more ostensively the meanings and uses I believe important. In any case, the words bear such heavy accumulations from centuries of everyday employment that it would be of little help or effect to legislate. And, of course, there remains Arthur Bentley's rather insouciant sentiment, "Who likes may snip verbal definitions in his old age, when his world has gone crackly and dry" (1908, p. 199).

THE CONCEPT OF INTEREST

Toward what end is political activity directed? At one level we might speak of justice, equity, or the redress of grievances. In a more neutral vein, a number of terms are employed, often more or less interchangeably; e.g., values, objectives, and interests. But it is interest that is most often incorporated into our skeins of theory and thus merits special attention. Interest refers to attitudes, of course (Truman, 1951; cf. MacIver, 1932). It involves values and preferences. But it is the perceived or anticipated effects of policy—government action or inaction including all its symbolic forms as well as more tangible allocations—upon values

that create politically relevant interests. Similarly, interested behavior expresses policy-related purpose, sometimes very broadly defined and sometimes highly specific and detailed. To be sure, preferences may be inert, quiescent, held *in pectore,* or otherwise unattached to any visible action. Yet it is often risky for an outside observer to impute interests, asserting that a given policy *ought* to be seen as having such-and-such an effect on certain values, thus producing interests and, perhaps, eventual political action. Finally, interests are certainly perceived by individuals, one at a time and sometimes uniquely, but it is also possible for other reasonably "unitary" actors to perceive and act politically upon interests. Here we come to the institutional actor, and in examining institutions and their interests we must consider how, if at all, they differ from more conventional notions of organized interest groups.

HOW INTERESTS ARE ORGANIZED INTO GROUPS

Until the publication of Mancur Olson's *The Logic of Collective Action* (1965), comparatively little serious attention had been given to the question of how and whether interests would become organized into associations capable of politically interesting action. Some commentators (e.g., Hagan, 1958), following Bentley's lead, refused to make a distinction between interest and group, treating them as identical phenomena, two words for the same observable activity. In this tradition the main intellectual task was one of mapping, locating the actors involved in the political situation and specifying the policy direction they took. Once all the interests were thus plotted, one would have a complete picture (Bentley, 1908, p. 269), and such a picture, it seems, was expected to yield satisfactory understanding. In any case, Bentley was so anxious not to step outside a strict empirical frame of analysis that little attention was given to the question of how interests developed, or failed to, and why some were more readily mobilized than others.

David Truman, building on and sometimes departing from Bentley, did ask specifically how groups emerged. He specified an initial condition, the sharing of attitudes or interests among potential members, and suggested that these shared values would most often be brought into being by some exogenous disruption of a social equilibrium, such as war or technological change. Formal association for Truman, as for Bentley, was a matter of "mere technique," and not given special theoretical status, but as a practical matter the discussion of group emergence focused mainly on organized groups. Truman went on to suggest that group formation was often a "wave-like" process with organization begetting counter organization until some new equilibrium was reached within the broad social sector in which the interests were located. In addition to this "homeostatic hypothesis," Truman presented a broader argument to the effect that groups proliferate as a consequence of the processes of social fission that result from the growing complexity of modern society (1951, p. 57).

Homeostatic and proliferation models both operate on a macrosocial level, and neither has anything directly to say about the specific formation of particular organizations. Truman assigned a functional meaning to group organizing—the stabilization of tangent relations—but he did not seem to regard the actual organizational process as problematic. He may well have shared the view that seems to have been the pervasive wisdom before 1965, namely, that like minded people join together to enhance their political power in order to achieve public policies that serve their common interests. It was this conventional view, of course, that Mancur Olson sought to redress.

Olson challenged the assumption that individuals would join an organization in order to press for public policies, the benefits of which they would enjoy whether they had joined or not. Philanthropy, coercion, or downright irrationality might lead some people to join some groups, but those considerations could not be expected to hold for the discernible profusion of extant organizations. It was Olson's central insight that interest groups, at least those concerned with economic interests, are not in the first instance organized for public policy-related reasons at all. Rather, they are constructed around the provision to members of selective incentives, material benefits unavailable outside the organization. Lobbying on public policy, if it occurs, is a by-product, an activity made possible by the internal exchange of selective benefits, but not necessarily given purposive direction by the values of the group's members. For example, a UAW member may or may not support the leadership's stand on a nuclear freeze or extension of the Voting Rights Act so long as his or her group membership is assured by a job and a union contract, and a doctor may read the *Journal of the American Medical Association* without sharing A.M.A. politics.

Walker (1983) has shown that in many cases some kind of subsidy, either from other groups or from the government, underwrites some part of the cost of creating and sustaining the organization. Nevertheless, one must still account for the ability of a group to attract members to that group and not some other, and for this problem Olson's argument still holds.

In subsequent revisions of Olson's original thesis, I (Salisbury, 1969, 1975) and others (Berry, 1977; Moe, 1980) contended that, although Olson excluded them, his argument applied fully as well to all the many groups that were organized around public policy goals. These, too, were vulnerable, highly vulnerable indeed, to the free rider problem. Why should any particular environmentalist join the Sierra Club or the Wilderness Society?

Each organization must provide selective incentives, different from the competition and compelling enough to attract the potential free rider, or go out of business. These incentives might include a distinctive formulation of policy purposes—a better "line"—as well as some combination of material and solidary attractions. In more intimate settings interpersonal pressures may supplement the advantages of membership. Moreover, as Olson argued, relatively small groups may be created out of the self-interest of a few large powerful members willing to bear the costs of organization in order to gain the political advantages of group expression.

In all of these cases, however, the political strength of the organization is derived from the support of its members, whatever the means by which that support may have been secured; that is, we grant an organization legitimacy and pay attention to its policy requests because we assume that in some sense the spokesmen for the group represent the interests of the members. To be sure, this assumption is often challenged; we may charge the group with oligarchical tendencies, or in other ways suspect that the leadership is not representative of rank-and-file opinion. Many groups go to elaborate constitutional and procedural lengths to obviate such doubts and establish their *bona fides* as to the reflection of membership sentiment in the group's policy stands (see, for example, McFarland, 1976). The widespread use of mechanisms providing a "democratic mold" (Truman, 1951, pp. 129–139) clearly indicates that groups which are believed to represent organized membership constituencies have both a legitimacy in the policy-making arenas and potential clout, especially through votes and campaign funds, which "unrepresentative organizations lack. Further, it is assumed that the policy interests expressed reflect either explicit or tacit concerns of the members, for otherwise they would leave the organization.

In fact, there are several modes of "interested activity" in which the assumption that group policy actions are driven by member preference might be unwarranted. Under some circumstances, one example would be Olson's by-product situation. Conceivably the internal exchange of selective benefits might be so secure that no public policy inanity the leadership commits will alienate the faithful. Quite often group leaders espouse policy positions with only tenuous support from their members, although *severe* discrepancies between leader actions and member wishes are probably rare and generally short-lived. A second type of deviant case is the organization that is nothing more than a letterhead, lacking membership altogether. Interest groups to which no one belongs and which do not even provide for the possibility of membership are quite common among public interest groups to Berry (1977) has shown. Similarly, Sorauf (1976, p. 19) has noted that in the field of church-state politics a good many "groups" are little more than institutionalized personalities. Leaders without organized followings may claim to have the sympathy of millions, of course, or at least to represent their "true interests," but such claims are likely to be received at a heavy discount.

At the other end of the spectrum there is the political movement, a congeries of organizations and individuals, participating in various ways in an effort to achieve a common set of policy goals (Asch, 1972; Gamson, 1975; Gusfield, 1963; McCarthy & Zald, 1973). It is characteristic of movements that many of the formal organizations within them have brief and highly volatile lives, and a large share of the sympathetically inclined individuals takes part only sporadically, if at all. Consequently, even though a movement may be very large in sympathy, it is typically uncertain in its mobilizable strength. Political movements are often characterized by great uncertainty also concerning who authentically speaks for those who identify themselves with the cause, with or without some formal membership, and typically there is considerable competition among several would-be spokespersons. Despite disputes over the correct line to take on a particular policy question, however, there is little doubt that the interests a movement represents are those of the "members," however that constituency is defined. Hence, all the norms and apparatus of representative democracy are applicable, and, in a society in which those norms are widely admired, that in turn places constraints on the tactical options available to movement leaders.

The several kinds of groups we have been discussing—political movements, voluntary organizations of members recruited through the use of selective incentives, and institutionalized personalities—all face the problem of establishing the legitimacy of their representational claims. The policy interests or values addressed are said to consist of the values of the group members, supporters, and identifiers. Mechanisms to allow consultation and display responsiveness are adopted. Moreover, since representational claims are so central to group legitimacy, the designation of group spokesman or representative is also a matter of critical importance. Many lobbying tasks can be performed by any competent hired hands, to be sure, but public articulation of group positions, if they are to be taken seriously, are inevitably caught up in the legitimation process and therefore cannot lightly be delegated or farmed out. The central point to be made is that in crucial respects the representation of membership-based interest groups differs significantly from the representation of institutional interests. Let us turn to the other side of this pairing to examine the difference further.

HOW INSTITUTIONS DIFFER FROM GROUPS

In an earlier phase of the political science discipline a great deal of attention was paid to the theoretical meaning and position of institutions. Nearly all of this discussion, however, was focused on governmental institutions; the state and its parts and subdivisions. Very little mention was made of nongovernmental institutions except occasionally when it was noted that private groups also have governing structures and may exercise power over their members as well as influencing the larger society. Even this observation makes no distinction between voluntary associations of members and hierarchical structures which exercise authority over people within their jurisdiction. A corporation, a local government, most churches, and even universities are different, not totally but in crucial ways, from our conventional notion of interest groups, and the traditional literature on the nature of institutions does not tell us about the difference.

First of all there is the question of interests. We presume that people who join interest groups respond to selective incentives that appeal to their particular values and that whenever the incentives lose their appeal or their personal resources fail, they will drop out—voluntarily. Exit is obviously possible as well from any particular institutional setting (cf. Hirschman, 1970). One may quit one's job (or be laid off), move to another town, be graduated from school, or otherwise depart. Yet in most cases these acts send no message to the institution's leaders, nor are they intended to. To be sure, if half the population leaves, the city fathers may search for a new service formula; if a large number of students transfer, the college will be in trouble. Institutions of this kind must satisfy the needs and serve the interests of those who "belong." But when a corporation seeks to affect public policy—regarding pollution standards, for example—it does not justify its effort by alleging that it is reflecting the values of its employees. Nor does a university seek increased student loan funds on the grounds that its student body has expressed its desire for the money. It is not member interests as such that are crucial, but the judgments of organizational leaders about the needs of the institution as a continuing organization.

A central distinction between an institution and an interest group is that institutions have interests that are politically and analytically independent of the interests of particular institutional members. In part this derives from the continuing nature of a corporate institution. For example, it is presumed in both law and fact that a university has an existence transcending any agglomeration of individuals who happen presently to occupy its diverse roles. Inasmuch as students surely, and faculty often, are "mere birds of passage," trustees are admonished to be careful not to mortgage the future or rashly to spend the endowment. Similarly, the directors of a corporation can be held liable if they distribute to the stockholders everything not nailed down, with no thought of the long run. A voluntary association does not have the same expectation of eternal life. It must recruit members every year to stay alive.

Unless liquidation or merger destroys its identity, a corporate institution not only has a continuing existence, but it also possesses significant assets which belong to the corporate entity, not to the individual members thereof. It is from this foundation that institutional interests in public policy arise. Institutional leaders are charged with protecting, strengthening, and otherwise enhancing the assets of their institutions, both in the short run and to assure reasonable financial safety and stability for the institution in the future. Much of what they do has no direct political significance, of course. But in the latter twentieth century public policy is of such immense scope that issues continually arise which affect the assets of particular institutions, thus generating politically relevant interests (Salisbury, 1980). Environmental regulation, safety and health regulation, rules regarding

employment practices, the host of grants and entitlement programs, tax policies—the list is long. Even an institution of the most modest size and aspiration will encounter both threats and opportunities in this policy array, and insofar as its resources permit may seek to increase its understanding of these possibilities and to influence them.

An institution can monitor public affairs and lobby to affect them only to the extent that it can afford to, of course. It must have resources available for such purposes. What we are calling institutions are generally complex organizations, highly differentiated and often with multiple functions. Such organizations typically command substantial and diverse resources and within limits a meaningful fraction may be allocated to policy-relevant tasks if and when these are perceived as useful to the maintenance and enhancement of the enterprise. Moreover, in most cases such allocations may be made without extensive consultations with members, employees, stockholders, or other constituent groups. They are, in effect, management decisions. And here lies a key distinction between institutions, as we use the term, and interest groups. Institutions are managed organizations. They are primarily hierarchical in their internal structures of authority, at least with regard to when and how far to become involved in the policymaking process. Membership groups must look far more carefully to the desires of their members, both to assure political legitimacy and to keep their supporters happy.

In distinguishing membership groups from institutions we do not mean to suggest that they are completely unlike. Most interest groups hope to survive into the indefinite future and thus take on institutional characteristics. Many possess substantial assets which they manage with a view to their long-term organizational health, and whenever public policy affects their institutional concerns, appropriate political action may be taken. Similarly, corporations and other hierarchies are not completely unconstrained by the views and needs of various groups both inside and outside the organizational boundaries (see, for example, Vogel, 1978). Demands for "socially responsible" behavior and for adoption of mechanisms to ensure democratic control are part of the political environment of all organizations in the United States, not just of membership groups. Nevertheless, there are important differences. Institutions have greater latitude—more discretionary resources and more autonomous leadership authority—to enter the political arena. Institutions have less need to justify their political efforts by reference to membership approval or demand. Institutions may also have a wider range of specific policy concerns. The instances in which policy impinges upon institutional interests will be numerous indeed for large complex organizations.

One result of these differences ought to be that institutions, not conventionally defined interest groups, will have come to dominate the roster of nongovernmental actors in Washington. This should follow inexorably upon the growth of government and of the scope and impact of policy. Before we turn to some examination of the empirical situation, however, let us consider briefly and in general terms the modes and motives of entering the political arena.

ENTRY INTO THE
POLITICAL ARENA

Until the publication of Olson's *Logic,* the question of how and why groups undertake political activity was scarcely acknowledged to be problematic. Interest groups were essentially defined by their political presence, and although perceptive students clearly understood how much ebb and flow there was in the vigor and

direction of political action, they gave it little theoretical attention. Olson showed that the mere existence of politically relevant shared values or interests could not account for the effective mobilization of those interests into politically relevant action; i.e., action aimed at effecting policy decisions that would supply collective policy benefits. Olson, as we have seen, did provide for the possibility that small homogeneous groups might so act, especially when one or a few members of the group had a particularly large stake in the collective good outcome. Otherwise, however, while persuading us that much lobbying had to be seen as a by-product of the internal organizational exchange of selective benefits, Olson did not explain why groups should bother to engage in political action. Why should the "by-product" of successful group formation be "spent" on political purposes rather than, say, on increased perquisites for the leadership?

One possibility is that securely entrenched group leaders act out of personal whim or conviction, unconstrained by member preferences, institutional needs or factional threats. Some of the late George Meany's positions on foreign policy come to mind in this connection (cf. Radosh, 1969), but it is probably very rare for leadership autonomy to be complete. More often, one suspects, group leaders lobby because they perceive potential effects of some government action on their members or members' values which the members might urge trying to influence if they were fully informed. A second and far more significant explanation is that group leaders are active on policy questions because that is why their members or followers support them in the first place. Here we speak of purposive or expressive groups. Despite Olson's reluctance to include such consumption values among the incentives that organizations offer their adherents, it is clear from subsequent empirical work, as well perhaps as being intuitively pleasing and logically persuasive, that members do often support organized efforts to secure collective public benefits, whether it is truly rational to do so or not. In any case, such purposive group activity presents no mystery regarding why political action is undertaken; it is of the very essence.

A third motive for action is institutional; that is, institutional leaders estimate that investment in political representation would be beneficial to the interests of the organization. One might treat this kind of decision as a rational calculus problem essentially like that faced by individuals in determining whether or not to participate politically, in groups or otherwise. Three considerations make it inadvisable to do so. One is that institutions are *far* more likely to be part of relatively small, similarly situated groups—Olson's privileged groups—and thus be able to organize more readily and to anticipate being more effective politically than most individual citizens can expect. Second, although a given individual may hold a large number of distinct values or interests and even embrace a considerable set of political causes, available resources for participation are quickly exhausted, and multiple modes of individual participation are comparatively uncommon. Institutions possess more resources which, combined with a greater sense of efficacy in political action, lead to a considerably increased probability of participation at any given level of intensity of interest or concern.

Finally, the very size and complexity of an institution renders it vulnerable to a much broader array of specific policy impacts, positive and negative, present and prospective. Indeed, insofar as individual citizens are themselves embedded for work and play in large institutional settings, as so many are, they experience many of the effects of policy only indirectly, through their respective institutions, rather than immediately and in person. This would largely be true for much of the "new regulation" of environment and job safety, for example, as well as for national programs affecting state and local government budgets and services. A given corporation is quite likely to find itself in several encounters at once, on different policy issues, being worked on in different institutional settings, and requiring different modes of political action. Perhaps individual level interests also possess such complexity in principle, but in actual practice they do not generate comparable diversity of interest representation.

The forms of political action undertaken by institutions are indeed diverse, although none is exclusively utilized by institutions rather than membership groups or even, in some cases, individuals. One common form is to join organizations of similarly situated institutions. Some of these are trade associations organized along specific industry lines. Others may be closer to "peak associations," attempting to encompass an entire sector of economic activity. A large research university might belong to several organizations of universities—AAU, NASULGC (if public) or NAICU (if private), AAMC (if they have a medical school) and other professional school groups, ACE (as the peak association for higher education), and perhaps some others (King, 1975). A manufacturing corporation may belong to several trade associations, depending on how complex its product line is, as well as the NAM, the U.S. Chamber of Commerce and the Business Roundtable. Part of these memberships may be expressive (the NAM would seem often to have been a forum for venting spleen regarding public policy rather than seeking realistically to affect it), and part may be more conventionally political, lobbying by small groups for beneficial collective policy goods.[3]

A mode of political involvement that has recently taken on Brobdingnagian proportions is the Political Action Committee (Conway, 1983; Malbin, 1980). Not all PACs have been created by institutions, but most of them have, and the prominence of PACs in campaign finance further illustrates how important institutional actors have become in our political life. Again, it must be stressed that although some PACs have raised significant sums from individual enthusiasts of liberal and, especially, conservative causes, business corporations, trade associations and, to a much lesser extent, labor unions dominate this form of activity, constituting nearly 78% of 3,371 members active at the beginning of 1983 (*National Journal,* 1983).

Finally, institutions enter the political arena directly. Several thousand corporations maintain permanent Washington offices to monitor the political scene and to help represent organizational interests.[4] Corporate divisions of public or government affairs are standard organizational components, not only of business enterprises but on a smaller scale of universities and many other institutions of contemporary American society. Further, many of these institutions retain outside firms, primarily lawyers and public relations counsel, to represent them in Washington in particular aspects of their wide-ranging institutional encounters with the federal government. The key word here is "represent," for it carries some current meanings that have not adequately been incorporated into the formulations of political science discourse in representation. Let us turn next to that issue.

WASHINGTON REPRESENTATIVES AND THE NATURE OF REPRESENTATION

It is rather startling to pick up a large volume entitled *Washington Representatives, 1982* (Close, 1982) and find that among the thousands of individuals listed, not one is a member of Congress. Yet, although these representatives are not accorded that status by customary formulations of social scientists and philosophers (Eulau, 1959, 1967; Pitkin, 1967; Wahlke et al., 1962), they clearly are so designated by the world. There are some differences in functions and activities, of course, between nongovernmental representatives and those who hold authoritative office. Let us consider of what these differences consist.

First, an official representative is said to have a constituency to which he is (or is not) responsive. An elected representative has a legally defined constituency, but he also has an effective one, those who supported him and those whose preferences he actually seeks to advance in policy-related actions. In this second sense, every official may be said to represent a constituency, i,e., to reflect some values rather than others in decisions. A "Washington Rep," on the other hand, typically represents a client, an organization, group, or individual (and occasionally only himself) who retains the representative and defines the scope of interests to be represented. The concept of client ordinarily implies a narrower range of policy concerns and a more limited set of representational activities than are contained in the idea of constituency representation. A corporation may retain a lawyer to represent it before the Federal Communications Commission on a specific licensing case, or alternatively to monitor the Federal Energy Regulatory Commission decisions on a continuing basis. Client representation may take many forms, but generally it is more specialized in subject matter, more limited in both scope and time, than constituency representation. At the margin the differences grow indistinct. The AFL–CIO is represented in Washington by a substantial crew of people and is actively interested in a range of questions that very nearly matches the full congressional agenda. Nevertheless, labor lobbyists have broad discretion to choose whether or not to get actively involved, whereas congressmen can hardly pick and choose so as to avoid all the issues about which their constituents disagree or are indifferent.

Client representation is relatively specialized and often quite discontinuous. Any specific representative may work on behalf of a particular client for a purpose that has a short life of relevance. Often, moreover, the representation is directed toward a specific agency, committee, or other unit of government, and once the policy issue moves away from that institutional setting to another, a different representative more familiar with the new arena may be brought in. Thus, specialized client representation often results in a given client retaining several representatives to perform highly focused representative services. The corollary of this is that a given representative often specializes in working with a particular piece of the governmental policy machinery and may represent numerous clients with problems involving that agency or committee.

Implicit in the foregoing discussion is the notion that representation involves three essential components rather than two, as conventional discussions of the topic assert. In addition to the representative and the represented, there is also the agency of government to which the representation is directed. Actually there are several prepositions employed to describe this side of the relationship. A lawyer may speak for a client *to* a congressional staffer; he may testify *in* court, *before* a judge; he may negotiate *with* an agency over a compliance schedule; indeed, he may only monitor what government does and counsel the client, in which case no prepositional connection with government is made. Even this last is seen as a form of representation, however, and requires the third party's presence to be meaningful.

It is not clear whether a third party is necessarily implied in traditional conceptions of representation. It is rarely if ever mentioned explicitly, but apart from descriptive representation, which can occur simply by possessing the appropriate personal characteristics, representation of constituency interests cannot logically occur unless there is some sort of "other." A legislator does not achieve his or her constituents' interests or even express them meaningfully without official status in an institutional arena where negotiations may be undertaken to accomplish his or her representational purposes. Nevertheless, ordinary speech vocabulary does not force us to recognize the institutional arena as a separate element in constituency representation as it does in considering client representation.

A full analysis of Washington representation requires us then to identify individual clients as well as broader constituencies, to examine who the representatives are and the diverse terms and conditions governing their service, and to understand the specific governmental institutions that serve as the focus of any particular representation activity. As we have said, much of that activity, although by no means all, is highly specific as to client, representative, and agency. It is often short-lived in duration and limited, even imperceptible, in its impact on any part of public policy or the world. Representational activity is very often ineffectual, redundant, or otherwise useless. Moreover, like the dog that Sherlock Holmes realized had not barked in the night, effective representation may entail doing nothing. In any case, however, this conception of representation is broader and more highly differentiated than either of two traditions in mainstream political science to which it is related, legislative representation and interest group lobbying.

Nevertheless, there remains a profound difference between the governmental official who, in either a Bentleyan or a Burkean sense, represents some interest in a specific authoritative choice among policy alternatives and the nongovernmental representative who can never do more than advocate that interest. Each may represent a client or constituency, but there remains a significant gulf between their respective capacities to act. Thus, even though only one key word is used, there are two quite different component processes involving two quite distinct sets of people, a nongovernmental set engaged in policy advocacy and a governmental set engaged in policy determination. If ordinary parlance calls both groups representatives, can we mitigate the confusion somewhat by using sharply distinct terms for the two processes? The answer is probably yes, but not if the advocacy process is called lobbying. That much-abused word is so fraught with ordinary language meaning, most of it unsavory, as to defy rehabilitation anyway, but it is also true that none of its historic uses comfortably fits what many Washington representatives do. The word lobbying does not well convey the meaning of a presentation by a drug company representative seeking approval of a new drug from the Food and Drug Administration. Nor does it capture the character of discussions between a committee on technical standards of the Aerospace Industries Association and Pentagon procurement officials. *Amicus curiae* briefs presented to the Supreme Court have sometimes been called "lobbying" instruments (Barker, 1967; Krislov, 1963), but they are different in much more than tactical form from the efforts of the National Rifle Association to prevent gun control legislation or of Chrysler to secure financial help. The latter are surely examples of lobbying; amicus briefs and FDA appearances involve a much more restricted kind of policy advocacy, by representatives acting in behalf of clients.

Interest representation is an encompassing term that embraces lobbying in its ordinary use as well as narrower, more rule-bound forms of policy advocacy. Interest representation incorporates the client-representative relationships of a corporation and its lawyer, the membership group and its president, and the congressman and his constituents. Within that conceptual frame we distinguish governmental officials from those outside, policy formulation and enactment from advocacy. Within both those distinctions we may wish also to distinguish among specific institutional settings in which representational activity occurs. The forms of policy advocacy in courts are different from those in legislatures and so are the forms and norms of policy making. One reason that the term lobbying is so awkward is that it was developed initially to characterize policy advocacy in and around legislative settings where its connotations made sense and only later applied to other contexts. In any case, we should try to establish a vocabulary that is compatible with observable political life and is as consistent and straightforward as possible.

If we turn from a focus on process to a focus on role, we find, to begin with, the same confusion between lobbyist and representative as between the equivalent verb forms. The two words have vastly different connotations in the American lexicon but frequently refer to the same phenomena. Again, lobbyist more often is used with reference to policy advocacy in and around legislative bodies (Milbrath, 1963; Ziegler & Baer, 1969). A less clearcut but not uncommon distinction uses *lobbyist* to refer to an organizational employee, subordinate to those who make policy for the organization, whereas *representative* connotes a free-standing agent, retained on a fee-for-service basis and often on the assumption that the agent possesses particular skills or credentials of relevance to the advocacy role that are not readily available within the interested

Table 14.1 Organizational Forms of Washington Representation

	Agriculture	Labor	Health	Energy
Law firms	17.9%	18.1%	16.8%	15.9%
Consulting and public relations firms	6.6	4.9	6.4	5.7
Corporations, trade associations and other institutions	75.5	77.0	76.8	78.4
N	832	304	722	1574

SOURCE: *Washington Representatives, 1981.*

organization, whether institution or membership group. Even when we do not distinguish between the two *words* in that manner, however, the two *roles* are distinguishable and of both theoretical and descriptive interest.

As a first approximation of our descriptive needs it will be helpful to know what proportion of the very large community of Washington representatives are employees of the organizations whose interests they represent. Milbrath (1963, p. 150) found that as of 1956, 74.6% of the 114 registered lobbyists he interviewed were employed by the organizations represented. Of the remainder, 21% were outside lawyers, hired on a fee basis, and 4.4% were non-lawyer consultants. Table 14.1 reports comparable data compiled from the listings in *Washington Representatives,* 1981 in four broad policy areas, selected to reflect reasonable diversity in subject matter and styles of representation. Not only are the 1981 proportions remarkably similar to those Mibrath found 25 years before, they are essentially constant across the four policy domains.

This consistency is all the more impressive when we remember that it has survived an explosive growth in the numbers of groups and institutions seeking Washington representation as well as in the numbers of individuals providing it. Estimates of raw numbers for earlier years are neither plentiful nor, probably, very reliable. Schlesinger (1949, p. 46)

claimed that in 1942 some 628 organizations maintained offices in Washington whereas Albig (cited in Blaisdell, 1957, p. 59) counted 1,180 organizations located there in 1947–1948. By 1981 there were approximately 1,600 trade and professional associations, about 100 labor unions, over 200 individual states, cities, counties, and other units of government, numerous foreign governments, more than 4,000 corporations, and membership interest groups numbering well over 1000, all located in the Washington area. Temporary and ad hoc issue coalitions and other short-lived organizational efforts make it difficult to establish exact magnitudes, but it seems reasonable to suppose that the contemporary Washington community of interest representation includes more than 7,000 organizations in more or less permanent residence.

When we turn to individual representatives, the numbers are even more startling. In 1981 the total capital area employment of trade and professional associations headquartered there was estimated to be more than 40,000 (Helyar, 1981).[5] In addition, as is well known, the number of lawyers in Washington has grown enormously. Membership in the District of Columbia Bar Association became mandatory in 1973, and between then and September, 1981, it went from 10,925 to 34,087. This number is somewhat misleading. Significant numbers of lawyers belong to the D.C. Bar who live elsewhere in the country. At the same

Table 14.2 Lawyers and Non-Lawyers, In-House and External Representatives

	LAWYERS		NON-LAWYERS	
	In-house	**External**	**In-house**	**External**
	%	%	%	%
Agriculture	12.4	79.4	87.6	20.6
Labor	8.3	71.4	91.7	28.6
Health	15.2	84.1	84.6	15.9
Energy	18.9	73.7	81.1	26.3

SOURCE: *Washington Representatives,* 1981; Martindale-Hubbell.

time, however, a considerable number of people with law degrees who work in Washington do not actually practice law; many work for the federal government. Hence, the total number of lawyers residing in the capital may well exceed 40,000.

We may easily be overwhelmed by these numbers, and they are truly impressive, but we should remember that by no means all trade association employees or all lawyers in Washington are really representing politically meaningful interests. A sizable percentage of the lawyers are engaged in the private practice of private law. The so-called "Fifth Street Bar," for instance, centers around the local District of Columbia courts, and its members never have occasion to lobby on Capitol Hill. Similarly, many association employees are engaged in internal administration and support and are not really relevant to our concerns here. On the other hand, an unknown but substantial number of representatives come to Washington from elsewhere, some often and some only occasionally, advocating policy positions but never becoming part of any register or roster of representatives. If we look only at the Washington-based individuals actually performing policy representation roles, again drawing on our examination of the listing in *Washington Representatives,* we can observe that in our four broad policy areas, 4,227 individuals were listed,

of whom 35.6% were lawyers. This proportion is remarkably close to that reported by Milbrath and also to the proportion of lawyers among public interest group lobbyists of the early 1970s examined by Berry (1977, p. 88). In the 1981 listings the labor area had a significantly smaller percentage of lawyers (17.1%), but in the other three policy domains the lawyer presence ranged from 31% to 39%.

We pay particular attention to the prominence of lawyers, in part because of the considerable publicity that has been given to them in recent years, but in greater part because the concept of the lawyer as representative carries some interesting connotations. Lawyers traditionally and predominantly operate as free-standing professionals retained by clients for relatively specific defined services and compensated by fee. Although many lawyers actually work in large organizational settings on a salaried basis, we would still expect that lawyers will, more often than non-lawyers, be found outside the organizations retaining them. Table 14.2 indicates that this is indeed true and that the proportions of lawyers who are in-house employees remain quite similar across the policy domains.

One consequence of the large number of lawyers around Washington may well be increased specialization in the representation process, possibly because lawyers are typically hired as outside counsel. Their services are sought when, and only when, the client firm requires those services, and their billing is ordinarily based on hourly charges. In-house counsel might work on anything the organization requires, but external representatives typically have a more limited assignment in both the time to be given and the official governmental segments to which the representation is made. A law firm might attempt to provide full representational services to a given client, advocating policy positions before all the legislative, executive, and judicial agencies that affect the client's interests, but no individual representative can hope to do so. The ever-increasing scope and variety of government and policy impact make this strategy a difficult one for even a large firm to employ successfully, however, and the more common response is the use of multiple representation by a given client. Ford, General Electric, IBM, GM, Exxon, and other giants may hire eight or ten separate outside representatives in addition to working through trade associations and their own substantial governmental relations staffs. The government of Japan in 1982 retained nine different representatives for its embassy and four for other parts of its government, while several dozen others work for specific Japanese firms and associations (Madison, 1982).

The heavy reliance on representatives, typically lawyers, chosen to speak to government officials on behalf of a limited set of client interests is more characteristic of institutional representation than of membership groups, especially when the membership is composed of individuals. Such groups seldom can afford the investment in hourly legal fees that such specialized representation calls for, and they are much more likely to adopt a jack-of-all-trades style. The sheer financial scale of institutional representation vastly exceeds the magnitude of

purposive group activity, and the respective personnel pools reflect this differential investment level. Only about 1,200 of the nearly 8,000 individuals listed in the 1982 *Directory* worked for purposive groups, and as numerous case studies attest, the salary and support levels enjoyed by this disparate group of advocates are hardly commensurate with the resources available to most institutional representatives.

We can round out this part of our discussion by reporting one other set of data demonstrating the importance of institutional representatives, especially of business corporations. For a single policy area, agriculture, Table 14.3 compares, first, the representational presence in Washington of different kinds of organizations declaring significant concerns with agricultural policy; private business corporations, rural cooperatives, governmental institutions, nonprofit private institutions, foreign interests, agri-business trade associations, general farm organizations and commodity groups, and other groups with purposive interests in agricultural policy. Only the last three categories are in any sense membership groups, and only in the last two sets are individuals enrolled. Thus, individual membership groups constitute only one-sixth of the community of agriculture interests more or less continuously represented in Washington. It should not be assumed that individuals listed are equal in political importance or policy input. On the other hand, the representational presence reflected in column 1 permits a wide array of interest-serving activities to undertaken. Informal lobbying, monitoring and grass-roots mobilization, and representation before administrative agencies are all greatly enhanced by an organizational presence on the scene. Rather than organizations of farmers, it is institutions, especially those of business, which clearly dominate that presence.

In more public and visible arenas, however, the picture changes. In testimony

Table 14.3 Agricultural Interest Representatives in Washington

	Washington Representatives, 1981	Congressional Committee Testimony, 1977, 1979, 1981	New York Times, References, 1977–1982
Business corporations	33.5%	10.3%	16.8%
Rural cooperatives	4.3	10.7	6.3
Governmental institutions	1.5	12.8	5.2
Non-profit private institutions	.4	6.4	4.7
Foreign interests	12.2	.6	1.6
Business trade associations	29.8	16.0	14.1
Farm organizations	9.9	30.7	22.5
Citizens groups, including labor	6.3	9.5	27.8
Not classified	2.1	3.1	1.0
Total	100.0%	100.1%	100.0%
N	466	2579	191

SOURCES: *Washington Representatives* (Close, 1981), Congressional Index Service, *New York Times* Index Service[6]

before congressional committees on matters of farm policy (column 2), farm organizations play the most prominent role. Newspaper mentions of organizations in connection with farm issues (column 3) are even more fully dominated by membership groups. Business corporations and trade associations recede. The lesson to be drawn is partly one concerning legitimation. The public process of policymaking gains more legitimacy through hearing and appearing responsive to self-interested individuals and groups than by deferring to organized institutions and institutional interests. In addition, however, it is probably the case that much of the substantive policy concerns motivating institutional advocacy consists of quite small items of no interest to most groups of farmers or the general public. This is especially likely when, because of the multiple representation phenomenon we have described, a corporation or trade association retains a representative for a

single, highly specialized task. This kind of thing counts in column 1 but is not otherwise noticed. When all the small specific policy items are added together the list can be formidable indeed, of course, but few of them may have attracted the attention of the *New York Times* or congressional committee hearings. Nevertheless, we can surely say that for much of what happens in Washington to influence the authoritative allocation of scarce resources in agricultural policy, the general farm organizations, such as AFBF, NFU, Grange, and NFO, once thought to be so powerful, are less prominent than conventional textbook treatments suggest.

The importance of institutional representation has some significant implications for the likely course of public policy as well as for our theories of how and why things work. The use of multiple representatives, each concentrating on a specialized set of policy concerns, surely must intensify the fragmenting, disaggregating tendencies in public policy so often alluded to in recent literature. Secondly, institutional representation may be expected to be far more durable and persistent in policymaking circles than most purposive groups or even membership groups based on material incentives. Institutional resources are not infinite, of course, but neither are they as often subject to membership demands for review or as vulnerable to shifts in political tides and entrepreneurial fortunes. Institutional representation may be more durable, but it is also typically more prosaic, more pragmatic, than purposive group advocacy. Institutional interests more often concern export licenses than anti-Communism, city budgetary assistance more than a war on poverty. (Corporate PACs continue to give significant financial support to their supposed ideological enemies, liberal Democrats. Surely this is a prime example of the pragmatism of institutions (Handler & Mulkern, 1982, esp. pp. 20–27).) In a very important sense, the conservative bias that Schattschneider (1960), McConnell (1966), and other critics of pluralist America have long attributed to interest groups is rooted far more in the power of institutional representation than in conventional membership groups. Indeed, it is the comparative weakness and fragility of membership interest groups of every point of view and persuasion, not their strength, that may be argued to be responsible for whatever malaise the American polity has lately suffered from interest-based politics.

This effort to clarify the conceptual map of American policymaking processes has yielded three main conclusions. First, I distinguish between institutions, institutional interests, and their representation, on the one hand, and what we have rather awkwardly called membership interest groups on the other, and I argue that important theoretical differences exist between the two. Second, I note that both these organizational forms of

nongovernmental interests are represented in Washington by large numbers of people whose roles have many conceptual similarities to those in formal policymaking positions and who, like their official counterparts, are called representatives in everyday usage. Nevertheless, there remains a critical difference in status and function between policy advocates and policymakers which the fuzziness of language should not be allowed to obscure. Washington terminology is not more precise than that used by political scientists to describe and analyze what happens there, but it is somewhat different and in recent years has grown more so with regard to interest representation and policy advocacy. Finally, we urge that the power and scope of institutional representation is such that our teaching, our research and our normative evaluations will all go awry unless we make the appropriate corrections in analytic focus.

NOTES

1. Business corporations are sometimes considered sensibly enough, among business interests, but the profound differences in organizational structure and motivation between, for example, General Motors and the Chamber of Commerce have not been remarked, nor has the implication these differences have for interest group theory.

2. I make no effort in this article to compare American patterns of interest representatives with those of other advanced industrial democracies. Membership associations with high rates of sectoral participation are considerably more common in European systems, and individual institutions may therefore have less room for assertive advocacy. Some aspects of "American exceptionalism" are treated in Salisbury (1979) and in Wilson (1981). See also Berger (1981).

3. Trade associations present some special complexities for our argument. They themselves are membership organizations, but their members are corporate institutions. The members must be kept satisfied with association policy, selective benefits of other kinds,

or both, but being institutions, their calculus regarding membership benefits may contain considerable slack. Moreover, corporate institutions may seldom confine their policy-related activity to association membership. That trade associations do operate under member-induced constraints has recently been illustrated by the cutbacks in association staff and programs brought about as a consequence of the economic recession (Teeley, 1983). Trade associations, like other groups, are often fragile organizations financially, begun with very shadowy support out of an enterprising lawyer's office, or on some otherwise flimsy basis. One result of this is the appearance of association management companies, interest group wholesalers, which manage the affairs of several small organizations. For example, Smith and Bucklin, a Chicago firm, operates more than 70 trade associations, and the National Center for Municipal Development assists dozens of local governments in their quest for federal support.

4. Governmental affairs offices have existed for a considerable time, of course. The Public Affairs Council, an organization composed mainly of corporate government affairs officers, was formed in 1954, and the Brookings Institution sponsored a roundtable discussion among 19 of them in 1958 (Cherington & Gillen, 1962). Little notice has been taken by political scientists, however; the Cherington and Gillen volume was never reviewed in the *American Political Science Review.*

   Dexter (1969) discusses Washington representatives in some detail, but unlike his earlier work (Bauer, Pool, & Dexter, 1963), this book does not seek to tie his discussion into more general theories of interest group performances.

5. Twenty-nine percent of all such organizations are located in the Washington area, up from 19% in 1971 (Close, 1981).

6. References in congressional committee testimony and *New York Times* references were calculated by reference to keywords "agriculture" and "farm," combined with "policy" and "legislation." *New York Times* references covered the period from January 1, 1977 to June 30, 1982.

REFERENCES

Asch, R. *Social movements in America.* Chicago: Markham, 1972.

Barker, L. J. Third parties in litigation. *Journal of Politics,* 1967, *29,* 41–69.

Bauer, R., Pool, I. de S., and Dexter, L. A. *American business and public policy.* New York: Atherton, 1963.

Bentley, A. *The process of government.* Chicago: University of Chicago Press, 1908.

Berger, S. *Organizing interests in western Europe: pluralism, corporatism and the transformation of politics.* Cambridge: Cambridge University Press, 1981.

Berry, J. M. *Lobbying for the people.* Princeton, N.J.: Princeton University Press, 1977.

Blaisdell, D. C. *American democracy under pressure.* New York: Ronald, 1957.

Cherington, P. W., & Gillen, R. L. *The business representative in Washington.* Washington, D.C.: Brookings Institution, 1962.

Close, A. C. (Ed.). *Washington representatives, 1981* (5th ed.). Washington, D.C.: Columbia Books, 1981.

Close, A. C. (Ed.). *Washington representatives, 1982* (6th ed.). Washington, D.C.: Columbia Books, 1982.

Conway, M. M. PACs, the new politics, and congressional campaign. In A. J. Cigler & B. A. Loomis (Eds.). *Interest group politics.* Washington, D.C.: Congressional Quarterly Press, 1983.

Dexter, L. A. *How organizations are represented in Washington.* Indianapolis: Bobbs-Merrill, 1969.

Eulau, H. The role of the representative: some empirical observations on the theory of Edmund Burke. *American Political Science Review,* 1959, *53,* 742–756.

Eulau, H. Changing views of representation. In I. de Sola Pool (Ed.). *Contemporary political science: toward empirical theory.* New York: McGraw-Hill, 1967.

Gamson, W. A. *The strategy of social protest.* Homewood, Ill.: Dorsey, 1975.

Gilbert, C. E. Operational doctrines of representation. *American Political Science Review,* 1963, *57,* 604–618.

Gusfield, J. R. *Symbolic crusade: status politics and the American temperance movement.*

Urbana, Ill.: University of Illinois Press, 1963.

Hagan, C. B. The group in a political science. In R. Young (Ed.). *Approach to the study of politics.* Evanston, Ill.: Northwestern University Press, 1958.

Handler, E., & Mulkern, J. R. *Business in politics: campaign strategies of corporate political action committees.* Lexington, Mass.: Lexington Books, 1982.

Helyar, J. Capital's service sector gives area economy a safety net. *Wall Street Journal,* April 28, 1981.

Hirschman, A. O. *Exit, voice and loyalty.* Cambridge, Mass.: Harvard University Press, 1970.

Key, V. O. Jr. *Politics, parties and pressure groups* (5th ed.). New York: Crowell, 1964.

King, L. R. *The Washington lobbyists for higher education.* Lexington, Mass.: Lexington, 1975.

Krislov, S. The *Amicus Curiae* brief: from friendship to advocacy. *Yale Law Journal,* 1963, *72,* 694–721.

MacIver, R. M. Interests. In E. R. A. Seligman (Ed.). *Encyclopedia of the social sciences.* New York: Mac-millan, 1932.

Madison, C. Is Japan trying to buy Washington or just do business capital style? Washington: *National Journal,* October 9, 1982.

Malbin, M. J. (Ed.). *Parties, interest groups, and campaign finance laws.* Washington, D.C.: American Enterprise Institute, 1980.

McCarthy, J. D., & Zald, M. N. The trend of social movements. In J. D. McCarthy & M. D. Zald, *American: professionalization and resource mobilization.* Morristown, N.J.: General Learning Press, 1973.

McConnell, G. *Private power and American democracy.* New York: Knopf, 1966.

McFarland, A. S. *Public interest lobbies: decision making on energy.* Washington, D.C: American Enterprise Institute, 1976.

Milbrath, L. W. *The Washington lobbyists.* Chicago: Rand McNally, 1963.

Moe, T. M. *The organization of interests.* Chicago: University of Chicago Press, 1980.

Olson, M. J. *The logic of collective action.* Cambridge, Mass.: Harvard University Press, 1965.

Pitkin, H. F. *The concept of representation.* Berkeley: University of California Press, 1967.

Proliferating political action committees. *National Journal,* January 29, 1983.

Radosh, R. *American labor and U.S. foreign policy.* New York: Random House, 1969.

Salisbury, R. H. An exchange theory of interest group *Midwest Journal of Political Science,* 1969, *13,* 1–32.

Salisbury, R. H. Interest groups. In N. Polsby & F. Greenstein (Eds.). *Handbook of political science.* Reading, Mass.: Addison-Wesley, 1975.

Salisbury, R. H. Why no corporatism in America. In P. C. Schmitter & G. Lehmbruch (Eds.). *Trends toward corporatist intermediation.* Beverly Hills, Calif.: Sage, 1979.

Salisbury, R. H. Are interest groups morbific forces. Paper presented to the Conference Group on Political Economy of Advanced Industrial Societies Washington, D.C., 1980.

Schattschneider, E. E. *The semi-sovereign people.* New York: Holt, Rinehart and Winston, 1960.

Schlesinger, A. M. *Paths to the present.* New York: Macmillan, 1949.

Sorauf, F. J. *The wall of separation.* Princeton, N.J.: Princeton University Press, 1976.

Teeley, S. E. Trade associations are shrinking with economy. *Washington Post,* January 31, 1983, P. B1.

Truman, D. B. *The governmental process.* New York: Knopf, 1951.

Vogel, D. *Lobbying the corporation.* New York: Basic Books, 1978.

Wahlke, J. C., Eulau, H., Buchanan, W., & Ferguson, L. C. *The legislative system: explorations in legislative behavior.* New York: Wiley, 1962.

Walker, J. The origins and maintenance of interest groups in America. *American Political Science Review,* 1983, *77,* 390–406.

Wilson, G. K. *Unions in American national politics.* London: Macmillan, 1977.

Wilson, G. K. *Interest groups in the United States.* New York: Oxford University Press, 1981.

Wilson, J. Q. *Political organizations.* New York: Basic Books, 1973.

Ziegler, H., & Baer, M. A. *Lobbying: interaction and influence in American state legislatures.* Belmont, Calif.: Wadsworth, 1969.

PROJECT

Determine how your university, church, or municipality is represented in your state's capital or in the nation's capital. Do lobbyists work on the institution's behalf? Do you believe that the institution is achieving representation for the individuals within the institution?

15

More of the Same: Washington Pressure Group Activity in a Decade of Change

KAY SCHLOZMAN
JOHN TIERNEY

Schlozman and Tierney's article examining the tactics and strategies of inter-est groups provides an in-depth glimpse into the activities of groups in Washington. Their survey of Washington lobbying organizations reveals that groups in the nation's capital engage in a wide variety of tactics to maintain their organizations and influence public policy. Many of the groups reported that they were more active in various areas than they had been in the past. In particular, they find growth in group usage of grassroots lobbying tactics and media-related strategies. Schlozman and Tierney's research goes a long way in describing and assessing the level of group activity in American politics.

QUESTIONS TO CONSIDER

1. What are the groups' most common activities, according to the survey? Why do you think this is?
2. What are the groups' least common activities, according to the survey? Why do you think this is?
3. What areas of activity show the largest increases among groups? Do you think this is more or less true today? Why?
4. Why does it matter if groups report doing "more of the same"?
5. How is Schlozman and Tierney's article related to "Federalist No. 10"? Pluralism?

The past two decades have been an era of pervasive change in American politics. Political scientists have been admirably sensitive to various modifications in the conduct of our politics. But if they have noted and documented the alterations in the voting habits of citizens, the financing of campaigns, the staffing of Congress, or the structure of the bureaucracy, they have paid less attention to the realm of pressure group activity.

This neglect of interest groups in assessing the contemporary political scene is perhaps ironic, for interest groups once figured prominently in the scholarly understanding of the American political process, and some of the most provocative academic interpretations of American politics since the turn of the century place competition among these groups at the heart of the political process. Following the tradition laid out early in the century by Arthur Bentley (1908), analysts of American politics during the 1950s—among them David Truman (1951), Earl Latham (1952), and Robert Dahl (1961)—characterized the political process not so much in terms of the static relations among institutions, as in terms of the dynamic relations among a plurality of contending groups.

It is not simply that scholars recognized the centrality of interest groups to policymaking in America. Rather, this empirical observation gave rise to a normative debate about the meaning of a vigorous group process for democratic governance. Champions of group politics argued that it enhances the mechanisms of representation, guaranteeing to ordinary citizens an effective voice in the halls of government; protects them from the coercive exercise of governmental power; precludes majority tyranny by accommodating the preferences of the most intensely concerned; ensures moderate policies and, therefore, political stability; and promotes political outcomes that approximate the public interest.

In the ensuing decade critics of the group process (Schattschneider, 1960; Olson, 1965; McConnell, 1966; Lowi, 1969) regarded much less optimistically pressure group dominance of policy. Oriented to justice rather than to liberty, and to change rather than to stability, these observers made a number of arguments to counter the advocates of interest group competition. They contended that, as interest groups usurp public authority, the boundaries between public and private spheres erode; that the resultant exercise of private power can be just as coercive—and much less accountable—than the exercise of public power; and that, because the pressure system is not universal, the interests of those groups not represented in the process—most notably, those of the poor and diffuse publics—are ignored in government policymaking. Given the degree to which such themes go to the heart of thinking about democracy, it is no wonder that a generation of academic observers of American politics took so seriously the role of interest groups.

Whether one's sympathies lie with the group theorists or their critics, this debate makes very clear that it matters crucially how active groups are in the political process. Therefore, it is central to know just how much group activity there is and what forms it takes. There have been several thoughtful treatments of interest groups in recent years (Wilson, 1973; Berry, 1977; Moe, 1980; Hayes, 1981). Unfortunately, however, with the exception of Walker (1981) and Gais,

SOURCE: From Kay Lehman Schlozman and John T. Tierney, "More of the Same: Washington Pressure Activity in a Decade of Change," Journal of Politics 45 (1983): 351–377 (including the tables). Reprinted with permission from Blackwell Publishing Ltd. This work was partially supported by research funds made available to Boston College by the Mellon Foundation. We gratefully acknowledge the support. We also wish to express our thanks to several persons who made helpful comments on earlier versions of this article: Terry Moe, Jack L. Walker, Sidney Verba, and the anonymous reviewers.

Peterson, and Walker (1982), there has been a paucity of new data collected—either of the systematic sort that Lester Milbrath (1963) amassed or of the in-depth kind that Bauer, Pool, and Dexter (1963) assembled two decades ago. Thus, although we have an old debate providing guideposts for the understanding of the republic's governance, we lack an empirical basis for judging whether the new realities accord with the old description. In this paper we use the results of our recently completed survey of 175 interest groups having offices in Washington to furnish descriptive data about changes in the Washington pressure group scene and to acquire some understanding of those changes. In particular, we use systematic data to probe *how* interest groups go about trying to influence the federal government. We assess not only *how much* group activity there is but also *what kind*; that is, we consider both the volume of group activity and the specific techniques employed. Furthermore, we shall probe the degree to which what we find constitutes change and inquire into the sources of any changes we isolate.[1]

AN EXPLOSION IN GROUP ACTIVITY?

In what *Time* called "an era of the strenuous clique and the vociferous claque" and *Newsweek* labeled an age of "Me-first factionalism," journalists and politicians have noted—and often lamented—the recent explosion in interest group activity.

Although journalists and politicians seem ready to declare this the age of "the imperial pressure group," their impressions have yet to be sustained by any systematically gathered data. After all, there is always the possibility that the expansion in group activity is merely illusory. It may be that the most successful lobbying traditionally has been that which is least overt—groups operating, largely unnoticed by the public, through regularized interactions with government officials. Perhaps what has happened is that a few noisy groups have arrived on the scene, exploiting new technologies (such as direct mail) and generating media coverage to bring their message to the public. Thus, perhaps what has changed is not the amount of activity but its visibility.

This line of argument also raises the possibility that we are witnessing *both* an expansion in group activity *and* a transformation of its character. Two of the principal changes in our larger political environment—the revolution in assorted electronic technologies and reinforcement of the nexus between the congressman and his district—may well be giving rise not simply to more group activity, but to entirely new kinds of activity or at least to enhanced salience of some forms of activity at the expense of others.

Let us elaborate. We might reasonably expect recent developments in mass-communication and data-processing technologies to add new weapons to a pressure group's arsenal, facilitating its use of indirect forms of lobbying in order to influence the decisions of government officials. The electronic and print media make it easier than ever to reach not only the public at large but also special publics with messages specially designed to maximize their popular appeal. Given the sophistication and effectiveness of these communication technologies, we might expect to find organizations relying increasingly on methods such as direct-mail fund raising, efforts to generate letters and telegrams to public officials, and advertising campaigns in the media to explain positions on issues.

Similarly, we might expect the approaches taken by interest groups to be altered by the strengthening of the ties between the congressional representative and his district. Academic observers of Congress—among them, Ferejohn (1974), Mayhew (1974), Fiorina (1977), Fenno (1978), and Roberts (1981)—point to a cluster of phenomena to demonstrate that the modern legislator in recent times is not so much an instructed delegate as a parochial advocate, attentive both to the expressed preferences and the particularistic needs of constituents. Given this enhanced sensitivity to what the folks back home are telling legislators, we would expect interest groups to place special emphasis upon certain strategies and methods: for example, framing appeals to legislators in terms of the specific effects of a proposed measure upon their own districts; bringing influential constituents from the district to Washington in order to present a case to their own representatives rather than relying upon the persuasiveness of their permanent Washington lobbyists; generating communications from constituents. Here, our expectations of the effects of changes in the nature of congressional representation reinforce our expectations of the effects of new technologies. Both point in the direction of increased salience of indirect lobbying techniques in which groups mobilize citizens at the grassroots to communicate with policymakers.

We can use the results of our recently completed survey of government-affairs representatives in a sample of 175 Washington-based organizations to shed light on these matters. In order to construct a sample in which large and active organizations would have a greater probability of being selected than smaller, less active ones, we devised a somewhat unusual sampling procedure (elaborated in much greater detail in the Appendix). Twice a year the *National Journal* publishes an index listing the private organizations mentioned in its articles during the preceding six months. We assembled indexes over a four-year period (1977–80) and sampled randomly from them by line, thus giving the more frequently mentioned groups a greater probability of being selected. Of the 200 organizations chosen—corporations, trade associations, unions, professional associations, civil rights groups, and so on—we were able to contact and interview 175 of them. Within each organization we sought to interview the individual having the broadest understanding of that organization and its involvement in politics. The interviews included both open- and closed-ended questions and lasted roughly two hours each.

We use the results of our survey as the primary data base for the tripartite inquiry that follows. First, we consider whether there in fact has been an explosive increase of late in pressure group activity and also whether technological and political changes have led to particular increases in certain kinds of techniques. Second, we probe further into two specific features of contemporary group activity—an emphasis on grassroots lobbying and the enhanced professionalism of Washington representation—that have received particularly great attention. Finally, we draw further on our survey to explore the primary reasons for the growth in pressure group activity.

HOW MUCH ACTIVITY?

Our initial concern is to investigate changes over time in the volume of group activity and to determine whether the perceived growth spurt is real or illusory. We can take a first, tentative stab at these questions by considering data we assembled (using information in the *Encyclopedia of Associations* [1979] and in the various volumes put out by Moody's Investors Service) about the birth dates of over 2100 of the nearly 2700 organizations listed in the 1981 *Washington Representatives* directory as having their own offices in Washington. Fully 40 percent of these organizations have been founded since the beginning of the 1960s;

in fact, 25 percent have been founded since the beginning of the 1970s.[2] Thus, there are clearly many new organizations on the scene. We should note, of course, that the total number of organizations active in Washington politics has probably not grown proportionally in the same period because some organizations have presumably gone out of business during the period. We know, after all, that some groups are meant to be temporary from the outset because their founders are concerned about a particular piece of legislation or an isolated regulatory matter. However, what we know about the tendencies of organizations to persist—coupled with the fact that organizations listed in one edition of the *Washington Representatives* directory have a high probability of appearing in successive ones—leads us to the conclusion that there are many more organizations around than in the past.

But that is only half the picture. Not only are there many *new* organizations, but there are many more organizations in *Washington*. In the past two decades there has been a massive immigration of organizations to Washington. There are no data, analogous to those just cited for organizational births, about when these organizations first established offices in the national capital. However, we do have such figures for most of the 175 organizations in our sample. Sixty-one percent of our organizations have opened a Washington office—often a national headquarters—since 1960, 38 percent since 1970. This indicates, presumably, the increased salience of national politics both to groups originally established for other purposes and to groups long active in politics whose political interests are now so compelling that they have established a permanent beachhead in Washington.

The figures just cited require further amplification. Our Washington sample, in fact, underrepresents younger organizations. While 40 percent of all organizations having Washington offices have been established since 1960, only 20 percent of the groups in our sample are so young. Given that we deliberately attempted to sample large and active organizations, this discrepancy is not surprising. Although many recently formed organizations—for example, Common Cause and the Business Roundtable—have quickly established a substantial Washington presence, it is hardly astonishing that, in seeking active and powerful groups, we also netted a disproportionate number of older ones. Since our sample underrepresents new organizations, it presumably also underrepresents the number of groups opening offices in Washington in the past two decades. However, we can arrive at a reasonable estimate of the number of new arrivals in Washington by weighting the data from our survey by the broader data we assembled on organizational birth dates. On the basis of those calculations, we speculate that roughly 70 percent of all groups have opened their Washington offices since 1960, and that just under half have established their Washington offices since 1970.

Techniques of Influence

Let us look more directly at the level of group activity. In an effort to piece together a comprehensive picture of exactly what techniques groups use in their efforts to influence, either directly or indirectly, what goes on in government, we devised an encompassing list of 27 such techniques. We presented our respondents with this list and asked them to tell us, with respect to each one, whether or not the group uses it. We show the results of that inquiry in Table 15.1 in which we list in descending order the proportion of groups using each of the 27 methods. At the top of the scale, virtually all our respondents, 99 percent of them, testify at hearings; 98 percent contact officials directly; and 95 percent talk shop with officials in informal settings. At the bottom, only 20 percent engage in protests and demonstrations. Surely,

Table 15.1 Percentage of Groups Using Each of Techniques of Exercising Influence

1.	Testifying at hearings	99%
2.	Contacting government officials directly to present your point of view	98
3.	Engaging in informal contacts with officials—at conventions, over lunch, etc.	95
4.	Presenting research results or technical information	92
5.	Sending letters to members of your organization to inform them about your activities	92
6.	Entering into coalitions with other organizations	90
7.	Attempting to shape the implementation of policies	89
8.	Talking with people from the press and the media	86
9.	Consulting with government officials to plan legislative strategy	85
10.	Helping to draft legislation	85
11.	Inspiring letter-writing or telegram campaigns	84
12.	Shaping the government's agenda by raising new issues and calling attention to previously ignored problems	84
13.	Mounting grassroots lobbying efforts	80
14.	Having influential constituents contact their congressman's office	80
15.	Helping to draft regulations, rules, or guidelines	78
16.	Serving on advisory commissions and boards	76
17.	Alerting congressmen to the effects of a bill on their districts	75
18.	Filing suit or otherwise engaging in litigation	72
19.	Making financial contributions to electoral campaigns	58
20.	Doing favors for officials who need assistance	56
21.	Attempting to influence appointments to public office	53
22.	Publicizing candidates' voting records	44
23.	Engaging in direct-mail fund raising for your organization	44
24.	Running advertisements in the media about your position on issues	31
25.	Contributing work or personnel to electoral campaigns	24
26.	Making public endorsements of candidates for office	22
27.	Engaging in protests or demonstrations	20

SOURCE: Kay Lehman Schlozman and John T. Tierney, "More of the Same: Washington Pressure Groups Activity in a Decade of Change," *Journal of Politics* 45 (1983): 357, Table 1. Reprinted with permission from Blackwell Publishing Ltd.

the nature of our sample affects the results shown in Table 15.1. Given our deliberate attempt to sample active organizations, it is not surprising that Table 15.1 shows a great deal of activity. Still, what is striking about the figures in Table 15.1 is just *how much* interest groups do. Seventeen of these techniques are used by at least three-quarters of the groups, and 21 are used by at least half. Turning

it upside down, we can cite figures not contained in Table 15.1 to the effect that the median number of techniques used by a group is 17, and the modal number of techniques is 21.

It seems useful to digress to inquire whether different kinds of groups are specialists in different kinds of activities. Four kinds of organizations—corporations, trade associations, unions, and public interest groups—are sufficiently numerous in our sample to make possible further investigation. When we cross-tabulated these twenty-seven activities by these four categories of organizations, what was striking was the overall similarity among the four categories with respect to the various techniques they employ. (Table 15.4 upon which the following remarks are based is contained in the Appendix.) Among the most heavily used activities (those on the top half of the list, employed by at least 80 percent of all organizations), in only two cases do fewer than 70 percent of the organizations in a specific category use it. (Only 67 percent of the corporations report that they talk with people from the press and the media, and only 58 percent of the public interest groups indicate that they mobilize influential constituents to contact legislators.)

Further down the list some differences do appear. Public interest groups seem substantially less likely than the other kinds of groups to make financial contributions to candidates (partly, we assume, because of their tax-exempt status and the restrictions that places on their political activity). In addition, there are several techniques that seem to be employed more frequently by certain groups. Unions and public interest groups seem to be much more likely to publicize candidates' voting records and, not surprisingly, to engage in direct-mail fund raising. Furthermore, there are several techniques—donating manpower to campaigns, endorsing candidates, and engaging in protests—which are within the virtually exclusive preserve of the unions. Still, with respect to techniques used, it is the similarities across types of groups that are striking.

MORE ACTIVITY?

Of course, "a lot" of activity is not necessarily more activity. However, our data provide ample evidence not only of the large volume of group activity but also of recent expansion in that activity. Among the first questions we asked our respondents was an open-ended one inquiring about the changes over the past decade in the way their groups went about trying to influence what goes on in Washington. The question, not surprisingly, netted dozens of answers going off in many directions. However, the single most frequent reply—articulated by 32 percent of the respondents—was some variation on the simple theme of "We are more active than we used to be."[3] For example, the representative for a major peak association of businesses explained his organization's escalating political involvement by reference to the expanding range of matters that demand attention:

> There are more people in the act and more issues to deal with. For example, in the 93rd Congress, we had 40 issues; in the 94th, 71 issues; in the 95th, 101 issues; in the 96th, 132 issues. Hopefully, that's tapering off now.

Our open-ended question was followed immediately by a closed-ended item asking about changes in the group's level of activity over the past decade. A remarkable 88 percent of the respondents indicated that their groups had become more active in recent years. Nine percent said that their activity level was largely unchanged, and a mere three percent said that their activity had diminished.[4]

We can probe this issue further by returning to our list of 27 methods of political influence. Each time a respondent indicated that his group utilized a given technique, we inquired whether its use of that method had increased, decreased, or remained the same in recent years. We present the results in Table 15.2 which shows, once again in descending order, the proportion of groups reporting increased use of a particular technique in recent years. Again there is a

Table 15.2 Percentage of Pressure Groups Using Each of Techniques More Than in Past

1.	Talking with people from the press and the media[1]	68%
2.	Entering into coalitions with other organizations	67
3.	Contacting government officials directly to present your point of view[3]	67
4.	Testifying at hearings[3]	66
5.	Sending letters to members of your organization to inform them about your activities[1]	65
6.	Presenting research results or technical information	63
7.	Mounting grassroots lobbying efforts[1,2]	59
8.	Inspiring letter-writing or telegram campaigns[1,2]	58
9.	Engaging in informal contacts with officials—at conventions, over lunch, etc.[3]	57
10.	Attempting to shape the implementation of policies	56
11.	Helping to draft legislation	54
12.	Shaping the government's agenda by raising new issues and calling attention to previously ignored problems	54
13.	Consulting with government officials to plan legislative strategy[3]	54
14.	Having influential constituents contact their congressman's office[2]	52
15.	Making financial contributions to electoral campaigns[2]	49
16.	Alerting congressmen to the effects of a bill on their districts[2]	45
17.	Helping to draft regulations, rules, or guidelines	44
18.	Filing suit or otherwise engaging in litigation	38
19.	Serving on advisory commissions and boards	32
20.	Engaging in direct-mail fund raising for your organization[1]	31
21.	Attempting to influence appointments to public office	23
22.	Doing favors for officials who need assistance[3]	21
23.	Running advertisements in the media about your position on issues[1]	19
24.	Publicizing candidates' voting records	19
25.	Contributing work or personnel to electoral campaigns	18
26.	Making endorsements of candidates for office	14
27.	Engaging in protests or demonstrations	9

[1] Facilitated by modern electronic technology.
[2] Relevant to strong representative-constituent relationship.
[3] Classic direct lobbying.

SOURCE: Kay Lehman Schlozman and John T. Tierney, "More of the Same: Washington Pressure Groups Activity in a Decade of Change," *Journal of Politics* 45 (1983): 361, Table 2. Reprinted with permission from Blackwell Publishing Ltd.

range: 68 percent of the groups in our sample are having more contact with people from the press and the media, while only 9 percent are engaging more frequently in protests and demonstrations. What is noteworthy, however, is how much increase there has been. In 14 of the 27 cases, at least half our respondents reported they were using a technique more in recent years. Viewed from another perspective, the median group reported increased utilization of 13, or just under half, of these methods.

The other side of this coin is perhaps even more striking. Our data on the proportion of groups reporting *decreased* use of a particular technique in recent years reveal a very narrow range: for each of the 27 techniques, the proportion of groups reporting a decrease in use was 5 percent or less. (The average across all 27 techniques was a decreased use by only 2 percent of the groups.)

MORE OF EVERYTHING?

On this basis we feel secure in concluding that the apparent explosion in group activity is not merely illusory, a by-product of the realization by a few groups that the media will cover whatever is noisy and interesting. In our introductory discussion, we posited that certain changes in the environment in which pressure groups operate—most importantly the revolution in electronic technologies and the strengthening of the connection between representative and constituency—would have the effect of not merely escalating group activity but transforming it. More specifically, we expected especially rapid rates of growth for certain techniques: those engaging the use of the media (for example, talking to people from the press and electronic media or running ads to publicize group positions); those facilitated by the use of computers (for example, direct-mail fund raising, communicating with organization members, and inspiring letter-writing campaigns); and those exploiting the links between legislator and constituency (for example, mounting grass-roots lobbying efforts, alerting representatives to the effects of legislation on their districts, and arranging communications from influential constituents about policy matters).

Table 15.2 indicates differences among the techniques in the extent to which their use by interest groups has increased. However, superficial inspection of Table 15.2 does not indicate selective increases among the clusters of techniques that are either electronically relevant or constituency-based.

Certainly, at the top of the list is one method of influence for which we would anticipate huge increases in an electronic age—talking with people from the press and media. However, two others that might also be related to new communications technologies—engaging in direct-mail fund raising and running ads in the media—are near the bottom. Techniques specified as particularly relevant to an era of close links between legislators and constituents seem anchored in the upper-middle ranges of the list, far from the bottom but not at the top.

To make some sense of these observations, we attempted to contrive some summary figures. We scanned the list of 27 methods and designated six (indicated on Table 15.2) that seemed most clearly linked to electronic technology and five that seemed most clearly linked to a strong representative-constituent bond. (As anticipated by our earlier discussion, two techniques—mounting grassroots lobbying efforts and inspiring letter-writing campaigns—fell into both of these categories.) Then we specified five other techniques that seemed to conform to the classical stereotype of lobbying in Washington as it has been conducted for over a century. Finally, for each of these three broad categories, we found the average proportion of groups indicating increased use of the individual techniques in that category, with the following results:

Mean Percentage of Groups Using Techniques More Often

Electronically relevant techniques:	50%
Constituency-based techniques:	53%
Classic direct lobbying techniques:	53%

Let us not endow these figures with more meaning than they merit. We wish neither to reify these categories nor to maintain that our choice of which specific techniques belong in which categories is beyond argument.

What we have found, however, is substantiation of our earlier observation about the nature of the growth in pressure group activity—a variant of the theme "more of everything." We are not saying that there has been a uniform expansion across each of the many techniques groups employ. However, our expectation that the advent of television and computers or the importance of advocacy representation would transform pressure group activity is not borne out. We did not find selective increases in either electronically related or constituency-based modes of interest group activity. Use of these forms of interest representation, of course, has skyrocketed, but so too has the use of the time-honored direct methods of contact and consultation.[5] Thus, the massive increase in group activity is built upon expanded use of all kinds of techniques.

MORE OF THE SAME?

Our respondents—and the journalists who chronicle their doings—might read the foregoing and point out with a sigh that our statistical summaries reveal little of the texture of political life, that we have overlooked the many subtle changes in kind as well as degree of activity. We can use our respondents' answers to an open-ended question about changes in how their groups go about influencing what goes on in Washington to suggest some areas in which to investigate subtle alterations. As we have mentioned, the largest proportion of our respondents (32 percent) reported simply that their group was more active. However, shedding additional light on the significant ways in which group activity may have changed, roughly 20 percent of our respondents spoke of changes in the nature of grassroots lobbying, and another 20 percent pointed to what they regard as the enhanced professionalism of

Washington lobbying, particularly as evidenced by a greater reliance on technical information.

To discern whether the changes identified by our respondents are in fact real, we needed a fuller understanding of the nature of group activity before the dawn of the new era. Accordingly, we consulted historical accounts of the Washington lobbying scene. We discovered that the absence of a systematic approach in the scholarly and journalistic works of previous eras would make it difficult to use these works to establish any kind of historical benchmark. We have no way of knowing whether the examples cited by these observers are typical or merely striking. Still, as we delved into this historical literature we were surprised to find precedents for techniques often considered unique to our modern era. Thus, we began to realize that we had found in our survey not only "more" but "more of the same."

Grassroots Lobbying

Grassroots lobbying it seems is not the invention of our era—one that enjoys the kind of data-processing and communications technologies that make this technique so easy to use. Rather, this is an ancient weapon in the pressure group arsenal. At the start of the century, without so much as a microchip to aid it, the Anti-Saloon League had a mailing list of over half a million people (Odegard, 1928, p. 76). Lest one assume that this powerful organization was unique in its resources, we find in the 1929 writings of Pendleton Herring every indication that this form of interest-group behavior was quite common at the time (Herring, 1929, p. 70).

Although it may be that the techniques of grassroots lobbying are less innovative than sometimes believed, the way grassroots communications are received and interpreted may have changed. The common wisdom among political scientists is that an official who gets even so much as a whiff of suspicion that communications have been orchestrated immediately discounts them. As a matter of fact, such stimulated communications have been labeled "probably the least effective and most relied on lobbying technique" (Zeigler and Peak, 1972, p. 153).

We asked our respondents about this problem with letter-writing campaigns. Because of the rich responses they provided, it is difficult to give statistical summaries of their replies. Nevertheless, several themes emerge with clarity. First, very few of our respondents said that because of the skepticism with which officials may greet such communications, their organizations eschew the use of grassroots lobbying techniques. Instead, groups seek ways to render those communications credible. Over two-thirds of the organizations using these methods mentioned attempts on their part to make the letters or contacts seem spontaneous and sincere. Typically, our respondents indicated that it helped to supply their members with a summary of salient points and to instruct them to compose their own letters, perhaps even to write in longhand. The comments of a vice president of Washington operations of a large membership organization indicate a typical approach:

> We try to avoid form letters. We send them the information and ask them to tailor it to themselves and make it personal. It depends on the issues. Mass mailings work for the unions, but not for us.

In an interesting twist, the Washington bureau director of a leading civil rights group indicated that the more illegible and ungrammatical the letters generated by her organization, the greater the likelihood they would be taken seriously.

In addition, many of our respondents indicated that, if the communications arrive in sufficient quantity in congressional offices, they will be heeded no matter how orchestrated they seem. As the chief lobbyist for a large natural

gas corporation (and son of a former congressman) told us:

> Members have to care about this mail, even if it's mail that is almost identically worded. Labor unions do this sort of thing a lot. The member [of Congress] has to care that *somebody* out there in his district has enough power to get hundreds of people to sit down and write a postcard or letter—because if the guy can get them to do *that,* he might be able to influence them in other ways. So, a member has no choice but to pay attention. It's suicide if he doesn't.

Confirmation of this view emerges from the results of a recent survey of Capitol Hill staff aides. The results of that study show that "orchestrated mail from constituents" ranks eleventh overall on a list of *ninety-six* types of communications that may influence the decisions of members of Congress (*STAFF,* 1981, p. 7).

Professionalism in Washington Representation

The other aspect of modern interest group politics that merited special mention from our respondents is the notion that the whole enterprise of Washington representation has become both more sophisticated and more professional. They indicated over and over that it was no longer sufficient just to know the right people. Now they must also marshall complicated and well-reasoned arguments. As the vice president of governmental affairs for an international airline told us:

> The lobbying process has become more complex and requires more sophistication. The old boy network has broken down. Now a lobbyist has to be much more articulate about the issues.

Furthermore, lobbyists increasingly buttress their arguments with complex technical information and research findings that not only aid the government in making policy but help to present a group's case in favorable light. A senior lobbyist for a large chemical company summed up the situation she and her colleagues face:

> Insofar as a great deal of the legislation we deal with is technical, we're doing a lot more providing of research results and technical information. We often think of ourselves as educators. Up until ten or twelve years ago, the issues were not so technical and complex. As the issues increased in technicality, no one congressman could be expected to know all the technical information about the issues. As a result, there is a greater reliance on staff by congressmen, and, in turn, the staffs rely on special interest groups for information.

This activity is clearly an important one, ranking high on our list of 27 techniques for exerting influence: 92 percent of our respondents indicate that they present research results and technical information as one of their activities; and 63 percent are doing more of it recently.

To some the corollary of the new sophistication and complexity of lobbying is a decline in the amount of the sleazy activity that we associate with lobbying in the era of the robber baron. According to the vice president for governmental affairs at a large corporation:

> To a large extent, the three B's— booze, bribes, and broads—have disappeared. Not altogether, you understand. But today a good lobbyist must have the ability to draw up factual information—a lot of it—in a short period of time for people on the Hill who want it. . . . Nowadays, taking somebody to a football game or a goose hunt just doesn't quite make it.

On this particular subject most of our other respondents were less forthcoming. Still, we can make a few observations. Most obviously, a more professional demeanor in presenting arguments and technical information does not preclude the use of illegal and quasi-illegal techniques.

With respect to outright bribery, nothing in our interviews contradicts the common wisdom among political scientists (for example, Milbrath, 1963, pp. 274–282) that there are so many legitimate avenues of influence in Washington politics that bribery is unnecessary. Nevertheless, our survey revealed that there are still many transactions between lobbyist and politician at the penumbra of what is legal. For example, 56 percent of our respondents indicated that they do favors for officials who need assistance, although no one ranked it as an activity consuming a great deal of time and resources. Moreover, only 21 percent reported an increase in their use of this tactic. Still, they do perform favors, and no respondent indicated a decrease in this activity. In fact, we gathered quite a bit of anecdotal evidence of the kinds of services rendered. For example, one corporate lobbyist admitted some regret at having lent the company limousine to a congressman for his daughter's wedding. Commenting more generally about the nature of some commonly used blandishments, the manager for government relations of a large professional association remarked:

> There's not much of the illegal stuff but *a lot* of things that border on it: hunting lodges and fishing trips and golf vacations to Florida; big dinners. . . . What's the real difference between a $10,000 cash payment to a senator and arranging for and paying for a $10,000 dinner party to which the senator is free to invite his favored constituents and friends?

What are we to make of this? It is clear that as congressional policy making becomes ever more complex and specialized, there is greater demand for lobbying that is professional and substantively informed. However, a more professional posture and reliance on complex information does not preclude the use of favors or other techniques of influence that may be of more dubious legality. Although our conclusion is tentative, it is our impression that while the three Bs have hardly disappeared, their usage does not seem to have accelerated as quickly as the employment of other techniques. Lest we consider this to be an entirely novel state of affairs, however, we can point out that a similar revolution was proclaimed over half a century ago when Richard Boeckel asserted that "the title 'legislative agent' [had acquired] something of a professional standing" and suggested that congressional efforts to register lobbyists constituted "a welcome recognition by Congress of the new dignity of their calling" (Boeckel, 1928, pp. 2–3). Thus, there is even precedent for the self-satisfaction with which many modern lobbyists seem to regard their vocation.

We have found instructive our brief foray into the historical accounts of Washington pressure politics: it has shown us that there is ample precedent for what often is proclaimed to be so new. What we see, in fact, is not only that there is more group activity now, but the *same kinds* of activities have been in use for many decades. Our remaining task is to try to understand why there is more pressure activity now.

WHY MORE ACTIVITY?

Useful as our data are in demonstrating an increase in interest group activity, they are less helpful in clarifying just why this expansion has taken place. However, we at least can draw some suggestions by looking at the remarks made by our respondents: in addition to the third of them who reported more activity over the past decade, many others pointed to some specific change

in the Washington scene that had spurred them to increased efforts. These responses are useful for providing clues as to some of the sources of the recent escalation in pressure group activity.

We looked to see, for example, if our respondents mentioned that they are more active in recent years as a reaction to increased activity by groups they consider antagonistic to their interests. This explanation is posited often by group theorists who assume that groups will inevitably coalesce and act in defense of their own interests—especially in the face of organized threats.[6] Given the importance of this stimulus-response concept in group theory, we were surprised to find that only 5 percent of our respondents volunteered that they are more active today because their antagonists—whether business or public interest groups—are more active. Groups in fact may escalate their efforts in response to what their opponents do, but our results indicate that group representatives do not perceive this to be a cause for their actions.

Governmental Activity as a Spur?

A theme that arose more often—discussed by 14 percent of those replying to our open-ended question—is that because the government has grown so much and become so much more intrusive, their organizations have become more politically involved.[7] Commenting on the expanded scope of federal involvement, a lobbyist for a major corporation observed:

> More and more groups and companies have recognized the increasing size of government and have therefore stepped up their involvement. Economically, the government is much more important these days than it was ten years ago. Great Society legislation and the environmental and consumer laws have all combined to make companies feel they need to be more active in Washington.

The current administration, however, is trying aggressively to diminish the size of the federal government. In view of the connection some of our respondents drew between federal expansion and interest group activity, what can we expect to happen to pressure group activity as the government shrinks? Insofar as the retreat means withdrawal of support for their favored programs, we can expect even louder clamor from interest groups. Discussing budget cuts in a program from which the reader may have benefited, the executive director of a professional association to which the reader may belong remarked:

> Just in this past year the whole nature of our involvement has undergone change. The government's efforts to reduce social science funding through NSF by 75 per cent forced us to become more active. We even joined with ten other organizations to form the Consortium of Social Science Associations.

It is not surprising that government reductions would engender pressure activity as groups rise to defend subsidy programs from which they have benefited. But what about deregulation? Can we expect corporate political activity to constrict as the government lifts the regulatory crown of thorns that has (at least in the eyes of businessmen) rested so oppressively on the corporate brow? Before we leap prematurely to the conclusion that, if the government gets out of the business of economic regulation, corporations will get out of the business of political influence, let us consider what we learned in our interviews with four corporations in a recently deregulated industry, the airlines.

Although our respondents from all four airlines indicated that deregulation makes life easier for their companies, they all remain very active politically, utilizing an average of 20 out of our 27 techniques of political influence. (For all corporations in the sample the average was 18.) Not only are they very active, these companies are *more* politically active now. All four said that their activity had risen in recent years. Furthermore, on average they have increased their usage of 16 of the 27 techniques. (Across the sample, the corporate average was 13.) This is not to say, however, that nothing has changed. The issues have changed—from routes and fares to airports and airways. The principal target has changed—from the Civil Aeronautics Board to the Federal Aviation Administration. But our discussions with airline executives make clear that their corporations remain highly active politically. Thus, if the experience of the airlines is any indication, substantial deregulation may not result in a wholesale contraction in corporate attempts to influence government—at least not in the short run.

Changes in Congress

We were not surprised to be told that increased pressure group activity is fostered by new threats either from organizational opponents or from the government. After all, the literature on interest groups has long since raised these points. We were struck, however, when twice as many of our respondents— 28 percent—attributed their increased activity to the reforms of congressional organization and procedure since 1974. The many changes on Capitol Hill over the past decade—the proliferation of subcommittees, the diminished importance of congressional staff, the greater number of policy entrepreneurs, the requirements for open meetings, the rapid turnover in congressional membership— have altered the environment of legislative lobbying and have left pressure groups bent on influencing officials with little choice but to escalate the range and volume of their activities. These changes in Congress have evoked more pressure activity primarily by multiplying the number of access points and expanding the variety of opportunities interested parties have to exert their political will. Because the patterns evidenced are somewhat intricate, we wish to elaborate.

In the aftermath of procedural reforms in Congress that diminished the powers of committee chairmen and multiplied the number of subcommittees, it is no longer possible for a group to make its case effectively by contacting only a few powerful legislators (see Davidson, 1981). Lobbyists must cultivate a broader range of contacts not only because there are more subcommittees whose jurisdictions touch each group's interests, but also because single committees and subcommittees no longer exercise as complete control over legislation as they once did. With the growing tendency to refer bills to multiple committees, and with the general relaxation of the norms inhibiting floor challenges to committees, threats to a group's legislative interests may come from anywhere in the chamber and at many more points over a bill's progression through the legislative labyrinth.[8]

By increasing the number of people with whom groups need to establish contacts, the expansion and professionalization of congressional staff also have led to more work for interest groups. Because staff members can provide valued access to the legislators and increasingly act as a policy making force in their own right (Malbin, 1980), groups find it desirable to cultivate good working relationships with them.

Sunshine rules which open oncesecret meetings to public scrutiny, were mentioned—although substantially less frequently—by our respondents as having similar effects: creating new opportunities for influence and thereby escalating the work load. According to the legislative counsel for one of the major hospital associations:

> It's great for the lobbyists, but the members of Congress hate it. There is in the back of the hearing room are

all these lobbyists watching a markup session and giving a thumbs-up or a thumbs-down to specific wordings or provisions. It's a fishbowl for them.

A final development in congressional politics that has meant more work for many groups is the accelerated turnover in congressional membership. In 1971 the ratio of newcomers to veterans was 1.2 to 1. By 1981 that ratio had risen to more than 3 to 1. The rate of turnover by 1981 had led to a decidedly junior Congress. By 1981 a majority of House members had served six terms or less, and 54 percent of the senators were in their first term (figures from Ornstein, 1981, p. 374). Many of our respondents commented that the absence of institutional memory that follows from such a rapid turnover has forced them to intensify their educational efforts as they patiently inform, programmatically, ignorant legislators and their staff members about the purposes, operation, and benefits of cherished programs. The director of a feisty social welfare action group described the Sisyphean task this way:

> One problem is that half the Congress has served fewer than six years. Much of the case made for food programs in the late 1960s was made to people who are no longer on the Hill. Current members of Congress only see the success of those earlier efforts; they look around now and, finding less malnutrition, don't see there's *still* a problem. Consequently, our lobbying task is being willing to tell the same story time after time to one legislator after another— making them see that hunger and malnutrition are reduced now *because* those programs [food stamps, school lunches, etc.] are in place, and that we can't afford to eliminate them. You have to have stamina to tell the story over and over—to persuade people who don't understand.

Thus, in yet another way the impact of changes on Capitol Hill is to demand that a conscientious group augment its efforts.

We consider it worth noting that although the architects of the congressional reforms of the 1970s had many purposes in mind, inducing more vigorous pressure from groups was not among them. Had the reformers paid attention to the lessons of history, they would have realized that this unintended consequence has precedent. Writing in 1929, in terms foreshadowing today's literature, Herring pointed to changes in Congress that invigorated group activity and altered the scope and methods of lobbying. In particular, he cited the reform of rules of procedure in the House of Representatives in 1911 that broke up the power center and distributed control more generally in the House; he also pointed to the adoption, at about the same time, of open congressional committee hearings as being a spur to group activity (Herring, 1929, pp. 41–43).

What we have learned about the impact of changes in Congress upon interest group activity helps us to solve an earlier puzzle. To review briefly, we originally expected to find selective escalation in the use of certain group techniques—those facilitated by electronic technologies and those capitalizing upon the close relationship between representative and district. We did, indeed, uncover increased employment of those methods of influence. However, we also found enhanced use of old-fashioned methods of direct lobbying.

The foregoing analysis of the implications for pressure groups of congressional reforms helps to explain why. These changes, taken collectively, spell both more opportunities for influence and more work for interest groups: more policymakers with whom one must consult and to whom one must present a case; more freshmen and issue amateurs requiring education; more meetings to attend; more hearings at which to testify and present technical information; more campaigns demanding contributions. These developments imply an increase in virtually all of the techniques relevant to legislative influence. In particular, however, they imply an increase in the use of those techniques we associate with old-fashioned lobbying. Thus, we now understand why the employment of these traditional methods has risen as quickly as the use of the clusters of electronically related or constituency-based methods.

CONCLUSION

In this paper we have trained for the first time in two decades systematic data on the question of what Washington-based pressure groups are doing. We were able to assess the journalistic common wisdom that there has been recently a vast expansion in the amount of interest group activity; we have found that, indeed, such an expansion has taken place. Not only are there more groups active in Washington, but they are doing more. The explosion in pressure group activity, however, is not confined to those methods peculiarly appropriate to an age either of electronic media and data processing or of stronger links between legislators and constituents. Rather, the increase has taken place across all categories of interest group techniques, the old-fashioned as well as the modern. Hence, we concluded, "more of everything."

In addition, when we probed more deeply, we learned that for each much-vaunted alteration in the nature of group activity there is historical precedent. It is the dimension not the substance that has been modified. Hence, "more of the same." Finally, we looked into the possible sources of this explosion in attempts to influence government and found the sources with government itself. Two developments seem to have fostered this growth: the tendency of the government to become involved in more and more areas of economic and social life; and the recent reforms in Congress which have multiplied the number of bases to be touched and meetings to be attended.

Because the modes of interest group activity have remained in balance—that is, because there have been no selective increases in certain forms of group influence relative to others—it might be argued that "more of the same" is really simply "the same." We disagree. We only need recall the normative underpinnings of the debate between the group theorists and their critics to understand that an expanded group process is fraught with implications for democratic governance. Even if there is more of all kinds of activity, not just some kinds, and even if there is precedent for that which is presumed to be innovation, we must take seriously the meaning of this proliferating activity. (This observation is particularly germane for the explosive growth of political action committees—a development that has received a great deal of both scholarly and journalistic attention.)

In the 1950s and 1960s academic analysts of American politics debated the implications for democracy of a political process in which private groups play a dominant role. Today a similar dialogue is taking place although the terms of the discussion are somewhat different and the discussants are less likely to be drawn from the ranks of political science. Still, as before, it is a matter of some contention whether a clamorous group process is salutary for democracy. To some, the cacophony of interest articulation is the fulfillment of the pluralist promise, indicating that many hitherto silent voices are being heard. In their view, to suggest that the din be hushed is to attack one of the most fundamental of liberties in a republic: the right of citizens, acting collectively, to appeal to government. To others, the cacophony is the application to politics of the "Me-decade" philosophy: with the clamor comes an increasingly divided and

fragmented society, a paralysis in national policymaking, and a politics in which statesmanlike concern with the common good yields to the tunnel vision of the narrowly interested.

Because the escalation in special-interest politics so complicates their lives, many members of Congress incline to the latter view. Their distaste for a politics of fractious interest groups is perhaps ironic since the structural and procedural reforms initiated by Congress itself appear to have played an important part in spawning more interest group activity. Whether or not members of Congress like the higher decibel level, they have to assume some of the responsibility for having raised the volume.

NOTES

1. In outlining our project in this way we are deliberately neglecting the important question of who is involved in the process. We are leaving for a subsequent paper the complicated— and perhaps more interesting—task of evaluating whether there has been a transformation in the nature of the interests that are represented by pressure groups, the question posed by Schattschneider (1961) about the nature of the "scope and bias of the pressure system."

2. It is interesting to note in this context that this growth has not been uniform across the various groups. Only 14 percent of the corporations have been established since 1960, 6 percent since 1970. The analogous figures for trade associations and other business groups are 38 percent since 1960, 23 percent since 1970; for professional associations, 30 percent and 14 percent; for unions, 21 percent and 14 percent; for public interest groups, 76 percent and 57 percent; for civil rights groups and organizations representing minorities, 56 percent and 46 percent; and for social welfare organizations and groups representing the poor, 79 percent and 51 percent.

3. This figure underrepresents the number of references to this theme because it does not include the many additional respondents who amplified this theme by citing some *specific*

change, such as the growth of government activity, that has had the effect of increasing their involvement in politics. These responses will be discussed further below.

4. We should point out that we are unsure of the effect of our sampling technique upon these figures. It is difficult to know whether, in systematically sampling organizations with *high* levels of Washington activity we also sampled organizations with *increasing* levels of Washington activity. We do not know whether the *National Journal* is systematically less likely to report on an active organization whose activity is, nonetheless, not growing. (See the Appendix for a discussion of related matters.)

5. We can further substantiate this conclusion with additional evidence. We asked our respondents to scan the entire list and choose those three that consume the largest share of the group's time and resources. As shown by the data in the following table, the classic direct lobbying techniques (3) actually outrank the electronically relevant (1) or constituency-based methods (2).

PERCENTAGE OF GROUPS FOR WHOM TECHNIQUE CONSUMES TIME AND RESOURCES

1. Contacting officials directly (3)	36%
2. Testifying at hearings (3)	27%
3. Presenting research or technical info	27%
4. Mounting grassroots lobbying (1, 2)	26%
5. Shaping the government's agenda	20%
6. Entering into coalitions	20%
7. Consulting to plan legislative strategy (3)	19%
8. Shaping implementation	17%
9. Alerting reps to effects (2)	14%
10. Sending letters to org. members (1)	12%
11. Drafting legislation	12%
12. Informal contacts (3)	10%
13. Talking with people from the press and media (1)	10%
14. Inspiring letter-writing campaigns (1, 2)	10%
15. Making contributions to campaigns (2)	8%
16. Drafting regulations	7%
17. Having influential constituents contact (2)	6%
18. Direct-mail fund raising (1)	5%
19. Serving on advisory commissions	4%
20. Filing suit	4%
21. Running ads in the media (1)	3%
22. Publicizing voting records	2%
23. Contributing manpower to campaigns	2%
24. Doing favors (3)	2%
25. Engaging in protests or demonstrations	1%
26. Influencing appointments	0%
27. Making endorsements	0%

6. This theme is a common one in the literature of group theorists of politics of the 1950s. Its most articulate exponent, however, is Truman (1951, chs. 1–3).

We ought to mention in passing another possible source of increased activity to which our respondents gave no voice. Although the empirical evidence is ambiguous, it often is alleged that the vacuum created by weak parties invites pressure group activity. In their answers to our open-ended question 3 percent of our respondents did discuss the enfeeblement of the parties. However, in so doing they were making no direct connection between party weakness and their own activity. Rather, disregarding the directive of the question, they simply were commenting on how the Washington scene has changed. Nevertheless, it is not surprising that our respondents did not make this link. From the vantage point of an organization's office of government affairs in downtown Washington, even the most perceptive observer would not have the kind of perspective to make such global inferences.

7. In this context it is interesting that although 13 percent of the membership organizations (that is, 13 percent of all organizations interviewed except corporations) rely upon federal grants or contracts for at least 10 percent of their budgets, no one mentioned this government subsidy as being a source of their organization's increased activity. Growth in government activity was always identified as being a hindrance to group interests and thus a spur to defensive activity; government actions were never mentioned as having sponsored group activity.

8. Our respondents' comments about the increasing number of committees and subcommittees they must deal with are germane to a subject we expect to treat in another context—theories about the dominance in the policy process of so-called subgovernments. Our findings suggest that self-contained and impermeable "iron triangles" have given way to many-sided polygons. Moreover, any such geometric metaphor is probably less appropriate than Hugh Heclo's (1978) concept of relatively more porous "issue networks" that are based on information and specialized knowledge.

APPENDIX: THE WASHINGTON REPRESENTATIVES SURVEY

Our sampling procedure bears elaboration. We wished to devise a technique that somehow would sample randomly from Washington interest group *activity*, not to sample Washington lobbyists or even the universe of organizations represented. In practical terms this meant that we wished to construct a sampling procedure in which the active and well-funded organizations that build a large Washington operation—for example, General Motors, the Petroleum Institute, or the American Medical Association—would have a greater probability of being selected than smaller, less active, and affluent groups like the Moped Association of America, the Frozen Pizza Institute, and the American Association of Sex Educators and Counselors.

We were able to locate a surrogate measure of a group's Washington activity by using the *National Journal's* Index to Private Organizations. Twice a year the *National Journal* publishes three separate indexes—one listing the subjects, one listing the names of individuals, and one listing the private organizations mentioned in its articles during the preceding six months. In any one index to organizations, the AFL-CIO might occupy several inches of column space whereas the American Hotel and Motel Association might merit only a single entry. We assembled indexes over a four-year period (1977–80) and sampled randomly from them by line, thus giving the more frequently mentioned groups a greater probability of being selected.

Not all the organizations listed in the *National Journal's* index have their own offices in Washington. We included in our sample only those organizations listed in *Washington Representatives—1981* (1981) as having their own Washington offices. We eliminated those having only Washington-based legal counsel or consultants. Practical considerations dictated this decision. We deemed full-time organizational employees to be more likely to be intimately involved in many aspects of the organization's affairs and also, as salaried employees, more likely than those who bill clients by the hour to share their time with us. Furthermore, focusing exclusively on organizational employees allowed us to obviate problems of professional/client confidentiality.

We also eliminated from the sample research organizations like the Gallup Poll, foreign governments, and foreign corporations (these two because they are legally barred from lobbying Congress directly), and representatives of American subnational governments such as the City of Provo, Utah, or the State of New Jersey. The issue of how to treat organizations of government workers is somewhat complicated. We decided to exclude those who lobby on behalf of *governments,* such as the Council of Chief State School Officers, but to retain those who lobby on behalf of their own private interests as public employees, such as the National Treasury Employees Union. What this meant in fact is that we eliminated organizations in which it is a governmental unit (state, regional authority, city, etc.) that joins, but included those in which the individual himself joins.

The resulting sample contained 200 organizations—corporations, trade associations, unions, professional associations, civil rights groups, public interest groups, and so on. We ultimately conducted interviews in 175 of these organizations. Our sample includes a broad range of organizations extending from the Liberty Lobby and the Child Welfare League to the Chamber of Commerce, the American Legion, and the United Mine Workers.

In selecting the person within the organization to interview we searched the personnel listing in the *Washington Representatives* directory for the one person whose job title indicated that he or she would have the broadest understanding of that organization's involvement in politics. If, after an introductory letter and follow-up phone calls, that person was unable or unwilling to be interviewed, we asked to be put in touch with someone else in the organization having

Table 15.3 The Washington Pressure System

	All Organizations Having DC Offices	National Journal Random Sample	National Journal Weighted Sample	Actually Interviewed
Corporations	22%	52%	30%	30%
Trade Associations and Other Business	32	21	24	26
Professional Associations	15	5	8	7
Unions	4	8	12	11
Public Interest Groups	9	13	15	13
Civil Rights/Social Welfare	3	4	4	5
Other/Unknown	16	10	8	7
	101%	100%	101%	99%
N =	(2694)	(200)	(200)	(175)

SOURCE: Kay Lehman Schlozman and John T. Tierney, "More of the Same: Washington Pressure Group Activity in a Decade of Change," *Journal of Politics* 45 (1983): 376, Table 3. Reprinted with permission from Blackwell Publishing Ltd.

Table 15.4 Percentage of Groups in Each Category Using Techniques of Exercising Influence

	Sample	Corporations	Trade Associations	Unions	Public Interest Groups
1. Testifying at hearings	99 %	98 %	100 %	100 %	100 %
2. Contacting officials directly	98	100	97	100	100
3. Informal contacts	95	98	97	95	96
4. Presenting research results	92	94	89	90	92
5. Sending letters to members	92	85	97	95	86
6. Entering into coalitions	90	96	91	100	92
7. Shaping implementation	89	90	91	85	92
8. Talking with press and media	86	67	89	95	96
9. Planning legislative strategy	74	81	85	85	83
10. Helping to draft legislation	85	86	94	85	74
11. Inspiring letter-writing campaigns	84	83	89	100	83
12. Shaping the government's agenda	84	79	77	85	100
13. Mounting grassroots lobbying	80	79	80	100	71
14. Having constituents contact	80	77	94	85	58
15. Drafting regulations	78	85	83	75	75
16. Serving on advisory commissions	76	74	74	95	67
17. Alerting congressmen to effects	75	92	74	85	57
18. Filing suit	72	72	83	95	79
19. Contributing to campaigns	58	86	66	90	29
20. Doing favors for officials	56	62	56	68	46

21. Influencing appointments	53	48	49	80	47
22. Publicizing voting records	44	28	37	90	75
23. Direct mail-fund raising	44	19	37	65	75
24. Running ads in the media	31	31	31	55	33
25. Contributing Manpower to campaigns	24	14	23	70	33
26. Endorsing candidates	22	8	9	95	25
27. Engaging in protests	20	0	3	90	25
Average Number of Techniques	19 %	18 %	19 %	24 %	19 %
N =	(174)	(52)	(35)	(20)	(24)

SOURCE: Kay Lehman Schlozman and John T. Tierney, "More of the Same: Washington Pressure Group Activity in a Decade of Change." *Journal of Politics* 45 (1983): 377, Table 4. Reprinted with permission from Blackwell Publishing Ltd.

extensive experience in the organization and a comprehensive knowledge of its Washington activity. These interviews lasted approximately two hours each. The questionnaire included both open- and closed-ended questions, and encompassed a wide range of subjects.

In order to ascertain what kinds of bias we had introduced by using our somewhat unusual sampling procedure, we conducted some further checks. Our concerns were dual: with respect to the various categories of Washington organizations, we wished to assess the effects, first, of having established as our sampling frame only those organizations mentioned in the *National Journal,* rather than all those listed in the *Washington Representatives* directory; and, second, of having increased the probability that more frequently mentioned organizations would be chosen. To do so we made an enumeration of the nearly three thousand organizations meeting our criteria that were listed in the directory as having Washington offices. We also chose an unweighted random sample of two hundred organizations from the *National Journal.* Table 15.3 allows us to compare the distributions thus obtained with the weighted sample we originally drew from the *National Journal.*

Our weighted sample of two hundred organizations—and the one hundred seventy-five we actually interviewed—do not differ appreciably from the random sample of *National Journal* organizations in terms of the distribution of organizations into rough categories. There are some differences between the various *National Journal* samples and the distribution of the universe of organizations having Washington offices; however, the differences are exactly the opposite of what we had expected. When we drew our weighted sample, we were dismayed that 54 percent of the organizations represented business and assumed that the *National Journal's* thorough coverage of economic affairs was responsible. In fact, although we oversampled corporations and undersampled trade associations somewhat, the overall total for business organizations was right on target. Contrary to our initial concerns that our sample did not capture sufficient numbers of the antagonists of business—unions and public interest groups— we actually oversampled these two categories substantially. (This is perhaps a consequence of the journalistic ethic of giving each side of the story more or less equal coverage, regardless of whether there is equal pressure activity on both sides.) We should note that our sample is deficient

in professional associations and in groups that defied classification. All told then, our sample is quite representative of the categories of groups having offices in Washington.

REFERENCES

Bauer, Raymond A., Ithiel De Sola Pool, and Lewis Anthony Dexter (1963). *American Business and Public Policy.* New York: Atherton Press.

Bentley, Arthur F. (1908). *The Process of Government.* Chicago: The University of Chicago Press.

Berry, Jeffrey M. (1977). *Lobbying for the People.* Princeton, NJ: Princeton University Press.

Boeckel, Richard (1928). *Regulation of Congressional Lobbies.* Washington, D.C.: Editorial Research Reports.

Dahl, Robert (1961). *Who Governs?* New Haven: Yale University Press.

Davidson, Roger (1981). "Subcommittee Government—New Channels for Policymaking." In Thomas E. Mann and Norman J. Ornstein (eds.), *The New Congress.* Washington, D.C.: American Enterprise Institute for Public Policy Research.

Encyclopedia of Associations (1979). Edited by Denise S. Akey and Nancy Yakes. 13th ed. Detroit: Gale Research Co.

Fenno, Richard F. (1978). *Home Style.* Boston: Little, Brown and Co.

Ferejohn, John A. (1974). *Pork Barrel Politics.* Stanford: Stanford University Press.

Fiorina, Morris (1977). *Congress—Keystone of the Washington Establishment.* New Haven: Yale University Press.

Gais, Thomas L., Mark A. Peterson, and Jack L. Walker (1982). "Interest Groups, Iron Triangles, and Representative Institutions in American National Government." Unpublished manuscript.

Hayes, Michael T. (1981). *Lobbyists and Legislators.* New Brunswick, NJ: Rutgers University Press.

Heclo, Hugh (1978). "Issue Networks and the Executive Establishment." In Anthony King (ed.), *The New American*

Political System. Washington, D.C.: American Enterprise Institute for Public Policy Research.

Herring, Pendleton (1929). *Group Representation Before Congress.* Baltimore: The Johns Hopkins University Press.

Latham, Earl (1952). *The Group Basis of Politics.* Ithaca, NY: Cornell University Press.

Lowi, Theodore (1969). *The End of Liberalism.* New York: W. W. Norton and Co.

McConnell, Grant (1966). *Private Power and American Democracy.* New York: Alfred A. Knopf.

Malbin, Michael (1980). *Unelected Representatives: Congressional Staff and the Future of Representative Government.* New York: Basic Books.

Mayhew, David (1974). *Congress: The Electoral Connection.* New Haven: Yale University Press.

Milbrath, Lester W. (1963). *The Washington Lobbyists.* Chicago: Rand McNally and Co.

Moe, Terry M. (1980). *The Organization of Interests.* Chicago: The University of Chicago Press.

Newsweek (November 6, 1978): 48.

Odegard, Peter (1928). *Pressure Politics: The Story of the Anti-Saloon League.* New York: Columbia University Press.

Olson, Mancur (1965). *The Logic of Collective Action.* Cambridge: Harvard University Press.

Ornstein, Norman (1981). "The New House and Senate in a New Congress." In Thomas E. Mann and

Norman J. Ornstein (eds.), *The New Congress.* Washington, D.C.: American Enterprise Institute for Public Policy Research.

Roberts, Steven V. (1981). "Congressmen and their Districts: Free Agents in Fear of the Future." In Dennis Hale (ed.), *The United States Congress: Proceedings of the Thomas P. O'Neill, Jr., Symposium on the U.S. Congress.* Boston: Boston College.

Schattschneider, E. E. (1960). *The Semisovereign People.* New York: Holt Rinehart and Winston.

STAFF: The Congressional Staff Journal (1981). "Orchestrated Mail Does Influence Staff—Who Says So?" (No. 6 of 97th Congress, December). Washington, D.C.: U.S. Government Printing Office.

TIME (October 23, 1978): 73.

Truman, David B. (1951). *The Governmental Process.* New York: Alfred A. Knopf.

Walker, Jack L. (1981). "The Origins and Maintenance of Interest Groups in America." Paper presented at the Annual Meeting of the American Political Science Association, September, New York.

Washington Representatives—1981 (1981). Edited by Arthur C. Close. Washington, D.C.: Columbia Books, Inc.

Wilson, James Q. (1973). *Political Organizations.* New York: Basic Books.

Zeigler, L. Harmon, and Wayne G. Peak. (1972). *Interest Groups in American Society.* 2d ed. Englewood Cliffs, NJ: Prentice-Hall, Inc.

PROJECT

Imagine you are a budding political scientist. Using Schlozman and Tierney's survey, call three different types of interest groups and ask them about their activities. How do your results compare to Schlozman and Tierney's? Be sure to explain your findings.

PART III

Group Influence

Power is central to the study of politics. In the end, most groups seek power, or at least a level of influence. This final part of the text examines interest-group influence. Several of the articles draw upon the pluralist–elitist frameworks described in earlier chapters. Others rely upon formal empirical models to assess group power. You will see that there is no unanimous verdict on the power of interest groups in American politics. As you read these articles, pay close attention to the role of context in determining group power. You will find that a multifaceted approach to examining interest groups will serve you better than reliance upon any one investigative approach.

GENERAL QUESTIONS TO CONSIDER

1. How do these authors relate to one another?
2. How do these authors differ from one another?
3. What is the unit of analysis each author uses to examine group influence? Does this matter? Why?
4. In your opinion, how does one accurately assess the power of interest groups in America? Refer to Table 1.4 in Chapter 1. In what ways do these groups conform to the analyses presented in Part III? In what ways do they differ?

16

Toward Juridical
Democracy

THEODORE J. LOWI

The following selection from *The End of Liberalism* derisively attacks the effects of interest groups in the American political system. Much of what Lowi criticizes is directly related to the arguments posed by Madison, Truman, Dahl, and Mills. I have chosen to place Lowi's argument in this section on group power because he squarely confronts the problems associated with what he calls "interest-group liberalism." He argues that the interest-group system is inimical to democracy. For Lowi, pluralism has been replaced by a hyperpluralist world in which too many groups have influence on public policy. This results in an unfocused, ineffectual government.

QUESTIONS TO CONSIDER

1. What is "interest-group liberalism"?
2. What is "juridical democracy"?
3. Why does Lowi believe interest groups are a threat to democracy?
4. What are Lowi's criticisms of pluralism?
5. What does Lowi propose as solutions to the problems caused by interest groups? Do you believe these changes have occurred since Lowi made his arguments in 1969?
6. Why is juridical democracy better than interest-group liberalism?

Assume that all developments of ideology, public philosophy, and public policy are part of some irresistible historical process. Epochs have no alternatives. Interest-group liberal ideology merely reflects the realities of power and rationalizes them into public policies. Criticism is irrelevant. All literature is a gigantic act of memorialization.

Fortunately, the influence of history and power over the human element is merely an hypothesis. To deny it is to wait for the long run. But to accept it is to confirm it. Ultimately, denial is the only choice, because acceptance is no test of hypothesis at all. History is much like a prison or a ghetto. It is difficult to escape, but the captive may succeed—unless he does not try. The only test of a deterministic hypothesis is whether real-world attempts to deny it fail.

THE END OF LIBERALISM:
THE INDICTMENT

The corruption of modern democratic government began with the emergence of interest-group liberalism as the public philosophy. Its corrupting influence takes at least four important forms, four counts, therefore, of an indictment. . . . Also to be indicted, on at least three counts, is the philosophic component of the ideology, pluralism.

SUMMATION I: FOUR COUNTS
AGAINST THE IDEOLOGY

(1) Interest-group liberalism as public philosophy corrupts democratic government because it deranges and confuses expectations about democratic institutions.

SOURCE: From Theodore J. Lowi, "Toward Juridical Democracy," in *The End of Liberalism* (New York: Norton, 1969), 287–314. Copyright 1969 by W. W. Norton & Company, Inc. Used by permission of W. W. Norton & Company, Inc.

Liberalism promotes popular decision-making but derogates from the decisions so made by misapplying the notion to the implementation as well as the formulation of policy. It derogates from the processes by treating all values in the process as equivalent interests. It derogates from democratic rights by allowing their exercise in foreign policy, and by assuming they are being exercised when access is provided. Liberal practices reveal a basic disrespect for democracy. Liberal leaders do not wield the authority of democratic government with the resoluteness of men certain of the legitimacy of their positions, the integrity of their institutions, or the justness of the programs they serve.

(2) Interest-group liberalism renders government impotent. Liberal governments cannot plan. Liberals are copious in plans but irresolute in planning. Nineteenth-century liberalism was standards without plans. This was an anachronism in the modern state. But twentieth-century liberalism turned out to be plans without standards. As an anachronism it, too, ought to pass. But doctrines are not organisms. They die only in combat over the minds of men, and no doctrine yet exists capable of doing the job. All the popular alternatives are so very irrelevant, helping to explain the longevity of interest-group liberalism. Barry Goldwater most recently proved the irrelevance of one. The *embourgeoisement* of American unions suggests the irrelevance of others.

The Departments of Agriculture, Commerce, and Labor provide illustrations, but hardly exhaust illustrations, of such impotence. Here clearly one sees how liberalism has become a doctrine whose means are its ends, whose combatants are its clientele, whose standards are not even those of the mob but worse, are those the bargainers can fashion to fit the bargain. Delegation of power has become alienation of public domain—the gift of sovereignty to private satrapies.

The political barriers to withdrawal of delegation are high enough. But liberalism reinforces these through the rhetoric of justification and often even permanent legal reinforcement: Public corporations—justified, oddly, as efficient planning instruments—permanently alienate rights of central coordination to the directors and to those who own the corporation bonds. Or, as Walter Adams finds, the "most pervasive method . . . for alienating public domain is the certificate of convenience and necessity, or some variation thereof in the form of an exclusive franchise, license or permit. . . . [G]overnment has become increasingly careless and subservient in issuing them. The net result is a general legalization of private monopoly. . . ."[1] While the best examples still are probably the 10 self-governing systems of agriculture policy, these are obviously only a small proportion of all the barriers the interest-group liberal ideology has erected to democratic use of government.

(3) Interest-group liberalism demoralizes government, because liberal governments cannot achieve justice. The question of justice has engaged the best minds for almost as long as there have been notions of state and politics, certainly ever since Plato defined the ideal as one in which republic and justice were synonymous. And since that time philosophers have been unable to agree on what justice is. But outside the ideal, in the realms of actual government and citizenship, the problem is much simpler. We do not have to define justice at all in order to weight and assess justice in government, because in the case of liberal policies we are prevented by what the law would call a "jurisdictional fact." In the famous jurisdictional case of *Marbury v. Madison* Chief Justice Marshall held that even if all the Justices hated President Jefferson for refusing to accept Marbury and the other "midnight judges" appointed by Adams, there was nothing they could do. They had no authority to judge President Jefferson's action one way or another because the Supreme Court did not possess such jurisdiction over the President. In much the same way, there is something about liberalism that prevents us from raising the question of justice at all, no matter what definition of justice is used.

Liberal governments cannot achieve justice because their policies lack the *sine qua non* of justice—that quality without which a consideration of justice cannot even be initiated. Considerations of the justice in or achieved by an action cannot be made unless a deliberate and conscious attempt was made by the actor to derive his action from a general rule or moral principle governing such a class of acts. One can speak personally of good rules and bad rules, but a homily or a sentiment, like liberal legislation, is not a rule at all. The best rule is one which is relevant to the decision or action in question and is general in the sense that those involved with it have no direct control over its operation. A general rule is, hence, *a priori*. Any governing regime that makes a virtue of avoiding such rules puts itself totally outside the context of justice.

Take the homely example of the bull and the china shop. Suppose it was an op art shop and that we consider op worthy only of the junk pile. That being the case, the bull did us a great service, the more so because it was something we always dreamed of doing but were prevented by law from entering and breaking. But however much we may be pleased, we cannot judge the act. We can only like or dislike the consequences. The consequences are haphazard; the bull cannot have intended them. The act was a thoughtless, animal act which bears absolutely no relation to any aesthetic principle. We don't judge the bull. We only celebrate our good fortune. Without the general rule, the bull can reenact his scenes of creative destruction daily and still not be capable of achieving, in this case, aesthetic justice. The whole idea of justice is absurd.

The general rule ought to be a legislative rule because the United States espouses the ideal of representative democracy. However, that is merely an extrinsic feature of the rule.[2] All that counts is the character of the rule itself. Without the rule we can only like or dislike the consequences of the governmental action. In the question of whether justice is achieved, a government without good rules, and without acts carefully derived therefrom, is merely a big bull in an immense china shop.

(4) Finally, interest-group liberalism corrupts democratic government in the degree to which it weakens the capacity of governments to live by democratic formalisms. Liberalism weakens democratic institutions by opposing formal procedure with informal bargaining. Liberalism derogates from democracy by derogating from all formality in favor of informality. Formalism is constraining; playing it "by the book" is a role often unpopular in American war films and sports films precisely because it can dramatize personal rigidity and the plight of the individual in collective situations. Because of the impersonality of formal procedures, there is inevitably a separation in the real world between the forms and the realities, and this kind of separation gives rise to cynicism, for informality means that some will escape their collective fate better than others. There has as a consequence always been a certain amount of cynicism toward public objects in the United States, and this may be to the good, since a little cynicism is the father of healthy sophistication. However, when the informal is elevated to a positive virtue, and hard-won access becomes a share of official authority, cynicism becomes distrust. It ends in reluctance to submit one's fate to the governmental process under any condition,

as is the case in the United States in the mid-1960's.

Public officials more and more frequently find their fates paradoxical and their treatment at the hands of the public fickle and unjust when in fact they are only reaping the results of their own behavior, including their direct and informal treatment of the public and the institutions through which they serve the public. The more government operates by the spreading of access, the more public order seems to suffer. The more public men pursue their constituencies, the more they seem to find their constituencies alienated. Liberalism has promoted concentration of democratic authority but deconcentration of democratic power. Liberalism has opposed privilege in policy formulation only to foster it, quite systematically, in the implementation of policy. Liberalism has consistently failed to recognize, in short, that in a democracy forms are important. In a medieval monarchy all formalisms were at court. Democracy proves, for better or worse, that the masses like that sort of thing too.

Another homely parable may help. In the good old days, everyone in the big city knew that traffic tickets could be fixed. Not everyone could get his ticket fixed, but nonetheless a man who honestly paid his ticket suffered in some degree a dual loss: his money, and his self-esteem for having so little access. Cynicism was widespread, violations were many, but perhaps it did not matter, for there were so few automobiles. Suppose, however, that as the automobile population increased a certain city faced a traffic crisis and the system of ticket fixing came into ill repute. Suppose a mayor, victorious on the Traffic Ticket, decided that, rather than eliminate fixing by universalizing enforcement, he would instead reform the system by universalizing the privileges of ticket fixing. One can imagine how the system would work.

One can imagine that some sense of equality would prevail, because everyone could be made almost equally free to bargain with the ticket administrators. But one would find it difficult to imagine how this would make the total city government more legitimate. Meanwhile, the purpose of the ticket would soon have been destroyed.

Traffic regulation, fortunately, was not so reformed. But many other government activities were. The operative principles of interest-group liberalism possess the mentality of a world of universalized ticket fixing: Destroy privilege by universalizing it. Reduce conflict by yielding to it. Redistribute power by the maxim of each according to his claim. Reserve an official place for every major structure of power. Achieve order by worshiping the processes (as distinguished from the forms and the procedures) by which order is presumed to be established.

If these operative principles will achieve equilibrium—and such is far from proven[3]—that is all they will achieve. Democracy will have disappeared, because all of these maxims are founded upon profound lack of confidence in democracy. Democracy fails when it lacks confidence in its own authority.

Democratic forms were supposed to precede and accompany the formulation of policies so that policies could be implemented authoritatively and firmly. Democracy is indeed a form of absolutism, but ours was fairly well contrived to be an absolutist government under the strong control of consent-building prior to taking authoritative action in law. Interest-group liberalism fights the absolutism of democracy but succeeds only in taking away its authoritativeness. Whether it is called "creative federalism" by President Johnson, "cooperation" by the farmers, "local autonomy" by the Republicans, or "participatory democracy" by the New Left, the interest-group liberal effort does not create democratic power but rather negates it.

SUMMATION II: THREE COUNTS AGAINST THE INTELLECTUAL COMPONENT

It ought to be clear from many sources that liberal leaders operate out of a sincere conviction that what they do constitutes an effort to respond to the stress of their times in ways best calculated to further the public interest. If the results are contrary to their hopes, it is because their general theory of cause and effect must be wrong. Everyone operates according to some theory, or frame of reference, or paradigm—some generalized map that directs logic and conclusions, given certain facts. The influence of one's paradigm over one's decisions is enormous. It helps define what is important among the multitudes of events (i.e., it "sets one's attention"). And it literally programs one toward certain kinds of conclusions. Men are unpredictable if they do not fully understand their own theory, and no theory is explicit enough on all issues to provide predictable guidance. But no thinking man operates without one. Pragmatism is merely an appeal to let theory remain implicit. The truth lies in Lord Keynes's famous aphorism. . . . History influences one's choice of paradigm. But one's paradigm influences what aspects of history will be most influential—unless everything is already locked in a predetermined secular trend.

Interest-group liberals have the pluralist paradigm in common, and its influence on liberal policy and liberal methods of organization has obviously been very large and very consistent. Discrediting the pluralist component of interest-group liberalism has been one of the central purposes of this volume, in the hopes that a change of theory can have some small impact on history. Nothing seems to be more evident than the observation that present theory is inappropriate for this epoch. Among the many charges made against pluralism, the following three seem relevant to a final effort at discrediting the entire theoretical apparatus.

(1) The pluralist component has badly served interest-group liberalism by propagating and perpetuating the faith that a system built primarily upon groups and bargaining is perfectly self-corrective. This is based upon assumptions which are clearly not often, if ever, fulfilled— assumptions that groups always have other groups to confront them, that "overlapping memberships" will both insure competition and keep competition from becoming too intense, that "membership in potential groups" or "consensus" about the "rules of the game" are natural and inevitable, scientifically verifiable phenomena that channel competition naturally toward a public interest. It is also based on an impossible assumption that when competition does take place it yields ideal results. As has already been observed, this is as absurd as a similar assumption of laissez-faire economists about the ideal results of economic competition. One of the major Keynesian criticisms of market theory is that even if pure competition among factors of supply and demand did yield an equilibrium, the equilibrium could be at something far less than the ideal of full employment. Pure pluralist competition, similarly, might produce political equilibrium, but the experience of recent years shows that it occurs at something far below an acceptable level of legitimacy and at a price too large to pay—exclusion of Negroes from most of the benefits of society.

(2) Pluralist theory is outmoded and unrealistic in still another way comparable to the rise and decline of laissez-faire economics. Pluralism has failed to grapple with the problem of oligopoly or imperfect competition as it expresses itself in the political system. When a program is set up in a specialized agency, the number of organized interest groups surrounding it tends to be reduced. Generally it tends to be reduced precisely to those groups and factions to whom the specialization is most salient. That in turn tends to reduce the situation from one of potential competition to potential oligopoly. That is to say, one can observe numerous groups in some kind of competition for agency favors. But competition tends to last only until each group learns the goals of the few other groups. Each adjusts to the others. Real confrontation leads to net loss for all rather than gain for any. Rather than countervailing power there will more than likely be accommodating power.

Galbraith has assumed that each oligopoly will be checked by an oligopsony— an interest from the opposite side of the market rather than a competitor for a share in the same market. This notion of countervailing power—competition between big labor and big industry, big buyers against big sellers, etc.—was to explain economic and political phenomena. But not only is this new kind of confrontation an unfounded assumption. It was to be created by public policy: ". . . the support of countervailing power has become in modern times perhaps the major peacetime function of the Federal government."[4] Countervailing power, in old or new form, can hardly be much of a theory of the way the industrial state naturally works if it requires central government support. And it hardly warrants government support if its consequences, as already proposed, do not produce the felicitous results claimed for them.

(3) Finally, the pluralist paradigm depends upon an idealized and almost totally miscast conception of *the group*. Laissez-faire economics may have idealized the firm and the economic man but never to the degree to which the pluralist thinkers today sentimentalize the group, the group member, and the interests. Note the contrast between the traditional American notion of the group and the modern pluralist definition. Madison in Federalist 10 defined the group ("faction") as "a number of citizens, whether

amounting to a majority or minority of the whole, who are united and actuated by some common impulse of passion, or of interest, *adverse to the right of other citizens, or to the permanent and aggregate interests of the community.*" (Emphasis added.) David Truman uses Madison's definition but cuts the quotation just before the emphasized part.[5] In such a manner pluralist theory became the complete handmaiden of interest-group liberalism, in a sense much more than laissez-faire economics was ever a handmaiden to big capitalism. To the Madisonian, and also to the early twentieth-century progressive, groups were necessary evils much in need of regulation. To the modern pluralist, groups are good; they require accommodation. Immediately following his definition in Federalist 10, Madison went on to say: "The regulation of these various interfering interests forms the principal task of modern legislation. . . ." This is a far cry from Galbraith's "support of countervailing power," or Schlesinger's "hope of harnessing government, business and labor in a rational partnership . . .," or the sheer sentimentality behind the notion of "maximum feasible participation," and "group representation in the interior processes of. . . ."

A revived feeling of distrust toward interests and groups would not destroy pluralist theory but would only prevent its remaining a servant of a completely outmoded system of public endeavor. Once sentimentality toward the group is destroyed, it will be possible to see how group interactions might fall short of creating an ideal equilibrium. Such distrust of prevailing theory might then lead to discomfort with the jurisprudence of delegation of power, for it too rests mightily upon an idealized view of how groups make law today. In such a manner the theoretical foundations of interest-group liberalism can be discredited. Some progress will then have been made toward restoration of an independent and legitimate government in the United States.

Until that occurs, liberalism will continue to be the enemy rather than the friend of democracy.

THE ENDS OF JURIDICAL DEMOCRACY: PROPOSALS FOR RADICAL REFORM

These proposals are written for the time when men of influence come to see that the Consensus of 1937 is finished. At the moment they continue to search for distant sociological causes of American distress. But ultimately they must come to see that they and their belief system constitute the pathology. When this is fully realized, all leaders—the ins as well as the outs—will begin to search for new goals rather than merely to express dissatisfactions. This basic shift of attitudes will be fruitless unless it yields fundamental institutional change. To accomplish that they will need a new paradigm. And, since a good cry is half the battle, I offer Juridical Democracy as the candidate. The following proposals provide the platform for such a movement. As is true of all radical platforms, each proposal is deceptively simple, each would be enormously effective, each would be politically extremely difficult to accomplish. However, as is also true of radicalism in America, once the first step is taken, the rest suddenly seems no longer radical.

Restoring Rule of Law
The first and most important step would be the easiest to accomplish but would probably excite the strongest opposition and fear if anyone ever took it seriously. This is mere revival of the still valid but universally disregarded *Schechter* rule. To accommodate interest-group liberal programs the Supreme Court created a basic line of jurisprudence by giving official and complete faith and credit to all expressions formally passed along by the legislature. The Court's rule must once again become one of declaring

invalid and unconstitutional any delegation of power to an administrative agency
that is not accompanied by clear standards
of implementation.

Restoration of the *Schechter* rule
would be dramatic because it would
mean return to the practice of occasional
Supreme Court invalidation of congressional acts. Nothing is more dramatic
than the confrontation of these two jeal-
ous Branches, the more so due to its
infrequent occurrence in recent years.
But there is no reason to fear judicial
usurpation. Under present conditions,
when Congress delegates without a shred
of guidance, the courts usually end up
rewriting many of the statutes in the
course of "construction." Since the Court's
present procedure is always to try to find
an acceptable meaning of a statute in
order to avoid invalidating it, the Court
is legislating constantly. A blanket invalidation under the *Schechter* rule is a Court
order for Congress to do its own work.
Therefore the rule of law is a restraint
upon rather than an expansion of the
judicial function.

There is also no reason to fear reduction of government power as a result of
serious application of the Schechter rule.
Fortunately, interest-group liberals have
less to fear from the rule-of-law requirement than they might have thought.
Rather than study the problem they have
simply allowed their defenses against rule
of law to be defined by the fact that it has
been the nineteenth-century liberals who
have championed its cause.[6] But the
laissez-faire hope that such a requirement
would help keep government small is
based on a misunderstanding of the principle or upon some definition of it quite
different from the one employed all
through this volume. Historically, rule of
law, especially statute law, is the essence of
positive government. A bureaucracy in
the service of a strong and clear statute is
more effective than ever. Granted, the
rule-of-law requirement is likely to make
more difficult the framing and passage of

some policies. But why should any program be acceptable if the partisans cannot
fairly clearly state purpose and means? We
ask such justification even of children. It
may also be true that requirement of rule
of law will make government response to
demands a bit slower and government
implementation of goals less efficient.
Good statistical analysis of the record
would probably not support such a
hypothesis; but even if the hypothesis
were fully confirmed, one must still ask,
What good is all our prosperity if we
cannot buy a little more law with it?

Rule of Law by
Administrative Formality

The Schechter rule, even forcefully
applied, could not eliminate all vagueness in legislative delegation of power.
Ignorance of changing social conditions
is important, although it is a much over-
used congressional alibi for malfeasance
in legislative drafting. It is also true that
social pressure for some kind of quick
action prevents a full search for a proper
rule in a statute once in a great while.
But fortunately reform can be realistic,
because there is a perfectly acceptable
way to deal with the slippage within the
dictates of rule by law. This is the simple
requirement for early and frequent
administrative rule-making.[7]

Most of the administrative rhetoric
in recent years espouses the interest-group
liberal ideal of administration by favoring
the norm of flexibility and the ideal that
every decision can be bargained. Pluralism
applied to administration usually takes the
practical form of an attempt to deal with
each case "on its merits." But the ideal
of case-by-case adjudication is in most
instances a myth. Few persons affected
by a decision have an opportunity to be
heard. And each agency, regulatory or
non-regulatory, disposes of the largest
proportion of its cases without any
procedure at all, least of all a formal
adjudicatory process. In practice, agencies
end up with the worst of case-by-case

adjudication *and* of rule-making. They try to work without rules in order to live with the loose legislative mandate. They then treat their cases in practice as though they were operating under a rule. For example, most of the applications to the Civil Aeronautics Board are disposed of without hearings, even where applicants are entitled to them.[8] The so-called flexibility of a case approach is an unconvincing rationalization. Bargaining is involved, but it is reserved for leaders in the field who will not accept mere processing.

In contrast, treatment of the same cases by a real administrative rule has most of the advantage claimed for the case-by-case approach, yet possesses few of the disadvantages. Davis observes that rule-making is especially superior to formal adjudication or informal bargaining when more than a handful of parties will be affected. A rule can be general and yet gain clarity through examples drawn up with known cases in mind. It was precisely this ability to perceive the public policy implications in complex phenomena that underlies reliance on expert agencies. The rule can be further refined by taking large numbers of potential cases into account. And even with this specificity the rule can become a known factor in every client's everyday life. In contrast, there is an implicit rule in every bargained or adjudicated case, but it cannot be known to the bargainer until he knows the outcome, and its later application must be deciphered by lawyers representing potential cases.

All these are important advantages to clients. But most important of all are the improvements rule-making would bring to administration and to legislative-administrative relationships. First, administrators should want to make rules deliberately focusing broad delegations of power, because broad delegations are a menace to formal organization and to the ideal of the Neutral Civil Servant. The pluralistic principle impairs the rational ordering of tasks and the rou-

tinization of routines. Broad discretion makes a politician out of a bureaucrat. Many bureaucrats are good politicians, but when such skills and talents become the prime criterion of appointment and promotion they tend to negate the original *raison d'être* and justification of administrative independence—expertise.

Rule-making would improve the administrative process still further by making administrative power more responsible as well as more efficient. When an agency formulates a rule, it is indeed formulating legislation. But it is not usurping legislative power this way any more than the Supreme Court would be usurping power if it went back to declaring bad delegations unconstitutional. When an agency formulates a rule it is merely carrying out what Congress delegated to it and what was expected of all such agencies by the Administrative Procedure Act passed by Congress.[9] Moreover, formulation of a rule will most likely lead the agency back to Congress more frequently. This is part of what [is] referred to as "bargaining on the rule". . . . In contrast . . . "bargaining on the decision" is more likely to keep the political process down on the line far away from political responsibility. Thus it seems clear that avoidance of rule-making is more of a usurpation than rule-making. When there are good administrative rules, legislative evaluation of whole programs becomes possible; Congress need no longer depend wholly upon piecemeal committee oversight and narrow appropriations subcommittee scrutiny. Still further administrative responsibility is secured by the fact that rule-making early in the life of a statute brings on some judicial evaluation before the agency is too committed to its own existence or before some flaw in the agency's makeup becomes too demoralizing to the clientele.

In a sense, Woodrow Wilson was correct when he argued in 1886 for centralized administration as a necessity for modern democracy. He was also probably correct in observing that large delegations of power end up more responsibly administered than small delegations. But his recommendations must be understood in the proper context. Broad delegation to Wilson must have meant well-guided delegation. Otherwise centralization and responsibility would be impossible; for broad, unguided delegation means the very opposite of centralization. On the other hand, centralization does not have to mean stern, hierarchical subordination, as in the classic Prussian system. Administrative centralization and responsibility can be achieved by centralization around rules: *Lesser authority can be subject to higher authority through criteria relevant to the programs themselves.*

An illustration from the judicial process may serve better than abstract elaboration of the point. Is a leading opinion by the Supreme Court a centralizing or a decentralizing force in judicial administration? Obviously it is both, in the best sense of both terms. A strong and clear ruling is an act of centralization by the Supreme Court. Yet at the same time it leads to significant decentralization of caseload and a good deal of self-administration by lower courts and counsel. To look at it in a slightly different way, an area with good leading opinions is an area of "easy law" in which there are few appeals to the top; nonetheless the area is centralized too, in the sense that each decision in each lower judicial unit becomes more consistent with all other comparable decisions, because the clear rule is a good criterion, departures from which are easily detectable by higher courts and clients. In contrast, the Supreme Court can inundate itself in areas of "hard law" where it cannot or will not enunciate a leading opinion expressing good governing rules. In such an area there is even greater centralization, but in the worse sense of the word because

responsibility can be maintained only through regular, bureaucratic supervision (in judicial administration this takes the form of appeals and certiorari).

In 1958 Professor Davis concluded his analysis of delegated legislation with the widely-quoted observation that the typical statute was telling the agency. "Here is the problem; deal with it." Seven years later, following a period of unprecedented government expansion, Davis went further: "Sometimes [the statute] has not even said 'Here is the problem.' It does less than that. It says, instead: 'We the Congress don't know what the problems are; find them and deal with them.'"[10] To Davis, the period between 1958 and 1965 had "passed without a significant development in the law of delegation."[11] This is a strong sign of retrogressive tendencies. But they can be reversed when and as the need for reversal has been perceived. The advantages to a more formal and rule-bound administrative process ought to be obvious to anyone not blinded by an ideology framed for a period when perhaps we could not afford legality. But now, when legality and efficiency tend to go together, it would be foolish not to grasp them.

The Senior Civil Service Versus the Ombudsman

Efforts to make a virtue of loose administration are known by many labels and are all doomed to dismal failure. At this point further critical commentary is hardly necessary on the administrative or political implications of such notions as interest representation, participatory democracy, community action, and the like. However, there is one other, a technique that at first seems appealingly different as a means of making administration more responsible and legitimate while yet allowing it to remain unbound by rules. This is the Ombudsman.[12] This device was in use for a century in its home country, Sweden, before its recent flush of popularity in the United States and elsewhere. The Ombudsman is a man and an office whose responsibility has generally been to respond to complaints of maladministration.

At first glance the Ombudsman may appear as the knight in shining armor, but that is unfortunately not at all the case. The idea of the Ombudsman has appealed to mayors and reformers in many American cities and to many serious observers of American national problems, as well as to thoughtful dissidents in the U.S. and many other countries, because there is a widespread expectation that government power is inevitably maladministered. But the Ombudsman would improve little and would in fact interfere with substantial progress during the course of the experiment. First, to handle the complaint load in a single American city today would require an office of many hundreds of assistants, clerks, and perhaps even a few assistant Ombudsmen.[13] Its size would vitiate its purpose. We would soon have to have an auxiliary Ombudsman just to handle complaints against the Ombudsman. Second, the Ombudsman would relieve the administrative process precisely where pressure is needed to expose problems that need central agency attention. Third, the Ombudsman would be a redundancy. He would perform functions that would duplicate congressional committees, courts, political parties. Fourth, and most important, he would not do the one thing the system really needs having done: He would not give agencies any more law or justification. Our problems go beyond the Ombudsman. We must reinstate a legitimate regime before we again concern ourselves with the details of equity.

A far more meaningful administrative reform in the United States would be the fostering of a truly independent and integrated administrative class—a Senior Civil Service. A profession of public administration, as distinct from a career within a specific agency, is vital to

the proper centralization of a democratic administrative process. The independent Senior Civil Servant can be designed for weak loyalty to any one agency. He comes closer to the intellectual who prefers to generalize, yet he is an activist. The makings of a Senior Civil Service lie already within the grasp of the Civil Service Commission if it will but perceive the opportunity in its interrelated Bureau of Executive Manpower, its Executive Assignment System and its Executive Seminar Centers. Through these units, recruitment of such a class out of the ranks, rather than through an Oxford or an Ecole Nationale d'Administration, would provide a balance of legal and technological considerations. If such a class were combined with court-imposed, Congress-imposed, and administratively-imposed standards of law, the administrative process would inevitably be more centralized without any loss of real pluralism in the larger system. Centralizing through law and formalizing through administrative recruitment would only centralize the places where groups must seek access. This would serve all the better to insure that conflicting groups be thrown together in public competition rather than kept apart within the almost secret confines of their respective programs.

If adopted, all of the foregoing proposals would definitely increase formalism, and yet they would also contribute to real competition. They would help restore emphasis upon the competition component rather than the group component of the pluralist paradigm. Inevitably this increases the frequency of congressional as well as presidential opportunities to enter the act. The price is a certain additional instability and perhaps in the short run a bit less efficiency. But due process and legitimacy are after all system values of some importance. Moreover, this type of instability was precisely what was supposed to make a pluralistic system work. It is distressing how many 1930's left-wing liberals become 1960's interest-group liberals out of a concern for instability.

Restore Regional Government: How to See Virtue in the States

Part of the reform program bears some resemblance to an old-line constitutional argument, for restoration of the rule of law provides a basis for establishing some practical limitations on the scope of Federal power. If an applicable and understandable set of standards must accompany every Federal program, Federal power could not extend to those objects for which no general rules are either practicable or desirable. Thus, where regional or local variation is desired, the Federal government is not even the appropriate unit. Unconditional rebates would be infinitely preferable. When regional variation is not desirable it is usually because some problem uniformly distributed across the country has been identified and is well known—as for example civil rights, military service, tax liability, access to the airwaves, obligations of contracts, free speech and petition—in which case there is no barrier, except fear, to prevent enactment of statutes in which clear and effective standards can accompany delegations of vast public power.

It matters little whether the delegation is to a Federal agency or to a State government, so long as standards flow with delegations. And in many, if not most, of our contemporary social problems State government would be superior to Federal units. This argument is not based on mere antiquarian admiration of federalism or fear of federal domination. It is based on an appreciation of the practical advantages of differentiation of functions. State governments have been systematically weakened by Home Rule, by Federal absorption of tax base, by the poor reputation given them by the abuses of southern State governments, and by the expansion of direct Federal-local relations. Now that cities have proven

that they cannot cope with urban problems; even with Federal help, we have, in any case, no other place but the States to turn to. But relying on the State need not be thought of as an act of desperation. As already argued, the State possesses all the powers of its cities plus the advantage of containing most of the metropolitan realities that are beyond the reach of cities.

The proposition that the State may be the only governmental unit capable of coping with contemporary problems can be better appreciated by French and British scholars and planners, who feel seriously weakened by not having an established unit of government at a regional level. Perhaps we have held on to our old model long enough for it to appear suddenly as the latest fashion. If so, it provides the further benefit, without extra charge, of restoring the practice of approaching persons through their citizenship, of defining persons according to their rights and obligations rather than according to their location in a group, a class, or a race.

Fiscal Policy as an Instrument of Control: Toward an Expansion

Limiting Federal power to programs for which it can provide acceptable standards of law is a limitation that could turn the Federal government toward far greater use of its fiscal and monetary techniques. (For simplicity, I shall refer to the category as fiscal.) This would be a very good reform in itself. Manipulating the entire system in order to influence conduct may sound insidious at first glance. The citizen may not know he is being manipulated. He may fear manipulation as he fears subliminal advertising. But that is a mistaken notion. Most fiscal techniques are very noticeable at the time of their adoption and tend only afterwards to recede into the subliminal. That, in fact, is the most outstanding advantage of the typical fiscal techniques. They are very noticeable in the threat but, once installed, tend to

Table 16.1 Legislative Creativity of Congress on Subsidy Bills and Fiscal Bills*

	(1) Average No. of Amendments Proposed Per Bill	(2) % Passed	(3) % Significant Amendments Passed Over Objections of Sponsoring Committee	(4) Scale Score Summary of 8 Attributes of Amendments	
				House	Senate
Subsidy and Porkbarrel Bills (N = 22)	5.8	41.8	0	1.09	2.12
Fiscal and Redistributive Bills (N = 25)	9.1	61	24	1.81	4.50

*SOURCES: L. John Roos (Unpublished Master's thesis, University of Chicago, 1968); and my forthcoming *Arenas of Power*. The bills included: (1) all bills in 87th Congress, 1st Session, that received roll call votes in House and Senate, and (2) 13 major bills since 1948 on which major case studies were published. Mr. Roos worked out an ingenious scaling device based upon 8 possible amending actions on a bill. Bills were then scaled along these 8 attributes, which included Columns 1, 2, and 3 on the table plus 5 others. For Column 4, Coefficients of Reproducibility averaged over 95, indicating excellent scales. The scores on Column 4 can be interpreted as follows: The higher the score the easier it was for the parliamentary body of Congress (the floor) to take some legislative functions back from its Committees. In other words, only on distributive bills can it truly be said that "congressional government is committee government." For a full discussion of the categories, see "American Business," Thesdore Lowi, *World Politics* 16 (July 1964), 677–715.

become part of a person's *modus operandi.* Fiscal techniques, in sum, tend to be administered according to clear general rules about which a person can learn and to which he can adjust. They tend to affect large aggregates of persons. Fiscal techniques cut across organized groups. It is difficult to imagine adoption of a major fiscal activity that is not the occasion of considerable debate and publicity. These actions range from an announced deliberate budget deficit to a decision to cut taxes at an unusual time, from the mere administrative decision to change slightly the Federal Reserve discount rate to a decision to alter the price of gold (devaluation), from decisions to manipulate aggregates of industry (investment tax credit) to decisions to redistribute regional wealth (block grant-in-aid criteria).

Fiscal policies immediately possess broad and noticeable social significance.

They are once or twice removed from constituencies at the level of formulation, yet they engage the best of constituency behavior in comparison to subsidy policies. Although at first glance subsidy and porkbarrel programs may appear closer to the public and the people, it is well known that legislative action on subsidy policies is contained almost completely inside the committee system, insulated from the parliamentary level of Congress as well as from the President.[14] Fiscal policies are a great deal more public. Using amending activity as a measure of open parliamentary creativity vis-à-vis committee control, note on the Table the dramatic contrast between action on subsidy and porkbarrel bills as compared to fiscal and other "redistributive bills." There is no question that political processes are far more exposed to public view on the latter than on the former.

Most of the implementation of fiscal policy is purely executive, but that too accords with the classic democratic formalisms.[15] Most fiscal policy implementation is in fact controlled at the very highest reaches of the executive—the President acting in concert with the Budget Director and Council of Economic Advisers, the Secretary of the Treasury, the top echelons of the Federal Reserve System. This too is a tremendously attractive feature of fiscal policy—a model of responsibility in comparison both to subsidy programs and to regulatory programs. It is all the more attractive because these decisions, unlike regulatory decisions, can be translated into rates through which very small changes can bring about large changes in behavior. As a result, fiscal policy is really the only type of policy that can achieve a high degree of rationality through the incremental approach so dear to pluralists.

Fiscal policy is not a panacea, for only rarely is a fiscal technique appropriate as a direct replacement for a subsidy or a regulatory policy. Each may be desirable or undesirable on its own terms, the criteria being need, result, and, above all, the accompaniment of a good general rule.[16] A negative income tax, for example, might well become a good addition to or replacement for Old Welfare, but that involves substitution of one fiscal technique for another. Meanwhile, neither the negative income tax, Old Welfare, or New Welfare can adequately fight civil wrongs. For that, only a stiff regulatory statute with inviolable standards and strong enforcement will work. However, fiscal policy, although not a panacea, is an area where federal expansion is most desirable.

A Tenure-of-Statutes Act

The final proposal for reform is for a statute setting a Jeffersonian limit of from five to ten years on the life of every organic act. As the end of its tenure

approaches, an agency is likely to find its established relations with its clientele beginning to shake from exposure, new awareness, and competition. This may ultimately be the only effective way to get substantive evaluation of a program and an agency. There is a myth that programs are given evaluation at least once a year through a normal appropriations process that extends through the Executive Office of the President to the two appropriations committees of Congress and their specialized subcommittees. However, these yearly evaluations get at only the marginal and incremental aspects of most programs. Substantive questions are most often treated as off limits; while individual members of Congress often ask substantive questions, they are likely to be disregarded or ruled out of order. Here indeed is a good illustration of the distinction between functional and substantive accountability. The very cost-consciousness and care for detail that makes appropriations review functionally rational is the source of its weakness as a means of achieving any substantive conclusions. Those who prefer formulation and evaluation of laws by democratic institutions rather than by courts should strongly favor statutory tenure.

THE FUTURE AS JURIDICAL DEMOCRACY

When this inquiry was undertaken several years ago the problem of interest-group liberalism seemed limited to a few areas, and the chances for changing the practices of politicians and beliefs of intellectuals regarding those areas seemed slim. Further familiarity revealed that a far wider range of government had been affected by interest-group liberalism but that nevertheless it had become possible to be optimistic about the prospects for reform.

The interest-group liberal phenomenon no longer appeared limited after the discovery that pluralistic government depended upon policy without law and that underlying pluralist political theory provided reasoning for the necessity and the justification of policy without law. This meant that mere group representation was not the only manifestation of the new liberal state. It could often be merely a byproduct of a far broader phenomenon. This also meant that the ideology of interest-group liberalism was not actually confined to a few intellectuals who were influencing the verbalisms of a few Democratic Party politicians. It meant, rather, that this ideology had long since escaped its earlier confines and had become the new public philosophy. While fortunately it was not applied with 100 per cent consistency to all actions of government, it is nevertheless clear that interest-group liberalism had become the public philosophy, that it clearly dominated all other ideologies. It had its controlling establishments in both major political parties. It had its own jurisprudence. The Supreme Court was seeing to its enforcement with almost total consistency.

At this advanced stage in the failure of interest-group liberalism to cope with the problems of our time, it is possible nevertheless to be optimistic, because interest-group liberalism combines all of the worst traits of pluralist society and is therefore weak enough to be subject to radical reform and even, perhaps, complete replacement as public philosophy. Interest-group liberalism arose out of weakness. It was the New Deal rationalized. It was making the best of one of our worst periods of history by buying time and support with sovereignty. Big rationalizations are durable, and in the 1960's interest-group values are applied almost habitually even in periods of national strength. Yet one can be optimistic if the practical alternative, juridical democracy, can be shown to combine all the best traits of the pluralist society:

(1) Interest-group liberalism cannot plan. Juridical democracy can. Law is a plan. Positive law guides and moves in known ways. Its flexibility is not a flabby bargain but its capacity to be changed in known ways. That is also the basis of the superior rationality and administrative efficiency of juridical democracy.

(2) Interest-group liberalism cannot achieve justice. Juridical democracy can, because its actions can be judged. Requirement of a rule of law leads to a justice-oriented politics just as automatically as the requirement of unguided delegation leads to a pluralistic, bargain-oriented politics. The juridical approach to politics produces increments of justice just as surely as the interest-group liberal approach produces increments of equilibrium. And yet, while pluralism eliminates justice from all consideration, the juridical approach does not eliminate pluralist patterns or principles. The juridical approach does not dictate a particular definition of justice, of virtue, or of the good life. It is not popular totalitarianism in disguise. The juridical principle can convert a consumer economy into a just society without altering in any way the virtue of consumption or the freedom to consume. It does not reduce the virtue of political competition but only makes access to some areas a bit more difficult to acquire.

(3) Interest-group liberalism weakens democratic forms. Juridical democracy strengthens them. Rule of law may have become unpopular to contemporary liberals because of a widespread idea that it operates as a "check against democracy." The truth lies almost altogether the other way. The decline of Congress, supposedly the popular branch, began with the expansion of delegation of power. The emergence of control by congressional committee absolutely parallels those developments. Congress is at its classic best when a proposed bill embodies a good rule. Good recent cases include Landrum-Griffin, the 1962 Trade Act, Medicare, and Civil Rights. Taking 10 years to pass a good civil rights law is no reflection on

Congress as a parliamentary body but only upon the frailty of the urban-liberal forces in the country until 1964. . . . The role of the Supreme Court is instructive here. Congress did not become a real parliament on civil rights until it had a rule of law to debate, *and that was a rule forced upon it by the Supreme Court's exercise of its power to declare legislative acts unconstitutional.* Rule of law is no check against democratic forms. The one will not endure without the other.

(4) Interest-group liberalism also weakens democratic power. Juridical democracy strengthens it. Here too its reputation as a check against government contributed to the contemporary unpopularity of the juridical principle. But again, most of the evidence lies the other way. No government is more powerful than one whose agencies have good laws to implement. Much is spoken and written of the problem of "bureaucratic power" and how to keep it under presidential control or how to be sure it is effective. But nothing serves better to direct bureaucracy than issuing it orders along with powers. One can hardly avoid being impressed with how effective a clear statute or a clear presidential order is. Students of Congress are struck by how effective a hearing or threatened investigation can be. Such orders and inquiries are least effective upon agencies that traditionally operate in the absence of rules of law—for example, the Corps of Engineers, the Armed Services, the public works and other subsidizing agencies. A grant to an agency of powers without rules or standards leads to the bargaining, the unanticipated commitments, and the confusions that are the essence of the illegitimate state. Juridical democracy tends to reduce the inconsistency between power and legitimacy.

(5) Finally, interest-group liberalism produces an apologetic political science. Juridical democracy produces an independent and critical political science. Interest-group liberalism's focus on

equilibrium and the paraphernalia of its establishment is apology. The focus on the group is a commitment to one of the more rigidified aspects of the social process and is, therefore, another kind of apology. Stress upon the incremental is also apology. The separation of facts from values is apology.

Is the apologetic a price required for science? Most assuredly the price need not have been paid. There is no denying that modern pluralistic political science brought science to politics. And that is a good thing. But it was pluralism and not science that required the absolute separation of facts and values. Pluralism required the separation because it could not live with the fact that governments make actual substantive choices. In embracing facts it embraced the ever-present. In thus embracing science from this viewpoint it took rigor without relevance. Juridical democracy need be no less scientific in its tendency to work toward fusion of facts and values. All that really amounts to in practice is a fusion of political behavior, public administration, and public law. Rules of law and their consequences— rights, justice, legitimacy—are just as susceptible of scientific generalization as their behavioral equivalents—bargaining, equilibrium, and opinions.

Juridical democracy could produce a superior science of politics because it allows rigor but is no enemy of relevance. The juridical approach permits apology. It simply does not make apology obligatory. The juridical principle does not destroy the idea of equilibrium. It simply does not indoctrinate students into believing that equilibrium is the only goal of the political system. The juridical principle does not erect barriers to the scientific study of behavior. It only insists that political behavior not destroy the scientific study of other dimensions of the polity. The juridical principle treats pathology and physiology as equal sciences and insists further that neither is impaired by efforts to define a healthy body.

Quite properly, *The End of Liberalism* concludes with an academic issue, for this may turn out to be the most important issue of all—the influence of theories and the insidiousness of theories that mask outmoded ideologies. But it would be wrong to leave the impression that political science created interest-group liberalism or that political scientists will produce the future of theory beyond liberalism. The political theories that regimes and revolutions are made of are not written in academe. Theories are only systematized and propagated there. In the United States the history of political theory since the founding of the Republic has resided in the Supreme Court. The future of political theory probably lies there too. A Court that can make a regime of interest-group liberalism can also unmake it. The Court has not done so, and so it surrounds itself in suspense: Is the Republic or is it not in good hands?

NOTES

1. Walter S. Adams and Horace Gray, *Monopoly in America* (New York: Macmillan, 1955), pp. 47–48.

2. ... There is a high probability that efforts to make rules will lead to the legislature. A general rule excites continuous efforts at reformulation, which tend to turn combatants toward the levels of highest legitimacy and last appeal. Contrary to the fears of pluralists, the statement of a good rule can produce more flexibility and more competition than the avoidance of the rule. These tendencies are still further developed under proposals for reform.

3. *Cf.* David Easton, *The Political System* (New York: Alfred A. Knopf, 1953), Chapter 11; *cf.* also Easton, *A Systems Analysis of Political Life* (New York: John Wiley, 1965), Chapter 2.

4. Galbraith, *American Capitalism: The Concept of Countervailing Power* (Boston: Houghton Mifflin, 1952), p. 136. *Cf.* Melvin Anshen and Francis D. Wormuth, *Private Enterprise and Public Policy.* (New York: Macmillan, 1954), p. 18 and p. 132. For the best case of accom-

modation, see any study of the cigarette industry, especially Chapter 10 of *The Structure of American Industry,* ed. Walter Adams (New York: Macmillan, 1961).

5. David B. Truman, *The Governmental Process* (New York: Knopf, 1951), p. 4.

6. See, for example, F. A. Hayek's superb essay "The Rule of Law," in his *Road to Serfdom* (Chicago: University of Chicago Press, 1944).

7. I am grateful to Professor Kenneth C. Davis for forcefully urging this dimension upon me and for providing the best possible guidance in his *Administrative Law Treatise* (St. Paul: West Publishing Company, 1958), especially pp. 9–53 and 144 ff. of the 1965 *Supplement.* See also Henry J. Friendly, *The Federal Administrative Agencies* (Cambridge: Harvard University Press, 1962), pp. 141 ff.

8. Davis, *Supplement,* p. 151.

9. 60 Stat. 237 (1946), Sec. 2(c) and Sec. 3(a): "Every agency shall separately state and currently publish in the Federal Register ... (3) substantive rules as authorized by law and statements of general policy. ... No person shall in any manner be required to resort to organization or procedure not so published."

10. Davis, pp. 43–44 of 1965 Pocket Part.

11. *Ibid.*, p. 54.

12. For an excellent brief treatment, comparing this device to the French Conseil d'Etat, see Andrew Shonfield, *Modern Capitalism* (New York: Oxford University Press, 1965), pp. 421 ff.

13. Shonfield reports an average of only 1,000 complaints per year in all of Sweden. Andrew Shonfield, *Modern Capitalism: The Changing Balance of Public and Private Power* (London: Oxford University Press, 1965), p. 423.

14. For the best case study of this, see Arthur Maass, *Muddy Waters* (Cambridge: Harvard University Press, 1951).

15. In contrast, congressional-committee meddling in public works, procurement, natural resources, etc., is notorious, but fortunately this pattern is not universal.

16. It is my opinion that subsidy policies are inherently amoral because it is almost impossible to formulate general rules for them. The great advantage of subsidy is the very absence of moral considerations. This

makes techniques of subsidy ideal for nation-building, when co-optation may be the only important criterion until a regime is well established. In mature nations the virtue of such policies seems to disappear. But these are only opinions at this point. They will be documented in a later volume, *Arenas of Power*.

PROJECT

Lowi argues that too many groups are active in the policy-making process; they subvert the democratic process to their narrow ends. Conduct research on the $80 billion appropriations bill for Operation Iraqi Freedom, approved by Congress in 2004. Do you find evidence supporting Lowi's thesis in this bill? How so?

17

From *Demosclerosis*

JONATHAN RAUCH

In *Demosclerosis,* Jonathan Rauch identifies what he calls the "silent killer" of American government. He defines *demosclerosis* as "government's progressive loss of the ability to adapt." He attributes this phenomenon to the rise of special interests and borrows from Mancur Olson's observations of economic rationality. What is good for the individual may have tragic consequences for the community—the numerous entitlement programs, pork-barrel projects, and benefits groups are able to obtain choke the democratic process. Like Lowi, Rauch finds that change will be difficult to achieve because of the entrenched interests that pervade the political system.

QUESTIONS TO CONSIDER

1. What are the main problems associated with demosclerosis?
2. What role do groups have in contributing to demosclerosis?
3. What does Rauch say about America's moral infrastructure in 1994? How is this related to interest groups?
4. What remedies does Rauch prescribe for demosclerosis?

Another election was just over, and again Bill Clinton stepped forward to speak to the public and press. This time, however, he was President Clinton rather than Governor Clinton and he stood not on the steps of the Old State House in Little Rock but in the East Room of the White House. In November 1992 he had announced that he would retake Washington from the special interests and return it to the people. Now, two years later, he was trying to explain why the public has thrashed him and his party for failure. Actually, he argued, he had not failed; he had gotten some things done, the economy had improved, federal employment had been slightly reduced. However, there had been no reform of the political process, no reform of the health care system, no major reform of the bureaucracy, no discernible change in the way Washington worked, or didn't. In 1994 a bill containing dozens of proposals for streamlining federal agencies foundered in the Senate, which approved only a sorry remnant requiring (for instance) that twenty-four federal agencies submit annual financial statements beginning in 1997. An attempt to overhaul archaic telecommunications laws fell off the tracks; so did an attempt to reform the 1872 law governing mining on federal land; so did an attempt to reform the wildly inefficient "superfund" program for toxic-waste cleanup, which had become a public-works jobs program for lawyers. Congress boasted of having killed forty-one programs, but a phone call to the Appropriations Committee revealed that the grand total for these was less than $1.3 billion: less than a tenth of 1 percent of the budget. Routine. Reforms would be tried again later, but at the present moment that was beside the point. The point was that Washington

SOURCE: From Jonathan Rauch, afterword to *Demosclerosis: The Silent Killer of American Government*. (New York: 1994) Times Books, pp. 236–257. Reprinted with permission.

was still Washington, demosclerosis was still demosclerosis, government was disliked more than ever. And the enraged electorate had exploded a kind of partisan neutron bomb that killed only Democrats while leaving Republicans standing. The Republicans had taken over the House, the Senate, and a majority of the governorships; and the man who started out confident that a fresh leader with ambitious plans could master Washington all but admitted that Washington had mastered him instead.

He sounded chagrined, humbled, the wind knocked out of him. "I agree with much of what the electorate said yesterday," he said. "They still believe that government is more often the problem than the solution. They don't want any party to be the party of government. They don't want the presumption to be that people in Washington know what's best. They do want the government to protect their interests, to promote their values, I think, and to empower them, and then they want people to be held accountable. So I'm saying that to that extent, that message: I got it. I accept responsibility for not delivering to whatever extent it's my fault we haven't delivered."

It was hard to imagine, watching the president choke down a full supper of crow, that even his political enemies did not feel a pang of empathy for him. In any case, they would have been unwise not to feel nervous in their own right. For the plight was not just Bill Clinton's. No sooner had the ballots been counted than pundits were warning that the Republicans' breathtaking sweep revealed no deep public admiration for Republicans. Rather, they said, it showed that the public pitches this way and that in its fits of rage and frustration with government's sclerosis and malperformance. If Democrats cannot make government work, cannot cut an ever growing parasite economy down to size, then maybe Republicans can. If Republicans can't, then maybe . . . . well, maybe what, exactly?

By Election Day of 1994, the government's fever chart showed that public confidence in Washington was if anything lower than ever. Only about one in five expressed trust in Washington to do what's right always or most of the time. One poll showed almost one out of ten volunteering, unprompted, that Washington could *never* be trusted. The disillusionment was thoroughly bipartisan: Democrats were only slightly more confident in government than were Republicans. In a poll for Cable News Network and *Time* magazine, the percentage saying they had "little confidence" or "no confidence" in Washington to deal with the nation's problems was 95 percent among Republicans, 88 percent among Democrats. That was typical. True, members of each party tended to favor their own, and Democrats preferred more government activism than Republicans; but none of that affected the sad fact that whatever it was people wanted from government, they believed they were not getting it. Two-thirds of Democrats, Republicans, and independents alike all said that people like themselves had "not much" say about what government does. "I don't feel the people of this country have any control over what's going on, even if we voted in the person we wanted," a thirty-five-year-old Indiana woman told *The New York Times*. People increasingly believed that Washington was in business for itself—which, increasingly, it was. But they spoke as though Washington was in business *only* for itself, rather than brokering endlessly escalating conflicts between ever-proliferating groups—as though the people themselves had nothing to do with this. Here was the central paradox of American democracy in its throes: the public was, at one and the same time, deeply implicated and utterly alienated.

In a particularly revealing vein, pollsters for ABC News asked people what politicians should and should not do. Predictably, a heavy majority (77 percent) blamed "special interest groups" for Congress's failure to get more done; an almost equally heavy majority (63 percent) piously said that their own representative should be more interested "in doing what's best for the country" than "in doing what's best for your own congressional district where you live." No surprise. People forever demand that politicians push the special interests aside and do what's best for the country as a whole—which is what politicians forever promise to do. But generally people decline to believe that there may be a conflict between their own program or district and the national interest. Pressing on, the ABC pollsters asked again what it is that members of Congress should be doing, but this time they did not imply a conflict between parochial interests and the larger good. In effect, they asked the question the way it is asked in the voting booth, without an "either-or." ("For each item I name, please tell me if that's something your own representative in Congress should or should not be doing.") Should your representative be "trying to direct more government spending to your congressional district"? Yes! said 58 percent. Should he be "trying to bring federal projects to your district"? Yes! yes! said 73 percent. And should he be "trying to help create jobs in your district"? Yes again! Said 90 percent.

Here you have a portrait of an electorate saying "Gimme—don't subvert the national interest, mind you, but gimme." Here you have a country dominated by groups believing fervently that whatever they happen to demand is in the national interest while blaming other groups for the country's problems. Here you have a public joining and empowering such groups in ever greater numbers while bitterly resenting the results, yet not quite understanding—and indeed often actively denying—the deep connection between personal political expectations and public political pathology. Here, in short, you have a picture of a country becoming gradually ungovernable.

For a majority to despise a majority-elected government is a very worrisome thing. It implies that the electorate is coming to regard its own sovereignty as a sham and its own government as an imposition. The United States government is fast headed toward a crisis of legitimacy.

To change course means understanding and overcoming an obstacle that I didn't fully appreciate when I first wrote this book. It may be, where demosclerosis is concerned, the stubbornest obstacle of all. The mechanical problem, of course, is that the broad public never cares about eliminating any given program as much as its beneficiaries care about saving it. So, for anyone trying to get rid of any program, the fight is always uphill. But that mechanical imbalance is rooted in, and compounded by, an attitudinal imbalance: a mind-set which, if not counterbalanced, is as destructive of government as it is morally enticing. The electorate is at war with its government (and with itself) because it demands both the security of entitlement and the effectiveness of experiment. It can't have both, and the demand for the one is obliterating the very possibility of the other. Cutting entitlement programs is indispensable for budgeting, and that's important. But cutting through the entitlement mentality is much more important still, because it's indispensable for governing.

At the core of entitlement politics is this presumption: whatever benefits me (or my group) belongs to me. Programs are property. Maybe, in a pinch, I'll let you reduce my benefits; after all, we pay taxes on our property, and likewise we

may need to give back some of our benefits. But if you cut my program without my permission, that's theft. I have every reason to be outraged.

The politics of entitlement is a way of thinking, not just of behaving. And if you think about it, entitlement thinking has profound consequences in the real world, where experimentation is so important for success. In fact, the difference between the politics of entitlement and the politics of experiment could hardly be more stark. The two make war on each other. Consider:

- Entitlements imply permanence. Since programs are property, they should be seen as permanent unless someone can show that they absolutely must be gotten rid of. It's your burden to show why I should ever give up a program. Experiments, by contrast, imply transience. Experimental thinking says that each program should be continued only until something more effective or more important comes along in a rapidly changing world. Programs should be regarded as provisional. It's my burden to show why I should keep one.

- Entitlements imply that programs should be inclusive. If programs are property, surely government should spread the wealth. So every program should try to help as many worthy groups and causes as possible. Experiments, by contrast, imply that programs should be focused. You can't make a program work, or even figure out whether it works, if it's trying to do everything at once. So each program should try to take aim at a specific problem, using a clean, straightforward design and aiming at clear, focused goals. Clean, clear programs are likelier to work and easier to evaluate.

- Entitlements imply that the criterion for culling is fairness. If our programs are our property, then any scheme that takes from one should take from all, or else government is unfairly singling out someone for sacrifice. Experiments, by contrast, imply that the criterion for culling is effectiveness. If programs are experiments, then obviously the whole point of culling is to end the experiments that fail (or else they're not experiments at all). Of course the culling process will affect different people and groups differently. But that is inevitable, because it's silly to suppose that all programs and policies are equally successful or important.

I am not saying that entitlements have no place in government. One reason we have government is to offer security in an uncertain world. I am also not saying that entitlement thinking is always wrong or inappropriate. Social Security should not be overhauled twice a year in hopes of making it perfect. What must not happen, however, is for the politics of entitlement to become all-encompassing and obliterate the politics of experiment. But that is exactly what has happened.

In Washington, a standard and generally useful distinction is between entitlement programs and discretionary ones. In the argot of budgeting, entitlements are permanent grants written into law; unless the law is changed, you automatically get your benefits every year. Discretionary programs are the ones that come up for annual review; unless the law is renewed, the programs stop spending. Anyway, that's the theory. With it goes the conventional wisdom that the entitlement programs— really a euphemism for big subsidies for the middle class, things like Social Security and Medicare—are the driving force behind today's budget crisis, if only because they are where most of the money is. And the conventional wisdom is right. But it breezes past a curious truth: in the real world today, *every federal program is an entitlement*. Not every program

technically is an entitlement, but every program behaves as though it were. It lasts forever and it's viewed as a right by the people who benefit from it.

This is a disaster for government. Once a program is snared by the logic of entitlement, it is driven mercilessly to include everyone and everything forever, sometimes to the point of self-destruction. In the 1970s and 1980s, Congress got in the habit of passing regular disaster-relief bills for farmers. By doing so, it undercut the government's own crop-insurance program (why buy insurance if Uncle Sam will bail you out anyway?). Worse, disaster relief began as targeted assistance but wound up being a thin film of federal money spread across the whole country. Every year in every congressional district, someone loses some kind of crop. Congress gradually expanded disaster aid until it included pretty nearly every kind of vegetation, from wheat and corn to kumquats and rosebushes and ornamental trees; eventually even fish farms got on the list.

When Hurricane Andrew leveled a swath of Florida in 1992, it seemed sensible to focus relief on devastated farmers there, but the chairman of the House Agriculture Committee warned *against* doing that on the principal of maximum possible inclusiveness (often known as "fairness"): "Congress should strive to ensure the fair and equitable treatment of producers who receive this assistance." That's entitlement-think: if something is worth doing for someone somewhere, then it's worth doing for everybody everywhere. The problem, of course, is that funds are limited, so the more widely federal money is dispersed, the more thinly it's spread. The government ended up throwing pennies at stricken farmers, who got neither effective crop insurance nor sufficient bail-out money. In desperation, in 1994 Congress made crop insurance virtually universal and passed a bill forbidding itself from passing disaster-aid bills.

For another example I'm indebted to the political scientist James Q. Wilson.

In 1956, he points out, the law creating the national highway system ran to twenty-eight pages. The reauthorization of the system thirty-five years later (notes Wilson) "was over ten times as long as the original one and not only told the secretary of transportation to 'finish the interstate highway system' but gave him, by my count, over twenty new goals and constraints. Among these were: preserve historic sites, reduce erosion, encourage the use of seat belts, control outdoor advertising, hire Indians, reduce drunken driving, use recycled rubber in making asphalt, give 10 percent of the construction money to businesses owned by women or other 'disadvantaged' individuals, buy iron and steel from American suppliers, require metropolitan area planning, and limit the use of calcium acetate in performing seismic retrofits on bridges." Thirty-five years from that world to this one: now that's what I call reinventing government!

Or again: in 1994, Congress took a stab at rewriting the Depression-era laws governing the American telecommunications industry. The laudable idea was to open the market so that local phone companies, long-distance carriers, and cable television companies could all compete. As the bill's sponsors tried to shore up support from lobbies on every side, the bill became more and more complicated. "The original draft swelled from 104 pages to nearly two hundred," reported *The New York Times,* "with provisions on topics as wide-ranging as high-definition television and special provisions to reserve space on new networks for nonprofit broadcasters." The bill became a Christmas tree for every lobby and its brother. Had it passed, it would have become an entitlement program for all its various beneficiaries. So it would have been born as an almost-unalterable sprawling mess.

The story here, of course, is that the government of today—Republican or Democrat—faces literally thousands of organized lobbies that its counterpart of thirty years ago never even imagined. More lobbies equals more demands equals more tollbooths and veto points that any particular program or piece of legislation must safely pass. The result is programs with dozens of complex and often conflicting missions and mandates and appendages and outcroppings, each clung to by whatever groups have found a purchase there. The political power of those lobbies comes from their money, their members, their passion. That's the mechanism of demosclerosis. But the moral power of the lobbies comes from the entitlement mentality. That's the mind-set of demosclerosis.

I've given some small examples of the real-world damage wrought on government by entitlement thinking. But the damage isn't small. Give the entitlement mentality a big program to work its mischief on and the effect is devastating.

In 1993, practically everyone agreed that the American health-care system needed reform. Prices were rising out of sight while more and more people went without health insurance. In the "gridlock" view of the world, the most revealing aspect of the subsequent reform effort was that no reform was enacted. From the demosclerosis point of view, even more revealing was the way entitlement politics seized control of the whole process and then twisted and blighted it, right from the day it began.

Take that day as September 22, 1993. That was when President Clinton convened a joint session of Congress to announce his health-care reform plan. For now, never mind the details. Consider the president's rhetoric and the expectations it generated.

About security, the president made this promise: "Those who do not now have health-care coverage will have it, and for those who have it, it will never be taken away." Here he was promising, not just a program of breathtaking scope and complexity, but an entitlement. Enact it today, it is yours forever. Permanence is the premise, the promise, the very moral foundation. The president might have said, "Let us try a universal program, or at least move toward one, and see how it works—always being prepared to change course if we steer ourselves up a creek." But the public, he believed, wanted iron-clad security, not tentative trial and error. "Health care that can never be taken away, health care that is always there": with those words, Clinton delivered the health initiative wholly and bodily into the custody of entitlement politics. He foreclosed the possibility—repudiated even the morality—of experimentation.

About results, he made a cluster of promises. He promised "a comprehensive package of benefits over the course of an entire lifetime, roughly comparable to the benefit package offered by most Fortune 500 companies." He promised to make the system simpler: "simpler for the patients and simpler for those who actually deliver health care." He promised less red tape and paperwork. He promised to cut down on fraud and abuse. He promised to increase the quality of care, of medical research, and of health information. And he promised to do all of that at effectively no cost. "The vast majority of the Americans watching this tonight will pay the same or less for health-care coverage that will be the same or better than the coverage they have tonight. That is the central reality."

Reality? On that night, the president attained a pinnacle of unreality that was positively dizzying. Coverage for everyone forever, complete with Fortune 500 benefits—at lower cost! Increased accountability, less fraud, better quality control—all with less red tape! Surely those numbered among the most reckless political promises of our century.

Although a good program might squeeze some waste from the system, over the longer term no program of any sort can increase quantity, increase quality, and decrease cost all at once. Clinton was promising to defy the economic laws of gravity. Combine this promise with his pledge that the system, once established, can "never be taken away," and you have a degree of disregard of government's limits that bordered on malfeasance. That a politician in late-twentieth-century America would so profligately spend government's scarce credibility was depressing. That he seemed to believe his own pie-in-the-sky rhetoric was even more so.

The plan's details confirmed that the president was only dimly aware of government's limits, if indeed he was aware of any limits at all. For example, the plan set up an entity called the National Health Board. This "would have many difficult tasks to perform," noted the Congressional Budget Office in its analysis of the plan: "establishing a national program for managing the quality of care, developing a national information system for health care, establishing the initial target for the per capita premium for each regional alliance, determining the inflation factor for each regional alliance, estimating the market shares for each health plan in each regional alliance, developing risk-adjustment factors, and recommending modifications to the benefit package." That was just one entity's portfolio. The proposed regional health alliances would have had "an even broader, and possibly more demanding, set of responsibilities." They would have to be purchasing agents, contract negotiators, welfare agencies, financial intermediaries, payment collectors, and more. Students of government found no example of any existing agency administering a portfolio of responsibilities as dense and as internally conflicted as was envisioned for Clinton's health alliances. "Any one of these functions," said the CBO dryly, "could be a major undertaking for an existing agency with some experience, let alone for a new agency that would have to perform them all."

In 1994, a proposal that required the government to do so much at once might as well have been written on Mars. Here was the everything-for-everybody-simultaneously vision of government run wild, promising whatever anyone wanted forever and serenely untroubled by such details as government's actual condition on the planet earth in 1994. And those were the terms on which the debate *began*. Then came the lobbies.

I've said several times now that lobbies aren't evil—or if some are, we can't agree on which. They are doing their job, which means both stirring the pot for new benefits and making sure they don't get left behind as others mobilize. When Washington cranks up an effort to rejigger a seventh of the economy at a single blow, every group in the country is potentially affected, and so every lobby faces the same stark choice: get in or get trampled. The Center for Public Integrity, a Washington research group, did some counting and concluded that the health-care reform was, as of that time, "the most heavily lobbied legislative initiative in United States history." Hundreds of groups spent cumulatively more than $100 million to influence the reform effort, according to the center's rough estimate; about a hundred law firms, lobbying firms, and public-relations companies were retained; dozens of former officials of at least three administrations went to work for health-care interests. Political donations from health groups grew by a third, reported Citizen Action. Exemplifying the Newtonian law of transfer-seeking (on average, every lobbying effort creates a parallel or opposing lobbying effort of equal or greater expense), when the Clinton Administration staged a "Health Care Security

Express" bus tour, a coalition called Citizens Against Rationing Health mounted a counteroffensive bus tour of its own. Groups scrambled desperately, and expensively, to be included in the package of government-assured health benefits. The chiropractors' lobby spent $2.8 million on advertising and lobbying and it nearly tripled its campaign contributions, reported Jim Drinkard of the Associated Press. It "also produced videos for its members to show in waiting rooms to their patients," Drinkard wrote. "And it compiled a massive database of 350,000 patient names in twenty congressional districts and four states." All of that was modest compared to the permanent lobbying establishment that would have grown up around the health plan had it passed. The decisions of any large health-entitlement program centered in Washington would be life-and-death matters for health interests of every stripe. The new health program was really the New Lobbies and Lobbyists Act of 1994.

Think about trying to enact a coherent, clean reform in this climate. Think about trying to correct it *after* enactment, or even preserving some modicum of flexibility as a million frantic groups descend. Try rearranging any of the pieces or reducing any of the benefits, and the National Lithotripter Users Group or the American Society of Left-Handed Dentists comes roaring down on your head with a dozen lobbyists, a hundred legal briefs, a thousand constituents, ten thousand postcards. Astonishingly, the Clintonites seemed never to have taken account of how their program would fertilize lobbies or how those lobbies might subsequently overrun the program. They had been so intent on designing a politically appealing entitlement program—one which offered something for everybody and covered all the bases—that they forgot about the real world, or just plain ignored it.

President Clinton gambled the whole government in a wildly extravagant gesture of denial. He risked straining an already overstressed, overextended government to the breaking point. What was just as bad, by making promises which God Himself would have been hard-pressed to keep, he also risked dragging Washington's already low credibility to fathomless new depths. (If you thought people hated government before, just wait until they could blame it for whatever they didn't like about their health care.) Whether the program would have damaged the health-care system was a contentious question, but in any case it would almost certainly have wrecked the government.

With luck, that fiasco and the electoral punishment that it brought down on Democrats will be a turning point instead of a way station—a grand finale to a period when politicians and voters have preferred denying demosclerosis to dealing with it. The worst way to deal with demosclerosis is to pretend it isn't there and behave as though government still had the flexibility of the 1940s and the public confidence of the 1960s. Maybe more people, especially liberals, will now realize that none of government's enemies are more deadly than well-intentioned reformers who defy the limits on what Washington can do. Maybe more will realize, too, that the course from here is not to demand more of government while diminishing its problem-solving capacity but to unburden it while expanding its problem-solving capacity. Until we confront demosclerosis, it is futile to insist that government straighten out the world. The first priority must be to straighten out the government.

I have no illusions that straightening out government—or even arresting its deterioration—is an easy thing to do. The biggest single criticism of *Demosclerosis* is that it's weak on solutions. And so it is. Let me re-emphasize what I've said before: compared to the depth of the problem, the solutions that we know

about now *are* weak. But if we think about treating this problem instead of curing it, we can make important headway, especially as we learn more about the problem and think more about remedies. Remember, demosclerosis in its current form is a relatively new problem that people have only just begun to think about in any concentrated way. And even the noncurative answers already at hand will be helpful, if only we would use them. For that matter, it would help a lot if intelligent, well-meaning people like Bill Clinton would just quit the hysterical denial. If they would think twice before framing diabolically complex new programs that feed zillions of lobbies, can't adapt, and "can never be taken away," that in itself would be a step in the right direction.

Another small step that would make a big difference would be to retire the hackneyed and misleading "gridlock" diagnosis, once and for all. A few weeks before the 1994 election, Bill Clinton had this advice for Democrats: "We have to go home and say, 'Look, you know, we've done a lot of stuff up there. You may not have liked it all, but we're finally getting something done.'" Clinton was judging his success by Washington's productivity level—but that's like boasting about driving faster when your wheels are dangerously out of alignment. The problem is not that the system is slow but that it is unbalanced. "Getting things done" only makes matters worse if nothing else gets undone or redone. President Clinton's apparent failure to understand this was, as much as anything, what marked him as more an old-style Democrat than a new one. "He's a get-along, go-along kind of guy, fundamentally," said Timothy J. Penny, a Minnesota Democrat who retired from Congress in 1994. "He's transitional in that he doesn't so much disagree with the old agenda, but he's got a new approach. He's trying to layer the new on top of the old." That

method of governing just will not do—
not any more.

Here's a bright spot of a sort: as important as demosclerosis is, it really isn't the
end of the world. One reason, which I
mentioned earlier, is that nongovernmental institutions may be able to compensate
to some degree. Another reason, I think,
is also important, and pausing to discuss it
helps put demosclerosis in context. In a
way, if demosclerosis had to happen, it
could have picked a worse time than now.
Although America's government is decreas-
ingly flexible and adaptive, America's
leading problems are increasingly nongovernmental. Strangely, demosclerosis
may have the perverse but positive side
effect of forcing Americans to focus less
on Washington at a time when our
problems have become singularly unre-
sponsive to Washington solutions.

A few years ago, at an embassy party
on a sticky summer day, I ran into a man
whom I think of as one of Washington's
leading analysts of public policy—a
scholar and government official who
leans liberal and Democratic but is well
respected by members of both parties.
(I keep his name confidential here
because public officials aren't supposed
to talk as honestly as he did.) We got onto
the subject of the country's social problems and the way his outlook had changed
over two decades, since the early 1970s.
Even back then, he considered himself a
realist: he thought well-designed government programs might be able to improve
social conditions by—oh, maybe 40 percent. And today? He pondered a minute,
sipped his drink. And said: Probably more
on the order of 5 percent.

Although he was well aware of government's weakening record of solving
problems, at that moment he wasn't
thinking about demosclerosis. In fact, he
wasn't really thinking about government.
He was thinking about a profound change
in the nature of the country's problems.

As a rule of thumb, large, central
governments are best at four kinds of
missions. First, they can wage or prepare
for war—something no other institution
can do. Fighting two world wars and
then the Cold War was easily the most
important thing the federal government
did in this century, and also the most
successful. Second, governments can build
big national infrastructure projects: giant,
one-shot bricks-and-mortar programs
that are designed to leave tracks or roads
on the ground for years. The federal
government built the interstate highway
system, ran the Manhattan Project, flew
men to the moon. Insofar as those were
focused, do-it-once projects, they succeeded. (By contrast, when the government tried to turn NASA into an ongoing
concern, expecting it to adapt without
giving it a clear mission, the space program
ran into trouble.) Third, though government is lousy at providing services or del-
icately manipulating human behavior, it is
pretty good at writing checks. By doing
so, it set up the basic safety-net programs,
such as Social Security and unemployment insurance. Finally, government is
good at setting minimum standards of
political and social freedom. Thus it struck
down local barriers to opportunity for
blacks, something that no other institution
could have done.

On balance, government did all
those things quite well. And then, having
done them, it looked down at itself and
found that it had been transformed; and
it looked around and saw that the world,
too, had been transformed. Today we
meet the result of both transformations:
the golden age of government, a roughly
thirty-year period beginning with the
New Deal, is over, probably for good.

Government was transformed partly
by its own prior successes, a victim of
its own brand of imperial overstretch.
Encouraged by the successes of a relatively
flexible government doing relatively
manageable tasks, people began to say

things like, "If we can send a man to the moon, then by God we can solve [here insert favorite unmet social need]"—as though because government can do some things well, it should be expected to do all things well. People didn't see that a government which is good at mailing Social Security checks is not necessarily good at running a health-care system, nor did they see how they might calcify government by demanding too much of it. A million intricate social and human missions were heaped on government's docket, each to be accomplished by many programs defended by countless constituencies—all at a time when government's adaptability had been gravely diminished. That, of course, is the story of demosclerosis.

Meanwhile, the world was changing, too. Much as viruses mutate to resist vaccines, so the country's problems changed in ways that defeat the postwar toolbox of centralized government programs. Today America's leading problems—hardly the only problems, but certainly the most important ones right now—relate not to the physical infrastructure but to the moral infrastructure.

I use that term in a generalized, non-sectarian sense to mean a set of social behaviors and values which, when intact, build the future: hard work, lawfulness, education, thrift, and devotion to family (especially children). Call them bourgeois values, call them the Protestant work ethic, call them "traditional" or "basic"—whatever you call them, they can be practiced or abandoned by people of any religion, creed, race, sexual orientation, social class, party, or country; and they are collectively the key to a better future. Individuals or societies that get them right cannot be stopped, absent bad luck; individuals or societies that get them wrong cannot be saved, absent good fortune.

The work ethic can't be measured directly, but the other four values can. What the measurements show are sharp declines over the last thirty or so years. The murder rate has about doubled since the early 1960s, and would be higher still if not for improved medical care (a homicide only happens if the victim dies). A young black man in Watts or the South Side of Chicago is likelier to be killed in violence than was a soldier during an average tour in Vietnam. Test scores are stuck well below where they were twenty-five years ago, and the stories of what the average American student doesn't know are infamous; Japanese students do about as much homework in a single day as their American counterparts do all week. Early in this century, America saved more than almost any other developed country (as Japan does now); today it is at the bottom of the heap, partly but not wholly thanks to the federal budget deficit. Family is in the worst way of all. The divorce rate more than doubled between 1960 and 1980; since 1960, the illegitimacy rate has risen from 5 percent to 30 percent. In 1970, one in nine American children lived in a fatherless home; by 1990 one in four did (including 60 percent of black children!). The link between fatherlessness and pathology—poverty, violence, crime, mental illness, poor education, you name it—is now beyond denying.

In 1960, a teenager was twice as likely to die of cancer as to be killed by somebody else; only twenty years later, the odds were reversed. Not only did cancer go down, killing went up. While we developed the medical technology to prevent and treat cancer, we lost our grip on the social technology to prevent and treat violence, which in theory is more preventable. This seems almost crazy. Who could ever have imagined?

Government no doubt had some role in creating and complicating (as well as ameliorating) these problems; no doubt it must play some role in reducing them. But in comparison to family, community, church, school, and self, government is the social institution that is least well adapted to solving them. Washington can write a check and build a bomb, but moral rot is not the kind of problem that you throw money at or solve with a crash development program. Democratic regimes are always eager to pander, and pandering is not the way to persuade students to work harder and citizens to behave better.

Of course, an adaptive government will always be more useful than a maladaptive one, but even an adaptive government cannot rebuild character the way it can rebuild roads. Indeed, Americans' peculiar postwar obsession with government—"governmentalism," as I've called it in Chapter 9—has itself become an obstacle to problem solving. Every social argument becomes an argument about government, politics, or law; every idea and ideology is defined by its relation to government. If you find a problem and then fail to propose a government solution, liberals say that you are, perforce, "doing nothing." If you find a problem whose solution does not entail blaming, shrinking, or reorienting government, conservatives yawn and look for a more exciting problem. The obsession with government monopolizes attention and usurps energy at a time when attention and energy need to be refocused.

If demosclerosis renders government largely incompetent, that is certainly bad, and I don't mean to minimize the consequences. Straightening out government is very important. But if demosclerosis forces people to look harder at nongovernmental methods in an increasingly postgovernmental age, then in an odd, indirect way it may yet do some good.

With demosclerosis, as with so many social problems, good and bad news seem always to come mixed together. The election of 1994, for instance, brought both. It brought the curious spectacle, here and there, of politicians campaigning against pork-barrel projects for their own districts. In New Jersey, two congressional candidates vied to oppose $1.4 billion in federal spending for a local water project. "We need people in Congress who will say, 'This is wasteful spending in our own district, and I don't want it,'" said the Republican. (He won, but the Democrat also opposed the project.) More members of the public seemed to be fed up with the standard way of talking, and some seemed to be figuring out that along with the game of "bring home the bacon" comes a large and expensive class of professional pork merchants. At the same time, poll numbers like the ones I cited above showed that things had changed only a little, not a lot—which, of course, is much better than not at all.

The 1994 elections brought to power a tough-talking and ambitious crowd of antigovernment Republicans. Their sudden rise gave them a chance to put their money where their mouths were—big mouths, to be sure. The election also took a broom to a largely brain-dead congressional Democratic party, forcing the survivors to think harder about new ways of doing things. On the other hand, the Republicans swept to power on a platform of more defense, lower taxes, and a balanced budget—all based on vague talk about cutting someone's (read: someone else's) spending programs. Stale, sorry stuff, and the Democrats' mindless reply was no less so: Republicans (they charged) are secretly plotting to cut entitlement benefits for the elderly! "The Republican Contract could devastate Social Security and senior citizens," shrilled the president. Business as usual.

The cascade of legislation in the House of Representatives following the election was certainly not business as usual. Newt Gingrich, the electrifying speaker of the House, pushed through the Contract with America—a miscellany of reforms promised by Republicans before the elections—with breathtaking speed and discipline. Here again, from the point of view of demosclerosis, the news was mixed.

Substantively, the Contract was much stronger on sizzle than steak. Its main focus was on process reforms: a balanced-budget amendment to the Constitution (which was defeated in the Senate), restrictions on Congress's ability to require that states and localities spend money on Washington's behalf (so-called unfunded mandates), requirements that new regulations be subject to cost-benefit analysis (a good idea, but already generally in practice), and so on. Process reforms may be worth doing, but they are no substitute for the kinds of substantive choices that fill Congressmen's mailbags with irate postcards from members of offended groups. Where substance was concerned, the Contract was soft-centered. The House Republicans' reforms of welfare—of welfare for the poor, that is, as opposed to welfare for everybody else—were real if slapdash. But their crime bill was old-fashioned grandstanding, and their tax cuts old-fashioned pandering—as the public itself seemed to sense.

If the Contract's substance was discouraging, however, the budgetary plans that Republicans in Congress proposed in May 1995 were heartening. They called for reducing deficits by more than $500 billion over five years—and doing so partly by killing a wide variety of subsidy programs. Most of those programs were small (though well defended), and many were familiar from their ritual appearances on presidential hit-lists going back to the Reagan years. Yet there was no gainsaying that the Republicans' attack on entrenched programs was larger and more serious than anything seen in years. As I write, it is too early to know how many of the proposed reforms will find their way to enactment—but the very fact of their proposal demonstrated that electoral upheaval can weaken the grip of entrenched lobbies.

The tax reform of 1986 had shown that clever political leadership inside Washington could divide and conquer the armies of groups that stand watch over their thousand secret subsidies. And the legislative whirlwind of early 1995 showed that a restive electorate outside Washington could still radicalize politics, at least temporarily, and shake the very ground of the capital. Despite all the little gray groups and politicians and lobbyists and claques that occupy and ossify the government, the broad electorate proved more than able to coil itself and strike back.

What's lacking in the system isn't energy but direction. The hard part is to convert the electorate's shuddering waves of discontent into the kinds of subtle and persistent changes in law and behavior that can counteract the insidious, ever-present forces of demosclerosis. That is like converting earthquake energy into steam power: possible but not easy. It requires the electorate to be not just angry but mature, especially about the limits of government and the dangers of entitlement. And it requires changing our mind-set three ways at once. First, stop thinking about "gridlock" and how hard it is to get things done. Instead, start thinking about demosclerosis and how hard it is to get things *un*done. Second, stop assuming automatically that cutting programs is an antigovernment thing to do. It isn't, any more than revising product lines is an anti-business thing do to. Third, remember that the main problem is no longer government's size, as such, but its flexibility. When thinking about a new program, don't just ask "How much bigger will it make government?" or "Does it do more than government has a right to do?" or "Does it do as much as government should do in an ideal world"? Ask also: "How many new lobbies will this program create? Is it relatively reversible if it doesn't work? Does it do more than government has the ability to do, right now in the real world?"

People say this book is pessimistic. I don't mean it to be; I see it as realistic. We can't hope to win until we fully appreciate what we are up against. The secret of success against demosclerosis is in our heads, first of all. And then in understanding that this is going to be a long, long fight—and embracing it. Of course that's difficult. But Americans have done difficult things before.

PROJECT

Since Rauch wrote *Demosclerosis,* many things have changed in American politics. Perhaps the biggest change is the creation of a new cabinet-level agency—the Department of Homeland Security. Conduct a case study of this department. You should pay particular attention to how it relates to all levels of government (federal, state, and local). What role do interest groups play in this new agency? How does this fit with Rauch's analysis?

18

Issue Networks and the Executive Establishment

HUGH HECLO

Hugh Heclo's examination of issue networks provides a novel approach to understanding the role of interest groups in the policy-making process. Heclo extends the notion of iron triangles and develops the idea of issue networks. He contrasts these two approaches to policy making and finds that the growth of government agencies has necessitated a form of policy making that is more open, fluid, changeable, and grounded in the ability to provide information to policy makers. The explosion of government programs has forced administrative agencies to deal with increasingly complicated issues that require specialization and expertise. Heclo notes that the size of bureaucratic agencies has not grown as the agencies' responsibilities have. Consequently, interest groups serve as purveyors of information. Heclo suggests that groups working within issue networks seek information and understanding rather than influence. The resulting relationship is qualitatively different from that described under the old construct of iron triangles.

QUESTIONS TO CONSIDER

1. What is an issue network?
2. Why did issue networks arise?
3. How do issue networks differ from iron triangles?

4. If Heclo is right in his description of policy making, what does this say about interest-group influence?
5. Are issue networks supportive of pluralism or elitism? Why?

The connection between politics and administration arouses remarkably little interest in the United States. The presidency is considered more glamorous, Congress more intriguing, elections more exciting, and interest groups more troublesome. General levels of public interest can be gauged by the burst of indifference that usually greets the announcement of a new President's cabinet or rumors of a political appointee's resignation. Unless there is some White House "tie-in" or scandal (preferably both), news stories about presidential appointments are usually treated by the media as routine filler material.

This lack of interest in political administration is rarely found in other democratic countries, and it has not always prevailed in the United States. In most nations the ups and downs of political executives are taken as vital signs of the health of a government, indeed of its survival. In the United States, the nineteenth-century turmoil over one type of connection between politics and administration— party spoils—frequently overwhelmed any notion of presidential leadership. Anyone reading the history of those troubled decades is likely to be struck by the way in which political administration in Washington registered many of the deeper strains in American society at large. It is a curious switch that appointments to the bureaucracy should loom so large in the history of the nineteenth century, when the federal government did little, and be so completely discounted in the

twentieth century, when government tries to do so much.

Political administration in Washington continues to register strains in American politics and society, although in ways more subtle than the nineteenth-century spoils scramble between Federalists and Democrats, Pro- and Anti-tariff forces, Nationalists and States-Righters, and so on. Unlike many other countries, the United States has never created a high level, government-wide civil service. Neither has it been favored with a political structure that automatically produces a stock of experienced political manpower for top executive positions in government.[1] How then does political administration in Washington work? More to the point, how might the expanding role of government be changing the connection between administration and politics?

Received opinion on this subject suggests that we already know the answers. Control is said to be vested in an informal but enduring series of "iron triangles" linking executive bureaus, congressional committees, and interest group clienteles with a stake in particular programs. A President or presidential appointee may occasionally try to muscle in, but few people doubt the capacity of these subgovernments to thwart outsiders in the long run.

Based largely on early studies of agricultural, water, and public works policies, the iron triangle concept is not so much wrong as it is disastrously incomplete.[2] And the conventional view is especially inappropriate for understanding changes in politics and administration during recent years. Preoccupied with trying to find the few truly powerful actors, observers tend to overlook the power

SOURCE: From Hugh Heclo, "Issue Networks and the Executive Establishment," in *The New American Political System,* ed. Anthony King (Washington, DC: American Enterprise Institute, 1978), 87–124. Reprinted with permission from the American Enterprise Institute for Public Policy Research.

and influence that arise out of the configurations through which leading policy makers move and do business with each other. Looking for the closed triangles of control, we tend to miss the fairly open networks of people that increasingly impinge upon government.

To do justice to the subject would require a major study of the Washington community and the combined inspiration of a Leonard White and a James Young. Tolerating a fair bit of injustice, one can sketch a few of the factors that seem to be at work. The first is growth in the sheer mass of government activity and associated expectations. The second is the peculiar, loose-jointed play of influence that is accompanying this growth. Related to these two is the third: the layering and specialization that have overtaken the government work force, not least the political leadership of the bureaucracy.

All of this vastly complicates the job of presidential appointees both in controlling their own actions and in managing the bureaucracy. But there is much more at stake than the troubles faced by people in government. There is the deeper problem of connecting what politicians, officials, and their fellow travelers are doing in Washington with what the public at large can understand and accept. It is on this point that political administration registers some of the larger strains of American politics and society, much as it did in the nineteenth century. For what it shows is a dissolving of organized politics and a politicizing of organizational life throughout the nation.

GOVERNMENT GROWTH IN AN AGE OF IMPROVEMENT

Few people doubt that we live in a time of big government. During his few years in office, President Kennedy struggled to avoid becoming the first President with a $100 billion budget. Just seventeen years later, President Carter easily slipped into history as the first $500 billion President. Even in constant prices, the 1979 federal budget was about double that of 1960.[3] The late 1950s and the entire 1960s witnessed a wave of federal initiatives in health, civil rights, education, housing, manpower, income maintenance, transportation, and urban affairs. To these, later years have added newer types of welfare concerns: consumer protection, the environment, cancer prevention, and energy, to name only a few. Whatever today's conventional skepticism about the success of these programs, posterity will probably regard the last twenty-odd years as an extraordinarily ambitious, reform-minded period. The dominant feeling behind our age of improvement was best expressed by Adlai Stevenson in 1955 when he sensed a new willingness "to feel strongly, to be impatient, to want mightily to see that things are done better."[4]

However, we need to be clear concerning what it is that has gotten big in government. Our modern age of improvement has occurred with astonishingly little increase in the overall size of the federal executive establishment. Figure 18.1 traces changes in the raw materials of government: money, rules, and people from 1949 to 1977. The year 1955 represented a return to more normal times after the Korean conflict and may be taken as a reasonable baseline. Since that year national spending has risen sixfold in current dollars and has more than doubled in constant terms. Federal regulations (as indicated by pages in the *Federal Register*) have also sextupled. In the cases of both money and regulations, it was during the second Eisenhower administration that a new and expensive activism in public policy began to sweep through the national government. The landslide congressional victory by liberal Democrats in 1958, the challenge of Sputnik, the new stirrings of the civil rights movement—these and other factors created a wave of government spending and regulation that has continued to roll ever since. The force

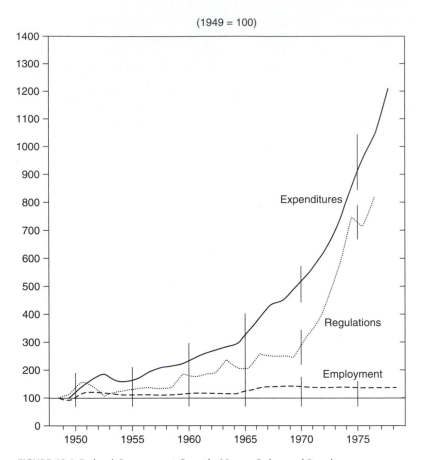

(1949 = 100)

FIGURE 18.1 Federal Government Growth: Money, Rules, and People

NOTE: Federal spending on income and product account. Figures are on an accrual basis and include trust account transactions with the public as well as grants-in-aid to state and local governments. Employment covers total end-of-year civilian employees in full-time, permanent, temporary, part-time, and intermittent employment in the executive branch, including the Postal Service. Regulations are indicated by numbers of pages in *The Federal Register.*

SOURCE: The Tax Foundation, *Facts and Figures on Government Finance,* 1977, table 20, p. 33; U.S. Office of Management and Budget, *Special Analyses, Budget of the U.S. Government, 1979,* p. 210. Figures are taken from an unpublished table compiled by the Executive Agencies Division, Office of the Federal Register, Washington, D.C. I wish to express my gratitude to this division for their cooperation in supplying information.

of this growth was felt at least as much in the Nixon-Ford years as in the earlier decade of New Frontier/Great Society programs under Democratic Presidents.

Yet federal employment grew hardly at all in comparison with spending and regulations (up by less than one-fifth since 1955). Despite widespread complaints about the size of government, the federal bureaucracy is entitled to join

foreign aid as one of that small band of cases where close to zero-growth has been the norm for the last twenty-five years.

The paradox of expanding government and stable bureaucracy has two explanations. In purely budgetary terms, much of the increase in federal outlays has been due to higher costs of existing policies. It does not necessarily require more bureaucrats to write larger checks. Such cost increases have been especially important in the area of income maintenance programs. Federal payments to individuals (social security, medical care, veterans' pensions, unemployment insurance, and public assistance) increased from $22 billion in 1960 to $167 billion in 1977, accounting for well over half of the total increase in federal domestic spending during these years.[5] Much of this increase came not from adding new programs but from higher bills of existing programs, particularly social security. Thus at the end of 1977, when federal outlays were at $402 billion, President Carter proposed a $500 billion budget for fiscal year 1979. Of the $98 billion increase, about 90 percent was due to the higher cost of existing policies and only 10 percent to new spending recommended by the President.[6] About one-quarter of the total cost increase was due simply to income security programs.

This sort of momentum in government obviously presents serious challenges to politicians in general and to politically appointed executives in particular. These are the people who tend to feel they have a mandate to "change things, shake up the bureaucracy" and who even in the best of circumstances have only a few years in which to do so. But there is a second and at least equally important explanation for the stability of the national bureaucracy in an era of increased policy interventionism. This factor creates even more profound problems for government leadership.

In the main, Washington has not attempted to apply its policies by administering programs directly to the general population. It has therefore been able to avoid bureaucratic giantism. This is true in many programs classified as payments to individuals (for example, Medicare and Medicaid funds pass through large numbers of administrative middlemen), and it is especially true in several of the policy areas that have grown the fastest since the mid-fifties. One such area is investment and subsidies for the physical environment. Grants for mass transit, waste treatment plants, highways, and the like have tripled in real terms since 1960. Another area rich in indirect administration falls under the heading of social investment and services; spending for education, health care, employment training, urban development, and social services has risen more than tenfold since 1960.[7] Rather than building and staffing its own administrative facilities for these programs, the federal government has preferred to act through intermediary organizations—state governments, city halls, third party payers, consultants, contractors, and many others. Administratively, the result is that what was true during the Eisenhower administration remains true today: despite huge increases in government programs, about the only time an ordinary citizen sees a federal bureaucrat is when his mail is delivered, his taxes are audited, or a trip to the local social security office becomes necessary (unless of course an FBI agent knocks on his door).

New policies associated with our modern age of improvement have tended to promote the idea of government by remote control. Political administration in Washington is heavily conditioned by an accumulation of methods for paying the bills and regulating the conduct of intermediary organizations. This pattern is consistent with a long tradition of fragmented and decentralized administration. Moreover, it offers important political and bureaucratic advantages. Spreading cash grants among various third party payers is an important way of building support for policies, translating otherwise indivisible collective goods into terms suitable for distributive politics. Rather than having to convince everyone of the value of a clean environment, government administrators can preside over a scramble for federal funds to subsidize construction of local sewage treatment plants. Likewise, in spending for health, manpower, transportation, and so on, the federal government has sidestepped the tremendously difficult task of creating a broad national consensus for its own administered activities. It has done so by counting on third parties to crave the funds which the national government makes available to serve its purposes. Recently Charles Schultze has argued that Washington should make greater use of market incentives to meet public ends.[8] Yet as far as fiscal relations in the political marketplace are concerned, a strong case could be made that in fact the federal government has done little else.

In terms of using intermediaries to administer the new melioristic policies, the mushrooming of federal regulations has much in common with federal spending. Rather than having to work at building and policing its own delivery mechanisms, the Washington bureaucracy can use regulations and then rest content with telling other public and private bureaucracies what should be done. This has the added advantage of allowing federal policy makers to distribute not only funds but also much of the blame when things go wrong.

One might suppose that the executive establishment in Washington has put itself in an extremely comfortable position, retailing the promise of improved policies and wholesaling the administrative headaches connected with delivery. Unfortunately, life has not been so kind. People increasingly expect Washington to solve problems but not to get in anyone's way in the process. The result is that policy goals are piled on top of each other without generating any commitment to the administrative wherewithal to achieve them. Even in the depths of anti-Washington sentiment, the overwhelming majority of Americans agreed that the federal government should control inflation, prevent depressions, assure international peace, regulate private business,

and also ensure that the poor are taken care of, the hungry fed, and every person assured a minimum standard of living. A comparably large majority also felt that the federal government was too "big and bureaucratic."[9] As it turns out, therefore, the executive establishment in Washington tends to get the worst of both worlds—blamed for poor delivery by its public customers and besieged with bills from its middlemen.

FRAYING AT THE CENTER

The strategy of responding to aspirations for improvement while maintaining a no-growth national administrative machine and relying on middlemen has succeeded in doing one thing. It has saved Washington policy makers from having to cope with what would otherwise have been an immense, nationwide bureaucracy. Yet far from simplifying operations, this "success" has vastly complicated the connection between administration and politics in Washington. Lacking their own electoral mandates, political administrators have always been in an ambivalent position in American government. Every ambitious new program, every clever innovation in indirect administration has merely deepened this ambivalence.

What is occurring at the national level is a peculiar "push-pull effect" on the relation between democratic politics and the executive establishment. On the one hand, government growth has pushed more and more policy concerns out of the federal government's own structure and into masses of intermediary, issue-conscious groups. On the other hand, the requirements for managing such a complex system are pulling government leadership further and further away from the nontechnical, nonspecialist understanding of the ordinary citizen and politician. It is worth looking more closely at how it is possible to be both politicizing organizational life and depoliticizing democratic leadership.

All Join in

During 1977–1978, Harvard University hired a Washington lobbyist and joined a loose group called Friends of DNA in an effort to influence federal regulation of research into the creation of new forms of life. The same year, the former militant chairman of the Black Panther party, Bobby Seale, founded a new Washington organization to lobby for community-controlled poverty programs. And the president of the national machinists' union convened a National Energy Coalition composed of environmentalists, neighborhood organizers, and consumer advocates. Perhaps not coincidentally, forty-seven congressmen announced their retirement, citing as the major reason a lack of enjoyment in the job.

Trivial in their own right, these incidents suggest something deeper than the feeling (probably true) that exercising power is not as much fun as it used to be in the clubby days of Washington politics. As more and more puzzling, unfamiliar policy issues have been thrust on government, more and more fluid groups have been unexpectedly mobilized. As proliferating groups have claimed a stake and clamored for a place in the policy process, they have helped to diffuse the focus of political and administrative leadership.

What has happened at the subnational level of government is a striking illustration of this process. Much of the bureaucratic expansion that might otherwise have occurred nationally has taken place in state and local governments. Between 1955 and 1977 state and local public employment grew by more than two and one-half times, to 12 million people, while federal employment hovered at around 2.5 million.[10] The increased interdependence of subnational and national bureaucracies has led to the growth of what Samuel H. Beer has termed the intergovernmental lobby.[11] Those in Washington whose memories go back a generation or more can recall a time when it was something of an occasion for a governor to undertake a mission to Washington. As Senator Moynihan (who was a junior aide to Governor Averell Harriman in the 1940s) put it, "You'd spend time planning how many shirts to take. Going to Washington was a very big deal."[12] Today, not only do governors or mayors as groups have their own specialized staffs permanently stationed in Washington, but large state governments, major units within state governments, and individual cities frequently have their own Washington offices or hired representatives. In addition to umbrella organizations such as the National Governors' Conference, the Conference of State Governments, the U.S. Conference of Mayors, the National League of Cities, the National Conference of State Legislatures, and the National Association of Counties, one finds the intergovernmental lobby peopled with representatives from groups such as the New York State Association of Counties, cities such as Detroit and Boston, major counties, various state water districts, boards of regents, and so on and on and on.

Similarly, an even larger number of private and semi-private organizations have grown up as important extensions of the new federal policies. One of the enduring legacies of every reform movement in the United States—whether it was the Progressives' good government movement, Hoover's attempts at engineering voluntarism, or FDR's New Deal—has been to create new groups with a stake in the reformed processes and programs.[13] So too our own age of improvement has encouraged a blossoming of policy participants and kibitzers. In this instance (and this differentiates it somewhat from earlier periods) virtually everyone has accepted the idea that the national government in Washington is the decisive arena and will continue to be so indefinitely.

Some groups are nurtured by the government's own need for administrative help. For example, new neighborhood associations have been asked to take a major part in Washington's urban and housing programs. Or when the Consumer Product Safety Commission sets new standards for extension cords, the National Electrical Manufacturers' Association plays a major part in drawing up the new designs. Some groups are almost spontaneously called into being by what they can gain or lose from new federal policies or—perhaps just as often—the unforeseen consequences of these policies. For example, in the early 1970s Washington launched vigorous new efforts to promote grain exports. This generated not only new borrowing by farmers to expand production but also a new, militant farmers' organization (American Agriculture) when prices later fell from their export-led highs.

A key factor in the proliferation of groups is the almost inevitable tendency of successfully enacted policies unwittingly to propagate hybrid interests. The area of health care is rich in examples. Far from solidifying the established medical interests, federal funding and regulation of health care since the mid-1960s have had diverse impacts and therefore have tended to fragment what was once a fairly monolithic system of medical representation. Public policy has not only uncovered but also helped to create diverging interests among hospital associations, insurance companies, medical schools, hospital equipment manufacturers, local health planning groups, preventive medicine advocates, nonteaching research centers, and many others.[14] This does not necessarily mean that every group is in conflict with all of the others all of the time. The point is that even when government is not pursuing a deliberate strategy of divide and conquer, its activist policies

greatly increase the incentives for groups to form around the differential effects of these policies, each refusing to allow any other group to speak in its name.

While nothing should necessarily be assumed about their political power, trade and professional associations offer a revealing pattern of growth. The number of such groups has grown sharply during three periods: during the First World War, the first half of the 1930s, and the Second World War. Since 1945 the total number has been continuously increasing, and in recent years more and more of these groups have found it useful to make their headquarters in Washington. During the 1970s the number of trade and professional associations headquartered in Washington surpassed that in New York for the first time, climbing to 1,800 organizations with 40,000 employees in 1977. Well over half of the nation's largest associations (those with annual budgets of over $1 million) are now located in the Washington metropolitan area.[15] This takes no account of the large number of consumer and other public interest groups that have sprouted all over the nation's capital since the early 1960s.[16]

Of course Americans' love affair with interest groups is hardly a new phenomenon. From abolitionists to abortionists there has never been a lack of issue-conscious organizations; in the 1830s, Tocqueville described how the tariff question generated an early version of local consumer groups and a national lobbying association.[17] Yet if the current situation is a mere outgrowth of old tendencies, it is so in the same sense that a 16-lane spaghetti interchange is the mere elaboration of a country crossroads. With more public policies, more groups are being mobilized and there are more complex relationships among them. Since very few policies ever seem to drop off the public agenda as more are added, congestion among those interested in various issues grows, the chances for accidental collisions increase, and the interaction tends to take on a distinctive group-life of its own in the Washington community. One scene in a recent Jacques. Tati film pictures a Paris traffic circle so dense with traffic that no one can get in or out; instead, drivers spend their time socializing with each other as they drive in endless circles. Group politics in Washington may be becoming such a merry-go-round.

How these changes influence the substance of public policy processes depends on what it is that the burgeoning numbers of participants want. Obviously their wants vary greatly, but to a large extent they are probably accurately reflected in the areas of greatest policy growth since the late 1950s—programs seeking social betterment in terms of civil rights, income, housing, environment, consumer protection, and so on—what I will simply refer to as "welfare policies." The hallmark of these policies seems to reflect attitudes in the general public.[18] What is wanted is not more equal outcomes or unfair preferences. No, if there is a theme in the clamor of group politics and public policy, it is the idea of compensation. Compensation for what? For past racial wrongs, for current overcharging of consumers, for future environmental damage. The idea of compensatory policy—that the federal government should put things right—fits equally well for the groups representing the disadvantaged (special treatment is required for truly equal opportunity to prevail) and for those representing the advantaged (any market-imposed loss can be defined as a special hardship). The same holds for newer public interest groups (government action is required to redress the impact of selfish private interests). If middle-class parents have not saved enough for college costs they should be compensated with tuition tax credits. If public buildings are inaccessible to the physically handicapped, government regulations should change

that. If farmers overinvest during good times, they should be granted redress from the consequences of their actions. The old American saying "there oughtta be a law" had a negative connotation of preventing someone from getting away with something. Today the more prevalent feeling is "there oughtta be a policy," and the connotation of getting in on society's compensations is decidedly positive.

In sum, new initiatives in federal funding and regulation have infused old and new organizations with a public policy dimension, especially when such groups are used as administrative middlemen and facilitators. Moreover, the growing body of compensatory interventions by government has helped create a climate of acceptance for ever more groups to insist that things be set right on their behalf. What matters is not so much that organizations are moving to Washington as that Washington's policy problems are coming to occupy so many different facets of organizational life in the United States.

Policy as an Intramural Activity

A second tendency cuts in a direction opposite to the widening group participation in public policy. Expanding welfare policies and Washington's reliance on indirect administration have encouraged the development of specialized subcultures composed of highly knowledgeable policy-watchers. Some of these people have advanced professional degrees, some do not. What they all have in common is the detailed understanding of specialized issues that comes from sustained attention to a given policy debate.

Certain of these changes are evident in the government's own work force. Employees in the field and in Washington who perform the routine chores associated with direct administration have become less prominent. More important have become those officials with the necessary technical and supervisory skills to oversee what other people are doing. Thus the surge in federal domestic activities in the 1960s and 1970s may not have increased the overall size of the bureaucracy very much, but it did markedly expand the upper and upper-middle levels of officialdom. Compared with an 18 percent rise in total civilian employment, mid-level executive positions in the federal government (that is, supergrade and public law 313 equivalents) have increased approximately 90 percent since 1960. Some of these changes are due to a slow inflation of job titles and paper credentials that can be found in private as well as public organizations. But case studies in the 1960s suggested that most of this escalation occurring in the Washington bureaucracy could be traced to the new and expanded public programs of that decade.[19] The general effect of these policy changes has been to require more technical skills and higher supervisory levels, overlaying routine technicians with specialist engineers, insurance claims examiners with claims administrators, and so on. Approximately two-fifths of mid-level executives in the bureaucracy (grades 16–18 or the equivalent) are what might loosely be termed scientists, though frequently they are in fact science managers who oversee the work of other people inside and outside of the government.

Increasing complexity and specialization are affecting leaders in all modern organizations, even profit-oriented enterprises with stable sets of clear goals. For decision makers in government—where the policy goals have been neither stable nor clear in the last twenty years—the pressures for more expert staff assistance have become immense. This is as true for legislators as it is for public executives. President Nixon estimated that he personally saw no more than 200,000 of the 42 million pieces of paper in his own presidential materials. Recent studies of Congress estimate that the average member of the House of Representatives

has, out of an eleven-hour workday, only eleven minutes to devote personally to reading and only twelve minutes in his or her own office to spend personally on writing legislation and speeches.[20] Congress, like the executive branch, has responded to the pressures by creating more specialists and topside staff. Since 1957 the total number of personal and committee staff on the Hill has climbed from 4,300 to 11,000 and over 20,000 more persons service the legislature from institutional staff positions (the General Accounting Office, Congressional Budget Office, and so on).[21] At the core of this blossoming congressional bureaucracy are bright, often remarkably young, technocrats who are almost indistinguishable from the analysts and subject matter specialists in the executive branch.

There are many straws in the wind to indicate the growing skill base of policy professionals in Washington. Executive search firms (so-called headhunters) have found a booming market in recent years, with many new firms being founded and prestigious New York organizations opening up Washington offices. One indicator of this movement, the amount of "professional opportunity" advertising in the press, now puts Washington on a par with Los Angeles and New York as an executive hunting ground for the private sector. The reason is clear. As government activities and regulations have grown, the value of policy specialists who understand the complex Washington environment has appreciated in the eyes of all of the private organizations with a stake in government activity. Another indicator is the mushrooming of new Washington law firms. Typically these firms are headed by former government officials and practice in substantive areas of law and policy that did not exist twenty years ago. Table 18.1 gives some idea of this trend.

Again it is tempting to borrow a term from Professor Beer and to refer to these groups of policy specialists as constituting a "professional-bureaucratic complex."

Table 18.1 The New Washington Law Firms

Firm	Year Founded	Area of Activity	Background of Leading Partners
Beveridge, Fairbanks and Diamond	1974	environmental law	former head of Environmental Protection Agency; official in tax division of Justice Department; assistant in EPA and White House adviser on energy and environmental policy
Epstein and Becker	1972	health care	official in Health Maintenance Organization Service of Department of Health, Education, and Welfare
Blum, Parker and Nash	1977	energy, international business	associate counsel of Senate subcommittee on multinational corporations; appellate attorney in tax division of Justice Department; assistant counsel, Senate anti-trust subcommittee
Brownstein, Zeidman, Schomer and Chase	1970	housing and urban development	assistant secretary of Department of Housing and Urban Development; commissioner of Federal Housing Administration; general counsel of Small Business Administration
Lobel, Novins and Lamont	1972	consumer litigation	legislative assistant to senator; official in Justice Department; assistant counsel to Senate subcommittee on small business
Garner, Carton and Douglas	1977	defense	general counsel of Defense Department; secretary of the army
Bracewell and Patterson	1975	energy	former assistant administrator of Federal Energy Administration
Breed, Abbott and Morgan	1976	general	former solicitor of Labor Department; head of Office of Federal Contract Compliance Programs
Lane and Edson	1970	housing	general counsel of U.S. National Corporation for Housing Partnerships; former Justice Department official; former official in Department of Housing and Urban Development

SOURCE: "The Boom in Small Law Firms," *National Journal*, February 4, 1978, p. 172.

Certainly there are many core groups with scientific or professional training which have carved out spheres of bureaucratic influence over health, highways, education, and so on. Likewise the familiar nexus of less professional, economic interests can still be found linking various parts of the Washington community. But the general arrangement that is emerging is somewhat different from the conventional image of iron triangles tying together executive bureaus, interest groups, and congressional committees in all-powerful alliances.

Unfortunately, our standard political conceptions of power and control are not very well suited to the loose-jointed play of influence that is emerging in political administration. We tend to look for one group exerting dominance over another, for subgovernments that are strongly insulated from other outside forces in the environment, for policies that get "produced" by a few "makers." Seeing former government officials opening law firms or joining a new trade association, we naturally think of ways in which they are trying to conquer and control particular pieces of government machinery.

Obviously questions of power are still important. But for a host of policy initiatives undertaken in the last twenty years it is all but impossible to identify clearly who the dominant actors are. Who is controlling those actions that go to make up our national policy on abortions, or on income redistribution, or consumer protection, or energy? Looking for the few who are powerful, we tend to overlook the many whose webs of influence provoke and guide the exercise of power. These webs, or what I will call "issue networks," are particularly relevant to the highly intricate and confusing welfare policies that have been undertaken in recent years.

The notion of iron triangles and subgovernments presumes small circles of participants who have succeeded in becoming largely autonomous. Issue networks, on the other hand, comprise a large number of participants with quite variable degrees of mutual commitment or of dependence on others in their environment; in fact it is almost impossible to say where a network leaves off and its environment begins. Iron triangles and subgovernments suggest a stable set of participants coalesced to control fairly narrow public programs which are in the direct economic interest of each party to the alliance. Issue networks are almost the reverse image in each respect. Participants move in and out of the networks constantly. Rather than groups united in dominance over a program, no one, as far as one can tell, is in control of the policies and issues. Any direct material interest is often secondary to intellectual or emotional commitment. Network members reinforce each other's sense of issues as their interests, rather than (as standard political or economic models would have it) interests defining positions on issues.

Issue networks operate at many levels, from the vocal minority who turn up at local planning commission hearings to the renowned professor who is quietly telephoned by the White House to give a quick "reading" on some participant or policy. The price of buying into one or another issue network is watching, reading, talking about, and trying to act on particular policy problems. Powerful interest groups can be found represented in networks but so too can individuals in or out of government who have a reputation for being knowledgeable. Particular professions may be prominent, but the true experts in the networks are those who are issue-skilled (that is, well informed about the ins and outs of a particular policy debate) regardless of formal professional training. More than mere technical experts, network people are policy activists who know each other through the issues. Those who emerge to positions of wider leadership are policy politicians—experts in using experts, victuallers of knowledge in a world hungry for right decisions.

In the old days—when the primary problem of government was assumed to be doing what was right, rather than knowing what was right—policy knowledge could be contained in the slim adages of public administration. Public executives, it was thought, needed to know how to execute. They needed power commensurate with their responsibility. Nowadays, of course, political administrators do not execute but are involved in making highly important decisions on society's behalf, and they must mobilize policy intermediaries to deliver the goods. Knowing what is right becomes crucial, and since no one knows that for sure, going through the process of dealing with those who are judged knowledgeable (or at least continuously concerned) becomes even more crucial. Instead of power commensurate with responsibility, issue networks seek influence commensurate with their understanding of the various, complex social choices being made. Of course some participants would like nothing better than complete power over the issues in question. Others seem to want little more than the security that comes with being well informed. As the executive of one new group moving to Washington put it, "We didn't come here to change the world; we came to minimize our surprises."[22]

Whatever the participants' motivation, it is the issue network that ties together what would otherwise be the contradictory tendencies of, on the one hand, more widespread organizational participation in public policy and, on the other, more narrow technocratic specialization in complex modern policies. Such networks need to be distinguished from three other more familiar terms used in connection with political administration. An issue network is a shared-knowledge group having to do with some aspect (or, as defined by the network, some problem) of public policy. It is therefore more well-defined than, first, a shared-attention group or "public"; those in the networks are likely to have a common base of information and understanding of how one knows about policy and identifies its problems. But knowledge does not necessarily produce agreement. Issue networks may or may not, therefore, be mobilized into, second, a shared-action group (creating a coalition) or, third, a shared-belief group (becoming a conventional interest organization). Increasingly, it is through networks of people who regard each other as knowledgeable, or at least as needing to be answered, that public policy issues tend to be refined, evidence debated, and alternative options worked out—though rarely in any controlled, well-organized way.

What does an issue network look like? It is difficult to say precisely, for at any given time only one part of a network may be active and through time the various connections may intensify or fade among the policy intermediaries and the executive and congressional bureaucracies. For example, there is no single health policy network but various sets of people knowledgeable and concerned about cost-control mechanisms, insurance techniques, nutritional programs, prepaid plans, and so on. At one time, those expert in designing a nationwide insurance system may seem to be operating in relative isolation, until it becomes clear that previous efforts to control costs have already created precedents that have to be accommodated in any new system, or that the issue of federal funding for abortions has laid land mines in the path of any workable plan.

The debate on energy policy is rich in examples of the kaleidoscopic interaction of changing issue networks. The Carter administration's initial proposal was worked out among experts who were closely tied in to conservation-minded networks. Soon it became clear that those concerned with macroeconomic policies had been largely bypassed in the planning, and last-minute amendments were made in the proposal presented to Congress, a fact that was not lost on the networks of leading economists and economic correspondents. Once congressional consideration began, it quickly became evident that attempts to define the energy debate in terms of a classic confrontation between big oil companies and consumer interests were doomed. More and more policy watchers joined in the debate, bringing to it their own concerns and analyses: tax reformers, nuclear power specialists, civil rights groups interested in more jobs; the list soon grew beyond the wildest dreams of the original energy policy planners. The problem, it became clear, was that no one could quickly turn the many networks of knowledgeable people into a shared-action coalition, much less into a single, shared-attitude group believing it faced the moral equivalent of war. Or, if it was a war, it was a Vietnam-type quagmire.

It would be foolish to suggest that the clouds of issue networks that have accompanied expanding national policies are set to replace the more familiar politics of subgovernments in Washington. What they are doing is to overlay the once stable political reference points with new forces that complicate calculations, decrease predictability, and impose considerable strains on those charged with government leadership. The overlay of networks and issue politics not only confronts but also seeps down into the formerly well-established politics of particular policies and programs. Social security, which for a generation had been quietly managed by a small circle of insiders, becomes controversial and politicized. The Army Corps of Engineers, once the picturebook example of control by subgovernments, is dragged into the brawl on environmental politics. The once quiet "traffic safety establishment" finds its own safety permanently endangered by the consumer movement.

Confrontation between networks and iron triangles in the Social and Rehabilitation Service, the disintegration of the mighty politics of the Public Health Service and its corps—the list could be extended into a chronicle of American national government during the last generation.[23] The point is that a somewhat new and difficult dynamic is being played out in the world of politics and administration. It is not what has been feared for so long: that technocrats and other people in white coats will expropriate the policy process. If there is to be any expropriation, it is likely to be by the policy activists, those who care deeply about a set of issues and are determined to shape the fabric of public policy accordingly.

THE TECHNOPOLS

The many new policy commitments of the last twenty years have brought about a play of influence that is many-stranded and loose. Iron triangles or other clear shapes may embrace some of the participants, but the larger picture in any policy area is likely to be one involving many other policy specialists. More than ever, policy making is becoming an intramural activity among expert issue-watchers, their networks, and their networks of networks. In this situation any neat distinction between the governmental structure and its environment tends to break down.

Political administrators, like the bureaucracies they superintend, are caught up in the trend toward issue specialization at the same time that responsibility is increasingly being dispersed among large numbers of policy intermediaries. The specialization in question may have little to do with purely professional training. Neither is it a matter of finding interest group spokesmen placed in appointive positions. Instead of party politicians, today's political executives tend to be policy politicians, able to move among the various networks, recognized as knowledgeable about the substance of issues concerning these networks, but not irretrievably identified with highly controversial positions. Their reputations among those "in the know" make them available for presidential appointments. Their mushiness on the most sensitive issues makes them acceptable. Neither a craft professional nor a gifted amateur, the modern recruit for political leadership in the bureaucracy is a journeyman of issues.

Approximately 200 top presidential appointees are charged with supervising the bureaucracy. These political executives include thirteen departmental secretaries, some half a dozen nondepartmental officials who are also in the cabinet, several dozen deputy secretaries or undersecretaries, and many more commission chairmen, agency administrators, and office directors. Below these men and women are another 500 politically appointed assistant secretaries, commissioners, deputies, and a host of other officials. If all of these positions and those who hold them are unknown to the public at large, there is nevertheless no mistaking the importance of the work that they do. It is here, in the layers of public managers, that political promise confronts administrative reality, or what passes for reality in Washington.

At first glance, generalization seems impossible. The political executive system in Washington has everything. Highly trained experts in medicine, economics, and the natural sciences can be found in positions where there is something like guild control over the criteria for a political appointment. But one can also find the most obvious patronage payoffs; obscure commissions, along with cultural and inter-American affairs, are some of the favorite dumping grounds. There are highly issue-oriented appointments, such as the sixty or so "consumer advocates" that the Ralph Nader groups

claimed were in the early Carter administration. And there are also particular skill groups represented in appointments devoid of policy content (for example, about two-thirds of the top government public relations positions were filled during 1977 with people from private media organizations). In recent years, the claims of women and minorities for executive positions have added a further kind of positional patronage, where it is the number of positions rather than any agreed policy agenda that is important. After one year, about 11 percent of President Carter's appointees were women, mainly from established law firms, or what is sometimes referred to as the Ladies' Auxiliary of the Old Boys' Network.

How to make sense of this welter of political executives? Certainly there is a subtlety in the arrangements by which top people become top people and deal with each other. For the fact is that the issue networks share information not only about policy problems but also about people. Rarely are high political executives people who have an overriding identification with a particular interest group or credentials as leading figures in a profession. Rather they are people with recognized reputations in particular areas of public policy. The fluid networks through which they move can best be thought of as proto-bureaucracies. There are subordinate and superordinate positions through which they climb from lesser to greater renown and recognition, but these are not usually within the same organization. It is indeed a world of large-scale bureaucracies but one interlaced with loose, personal associations in which reputations are established by word of mouth. The reputations in question depend little on what, in Weberian terms, would be bureaucratically rational evaluations of objective performance or on what the political scientist would see as the individual's power rating. Even less do reputations depend on opinions in the electorate at large. What matters are the assessments of people like themselves concerning how well, in the short term, the budding technopol is managing each of his assignments in and at the fringes of government.

Consider, for example, the thirteen department secretaries in Jimmy Carter's original cabinet. In theory at least, one could spin out reasons for thinking that these top political appointments would be filled by longstanding Carter loyalists, of representatives of major Democratic party factions, or recognized interest group leaders. In fact, none of these labels is an accurate characterization. One thing that stands out clearly is the continuation of a long-term trend away from relying on party politicians, others active in electoral politics, or clientele spokesmen, to fill executive positions. Nelson Polsby has concluded that at most, three members of the original Carter cabinet fell into the clientele or party political category.[24] Polsby goes on to divide the remainder into specialists and generalists, but a closer look at individual careers suggests how almost all of them—the Vances and the Califanos, the Browns and the Schlesingers—came out of or had a lasting affinity to particular issue networks.

The background of Carter's cabinet can be described in terms of movement among four great estates: academia, corporate business and the law, the government bureaucracy, and (to a lesser extent) elective politics. To represent these movements on a motionless page is difficult, but even a rough, schematic presentation of top public executives' careers reveals several outstanding features (see Table 18.2). Obviously no one estate is able to dominate all of the top positions. Moreover, every cabinet secretary has been service in more than one of the major sectors. While there is movement from lower to higher positions, few people move up through the ranks of a single organization or sector in order to reach

the top slots. Rather they move in hierarchies that stretch across the estates. Lower academic or business positions are parlayed into higher political appointments; lower political appointments into higher business positions; and so on.

Finally, and most importantly, all of President Carter's new cabinet secretaries had established reputations for handling leading problems that were regarded by issue-watchers as having a place on the public agenda. The secretary of interior had an outstanding record in dealing with conservation and environmental issues. The secretary of labor was a recognized expert in labor economics, particularly the problems of minorities. The secretary of health, education, and welfare had presided over the creation of the Johnson Great Society programs a decade earlier. The secretary of defense was one of the insiders in the arcane world of defense technology. The secretary of commerce had a well established reputation as an advocate for consumer, minority, and women's issues. And so it went. For the one new field where issues and networks were poorly formed, the Energy Department, Carter chose a respected technocrat's technocrat with a strong track record in strategic theory, defense management, and bureaucratic politics.

The emergence of the policy politicians in our national politics goes back many years, at least to the new policy commitments of the New Deal era. Policy initiatives undertaken in the last generation have only intensified the process. For example, since 1960 the selection process for presidential appointees has seen important changes.[25] Using somewhat different techniques, each White House staff has struggled to find new ways of becoming less dependent on the crop of job applicants produced by normal party channels and of reaching out to new pools of highly skilled executive manpower. The rationale behind these efforts is always that executive

Table 18.2 Career Patterns of Selected Members of Carter's First Cabinet

Cabinet Member	Academia	Government	Corporate Business/Law	Elective Politics
Michael Blumenthal (Treasury)	Ph.D. economics teacher 1953–57			
		deputy assist. secretary 1961–63 U.S. trade representative 1964–67	manager 1957–59 vice president 1959–61	
		cabinet secretary	executive 1967–72 president and chairman 1973–76	
Harold Brown (Defense)	Ph.D. physics teacher 1947–49 research scientist 1949–52 laboratory manager 1952–60	consultant 1956–61 director of research office 1961–65 air force secretary 1965–69		
	university president 1969–77	cabinet secretary		

Table 18.2 Career Patterns of Selected Members of Carter's First Cabinet (*continued*)

Joseph Califano (Health, Education, and Welfare)	LL.B.
	Judge Advocate General's Office 1955–58
	law practice 1958–61
	special assistant 1961–63
	general counsel 1963–64
	deputy secretary 1964–65
	presidential assistant 1965–68
	law practice 1969–71
	law firm partner 1971–76
	cabinet secretary

Bob Bergland (Agriculture)	
	(independent farmer)
	regional official 1961–62
	regional director 1963–68
	(independent farmer) 1968–70
	congressman 1971–76
	cabinet secretary

Juanita Kreps (Commerce)

instructor 1942–43
economist 1943–44
instructor 1945–46
Ph.D. 1948
lecturer 1952–55
associate professor 1963–68
various advisory positions 1963–76
dean 1969–72
vice president 1973–76
cabinet secretary

Patricia Harris (Housing and Urban Development)

LL.B.
attorney 1960–61
associate dean 1962–65
ambassador 1965–67
dean 1967
law firm partner 1967–76
various part-time party positions 1960–76
cabinet secretary

NOTE: Part-time membership on corporate boards is not included.

SOURCE: Compiled by the author from biographies supplied by the respective cabinet secretaries' offices.

leadership in the bureaucracy requires people who are knowledgeable about complex policies and acceptable to the important groups that claim an interest in the ever growing number of issue areas. Not surprisingly, the policy experts within the various networks who are consulted typically end by recommending each other. Thus over half of the people President-elect Carter identified as his outside advisers on political appointments ended up in executive jobs themselves. Similarly, while candidate Carter's political manager promised to resign if establishment figures such as Cyrus Vance and Zbigniew Brzezinski were given appointments after the election, at least half of the candidate's expert foreign policy advisers (including Vance and Brzezinski) wound up in major political positions with the administration.

Historical studies tend to confirm the impression of change in the political executive system. In the past, there have generally been short-term fluctuations in a few social attributes (religion, types of school attended) that can be associated with changes in party control of the presidency. But, especially since the early 1960s, changes in party control of the White House have produced few distinctive differences in the characteristics of political appointees. Instead, the longer-term trend toward specialized policy expertise tends to wash over the short-term political fluctuations. Law, the traditional career base for generalists, has become progressively less important in filling the ranks of political executives. Academia, think tanks, and people with specialized credentials have been gaining in importance. If law itself were broken down into general versus specialized practice, the trend would probably appear even more sharply. In any event, the historical findings tentatively support the view that "there is a growing distance between electoral coalitions and governing coalitions . . . The bases a

presidential candidate needs to touch in order to win election are progressively unrelated to the bases a president needs to govern."[26]

Below the level of cabinet secretaries, the same changes in political administrators stand out even more sharply. Fifty years ago there were few political subordinates to the top executives in the departments, and scholars dismissed the career background of those who were there as a "miscellany of party assignments and political posts."[27] Today the people filling the much larger number of subordinate political executive positions are rarely partisan figures with any significant ties to party or electorate. Instead they are part of a political bureaucracy of policy specialists that sits atop and beside the permanent career bureaucracy in Washington. The key indicators for these changes are not just the obviously larger numbers of appointees. More revealing of the political bureaucracy is the growing compartmentalization by functional specialty and the increased layering of appointed executives. Figure 18.2 offers three snapshots of the top political manpower in one department: before the arrival of the New Deal, before the Kennedy-Johnson Great Society, and at the present time. Despite the picture that Figure 18.2 presents of bureaucratic expansion in political manpower, the Labor Department is actually among the smallest agencies, with a reputation for one of the leanest staff structures, in Washington.

The Agriculture Department offers another good example of change in one of the oldest and most traditional domestic departments. At one time, agricultural policies could be accounted for fairly economically in terms of general purpose farmers' organizations, particular bureaus in the Department of Agriculture, and a congressional farm block in legislative committees and subcommittees. Today one would have to feed into the equation

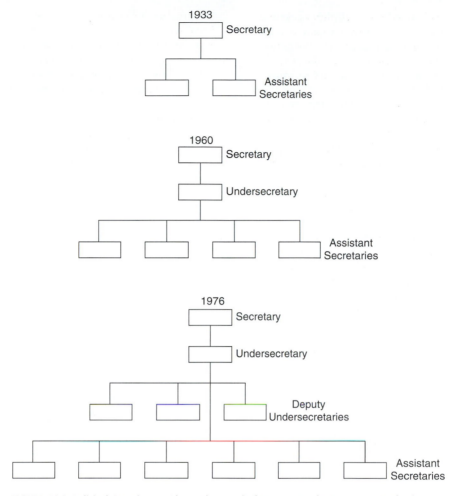

FIGURE 18.2 Political Appointees Above the Level of Bureau Heads, Department of Labor, 1933, 1960, and 1976

SOURCE: U.S. Congress, Senate, Committee on Civil Service, *Positions Not Under the Civil Service*, document no. 173, 72d Cong., 2d sess., January 1933, pp. 4 and 19; U.S. Congress, Senate, Committee on Post Office and Civil Service, *United States Government Policy and Supporting Positions*, committee print, 86th Cong., 2d sess., 1960, p. 92; U.S. Congress, House, Committee on Post Office and Civil Service, *United States Government Policy and Supporting Positions*, 94th Cong., 2d sess., 1976, pp. 64–65.

not only more specialized expressions of agricultural interests (different associations for particular commodities, corporate "farmers," grass-roots family farm groups, and so on) but also environmentalists, international economic and foreign policy advocates, and civil rights, nutritional, and consumer groups.

Whereas a previous agriculture secretary might have surrounded himself with a few political cronies and a clutch of Farm Bureau (or National Farmers' Union) insiders, the current secretary's inner circle is described as including "three women (one of them black), a Mexican-American, an environmentalist, two economists, and a politician."[28] Within a year of his appointment the politician was gone after reported fights with one of the "women," who was also the former executive director of the Consumer Federation of America.

Of course, if appointed executives were part of a coherent political team, the larger numbers and deeper issue specialization might suggest a stronger capacity for democratic leadership in the bureaucracy. But as participants themselves often come to realize, this is not the case. Political executives' tenure in a given position is short. Their political bases of support in the electorate at large are ambiguous at best. Any mutual commitment to each other is problematic. Thus coherent political leadership in the bureaucracy—especially leadership with any ties to ordinary democratic politics— is normally at a premium. What one can count on finding in and at the fringes of every specialized part of the political bureaucracy are policy networks. It is likely to be in these that judgments about performance are made, reputations established or lost, and replacements for appointees—whoever may be the President—supplied.

THE EXECUTIVE LEADERSHIP PROBLEM

Washington has always relied on informal means of producing political leaders in government. This is no less true now than in the days when party spoils ruled presidential appointments. It is the informal mechanisms that have changed. No doubt some of the increasing emphasis on educational credentials, professional specialization, and technical facility merely reflects changes in society at large. But it is also important to recognize that government activity has itself been changing the informal mechanisms

that produce political administrators. Accumulating policy commitments have become crucial forces affecting the kind of executive leadership that emerges. E. E. Schattschneider put it better when he observed that "new policies create new politics."[29]

For many years now the list of issues on the public agenda has grown more dense as new policy concerns have been added and few dropped. Administratively, this has proliferated the number of policy intermediaries. Politically, it has mobilized more and more groups of people who feel they have a stake, a determined stake, in this or that issue of public policy. These changes are in turn encouraging further specialization of the government's work force and bureaucratic layering in its political leadership. However, the term "political" needs to be used carefully. Modern officials responsible for making the connection between politics and administration bear little resemblance to the party politicians who once filled patronage jobs. Rather, today's political executive is likely to be a person knowledgeable about the substance of particular issues and adept at moving among the networks of people who are intensely concerned about them.

What are the implications for American government and politics? The verdict cannot be one-sided, if only because political management of the bureaucracy serves a number of diverse purposes. At least three important advantages can be found in the emerging system.

First, the reliance on issue networks and policy politicians is obviously consistent with some of the larger changes in society. Ordinary voters are apparently less constrained by party identification and more attracted to an issue-based style of politics. Party organizations are said to have fallen into a state of decay and to have become less capable of supplying enough highly qualified executive manpower. If government is committed to intervening in more complex, specialized areas, it is useful to draw upon the experts and policy specialists for the public management of these programs. Moreover, the congruence between an executive leadership and an electorate that are both uninterested in party politics may help stabilize a rapidly changing society. Since no one really knows how to solve the policy puzzles, policy politicians have the important quality of being disposable without any serious political ramifications (unless of course there are major symbolic implications, as in President Nixon's firing of Attorney General Elliot Richardson).

Within government, the operation of issue networks may have a second advantage in that they link Congress and the executive branch in ways that political parties no longer can. For many years, reformers have sought to revive the idea of party discipline as a means of spanning the distance between the two branches and turning their natural competition to useful purposes. But as the troubled dealings of recent Democratic Presidents with their majorities in Congress have indicated, political parties tend to be a weak bridge.

Meanwhile, the linkages of technocracy between the branches are indeliberately growing. The congressional bureaucracy that has blossomed in Washington during the last generation is in many ways like the political bureaucracy in the executive branch. In general, the new breed of congressional staffer is not a legislative crony or beneficiary of patronage favors. Personal loyalty to the congressman is still paramount, but the new-style legislative bureaucrat is likely to be someone skilled in dealing with certain complex policy issues, possibly with credentials as a policy analyst, but certainly an expert in using other experts and their networks.

None of this means an absence of conflict between President and Congress.

Policy technicians in the two branches are still working for different sets of clients with different interests. The point is that the growth of specialized policy networks tends to perform the same useful services that it was once hoped a disciplined national party system would perform. Sharing policy knowledge, the networks provide a minimum common framework for political debate and decision in the two branches. For example, on energy policy, regardless of one's position on gas deregulation or incentives to producers, the policy technocracy has established a common language for discussing the issues, a shared grammar for identifying the major points of contention, a mutually familiar rhetoric of argumentation. Whether in Congress or the executive branch or somewhere outside, the "movers and shakers" in energy policy (as in health insurance, welfare reform, strategic arms limitation, occupational safety, and a host of other policy areas) tend to share an analytic repertoire for coping with the issues. Like experienced party politicians of earlier times, policy politicians in the knowledge networks may not agree; but they understand each other's way of looking at the world and arguing about policy choices.

A third advantage is the increased maneuvering room offered to political executives by the loose-jointed play of influence. If appointees were ambassadors from clearly defined interest groups and professions, or if policy were monopolized in iron triangles, then the chances for executive leadership in the bureaucracy would be small. In fact, however, the proliferation of administrative middlemen and networks of policy watchers offers new strategic resources for public managers. These are mainly opportunities to split and recombine the many sources of support and opposition that exist on policy issues. Of course, there are limits on how far a political executive can go in shopping for a constituency, but the general tendency over time has been to extend those limits. A secretary of labor will obviously pay close attention to what the AFL–CIO has to say, but there are many other voices to hear, not only in the union movement but also minority groups interested in jobs, state and local officials administering the department's programs, consumer groups worried about wage-push inflation, employees faced with unsafe working conditions, and so on. By the same token, former Secretary of Transportation William Coleman found new room for maneuver on the problem of landings by supersonic planes when he opened up the setpiece debate between pro- and anti-Concorde groups to a wider play of influence through public hearings. Clearly the richness of issue politics demands a high degree of skill to contain expectations and manage the natural dissatisfaction that comes from courting some groups rather than others. But at least it is a game that can be affected by skill, rather than one that is predetermined-by immutable forces.

These three advantages are substantial. But before we embrace the rule of policy politicians and their networks, it is worth considering the threats they pose for American government. Issue networks may be good at influencing policy, but can they govern? Should they?

The first and foremost problem is the old one of democratic legitimacy. Weaknesses in executive leadership below the level of the President have never really been due to interest groups, party politics, or Congress. The primary problem has always been the lack of any democratically based power. Political executives get their popular mandate to do anything in the bureaucracy second-hand, from either an elected chief executive or Congress. The emerging system of political technocrats makes this democratic weakness much more severe. The

more closely political administrators become identified with the various specialized policy networks, the farther they become separated from the ordinary citizen. Political executives can maneuver among the already mobilized issue networks and may occasionally do a little mobilizing of their own. But this is not the same thing as creating a broad base of public understanding and support for national policies. The typical presidential appointee will travel to any number of conferences, make speeches to the membership of one association after another, but almost never will he or she have to see or listen to an ordinary member of the public. The trouble is that only a small minority of citizens, even of those who are seriously attentive to public affairs, are likely to be mobilized in the various networks.[30] Those who are not policy activists depend on the ability of government institutions to act on their behalf.

If the problem were merely an information gap between policy experts and the bulk of the population, then more communication might help. Yet instead of garnering support for policy choices, more communication from the issue networks tends to produce an "everything causes cancer" syndrome among ordinary citizens. Policy forensics among the networks yield more experts making more sophisticated claims and counterclaims to the point that the non-specialist becomes inclined to concede everything and believe nothing that he hears. The ongoing debates on energy policy, health crises, or arms limitation are rich in examples of public skepticism about what "they," the abstruse policy experts, are doing and saying. While the highly knowledgeable have been playing a larger role in government, the proportion of the general public concluding that those running the government don't seem to know what they are doing has risen rather steadily.[31] Likewise, the more government has tried to help, the more feelings of public helplessness have grown.

No doubt many factors and events are linked to these changing public attitudes. The point is that the increasing prominence of issue networks is bound to aggravate problems of legitimacy and public disenchantment. Policy activists have little desire to recognize an unpleasant fact: that their influential systems for knowledgeable policy making tend to make democratic politics more difficult. There are at least four reasons.

Complexity

Democratic political competition is based on the idea of trying to simplify complexity into a few, broadly intelligible choices. The various issue networks, on the other hand, have a stake in searching out complexity in what might seem simple. Those who deal with particular policy issues over the years recognize that policy objectives are usually vague and results difficult to measure. Actions relevant to one policy goal can frequently be shown to be inconsistent with others. To gain a reputation as a knowledgeable participant, one must juggle all of these complexities and demand that other technocrats in the issue networks do the same.

Consensus

A major aim in democratic politics is, after open argument, to arrive at some workable consensus of views. Whether by trading off one issue against another or by combining related issues, the goal is agreement. Policy activists may commend this democratic purpose in theory, but what their issue networks actually provide is a way of processing dissension. The aim is good policy—the right outcome on the issue. Since what that means is disputable among knowledgeable people, the desire for agreement must often take second place to one's understanding of the issue. Trade-offs or

combinations—say, right-to-life groups with nuclear-arms-control people; environmentalists and consumerists; civil liberties groups and anti-gun controllers—represent a kind of impurity for many of the newly proliferating groups. In general there are few imperatives pushing for political consensus among the issue networks and many rewards for those who become practiced in the techniques of informed skepticism about different positions.

Confidence

Democratic politics presumes a kind of psychological asymmetry between leaders and followers. Those competing for leadership positions are expected to be sure of themselves and of what is to be done, while those led are expected to have a certain amount of detachment and dubiety in choosing how to give their consent to be governed. Politicians are supposed to take credit for successes, to avoid any appearance of failure, and to fix blame clearly on their opponents; voters weigh these claims and come to tentative judgments, pending the next competition among the leaders.

The emerging policy networks tend to reverse the situation. Activists mobilized around the policy issues are the true believers. To survive, the newer breed of leaders, or policy politicians, must become well versed in the complex, highly disputed substance of the issues. A certain tentativeness comes naturally as ostensible leaders try to spread themselves across the issues. Taking credit shows a lack of understanding of how intricate policies work and may antagonize those who really have been zealously pushing the issue. Spreading blame threatens others in the established networks and may raise expectations that new leadership can guarantee a better policy result. Vagueness about what is to be done allows policy problems to be dealt with as they develop and in accord with the intensity of opinion among policy specialists at that time. None of this is likely to warm the average citizen's confidence in his leaders. The new breed of policy politicians are cool precisely because the issue networks are hot.

Closure

Part of the genius of democratic politics is its ability to find a nonviolent decision-rule (by voting) for ending debate in favor of action. All the incentives in the policy technocracy work against such decisive closure. New studies and findings can always be brought to bear. The biggest rewards in these highly intellectual groups go to those who successfully challenge accepted wisdom. The networks thrive by continuously weighing alternative courses of action on particular policies, not by suspending disbelief and accepting that something must be done.

For all of these reasons, what is good for policy making (in the sense of involving well-informed people and rigorous analysts) may be bad for democratic politics. The emerging policy technocracy tends, as Henry Aaron has said of social science research, to "corrode any simple faiths around which political coalitions ordinarily are built."[32] Should we be content with simple faiths? Perhaps not; but the great danger is that the emerging world of issue politics and policy experts will turn John Stuart Mill's argument about the connection between liberty and popular government on its head. More informed argument about policy choices may produce more incomprehensibility. More policy intermediaries may widen participation among activists but deepen suspicions among unorganized nonspecialists. There may be more group involvement and less democratic legitimacy, more knowledge and more Know-Nothingism. Activists are likely to remain unsatisfied with, and nonactivists uncommitted to,

what government is doing. Superficially this cancelling of forces might seem to assure a conservative tilt away from new, expansionary government policies. However, in terms of undermining a democratic identification of ordinary citizens with their government, the tendencies are profoundly radical.

A second difficulty with the issue networks is the problem that they create for the President as ostensible chief of the executive establishment. The emerging policy technocracy puts presidential appointees outside of the chief executive's reach in a way that narrowly focused iron triangles rarely can. At the end of the day, constituents of these triangles can at least be bought off by giving them some of the material advantages that they crave. But for issue activists it is likely to be a question of policy choices that are right or wrong. In this situation, more analysis and staff expertise—far from helping—may only hinder the President in playing an independent political leadership role. The influence of the policy technicians and their networks permeates everything the White House may want to do. Without their expertise there are no option papers, no detailed data and elaborate assessments to stand up against the onslaught of the issue experts in Congress and outside. Of course a President can replace a political executive, but that is probably merely to substitute one incumbent of the relevant policy network for another.

It is, therefore, no accident that President Carter found himself with a cabinet almost none of whom were either his longstanding political backers or leaders of his party. Few if any of his personal retinue could have passed through the reputational screens of the networks to be named, for example, a secretary of labor or defense. Moreover, anyone known to be close to the President and placed in an operating position in the bureaucracy puts himself, and through him the President, in an extremely vulnerable position. Of the three cabinet members who were President Carter's own men, one, Andrew Young, was under extreme pressure to resign in the first several months. Another Carter associate, Bert Lance, was successfully forced to resign after six months, and the third, Griffin Bell, was given particularly tough treatment during his confirmation hearings and was being pressured to resign after only a year in office. The emerging system of political administration tends to produce executive arrangements in which the President's power stakes are on the line almost everywhere in terms of policy, whereas almost nowhere is anyone on the line for him personally.

Where does all this leave the President as a politician and as an executive of executives? In an impossible position. The problem of connecting politics and administration currently places any President in a classic no-win predicament. If he attempts to use personal loyalists as agency and department heads, he will be accused of politicizing the bureaucracy and will most likely put his executives in an untenable position for dealing with their organizations and the related networks. If he tries to create a countervailing source of policy expertise at the center, he will be accused of aggrandizing the Imperial Presidency and may hopelessly bureaucratize the White House's operations. If he relies on some benighted idea of collective cabinet government and on departmental executives for leadership in the bureaucracy (as Carter did in his first term), then the President does more than risk abdicating his own leadership responsibilities as the only elected executive in the national government; he is bound to become a creature of the issue networks and the policy specialists. It would be pleasant to think that there is a neat way out of this trilemma, but there is not.

Finally, there are disturbing questions surrounding the accountability of a political technocracy. The real problem is not that policy specialists specialize but that, by the nature of public office, they must generalize. Whatever an influential political executive does is done with all the collective authority of government and in the name of the public at large. It is not difficult to imagine situations in which policies make excellent sense within the cloisters of the expert issue watchers and yet are nonsense or worse seen from the viewpoint of ordinary people, the kinds of people political executives rarely meet. Since political executives themselves never need to pass muster with the electorate, the main source of democratic accountability must lie with the President and Congress. Given the President's problems and Congress's own burgeoning bureaucracy of policy specialists, the prospects for a democratically responsible executive establishment are poor at best.

Perhaps we need not worry. A case could be made that all we are seeing is a temporary commotion stirred up by a generation of reformist policies. In time the policy process may reenter a period of detumescence as the new groups and networks subside into the familiar triangulations of power.

However, a stronger case can be made that the changes will endure. In the first place, sufficient policy-making forces have now converged in Washington that it is unlikely that we will see a return to the familiar cycle of federal quiescence and policy experimentation by state governments. The central government, surrounded by networks of policy specialists, probably now has the capacity for taking continual policy initiatives. In the second place, there seems to be no way of braking, much less reversing, policy expectations generated by the compensatory mentality. To cut back on commitments undertaken in the last generation would itself be a major act of redistribution and could be expected to yield even more turmoil in the policy process. Once it becomes accepted that relative rather than absolute deprivation is what matters, the crusaders can always be counted upon to be in business.

A third reason why our politics and administration may never be the same lies in the very fact that so many policies have already been accumulated. Having to make policy in an environment already crowded with public commitments and programs increases the odds of multiple, indirect impacts of one policy on another, of one perspective set in tension with another, of one group and then another being mobilized. This sort of complexity and unpredictability creates a hostile setting for any return to traditional interest group politics.

Imagine trying to govern in a situation where the short-term political resources you need are stacked around a changing series of discrete issues, and where people overseeing these issues have nothing to prevent their pressing claims beyond any resources that they can offer in return. Imagine too that the more they do so, the more you lose understanding and support from public backers who have the long-term resources that you need. Whipsawed between cynics and true believers, policy would always tend to evolve to levels of insolubility. It is not easy for a society to politicize itself and at the same time depoliticize government leadership. But we in the United States may be managing to do just this.

NOTES

1. Hugh Heclo, *A Government of Strangers: Executive Politics in Washington* (Washington, D.C.: Brookings Institution, 1977).

2. Perhaps the most widely cited interpretations are J. Leiper Freeman, *The Political Process* (New York: Random House, 1965); and Douglass Cater, *Power in Washington* (New York: Vintage, 1964).

3. Office of Management and Budget, *The United States Budget in Brief, 1979* (Washington, D.C., 1978), p. 21.

4. Adlai E. Stevenson, quoted in James L. Sundquist, *Politics and Policy* (Washington, D.C.: Brookings Institution, 1968), p. 385.

5. Office of Management and Budget, *The Budget in Brief, 1979,* p. 21.

6. Office of Management and Budget, *Special Analyses, Budget of the United States Government, 1979* (Washington, D.C., 1978), table A-4, p. 12.

7. Charles L. Schultze, "Federal Spending: Past, Present, and Future," in Henry Owen and Charles L. Schultze, *Setting National Priorities: The Next Ten Years* (Washington, D.C.: Brookings Institution, 1976), p. 335.

8. Charles L. Schultze, *The Public Use of Private Interest* (Washington, D.C. Brookings Institution 1977).

9. U.S. Congress, Senate, Subcommittee on Intergovernmental Relations of the Committee on Government Operations, *Confidence and Concern: Citizens View American Government,* committee print, 93d Cong., 1st sess., 1973, part 2, pp. 111, 117, 118–19, 238.

10. Office of Management and Budget, *Special Analyses, 1979 Budget,* p. 33.

11. Samuel H. Beer, "Political Overload and Federalism," *Polity,* vol. 10 (March 1977).

12. Unpublished talk at the Brookings Institution, June 8, 1977.

13. See for example Ellis Hawley, "Herbert Hoover and the Associative State," *Journal of American History,* June 1974; and Grant McConnell, *Private Power and American Democracy* (New York: Alfred Knopf, 1966), pp. 50, 69.

14. A similar tendency for public involvement to divide private interests occurred with earlier health initiatives in other countries. See Arnold Heidenheimer, Hugh Heclo, and Carolyn Adams, *Comparative Public Policy* (New York: St. Martin's Press, 1976).

15. Craig Colgate, Jr., ed., *National Trade and Professional Associations* (Washington, D.C.: Columbia Books, 1978).

16. For example, a statement issued by Ralph Nader on April 24, 1978, criticizing the Carter energy program included endorsements by the National Resources Defense Council Inc., Friends of the Earth Inc., the Environmental Policy Center, the Environmental Action Foundation, Environmentalists for Full Employment, the Wilderness Society, Consumer Action Now, the Sierra Club, the Environmental Defense Fund Inc., the National Parks and Conservation Association, and the National Consumers League.

17. Alexis de Tocqueville, *Democracy in America* (New York: Harper and Row, 1966), p. 176.

18. Seymour Martin Lipset and William Schneider, "The Bakke Case: How Would It Be Decided at the Bar of Public Opinion?" *Public Opinion* (March/April 1978), pp. 41–42.

19. McKinsey and Company, Inc., "Strengthening Control of Grade Escalation" (Office of Management and Budget Archives: processed, June 1966).

20. *Washington Post,* August 28, 1977, p. 1.

21. Harrison W. Fox, Jr. and Susan Webb Hammond, *Congressional Staffs* (New York: Free Press, 1977).

22. Steven V. Roberts, "Trade Associations Flocking to Capital as U.S. Role Rises," *New York Times,* March 4, 1978, p. 44.

23. For a full account of particular cases, see for example Martha Derthick, *Policy-Making for Social Security* (Washington, D.C.: Brookings Institution, forthcoming); Daniel Mazmanian and Jeanne Nienaber, *Environmentalism, Participation and the Corps of Engineers: A Study of Organizational Change* (Washington, D.C.: Brookings Institution, 1978). For the case of traffic safety, see Jack L. Walker, "Setting the Agenda in the U.S. Senate," *British Journal of Political Science,* vol. 7 (1977), pp. 432–45.

24. Nelson W. Polsby, "Presidential Cabinet Making," *Political Science Quarterly,* vol. 93 (Spring 1978). Brief biographies of the original Carter cabinet are given in Congressional Quarterly, *President Carter* (Washington, D.C.: Congressional Quarterly, 1977), pp. 17–22.

25. Changes in the presidential personnel process are discussed in Hugh Heclo, *A Government of Strangers* (Washington, D.C.: Brookings Institution, 1977), pp. 89–95.

26. Kenneth Prewitt and William McAllister, "Changes in the American Executive Elite, 1930–1970," in Heinz Eulau and Moshe Czudnowski, *Elite Recruitment in Democratic Politics* (New York: Wiley, 1976), p. 127.

27. Arthur W. Macmahon and John D. Millett, *Federal Administrators* (New York: Columbia University Press, 1939), pp. 295, 302.

28. Daniel J. Balz, "Agriculture under Bergland—Many Views, Many Directions," *National Journal,* December 10, 1977, p. 1918. For an interesting case study of the multifaceted play of influence in recent agricultural policy see I. M. Destler, *United States Foreign Economic Policy-Making* (Washington, D.C.: Brookings Institution, 1978).

29. E. E. Schattschneider, *Politics, Pressures and the Tariff* (Hamden: Archon, 1963), p. 288 (originally published 1935).

30. An interesting recent case study showing the complexity of trying to generalize about who is "mobilizable" is James N. Rosenau, *Citizenship Between Elections* (New York: The Free Press, 1974).

31. Since 1964 the Institute for Social Research at the University of Michigan has asked the question, "Do you feel that almost all of the people running the government are smart people, or do you think that quite a few of them don't seem to know what they are doing?" The proportions choosing the latter view have been 28 percent (1964), 38 percent (1968), 45 percent (1970), 42 percent (1972), 47 percent (1974), and 52 percent (1976). For similar findings on public feelings of lack of control over the policy process, see U.S. Congress, Senate, Subcommittee on Intergovernmental Relations of the Committee on Government Operations, *Confidence and Concern: Citizens View American Government,* committee print, 93d Cong., 1st sess., 1973, pt. 1, p. 30. For a more complete discussion of recent trends see the two articles by Arthur H. Miller and Jack Citrin in the *American Political Science Review* (September 1974).

32. Henry J. Aaron, *Politics and the Professors* (Washington, D.C.: Brookings Institution, 1978), p. 159.

PROJECT

Heclo describes the growing tendency that agency department heads possess expertise. Examine the current cabinet posts of the Bush administration. What is the background of each cabinet head? Are these cabinet appointments of a political or policy nature? In your opinion, how expert are these cabinet heads? How much expertise must agency heads hold? Which is more important—their ability to manage their agency or their policy expertise? Why?

19

Organized Interests
and Their Issue Niches

WILLIAM BROWNE

ollowing in line with Heclo's examination of issue networks, William
Browne finds that policy making had become even more complex by the
1990s. Relationships between interest groups and government officials evolved
into new arrangements called issue niches. Because group resources are scarce,
Browne suggests that groups must be strategic in how they deploy them. He
surmises that groups specialize in achieving recognizable, specific identities
within the increasingly crowded interest-group scene. Interest groups create
identities so that they can market themselves to legislators and administrators in
a competitive environment. They lack broad goals and instead focus on quite
specific issues. In the end, groups accommodate one another in order to accomplish their individual group goals. Browne's analysis fits into both elitist and
pluralist frameworks.

QUESTIONS TO CONSIDER

1. What is an issue niche?
2. How is an issue niche different from an issue network?
3. What changes in government have necessitated the rise of issue niches?
4. Do you believe issue niches are at work in all policy domains or only in
   select domains? Why?

G iven the complexities of deciding the many difficult issues of modern government, interest-group and pluralist theories have become conceptually intertwined as we shall see below. Yet, interest-group theory is not well founded on systematic data because they are so hard to collect. So the questions that remain unanswered about theoretical linkages are at least as consequential as the ones unraveled. Using data that link interest-group demands to the range of political issues contested, this study finds something that earlier analyses could not: that organized interests define themselves in terms of carefully constructed issue niches. These, in turn, govern their own selection of which issues to address. Issue niches are, in effect, necessary for organizations as lobbyists and other interest representatives differentiate one from the other in competition for policymakers' support. This self-restricting niche behavior, as it relates to a theory of interest-group services, severely limits the degree to which organized interests promote plural governance.

INTEREST GROUP THEORY AND PLURALIST THOUGHT

Pluralist political thought covers an immense range of topics and concerns, not to mention variation in the use of its terminology. Yet, going back to Dahl (1961) and other community power analysts (Vidich and Bensman 1960; Hunter 1953; Polsby 1963), the crux of their elitism/pluralism disagreements center around a simple theme with a complex premise. The generalized pluralist theme is that multiple interests (either organized at the community or national level) interacting together both

SOURCE: From William Browne, "Organized Interests and Their Issue Niches: A Search for Pluralism in a Policy Domain." *Journal of Politics* 52, no. 2 (May 1990): 477–509. Reprinted with permission from Blackwell Publishing Co.

inside and outside of government and effectively representing all components of a specific society—or, as shall be used here, a network of decision making—produce a democratic process for governing. This theme is premised on the assumption that those representing various private parties will in fact rationally mobilize their resources and play out their interests by active participation on some generally level field of contest.

We now understand that assumption as a most unrealistic one. The first part of this article explains why it is unrealistic in order to show the importance of using issue-level data having specified substantive context. The complexity of the pluralist premise as well as the improbability of meeting its ideal are made clear by numerous interest-group theorists who, over recent decades, looked at the institutional and structural features that distinguish one organized interest from another. All of these theorists brought us, acting independently but through the systematic development of their thought, to the point where we can now call the feasibility of the pluralist premise itself into question, at least for private interests exercising policy influence as the nongovernmental component of the equation.

As so often is the case in the general study of interest groups, the development of thought on this aspect of interest-group theory starts with Truman (1951). Truman called attention to the many types of resources available to interest groups in gaining the access needed to exercise influence. In so doing, he noted that the policy playing field is distinctly tilted, not level. Many of what he identified as resources had to do with the political standing that some organizations already enjoyed in governing circles rather than with such democratic criteria as membership size or its distribution. As both political scientists and sociologists have shown, organizations without such standing are disadvantaged in their representation. Accordingly, they are forced as challengers to engage in costly compensatory behavior in order to deal with inequality of opportunity (Wilson 1973, 281–302; Berry 1977; Tilly 1978; Useem and Zald 1982; Browne 1985). Things are far from fair from in the external decision-making environment in which interest groups operate, even as unspecified as Truman left it.

Olson (1965) and then Salisbury (1969), in moving from external to internal interest-group problems, called into question the democratic potential of interest-group structure from yet another perspective important to representation. Salisbury demonstrated that organizational entrepreneurs marketed group membership on the basis of selective non-policy goods rather than just collective policy benefits. Interest groups, as this view was reinforced by numerous subsequent studies, are now widely understood to be frequently devoid of active policy support from their members. In all likelihood, members often lack extensive knowledge of issues. Several indicators of this lack of policy awareness exist. Research, for example, showed the importance of staff who, by "farming the membership" to gain issue support, construct the interest-group agenda that determines which lobbying priorities will be set (Milbrath 1963; Zeigler and Baer 1969; Schlozman and Tierney 1986).

By the 1980s, scholars fairly well recognized that participatory democracy was not the driving force in interest-group politics. Later, as research pointed to the growing number and even dominance of institutions as organized interests (Salisbury 1984), they understood further that even tacit mass membership support has little to do with much of the activity in the whole of the interest-group system. But, other than those important observations, no operational consensus over the essential characteristics of interest-group pluralism appeared in group theory. Rather, many theorists now suggest, or hope, that some undetermined degree of proliferation and fragmentation of active interests promotes pluralism through some form of interactive bargaining among those who manage the organizations (Greenwald 1977, 306). In this way, the ideas that are valued—if not actively promoted—by all citizens can come into play as government makes decisions under interest-group pressure. The tentativeness with which that suggestion is advanced results primarily from the lack of quantifiable empirical data that characterized the study of interest groups and that only recently began to be rectified (Walker 1983). Hope, it seems, springs eternal in light of evidence to the contrary.

Hope can also guide analysis. To the degree that pluralism and organized interest politics can be intuitively linked in the absence of data from which to generalize, one is almost tempted to take the proliferation/fragmentation contention and hypothesize that the relative number of interests represented can be used to draw distinctions between elite versus pluralist control. The logic for that hypothesis would be based on the assumption that the presence of only a very few active interests within some network of decision making means the limited articulation of policy options. That is, elite factors in a single network discourage entrepreneurial efforts on behalf of otherwise viable or popular policy points of view. On the other hand, supposedly, the existence of multiple interests within a network would produce unrestrained behavior. This would give rise to the expression of a wide range of alternatives. These could each be brought by their entrepreneurs to the bargaining process within the network of decision making in which programs are developed. It is indeed that sort of contention about the effects of over- and underrepresentation that Sohlozman (1984) implied when she commented on the disproportionate presence—or the accent of the heavenly chorus—of business interests in Washington, a condition that elite theorist E. E. Schattschneider (1960) earlier described as the "upper class bias" of interest politics.

Yet the assumption of few-versus-more as a measure of pluralism already had been called into question by repeated observation. One factor stands out in explaining why. There appears to exist little in the way of a negotiating framework for the bargaining that should be going on. McConnell (1966) and Rose (1967), from different disciplinary perspectives, noted a balkanization of interests in U.S. public policy circles. These many interests share empowered places in the whole of government but still operate as so functionally distinct in their issue concerns that they never even contest on the same playing field. That is, in ways that Truman and subsequent interest-group theory long neglected, they are not in the same networks of decision making.

Lauman and Knoke (1987), in a more empirically sophisticated study that represents the new genre of data based interest-group analysis, shrewdly picked up on the importance of specifying which decisional network should be the unit of analysis. When they shifted the context of their analysis from the entire interest-group system to what they termed the policy domain level, they similarly observed private interest balkanization. Lauman and Knoke found a dozen or more subdomains in each of two domains that exist as distinct networks for interest interaction. Thus, as the relevant network of decision making shifts still further from the domain to the subdomain level in their analysis, the number of discernible interactive interests also shifts from many to a few. Lauman and Knoke then applied the distinctive but undistinguishing label "elite interest group pluralism" (377) to this situation. Once again the reason was the lack of central players that can integrate the

limited demands that only a few interests are bringing forth within each subdomain.

But interest-group theory, despite an increasing ability to compare group demands, still remains unclear as to whether patterns of interest interaction based on numerical entry into the decisional network bring elite or pluralist policy input. The concept of elite interest group pluralism, based as it primarily is on the absence of centralization rather than the hoped for interactive bargaining of proliferation and fragmentation, does not address whether interest representation brings with it the widespread articulation of policy alternatives in U.S. government. But the discovery of this omission certainly discourages us from hypothesizing, as we might have earlier, a linkage between numbers of organized interests and pluralism.

More recent and far more data-rich research by Salisbury, Heinz, Lauman, and Nelson (1987) went beyond the Lauman and Knoke findings. This research offered unique insights into the previously ignored dimension of considering alternative policies. In each of four policy domains, they found that networks of decision making are "defined by interaction among organized groups and between groups and public officials" (1218). Within each domain, moreover, interest representatives are generally able to identify both allies and adversaries from among other domain interests. Furthermore, there emerges recognizable patterns of alliances and adversary relationships among interests when representatives are asked about those organizations with whom they are likely to either cooperate or engage in issue contests. These patterns also exist within and between specific types of organizations in each domain.

The implications drawn by Salisbury et al. from their data are important to pluralist theory since they suggest the likelihood of a representational structure at the domain level in which the long hoped for policy options can freely develop. First, a multiplicity of interests are organized to compete for public policy rewards withinwhat can be observed, through recurring interaction, as a network of decision making. Second, within the resulting competition, organized interests target specific but different policy goals rather than cluster around encompassing and only bifurcated options. Organizations do not divide in any structured way over simple policy dichotomies such as an agricultural free market as opposed to a supply control position. Quite the contrary. Within the universe of organized interests in any single domain, representatives plot policy objectives that are far more varied and likely to be reflective of an extensive search for policy alternatives.

But, without resorting to theoretical extrapolation, do numerous policy options develop? We still do not know. However, early research by Lowi (1964), with later interpretation by Wilson (1973, 327–45), suggested that these options will not all, or even in large number, be pursued. Many patterns of decisions, such as distributive ones, are not formulated to encourage pluralist contests. Unfortunately, the Salisbury et al. research had other objectives than measuring either the degree of conflict or the likelihood of policy alternatives developing within the decisional network. As a result, they analyzed only a limited number of issues. They did not delve into the entire range of issue priorities of each organized interest within each domain. Were they to have done so, evidence would have been available to show the degree to which conflict and advancement of competing issues is characteristic of interest-group interaction within whatever are found to be the most relevant interactive networks for decision making, either at the domain or subdomain level. Only by collecting such an extensive amount of data can the level of analysis be shifted in context

from the domain or subdomain level to the actual issue level. And only at the issue level can a realistic measure of the degree of specialization and conflict be determined. Until such data are collected, we can never dispel the suspicions planted by McConnell, Rose, and cohorts about the unlikely survival of all policy ideas in the inherently inequitable universe of interest-group politics. Therefore, the general hypothesis that guides this study is a less hopeful one than pluralist theory so far suggests. It appears that numerous interests, despite their potential for bringing forth alternative policy options, are insufficient to encourage pluralist governance and its hoped for replication of both the most widely held and the most widely dispersed of social values.

THE RESEARCH

Policy universes, domains, and subdomains as networks of decision making are defined, by use and implication in the studies cited above, both by the players involved and by the range of issues being decided. The issues and the choices made about them, after all, are what prompt interest representatives to act and, therefore, interact among themselves. The data presented here follow the issue level analysis option that Salisbury et al. quite legitimately did not pursue when they focused on domain patterns. By design, this research advances the Salisbury et al. findings as to the potential of pluralism by examining, first, how extensive the alliances and adversary relationships are among and between organized interests and, second, what motivates these interactive relationships.

The analysis of issue data is in four sections. The first looks to see whether or not we can find organized interests that have a sufficiently broad issue interest to integrate demands within the domain. That is, are there central players? In the second section, the analysis turns to the types of issues dealt with by different interest groups. Are they sector-wide, narrow, or a mix of the two? Section three measures issue overlap and conflict among participating organizations. Finally, section four examines multi-interest coalition politics as a means of integrating domain demands in the absence of individual organizations that will do so.

Only one policy domain, agriculture, was selected for this analysis because of the immense difficulty in securing information about a nearly complete set of domain issues, their content, and outcomes.[1] However, despite being restricted to one domain, the choice provides an excellent test of the hypothesis. If it exists anywhere in U.S. government, we should be able to find pluralism in agriculture.

Agriculture represents nearly one-fifth of the gross national product in its farm, food, fiber, and trade policy concerns. As a result, there exist numerous interests to address a wide range of alternative policy options for government. In addition to the economic ones noted above, policy attention is also directed to sector-specific issues of farm and food environment and safety, rural development, and rural social welfare. And, even with such issue diversity in the policy domain, the interest politics of agriculture has been traditionally viewed as well integrated, even clustered around a farm bloc of peak associations (Zeigler 1964, 163–98). Thus, judging from interpretations about the past, we can reasonably expect some central players who might integrate the bargaining system of this domain.

Agriculture is also governed on the basis of fragmented rather than domain-wide concern. The distinct provisions of omnibus farm bills, since 1933, allocate most agricultural policy benefits to distinctly different areas of issue emphasis (Lowi 1969, 102–15). These are routinely updated, both annually and in a four- to five-year cycle of total review. Most farm bill provisions are subject to extensive criticism on this point by a near consensus opinion of agricultural economists. After major study, these uncoordinated provisions were found to be inappropriate in their comprehensive attention to a farm economy that is dramatically different from the one to which they owe their origins (Gardner 1985; Price 1985). Moreover, the proliferation and fragmentation of organized interests dramatically increased over time as more and increasingly specialized interest groups gravitated to a growing number of agricultural issues (Heinz 1962; Bonnen 1980, 1988; Browne 1988). This made for even more numerous narrow interests than existed before. Many of these should quite likely restrict their lobbying to identifiable sub-domains and only to selected issues as defined by the structure of agricultural legislation.

In addition, persuasive evidence exists that interest fragmentation brings with it at least one major cleavage that severely divides the policy goals of interest groups across the entire domain. There exist both traditional interests that generally favor ongoing programs and a newer wave of externality groups that contest the effects of present policies on third parties (Hadwiger 1982). As a result, the expectation of conflict within the agricultural domain is especially high.

In short, agriculture has been viewed as a network of decision making where both well-established patterns of organized interest cooperation and conflict exist around a commonly valued yet widely varying set of policy alternatives. Thus, although nothing can be firmly stated about trends over time, the domain is a good place to search for pluralism today. It seems quite representative of those long organized, or traditional, policy domains where peak associations have been joined by an array of newer, more narrowly and intensely directed organizations. Because of both the greater likelihood of rancor that this situation creates (as opposed to the less frequently found domains without peak associations, see Salisbury et al. 1987, 1229) and the other characteristic features of this policy domain cited above, conclusions made about levels of agricultural policy interaction appear to be at least somewhat generalizable across the spectrum of U.S. policy-making.

For this paper's analysis, two sets of data are employed to provide measures of issues pursued as policy alternatives: a "who wants what" list of all issues that a purposive sample of organized interests actively lobbied for over a recent three-year period; and a "who got what" list of legislative and administrative items that passed during the same period plus the preceding two years. The sample of organized interests was drawn to include 136 of 215 groups and firms previously identified as concerned with agricultural policy. The sample design allowed data to be collected from all the most active interest groups addressing agricultural policy in the first half of the 1980s. The procedures for sampling and data collection are included in detail in the appendix.

ORGANIZATIONS, ISSUES, AND THEIR NUMBERS

The analysis begins by determining whether or not any organizations exist that can integrate policy demands within the domain. The first indicator suggests that several try. The factor that stands out in differentiating organizations by their issue preference is the number of issues that each group states to be of active interest. In that sense, as was expected from previous studies of agriculture, there are two types of organized interests in the domain. Twenty-one of the sample organizations are either generalist peak associations (both farm and non-farm) or the disadvantaged challenger organizations involved with farm protest movements

and agrarian reform. Both types are expected to be concerned with integrating domain policies. At one time the peak associations were the dominant interests in agriculture, valued for their ability to aggregate under a common umbrella of policy demands the diffuse and plural interests of otherwise economically competitive farmers (Zeigler 1964; Hansen 1987a). They supposedly did so with great effectiveness into the 1950s (Heinz 1962; Cochrane 1979; Paarlberg 1980). The reform groups and peak associations of general farmers share a common history because, in earlier eras and with the farm protests of the 1980s, the latter frequently grew from the same sort of diffuse public policy concern. But, in their case, it was through generalized policy discontent expressed by challenger style protest during their initial periods of organizing (Browne and Dinse 1985, 229–32).

Using the "who wants what" list, the representatives of these interests claim to lobby actively on an average of nearly 24 agriculture and rural policy issues per year per organization. The range is from 12 to 38 issues, most of which are addressed annually as the issues recur from year to year on the policy agenda. Apparently then, as the Salisbury et al. research showed, organized interests of this multipurpose type do promote pluralist ideals. They each bring numerous demands to government and keep pursuing their array of long-lived issues as they adjust internally to the difficulties of representing many types of farmers.

Evidence about the amount of lobbying of other interests suggests that the above interest groups do exhibit domain-wide concerns, at least comparatively. The remaining organizations—representing farmers, agribusinesses, service institutions, and the third-party externality interests—all actively lobby on far fewer issues, eight or less per year. None of these are peak farm or farm equipment associations nor nationally organized protest groups.

Table 19.1 An Issue Involvement Profile of Organized Interests in the Agriculture Policy Domain

Type	Examples	Number of Interests	Issue Involvement
Multipurpose Organizations (Type I)	American Farm Bureau Federation, American Agriculture Movement, Food Marketing Institute	21	Numerous (12–38 per year; average of 24 issues per year per interest)
Unrestrained Investment Single-Purpose Organizations (Type IIb)	National Association of Wheat Growers, National Broiler Council, American Frozen Food Institute	44	Modest (5–8 per year; average of 6.5 issues per year per interest)
Restrained Investment Single-Purpose Organizations (Type IIa)	Agricultural Research Institute, Corn Refiners Association, Food Research and Action Center	65	Low (0–4 per year; average of 2 issues per year per interest)

A small number (3) are peak associations of businesses that are more active on issues outside the agricultural policy domain than they are within.

Two distinct subtypes of these narrowly focused groups exist though, an unexpected finding. Previous analyses have portrayed agricultural policy demands as either diffusely represented by peak style organizations or very narrowly sought after by a fragmented array of intensively focused single-purpose groups (Heinz 1962; Bonnen 1973; Moe 1980, 181–91; Browne 1982). The last were thought to be very much alike other than for sector differences between, for example, farm and business. Sixty-five organizations, reflecting indeed a narrow sense of single purpose, lobby for an average of only two domain issues per year (ranging from an average of 0 to 4). The remaining 44 interests behave differently in that they act on more numerous active policy concerns. Each lobbies for 5 to 8 issues per year; and they average 6.5 per group.

These findings suggest that the policy domain is a busy place where pluralist representation might well be found, one in which numerous policy alternatives could easily develop from interest-group demands. Moreover, the domain is populated by an array of rather specialized groups whose range of policy concerns are more extensive than might be expected. The more active of the narrow interests, in particular, do not restrict their lobbying to commodity price support policy or, for agribusiness, just issues of competitive product pricing. Only a small number of groups are intensely single purpose with only a very few items on their agenda.

Thus, as shown in Table 19.1, there exists empirically based conceptual categories that are directly related to the issue preferences of interest groups and, indirectly, to the elite/pluralist theme. Two distinct types of interests can be identified as active in the agricultural policy domain, with one type divisible in two: those likely to attempt to influence nearly any farm, food, fiber, trade, environmental, or welfare issue of agriculture policy (which will be called Type I or multipurpose interests); and those that restrict their involvement far more narrowly (which will be called Type II or single-purpose interests). The Type II groups can be subtyped

Table 19.2 Commodity, Business and Externality Groups Divided by Type II Issue Focus

Interests by Sector	Number of Type II Organizations	Number of Type IIa Organizations, Restrained Investment	Number of Type IIb Organizations, Unrestrained Investment
Commodity Groups[a]	23	13	10
Business Organizations	47	25	22
Externality Groups	21	18	3
All Others[b]	18	9	9
Total	109	65	44

[a]Includes marketing associations with both business and farm members.
[b]Institutional interests, smaller protest groups, and miscellaneous.

between those that lobby quite restrictively on only a very few issues (Type IIa or restrained investment single-purpose interests) and those that are somewhat more involved and necessarily devote more resources to lobbying (Type IIb or unrestrained investment single-purpose interests). The investment distinction comes solely from the broader scope of these organizations. A rather typically stated explanation was given by one Type IIb lobbyist as to why his organization addressed so many more issues than an otherwise similar group: "[We have] been fortunate in being able to convince those who pay our bills that a Washington investment produces numerous dividends. So we added staff and hired consultants to look into otherwise neglected problems." Pluralist values, on first glance, apparently are served by choices made about organizational structure (i.e., resource allocation, hiring specific types of personnel) by at least some interests.

ISSUE CONCERNS

Who best pursues what may be pluralist styles of representation? The answers show the imbalance in the playing field within the domain. By a nearly four-to-one

margin over business groups, farm organizations are the Type I interests exhibiting domainwide activity. Type II political behavior, on the other hand, characterizes groups found in each of the conventional, economic sector based interest-group categories (Zeigler 1964; Walker 1983; Salisbury et al. 1987). As shown in Table 19.2, farm, business, and miscellaneous groups tend to divide rather evenly between restrained and unrestrained investment categories.

But groups from the externality sector, previously described by Berry (1977) as financially plagued and by Salisbury (1986, 155) as limited in their ability to pay competitive Washington salaries, consistently restrain their agricultural issue involvement. None are Type I groups and only three are unrestrained in their investment. Thus, representatives of commodity, business, institutional, and a few assorted interests organize around issues in numerous ways. For example, all business interests do not act or choose alike. It appears that, when funding limitations are not a sectorwide problem within a domain, those choices about structuring issue selection may well be open to a broad array of group representatives. What do these choices mean? Do they frequently bring competing policy

Table 19.3 The Issue Emphasis of Agricultural Interests, Externality Groups Excluded

Type	Issue Selection: Emphasis on Selective Benefits	Policy Follow Through: Charac- terization of Policy Involvement	Policy Resolution: Likelihood of Eliminating Issues from Agenda
Multipurpose Organizations	Divided but Rather High (81% of all issues)[a]	Indiscriminate Issue Involvement on Proposals that Passed	Least Likely (85% of issues recur over three years)
Unrestrained Investment Organizations	Moderately High (89% of all issues)[a]	Issue Selection Reflects Imputed Interest. Addressed over 70% of Proposals that Passed[b]	Moderately Likely (76% of issues recur over three years)
Restrained Investment Organizations	Extremely High (98% of all issues)	Issue Selection Negligent of Imputed Interest. Addressed Less than 50% of Proposals that Passed[b]	Most Likely (69% of issues recur over three years)

[a]Below mean because of high multipurpose organization involvement with nonselective benefit issues.
[b]All organizations combined, not each interest group within the category.

ideas of the Type II interests forward for resolution by Type I interests or someone else? No. As we shall see, even the choice of doing so is largely illusion.

Who Wants What?

Promoting pluralist values, in part, depends on what sorts of issues group representatives choose to be involved with when they have the organizational resources to select. The analysis next turns to which issues interest groups select for active participation. Within the policy domain, issue demands are overwhelmingly framed very narrowly regardless of the interest group's degree of issue involvement. Ninety-two percent of the total number of issues (after controlling for multiple mentions) raised on the "who wants what" list, as lobbied for by commodity groups and Type II agribusiness interests, affect only (that is, proposals to resolve or conclude policy debates surrounding these issues selectively assigned policy benefits through) a specific commodity, product, or stage in the food and fiber delivery process. Restrained type commodity and business interests, which express the least policy involvement, lobby on those kinds of issues in 98% of the cases (see column 1, Table 19.3). The unrestrained investment interests have a somewhat broader agenda, with 11% of their issue concerns (for example, tax policy, pesticide regulation, export policy) being less specific to the imputed interest (see appendix) of the organization (that is, proposals to resolve these issues nonselectively assigned policy benefits to various commodity producers, business in general, or as the third-party clientele of several single purpose externality interests).

Institutional interests such as foundations, universities, and state departments of agriculture are even more inclined to address issues in order to obtain only their own selective rewards. One hundred percent of the issues on their "who wants what" lists enhance or bring specific programs, funding, or responsibilities to institutional affiliates. Thus, they too are affected by the politics of self-interest even though the end result of institutional expenditures, once attained, may pass through and then go for public goods.

While the externality groups—by the nature of their public interest identities—cannot be evaluated using the same criteria, the unique issue involvement that these groups do pursue is at least comparably narrow. Since some policy rewards go to an assignable third-party public (such as rural residents who live near farms or targeted Third World residents) while others go to an unassignable one (such as all those who breathe fresh air or who may inadvertently eat food with high levels of cholesterol), all public interest policies are not similarly broad-based in their intended service. Seventy-six percent of the issue selections on the externality group's "who wants what" list allocate benefits to a single assignable public as opposed to either two or more or to an unassignable one.

These findings suggest quite strongly that the large number of interests in the agriculture policy domain give rise primarily to very narrow and intensely directed issues. Even though many organizations are busier than expected, a distinctive sense of policy direction develops for most interests. Policy interest is characterized by obsessive focus on a single facet of agriculture production and food delivery. Even the multipurpose organizations (see column 1, Table 19.3) articulated 81% of their issue concerns as ones that allocate selective benefits to a single constituency, always one represented by a single-purpose organization. Not even externality groups, for all they might add to the pluralist goal of articulating competing policy options, are immune to this singularity of focus.

This narrow focus of political demands can be better illuminated by examining differences between the Type IIa and IIb single-purpose commodity and business interests. Their varying levels of issue involvement do not reflect

a desire on the part of the unrestrained groups to comment on every aspect of agricultural policy, even with that 11% of targeted issues that address collective problems. Unrestrained type interests become more involved through more extensive investments in both a greater number and greater variety of narrow issues of public policy. Their specific commodity, product, or delivery problems are also sometimes addressed by proposed policy solutions that achieve selective ends through collective means. While a restrained investment commodity group might, for example, restrict lobbying to the immediate economic gains of price support issues, an unrestrained investment commodity interest is different. It also lobbies for government research funds, nutrition standards, and public support for exports directed only to that single crop. To facilitate those selective benefit issues, the group might also find it necessary to lobby for increased research appropriations for the collective needs of all land grant universities and their multiple clientele. Likewise, a restrained investment farm supply association lobbies only for government supported purchases of lime as a soil treatment when its members can benefit through increased sales of that product. Meanwhile, a similar but unrestrained investment farm supply association increases its level of policy demands over that of the lime group by addressing acreage limits on planting, farm income policy, and groundwater contamination.

Some of these issues are advanced in policies that are structured as collective goods, such as lobbying against restrictions on price support payments to farmers who do not limit acreage use. Thus there is some integration of domain problems going on. But, in neither instance does the unrestrained organization choose to address public policy in an encompassing or comprehensive fashion to produce a general agricultural good. Its support of an issue still reflects a narrow policy concern. That concern is determined in part by the expressed belief of 91% of the single-purpose lobbyists that they should keep proposals as narrow as possible in order to win. Thus, if these proliferating groups promote pluralism within the domain, they do so only by further fragmenting interests rather than by integrating policy demand through shared attention to common concerns.

Who Got What?

The same difference can be seen by examining which issues are addressed from the "who got what" list of commodity and Type II business interests. Whenever a specific imputed interest can be identified on an issue for a commodity group or trade association, unrestrained investment organizations are more likely than those of the restrained type to be active in lobbying Congress or USDA. This strongly suggests that organized interests in agriculture do not vary in their active policy involvement or investment (as opposed to simple policy concern) because their representatives are reacting systematically, by choice, to the entire range of issues on the agricultural policy agenda. Rather they are responding to decisions made about how many issues can be addressed effectively. Group representatives show no evidence that they really have choices available to them which shift their attention from the organization's distinct need to that of the domain.

Further underscoring the importance of the numerically based typology of issue involvement is the comparative behavior of the 21 multipurpose interests and the Type II organizations (see column 2, Table 19.3). At least one of the relatively small number of multipurpose organizations is involved in 171 of 180 sample decisions (100% for Congress, 79% for USDA). On the contrary, even for decisions that obviously affect only the specific commodities, commodity

group representatives lobby on only 88% of congressional bills and 56% of USDA rulings. Where specific products or stages in the food/fiber delivery process can be identified, the directly affected business interests are involved in only 72% of congressional actions and in 46% of USDA actions. Externality groups, with their resource limitations, are no better watchdogs for those assignable publics they work for on their "who wants what" priorities. When their most frequent assignable publics are affected by a bill or ruling, the expected externality group lobbies but 35% (Congress) and 22% (USDA) of the time.

While there is an important degree of difference in the selective benefit focus of restrained and unrestrained type single-purpose organizations on issues of imputed interest (column 2, Table 19.3), the behavior of the multipurpose groups shows comparatively indiscriminate policy activity. At the other extreme, more than other Type II interests, the externality groups are so highly discriminate that they miss the great majority of issues that would be predicted to be their own (Hadwiger 1982). Interest groups, thus, show additional evidence of identifying first and foremost with a predetermined range of issues that their representatives somehow feel they should address. Whatever values they attach to issues are specific, not generalized to the domain.

A small number of multipurpose organizations promote pluralism through their policy behavior, apparently willing to contest an array of both narrow and encompassing policy issues. However, a far greater number of interests—and ones that are representative of a far broader range of distinct social and economic values—are unwilling to joust even with all of the ongoing issues before government that affect some conceptual idea of their own organizational goals. Organized agricultural interests, as can be seen, evidence a far more restricted and perhaps sophisticated—but to this point still unexplained—issue selection strategy than McConnell (1966), Rose (1967), and Lauman and Knoke (1987) suggest when they raise the specter of elitist behavior.

ISSUE OVERLAP AND THE MINIMIZING OF INTEREST CONFLICT

So far we have two findings of general consequence—those that categorize interest groups by differences in their issue involvement, and those that show how limited and narrow organizations are in defining their policy goals. They have important but countervailing implications for pluralist thought. On the one hand, the agricultural policy domain is busier than expected, especially with numerous single-purpose organizations that do not restrict their involvement to only a single intensely focused issue. As such, policy alternatives are likely to be articulated far more broadly than earlier reported in a public domain where highly integrated interests once ruled (Paarlberg 1980; Hansen 1987a). Yet, on the other hand, there exists a great deal of issue avoidance as policy interests become focused.

The selectively narrow and unencompassing nature of interest demands imply a bias against pluralist tendencies. While many alternatives may be proposed and are seriously considered by policymakers, demands may be so narrow that issues seldom overlap from interest to interest. Therefore, the proliferation of issues may not bring with it conditions of routine interorganizational cooperation and conflict along with the eventual multi-interest policy review that comes most likely, as pluralism would suggest, from such interaction. Indeed, as the following data on issue overlap demonstrate, nonreview is the prevailing pattern.

Most organizations avoid issues that bring them either cooperation or conflict with one another. The give and take so critical to the pluralist assumption is surprisingly absent.

Single-Purpose Organizations
Avoiding cooperative entanglements and conflict typifies the behavior of the entire spectrum of single-purpose, Type II groups. Representatives of these 109 organizations identify, including multiple mentions of the same issues, a total of 418 issues per year that their groups actively lobbied for in each of the past three years. For each interest, 74% of these issues recur (column 3, Table 19.3). That is they reappear similarly in form and substance as an active item of involvement over the entire period. Twenty-six percent of their issues either are, in one way or another, resolved and removed from a group's policy agenda, or they are ones that are raised anew.

However, when the issue mentions are aggregated to check for overlapping involvement, the single-purpose organizations claim to have addressed 402 distinct issues (with regional or state subset issues of a general policy concern aggregated to count as a single issue, see appendix and footnote 7) over that entire period. Sixty-eight percent of these are mentioned by only one Type II organized interest (see Table 19.4). Of the remaining 32% of identified issues, 28% of those show potential Type II alliance activity with mentions of the same position on the same issue. Only 16% reveal adversary positions where two or more groups note competing positions on the same issue. Among Type II groups, 65% address the same issue in additive or accommodating fashion, wanting neither the same nor competing benefits from a pending policy decision. Only 15 of the 402 issues were policy concerns of five or more single-purpose interests. Quite clearly, even the externality interests (which account for

Table 19.4 Targeted Issues of Agricultural Interests

Between Category Comparisons	Single-Purpose Organizations (109)	Multipurpose Organizations (21)
Total number of targeted issues of all groups over a three-year period, all mentions	1,255 (418/year)	1,509 (503/year)
Number of target issues of all groups recurring all three years, all mentions	929	1,283
Number of distinct issues for all groups, aggregated mentions[a]	402	82
Within Category Comparisons		
Issues of only a single organization	273	0
Distinct issues showing potential alliance activity	36	68
Distinct issues showing competing policy positions	21	51
Distinct issues that overlap among groups but address different policy benefits or goals	84	76

[a]Eliminates multiple mentions (more than one organization); regional or state issues are counted not as distinct but as a subset of national issues whenever they occur (see appendix, footnote 7).

approximately 35% of the conflict) do not emphasize policy competition and direct challenge as the dominant part of their workload.

For the single-purpose groups, self-selecting issue attention rather than systematic attention to all items that appear on the policy agenda of government structures conflict. This conclusion is all the more apparent if one additional set of data is added, the imputed interests of each single-purpose organization for each of the 402 issues. More than 80% of these issues are rated as affecting the imputed interests of five or more such organizations. Active issue involvement, as can be seen above, is far more limited than would be thought. That is, at least in the view of the informed agricultural observers who judged imputed interest, most interest groups conspicuously avoid the challenges of pluralist government.

Multipurpose Organizations

Other agricultural interests do emphasize issue interaction between groups though, an observation that fits with and explains the policy rancor that Salisbury et al. (1987) identify with peak associations. Representatives of the 21 multipurpose organizations claim to be involved with a total of 503 issues per year (see Table 19.4). Moreover, after overlap is controlled, each distinct issue is of expressed concern to at least five multipurpose groups; and eight or more of them are active on 43% of these issues. But these interests are not the dominant policy players that the above might indicate if all issues are considered.

First, as seen in Table 19.4, when the issues are aggregated for multiple mentions, these groups are involved with a total of only 82 actual agricultural and rural policy issues over the three-year period (all of which are also issues for at least one single-purpose organization). Second, a considerably smaller percentage of issues are resolved (that is, they disappear from an interest's active policy agenda from one year to the next) for the multipurpose interests than for the other types of groups. Approximately 85% of these issues recur as a similar active policy demand for each organization over the entire three-year period. The multipurpose groups—whether they be farm, agribusiness, institutional, or externality interests—follow issue selection practices that demonstrate a broad and diffuse policy focus. They become lightning rods for multi-interest alliances and conflicts. But they still fail to address anywhere near the wide range of issues being articulated within the policy domain. While multipurpose groups may be good representatives of pluralist values because they act *throughout* the domain, their impact is not widely felt by the entire set of players *within* the domain as measured by total issue involvement or by issue resolution.

Nor do these multipurpose organizations possess a special prominence because they seek active involvement in what might be considered subjectively the most important issues of the domain. While these interests are obviously involved in all high conflict issues, they are by no means involved in all of the highest financial cost issues. In fact, one or more of the multipurpose organizations are actively involved in only 14% of the issues targeted by single-purpose organizations in the four highest cost program areas of agriculture policy: commodity price supports, research, food stamps, and international trade/assistance. By contrast, one or more of the Type I organizations are actively involved with 20% of all the issues targeted by Type II interests.

As a result, there do exist patterns of conflict between regularly contesting agricultural interests, as Salisbury et al. discovered (1987, 1225). Multipurpose groups, as they suggest and as can be seen in Table 19.4, disagree among themselves routinely. Externality interests and the American Farm Bureau Federation, for example, also take opposing views quite frequently. Patterns of alliances to obtain related policy benefits also exist. However, for most interest

groups and for most issues, neither cooperation among nor conflict between groups is a primary feature of the private interest demand process within the agriculture domain. Pluralist patterns of interest interaction, thus, are not as common across the wide range of issues affecting agriculture as either Hadwiger (1982) or Salisbury et al. (1987) would suggest on the basis of their sample issues.

THE FRAIL COALITION

To this point, cooperation has been defined in terms of issue congruence, the desire of two or more organized interests to identify or to have identified the same benefits from a hoped for or previously obtained policy decision. As was noted, and as can be seen in Table 19.4, most instances of issue overlap show what will be called "additive involvement." That is, two or more interests accommodate one another by pursuing the same policy question for unrelated reasons. Usually each hopes to address unique parts of a single regulation, bill, or even provision of a bill for purposes of obtaining different policy benefits.

However, there exists a second and perhaps related form of cooperative multi-interest behavior, the coalition. Coalitions can be seen as collectivist associations, voluntarily organized in pursuit of a goal that several interests hold in common. As two analyses by journalists demonstrated, however, lobbying coalitions also are frequently assembled to pursue additively a variety of selective policy goals through the construction of a single legislative act such as tax reform or trade policy (Birnbaum and Murray 1987; Victor 1988). That is, they do their own logrolling and present the agreement to Congress for review. Such relationships, carefully constructed through difficult negotiation, allow for two or more interests, for example, to trade the votes of supporters in Congress in order to enhance opportunities for winning on an issue. In agriculture, regular coalitions of feed grains groups work together to promote Midwestern congressional solidarity on commodity programs. Rice, tobacco, and peanut interests also lend and bring together mutual support to Southeast crop programs (Browne 1988, 183).

It may well be that coalition politics—especially given the earlier mentioned propensity of multipurpose organizations to engage overlapping issues—bring otherwise uninvolved groups together. By forcing interaction, multi-interest coalitions may resolve long-term disagreements among private interests to obtain short-term policy gains for each. To that extent, an otherwise limited form of pluralism may be played out through multi-interest coalition politics. This may be the as yet undiscovered negotiating framework that facilitates pluralist compromise. But issue evidence suggests that this is not usually the case. During the interviews, those closely allied commodity representatives acknowledged that the proposed content of wheat, corn, and soybean programs as well as those of rice, tobacco, and peanuts are developed independently as issues by each group without the review and comment of coalition partners. Each still gained support from the others, however.

Testing Coalition Support

Despite the interpretive interview data that was included with this study (see appendix), there was at the onset of the project a recognized need to apply a specific test of coalition support. The intent was to determine whether items on the "who wants what" list of each organization include the issues that bring the partners within notable agricultural coalitions together. That is, does each partner become actively involved in issues central to the coalition?

Prior to data collection, four broadly definable agricultural issues (each having the potential to satisfy the selective needs of several groups) were identified from press accounts as major ones dividing respondent organizations within this policy domain. These issues were: agricultural research, ethanol subsidies, sugar and dairy programs, and strengthened pesticide legislation. Two sets of proponents (ethanol and pesticides) and two sets of opponents (research and commodity programs) were determined by identifying public statements about support or opposition from the media, in-house organizational publications, and/or congressional hearings. While 94 respondent organizations assumed a public stance on those issues in such sources (25, 23, 30, and 6, respectively), only 22 respondent organizations (5, 5, 9, and 3, respectively), during the interviews, selected these as issues on which their representatives actively lobby. Thus, even on high profile policy questions, 77% of publicly announced issue claims are merely intended for posturing or position taking. As do members of Congress who take positions that they do not work toward, interest groups also assume public postures that do not translate into instrumentally useful, active lobbying on behalf of targeted issues (Mayhew 1974, 61–73).

There also exists very limited coalition support among participating interests whose representatives directly interact with one another when coalition partners actually meet in structured settings. Two of the issue controversies (pesticides and commodity programs) led to the emergence of regularly meeting coalitions. Of the 46 organizations taking public positions supportive of coalition goals, 38 acknowledged that their representatives also attend coalition meetings or signed off on statements of coalition support. Still only 12 organizations, or less than one-third of the coalition participants, lobbied policy-makers in any way beyond just attending interest-group meetings. Of the active interests, six are multipurpose or generalist organizations. So, while the multipurpose groups, as earlier data would indicate, are disproportionately active coalition players, there is little evidence that the coalitions themselves are important to the issue concerns of most participants. For most interests in these two coalitions, interorganizational arrangements are distinct from whatever determines the range and scope of their expressed issue concerns.

According to respondents who explain the above circumstances, most interests (and particularly single-purpose groups) hope to participate in coalitions for other than reasons of advancing their own targeted issues. They want, variously, to: keep commitments to long-term allies in other organizations by a public endorsement, show support for friends in policy-making positions by lending symbolic assistance, or address member pressures by falsely portraying the extensiveness of the group's issue involvement. Many also participate in coalitions simply to secure information about pending policies, another prime reason why many of these groups are in Washington to begin with (Browne 1988, 167–90). In this sense, much multi-interest coalition politics works toward maintaining internal and external political relationships as well as helping interests adjust to changing governmental conditions. It has the same issue substance as do the internal policy resolutions processes that produce unwieldy documents from the membership about what an organized farm interest should do in the unlikely event that lobbying time and resources were unlimited (Talbot and Hadwiger 1968; Browne and Wiggins 1978). As Bosso (1987) has shown for pesticide legislation, coalitions within the agricultural policy domain are tedious and disappointing fora for

transforming policy disagreement into interest group consensus. Participants do not, as this paper's data also suggest, want to consider a variety of policy alternatives that they would not otherwise target. Riker's (1962) warning of least winning size in coalition formation seems verified in the interest politics of agriculture. Effective coalitions are probably formed on the principle of integrating the least number of players needed to win rather than searching for encompassing policies that satisfy the widest range of policy claimants. Private interests, it appears, avoid strategies that would obtain private goals through a collective process that pluralistically integrates multiple demands.

ELITISM WITH A PLURALIST COMPONENT

The findings on narrow issue orientation, minimizing issue-based interaction, and avoiding commitment within coalitions suggest strongly that interest-group politics is essentially about gaining elite status over a small range of issues. The issues that groups control then go to government for resolution. Interest-group politics within a domain is not about the mobilization of all possible resources on all issues of logical interest (see summary Table 19.5). It is much more constrained behavior. Single-purpose organizations do not each promote one among several policy options as these combine to address common agricultural problems. Rather, their representatives choose and develop issues to meet the narrow goals of select clientele, defining their issues with the expectation that proposals will engender little active support or opposition from other lobbyists. In doing so, both farm and business interests as economic spokesgroups pick and choose equally among those issue goals that reflect the major philosophical divisions that economists identify as the disparate ones of

Table 19.5 Elite and Pluralist Interest Behavior in the Agricultural Policy Domain

	Type of Organization	Likelihood of Selecting Potential Alliance Issues	Likelihood of Selecting Issues of Conflict	Likelihood of Actively Supporting Coalitions
Pluralist Interests:	Multipurpose	Most Likely and Common	Most Likely and Common	Most Likely, Posturing on Common Issues is High
Elite Interests:	Single-Purpose, Unrestrained Investment	Generally Unlikely but Occurs	Generally Unlikely but Occurs	May Occur, Posturing Frequent
	Single-Purpose, Restrained Investment	Least Likely but Occurs	Least Likely and Rarely Occurs	Least Likely, Posturing Less Frequent

macroagricultural policy choice: either market defined or mandated control of commodity production. Perhaps, as Offe's (1985) structuralist elitism argument suggested, fragmented economic control brings with it fragmented political control.

This means, as earlier data show, that interest groups sequentially—as opposed to comprehensively—address some and only some of the series of agricultural policy decisions made by government. In doing so, they respond to no centralized private interest that either sets a general policy agenda for others or that integrates their diverse demands (Domhoff 1978). The collective or encompassing needs of agriculture, especially as criticized by economists and other agricultural policy reformers, are conspicuously ignored by organized interests in ways that Dahl (1961) and Polsby (1963) did not envision in their community-based networks of decision making. Nor, does it seem likely, is this what Dahl (1956) envisioned as the eventual result of polyarchal democracy as an "American hybrid" that allows a sort of domain control but still eschews elitism as unique decisions are made.

Only a handful of multipurpose organizations promote pluralism as that term has been applied in this article, the willingness to step into the political fray to either contest or compromise with competing private interests. Moreover, the issue selection of representatives who are contest-oriented is so limited (82 of 402 issues) that these generalist interests cannot hope to play an integrating role for the entire policy domain as it constitutes the relevant network of decision making. These organizations, when it comes to typical or routine issues, might well be an anachronism within the modern interest-group universe, especially in view of the Salisbury et al. (1987, 1227) finding that the health policy domain has evolved into a network where no organizations address the wide range of issues that they do in agriculture. At best, as was suggested by respondents to this study, the selective issue involvement of multipurpose groups promotes pluralism by reminding single purpose representatives that their issues may well be shifted into an arena of policy resolution where interaction and conflict are more present than usual.

Even then, however, multipurpose groups do not redesign or craft the initiatives and demands of single-purpose organizations. They assist; and their willingness to do so, respondents claim, brings multipurpose groups especially into three kinds of decisions (which it must be remembered will usually be selectively defined): those where budgetary restraints are discussed between interests, those where externality groups threaten components of an industrial sector within the domain, or those where issue demands must be clarified between single-purpose groups to avoid bifurcating ideological policy conflict. Since some multipurpose representatives are willing to interject themselves into exceptional policy problems that either reallocate narrow benefits under strict budgetary constraints, mediate the most visible cleavages within the domain, or address philosophical dimensions of policy in an otherwise conflict avoidance domain, they do bring a pluralist dimension to a generally elitist situation. But what explains this behavior?

ISSUE NICHES: EXPLAINING INTEREST-GROUP ELITISM

The narrowing of policy demands and the selection of only some among numerous issues has suggested, throughout this analysis, that interest-group politics is largely about restrictive choices. But what guides this self-selective choice of some issues from among many, especially the rejection of issues that knowledgeable observers believe to be in an organization's imputed interest? And how is this behavior consistent with elitism?

An answer that is both compatible with (1) the data and (2) the conclusion that interest-group politics is elitism tempered by some pluralist behavior can be advanced. To do so requires looking at how each organized interest identifies itself, and what it perceives as its issues of interest within the substantive context of policy-making. That is, the answer lies in the way organizations are defined by their own representatives as politically relevant to the overall structure of the domain and decisions that must be made within it.

The identity of organized interests and how they define their policy involvement has been treated by interest-group theorists rather like a maypole. Political scientists dance around the concept of identification, recognize its centrality, but seldom reflect on it. Numerous studies, however, imply that organized interests do worry about their own identities and how others see their group. Berry (1977) addressed externality group identity in terms of a funding dilemma in which they adjust issues to secure financing. Hayes (1981, 64–92) suggested that congressional members and staff have specific expectations of a group based on, among other factors, what points of view the interest is perceived to represent on issues. Even Truman's (1951) vague grappling with the meaning of a group being organized around its interest was such a recognition. Truman understood that much of the struggle for private representation has long revolved around deciding what each organization is all about in some highly specific public policy sense.

The Salisbury et al. (1987) research, suggesting as it does established patterns of policy interaction, is all the more important if one takes into consideration the need for an organizational identity as a prerequisite to providing recognizable services. Their research implied that organized interests behave with some degree of consistency over time on the issues they address. In some fashion, organizations that follow recognized patterns of behavior must also be sending out messages as to what their organizational identity is all about. Allies and adversaries can be categorized as a consequence. But, to do so, each organization must comprehend and act on its own issue identity.

One conceptual view of interest-group politics is especially useful in examining organizational identity, transactional theory. As advanced by Bauer, de Sola Pool, and Dexter (1963) and later by Hayes (1981, 17–18), the relationships between lobbyists and policymakers are based on market and exchange principles. That is, each policy domain is like a marketplace in which services are the interest group's unit of exchange. Within that market, the services of various interest-group suppliers (and their policymaker consumers) constitute worthwhile goods that are the basis for exchanges, or transactions, that facilitate policy-making. These external transactions, except that they center on staff/policymaker rather than staff/member relationships, are not at all unlike the maintaining internal exchanges that hold interest groups together by providing service incentives to membership and operating resources for the staff (Olson 1965; Salisbury 1969).

From the perspective of this study, transactional theory (like the Olson/Salisbury exchange analysis) is useful because it suggests that organized interests develop issue identities—indeed are compelled to do so—because their representatives must have something recognizable to market within some one or more relevant networks of decision making. Those with whom they interact, as Hayes (1981, 93–127) showed, gain noticeable transaction benefits from what organized interests supply to policy-making. But these beneficiaries gain only when the identifiable goods of an interest group meet a policymaker's specific demand, either by satisfying an old need or creating a new one. Quite obviously, and what is apparent in earlier transactional analyses, interest groups will keep supplying whatever specific goods to meet policymaker demand as

long as lobbyists have the resources to do so. To some extent, this explains why group representatives make restrictive and narrowly selective choices as to appropriate issues rather than attempt to market any and every compatible policy idea that may benefit some part of the organization or be what others would consider as its imputed interest. That is, for various reasons of political acceptability, some policy ideas simply have no marketable exchange value despite their inherent organizational worth. Given that no interest group has unlimited lobbying resources, supplying such valueless goods—or mobilizing scarce resources on every issue of imputed interest—is irrational.

However, still other restrictions on issue choices are imposed by transaction costs, and their still not well-defined relationship to production costs, as opposed to transaction benefits. Once again consider resource scarcity in determining which services an organization can provide to a relevant exchange partner. As both Williamson (1985) and North (1987) noted in their economic analysis of institutional interaction, there are in any transaction always obstacles. These, as losses, impose costs on what has previously been produced as an organization's resource base. For interest groups, the costs of both getting and being involved in the contracting and monitoring of an issue are often high while attainment of the desired issue benefit is at best uncertain and at worst unlikely.

Suggestive research by van Ravenswaay and Skelding (1985) indicated that some groups will not be as effectively represented as others in regulatory decisions when the production costs of entering into participation exceed expected benefits. The same holds true when transaction costs that are spent in the relationship diminish the value of these benefits. Organized interests must expend money, time, goodwill, credibility, and a myriad of other costs not only in starting-up new relationships but also in negotiating any resulting transactions through their active lobbying. New participants to a recurring issue have an entry problem because they have made no gains from production costs sunk as investments in previous deliberations. But long involved participants have maintenance problems because if they redefine or select a new issue during the course of the transaction, or allow either to be done for them, they may well lose their expertise and reputation as part of the settlement. If an interest's representative selects such inappropriate issue choices and loses, neither the investments made nor the benefits of the targeted issue can be recovered. Restricting issue choices is the only rational act. Organized interests look away and do not enter policy discussions—or invest production costs—on issues with potentially high transaction costs if they have other options.[2] Instead they look toward two kinds of issues: those that enhance or expand their internal resource base or those that can likely be won through low cost interaction with policy participants external to the organization.

As Lauman and Knoke (1987) and Salisbury et al. (1987) show, and as do the data presented here, issues are long-lived and tend to recur on the policy agenda. Things never stabilize, which produces an inherently high-cost network for doing lobbying business. A historical review of farm programs since the 1930s certainly confirms that observation for a long-term period within the agricultural policy domain (Bowers, Rasmussen, and Baker 1984). Because issues are relatively constant over time and subject to near constant review, organized interests can at least base their issue selection on the expectation that many of their expressed concerns will be appropriate—in demand and marketable—in the future. If that proves true, many organizations, once established, can devote lobbying

resources to the relatively low transaction cost behavior of dealing regularly with a very few easily understood (for them) issues, maintaining interactions with policymakers who govern programs affected by those issues, and watching diligently for new issues that others raise which overlap with their own. In addition, the more successful an organization is at defining recurring issues as narrow ones that selectively assign benefits to an assignable public that no one else represents, the lower go the transaction costs of representing the issue. This description, applied across the entire spectrum of Type II single-purpose agricultural issues, fits well most of the agricultural policy domain. Issue overlap is minimal there and conflict generally avoided.

An organized interest, in effect, gains a recognizable identity by defining a highly specific issue niche for itself and fixing its specified political assets (i.e., recognition and other resources) within that niche.[3] From that point on, various organized interests within a policy domain additively accommodate one another, usually by focusing on only their own increasingly narrow demands. When niches are not occupied, groups can move in with minimal production cost investment. For single-purpose groups, their behavior generally allows them to be, or at least they aim to be, the only niche occupant and the only active interest on the issue. That is, they want the network of decision making to be at the issue level; and they hope to operate far below the level of play of the domain. Commodity groups anticipate that no one else will attempt to assume the high production costs and sustain the high transaction costs of developing new commodity programs. Externality groups, in contrast, apparently hope to identify issues where they can move into a niche, gain credibility, and then create such high transaction costs for any challenging interests that opposition to them never seriously emerges (i.e., a group does not follow and even retreats from its imputed interest). The generalizable rule, from the organized interest's supply side of the transaction, is to shift the playing field away from domain and even subdomain consideration to one in which any challenge from another private interest takes place in an issue resolution situation that severely disadvantages the contesting organization. That is, single-purpose groups want—and, in agriculture at least, they most often get—elite control over issue representation by successful occupancy of a recognizable issue niche.

Because of the allocative nature of politics, however, all policy issues cannot be managed in this way. Nonetheless, organized interests do aim at issue containment rather than the free and open consideration of all points of view that may be on the public agenda of government officials. While unrestrained investment groups must raise greater resources to expend in lobbying on more issues, their issue niches are only incrementally larger and, as seen earlier, only somewhat more subject to interaction with other interests. Their lobbyists are seemingly as adroit at lowering the transaction costs of issue representation as are lobbyists for the restrained investment type. They need to be adroit, for example, when a beef organization feels compelled to address nutrition guidelines of the Food and Drug Administration or when a dairy group aims at sending large numbers of cows to slaughter even as that action lowers beef prices. In both instances, when those actions occurred during this research project, high levels of expected conflict did not materialize: fewer than 15% of imputed interests actively opposed either issue.

Even the multipurpose groups each address only a selective number of issues from among the numerous ones being contested in the domain. While those interests, as a set of unique organizations, bring pluralist styles of representation to the domain, they nonetheless occupy

restrictive but far broader issue niches as they go about the business of cost containment, externality conflicts, and ideology. While the time is past when multipurpose groups can effectively address comprehensive issues of agricultural policy change as sectorwide reformers, these groups still gain from having distinctive identities that identify the transaction benefits and associated costs of controversy for other interests. At least, in doing so, they still play a recognizable issue role within the well-structured domain—or occupy their own niche—rather than fade into oblivion.

CONCLUSION

Quite obviously, elitist issue niches in agriculture are conceptually dissimilar from C. Wright Mills' (1956) description of a power elite whose unrestricted supply of resources brought control over the few policy options that government considers. For one thing, the interests analyzed here are not in control of the policy-making agenda nor involved in the development of all institutional rules. Far from it. Patterns of interest-group elitism do not necessarily mean that interests *within* government will not compensate and bring plurally considered policies forward.

Private interest issue niches, however, allow for an almost unlimited number of interests to become organized around specific policy rewards within a single policy domain, or in several domains if their representatives choose to pursue other identities elsewhere (Cigler and Loomis 1986).[4] They proceed by staking out claims to increasingly narrower segments of public policy. As a consequence, the private interest politics of agricultural issue representation is organized around the accommodation of more and more players and the promulgation of what agricultural policy specialists (Bonnen 1973, 1980) see as a very fragmented, uncoordinated, and nonaggregated set of programs. But that politics does not promote open and freewheeling discussion of all relevant policy ideas and alternatives.[5]

Where Salisbury et al. (1987) noted the potential for pluralism, these data suggest fragmented elite dominance among the interest groups of the policy domain. Dominance exists because both the production and transaction costs of representing issues in conflict appear to be too high to be generally tolerable. As a result, interest representatives seek other strategic options; and, in the process, they also restrict comprehensive and encompassing debates over the appropriate direction or reform of agricultural policy. Whatever semblance of pluralism exists for the interest politics of agriculture is directed primarily at arbitrating between the differences of narrow interests. It does not effectively suggest the reallocation of the selective, elite supported benefits of present agricultural policies.

APPENDIX

The first data base (put together as the "who wants what" list) is responses to questions posed to representatives of a sample of 136 organized interests involved with agricultural policy. Respondents, during personal interviews, were asked questions about their own organization's policy concerns, prioritized policy positions, and activity on specific issues. The latter are what might be called the topics of policy actor concern as defined by Lauman and Knoke (1987, 107).[6] After the total number of distinct issues were identified from among all those expressed by group representatives, regional or state specific concerns were combined as subsets of a single issue.[7]

Respondents also were questioned about working relationships with other interests and with specific government officials. Questioning covered a three-year time period with some reference also made to 1981 farm bill positions.

The interviews were scheduled after policy briefings were held by the interviewer with legislative staff and U.S. Department of Agriculture (USDA) officials mostly from the department's policy analysis units, the Economic Research Service (ERS). The briefings provided background information on the substance of and controversies attendant with the many issues of agriculture policy. As a result, questions for the respondents were framed around specific policy decisions where proposals and alternatives had both passed and failed.

The sample of organizations was drawn, in three stages, from an earlier compiled list of organized interests articulating positions on agricultural policy and problems in the 1980s. The initial list of organizations was determined from previous research and from four other sources, using materials printed between January 1980 and October 1985. The sources were congressional hearings on agricultural issues, The *Washington Representatives* directory, the *New York Times,* and the *Washington Post.*[8]

The universe of 215 organizations was divided between those with a Washington office (128) and those without representatives in that city or its suburbs (87).[9] In order to disproportionately interview those from the most active interests, two random samples were drawn. The first sample was made up of 101 Washington organizations and the second of 25 from outside Washington. Later, while the interviews were being conducted in 1985 and 1986, 10 other organized interests from the initial roster were added to the respondent organization list. Discussions with legislators, legislative staff, USDA officials, and other interest representatives suggested that eight were exceptionally active lobbies. They were included in order to acquire complete data on issue alliances from all the most frequently referenced coalition players. Two other groups were sample replacements of Washington interests.

Interviews were conducted with one or more staff members from each of the 136 sample organizations. Specific respondents were selected after suggestions were made by USDA employees and after the study's purpose was explained to the initially selected contacts. Multiple interviews were necessary in many organizations because responsibilities, and thus knowledge of lobbying circumstances, were often divided among those who shared parts of an organization's policy identity. In total, 246 respondents were selected for interviews. Of these, 238 provided extensive interview data. They represented 130 of the 136 sample organizations. Although the other eight respondents (including the other six groups) were interviewed, they contributed little information because they had no substantive knowledge of lobbying and issue positions.[10]

The second set of data (or the "who got what" list) is on legislative acts and administrative rulings—each broken down by provision or title—affecting agriculture and closely related rural problems. A series of probe questions was asked of representatives of each organization about their group's concern, attention, and involvement on each of these items. All distinct provisions of congressional acts (40), excluding the omnibus 1981 farm bill, and a random sample of USDA rulings (140) were collected for a five-year period, January 1980 to June 1985.[11] These data were obtained from *Policy Research Notes* (Economic Research Service 1980–1985), a publication that updates agricultural policy specialists on changing events.

The intention of each provision was categorized as was the imputed interests affected (Scholzman and Tierney 1986, 21–23). Identifying imputed interest (that is, which policy concerns were most likely represented by whom) entailed judgments by informed observers as to how private organizations as equally capable lobbies would rationally determine which

issues to address. These judgments were made possible by policy briefings from ERS specialists. All of the acts and rulings fell within the jurisdiction of at least one ERS employee due to that agency's policy analysis responsibility. In some instances, additional information about intent, affected interests, and involved organizations was solicited from congressional staff. After this categorizing was complete, interest representatives were asked whether or not their organizations had been involved in decisions that others had defined to be an imputed concern.

NOTES

1. To gain access to information and policy experts, I obtained the position of visiting scholar with the Economic Research Service, U.S. Department of Agriculture. I worked on this project and solicited my interviews under their auspices from summer of 1985 through summer of 1986. The National Center for Food and Agricultural Policy, Resources for the Future also supported the project.

2. As a helpful reviewer pointed out, there are maintenance costs of keeping the organization going and opportunity costs affected by scarce resources as well as start-up costs. But protecting the previous investments made in what the niches vest as property rights to issue credibility is what appears to be the most important and avoided transaction cost of lobbying. This concept needs to be researched further.

3. Asset fixity and specificity are concepts suggested by agricultural economist Glenn L. Johnson. He and his colleague James T. Bonnen, both of Michigan State University, contributed greatly to my understanding of transaction costs.

4. This statement seems all the more appropriate in view of with whom these interest respondents claim to work. At least 91 organizations, including many Type IIa interests, lobbied policymakers from two or more subcommittees or two or more substantive government agencies. That suggests that fragmentation does not result from the existence

of tightly closed and enduring tripartite or iron policy triangles.

5. I cannot suggest or imply more or less pluralism today in the agricultural policy domain. There is no data to support either view. However, from the late 1930s to the 1950s, the American Farm Bureau Federation and National Farmers Union publicly addressed and usually contested each other on most issues of farm policy. In doing so they supposedly once integrated the demands of narrower organizations into their partisan camps. By way of speculation without data, if this description is accurate, this would have encouraged greater pluralism in the past.

6. A small number of interviews, nearly all with non-Washington interests, were conducted by telephone.

7. That is, for example, an application of set-asides in Montana could not have been counted as distinct from the resolution of national set-aside policy.

8. A few organizations were added after discussing my list with congressional and USDA officials.

9. In general, the Washington office sample commented extensively on agricultural policy. On the contrary, organized interests without Washington representation did not. The fact that the latter organizations were so publicly quiet is a notable one. It seems that frequent posturing on public policy is a learned Washington behavior, perhaps motivated by the staff's need to appear active and concerned.

10. The 100% response rate and the frankness of respondents can only be attributed to my ERS, USDA position at the time of the interviews. During this period, at the height of farm bill discussions, it was common knowledge among lobbyists that USDA officials were very curious as to who wanted what.

11. Farm bill data were being treated differently as another part of the project.

REFERENCES

Bauer, Raymond A., Ithiel de Sola Pool, and Lewis Anthony Dexter. 1963. *American Business and Public Policy.* New York: Atherton.

Berry, Jeffrey. 1977. *Lobbying for the People.* Princeton, NJ: Princeton University Press.

Birnbaum, Jeffrey H., and Alan S. Murray. *1987. Showdown at Gucci Gulch.* New York: Random House.

Bonnen, James T. 1973. "Implications for Agricultural Policy." *American Journal of Agricultural Economics* 55:391–98.

Bonnen, James T. 1980. "Observations on the Changing Nature of Agricultural Policy Decision Processes." In *Farmers, Bureaucrats, and Middlemen,* ed. Trudy Huskamp Peterson. Washington, DC: Howard University Press.

Bonnen, James T. 1988. "Institutions, Instruments and Driving Forces Behind U.S. Agricultural Policies." In *U.S.-Canadian Agricultural Trade Challenges: Developing Common Approaches,* ed. Kristen Allen and Katie Macmillan. Washington, DC: Resources for the Future.

Bosso, Christopher J. 1987. *Pesticides and Politics: The Life Cycle of a Public Issue.* Pittsburgh: University of Pittsburgh Press.

Bowers, Douglas E., Wayne E. Rasmussen, and Gladys L. Baker. 1984. *History of Agricultural Price-Support and Adjustment Programs, 1933–1984.* Washington, DC: Economic Research Service, U.S. Department of Agriculture.

Browne, William P. 1982. "Farm Organizations and Agribusiness." In *Food Policy and Farm Programs,* ed. Don F. Hadwiger and Ross B. Talbot. New York: Academy of Political Science.

Browne, William P. 1985. "Variations in the Behavior and Style of State Lobbyists and Interest Groups." *Journal of Politics* 47:450–68.

Browne, William P. 1988. *Private Interests, Public Policy, and American Agriculture.* Lawrence: University Press of Kansas.

Browne, William P., and John Dinse. 1985. "The Emergence of the American Agriculture Movement, 1977–1979." *Great Plains Quarterly* 5:221–35.

Browne, William P., and Charles W. Wiggins. 1978. "Resolutions and Priorities: Lobbying by the General Farm Organizations." *Policy Studies Journal* 6:493–98.

Cigler, Allan J., and Burdett A. Loomis. 1986. "Moving On: Interests, Power, and Politics in the 1980s." In *Interest Group Politics*, 2d ed., ed. Cigler and Loomis. Washington, DC: Congressional Quarterly Press.

Cochrane, Willard W. 1979. *The Development of American Agriculture: A Historical Analysis.* Minneapolis, MN: University of Minnesota Press.

Dahl, Robert H. 1956. *A Preface to Democratic Theory.* Chicago: University of Chicago Press.

Dahl, Robert H. 1961. *Who Governs?* New Haven, CT: Yale University Press.

Domhoff, G. William. 1978. *The Powers That Be.* New York: Random House.

Gardner, Bruce L., ed. 1985. *U.S. Agricultural Policy: The 1985 Farm Legislation.* Washington, DC: American Enterprise Institute.

Greenwald, Carol S. 1977. *Group Power: Lobbying and Public Policy.* New York: Praeger.

Hadwiger, Don F. 1982. *The Politics of Agricultural Research.* Lincoln: University of Nebraska Press.

Hansen, John Mark. 1987a. "Choosing Sides: The Development of an Agriculture Policy Network in Congress, 1919–1932." *Studies in American Political Development* 2:183–229.

Hansen, John Mark. 1987b. "The Ever-Decreasing Grandstand: Constraint and Change in an Agricultural Policy Network, 1949–1980." Paper presented at annual meeting of American Political Science Association, Chicago.

Hayes, Michael T. 1981. *Lobbyists and Legislators.* New Brunswick, NJ: Rutgers University Press.

Heinz, John P. 1962. "The Political Impasse in Farm Support Legislation." *Yale Law Journal* 71:954–70.

Hunter, Floyd. 1953. *Community Power Structure: A Study of Decision Makers.* Chapel Hill: University of North Carolina Press.

Lauman, Edward O., and David Knoke. 1987. *The Organizational State.* Madison: University of Wisconsin Press.

Lowi, Theodore J. 1964. "American Business, Public Policy, Case Studies and Political Theory." *World Politics* 16:677–715.

Lowi, Theodore J. 1969. *The End of Liberalism.* New York: W. W. Norton.

Mayhew, David R. 1974. *Congress: The Electoral Connection.* New Haven, CT: Yale University Press.

McConnell, Grant. 1966. *Private Power and American Democracy.* New York: Alfred A. Knopf.

Milbrath, Lester. 1963. *The Washington Lobbyists.* Chicago: Rand McNally.

Mills, C. Wright. 1956. *The Power Elite.* New York: Oxford University Press.

Moe, Terry M. 1980. *The Organization of Interests.* Chicago: University of Chicago Press.

North, Douglass C. 1987. "Institutions, Transaction Costs and Economic Growth." *Economic Inquiry* 25:419–28.

Offe, Claus. 1985. *Disorganized Capitalism.* Cambridge, MA: MIT Books.

Olson, Mancur, Jr. 1965. *The Logic of Collective Action.* Cambridge, MA: Harvard University Press.

Paarlberg, Don. 1980. *Farm and Food Policies: Issues of the 1980s.* Lincoln, NE: University of Nebraska Press.

Polsby, Nelson. 1963. *Community Power and Political Theory.* New Haven, CT: Yale University Press.

Price, Kent A., ed. 1985. *The Dilemmas of Choice.* Washington, DC: Resources for the Future.

Riker, William H. 1962. *The Theory of Political Coalitions.* New Haven, CT: Yale University Press.

Rose, Arnold M. 1967. *The Power Structure: Political Process in American Society.* London: Oxford University Press.

Salisbury, Robert H. 1969. "An Exchange Theory of Interest Groups." *Midwest Journal of Political Science* 13:1–32.

Salisbury, Robert H. 1984. "Interest Representation: The Dominance of Institutions." *American Political Science Review* 78:64–76.

Salisbury, Robert H. 1986. "Washington Lobbyists: A Collective Portrait." In *Interest Group Politics,* 2d ed., ed. Allan J. Cigler and Burdett A. Loomis. Washington, DC: Congressional Quarterly Press.

Salisbury, Robert H., and John P. Heinz, Edward O. Lauman, and Robert L. Nelson. 1987.

"Who Works With Whom? Interest Group Alliances and Opposition." *American Political Science Review* 81:1217–34.

Schattschneider, E. E. 1960. *The Semi-Sovereign People.* New York: Holt, Rinehart and Winston.

Schlozman, Kay Lehman. 1984. "What Accent the Heavenly Chorus? Political Equality and the American Pressure System." *Journal of Politics* 46:1006–1032.

Schlozman, Kay Lehman, and John T. Tierney, 1986. *Organized Interests and American Democracy.* New York: Harper and Row.

Talbot, Ross B., and Don F. Hadwiger. 1968. *The Policy Process in American Agriculture.* San Francisco: Chandler.

Tilly, Charles. 1978. *From Mobilization to Revolution,* Reading. MA: Addison-Wesley.

Truman, David B. 1951. *The Governmental Process.* New York: Alfred A. Knopf.

Useem, Bert, and Mayer N. Zald. 1982. "From Pressure Group to Social Movement: Organizational Dilemmas of the Effort to Promot Nuclear Power." *Social Problems* 30:145–56.

van Ravenswaay, Eileen O., and Pat T. Skelding. 1985. "The Political Economics of Risk/Benefit Assessment: The Case of Pesticides." *American Journal of Agricultural Economics* 67:971–77.

Victor, Kirk. 1988. "Step Under My Umbrella." *National Journal* 20:1063–67.

Vidich, Arthur, and Joseph Bensman. 1960. *Small Town in Mass Society.* New York: Doubleday.

Walker, Jack L. 1983. "The Origins and Maintenance of Interest Groups in America." *American Political Science Review* 77:390–406.

Williamson, Oliver E. 1985. *The Economic Institutions of Capitalism.* New York: Free Press.

Wilson, James Q. 1973. *Political Organizations.* New York: Basic Books.

Zeigler, L. Harmon. 1964. *Interest Groups in American Society.* Englewood Cliffs, NJ: Prentice-Hall.

Zeigler, L. Harmon, and Michael Baer. 1969. *Lobbying: Interaction and Influence in American State Legislatures.* Belmont, CA: Wadsworth.

PROJECT

Browne contends that groups are narrowly focused and lack broad policy agendas. Using his article, how do you explain such groups as AARP, the National Governors Association, and the American Medical Association?

20

PACs, Contributions, and Roll Calls: An Organizational Perspective

JOHN R. WRIGHT

Changes to campaign finance laws in the 1970s created a new political force—Political Action Committees (PACs). PACs grew dramatically throughout the 1970s and 1980s. Observers of American politics noticed their seemingly ubiquitous nature and their ability to skirt campaign finance laws. Conventional wisdom dictates that PACs wield considerable influence in the political process. John Wright's analysis of PAC influence is revealing for several reasons. First, he finds that, contrary to conventional wisdom, PAC influence is limited in a number of ways. Second, he notes that the relationships among PACs, members of Congress, and the citizenry can be tricky. When representatives consider their voting calculations, they often must take into account multiple constituencies, rather than focusing solely upon PAC money. Wright's analysis informs us that policy making and political influence are far more complicated than simply "follow[ing] the money."

QUESTIONS TO CONSIDER

1. Why does Wright select the PACs he does for this study?
2. What strategies do PACs use when making contribution decisions?
3. How does the federated structure of PACs affect fundraising?

4. Who dominates the allocation decisions of PACs? Why? Why is this important?

5. According to Wright, to what extent do PAC contributions affect roll-call voting?

Concern about the effects of campaign contributions on congressional voting has stimulated a growing collection of studies on contributions and roll calls. Scholarly interest in this issue is a natural outgrowth of representatives' increased dependence on money for electoral survival. From 1974 to 1980, political action committee (PAC) expenditures increased by 500%, and average total contributions to congressional candidates tripled (Jacobson, 1983). During just the 1981–1982 election cycle, 2665 nonparty PACs contributed over $87 million to federal candidates (Malbin & Skladony, 1984).

Because of the prominent role of money in congressional elections, a relationship between PAC contributions and congressional voting is often claimed.[1] The validity of such assertions, however, has been difficult to establish. More often than not, these claims have not been confirmed through rigorous empirical analysis, and even when they have been, researchers have failed to identify any theoretical forces that might constrain or limit PAC influence. Unfortunately, because such theoretical considerations are absent, our understanding about PACs and their ability to influence roll calls is extremely tenuous.

In the research reported here, I begin to examine organizational arrangements

in the PACs of five national associations that affect the ability of these PACs to influence roll call votes. Although organizational arrangements are thought to be important considerations in understanding interest groups generally (e.g., Berry, 1977; Truman, 1951; Wilson, 1973), the consequences of organizational arrangements in PACs have not been explored.[2] As a result, an important constraint on their activities and influence has been overlooked.

My objective in this article is to point out a fundamental paradox about an organizational arrangement common to many political action committees. The contradiction is that the organizational arrangement *most* conducive to raising money from individual contributors is also the organizational arrangement *least* conducive to influencing congressional voting. Paradoxically, the factors that allow some PACs to become very rich are the very same factors that undercut their potential influence. As a consequence, organizational arrangements are capable of limiting the ability of PACs to influence roll calls through money. This argument is assessed in light of empirical evidence drawn from a qualitative study of PAC organizations and a quantitative analysis of contribution patterns and roll calls.[3]

SOURCE: From John R. Wright, "PACs, Contributions, and Roll Calls: An Organizational Perspective," *American Political Science Review* 79, no. 2 (June 1985): 400–414. Reprinted with permission from Cambridge University Press.

I am especially grateful to Richard F. Fenno for his suggestions and support. In addition, I wish to thank Greg Caldeira, Samuel C. Patterson, Vernon Van Dyke, and three anonymous referees for their valuable comments.

PAC CONTRIBUTIONS AND ROLL CALLS

Empirical evidence about the influence of PAC contributions on congressional voting is filled with ambiguity and apparent contradiction. On the positive side, Silberman and Durden (1976) found that an increase in total labor contributions in 1972 led to a significant increase in congressmen's support for the minimum wage in the 93rd Congress. Chappell (1982), too, discovered a significant positive connection between contributions and votes: a connection between contributions from Rockwell International and votes on the B1 bomber. In a study using aggregate data, Kau and Rubin (1982) reported that total labor contributions in 1978 were significantly related to votes on such issues as the debt limit, the windfall profits tax, and wage and price controls in 1979. Frendreis and Waterman (1983) uncovered a significant relationship between contributions from the trucking industry and voting in the Senate on trucking deregulation, and Brown (1983) concluded that contributions from the National Automobile Dealers Association and the American Medical Association had "substantial" effects on votes pertaining to those two groups in the 97th Congress.

In contrast, however, Chappell's (1981) work indicates that the effects of campaign contributions from several maritime unions on votes in the 96th Congress were "unavoidably ambiguous." More conclusively, Welch (1982) has asserted that "contributions by dairy PACs were *not* a major influence" (p. 491) on votes for dairy price supports in 1975. Finally, in an analysis of the effects of PAC contributions on House votes for the Chrysler loan guarantee and the windfall profits tax, Yiannakis (1983) has concluded that the influence of money was "very limited."

This diversity in findings is not particularly surprising, because different researchers have analyzed different groups and different votes. Unfortunately, because of the excessive costs involved, a representative sample of PACs and roll calls has not been collected and analyzed, and as a result, the meanings of the

existing findings are difficult to interpret.[4] Are there really significant discrepancies in the various findings? Which findings are the aberrations—those that ascribe a positive and significant influence to PAC contributions or those that do not? How substantial is a "substantial" effect? Can even larger effects be expected?

The strategy of this research is to examine just five PACs, but five PACs that appear to have considerable influence on roll call decisions. Because this sample is both so small and skewed, it will not be possible to make generalizations about the influence of all PACs, or even a "typical" PAC. Yet an analysis of some of the most powerful PACs will permit generalizations about the upper bounds of PAC influence on roll call decisions. Given the present state of knowledge, an attempt to specify the range of possible empirical results, along with an explanation of why the range is as restricted as it is, represents a clear step forward in generalizing about PACs and roll calls.

DATA ON FIVE PACS

The five PACs included in this study are: The American Medical Political Action Committee (AMPAC), affiliated with the American Medical Association; the Dealers Election Action Committee (DEAC), affiliated with the National Automobile Dealers Association; BANKPAC of the American Bankers Association; the Realtors Political Action Committee (RPAC) of the National Association of Realtors; and the Associated General Contractors Political Action Committee (AGCPAC), affiliated with the Associated General Contractors.

The focus is on the PACs of national associations because many observers think they are among the most active and successful of all PACs in influencing roll call voting. Several factors contribute to this reputation. First, the national associations are generally well known for their strong lobbying organizations, and these organizations are alleged to work closely with the PACs (Malbin, 1979).[5] Second, the PACs of national associations tend to be among the largest PACs in terms of total dollars contributed to congressional candidates. As of 1982, RPAC was the largest of the association PACs; AMPAC ranked second; BANKPAC and DEAC ranked fourth and fifth, respectively; and AGCPAC was seventh largest among the association PACs. Moreover, RPAC, AMPAC, and DEAC were among the ten largest PACs, regardless of type (Cohen, 1983). If one assumes that congressmen will be more sensitive to large contributions than small ones, then large PACs are more likely to affect voting decisions.

A third reason for the strong reputation of the association PACs is the excessive publicity they have received from the news media. One of the most publicized cases of influence in the 97th Congress involved the House vote to overturn the FTC rule regulating used-car dealers. Campaign contributions from the National Automobile Dealers Association were thought to be instrumental in that vote (UPI, 1982). The alleged connection between AMPAC contributions and the House's decision to exempt professionals, physicians in particular, from FTC regulation also received attention in 1982 (Barone, 1983). Finally, campaign contributions from the American Bankers Association were thought to be a "major factor" in the effort to repeal the law requiring banks to withhold taxes on interest and dividend payments (Noble, 1983).

Last the national associations tend to lobby a lot of bills, so that at least one important bill for each group is likely to reach the House floor for a vote in any given session. Consequently, the possibility of a connection between money and votes is greater. Of the five PACs selected for this study, the Associated General Contractors is one of the more active groups. Although smaller and less well-known than some of the other groups, the AGC has traditionally played a leading role in lobbying major pieces of legislation (Ornstein & Elder, 1978). During the 97th Congress, the AGC lobbied extensively for passage of the Surface Transportation Assistance Act. That act involved several roll calls before final passage.

In summary, all five PACs selected for study here are either large PACs, PACs that were quite active in the 97th Congress, or PACs that had reputations for influencing legislation with their contributions. These five PACs certainly are not the only ones that meet these criteria; evidence of the effects of campaign contributions on voting might be found by studying other PACs. But if such evidence is to be found, it is likely to be found among these five.

In relation to the entire universe of PACs, the five PACs of this study fall under the rubric of "connected" PACs. A connected PAC, stated simply, is one that is affiliated with, and which coexists with, some extant organization, and this extant organization is commonly called the PAC's "parent" (Sorauf, 1982). Typical parents are trade and professional associations, membership organizations (such as the National Rifle Association), corporations, and labor unions. The vast majority of all nonparty PACs—more than 80%—are connected PACs. In contrast, unconnected PACs have no sponsoring organizations. Examples are the National Conservative Political Action Committee; National Committee for an Effective Congress, and Life Amendment PAC. Unconnected PACs generally, but not always, fall under the rubric of "ideological" PACs, and ideological PACs are generally, but not always, unconnected PACs (Latus, 1984).

Two types of data were collected for each of the five PACs. One type is from open-ended personal interviews; the other is quantitative data on actual contributions and roll calls. The interview data were collected in order to help *strategy Type I*

characterize the organizational structures of the PACs and to provide first-hand information about fundraising practices and allocation strategies.[6]

Fourteen officials were formally interviewed from the five PACs. Most of those interviewed were located in Washington, but several were in other offices of their committees (e.g., at the regional and state levels). In four of the five, the principal interview was conducted with the executive director, or the official in charge of the day-to-day operations of the PAC. In the fifth, the principal interview was conducted with a consultant to the PAC who was instrumental in its founding. For four of the PACs, lower-level Washington officials were interviewed in addition to the executive director. These formal interviews were then supplemented with a number of informal discussions with various officials in the PAC community in Washington.

The quantitative data on campaign contributions were provided by the Federal Election Commission. The data set includes all nonindependent contributions to all House candidates for the 1979–1980 and 1981–1982 election cycles. Excluded are candidates who received money but subsequently were defeated in a primary, retired, died, resigned, or ran for some other office. These data were combined with data on roll calls in the U.S. House of Representatives from the first and second sessions of the 97th Congress.

ORGANIZATION, FUNDRAISING, AND ALLOCATION STRATEGIES

Students of political action committees and campaign finance have theorized that PAC officials use one of two basic strategies when attempting to influence congressional outcomes through campaign contributions (Welch, 1980).

Under one strategy (call it Type I), PACs attempt to influence elections. This strategy gives priority to candidates in the closest contests, and the objective is to keep representatives in office, or to place new candidates in office, who by nature are most sympathetic to the PAC's policy goals. Under the other strategy (Type II), *Type II* PACs attempt to influence the behavior of incumbent representatives. Theoretically, this strategy gives priority to candidates who are likely to win, regardless of their initial policy positions, and to incumbents who are influential within the House. The objective is to persuade influential congressmen who are not always in agreement with the PAC's policy goals to become more agreeable and to maintain the support of already agreeable congressmen.

Although the goal of each strategy is to influence legislation, the means of accomplishing this goal and the assumptions underlying each strategy are quite different. Under the first strategy, congressmen's policy positions are assumed to be known, but fixed. As a result, voting decisions are not thought to be susceptible to manipulation or persuasion through campaign contributions, and thus the emphasis is on altering the membership of Congress rather than altering members' policy positions.

Under the second strategy, however, congressmen's policy positions are assumed to be variable, and congressmen are thought to be willing to exchange votes for campaign contributions.[7] PACs, therefore, pursue policy objectives by contributing to likely winners, who presumably will have flexibility in their policy positions, and to influential incumbents, who presumably are most capable of affecting the fate of proposed legislation.[8]

Both strategies assume that candidates need money, but the source of the need is different for each strategy. The Type I strategy presumes that the basis for financial need is immediate electoral competition, that is, a very close race. Implicit in the Type II strategy, however, is the notion that need derives from other considerations. Among these are the desire to establish or maintain a large war chest in order to deter future challenges, the desire to win by an exceptionally large margin in order to demonstrate viability for an attempt at a senatorial or gubernatorial seat, and the desire to make contributions to one's colleagues in order to solidify or expand one's influence within the House.[9]

Whether a PAC uses a Type I or Type II allocation strategy depends, in part, on the organizational resources available to the PAC. Theoretically, only those PACs that have the capacity to link contributions to congressional action can effectively employ a Type II strategy. Because Washington lobbyists are essential in establishing these links, a Type II strategy is much more viable for PACs associated with professional lobbying organizations—that is, connected PACs—than for unconnected, or ideological, PACs. In fact, research by Welch (1978, 1980) indicates convincingly that ideological PACs are much more likely to use a Type I than a Type II allocation strategy.

Because the PACs of national associations are affiliated with established lobbying organizations, contributions and lobbyists are often thought to be inextricably linked in the association PACs. Malbin (1979), for example, has suggested that the PACs of national associations are "special interest" rather than "general interest" groups. The hallmark of special interest groups is that they allocate their money "defensively," being concerned more with influencing legislative behavior than with influencing electoral outcomes. One reason the PACs of associations behave this way, says Malbin, is that national associations "tend to be headquartered in Washington, where lobbyists and PAC staffs work closely together" (p. 33). Similar views have been expressed by Fred Wertheimer, President

of Common Cause, who states flatly that "PAC money is tied to lobbying" (Hucker, 1978), and by Germond and Witcover (1983) who claim that, "It's left to a few professional lobbyists to steer that [PAC] money in the 'right' direction."

A popular belief about PAC contributions (particularly association PACs), then, is that they are controlled, or at least shaped to a considerable degree, by Washington lobbyists. Surprisingly, however, the analysis of decision-making patterns within the five PACs of this study yielded *very little support for this position*. Instead of allocation decisions being controlled by Washington lobbyists, the evidence suggests overwhelmingly that PACs' allocations are dominated by local inputs—recommendations of active members of the PACs at the state, congressional district, and county levels.[10] Interviews with PAC officials in Washington indicated that when local recommendations are made concerning the amount of money that the national office should allocate to different federal candidates, some *80 to 90% of these recommendations are approved without modification*. Within AMPAC, for example, 80% of all local recommendations are approved. For RPAC, the approval rate is 92%; and for DEAC, 95 to 98%.

Furthermore, there is very little evidence that PAC staffs and lobbying staffs work closely together. Historically, lobbying has been an activity of the parent organizations, not the PACs; and thus the two staffs have developed separately. Of the five PACs studied here, only in the case of the AGC does a single individual oversee both the lobbying activities and the PAC activities. Even physical distance often separates the PAC officials from the lobbyists. The NADA maintains an office for its lobbyists in downtown Washington, but the PAC operations are located in the organization's headquarters in McLean, Virginia. The headquarters for AMPAC have been located in

Washington only since 1982; before 1982, the AMPAC offices were located in Chicago.

So, in light of the conventional view about PAC contributions and lobbyists, these findings are indeed surprising, and, as with most unexpected results, they raise important questions. Why is it that allocation decisions are dominated so strongly by local officials rather than Washington lobbyists? Who are these individuals at the local levels whose recommendations carry so much weight? Answers to both of these questions require a short digression into the process by which political action committees raise money for distribution to political candidates.

ORGANIZATION AND FUNDRAISING

A continual and pressing problem for political action committees, as for any interest group, is the establishment and maintenance of a large contingent of active, dues-paying members (e.g., O'Brien, 1975; Olson, 1965/1971). Under federal law, corporations, labor unions, and other membership organizations are allowed to draw on their general treasury funds (e.g., funds from the parent organization, such as the AMA) to raise money for their PACs, but they are prohibited from drawing on their general treasury to make campaign contributions to federal candidates. National associations, as well as other organizations, must establish a "separate, segregated fund" (i.e., a political action committee) and make campaign contributions from this separate fund rather than from the general treasury. As a result, a separate membership must be established for the PAC, and this membership is itself a subset of the membership of the parent organization.

The fact that the PAC draws its members from the parent association puts the PAC at a severe disadvantage, relative to the parent, in providing selective material incentives to attract contributors or members. Members of the parent association can enjoy all of the selective incentives provided by the parent without ever contributing a dime to the political action committee, and because PACs are nascent political organizations, generally having been formed some 50 or 60 years after their parents, they lag far behind their parents in the provision of material benefits to prospective members. The American Medical Association, for example, was founded in 1846, but AMPAC was not added until 1961; the National Automobile Dealers Association was founded in 1917, but DEAC was not established until 1975; and the National Association of Realtors was formed in 1908, but RPAC was not founded until 1969. The parent associations, therefore, have had a great deal of "lead time" in testing and adopting those incentives that are most efficient for encouraging membership. In effect, then, the parents have established a virtual monopoly on material incentives, posing a formidable problem for the PACs in their fundraising efforts.

The way the PACs have managed to overcome this obstacle is to take advantage of their basic organizational structures. A common characteristic of the five PACs of this study is that the organizations with which they are affiliated are federated, or decentralized, organizations. Because the PACs were formed so much later than their parents, the organizational lines of the PACs tend to run parallel to the organizational lines of their parent groups.[11] Under the aegis of each of the five national PACs of this study are state-level PACs which, in turn, comprise officials from congressional districts, counties, and, where appropriate, individual corporations.[12]

The federal, or decentralized, structure of the association PAC provides an extensive grassroots network through which contributions can be raised. Each national PAC has, in effect, a dedicated core of local activists who bear much of the responsibility for soliciting individual contributions. These local activists are neither professional lobbyists nor full-time, salaried officials of the PAC, but rather political amateurs, such as professional bankers, physicians, and realtors, who happen to have a strong interest in politics and who take an active role in the local PAC organization.

Because these activists operate at the local level through small constituent groups, solidary incentives (e.g., Salisbury, 1969) can be used effectively to stimulate membership. Instead of offering selective material incentives (e.g., Olson, 1965/1971), the basic approach to fundraising is to make persuasive appeals to an individual's sense of *citizen or professional* duty—the opportunity and obligation to join with other members of one's profession in order to create and sustain a political environment that is favorable to the maintenance and growth of the profession or industry. One PAC official characterized this approach as "an appeal to professional responsibility," and he stated that "it's how you market that approach that determines how successful you are going to be."

Persuasive appeals are made in a variety of ways: through direct mailings, presentations and speeches at small gatherings of staff and employees, phone calls, and personal visits. Because persuasive appeals of this sort are most effective when made in person, or in small group settings, the basic fundraising approach of the association PACs is ideally suited to a decentralized organizational structure. In fact, it is doubtful whether such an approach could be implemented successfully in any arrangement other than a decentralized one.

But in addition to persuasive appeals, the PACs also emphasize the effectiveness and legitimacy of contributing money to the PAC. PACs, it is argued, can and do influence election outcomes, and PACs frequently publish figures that emphasize the percentage of winning candidates they have supported. PAC officials also are quite sensitive to the perceived legitimacy of PACs, and they devote considerable effort—through speeches, cooperation with the news media, written editorials, and similar means—to stimulate contributions by portraying PACs in a positive light.[13]

The notion that large groups can be organized on the basis of factors other than selective material incentives is certainly consistent with the theoretical work of other scholars. Even Olson (1965/1971) has pointed out that federal groups may be able to bring about collective action through social incentives in the small constituent groups, and Moe (1980) has argued that

[It] would be a serious mistake to "understand" organizational politics by automatically pointing to whatever organizational structures exist for the production and distribution of economic selective incentives. Organizations can do much more than this to attract members, and attention must clearly be given to other means of generating support: e.g., the ideological appeals of leaders; peer and leader emphasis on responsibility or fairness; the structuring of meetings, committees or social activities; the organizational generation of social pressure; leader efforts to convince individuals that their contributions make a difference; and the role of newsletters and informal communications networks in shaping member perceptions and values.

Implications for Allocation Strategies

The great dependence on local activists of the PAC for raising money significantly enhances their influence over decisions about how to allocate money to political candidates. National officials of the PAC are acutely aware of the need to respect local recommendations when allocation decisions are made. To do otherwise would reduce the incentives of local officials to raise money. In an outline of guidelines for establishing an effective state PAC organization, one national PAC makes the following suggestion.

> Although [statewide] contribution decisions must finally be made by the state PAC, proper recognition of the role of leaders of local PAC support groups and others should be given. *This is the key to a harmonious PAC program, and an important stimulus to membership development.* (emphasis added)

The national executive director of another PAC explained that:

> If we have someone who raised 10,000 dollars at the local level, but wants to support someone who we don't think is especially deserving, we will usually go along with him. If we didn't, he might not raise that kind of money for us the next time around.

And an official from still a different PAC summed it up this way: "They [the local officials] raise the money; they ought to be the ones who spend it."

These observations suggest that, contrary to conventional wisdom, the best allocation strategy for the association PACs is a Type I rather than a Type II strategy. The dominance of local inputs emphasizes electoral considerations rather than lobbying considerations, because local PAC officials are much more likely to be familiar with electoral politics of geographic constituencies than with the mechanics of influencing legislation in the Congress. In addition, because allocation decisions are shaped largely by local PAC officials, congressmen who desire campaign contributions are better advised to cultivate favorable relationships with prominent local PAC officials than with Washington lobbyists. This arrangement tends to undercut substantially the value of money

as a bargaining tool for professional lobbyists, thereby undermining the effectiveness of a Type II allocation strategy.

CONTRIBUTION PATTERNS IN FIVE PACS: EMPIRICAL ANALYSIS

The fact that allocation decisions are dominated by local officials leads to testable propositions about allocation strategies and the impact of campaign contributions on congressmen's voting decisions. Specifically, the weak influence of Washington lobbyists relative to the strong influence of local PAC officials suggests that PACs' campaign contributions will be used to elect ideologically sympathetic candidates in close races rather than alter the policy positions of not-so-sympathetic candidates in safe races. As a consequence, campaign contributions are not likely to carry substantial weight in congressmen's roll call voting decisions. These two propositions are examined in this section and the next with the use of data on campaign contributions during the 1979–1980 and 1981–1982 election cycles, along with roll calls from the House during the 97th Congress.

In the analysis that follows, inferences about PACs' allocation strategies are made from information about the characteristics of the candidates to whom the PACs contribute. Under a Type I strategy, as defined previously, priority for contributions is given to congressmen who have the "correct" ideology and to those who face tough electoral competition. Under a Type II strategy, priority for contributions is given to likely winners who are influential within Congress. Theoretically, then, these three factors—ideology, institutional influence, and electoral security—can be used to distinguish between allocation strategies.

The measurement of institutional influence is accomplished through a cluster of variables indicating committee assignments and leadership positions within the party. The relationship between this cluster of variables and a Type II allocation strategy has been recognized by Green (1979).

> Special interest investors, who would not dream of pouring their money into dud stocks, are equally careful when it comes to choosing their legislative portfolios. A freshman legislator with a seat on a dull committee won't cost much, but won't yield much return either. The logical result is that the money goes to the men who rule Congress—the members of key committees, the party leaders of each of the houses, and the committee chairmen. (pp. 10–11)

The committee variables included in the present analysis are: AGRICULTURE, APPROPRIATIONS, BANKING, COMMERCE, JUDICIARY, and WAYS AND MEANS. These six committee variables were selected on the basis of the interviews with the PAC officials, who were asked explicitly whether or not members of certain committees were targeted routinely for contributions. Officials of BANKPAC mentioned Banking, Ways and Means, Agriculture, Commerce, Judiciary, and Appropriations, in that order of priority. An official of the realtors' PAC indicated that Ways and Means is sometimes important, and Commerce was mentioned by an official of DEAC. Neither AMPAC nor AGCPAC claimed to give special consideration to members of any particular committee. In addition to membership on these committees, institutional influence is also measured by whether or not a representative is a party leader (REP LEADER, DEM LEADER) or a committee or subcommittee chairman (CHAIRMAN). Complete definitions of these and other variables are given in the Appendix.

The ideology factor is operatinoalized through another cluster of variables—the congressman's party affiliation (PARTY)

and his score on the Americans for Democratic Action index of voting in 1979 (ADA79). And the electoral competition factor is measured by the closeness of the candidate's race and the electoral experience of his or her challenger (NEED).[14] In addition, the NEED variable involves the interaction between ideology and competition, because ideology should be a more important factor under a Type I strategy when competition is strong.

The importance of ideology, institutional influence, and electoral security for predicting allocation patterns should vary depending on whether a PAC uses a Type I or a Type II allocation strategy. Under a Type I strategy, larger campaign contributions should be associated with greater electoral need and more conservative ADA scores. If a Type I strategy is dominant, the coefficients for PARTY and NEED should be large and positive, and the coefficient for ADA79 should be large and negative (because high ADA79 scores denote liberalism). Also, the coefficients for the institutional influence variables should all be negative. Under a Type II strategy, larger contributions should be associated with institutional influence, less conservative ideological positions, and less competitive races. Although the coefficient for ADA79 will not necessarily be positive, it should be small if a Type II strategy is dominant. Similarly, the NEED coefficient should be small, but not necessarily negative, and all of the coefficients for institutional influence should be large and positive.

These hypotheses were tested by regressing the total contributions (minus independent expenditures) in actual dollars for each of the five PACs during the 1979–1980 election cycle on all twelve of the explanatory variables. The results of the regression analyses appear in Table 20.1

Generally, the signs of the coefficients in Table 20.1 are more consistent for the ideology and need variables than for the committee and leadership variables.

Table 20.1 Regression Results for Contributions to Incumbents

Variable	AGCPAC	AMPAC	BANKPAC	DEAC	RPAC
Intercept	245.1	2354.1	864.5	2163.1	3222.8
AGRICULTURE	−51.2	−118.9	409.5	−148.8	555.8
APPROPRIATIONS	−154.0	−365.3	17.2	12.5	−624.2
BANKING	−109.6	−405.8	1281.4	200.8	589.4
COMMERCE	−139.4	172.1	157.8	977.6	−40.7
JUDICIARY	−139.2	580.8	−196.2	86.0	73.7
WAYS AND MEANS	11.8	−225.8	963.6	372.1	−292.4
CHAIRMAN	70.0	−608.2	580.6	575.3	−401.8
REP LEADER	11.6	−475.5	562.4	369.6	195.2
DEM LEADER	178.8	−176.6	−102.2	631.5	−432.8
PARTY	121.5	196.7	13.9	−219.2	84.3
ADA	−2.0	−23.2	−7.9	−22.8	−33.6
NEED	423.6	1739.9	209.8	930.0	1153.0
R SQUARE	.17	.33	.23	.24	.41

N = 385

The sign of the NEED coefficient is always positive, indicating that all five PACs gave more money to candidates who generally agreed with them ideologically and who faced tough election fights. Similarly, the sign of the ADA coefficient is always negative, which indicates a clear preference among all five PACs for conservative candidates. Also, with the exception of DEAC, all five PACs gave more money to Republican than to Democratic candidates. The coefficients for the committee and leadership variables, however, do not exhibit such clear patterns. As expected, BANKPAC favored members of the Banking and Ways and Means Committees, and DEAC clearly favored members of the Commerce committee. But otherwise, there is little clear evidence that committee and leadership positions elicited larger contributions.[15]

Overall, then, the results of the regression analyses tend to provide greater support for a Type I allocation strategy than for a Type II strategy. The general pattern is for larger contributions to go to sympathetic candidates who need money rather than to candidates who are on influential committees or in positions of party leadership. Only the coefficients for the ideology and need variables, not the influence variables, are consistently strong and in the right direction. These are precisely the results one would expect when allocation decisions are dominated by local inputs.

The results in Table 20.1 can be carried a step further by using the regression coefficients to make predictions of the actual dollar amounts allocated under each type of strategy. Such an exercise yields a more concrete picture of allocation patterns—a picture in terms of dollar amounts rather than OLS coefficients.

The prediction of actual dollar amounts that follows is based on a conception of two hypothetical kinds of congressmen. One kind, Congressman A, is intended to represent the ideal target for a Type I allocation; the other, Congressman B, the ideal target for a Type II allocation.

Table 20.2 Predicted Contributions to Different Types of Congressmen

	Congressman A (conservative, non-leader, competitive)	Congressman B (moderate, liberal, leader, sale)
AGCPAC	$ 740	$ 223
AMPAC	3709	0
BANKPAC	891	2981
DEAC	2304	2857
RPAC	3619	0
Mean	$2253	$1212

Let Congressman A be a rank-and-file, conservative, Republican congressman from a competitive electoral district. Let Congressman B be a member of a strategic committee (Ways and Means and Banking for the ABA, Commerce for the auto dealers), a committee or subcommittee chairman, a Democratic House leader, a liberal, and electorally secure. Then, a PAC that uses a Type I allocation strategy should give larger contributions to Congressman A, and a PAC that uses a Type II strategy should give larger contributions to Congressman B.

The entries in Table 20.2 are the dollar amounts that each PAC, on the basis of its allocation strategy, is predicted to give to each kind of congressman.[16] Of the five PACs, only BANKPAC clearly places highest priority on a Type II allocation strategy.[17] Even though DEAC is predicted to give slightly more money to Congressman B, the PAC is also predicted to give a substantial contribution to Congressman A. Each of the other three PACs, however, is predicted to give a substantially larger contribution to Congressman A than to Congressman B, and on average across all five PACs, Congressman A is predicted to receive almost twice as large a campaign contribution as Congressman B. These results are quite consistent with the hypothesis that allocation decisions are a function of local discretion in the allocation process.

CAMPAIGN CONTRIBUTIONS AND ROLL CALL VOTES

Two necessary (but not sufficient) conditions for PAC contributions to influence roll call voter are that PACs allocate money with the intent of influencing roll calls, and congressmen are aware of that intent. The evidence presented thus far, however, suggests quite clearly that neither of these conditions will be satisfied. The evidence indicates that money is given with the intent of influencing election outcomes, not specific roll calls, and that congressmen and their staffs must cultivate relationships with local PAC officials, not Washington lobbyists. As a result, a strong causal relationship between PAC contributions and roll calls is unlikely.

To assess the influence of contributions on roll call decisions in the 97th Congress, the most important—or one of the most important—roll calls for each of the five PACs was selected for analysis. Information on important roll calls was obtained through communication with PAC and association officials and through a review of the lobbying priorities of each group as reported in the *Congressional Quarterly Weekly Reports*.

The most important vote for the NADA in the 97th Congress was the vote to overturn the Federal Trade Commission's rule that required used-car dealers to inform customers of known defects in used automobiles. On May 6, 1982, the House adopted a concurrent resolution (286-133) to disapprove the FTC rule.

A crucial vote for the Associated General Contractors was a vote on the rule governing floor consideration of the Transportation Assistance Act (HR6211). A closed rule was assigned to a Ways and Means tax package to be amended to the act, and the AGC supported the closed rule from fear that an open rule might destroy all prospects of passing a highway bill in any form. The House adopted a resolution approving the closed rule on December 6, 1982, by a 197-194 vote.

Votes on the Gramm-Latta budget proposal were important to the National Association of Realtors.[18] The realtors favored as deep a slowdown in the growth of spending as possible and opposed a rule governing consideration of Gramm-Latta-II that would have encouraged lower spending cuts. The rule was over-turned by a 210-217 vote (HR3982) on June 25, 1981.

For the AMA, the critical vote was on an amendment to exempt professionals—physicians in particular—from FTC reg-ulation. The AMA succeeded in getting the amendment (HR6995) passed in the House by a 245-155 vote margin in December, 1982, but the amendment subsequently failed in the Senate.

Finally, an important vote to the bankers (although not as important as in the next Congress) was a vote concern-ing the withholding of taxes on interest income from bank accounts. The ABA opposed a closed rule for consideration of the 1983 tax bill in hopes of amending the bill to exclude the withholding pro-vision. On August 19, 1982, the bankers ended up on the losing side of a 220-210 vote on the rule (HR4961).

Each congressman's votes on these issues was recorded, and various predictor variables, including PAC contributions, were collected in order to examine the impact of campaign contributions on roll call votes, with other factors held constant. The full array of predictor variables fall into four general cate-gories: constituency demographics (URBAN, BLUE COLLAR, INCOME, REAGAN), region (EAST, MIDWEST, WEST, SOUTH), ideology (ADA79, ADA81, PARTY), and contributions. Full definitions of these variables are given in the appendix.

The use of these particular indepen-dent variables to predict roll calls can be justified on several grounds. The inclusion of the demographic, or constituency, vari-ables is justified in that demographic char-acteristics serve as rough indicators of some of the basic needs and concerns of constituents. Fenno (1978), for example, reports that congressmen frequently dis-cuss demographic factors when talking about their constituencies. Even though the basic needs and concerns of a con-stituency are much more complex and heterogeneous than allowed for by demo-graphic variables, the absence of better measures helps justify their inclusion (Clausen, 1973).

Because the demographic factors are rather firmly fixed, whatever needs or preferences they represent can be assumed to be longstanding. In order to capture some of the more immediate or short-term policy concerns of voters in the dis-trict, the variable for support of Reagan in 1980, REAGAN, has been included. Presumably, this variable represents con-stituency support for the policies of the president or the president's party. Even though it is true that some voters cast their ballots devoid of any policy consid-erations, congressmen may perceive that the presidential vote percentage is an indi-cator of voters' policy preferences. If so, congressmen may be reluctant to vote against a bill supported by the president if the president appears to have consider-able support in the district, and empirical studies indicate that this is sometimes the case (Erikson & Wright, 1980; Kau & Rubin, 1982).

The region variables have been included to account for differences in outlook and behavior resulting from geographic and environmental constraints. The South, Midwest, East, and West have differed historically with regard to agricultural, environmental, and industrial concerns. Because of the geographic basis of representation in American politics, a congressman's first responsibility is usually to his district, not to the nation as a whole, and as a result, the geographic differences among districts should be reflected in congressmen's voting decisions (Jackson, 1974).

The ADA variables have been included as general measures of a congressman's ideological orientation. ADA79 is used to predict votes in the first session of the 97th Congress, and ADA81 is used to predict votes in the second session. The ADA score is a composite measure that reflects numerous voting decisions on different types of issues. Because the ADA score used here is always from the session preceding the vote being analyzed, it provides the most recent snapshot of the congressman's voting behavior. This snapshot captures not only a bit of the congressman's own personal ideological leaning, but also reflects the shared ideology of the congressman and his constituents. Because most congressmen have lived a good portion of their lives in the districts they represent, the beliefs of constituents and the beliefs of the congressman are likely to be similar owing to the common roots of both, and the ADA score is presumed to reflect these beliefs.

The contribution variables indicate the actual dollars contributed by each PAC to each congressman. Ideally, these variables should be weighted by their importance to the congressman, because all congressmen are not likely to attach the same significance to each dollar

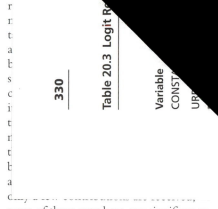

Table 20.3 Logit R

Variable
CONST
UR

none of them may have any significance.

Each congressman's vote on each of the five roll calls was predicted on the basis of the explanatory variables through a logistic estimation technique. The result of the logit analysis appear in Table 20.3.[19] The entries in Table 20.3 are logit coefficients which indicate the change in the log odds of voting "yea" given a unit change in an independent variable, the other independent variables remaining constant. The preferred position was "Yea" for all groups but BANKPAC and RPAC.

With the exception of the sign for AGC, all the signs of the coefficients indicate that contributions increased the probability of voting in the direction preferred by the contributing group. One explanation for the reversal of the sign for the AGCPAC coefficient is that the AGC gave most of its money to conservative Republicans who happened to oppose the rule because of their objections to any tax increases at the time. This finding, however, merely underscores the fact that the congressmen who received money from the AGC voted on the basis of their ideological and partisan convictions, not on the basis of contributions.

With a little manipulation, the logit coefficients can be combined with values of the independent variables to yield predicted probabilities of voting with a contributing group's position. Two probabilities of voting with the contributing

esults for Contributions and Roll Calls

	ROLL CALL VOTE FOR				
	AGCPAC	AMPAC	BANKPAC	DEAC	RPAC
ANT	−5.934	1.423	−2.2992	2.219	8.947
BAN	0.034	−0.13	0.014	−0.050	−0.009
BLUE COLLAR	0.049	0.034	0.030	0.0006	−0.038
INCOME	0.00019	−0.00002	0.0001	0.00023	−0.0003
REAGAN	−0.006	0.040	0.006	0.066	−0.078
EAST	0.741	−1.326	−0.634	−1.366	−1.746
MIDWEST	−0.139	−1.579	0.031	−0.330	0.480
WEST	0.652	−0.583	0.292	0.531	−1.982
SOUTH	0.567	−0.615	0.524	0.897	−2.204
ADA	0.007	−0.054	0.002	−0.060	0.100
PARTY	−0.838	−0.182	−0.796	−0.507	−7.189
CONTRIBUTION	−0.00023	0.00027	−0.00004	0.00024	−0.00006
N	348	358	419	416	347
−2 log L	369.41	226.4	537.4	211.69	82.96

group were computed for each congressman. One probability was based on the actual contribution received by the congressman, together with his or her actual values on the remaining independent variables. The other probability was based on a theoretical contribution of zero dollars, with no change in the other independent variables. The difference between these two probabilities indicates the theoretical increase in the probability of voting with the contributing group associated with a campaign contribution.

The mean increases in the differences between these two probabilities are reported in Table 20.4. Each entry in the table indicates the average (over all congressmen in the analysis) change in the predicted probability of voting with the contributing group's preferred position as a result of a campaign contribution. For example, if the auto dealers had made no campaign contributions in 1979–1980, then, on average, each congressman's probability of voting to overturn the FTC regulation on used cars would have been

lowered by .019 (e.g., from a .6 probability of supporting the NADA to a probability of support of .581). Clearly, the changes reported in Table 20.4 are rather paltry. The mean of the means across all five groups is a mere .0096. Moreover, in none of the cases were the effects of contributions great enough to change the voting outcome.[20]

The actual results in Table 20.4 are quite consistent with the anticipated results, which were that the relationships between campaign contributions and roll calls would be weak. This is clearly the case. In none of the five cases examined were campaign contributions an important enough force to change the legislative outcomes from what they would have been without any contributions.

Even more important, though, to the extent that the PACs under investigation here are among the most influential PACs, the effects exhibited by their contributions should be among the largest effects that campaign contributions can exert on roll call voting decisions. Results

Table 20.4 Mean Change in Probability of Voting with Contributing Group due to Difference between Zero Contributions and Actual Contributions

Political Action Committee	Change in Probability
AGPAC	−.022
AMPAC	.038
BANKPAC	.007
DEAC	.019
RPAC	.006
Mean	.0096

that scholars have labeled "substantial" or "significant," therefore, are substantial and significant only in the sense that they characterize the upper limits of PAC influence. But these upper limits pale in comparison to the unbounded influence that many scholars, journalists, and politicians have imputed to PACs.

Finally, as I suggested earlier, there is a sound theoretical reason for not expecting campaign contributions to exert effects on roll call voting any larger than those reported in Tables 20.3 and 20.4. Very simply, the organizational arrangements in which PACs raise and allocate money impose strong constraints on the ability of PACs to influence congressional voting through their campaign contributions. Thus, any time the fund raising operation and the locus of decision-making are structured as they are in the PACs of this study, contributions are not likely to carry much weight in congressional voting decisions.

CONCLUSIONS

The major finding of this research is that the ability of PACs to use their campaign contributions to influence congressional voting is severely constrained by the organizational arrangements through which money is raised. Paradoxically, the organizational arrangement that allows PACs to raise and allocate large sums of money

also restricts their ability to influence roll calls. Because money must be raised at a local, grassroots level, local PAC officials, not Washington lobbyists, are primarily responsible for making allocation decisions. Consequently, congressmen who desire contributions must cultivate favorable relationships with local officials, and this arrangement tends to undercut the value of contributions as a bargaining tool for professional lobbyists.

This finding is significant in two respects. First, in contrast to previous analyses, this analysis has demonstrated with marked clarity the limited nature of PAC influence. Of the numerous variables that influence the voting behavior of congressmen, the campaign contributions of PACs appear to take substantial effect only infrequently. Only when other cues, such as party, are weak can PAC contributions be expected to be important. The results presented here cannot support a claim that PACs never have, or never will, determine voting outcomes, but they do indicate the probable rarity of such influence.

Second, I have formulated an explanation for the limited nature of the influence of PAC contributions. This explanation adds a very substantial degree of confidence to the empirical results. Moreover, it moves the analysis in the direction of a more general understanding of the relationship between PAC campaign contributions and roll calls. Future efforts to understand roll calls in terms of campaign contributions should benefit substantially from a consideration of the organizational arrangements of PACs.

Additional tests of the explanation presented here need to be conducted. Not only is it important to investigate the frequency with which the organizational structures of the five PACs studied here characterize other PACs, but it is also important to explore the implications of quite different organizational arrangements—for example, the organization of "institutional" groups (Salisbury, 1984) or the differences between nascent and mature organizations (Hayes, 1981). Evidence of systematic and predictable differences across different organizational arrangements would put the explanation on even firmer ground.

Finally, evidence of the relative inability of PACs to determine congressional voting should not be construed as evidence that PACs in no way matter. The growth of PACs may have altered the way congressmen allocate their scarce resources of staff and time. Today, congressmen must spend a great deal of time courting past and potential contributors to their campaigns. If such efforts drain members' resources and energies so thoroughly that they can no longer devote themselves properly to important political issues and to formulating sound public policy, then prevailing methods of campaign finance might be considered highly inappropriate. The purpose of this article, however, has been neither to endorse PACs nor to indict them, but only to improve understanding of them.

APPENDIX

Table 20A.1 Variables Used for Predicting Contributions (Table 20.1)

Institutional Influence

AGRICULTURE	1 if the incumbent was a member of the Agriculture Committee in the 96th Congress; 0 otherwise.
APPROPRIATIONS	1 if the incumbent was a member of the Appropriations Committee; 0 otherwise.
BANKING	1 if the incumbent was a member of the Banking, Finance, and Urban Affairs Committee; 0 otherwise.
COMMERCE	1 if the incumbent was a member of the Interstate and Foreign Commerce Committee; 0 otherwise.
JUDICIARY	1 if the incumbent was a member of the Judiciary Committee; 0 otherwise.
WAYS AND MEANS	1 if the incumbent was a member of the Ways and Means Committee; 0 otherwise.
REP LEADER	1 if the incumbent was a floor leader, chairman or secretary of the party caucus or conference, a whip, deputy whip, or assistant whip; 0 otherwise.
DEM LEADER	same as for REP LEADER.
CHAIRMAN	1 if the incumbent chaired a standing or select committee; 0 otherwise.

Ideology

PARTY	1 if the incumbent is a Republican; 0 if a Democrat.
ADA79	the incumbent's score on the Americans for Democratic Action index in 1979; a score of 0 indicates conservatism; a score of 100 indicates liberalism.

(Continued)

Table 20A.1 Variables Used for Predicting Contributions (Table 20.1) (*Continued*)

Electoral Need

NEED — 1 if the incumbent was ideologically sympathetic to the PAC's policy goals (ADA79 less than or equal to 50) and faced strong electoral competition; 0 if the incumbent was not sympathetic or did not face strong competition.

Table 20A.2 Variables Used for Predicting Roll Calls (Table 20.3)

Constituency Demographics

URBAN — the percentage of residents in a district living in urban areas (as defined by the Bureau of the Census).

BLUE COLLAR — the percentage of blue collar workers in a district.

INCOME — the median income of a district.

REAGAN — the percentage of the presidential vote in a district in 1980 for Ronald Reagan.

Region

EAST — 1 if a district is in Maine, New Hampshire, Vermont, Connecticut, Rhode Island, Massachusetts, New York, Pennsylvania, New Jersey, or Delaware; 0 otherwise.

MIDWEST — 1 if Ohio, Michigan, Indiana, Illinois, Wisconsin, Minnesota, Iowa, North Dakota, South Dakota, Nebraska, Kansas; 0 otherwise.

WEST — 1 if Montana, Wyoming, Colorado, New Mexico, Utah, Idaho, Nevada, Arizona, California, Oregon, Washington, Alaska, Hawaii; 0 otherwise.

SOUTH — 1 if Virginia, North Carolina, South Carolina, Georgia, Florida, Alabama, Louisiana, Mississippi, Texas, Arkansas; 0 otherwise.

(BORDER) — (Missouri, Kentucky, Tennessee, Oklahoma, Maryland, West Virginia).

Ideology

ADA79 — the congressman's rating from the Americans for Democratic Action during the second session of the 96th Congress.

ADA81 — the congressman's ADA rating from the first session of the 97th Congress.

PARTY — 1 if a Republican; 0 if a Democrat.

Contributions

AGCPAC — total contributions from AGCPAC during the 1981–1982 election cycle.

AMPAC — total contributions from AMPAC during the 1981–1982 election cycle.

BANKPAC — total contributions from BANKPAC during the 1979–1980 election cycle.

DEAC — total contributions from DEAC during the 1979–1980 election cycle.

RPAC — total contributions from RPAC during the 1979–1980 election cycle.

NOTES

1. Representative Downey, Democrat of New York, for example, claims, "You can't buy a congressman for $5000. But you can buy his vote. It's done on a regular basis" (Isaacson, 1982, p. 20). Barber Conable, Republican of New York, suggests that "These new PACs not only buy incumbents, but affect legislation as well. It's the same crummy business as judges putting the arm on lawyers who appear before them to finance their next campaign" (Green, 1982, p. 18). Additional support for these positions can be found in Drew (1982).

2. Organizational arrangements have not been ignored altogether (e.g., Eismeier & Pollock, 1984; Sabato, 1984; Sorauf, 1982), but the importance of organization for congressional decision making has not received attention.

3. Naturally, roll call votes are only a rough indicator of the overall influence that contributions might have on legislative outcomes. Contributions may have considerable effects on other aspects of the legislative process such as decisions to report bills out of committee, or strategic considerations in scheduling.

4. Although Sabato (1984) has surveyed a random sample of 399 PACs, his data do not include roll call votes.

5. Even though many of the labor unions also have strong lobbying organizations, the labor PACs appear to be more interested in using their campaign contributions to influence election outcomes than the voting decisions of incumbent members of Congress (e.g., Budde, 1980).

6. For a fuller discussion of both types of data, see Wright (1983, pp. 13–21).

7. Congressmen are predicted to alter their votes, however, only up to the point where the gain in electoral support through additional contributions just offsets the losses in support that result from moving away from voters' preferred policy positions. For a mathematical formulation, see Ben-Zion and Eytan (1974).

8. In reality, PACs probably pursue some mix between the two strategies. Unfortunately, though, attempts to model mathematically behavior motivated by both approaches have been unsuccessful (Welch, 1980, p. 101). The two pure strategies, then, should be regarded as heuristic tools, not as perfect depictions of the real world.

9. These three rationalizations for money were described in the interviews with the PAC officials.

10. Handler and Mulkern (1982) make a comparable finding with respect to allocation decisions of corporate PACs. In 14 of 70 PACs surveyed, allocation decisions were said to be made by "nonspecialist amateurs."

11. For a more detailed description of organizational arrangements, see Wright (1983, pp. 50–56).

12. Member banks of the ABA generally, but not always, have their own political action committees. However, individual corporations of the AGC generally do not have their own PACs, although there are exceptions.

13. Additional discussion of the fundraising methods of the association PACs can be found in Wright (1984).

14. A congressman was determined to have had strong competition if he or she received less than 60% of the vote in a two-way race in 1978, or if the challenger in 1980 had held any elective office before the 1980 congressional election. Information on the experience of challengers was taken from "The 1980 Elections," Congressional Quarterly Weekly Report, Supplement, October 11, 1980, pp. 2965–3092.

15. Tests of statistical significance have been omitted here because there is no reason to believe that they would be meaningful. Significance tests are meaningful only when observations have been selected randomly from a larger population or when it can be assumed that the universe from which they have been selected is normally distributed. The universe of interest here is all Congresses from 1974 to 1980, because 1974 marked the first year that the FEC required full disclosure of campaign expenditures. But the observations of this study have not been selected randomly from this universe, and the Congresses since 1974 are certainly not normally distributed with respect to relevant variables, because they have all been controlled by Democrats.

16. The entries under Congressman B for AMPAC and RPAC have been entered as "0" rather than the negative values (−370 and −216) that actually were predicted. The reason for the negative values is that OLS is an inappropriate functional form when the dependent variable is truncated normal—that is, when there is a lower bound (i.e., zero contributions) with a large concentration of values, but no such concentration at the upper bound. Tobit analysis (Tobin, 1958), which provides an appropriate functional form, was also used to estimate coefficients for the independent variables. However, the results did not differ in any systematic ways from the OLS results, so the more familiar OLS results have been presented here.

17. BANKPAC also has the most centralized structure of the five PACs for making allocation decisions. The Washington office sends out a computer listing to all state PAC organizations with recommended contributions to all candidates. These recommendations are based primarily on the congressman's committee assignment, and local PAC officials usually, but not always, follow these recommendations.

18. Unfortunately, this issue is not as specific to the realtors as one might wish. It is a more general bill and, therefore, does not provide as strong a test of the effects of contributions as the bills selected for the other groups. For a discussion of the realtors' position, see Fair (1981).

19. Since the votes for AGCPAC and AMPAC occurred after the 1982 election, during the lame-duck session, 1982 contribution data were used. The Ns for the DEAC and BANKPAC equations include all members of the 97th Congress who were elected in 1980 and voted on the resolutions. The N for the RPAC equation includes only members of both the 96th and 97th Congresses who voted on the motion. Since this vote occurred relatively early in the first session of the 97th, there were not enough votes to construct an ADA score for the congressmen first elected in 1980. Hence they were excluded from the analysis. The Ns for the AGC and AMA equations include all members of the 97th Congress who were elected in 1980 with the exclusion of 58 lame duck congressmen.

20. This was determined by counting the number of congressmen on each roll call whose probability of support changed from less than .5 to greater or equal to .5 because of the contribution received.

REFERENCES

Barone, M. When the price is right. *The Washington Post*. March 9, 1983, A25.

Ben-Zion, U., & Eytan, Z. On money, votes, and policy in a democratic society. *Public Choice*, 1974, *17*, 1–10.

Berry, J. *Lobbying for the people*. Princeton, N.J.: Princeton University Press, 1977.

Brown, K. F. Campaign contributions and congressional voting. Presented at the Annual Meeting of the American Political Science Association, 1983.

Budde, B. Business political action committees. In M. J. Malbin (Ed.). *Parties, interest groups, and campaign finance laws*. Washington: American Enterprise Institute, 1980.

Chappell, H. Campaign contributions and congressional voting: A simultaneous probit–tobit model. *Review of Economics and Statistics*, 1982, *62*, 77–83.

Chappell, H. Campaign contributions and voting on the cargo preference bill: A comparison of simultaneous models. *Public Choice*, 1981, *36*, 301–312.

Clausen, A. *How congressmen decide: A policy focus*. New York: St. Martin's, 1973.

Cohen, R. E. Here are the big contributors. *The National Journal*. 1983, *15*, 974.

Drew, E. Politics and money—1. *The New Yorker*. Dec. 6, 1982, 54–149.

Eismeier, T. J., & Pollock, III, P. H. Political action committees: Varieties of organization and strategy. In M. J. Malbin (Ed.). *Money and politics in the United States*. Chatham, N. J.: Chatham House, 1984.

Erikson, R. S., & Wright, G. C. Policy representation of constituency interests. *Political Behavior*, 1980, *2*, 91–106.

Fair, R. Personal testimony in hearings before the subcommittee on housing and community development of the committee on banking, finance, and urban affairs. *Housing and community development amendments of 1981.* Washington: U.S. Government Printing Office, 1981, 1576–1618.

Fenno, R. F. *Home style.* Boston: Little, Brown, 1978.

Frendreis, J., & Waterman, R. PAC contributions and legislative behavior: senate voting on trucking deregulation. Presented at the Annual Meeting of the Midwest Political Science Association, 1983.

Germond, J., & Witcover, J. A pac-man in Congress won't heed constituents. *The Rochester Times Union.* March 7, 1983, 6A.

Green, M. Political pac-man. *The New Republic,* December 13, 1982, 18–25.

Green, M. *Who runs congress?* New York: Viking Press, 1979.

Handler, E., & Mulkern, J. R. *Business in politics: Campaign strategies of corporate political action committees.* Lexington, Mass.: Health, 1982.

Hayes, M. T. *Lobbyists and legislators: A theory of political markets.* New Brunswick, N.J.: Rutgers University Press, 1981.

Hucker, C. Organized labor takes a hard look at whom it will support this fall. *Congressional Quarterly Weekly Report.* 1978, *36,* 193–198.

Isaacson, W. Running with the PACs. *Time,* October 25, 1982, 20–26.

Jackson, J. E. *Constituencies and leaders in Congress: Their effects on Senate voting behavior.* Cambridge, Mass.: Harvard University Press, 1974.

Jacobson, G. C. *The politics of congressional elections.* Boston: Little, Brown, 1983.

Kau, J. B., & Rubin, P. H. *Congressmen, constituents, and contributors.* Boston: Martinus Nijhoff, 1982.

Latus, M. A. Assessing ideological PACs: From out-rage to understanding. In M. J. Malbin (Ed.), *Money and politics in the United States.* Chatham, N.J.: Chatham, House, 1984.

Malbin, M. J. Campaign financing and the special interests. *The Public Interest,* 1979, *56,* 21–42.

Malbin, M. J., & Skladony, T. W. Appendix: Selected campaign finance data, 1974–1982. In M. J. Malvin (Ed.), *Money and politics in the United States.* Chatham, N.J.: Chatham House, 1984.

Moe, T. A. calculus of group membership. *American Journal of Political Science,* 1980, *24,* 593–632.

Noble, K. B. Critics cite banks' aid in elections. *The New York Times,* March 14, 1983, D1.

O'Brien, D. *Neighborhood organization and interest-group processes.* Princeton, N.J.: Princeton University Press, 1975.

Olson, M. *The logic of collective action: Public goods and the theory of groups.* Cambridge, Mass.: Harvard University Press, 1965/1971.

Ornstein, N. J., & Elder, S. *Interest groups, lobbying and policymaking.* Washington: Congressional Quarterly Press, 1978.

Sabato, L. J. *PAC power: Inside the world of political action committees.* New York: Norton, 1984.

Salisbury, R. H. An exchange theory of interest groups. *Midwest Journal of Political Science,* 1969, *13,* 1–32.

Salisbury, R. H. Interest representation: The dominance of institutions. *American Political Science Review,* 1984, *78,* 64–76.

Silberman, J. I., & Durden, G. C. Determining legislative preferences on the minimum wage: An economic approach. *Journal of Political Economy,* 1976, *84,* 317–329.

Sorauf, F. J. Accountability in political action committees: Who's in charge? Presented at the Annual Meeting of the American Political Science Association, 1982.

Tobin, J. Estimation of relationships for limited dependent variables. *Econometrica,* 1958, *26,* 24–36.

Truman, D. B. *The governmental process: Political interests and public opinion.* New York: Knopf, 1951.

United Press International. Congress vetoes FTC rules on disclosure of car defects. *The New York Times.* May 27, 1982, 1.

Welch, W. P. The allocation of political monies: Economic interest groups. *Public Choice,* 1980, *35,* 97–120.

Welch, W. P. Campaign contributions and legislative voting: Milk money and dairy price supports. *Western Political Quarterly,* 1982, *35,* 478–495.

Welch, W. P. Patterns of contributions: Economic interest and ideological groups. In H. E.

Alexander (Ed.), *Political finance*. Beverly Hills, Calif.: Sage, 1978.

Wertheimer, F. Has Congress made it legal to buy congressmen? *Business and Society Review,* 1978, *27,* 29–32.

Wilson, J. Q. *Political organizations.* New York: Basic Books, 1973.

Wright, J. R. Fundraising by political action committees: The problems of collective action. Unpublished, 1984.

Wright, J. R. Pacs, contributions, and roll calls: Evidence for five national associations. Unpublished doctoral dissertation, University of Rochester, 1983.

Yiannakis, D. E. PAC contributions and house voting on conflictual and consensual issues: The Windfall Profits Tax and the Chrysler loan guarantee. Presented at the Annual Meeting of the American Political Science Association, 1983.

PROJECT

Place Wright's analysis in the context of the pluralism-elitism debate. How does his analysis conform to and refute the arguments made by each of these perspectives?

21

Legislators and Interest Groups: How Unorganized Interests Get Represented

ARTHUR T. DENZAU
MICHAEL C. MUNGER

Lay observers often claim that interest groups are powerful because they have vast sums of money and are able to "buy" the votes of representatives. You have already seen that policy making is far more complicated than this. Denzau and Munger investigate the relationships among interest groups, constituencies, and legislators, and find that rather than expend resources haphazardly, a group will seek out legislators who are sympathetic to its cause. Groups who argue for increased gun control, for instance, will not lobby legislators who have vowed to defend the Second Amendment.

Most citizens do not participate in the electoral process, but their needs are regularly met nonetheless. Groups lobby on behalf of candidates who support the interests of a given constituency. Agricultural interest groups, for example, are more likely to be active in agricultural legislative districts because the representatives are expected to devote their attention to agricultural issues. Denzau and Munger's analysis provides support for the pluralist scholarship dominant in the 1950s and 1960s.

QUESTIONS TO CONSIDER

1. How do these authors define "constituency"? Why is this important?
2. In what ways are interest groups strategic in whom they choose to lobby?
3. What is "rational ignorance"? Why is it important to understand?
4. What are the main factors interest groups take into consideration when seeking out legislators to lobby?
5. What normative implications do the authors conclude from their model?

The extent to which organized interest groups can affect policy is a matter of theoretical debate. Early pluralist theory in political science asserted that competition between groups is the sole process by which policy was formed, with the Congress (in the U.S.) as the passive referee in this struggle (see Bailey, 1950; Bentley, 1907; Latham, 1952; Schattschneider, 1935; and Truman, 1951, 1959; Niskanen, 1971, takes this view in discussing bureaucracy). "The legislative vote on any issue tends to represent the composition of strength, i.e., the balance of power among the contending groups at the moment of voting" (Latham, 1952, p. 36).

However, this view is clearly too simplistic. Congressmen are not ciphers, meekly responding to pressure-group activities. Partly as a reaction to the pluralist position, a dissenting school developed, marked by Matthews (1960), Bauer, Pool, and Dexter (1972), and others. Bauer et al. (1972, p. 478) assert that

congressmen have a great deal more freedom than is ordinarily attributed to them. The complexities of proce-

SOURCE: From Arthur Denzau and Michael Munger, "Legislators and Interest Groups: How Unorganized Interests Get Represented," *American Political Science Review*, 80, no. 1 (March 1986): 89–106. Reprinted with permission of Cambridge University Press.

dure, the chances of obfuscation, the limited attention constituents pay to any one issue, and the presence of countervailing forces all leave the congressman relatively free on most issues. He may feel unfree because of the great demands on his time, but, consciously or unconsciously, by his own decisions on what he chooses to make of his job he generates the pressures which impinge upon him. He hears from voters about those things in which he himself chooses to become involved.

The view of Congressional dominance did not completely replace the pluralist theory as the orthodox model of policy formation, but it was widely accepted. The new approach was of great importance because of the explicit recognition that policy formation is affected both by those who seek a certain outcome, as the pluralists claimed, and by those legislators who have discretion over who receives the benefits. More recent work views Bauer et al. as having overemphasized "supply" forces, giving Congress nearly complete discretion over policy and ignoring interest groups as demanders of policy. Efforts to explore the middle ground, where lobbyists and congressmen both share and compete with each other for decision power

(Hayes, 1981, p. 12) have spawned case studies and theoretical analyses involving "subgovernments," "policy subsystems," "iron triangles," and "clientelism," but offer few attempts to model these relationships formally, and provide few general conclusions.

One explicit model of the supply and demand components of the process is Miller and Moe's (1983) bilateral monopoly model. While conceptually appealing, the bilateral monopoly model has few predictions for outcomes beyond the fact that the greater a group's bargaining strength, the better able it is to improve its strength against the others. However, many political situations have competitive aspects that make a bilateral monopoly model inappropriate. There are a number of national, or at least multi-district, interest groups that may compete with other groups, or have the option of lobbying among several legislators.

Economists have generally used a different approach in attempting to discover, explain, and measure the effects that interest groups have in influencing legislators and legislation. For example, Stigler (1971), McPherson (1972), Pincus (1975), and Salamon and Seigfried (1977) all attempt to measure the effect of interest group power in obtaining favorable treatment. The same kind of technique has been used by Kau and Rubin (1982) and Peltzman (1982), using district-level aggregate data to measure the effect of demographic and other regularities of the constituency on roll-call voting behavior. While providing useful insights into the relationship between interest groups and congressmen, these studies are limited by the inability of survey or demographic data to measure accurately lobbying activity, constituent interests, and the preferences of legislators. Rather than explicitly modeling these disparate but important influences, the economic studies have simply identified regularities in the characteristics of interest groups and legislative voting behavior or policy outcomes.

This paper develops a theoretical model of the supply of public policy in the U.S. The model is shown to yield testable implications about which interest groups and which sets of voters are likely to be served. The basic logic of the supply model is as follows: Policy outcomes depend on the comparative advantages of the participants. Comparative advantage, in this context, depends on the value of what each set of agents in the model has to offer the others. We consider three sets of agents: voters, interest groups, and legislators. In order to simplify the analysis we focus on the implicit market for policy, in which interest groups offer contributions to legislators in exchange for legislators' efforts on each interest group's behalf. The contribution of this research is its derivation of an explicit *supply price* for policy. The amounts interest groups must offer a legislator for his services are shown to depend on that legislator's productivity and the preferences of the voters in his district.

Two extreme assumptions about voter preferences, which we distinguish by the name *rational ignorance* and *civics class,* are used to illustrate the comparative statics predictions of the model. The comparison of the results of these assumptions allows us to focus on the question of which factors influence the determination of groups to be served. Clearly, a variety of other comparative statics results are implied by the model, and these are discussed briefly in the conclusions.

The paper is divided into five parts. The first is a discussion of assumptions and definitions, followed by a version of the model that accounts for an incumbent legislator's choice of constituency. Section three examines the decision of interest groups to allocate their scarce resources among legislators. The fourth section examines the implications of the rationally ignorant and civics class assumptions about voter behavior for public policy outcomes. The last section is devoted to a summary and a discussion of extensions.

THE AGENTS

Legislators

Legislators are assumed to maximize the number of votes they receive in the next election. While not literally accurate, maximizing votes is a sensible proxy, because a large margin in any given election affects the margin in the following election. That is, even if the legislator cares only about winning in each of the next several terms, he still acts as if he were maximizing votes in any contest except the last. As Mayhew (1974, p. 46) said, the goal of the elected official is to

> stay in office over a number of future elections, which does mean that 'winning comfortably' in any one of them . . . is more desirable than winning by a narrow plurality. The logic here is that a narrow victory (in primary or general election) is a sign of weakness that can inspire hostile political actors to deploy resources more intensively the next time around. By this reasoning, the higher the election percentage, the better.

Thus, maximization of vote received is a concise way to capture the motivation of a candidate involved in a campaign in which he is unsure of the identity or even of the probable characteristics of his opponent(s). Under these circumstances, strategic choice of activities reduces to a game against nature: the legislator actively searches for new ways to serve constituencies, impelled not by an actual opponent, but by the knowledge that he will face an attractive, well-financed challenger if he does not behave in this way.[1]

In order to influence votes received, legislators can provide services to any of n organized interest groups, or provide constituency services to the voters in their geographic district, by allocating a limited amount of effort to producing these services. This taxonomy was chosen over that of Lowi (1964) and others because their approaches involve a demand-oriented categorization of types of policy. In order to model more closely the sources of the services, we chose to use types of effort. Services to interest groups may include actual legislation, private bills, influence on the way bills are written (or vetoed) at the committee level, and the assurance that the "right" sources will be called on to testify at important hearings. Constituency services include casework, dealing with bureaucrats on a voter's behalf, and other individual services (Loewenberg and Patterson, 1979, pp. 187–90).

Voters

Votes come from voters, a heterogeneous, unorganized group. They respond to the activities of the legislator, both in the legislature and in the district. In addition, because voters are assumed to be largely uninformed, resources devoted to advertising affect their responses. The type of advertising must be recognized as important. We acknowledge the legitimacy of Fiorina and Noll's (1979) criticism: "A major current area of inquiry in the legislative subfield is to explain the apparently overwhelming advantage of incumbency. Most . . . explanations seem to conflict with the basic spirit of rational choice majority rule models, in that citizens are implicitly assumed to respond to advertising regardless of content." It is our view that candidates do not accept this Galbraithian perspective, but rather have powerful incentives to control carefully the content of their advertising activities, both for unorganized groups and interest groups.

Interest Groups

Each interest group is assumed to be interested in only one policy. It offers a legislator campaign resources, in exchange for the expectation of future services. The definition of *resources* to be used here is Dahl's (1961, p. 226): "[A] resource is anything that can be used to sway the specific choices or the strategies of another individual." So resources include money, in-kind services, volunteer labor etc.

Each of these three agents is assumed to be a constrained maximizer: Legislators maximize votes, subject to the constraint of total effort they can allocate. Voters' utility maximization, for our purposes, is completely embodied in the way they cast their one vote. Interest groups allocate scarce resources in the way that best furthers their goals.[2] All are constrained by the rules of the legislative' institution, which is assumed to be a unicameral, majority-rule congress, with members elected from geographic districts.[3]

THE SINGLE
LEGISLATOR MODEL

Consider an individual legislator who chooses activities that maximize the number of votes he expects to receive in the next election. Suppose there are n organized single interest groups, each of which can provide the legislator with campaign resources. That is, each group, i, can provide campaign resources, R_i, that the legislator will use in his next election campaign. In addition, there is a large unorganized group, U, each member of which has a vote to cast; aggregating these votes gives us the total voting resources, V_U, of the unorganized group. The unorganized group is assumed not to contribute campaign resources. The legislator then can choose from $n + 1$ activities or types of policy services: constituency services—P_U—to group U, or policy services—P_1 through P_n—to the n single interest groups.

In order to decide which groups to serve, the legislator considers the total votes he will receive for each possible strategy. That is, he calculates whether he will devote effort, E_i, to produce each of the categories of service, P_i, where $i = 1$ to n. In making these calculations, he

considers the response of each group to his activities:

for single-interest groups:

$$V_i = 0, i = 1 \text{ to } n \tag{1}$$

$$R_i = R_i[P_i(E_i)], i = 1 \text{ to } n; \tag{2}$$

total campaign resources:

$$R = R_1 + R_2 + \ldots + R_n; \tag{3}$$

for the unorganized group:

$$R_U = 0 \tag{4}$$

$$V = V[P_U(E_U), P_1(E_1), P_2(E_2), \ldots$$
$$P_n(E_n), R]. \tag{5}$$

The explanation of the first four functions is straightforward. Equation (1) reflects the assumption that interest groups are nonvoting.[4] The second expression means that campaign contributions from interest group i depend on the level of services provided, where service P_i is a function of the effort E_i devoted to it. For example, E_1 is the legislator's effort devoted to serving the first group, $P_1(E_1)$ is the policy outcome the legislator can produce by E_1, and $R_1[P_1(E_1)]$ is the amount of contributions from group 1 the legislator would receive if he produces $P_1(E_1)$. If group 1 is the Sierra Club, E_1 might represent time spent in committee on an Acid Rain Prevention Bill; $P_1(E_1)$ the impact the legislator has on the bill through this effort; and $R_1[P_1(E_1)]$ the campaign contributions the legislator expects to receive from the Sierra Club as a result. The identity (3) claims that the total campaign resources the candidate receives are simply the sum of the resources contributed by each of the n interest groups. The assumption that the unorganized group contributes no campaign resources is reflected in equation (4).

In summary, the first five equations represent the assumptions of the model. The analysis is simplified greatly by dividing the activities of voting and of contributing campaign resources. Voters do not make contributions, and interest groups do not vote in this model. Interest group contributions are determined only by the promised level of effort of the legislator in the single dimension the group seeks to influence; there are no multiple-issue groups in the model.

The last function requires more careful scrutiny. Intuitively, equation (5) tells us that the unorganized group votes in response to three separate influences. First, effort devoted to producing constituency services, P_U, affects their votes. Next, the unorganized group responds also to all other policies 1 through n. That is, an individual, though not a member of the Sierra Club, may have strong preferences over the Acid Rain Prevention Bill. The vote cast by that individual may be affected by the legislator's activities in that direction, be it writing the bill, debating, or casting a roll-call vote. Third, the unorganized group responds to advertising or campaign expenditures made from R, the total resources contributed by interest groups, assuming each candidate uses the resources he receives in the optimal way.

Having developed the response functions of the groups, the next step is to characterize the strategy of the legislator to maximize votes, given a limit, $\overline{E}$, on the effort he has to allocate. For our purposes, *effort* is simply the amount of the legislator's time, the time spent by staff, and the amount of office resources a legislator allocates to an activity, and $\overline{E}$ is the total amount of effort he has available to allocate. The problem, then, is to choose the $n + 1$ levels of effort so as to maximize

$$V[P_U(E_U), P_1(E_1), \ldots, P_n(E_n), R],$$

providing that

$$\overline{E} = E_U + E_1 + E_2 + \ldots + E_n,$$

(total effort equals the constraint $\overline{E}$). For simplicity, let this symbol denote derivatives: '; let superscripts denote partial derivatives; and suppose there are but three groups, U, 1, and 2. The necessary conditions for a solution imply:

$$\lambda = (V^U)P_U' = (V^R R_1' + V^1)P_1'$$

$$= (V^R R_2' + V^2)P_2', \tag{6}$$

where λ is the *shadow price* of effort. The overall meaning of equation (6) is quite sensible: a unit of effort has the same marginal effect on total votes, regardless of which activity it is devoted to—the usual result in maximization problems. If E is large enough, effort has no alternative use ($\lambda = 0$) and the terms in equation (6) equal 0, meaning that the legislator gets every vote he possibly can. If the constraint is binding, then $\lambda > 0$, and devoting effort to one activity now has a positive opportunity cost in terms of votes foregone by not engaging in some other activity. In this case, the maximizing strategy is to devote effort to each activity until the marginal gains are all the same.[5]

Each term in parentheses in equation (6) is the marginal vote productivity of a type of policy—that is, the change in vote received in response to a change in policy. The last two are the most interesting: $V^R R_1'$ represents the vote-producing effects of a change in resources (V^R) multiplied by the total change in resources in response to a change in services to group 1 (R_1').[6] The term V^1 is the vote-producing effect of policy service to interest group 1. Each P_i', the change in the amount policy i produced with respect to the change in effort devoted to producing it, is a measure of the legislator's relative ability to produce policy services for each of the three groups. Thus, the equality of the four expressions means that the productivity of effort in producing outcomes multiplied by the productivity of outcomes in producing votes is the same, for all types of effort. In addition, each expression equals λ, reflecting the fact that devoting effort to one activity has the opportunity cost of not devoting that effort to some other activity.

The legislator's decision problem is to allocate effort, given the vector of effort productivities, so as to maximize the probability of winning the election, subject to the constraint that total effort expended, $\Sigma_{i=1}^{n} E_i$, is less than or equal to $\bar{E}$. There are two potential difficulties with this formulation: the question of how the limit is fixed, and the possibility that the legislator's staff provides much of the services that affect votes and resource contributions. Fenno (1978, p. 34) claims that

> time is a House member's scarcest and most precious political resource. If there is an exemplary congressional complaint, surely "there isn't enough time" must be it. In deciding how to spend his time . . . a member confronts his most difficult allocative dilemma. . . . Different representatives make different allocative choices and different allocative trades.

The setting of the effort level is beyond the scope of this paper. However, the existence of a binding constraint on the legislator's effort is not implausible. The implication is that the candidate's time has some opportunity cost and is not valued at zero at the margin.

Still, we must consider the question of staff effort. As Fenno points out (1978, p. 34), it is not true that

> "all" the congressmen has is time and himself. The office carries with it a large number of ancillary resources— a staff, office expenses allowances, free mailing privileges, personal expense accounts. . . . Each congressman chooses how he will use these resources. The most significant of these choices involve the use of staff.

The choice of staff size, like the constraint of effort, is not treated here. Staff effort is included within $\bar{E}$, the total effort the legislator has available. In sum, legislators choose how much time they themselves will spend working for reelection, and how large a staff they will retain once this choice is made. All of the available effort is allocated in such a way as to maximize the likelihood of reelection.

Choice of Constituency

It is important to understand the definitions of *constituency* used in this paper. The usual definition is those groups providing votes or campaign resources to the legislator. However, this definition does not really identify the choices available to the legislator in the decision about which set of groups to serve actively. There may well be groups that vote for, or donate resources to, the legislator, even though he does not actively serve them, and so these groups are not in his "constituency." In order to identify and separate the various constituencies, we will use the following definitions:

a) The *geographic constituency* is that part of the unorganized group of voters which votes for the legislator (see Loewenberg and Patterson, 1979, pp. 170–72; Fenno, 1978, pp. 1–8).

b) The *service constituency* is that set of groups the legislator actively devotes effort to serving.

c) The *resource-supplying constituency* is that set of groups supplying the legislator with campaign resources.

Notice that these are not necessarily the same: interest groups provide no votes, but may be served in exchange for resources; voters may not be actively served, but may vote for the legislator anyway. Further, interest groups may choose to offer resources to a legislator simply because of his views. Such a legislator receives resources not because of any expected quid pro quo, but because the group would like to see him stay in office.

Let $\hat{E} = (\hat{E}_U, \hat{E}_1, \hat{E}_2)$ be a solution to the three-group maximization problem. Suppose that, in addition to serving group U, the legislator also provides policy services to group 1, but not group 2. Notice that since the heterogeneous voter group responds to all policy dimensions, the *unorganized group* can affect the legislator's decision on whether or not to provide policy service to *interest groups*.

Let us examine next the case where one group is served and another is not. For example, if, contrary to equation (6), $\hat{E}_1 > 0 = \hat{E}_2$, we know that:

$$(V^1 + V^R R_1')P_1' > (V^2 + V^R R_2')P_2' \quad (7)$$

(policy service effort for group 1 produces more votes than it does from group 2). There are several cases where this might occur, the simplest of which is an absolute advantage in producing policy for group 1 ($P_1' > P_2'$, or, the marginal productivity of the legislator's effort is greater for P_1). That is, the legislator has some extra ability to produce P_1 as a committee member or chairman, a leadership position in the Congress. Also, he may have more knowledge about group 1 policy service because of prior experience, the location of his district office, etc.

If the legislator has no such advantage ($P_1' = P_2'$), equation (7) reduces to

$$(V^1 + V^R R_1') > (V^2 + V^R R_2') \quad (7')$$

Each of the remaining cases will be examined separately.

($V^1 > V^2$): The voting response of the unorganized group is greater for policy 1, completely separate from the interest group response in providing resources. Thus, in deciding which interest groups to serve, the legislator must consider the response of the large, unorganized group.

($R_1' > R_2'$): Interest group 1 will provide more campaign resources in response to policy service than will group 2. In this simple case, we are assuming that there is no backlash from the unorganized group against a legislator who accepts campaign contributions other than that summarized in V^1, which can be large and negative. That is, the unorganized group makes its voting decisions based not on whether the legislator accepts money, but on what he does in order to elicit the contributions in the first place. The implication is that $V^R R_1' > V^R R_2'$, or that the votes the legislator can get from the unorganized group by advertising, multiplied by the marginal resource response he gets by producing policy services, is greater for group 1 than for group 2.

We can graphically depict the overall decision process of the legislator in choosing which group(s) to serve, assuming no two interest groups seek to influence the same policy. This graphical solution is shown in Figure 21.1 Panel A: at a maximum, the marginal vote productivity of each type of effort must be the same, and it must equal λ, the opportunity cost or shadow price of using effort for an alternative. In Panel A, all groups are served with positive levels of effort, but this need not be the case. If the marginal vote productivity of serving some group is very low (always less than λ, the opportunity cost of using that effort somewhere else), then that group will not be served. This situation is depicted in Figure 21.1, Panel B, where the legislator provides no policy service to group 2. The previous discussion showed that this can occur when (a) the legislator is not very good at producing P_2, whether because he is not on the "right" committee, is not knowledgeable, etc.; (b) because the unorganized group is indifferent or opposed to policy 2, offsetting the benefits from providing it; (c) interest group 2 provides few campaign resources in exchange for policy 2.

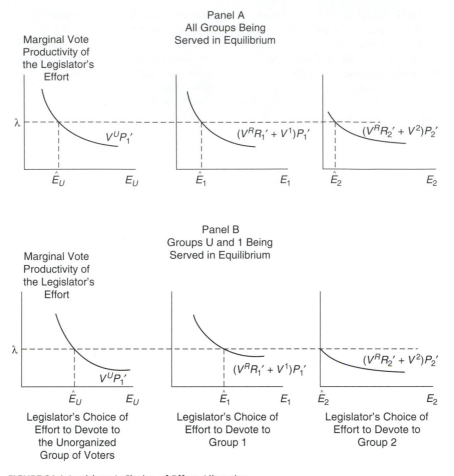

Panel A
All Groups Being
Served in Equilibrium

Marginal Vote
Productivity of
the Legislator's
Effort

λ

$V^U P_1'$

$(V^R R_1' + V^1) P_1'$

$(V^R R_2' + V^2) P_2'$

$\hat{E}_U$ E_U

$\hat{E}_1$ E_1

$\hat{E}_2$ E_2

Panel B
Groups U and 1 Being
Served in Equilibrium

Marginal Vote
Productivity of
the Legislator's
Effort

λ

$V^U P_1'$

$(V^R R_1' + V^1) P_1'$

$(V^R R_2' + V^2) P_2'$

$\hat{E}_U$ E_U

$\hat{E}_1$ E_1

$\hat{E}_2$ E_2

Legislator's Choice of
Effort to Devote to
the Unorganized
Group of Voters

Legislator's Choice of
Effort to Devote to
Group 1

Legislator's Choice of
Effort to Devote to
Group 2

FIGURE 21.1 Legislator's Choice of Effort Allocation

A SPECIAL INTEREST GROUP'S CHOICE OF LEGISLATORS

Thus far, we have modelled interest groups as supplying resources and votes in exchange for the policy and constituency services the legislator can provide. However, interest groups can be viewed as active seekers of those services from legislators. If interest groups are not passive, but actively seek legislators whom they believe can help them, then the situation looks quite different from that of the previous sections.

Suppose each interest group desires to achieve a set of goals, and makes its campaign resource contributions in the way it believes best accomplishes these goals. For example, the group may simply wish to have a legislator who will sponsor a bill when asked, which may be more effective if that legislator is on a particular committee or subcommittee. Alternatively, the group may want to be the first to know when legislation inimical to its interests is being considered. The group might want to be able to block or amend legislation. For other groups, it might suffice to be certain that the "right" people will be called to testify at committee hearings.

Recalling the earlier formulation, the maximization problem from the point of view of the legislator is: Maximize

$$V[P_U(E_U), P_1(E_1), P_2(E_2), \ldots, P_n(E_n), R]$$

subject to

$$\overline{E} = E_U + E_1 + E_2 + \ldots + E_n.$$

The first order conditions of this problem relating to interest groups are:

$$V^R R_i' + V^i) P_i' - \lambda = 0,$$
$$i = 1, \ldots, n. \tag{8}$$

From the earlier discussion, recall that the terms inside the parentheses are the vote productivities of the n types of policy service. P_i' is then the productivity of effort for each policy. If we again consider only a single legislator, these expressions can be manipulated to illustrate the minimum price the legislator will accept to provide a unit of effort. This is done by solving for R_i' in the above equation. Given the usefulness of campaign resources (V^R), the marginal productivity of effort P_i, the reaction of the voters (V^i), and the opportunity cost of effort (λ), the quantity of resources a legislator will require to provide one unit of effort to the ith group is:

$$R_i' = \frac{\lambda - P_i' V^i}{V^R P_i'} \tag{9}$$

This expression can be separated into two parts:

$$R_i' = \underset{(a)}{\frac{\lambda}{V^R P_i'}} - \underset{(b)}{\frac{V^i}{V^R}}; \tag{9'}$$

Part (a) of expression (9') is fairly easy to understand. Since λ is constant across interest groups, and assuming V^R is constant (voters everywhere react the same way to advertising), only P_i' differs across legislators. Remember that P_i' is the marginal productivity of the legislator's effort in policy service to group i. Since P_i' appears in the denominator,

the better the legislator at producing the ith policy service (i.e., the fewer hours he must devote to producing the same amount), the lower is the minimum price he will accept to provide that service. If we compare the legislator's price for services to groups 1 and 2, and look only at part (a), then if $P_1' > P_2'$ (the legislator is better at producing P_1 than he is at producing P_2) we have

$$R_1' = \frac{\lambda}{V^R P_1'} < \frac{\lambda}{V^R P_2'} = R_2'.$$

The more adept the legislator is at producing policy services for a group, the lower the minimum price he will require for doing so.

Part (b) adds an additional consideration; it is the ratio of the vote productivity of P_i to the vote productivity of resources. The larger this ratio, since it is subtracted, the smaller the supply price of that policy. Intuitively, this is what we would expect. The greater the voting response of the unorganized group to policy i, the fewer resources the legislator will demand to produce policy i. We might think of legislators whose geographic constituency is in favor of P_i as having a comparative advantage in producing P_i, at least from the point of view of interest groups.

Alternatively, if the unorganized group is very much opposed to policy i (that is, if $V^i < 0$), then this raises the supply price. Thus, the disadvantages of serving unpopular interest groups by producing policy helpful to them is built into the model.[7] Only if the interest group can provide large resource contributions will publicly unpopular policy service be provided.

A concrete extension of the problem of the interest group's choice of legislators is the case in which the interest group hopes to build a majority coalition of some group (a committee, subcommittee, etc.). If, for example, group 1 hopes to get a bill past the committee stage, it would form a ranking of the supply prices of the members of the committee. If there are k committee members, the ranking is from 1 (the lowest price) to k (the highest price). Notice that some of the lowest prices may be *negative*, meaning that the unorganized constituency of that legislator is so much in favor of that bill that he would have to be paid not to vote for it. Clearly, group 1 need allocate no resources to these legislators, because their support is "free." Beginning at the first price above zero, group 1 pays this price, and the next, until it has secured a majority. Suppose for example that there are seven committee members, and the supply prices are ranked as follows:

Legislator	Supply Prices
1	−$5000
2	−2000
3	−500
4	100
5	750
6	1500
7	2000

A majority on this committee can be had for $100; only this contribution to the fourth committee member need be made in order to gain a majority and ensure passage through the committee.

Unfortunately, the example thus far is flawed in an important respect: it assumes there are no competing interest groups, so that interest group 1 can act as a monopsonistic purchaser of policy services. Suppose there is a diametrically opposed group 2, so that $P_1 = -P_2$. That is, any policy service favorable to group 1 is unfavorable to group 2. For example, suppose the committee is the House Interior Committee, group 1 is the Sierra Club, and group 2 is the Chemical Manufacturers Association (CMA). The supply prices are the minimum the legislators will accept to provide P_1 or P_2; the actual price paid is likely to be bid up by the two competing groups.

To illustrate this, suppose the payoffs are the same as above, and that the committee must either report the bill to the floor ($P_1 = 1, P_2 = -1$), or not report the bill ($P_1 = -1, P_2 = 1$). Then the ranking is as follows:

Legislator	P_1 supply prices (lowest to highest)	P_2 supply prices (highest to lowest)
1	−$5000	$5000
2	−2000	2000
3	−500	500
4	100	−100
5	750	−750
6	1500	−1500
7	2000	−2000

If group 2 did not exist, then group 1 could buy $P_1 = 1$ for $100, because then L_1, L_2, L_3, and L_4 would vote for it. If group 2 did not exist, then the CMA could buy $P_2 = 1$ for free, because L_4, L_5, L_6, and L_7 all would have to be paid not to vote that way anyway. If, however, both groups do exist, and actively bid, it is quite conceivable that the legislators who are relatively indifferent (L_4, then L_3 and L_5, and so on) will receive a considerable amount of campaign resources.[8] The point of this example, however, is that although the unorganized group appears nowhere as an explicit agent in the bargaining over the policy outcome between the legislator and interest groups 1 and 2, the preferences and expected voting reaction of the unorganized group are implicitly embodied in the schedule of supply prices above, as we saw from (9) and (9′).

The results of this section can be summarized as follows. Interest groups choose among legislators based on the supply price of the service each group seeks. The supply price is determined by the "cost" to the legislator of providing the service. This cost depends first on the productivity of the legislator's effort.

Productivity is affected by committee assignments, seniority, and the legislator's skill in using legislative institutions. Thus, the first component of cost is whatever the legislator gives up by serving an interest group and not using his time on something else. The second component of cost reflects voter preferences. A legislator seeking reelection must be compensated for votes lost by serving an interest group before he will provide such services. The amount required varies with the distaste of voters for the policy. In sum, the supply price or cost of policy to an interest group varies across legislators. Legislators have a comparative advantage in supplying policy on issues in which either (1) their effort is highly productive, or (2) their own voters are relatively more favorable toward increases in the policy. The following section illustrates a comparative statics implication of the model, based on the reactions of voters to changes in policy.

RATIONAL IGNORANCE VS. CIVICS CLASS/FULL INFORMATION

The discussion to this point has been concerned with legislators and interest groups struggling to achieve their own goals, and the ways in which their success can be affected and constrained by the large unorganized group of voters. No dominance or control has been ascribed to any of these agents; instead, the general framework encompasses the possibility that any one group or more may have the major influence on policy outcomes. In the context of the model, outcomes are determined by the prices, or costs, at which policies are offered by legislators. In order to illustrate the comparative statics predications of the model, this section considers the supply price of policy under two alternative extreme assumptions about voter behavior. The

two assumptions we consider are (a) rational ignorance, and (b) civics class/full information.

Rational Ignorance

One possibility for voter behavior is that voters invest very little in political information gathering. Resource contributions are the primary vehicle for determining policy outcomes. Voters in the unorganized group are ignorant of the activities of legislators in serving interest groups. According to this view (Becker, 1976, p. 37):

> since each person has a fixed number of votes—either 1 or 0—regardless of the amount of information he has and the intelligence used in acting on this information, and since minorities are usually given no representation, it does not "pay" to be well-informed and thoughtful on political issues, or even to vote . . . candidates for many offices, such as the presidency and state governorships, must have enough resources to reach millions of voters. Many groups that would like to compete for these offices do not have sufficient resources to reach large numbers of voters.

Thus, legislators must depend primarily on interest groups to provide them with enough resources to be able to make themselves known to the uninformed voters. By actively serving interest groups, legislators ensure interest group primacy in policy. Because voters are completely ignorant (until provided with biased information—Calvert, 1982), legislators can use these resources to advertise themselves with little concern about adverse voter response.

In the context of the model developed in this paper, *rational ignorance* implies that voters respond only to resource expenditures, because they are "rationally ignorant" of everything else. Thus, since only resources can mobilize votes, each legislator maximizes the resources he receives from interest groups, each interest group chooses legislators to contribute to on the basis of their policy productivity alone, and voters respond passively to advertising expenditures. The response functions of the agents look as follows: for voters,

$$V = V(R)$$

(policy has no effect; votes exchange for resources); for special interest groups,

$$R_i = R_i[P_i(E_i)], i = 1 \text{ to } n$$

(payment for legislator's effort); and for legislators,

$$R_i' \geq \frac{\lambda}{V^R P_i'} - \frac{V^i}{V^R} = \frac{\lambda}{V^R P_i'}$$

(because $V^i = 0$; no voter policy response). Only P_i' differentiates legislators, because λ and V^R are assumed constant. Notice that, as before, voters do not make contributions and contributors do not vote.

In this model, interest groups can almost completely control the legislator's activities. Those who act to further what they believe are the interests of their geographic constituency are never reelected, unless it happens that some interest group is in favor of the policy as well, and contributes resources. Legislators who act against the interests of their geographic constituency, but in accordance with interest group wishes, can lose an election only if the challenger has a higher policy productivity of effort in those policies, and can thereby win resources away from those less able, or with a smaller endowment of valuable committee assignments. The predictions of the model for desired committee assignments and voting patterns are quite simple (see Peltzman, 1982): assuming voters are rationally ignorant, both committee assignments and voting patterns chosen by legislators will be those which maximize the campaign resources received. In fact, the best

strategy for a legislator is to keep his service constituency and his geographic constituency completely disjoint, so that voters are never served at all, unless they benefit from interest group resources spent in their districts.

The rational ignorance assumption model provides an interesting benchmark in extreme interest group influence, but is not a very useful view of the world. Notice that if voters are not ignorant about a legislator's policy activities in any policy category, interest group influence is affected. Putting this point in the context of the price an interest group must pay a legislator to provide effort on its behalf, let us reproduce (9'):

$$R_i' \geq \frac{\lambda}{V^R P_i'} - \frac{V^i}{V^R} \qquad (9')$$

Voter's policy preference appears in the V^i term, the change in vote received in response to a change in policy i. If, for some geographic constituency, this term is negative (voters are not ignorant and are violently opposed to this policy), the interest group may find it either very expensive or impossible to purchase that legislator's services. This point can be extended to account for the role of the media or potential competitors: even if voters are currently ignorant of the activities of a legislator in serving an interest group, the legislator's actions may be constrained by the knowledge that the media or a competitor will expend resources to make voters aware. That is, the legislator must consider not only the reaction of voters given their present knowledge, but also the expected reaction if voters were to find out. The role of potential competitors and the news media in policing the actions of incumbents in this way has been noted by Mayhew (1974) and others, including MacKuen (1981, 1983).

Thus, another consideration enters the interest group's choice of which legislators to contribute to—the preferences of a legislator's geographic constituency. Legislators whose geographic constituency has strong, informed preferences about some policy will receive resource contributions from an interest group only if voters and the interest group want the same thing; otherwise, the interest group will search out some other legislator whose geographic constituency is either ignorant or indifferent (Weingast and Marshall, 1984). Further, given the incentives for challenges and the media to monitor and report on the activities of legislators, the ignorance of the typical voter may still provide little room for discretionary behavior on the part of the legislator. In any case, the empirical prediction that the service constituency and the geographic constituency are disjoint is simply wrong: the intersection of the two groups is exactly those voters who are informed, have policy preferences, and who vote. The size of this group is an empirical matter; it is probably wrong to suggest a priori, as Becker (1976) seems to, that the group does not exist.

Civics Class/Full Information

The *civics class* model of voter behavior developed in this section is conceptually the opposite of the rational ignorance model just described.[9] The overriding concern of the legislator, under the assumption that voters act the way they are depicted in a high school civics class, is to discover the preferences of what we have called the geographic constituency, and then to act so as to serve these preferences. As shown below, interest groups have very little influence in such a scheme. Fully informed voters imply a model of legislative behavior where the service constituency and the geographic constituency are identical; interest group service is at most an artifact or coincidence resulting from the preferences the legislator is actually serving.

If voters are well-informed and have strong preferences, advertising has little

effect, so that V^R, the partial derivative of the vote function with respect to resource expenditures, is near zero. The response functions are then as follows: for voters,

$$V = V(P_U, P_1, \ldots, P_n, R);$$

for special interest groups,

$$R_i = R_i[P_i(E_i)], i = 1 \text{ to } n;$$

and for legislators,

$$R_i' \geq \frac{\lambda}{V^R P_i'} - \frac{V^i}{V^R}.$$

V_R goes to zero, and R_i (the legislator's minimum supply price) becomes very large, moving toward either positive or negative infinity. No legislator can be induced to serve an interest group he would not already be serving. But this is an obvious consequence of our assertion that legislators maximize the number of votes they receive, and that effort is limited. If advertising resources produce no votes, and the legislator is prevented from using these resources for his own consumption, then he will not devote any effort to obtaining resources.[10]

Implications of the Models

Having illustrated the implications of the alternative assumptions of complete voter ignorance and full information, it is possible to address the question of the behavior implied by each. First, if voters are ignorant, it is clear that preferred committee assignments for legislators bear no resemblance to geographical constituency interests. Seniority, committee chairmanships, etc., are important because of their value as capital assets, capable of generating resource flows that are indirectly translated into votes through advertising. If voters are informed, however, there are very different implications for committee preferences. The skills of the legislator, prior knowledge, and other factors are of secondary importance. The primary goal is a committee position which enables the legislator to serve his geographical constituency. Interestingly, however, seniority and committee leadership positions are still very valuable, even if they are not capital, or resource-producing, assets: these things can provide votes directly, because they increase the effectiveness of the effort devoted to serving the geographical constituency.[11]

The behavior of interest groups can be compared by examining the supply price of a legislator implied by each assumption. Uninformed voters imply that a legislator's willingness to exchange effort devoted to legislative services for resources is affected only by the response of his geographic constituency to advertising, the opportunity cost of effort, and the productivity of the legislator's effort:

$$R_i' \text{ (uninformed)} = \frac{\lambda}{V^R P_i'}$$

In this model, interest groups determine policy outcomes by bidding for a legislator's effort.

Interest group behavior under full information (assuming $V^R = 0$, or that advertising is ineffective) is quite different. A legislator's supply price, R_i' (when voters are fully informed) is simply:

$$\lim_{V^R \to 0} \frac{\lambda}{V^R P_i'} - \frac{V^i}{V^R} = \pm\infty$$

(depending on the sign of $\lambda - P_i' V^i$), and thus interest groups can have no independent effect whatsoever. Interest group preferences and offers of resources have no impact on legislators' behavior.

Thus, neither assumption is completely consistent with the two most noted "facts" about the relations among legislators, special interest groups, and geographic constituencies. First, legislators choose committees which have jurisdiction over matters important to the geographic constituency (Niskanen, 1971; Weingast and Marshall, 1984), contrary to the predictions of the rational ignorance assumption and consistent with full information. Second, as Dexter (1956, 1963) points out, interest groups

choose legislators whose geographic constituencies have similar demands. Legislators elected from homogeneous geographic constituencies will value committee assignments that are of direct importance to their voters: e.g., legislators from Kansas seek seats on the Agriculture Committee. To the extent that legislators elected from heterogeneous geographic constituencies need more resources in order to advertise, these legislators will pursue committee seats that help them affect legislation wealthy interest groups will notice. That is, optimal election strategies must vary at the margin with the composition and preferences of the voters in the geographic constituency.

Interest groups have a complicated problem in seeking out the legislator with the lowest supply price. However, as we have demonstrated, an interest group need not search very far for legislators with relatively low supply prices of effort, because those whose geographic constituencies are most in favor, or least opposed to, a policy are likely to be the cheapest source of interest group legislative services. The result, then, is that interest group policy manipulation is constrained by the preferences of the geographic constituency.[12] This constraint is imperfect, however, because voters are less than perfectly informed. Legislators themselves act in ways that do not perfectly represent their geographic constituency, in order to gain campaign resources from interest groups; these resources are used by each legislator both to portray himself in an attractive way and to inform voters. The voting group is not "organized" in Olson's (1965) sense, but legislators acting as political entrepreneurs can use the unorganized group to countervail interest group pressure (Wagner, 1966, p. 164).

The conclusion is that interest groups do not control this process, but neither are special interests powerless.

Contributions can have some influence on policies about which voters are divided, ignorant, or indifferent. The geographic constituency is not represented to the exclusion of all other groups, but departures by legislators from their voters' interests are constrained by the strong preferences voters have on some issues, and by the threat of informing and mobilizing public opinion that the news media and potential competitors always represent. In short, each of the extreme information assumptions offers a useful view of a small portion of the legislative process some of the time. Yet each is only part of a larger view of the complicated process exhibiting hidden, but very real, incentives that impel the activities of the political agents.[13]

SUMMARY AND CONCLUSIONS

This paper presents a model of the supply of government policy. The agents in the model include legislators, voters, and interest groups. The supply price, or cost, of policy is derived assuming that legislators seek to maximize votes, which can be obtained either by providing policy that voters favor or by serving interest groups in exchange for vote-producing campaign resources.

The price of policy for an interest group is shown to depend on the comparative advantage of the legislators offering to help provide the policy. The two factors determining comparative advantage are productivity and the preferences of the voters back home. Specifically, the more productive a legislator's effort, or the less hostile that voters are to a given policy, the lower the minimum price an interest group must pay in exchange. Since legislators differ in their productive capabilities (because of differences in committee assignment, seniority, and competence), and since the voters in their geographic constituencies

differ in their preferences, these prices vary in predictable ways across legislators. Interest groups can be expected to choose among alternative legislators on this basis.

Finally, an explicit comparative statics result of the model is derived. We ask under what circumstances will unorganized interests (i.e., voters) be represented. Two extreme alternative informational assumptions are considered. First, voters are assumed to be completely (though rationally) ignorant of the effects of a given policy on their welfare. The implications of this assumption are contrasted with a situation in which voters are fully informed. The supply price observed is demonstrated to differ, in a predictable way, between these two situations. To the extent that any voters are informed and opposed to a policy, an interest group seeking favorable treatment must pay a higher price than if all voters were indifferent or uninformed.

The conclusion is that unorganized, noncontributing voters may be effectively represented even in a situation in which interest groups are well organized and active. The representation of such voters, deriving from the institutional requirement of periodic reelection for legislators, tends to reduce the influence of organized but nonvoting economic interests in the political process. Thus, unorganized groups can shape and constrain decisions to a greater extent than that predicted by simple demand-oriented group theories of collective action.

Several extensions of the model presented above merit future consideration. The model is capable of addressing comparative statics questions such as the effects of changes in committee assignments or jurisdictions, or of changes in district boundaries. Committee assignments influence the policy productivity of legislators; redistricting modifies the vote functions that influence legislator and, implicitly, interest group decisions.

In addition, the model itself could be extended in at least two ways. First, the source of the vote functions, or what others have called "political support functions," can be explicitly derived using a model of consumer voter behavior similar to that of Denzau and Parks (1979).[14] Second, the equilibrium properties of the model, with voter preferences more clearly defined, can be explored in the context of a formal game to illustrate the implications for policy of interest groups competing directly against one another.

NOTES

The authors wish to thank Randall Calvert, William Dougan, Brian Humes, William Riker, Kenneth Shepsle, and Barry Weingast for helpful comments and suggestions.

1. Fiorina (1974, p. 48) demonstrates that when election is "assured," votes are not maximized if candidate resources have an opportunity cost. However, assuming the candidate hopes to win at least two elections, and that the constraint on effort accounts for opportunity cost, the election is not assured in Fiorina's sense; legislators in our model are "maximizers" rather than "maintainers."

2. At a more detailed level, this outcome is itself the outcome of a game involving members of the interest group. The very existence of one pattern or set of interest groups is an equilibrium of a complicated process that we take as exogenous. We will allow, however, for the possibility that an interest group has zero members, or that no organized group actually exists, for the reasons Olson (1965) discusses.

3. A model using assumptions similar to those described here has been developed by Cox, McCubbins, and Sullivan (1983). Using the reelection motivation for legislators and Fenno's taxonomy of constituent groups, they examine technological constraints on legislators' ability to choose forms of public policy implementation that improve their reelection chances. The orientation in the present paper, though arising from the same assumptions, is on the constraints placed on legislators' and interest groups' activities not by "technology," but by voters through the electoral mechanism itself.

4. The fact that interest groups provide no votes is not crucial to the results presented here. An earlier version of this paper included interest group voting, adding considerable complexity, but no qualitative difference in the results. Interest group voting was thus dropped for expositional simplicity. Dougan and Kenyon (1984) present a model in which interest groups provide both money and votes, and they obtain results qualitatively similar to ours.

5. Suppose this were not true, and that the last hour of effort devoted to service to the unorganized group produces 9 votes, while that devoted to group 1 produced only 6 votes. Then the legislator could increase his total votes by working one less hour on P_1 (he loses 6), one more on P_0 (he gets 9), so that there is a net gain of 3 votes.

6. This formulation is used for notational simplicity. Since $R = \Sigma R_i$, but only R_i is affected by a change in E_i, R_i' is the change in total resources in response to a change in the services provided to group i.

7. From the first order conditions, we can explicitly derive the conditions under which the candidate will "sell out." If $V^R R_i' P_i' > \lambda - V^i P_i'$ then $\hat{E}_i > 0$. Suppose $V^i P_i' < 0$ (geographic constituency is opposed). Then if serving group i produces more votes (through use of resources gained by $\hat{E}_i > 0$) than the sum of (1) the opportunity cost of legislator's time, and (2) the negative reaction of voters to policy i, the legislator will act directly against the interest of his geographic constituency. We would expect to see this occur when (a) the interest group being served is willing to pay large amounts, and (b) the legislator's marginal vote value of resources is high. Thus, poor campaigns are more likely to serve interest groups, to the detriment of voters.

8. William Riker points out that this example bears a striking resemblance to the reasoning used by Shapley and Shubik in deriving an abstract "power," or value index for use in predicting outcomes in small numbers bargaining games (see Schotter and Schwodiauer, 1980, for a review of the development of this concept, and

for references). While a game theoretic treatment of the bargaining between interest groups and legislators is beyond the scope of this paper, the similarity in results suggests both the generality and usefulness of Shapley and Shubik's result, and an interesting direction for further research.

9. Fenno (1973), and Shepsle (1978) portray legislators as seeking committee assignments that tend to further their personal goals, one of which is reelection. Since we have abstracted away from nonelection goals of legislators, this view is not here incorporated. A more sophisticated treatment, with legislators trading off votes against the ability to act on their own preferences, given some chance of reelection, could be incorporated as an extension of the present model (see note 1 above). For our purposes now, however, Fenno's (1978) description of a legislator's behavior is what we assume legislators believe about voters: that each has strong and informed preferences. In the present model, this problem is ignored: the $V(\cdot)$ functions are known. Clearly, an extension of the model is to allow some combination of the two extreme informational assumptions made in the text, perhaps allowing preferences to be unknown to the legislator, or else associated with some stochastic function.

10. The consideration of "political advertising" given here is at most a preliminary treatment of a complicated problem. If, as has been suggested in the economics literature (Benham, 1973, and other articles reviewed by Comanor and Wilson, 1979), advertising does not persuade, but instead activates or informs existing latent preferences, then the usefulness of campaign resources depends crucially on what is being advertised. While this effect is implicitly built into the present model, the role of advertising on outcomes requires a more sophisticated theoretical treatment than that developed so far.

11. Weingast and Marshall (1984) suggest that the present system has evolved because of the recognition by legislators that political "gains from trade" can be realized. Drawing on the industrial organization literature, Weingast and Marshall suggest that the costs of enforcing implicit contracts between voters and legislators create incentives for legislators to seek the "best" committee assignments out of personal self-interest. Earlier versions of our paper included a rather long section on committee assignments and optimal assignments rules. However, the section was removed for reasons of length. For an application of the idea, see Munger (1985).

12. Mancur Olson (1965) demonstrates that opposing interest groups, either existing or potential, cannot be expected to constrain interest group activity. The "free rider" problem arising from the shared benefits of organizing opposing interest groups implies the interest equilibrium of pluralist theory may well not occur at mean or median of all preferences; some groups will benefit at the expense of others, even if those others are partially organized.

13. An empirical implication of the model is that if it is cheaper and more effective for an interest group to try to affect those policies that the unorganized voters are in favor of, we would expect a pattern to develop over time in the growth of an interest group. A nascent interest group with a poorly developed resource base will try to affect those policies that are publicly popular and widely supported in the jurisdictions in which it organizes. As the interest group grows in the quantity of resources it can command, it should then begin to concentrate on less popular policy directions that provide more benefits for interest group members. In sum, interest groups may be public policy-oriented at the outset, but over time move toward more personal favors for interest group members. This proposition is to be developed and tested in future work.

14. The Denzau and Parks model expresses public sector preferences in terms of the private consumption possibilities set that they imply. The properties of these derived preferences appear quite tractable for incorporation within the present model.

REFERENCES

Bailey, Stephen K. 1950. *Congress Makes a Law: The Story Behind the Employment Act of 1946.* New York: Columbia University Press.

Bauer, Raymond A., Ithiel de Sola Pool, and Anthony Dexter. 1972. *American Business and Public Policy: The Politics of Foreign Trade,* 2nd ed. Chicago: Aldine-Atherton.

Becker, Gary S. 1976. *The Economic Approach to Human Behavior.* Chicago: University of Chicago Press.

Benham, Lee. 1973. The Effect of Advertising on the Price of Eyeglasses. *Journal of Law and Economics,* 16:337–52.

Bentley, Arthur F. 1907. *The Process of Government.* Chicago: University of Chicago Press.

Calvert, Randell L. 1982. The Rational Preference for Biased Information. Working Paper No. 75. Center for the Study of American Business. St. Louis: Washington University.

Comanor, William S., and Thomas A. Wilson. 1979. Advertising and Competition: A Survey. *Journal of Economic Literature,* 17:453–76.

Cox, Gary W., Mathew D. McCubbins, and Terry Sullivan. 1983. Policy and Constituency: Reelection Incentives and the Choice of Policy Intervention. Working Paper No. 02, Working Papers on Institutional Design and Public Policy. Department of Government, University of Texas at Austin.

Dahl, Robert A. 1961. *Who Governs?* New Haven: Yale University Press.

Denzau, Arthur T., and Robert P. Parks. 1979. Deriving Public Sector Preferences. *Journal of Public Economics,* 11:335–52.

Dexter, Lewis Anthony. 1956. Candidates Make the Issues and Give Them Meaning. *Public Opinion Quarterly,* 19:16–27.

Dexter, Anthony. 1963. The Representative and His District. In Robert Peabody and Nelson Polsby, eds., *Perspectives on the House of Representatives.* Chicago: Rand McNally.

Dougan, William and Daphne Kenyon. 1984. Pressure Groups and Public Expenditures: The Flypaper Effect Reconsidered. Unpublished manuscript.

Fenno, Richard F., Jr. 1973. *Congressmen in Committees.* Boston: Little, Brown, and Company.

Fenno, Richard F., Jr. 1978. *Home Style: House Members in Their Districts.* Boston: Little, Brown, and Company.

Fiorina, Morris P. 1974. *Representatives, Roll Calls, and Constituencies.* Lexington: D.C. Health and Company.

Fiorina, Morris P., and Roger G. Noll. 1979. Majority Rule Models and Legislative Elections. *The Journal of Politics,* 41:1081–1104.

Hayes, Michael T. 1981. *Lobbyists and Legislators. A Theory of Political Markets.* New Brunswick Rutgers University Press.

Kau, James B., and Paul H. Rubin. 1982. *Congressmen, Constituents and Contributors.* Boston: Martinus Nijhoff Publishing.

Latham, Earl. 1952. *The Group Basis of Politics: A Study of Basing-Point Legislation.* Ithaca, N.Y. Cornell University Press.

Loewenberg, Gerhard, and Samuel C. Patterson. 1979. *Comparing Legislatures.* Boston: Little, Brown and Company.

Lowi, Theodore J. 1964. American Business, Public Policy, Case Studies, and Political Theory *World Politics,* 16:677–715.

MacKuen, Michael B. 1981. Social Communication and the Mass Policy Media. In Michael B. MacKuen and Steven L. Coombs, eds., *More Than News: Two Studies of Media Power.* Beverly Hills: Sage.

MacKuen, Michael B. 1983. The Concept of Public Opinion. In Charles F. Turner and Elizabeth Martin, eds., *Surveys of Subjective Phenomena.* National Research Council Report. New York: Sage.

Matthews, Donald R. 1960. *U.S. Senators and Their World.* Chapel Hill: University of North Carolina Press.

Mayhew, David R. 1974. *Congress: The Electoral Connection.* New Haven, CT: Yale University Press.

McPherson, Charles P. 1972. Tariff Structures and Political Exchange. Ph.D. diss., University of Chicago.

Miller, Gary, and Terry Moe. 1983. Bureaucrats, Legislators, and the Size of Government. *American Political Science Review,* 77:297–322.

Munger, Michael C. 1985. A Ranking of the Direct Benefits Provided by House Committees: An Indirect Approach. Department of Economics, Washington University. Mimeo.

Niskanen, William A., Jr. 1971. *Bureaucracy and Representative Government.* Chicago: Aldine-Atherton.

Olson, Mancur. 1965. *The Logic of Collective Action: Public Goods and Theory of Groups,* 2nd ed. New York: Schocken.

Peltzman, Sam. 1982. Constituent Interest and Congressional Voting. University of Chicago, Mimeo.

Pincus, Jonathan J. 1975. Pressure Groups and the Pattern of Tariffs. *Journal of Political Economy,* 83:757–78.

Salamon, Lester M. and John J. Seigfried. 1977. Economic Power and Political Influence: The Impact of Industry Structure on Public Policy. *American Political Science Review,* 71:1026–43.

Schattschneider, Elmer E. 1935. *Politics, Pressures, and the Tariff: A Study of Free Enterprise in Pressure Politics as Shown in the 1929–1930. Revision of the Tariff.* New York: Prentice-Hall.

Schotter, Andrew, and Gerhard Schwodiauer. 1980. Economics and Game Theory: A Survey. *Journal of Economic Literature,* 18:479–527.

Shepsle, Kenneth A. 1978. *The Giant Jigsaw Puzzle: Democratic Committee Assignments in the Modern House.* Chicago: Univeristy of Chicago Press.

Stigler, George J. 1971. The Theory of Economic Regulation. *Bell Journal of Economics,* 2:3–19.

Truman, David B. 1951. *The Governmental Process.* New York: Knopf.

Truman, David B. 1959. *The Congressional Party.* New York: Wiley.

Wagner, Richard E. 1966. Pressure Groups and Political Entrepreneurs: A Review Article. *Papers on Non-Market Decision Making,* 1:161–70.

Weingast, Barry R., and William J. Marshall. 1984. The Industrial Organization of Congress. School of Business, Washington University, Mimeo.

PROJECT

Go to http://www.opensecrets.org. Look up your congressional representative. This website will enable you to see the sources from which he or she obtains money. Do you believe your representative is receiving money from groups that support the interests of your geographic constituency?

22

Buying Time: Moneyed Interests and the Mobilization of Bias in Congressional Committees

RICHARD L. HALL
FRANK WAYMAN

With the changing responsibilities placed upon government agencies, the role of government has expanded during the last seventy years; this expansion has changed the contours of interest-group influence. Schattschneider once said that "new policies create new politics." Contemporary legislators must be attentive to a wide array of public policies. Hall and Wayman suggest that no legislator can master all of the intricacies of policy making. They find that representatives are quite selective in the policies they actively pursue. To understand influence, one must look beyond roll-call votes toward a legislator's level (or degree) of participation. Hall and Wayman find that legislators use interest groups as resources to help them accomplish their policy-making goals. A group's ability to provide information enables it to have access to the legislator. It is groups who are "used" by legislators rather than groups who "use" legislators. Ultimately, Hall and Wayman find that a few active legislators dominate policy making in any given issue domain. At best, groups attempt to maintain access to and awareness among legislators rather than influence in the policy process. Like the pluralists of the 1950s and 1960s, Hall and Wayman find the power of interest groups to be relatively benign.

QUESTIONS TO CONSIDER

1. What is a "rational PAC"?

2. Why is it important to study what groups do in relation to congressional committees?

3. Who do PACs target with their money? Why?

4. What do Hall and Wayman say about the "intensity" with which groups attempt to get their messages heard? Why is this observation important?

A t least since Madison railed about the mischiefs of faction, critics of U.S. political institutions have worried about the influence of organized interests in national policy making. In this century, one of the most eloquent critics of the interest group system was E. E. Schattschneider, who warned of the inequalities between private, organized, and upper-class groups on the one hand and public, unorganized, and lower-class groups on the other. The pressure system, he argued in *The Semisovereign People* (1960), "mobilized bias" in national policy making in favor of the former, against the interests of the latter, and hence against the interests of U.S. democracy. Such concerns have hardly abated thirty years since the publication of Schattschneider's essay. In particular, the precipitous growth in the number and financial strength of political action committees has refueled the charge that moneyed interests dominate the policy making process. The current Congress is

SOURCE: Richard L. Hall and Frank Wayman, "Buying Time: Moneyed Interests and the Mobilization of Bias in Congressional Committees," *American Political Science Review* 84, no. 3 (Sep 1990): 797–820. Reprinted with permission from Cambridge University Press.

This research was supported in part by the National Science Foundation under Grant SES-8401505. For assistance or comments at various stages of this paper, we are indebted to Severin Borenstein, John Chamberlin, Cary Coglianese, David C. King, John Kingdon, Tim McDaniel, Mike Munger, Ken Organski, Randall Ripley, Robert Salisbury, Eric Uslaner, Carl Van Horn, Jack Wright, and participants in a faculty seminar at the Institute of Public Policy Studies, University of Michigan, Ann Arbor. For assistance in collecting and coding data, we thank Nick Greifer, Ed Kutler, Gary Levenson, and Dan Polsky. An earlier version of this paper was presented at the 1989 meeting of the Midwest Political Science Association, Chicago.

The Best Congress Money Can Buy according to one critic (Stern 1988), one where *Honest Graft* is an institutional imperative (Jackson 1988; see also Drew 1982; Etzioni 1984). "The rising tide of special-interest money," one close observer concludes, "is changing the balance of power between voters and donors, between lawmakers' constitutional constituents and their cash constituents" (Jackson 1988, 107).

Despite the claims of the institutional critics and the growing public concern over PACs during the last decade, the scientific evidence that political money matters in legislative decision making is surprisingly weak. Considerable research on members' voting decisions offers little support for the popular view that PAC money permits interests to buy or rent votes on matters that affect them. Based on an examination of 120 PACs in 10 issue areas over four congresses, one recent study concludes flatly that PAC contributions do not affect members' voting patterns (Grenzke 1989a). Another study, designed to explore the "upper bounds" of PAC influence on House roll calls, emphasizes "the relative inability of PACs to determine congressional voting" (Wright 1985, 412). Other studies have come to similar conclusions (see e.g., Chappell 1982; Wayman 1985; Welch 1982), though there are also dissenting voices (e.g., Kau and Rubin 1982; Silberman and Durden 1976). On the whole, then, this literature certainly leads one to a more sanguine view of moneyed interests and congressional politics than one gets from the popular commentaries. Does money matter?

Our approach to this question is two-pronged. In the first two sections, we revisit the question by developing a theoretical account of the constrained exchange between legislator and donor quite different from the one evident in the substantial literature cited above. In particular, we adopt the premise that PACs are rational actors, seeking to maximize their influence on the legislative outcomes that affect their affiliates; but we take issue with the standard account of PAC rationality. Our approach does not lead us to predict a strong causal relationship between PAC money and floor votes. House members and interest group representatives are viewed as parties to an implicit cooperative agreement, but the constraints on member behavior and the rational calculations of group representatives limit the extent to which votes become the currency of exchange. Instead, we advance two hypotheses about the effect of money on congressional decision making.

First, we suggest that in looking for the effects of money in Congress, one must look more to the politics of committee decision making than those of the floor. This view, of course, is neither original nor remarkable. Students of Congress have long contended that interest group influence flourishes at the committee level, and recent students of PAC influence invariably advocate that work move in this direction (e.g., Grenzke 1989a, 18; Schlozman and Tierney 1986, 256). To date, however, systematic studies of PACs and committee decision making have been altogether rare (for an important exception, see Wright 1989). We focus here at the committee level and emphasize the theoretical reasons for doing so.

Second, and more importantly, our account of the member-donor exchange leads us to focus on the *participation* of particular members, not on their votes.

This variable, we believe, is a crucial but largely neglected element of congressional decision making. It is especially important in any analysis of interest group influence in a decentralized Congress. In their famous study of lobbying on foreign trade policy, for instance, Bauer, Pool, and Dexter concluded that a member's principal problem is "not how to vote but what to do with his time, how to allocate his resources, and where to put his energy" (1963, 405). More recently, Denzau and Munger (1986) have modeled the interest group–member relationship as an exchange of contributions and electoral support for legislative services or effort. If money does not necessarily buy votes or change minds, in other words, it can buy members' time. The intended effect is to mobilize bias in congressional committee decision making.

We then develop and estimate a model of committee participation that permits a direct test of whether moneyed interests do mobilize bias in committee decision making. Analyzing data from three House committees on three distinct issues, we find that they do. In the final section we briefly discuss the implications of the findings for our understanding of money, interest groups, and representation in Congress.

THE RATIONAL PAC REVISITED

The interdependencies of legislators and moneyed interests have been widely discussed by political scientists and widely lamented by critics of pluralism (see esp. Hayes 1981). The basis for political exchange is clear. Each depends at least partially on the other to promote its goals. Interest groups seek, among other things, favorable action on legislation that will affect them; members of Congress seek financial and political support from particular groups. Like the relationship between legislators and bureaucrats, however, the relationship between legislators and interest groups is one of *implicit* exchange: the actors "trade speculatively and on credit" (Arnold 1979, 36; see also Denzau and Munger 1986; Hayes 1981). Contributions are marked somewhere in the invisible ledger, and a group's political strategists presumably can use them to their momentary legislative ends.

This account of the legislator–interest group relationship underpins the now-considerable literature on contributions and roll call voting. The working hypothesis is that contributions influence legislative outcomes by "purchasing" the votes of particular members or, less directly, by serving as "investments" that will pay dividends in legislative support at some later date (e.g., Chappell 1982; Jacobson 1980, 77, 82). The scientific evidence that such effects appear only infrequently may be cause for relief among critics of the system, but it is puzzling to theorists of institutional behavior. Why should PACs flourish, both in number and financial strength, when their legislative efficacy is so low? The payoffs would appear inadequate to sustain the cooperative relationship.

One possible explanation is that PACs raise and disburse money with local congressional elections, not specific legislative ends, in mind. Wright (1985) argues, in fact, that the decentralized nature of most PAC organizations inclines them to do just that. But this account simply moves the issue of PAC rationality to a second, institutional level. Why would PACs organize in this way? Wright suggests that the typical national PAC office permits local officials substantial discretion because it wants to encourage them to continue raising funds. But the organization's fund-raising and disbursement, presumably, are intended for some more ultimate purpose, namely, to increase the net political benefits associated with governmental action (or inaction) on issues that affect it. On the whole, using money solely to affect election outcomes is not likely to be a rational means to this end.

The probability that any single group's contribution will affect the outcome of a congressional election—in which a wide range of more powerful forces are at work—is almost certainly slight. In the aggregate it might affect the organization's political support within Congress by only a member or two (Wayman 1985). While organizational arrangements may create some inefficiency in the way PACs employ funds to promote their political ends, one should still expect to find systematic patterns of allocation that are driven by legislative considerations, even among PACs that are highly decentralized (and especially among those that are not). Indeed, there is growing evidence that this is the case (Grenzke 1989b).

If the principal value of contributions lies in their potential to affect floor roll calls, however, a second puzzle appears. One would expect to find contribution strategies that favor the swing legislators in anticipated floor battles, since these are the cases where the marginal utility in votes purchased per dollar spent is likely to be greatest (Denzau and Munger 1986). Money allocated to almost certain supporters (or almost certain opponents) should be counted as irrational behavior, evidence of scarce resources wasted. In fact, however, the evidence suggests that such "misallocations" systematically occur. The Business–Industry Political Action Committee (BIPAC) and the National Chamber of Commerce give overwhelmingly to conservative Republicans (Kau and Rubin 1982, 88; Maitland 1985). Labor PACs such as the AFL-CIO's Committee on Political Education give overwhelmingly to incumbent Democrats loyal to labor's agenda (Chappell 1982; Grier and Munger 1986; Jacobson 1980). Oil PACs give to conservative incumbents regardless of party and to friends regardless of ideology (Evans 1988). In general, PACs are prone to reward their friends—even when their friends are not in danger of defeat. In a specific test of the swing hypothesis, in fact, Welch found that if anything, dairy PACs were *less* likely to contribute to swing legislators on dairy issues, all other things being equal (1982).[1] On the whole, it would seem that if, as Schattschneider (1960) said, moneyed interests sing with an upper-class accent, they also spend a good deal of effort singing to the choir.

One oft-mentioned solution to these puzzles is that contributions buy not votes but "access" to members and their staffs (e.g., Berry 1984; Gopoian 1984; Schlozman and Tierney, 1986). But this solution only provokes a second query: If money buys access, what does access buy? (see esp. Herndon, 1982, 1017). Presumably, it gives the representatives of contributing groups important opportunities to directly lobby and potentially persuade legislators to the group's point of view. In this scenario the language of *access* may serve symbolically to launder the money going from group to roll call vote, but the effect of the group on the vote should still appear in systematic analysis (Grenzke 1989a). As we note above, it does not.

THE RATIONAL PAC REVISED

The literature on PAC contribution strategies and members' roll call voting behavior thus suggests two puzzles. First, if group strategists are reasonably rational, why would they continue to allocate scarce resources to efforts where the expected political benefits are so low? Second, if PAC allocation strategies are designed to influence members' votes, why do they contribute so heavily to their strongest supporters and occasionally to their strongest opponents? Is it the case that PACs are systematically irrational (e.g., Welch 1982, 492) and, by extension, that claims about the influence of money on legislative process almost certainly exaggerated? We believe that the premise of rationality need not be rejected but that theoretical work in this area requires a more

complete account of rational PAC behavior. We extend here an account developed formally in Denzau and Munger's model of a supply price for public policy (1986). Simply put, interest group resources are intended to accomplish something different from, and more than, influencing elections or buying votes. Specifically, we argue that PAC money should be allocated in order to *mobilize* legislative support and *demobilize* opposition, particularly at the most important points in the legislative process.

This argument turns directly on what we already know about the nature of legislators' voting decisions from a very rich literature. The simple but important point is that a number of powerful factors exist that predispose a member to vote a certain way, among them party leaders, ideology, constituency, and the position of the administration (Fiorina 1974; Jackson 1974; Kingdon 1981).[2] Kingdon notes, moreover, that members' votes on particular issues are also constrained by their past voting histories (1981, 274–78). Members attach some value to consistency, independent of the other factors that influence their voting behavior. A third and related point is that the public, recorded nature of the vote may itself limit the member's discretion: a risk-averse member may fear the appearance of impropriety in supporting major campaign contributors in the absence of some other, legitimate force pushing her in the same direction. Finally, the dichotomous nature of the vote acts as a constraint. Money must not only affect members' attitudes at the margin but do so enough to push them over the threshold between *nay* and *yea*. In short, the limits on member responsiveness to messages wrapped in money are substantial, perhaps overwhelming, at least insofar as floor voting is concerned.

Of course, almost all studies of PAC contributions and roll calls acknowledge the importance of such factors and build them into their statistical models of the voting decision. But it is also important to consider the implications of these findings for the vote-buying hypothesis itself. Interest group strategists tend to be astute-enough observers of the legislative process to appreciate the powerful constraints that shape members' voting behavior. To the extent that this is true the rational PAC should expect little in the way of marginal benefits in votes bought for dollars spent, especially when individual PAC contributions are limited by the Federal Election Campaign Act to ten thousand dollars—a slight fraction of the cost of the average House race. Individual votes, that is, simply aren't easy to change; and even if some are changed, the utility of the votes purchased depends on their net cumulative effect in turning a potentially losing coalition into a winning one. For the rational PAC manager, the expected marginal utility approximates zero in most every case. All other things being equal, scarce resources should be allocated heavily elsewhere and to other purposes.

How, then, should the strategic PAC distribute its resources? The first principle derives from the larger literature on interest group influence in Congress. Well aware of the decentralized nature of congressional decision making, interest groups recognize that resources allocated at the committee stage are more efficiently spent (e.g., Berry 1984; Grier and Munger 1986; Kingdon 1981, 170–71). Interest group preferences incorporated there have a strong chance of surviving as the bill moves through subsequent stages in the sequence, while provisions not in the committee vehicle are difficult to attach later. Second, the nature of the committee assignment process increases the probability that organized interests will find a sympathetic audience at the committee or subcommittee stage. Members seek and often receive positions that will permit them to promote the interests that, in turn, help them to get reelected (Shepsle

1978). Finally, the less public, often informal nature of committee decision making suggests that members' responsiveness to campaign donors will receive less scrutiny. Indeed, a long tradition of research on subgovernments emphasizes that such clientelism flourishes at the committee stage (e.g., Ripley and Franklin 1980; Shepsle 1978, chap. 10; but see Gais, Peterson, and Walker 1984). In short, groups will strategically allocate their resources with the knowledge that investments in the politics of the appropriate committee or subcommittee are likely to pay higher dividends than investments made elsewhere. Indeed, this principle is especially important in the House, where the sheer size of the chamber's membership, the greater importance of the committee stage, and the frequent restrictions on floor participation recommend a more targeted strategy (see, esp., Grenzke 1989b and Grier and Munger 1989).

If PACs concentrate at the committee level, what, specifically, do they hope to gain there? Purchasing votes is one possibility; and, in fact, the rationale for allocating campaign money to buy votes in committee is somewhat stronger than for vote-buying on the floor. But even within committee, PACs still tend to give to their strongest supporters. In addition, committee votes, like floor votes, are dichotomous decisions. And despite the lower visibility of committee decision making, the factors of constituency, ideology, party, and administration are almost certainly at work. In fact, while research on PACs and committee voting is just now beginning to emerge, there is little evidence that contributions influence voting in committee any more than they do voting on the floor (Wright 1989).

The alternative hypothesis that we test here is that political money alters members' patterns of legislative involvement, a point that emerges from an older literature on interest group influence in Congress (e.g., Bauer, Pool, and Dexter

1963; Matthews [1960] 1973, esp. 192–93) but is given its fullest theoretical expression in the recent work of Denzau and Munger (1986). Denzau and Munger suggest that interest groups provide political resources in an implicit effort to purchase policy-relevant "services" from members or their staffs. Stated somewhat differently, the object of a rational PAC allocation strategy is not simply the *direction* of legislators' preferences but the *vigor* with which those preferences are promoted in the decision making process. Such strategies should take the form of inducing sympathetic members to get actively involved in a variety of activities that directly affect the shape of committee legislation: authoring or blocking a legislative vehicle; negotiating compromises behind the scenes, especially at the staff level; offering friendly amendments or actively opposing unfriendly ones; lobbying colleagues; planning strategy; and last and sometimes least, showing up to vote in favor of the interest group's position. The purposes of PACs in allocating selective benefits, then, are analogous to the purposes that Arnold attributes to legislatively strategic bureaucrats: the goal is not simply to purchase support but to provide incentives for supporters to act as agents—at the extreme, to serve as "coalition leaders" on the principal's behalf (see Arnold 1979, 40–42 and esp. 98–100).

Several arguments support this view. First, participation is crucial to determining legislative outcomes; and voting is perhaps the least important of the various ways in which committee members participate (Hall 1989; Mayhew 1974, 95). Second, while members' voting choices are highly constrained, how they allocate their time, staff, and political capital is much more discretionary (Bauer, Pool, and Dexter 1963, 406–7). At any given moment, each member confronts a wide range of opportunities and demands, the response to any subset of which will serve one or more professional goals.

To be sure, the member must choose among them. Legislative resources are scarce, and their allocation to one activity results in other beneficial opportunities foregone (Bauer, Pool, and Dexter 1963; Hall 1987; Matthews [1960] 1973, 182–93). But for the most part, the purposive legislator is free to choose among the abundant alternatives with only modest constraints imposed by constituents, colleagues, or other actors. Hence, the member's level of involvement is something that a strategic PAC can reasonably expect to affect. The contribution need not weigh so heavily in a member's mind that it changes his or her position in any material way; it need only weigh heavily enough to command some increment of legislative resources. The minimum threshold that must be passed is thus a fairly modest one, and the potential effect of contributions on behavior is one of degree. Specifically, the member will allocate scarce legislative resources on the group's behalf so long as the marginal utility of the contribution to the member exceeds the expected marginal utility of the most valuable remaining use of the member's resources (see also Denzau and Munger 1986).

A third advantage of this view is that it explains the ostensibly anomalous tendency of PACs to contribute so heavily to members who are almost certain to win reelection and almost certain to support the group's point of view. Such behavior now appears quite rational. It is precisely one's supporters that one wants to mobilize: the more likely certain members are to support the group, the more active it should want them to be. Furthermore, this view of purposive PACs makes sense of the evidence that PACs sometimes contribute to members who will almost certainly oppose them and whose involvement in an issue stands to do the group harm. The PAC may have no hope of changing the opponent's mind, but it may, at the margin at least, diminish the intensity with which the member pursues policies that the organization does not like. The intent of the money, then, is not persuasion but demobilization: "We know you can't support us, but please don't actively oppose us." However, we should not expect the demobilizing effect of money to be nearly so strong as the mobilizing effect. The message provided through contributions to one's supporters is widely perceived as a legitimate one: in asking for help, the group is encouraging members to do precisely what they would do were resources plentiful. In contrast, contributions to opponents are meant to encourage them to go against their predispositions: the implicit message is to "take a walk" on an issue that they may care about. In short, the expected effects are not symmetric; the mobilization hypothesis is on stronger theoretical ground.

A final advantage of the view of rational action employed here is that it renders the matter of access more comprehensible. We have already noted that according to the standard account of PAC behavior, the importance that both legislators and lobbyists attach to the money-access connection makes little sense, given the evidence that money has little ultimate effect on votes. In light of the theory sketched here, however, access becomes an important, proximate goal of the interest group pursuing a legislative agenda. Access is central to stimulating agency. It gives the group the opportunity to let otherwise sympathetic members (and their staffs) know that some issue or upcoming activity is important to them. The ideal response they seek is not simply "I'll support you on this" but "What can I do to help?" Perhaps more importantly, access refers to the reciprocal efforts of the group. It is the pipeline through which the group effectively subsidizes the considerable time and information costs associated with their supporters' participation in the matters the group cares about. As

various accounts reveal, group representatives often serve as "service bureaus" or adjuncts to congressional staff (e.g., Bauer, Pool, and Dexter 1963, chap. 24; Kingdon 1981, 154–55). They provide technical information and policy analysis; they provide political intelligence; they draft legislation and craft amendments; they even write speeches or talking points that their supporters can employ in efforts on their behalf. Such subsidies to the "congressman-as-enterprise" (Salisbury and Shepsle 1981) do not necessarily persuade, but they should affect the patterns of activity and abdication that have a direct bearing on legislative deliberations and outcomes (Hall 1987, 1989).

THE DATA: MONEY AND MOBILIZATION ON THREE COMMITTEES

The data for this investigation are drawn from staff interviews and markup records of three House committees on three issues: (1) the Dairy Stabilization Act, considered by the Agriculture Committee in 1982; (2) the Job Training Partnership Act (JTPA), considered by Education and Labor in 1982; and (3) the Natural Gas Market Policy Act, considered by Energy and Commerce during 1983–84.

Several features of these cases make them particularly appropriate for exploring the effects of money on the participation of committee members. First, all were highly significant pieces of legislation, the stakes of each measuring in the billions of dollars. At issue in the Natural Gas Market Policy Act was the deregulation of natural gas prices, a proposal that would transfer billions of dollars from one region to another, from consumer to industry, and within the industry from interstate pipelines and distributors to the major natural gas producers (Uslaner 1989, chap. 5; Maraniss 1983).

Annual spending on the Job Training Partnership Act was expected at the time of its passage to be in the four-to-five-billion-dollar range (Donnelly 1982, 1035), and it replaced one of the most important domestic programs of the 1970s (Franklin and Ripley 1984). While more narrow than these in scope, the Dairy Stabilization Act also entailed significant economic effects. The principal purpose of the act was to adjust the scheduled support price for milk downward by as much as a dollar per hundredweight over two years, creating budget savings of 4.2 billion dollars for fiscal years 1983–85 and decreasing the profitability of milk production by as much as 30% for the typical dairy farmer. In each case, then, evidence of the influence of PAC money on congressional decision making can hardly be counted narrow or trivial. The deliberations in each case bore in significant ways on major interests, both public and private.

A second feature relevant to this investigation follows from the economic importance attached to these issues. All three were salient among actors other than the private groups immediately affected, a feature that the considerable research on roll call voting suggests should depress the effect of PAC contributions on congressional decision making (see, esp., Evans 1986). This was especially true for the natural gas and job training bills. While the Natural Gas Market Policy Act never received action on the House floor in the 98th Congress, it was a highly visible issue while still in committee. Consumer interest in the issue of natural gas pricing was unusually high. Gas heating costs had been climbing quickly in much of the country despite a substantial surplus of domestic natural gas (Davis 1984; Murray 1983; Uslaner 1989, chap. 5); and this fact was widely publicized through the efforts of the Citizen/Labor Energy Coalition (Pressman 1983). The *Washington Post,* in turn,

gave Commerce Committee deliberations front-page coverage, and the issue was a high priority for the Reagan administration. The job training bill, likewise, was one of the most important domestic initiatives of Reagan's first term and received considerable media attention. The principal purpose of the bill was to replace the much maligned but widely used public jobs program, the Comprehensive Employment and Training Act (CETA), at a time when the national unemployment rate threatened to exceed 10% for the first time in four decades. To a lesser degree, finally, the 1982 dairy bill was also salient among actors off the committee and outside the industry. While the interest of the general public in dairy policy was slight, the burgeoning budget deficit loomed large on Capitol Hill, and it clearly motivated the decision to change dairy policy only one year after passage of an omnibus farm bill (Wehr 1982a, 1982b). Indeed, relative to other domestic nonentitlements, dairy subsidies were widely perceived as a major budget offender. The administration thus counted the price adjustments a high priority, one that commanded considerable attention from Budget Director David Stockman, and the House Budget Committee was involved at every stage of the process.

Finally, each of the policy areas we examine here has received the attention of previous scholars studying PAC contributions and floor roll calls; and in each case the effects of PAC money were found to be slight. In a study of dairy legislation considered in the House in 1975, for instance, Welch (1982) concluded that dairy PAC contributions were the least important determinant of voting on milk price supports and that their effect on the legislation was negligible (see also Chappell 1982). Grenzke (1989a) estimated a dynamic model of members' voting behavior over four congresses and found that labor union contributions had either a negligible or a *negative* effect on members' propensity to take prolabor positions on the House floor (but see Wilhite and Theilmann 1987). And Wayman and Kutler (1985) found no effect of natural gas industry campaign contributions on members' votes during House consideration of natural gas deregulation in 1975.

At two levels, then, past research indicates that our selection of cases is biased against our argument. It suggests that high salience issues should exhibit little PAC influence on legislative behavior, yet each of the cases here commanded the attention of a wide range of political actors. Second, past research suggests that we will find little PAC influence in precisely these three policy areas. Should we find support for the hypothesis that money mobilizes support (or demobilizes opposition) at the committee level, we should be on reasonably solid ground to conclude that (1) the results of this exploration are apt to generalize to other committees and other issues and (2) the null results of past research are more likely to be artifacts of the legislative behavior and the legislative stage studied than evidence that moneyed interests do not matter in congressional decision making.

THE MODEL

The model of participation we use to test for the hypothesized effects is adapted from Hall 1987.[3] The model begins from the same motivational premise that we employed in our discussion of PAC contribution behavior. Members of Congress are purposive actors who allocate their time, staff, and other legislative resources in such a way as to advance certain personal goals or interests. There are several goals that commonly figure in these calculations. The one most prominently cited in the literature on legislative behavior is reelection or, more generally, service to the district (see, esp., Mayhew 1974);

but we report elsewhere that the relevance of any particular goal to a member's participation depends directly on the nature of the issue and the legislative context (Hall 1987). To use language borrowed from Kingdon (1981), goals are "evoked." Any particular issue may evoke several goals simultaneously or may evoke none at all. In the latter case, a member is simply uninterested, the expected benefits of participation slight; in the former, the level of interest is intense, the expected benefits of participation high.

In the three cases under study here, in fact, several goals were probably at work in the resource allocation decisions of most committee members. For instance, the natural gas bill raised issues of government intervention in the economy and the country's long-term dependence on foreign energy sources. The budgetary implications of the dairy bill undoubtedly evoked some committee members' concerns about good fiscal policy and its macroeconomic consequences. The Job Training Partnership Act concerned the government's obligation to redress inequalities of economic opportunity resulting from inadequate or outdated job skills. But the goal most consistently evident in staff interviews, markup debates, and secondary accounts of the three bills was promoting or protecting district interests. For the purposes of this analysis, then, we adopt the simpler and more tractable motivational assumption common to most models of legislative behavior.[4] In deciding whether and to what extent to participate on a particular issue, the member estimates both the expected benefits and expected costs, where benefits are a direct function of the issue's economic relevance to the district.[5]

If the interests of one's constituents motivate a member to become involved, the costs of participation are also important and highly variable: resources are scarce, and the allocation to one activity results in other profitable opportunities foregone.

Several factors affect the resources available to particular members on particular issues. First, assignment to the subcommittee of jurisdiction provides members both with greater formal opportunities to participate and access to an earlier stage of the sequential process. It also gives the member greater access to staff and to lines of communication with other interested actors both on and off the committee. For similar reasons, a committee or subcommittee leadership position subsidizes participation even more. The greater staff allocations that these positions bestow, the procedural control over the agenda, and the central place in the committee communication network diminish the time and information costs associated with meaningful involvement in the issue at hand. Finally, freshman status tends to increase the information costs and diminish the opportunities or resources a member enjoys for any particular bill.

The variable of greatest interest in this investigation, however, is the level of contributions each member receives from PACs interested in the issue at hand. To what degree, that is, does money affect members' decisions regarding whether and to what extent they will participate in the committee deliberations? Two points require emphasis here. First, the foregoing discussion suggests that the effects of money on participation should not be simply linear. The positive effect of contributions on participation should be contingent on probable support; this is the mobilization hypothesis. To the extent that contributions are given to probable opponents, on the other hand, they should diminish participation; this is the demobilization hypothesis.

Second, contributions may well be related to other activities that moneyed interests employ to further their legislative aims, making it difficult to isolate the effects of any particular part of their effort (Rothenberg 1989; Wright 1989). For instance, it may be the case that

those groups that organize PACs for the purpose of channeling money to candidates are also the most active in developing grass roots campaigns or direct lobbying efforts. While there is evidence to suggest that the correlation among these activities is modest for the cases under study here,[6] our data on interest group activity are limited to political action committee campaign contributions. Hence, while our model tests for the effect that money has on committee behavior, one might more accurately characterize our results as capturing the effect of the several resources that moneyed interests employ.[7]

The dependent variable is the participation of member i on bill j, where participation refers to a member's activity both during formal committee markups and committee action behind the scenes. Our data on activity are drawn from two sources: semistructured interviews with both the majority and minority staffers assigned to cover each bill and the largely unpublished but meticulously kept committee and subcommittee markup records. The summary measure of participation that we use for the purposes of this exploration is a simple scale score derived from a factor analysis of six activities: attendance; voting participation; speaking; offering amendments during committee markups; role in authoring the legislative vehicle or an amendment in the nature of a substitute; and negotiating behind the scenes at either the member or the staff level.[8] The measurement of the independent variables, in turn, follows directly from the preceding discussion. Members' institutional positions and status are measured with dichotomous variables that are set at zero except as the following conditions hold: subcommittee membership takes a value of one if a member sat on the subcommittee with jurisdiction over the bill; leadership position takes a value of one if a member was chair or ranking minority member of either the full or subcommittee; and freshman status takes a value of one for members in their first term in the House.

In measuring the relevance of each issue to committee members' districts, we assume that relevance is primarily economic in nature. In the natural gas case, this takes two quite different forms: total district-level natural gas production[9] and the economic effect of gas price increases on residential consumers in the member's district, which we measure using industry data on natural gas price increases and census data regarding congressional district natural gas use.[10] If high production and high inflation capture dimensions of intradistrict salience, however, the presence of both at once should produce intradistrict conflict. The member is torn between two significant economic interests, and activity on behalf of one may alienate the other. Indeed, Fiorina (1974) suggests that unrequited constituents are likely to punish more than the requited are to reward. As intradistrict conflict increases, in any case, the expected benefits of activity on the issue should diminish, ceteris paribus. In the natural gas case, then, intradistrict conflict occurs as the production and inflation variables both approach their upper limits. We measure this condition as the product of two terms: "high production" is the extent to which natural gas production in the district exceeds the mean district production for all members of the committee; similarly, "high inflation" is the extent to which the district inflationary effect exceeds the mean for all committee members. When either district gas production or inflationary effect is below the committee mean, then, intradistrict conflict is zero.

In the other two cases the measurement of district interest is uncomplicated by potential conflicts within members' geographic constituencies. In the dairy stabilization case district relevance is directly related to the importance of dairy farming, measured simply by the total number of dairy cows in the member's district as reported by the United States Department of Agriculture biennial census. Given that milk prices were not a salient consumer issue per se and that the Dairy Stabilization Act was not likely to affect retail prices in any significant way, we do not assume a more general public concern with this issue. For the Job Training Partnership Act, likewise, district relevance is directly related to the importance of federal jobs programs in addressing structural unemployment, which we measure as the current level of CETA expenditures in the member's district.[11] This variable not only taps the district-specific economic benefits of clients of the expiring job training program but (given that CETA allocations were directly tied to local unemployment rates) also captures the severity of structural unemployment in the district.

Consistent with the preceding theoretical discussion, we estimate the effect of group expenditures on participation by including pairs of interactions between group contributions (measured as the amount contributed during the two-year election cycle prior to committee action) and indicators of probable support or opposition. For each case, the exact specification of the interactions is straightforward. In the dairy stabilization case, we measure probable support or opposition using the ratings of the National Farmers' Union (NFU),[12] an organization that strongly supports federal intervention in the agricultural economy to control supply and support the commodity prices paid to farmers. Given that we expect very different effects for contributions on the behavior of likely supporters and opponents, however, the model requires two separate interactions: *Money to supporters* is the product of contributions[13] and the member's distance from the mean NFU score where the members' rating is greater than the mean; the money-support term is zero otherwise. *Money to opponents* is the product of contributions and the member's distance from the mean NFU score, where the member's rating is less than the mean; the money-opposition term is zero otherwise. Following the theoretical reasoning of the last section, then, the expected effect on participation is positive for money to supporters. The expected effect is negative for money to opponents in each case.

Any attempt to model the effect of contribution activity on legislative behavior cannot assume that a particular industry is necessarily unified, however: one segment of an industry may have different interests and work in ways that offset some other segment. In the case of the federal dairy legislation, no such split within the industry was apparent among the principal actors, thus permitting the fairly simple specification described above. But in general—and in the natural gas case in particular—an industry may not be so easily simplified. While the gas producers were by far the most visible and most vigorous among the corporate actors and gave by far the most money in campaign contributions among energy PACs, the natural gas industry was seriously divided (Pressman 1983; Uslaner 1989, chap. 5), a feature that we attempt to capture. The alignments were by no means perfect, but the principal issues at stake in the legislation before House Energy and Commerce pitted the major gas producers and intrastate pipelines against the interstate pipelines and distributors. As a result, different segments of the industry were likely to target different members to serve as legislative agents and identify different members as their likely opponents. Our first task therefore was to distinguish the various energy PACs according to the principal business activities of their affiliates. Using the detailed descriptions of individual companies provided by Moody's Investor Service (1983a and 1983b), we classified each affiliate according to its principal interests in the natural gas area.[14] We then divided the contributions a member

received according to whether they came from producers or intrastate pipelines on the one hand and interstates or distributors on the other. The measure of contributions that we employ, then, is the producer-intrastate contributions minus the interstate-distributor contributions, the value of which was positive in almost every case.

The operationalization of the interactions tapping the net producer-intrastate effects, in turn, was handled in a fashion analogous to the dairy stabilization case. In the natural gas case, however, members' Americans for Democratic Action (ADA) scores were more appropriate as an indicator of likely support or opposition. For the producer-intrastate segment of the gas industry at least, the issue of greatest concern was the extent to which the government continued its intervention in the natural gas market by controlling the price of old gas. The ADA score should tap members' historical tendency to support such federal interventions quite well. *Money to supporters*, then, is the product of net producer-intrastate contributions and the member's distance from the mean ADA score where the member's rating is less than the mean; the money-support term is zero otherwise; and *money to opponents* is the product of contributions and the member's distance from the mean ADA score where the member's rating is greater than the mean; the money-opposition term is zero otherwise.

Unlike the dairy and natural gas cases, finally, the job training bill did not involve issues specific to a particular industry. The organized interests most concerned with CETA and its prospective replacement were the national labor unions: public service employment and training programs were at the top of labor's agenda, especially in 1982, when unemployment was approaching postwar records. Moreover, labor unions were one of the single largest categories of contributors to congressional campaigns and gave to five-sixths of the members of House Education and Labor. It is the effect of these contributions on committee behavior with which we are primarily concerned. This is not to say, however, that labor unions were the only groups interested in mobilizing support on this bill.[15] On the business side, national business associations generally opposed any public service employment provisions and favored an expanded role for private industry councils so that federally subsidized training would be tailored to meet the changing needs of the private sector (Baumer and Van Horn 1985, 173). As in the natural gas case, we thus employ a net contributions variable, which takes the value of the member's total labor contributions less the total contributions received from national business organizations.[16] As in the other two cases, likewise, the indicator of probable support or opposition was constructed using the appropriate group rating, in this case, the AFL-CIO's Committee on Political Education (COPE) score. *Money to supporters*, then, is the product of net labor contributions and the member's distance from the mean COPE score, where the member's rating is greater than the mean; and *money to opponents* is the product of contributions and the member's distance from the mean COPE score where the member's rating is less than the mean.

RESULTS AND INTERPRETATIONS

In estimating the model of participation, we explicitly account for the possibility that contributions are effectively endogenous, that is, that in allocating contributions to committee members during the previous election cycle, a group may attempt to anticipate who the principal players will be on issues it cares about.[17] To the extent this is true, at least, the error term will be correlated with contributions

and the ordinary least squares coefficient on the latter will be upwardly biased. We thus estimate the participation model using two-stage least squares, with the second stage results reported in the tables.[18] In each of the three cases, the model performs quite well, explaining over 55% of the variance in participation. More importantly, the analysis provides solid support for the principal hypothesis of this study, that moneyed interests mobilize bias in committee decision making.

This finding is clear for all three cases.[19] The campaign contributions that dairy industry PACs gave to their likely supporters significantly increased their participation, even when we controlled for the importance of the issue to individual members' districts, whether they sat on the subcommittee of jurisdiction, and whether they held a leadership position, (Table 22.1). Such factors are reported elsewhere to be strong determinants of committee participation (Hall 1987), and each is also likely to affect contributions since interest groups tend to concentrate their resources on members who hold positions of institutional power (e.g., Grenzke 1989b; Grier and Munger 1986, 1989), as well as on members who have a district stake in their industry. That the mobilization coefficient remains positive and significant in the face of the multivariate controls reinforces the interpretation that the connection between group resources and mobilization is causal. When dairy PACs did give to their probable opponents, moreover, there is some evidence that the contributions diminished participation. While the coefficient on the money-opposition variable is statistically insignificant, its size is substantively nontrivial, and the negative sign is consistent with the demobilization hypothesis. In short, the more money a supporter received from the dairy PACs and the stronger the member's support, the more likely he or she was to allocate time and effort on the industry's behalf (e.g., work behind the scenes, speak on the group's

Table 22.1 PAC Money and Committee Participation: 1982 Dairy Stabilization Act

Independent Variables	Unstandardized 2SLS Coefficient	t-statistic
Intercept	.01	.05
Number of dairy cows in district	.27**	2.21
Dairy PAC contributions to supporters	.26**	2.42
Dairy PAC contributions to opponents	−.11	−.61
Membership on reporting subcommittee	.17**	3.54
Committee or subcommittee leadership position	.35**	4.50
Freshman status	−.02	−.31

NOTE: Adjusted R-squared = .60; number of observations = 41. All variables are measured on a 0–1 scale. The contributions term is the predicted value from the first-stage equation.

**Statistically significant at .05 level; one-tailed test.

behalf, attach amendments to the committee vehicle, as well as show up and vote at committee markups). Alternatively, money may have diminished the intensity of the opposition. The effect of money on decision making in the House Agriculture Committee, then, was to encourage industry supporters to be active and, if anything, to encourage industry opponents to abdicate.

The results of the job training case are also clear, and the specific estimates are striking in their similarity to the dairy stabilization case. As Table 22.2 shows, the contributions that labor groups made to their supporters had a substantial, statistically significant effect on participation during Education and Labor deliberations. Remarkably, the unstandardized coefficient for the money support variable is almost identical in size to the analogous coefficient in the dairy stabilization model despite the fact that the two cases are drawn from different committees with qualitatively different jurisdictions and policy environments (Smith and Deering 1984). In each case, a change in the money support variable from its minimum to its maximum value moves a member approximately one-fourth of the way along the participation scale, almost exactly one standard deviation. In both cases, likewise, this coefficient is greater

than that for subcommittee membership, a variable generally considered central to understanding participation in the post-reform House. As in the dairy stabilization case, finally, the Education and Labor bill provides some support for the demobilization hypothesis. While it fails to meet conventional levels of statistical significance, the size of the money-opposition term proves negative and substantively significant, nearly matching the size of subcommittee membership.

The results regarding moneyed interests and mobilization are only slightly less compelling in the natural gas case, a case complicated both by divisions within the industry and the apparent importance of both organized and unorganized interests. As we note above, such conditions are likely to mitigate the efficacy of interest group efforts, and they complicate the measurement of anticipated support and opposition. Still, the mobilization hypothesis finds strong support in the behavior of Energy and Commerce members. While the size of the unstandardized coefficient for the money support variable is somewhat smaller than for the other two cases, it is still substantial and statistically significant at the .05 level. A change in the money support variable from its minimum to its maximum moves a Commerce

Table 22.2 PAC Money and Committee Participation: 1982 Job Training Partnership Act

Independent Variables	Unstandardized 2SLS Coefficient	t-statistic
Intercept	.13	.77
CETA expenditures in district	.03	.23
Labor union net contributions to supporters	.25*	1.62
Labor union net contributions to opponents	−.18	−.80
Membership on reporting subcommittee	.19**	2.61
Committee or subcommittee leadership position	.47**	4.55
Freshman status	−.05	−.51

NOTE: Adjusted R-squared = .56; number of observations = 32. All variables are measured on a 0–1 scale. The net contributions term is the predicted value from the first-stage equation.

*Statistically significant at .10 level, one-tailed test.

**Statistically significant at .05 level, one-tailed test.

Committee member approximately one-sixth of the way along the participation scale. By way of illustration, this amounts to the difference between Minnesota Representative Gerry Sikorski, who did little more than faithfully attend and vote during formal markups, and Alabama Representative Richard Shelby, whose staff participated in behind-the-scenes negotiations and who offered two substantive amendments during subcommittee markup, both of which passed.

As Table 22.3 shows, finally, the demobilization hypothesis is not supported in the natural gas case. While the coefficient on the money opponents interaction is slight, its positive sign is inconsistent with our prediction. The foundation for the demobilization hypothesis being theoretically weaker, however, the null result here, as well as the weak results in the dairy and job training cases, are not altogether surprising. The theoretically stronger hypothesis, that money mobilizes a pro-PAC bias at the committee level, is confirmed in all three.

For the most part, the other variables in the model also perform as predicted and suggest interesting implications for the politics of representation in a decentralized Congress. The rele-

vance of an issue to the member's district enhances member participation in two cases, providing evidence that Agriculture and Commerce members purposively allocate their legislative time and resources to promote the interests of their constituencies. On House Agriculture, the more important dairy farming was to the member's district, the more likely he or she was to participate in committee deliberations. Likewise, the greater the presence of natural gas production in the district, the more likely the Energy and Commerce member was to participate in deliberations on the Natural Gas Market Policy Act. Indeed, a change in gas production from its minimum to its maximum corresponds to a 32% change along the participation scale, the difference between simply showing up and being a major player on the bill. By comparison, however, the effect of natural gas price increases on district consumers appears smaller by half. And the importance of structural unemployment and program spending in the districts of Education and Labor members had at best a slight effect on their involvement in the Job Training Partnership Act.

Pending better measurement of unorganized constituents' interest at the district level, of course, we cannot draw

Table 22.3 PAC Money and Committee Participation: 1984 Natural Gas Market Policy Act

Independent Variables	Unstandardized 2SLS Coefficient	t-statistic
Intercept	.08	.40
Natural gas production in district	.32*	1.65
Natural gas price increase effect on district	.17*	1.35
High production/high inflation interaction	−.18	−1.28
Producer-intrastate net contributions to supporters	.17**	1.69
Producer-intrastate net contributions to opponents	.01	.06
Membership on reporting subcommittee	.23**	3.17
Committee or subcommittee leadership position	.54**	4.77
Freshman status	.13*	1.31

NOTE: Adjusted R-squared = .57; number of observations = 42. All variables are measured on a 0–1 scale. The net contributions term is the predicted value from the first stage equation.

*Statistically significant at .10 level, one-tailed test.

**Statistically significant at .05 level, one-tailed test.

unqualified conclusions regarding their importance in shaping committee behavior. Should such patterns hold up under subsequent analysis, however, the implications for member responsiveness to industry interests and industry money relative to more general constituency concerns would be several and important. If members allocate their scarce legislative time and resources with district interests in mind, they perceive their districts in terms of different constituencies; and these perceptions affect their behavior as representatives (Fenno 1978). In part, the results presented here suggest that organized economic interests within districts figure more prominently in the psychology of representation than the diffuse and unorganized interests of rank-and-file voters. Such was the charge that Schattschneider made thirty years ago, one which critics of pluralism have echoed repeatedly since.

At the same time, however, the findings in the natural gas case also suggest that the preferences of unorganized interests sometimes constrain the responsiveness of members to organized groups, thus confirming the thesis of Denzau and

Munger (1986) regarding how unorganized interests get represented. Beyond the positive coefficient for the inflationary effect variable, this is evident in the size and significance of the coefficient on the high production–high inflation interaction. Even if members are inclined to respond to producer interests, in short, this tendency is mitigated when consumer interests are also high. However, we should point out two things. First, the simultaneous occurrence of both strong producer interests and high consumer-voter salience is rare. Indeed, this distinguishes the natural gas issue from most of the issues with which members of Congress typically deal, and even in this case only 4 of the 42 members of Energy and Commerce were seriously cross-pressured. Second, we found no such constraint on the behavioral effect of producer contributions. One might expect, for instance, that the mobilizing effect of producer contributions would be diminished for a member who also represents a high inflation district. In one variant of the model tested here we included an interaction between the money support and high inflation variables, with the result that the coefficient was correct in sign (negative) but very near zero and the money-support coefficient was unchanged.

Finally, most of the variables that tap members' institutional positions prove to be strong determinants of committee participation. While the coefficients on freshman status differ in sign, both subcommittee membership and leadership position are positive, statistically significant, and substantively large in all three cases. Even on issues that are widely perceived among the committee membership to be important, issues where the organized interests in the policy environment are themselves active, the opportunities and resources provided by formal institutional position are major factors in determining who makes the laws at the committee stage. Such findings are generally consistent with findings from other committees and larger samples of issues (Evans n.d.; Hall 1987, 1989; Hall and Evans 1990) and reinforce the assumption that the model of participation employed here is specified correctly.

CONCLUSION

We have elaborated a theory of the member-group exchange relationship that comprehends the general patterns of PAC contributions reported in the literature. House members and interest group representatives are parties to an implicit cooperative agreement, but the constraints on member behavior and the rational calculations of group strategists limit the extent to which votes become the basis for exchange. This view suggests expectations about the effects of money on congressional decision making quite different from the ones that motivate the substantial research on the subject. We should find little causal connection between contributions and votes, especially on the floor—an expectation generally supported, although not adequately explained, in the

literature. We should expect to find an important connection between contributions and the legislative involvement of sympathetic members, especially in committee—a relationship that empirical research to date has altogether ignored.

In order to test this view of moneyed interests and congressional decision making, we investigated the participation of House members on three issues in three committees. In each case, we found solid support for our principal hypothesis: moneyed interests are able to mobilize legislators already predisposed to support the group's position. Conversely, money that a group contributes to its likely opponents has either a negligible or negative effect on their participation. While previous research on these same issues provided little evidence that PAC money purchased members' votes, it apparently did buy the marginal time, energy, and legislative resources that committee participation requires. Moreover, we found evidence that (organized) producer interests figured more prominently than (unorganized) consumer interests in the participation decisions of House committee members—both for a case in which the issue at stake evoked high district salience and one where it did not. And we found little evidence that committee members respond to the interests of unemployed workers except insofar as those interests might be represented in the activities of well-financed and well-organized labor unions. Such findings suggest several implications for our understanding of political money, interest groups, and the legislative process.

The first and most important implication is that moneyed interests *do* affect the decision-making processes of Congress, an implication that one does not easily derive from the existing political science literature on contributions. In fact, it matters most at that stage of the legislative process that matters most and for a form of legislative behavior likely to have a direct bearing on outcomes. As

David Mayhew has suggested (1974, 95), parliamentary suffrage gives a member relatively little leverage over the shape of legislation, especially at the committee stage. Only a small fraction of the decisions that shape a bill ever go to a vote, either in committee or on the floor. The vast majority are made in authoring a legislative vehicle, formulating amendments, negotiating specific provisions or report language behind the scenes, developing legislative strategy, and in other activities that require substantial time, information, and energy on the part of member and staff. While such efforts by no means guarantee that a particular member will influence the final outcome, they are usually a precondition for such influence (Hall 1989).

A second and related implication of this investigation, then, is that empirical research should expand its view of the legislative purposes of political money and the other group resources that may accompany it (see also Salisbury 1984, esp. 70–72). We focus here on committee participation; but the more general implication is that group expenditures may do much more than buy votes, or they may buy votes under certain conditions and affect other forms of legislative behavior under others. Such a suggestion, of course, usually appears in the various studies that examine the relationship between contributions and floor roll calls, but it needs to be elevated from the status of footnote or parenthetic remark to a central element of future research designs. Even for a small set of issues and a single group, the legislative strategies available are several, sometimes mixed. To speculate beyond the research reported here, for instance, we believe groups allocate their various resources (1) to mobilize strong supporters not only in House committees but also on the Senate floor, in dealings with executive agencies, and in various other decision-making forums relevant to the group's interests; (2) to demobilize strong

opponents; and (3) to effect the support of swing legislators. We require greater knowledge of the frequency and efficacy of such strategies, in any case, before we denigrate the role of moneyed interests in Congress, especially when the overwhelming weight of the evidence provided by Washington journalists and political insiders suggests that they matter a great deal.

Finally, the argument presented here provides a very different slant on the role of interest groups as purveyors of information in the deliberations of representative assemblies. A common defense of group lobbying activity, in fact, is that it provides ideas and information although its effect on member preferences is slight. Members (and their staffs) tend to consume information selectively, relying on sources with whom they already agree and discounting sources with whom they usually disagree (e.g., Milbrath 1963). The view that we have advanced here suggests that while this may in fact describe how such information is used, it does not render it inconsequential. In light of the extraordinary demands on each congressional office, information—gathering it; analyzing it; turning it into speeches, amendments, and bills; using it to develop legislative strategy—can be very costly. Such costs, more than anything, limit the extent to which a nominal member will be a meaningful player in the decision-making process on a particular bill. At the very least, then, money-induced activity will distort the "representativeness of deliberations," a standard that democratic theorists since John Stuart Mill have used to evaluate the legitimacy of legislative assemblies (Chamberlin and Courant 1983). But it may also affect the "representativeness of decisions." By selectively subsidizing the information costs associated with participation, groups affect the *intensity* with which their positions are promoted by their legislative agents. In short, not all preferences weigh equally in legislative deliberations; and the resources of moneyed interests at least partly determine the weights.

The extent to which such efforts are damaging to representative government, as Schattschneider claimed, depends in part on the balance of interests and resources apparent in the relevant set of groups that are organized for political action. On any given issue, the efforts of one interest to mobilize supporters in Congress may be at least partially offset by the efforts of some competing group to mobilize its own supporters; indeed, there is some evidence that such countervailing efforts occurred in the natural gas case. But for those who believe that money is an illegitimate resource in such efforts—that pluralism requires something more than a competition among moneyed interests—the results of this study can only be disturbing.

NOTES

1. Rothenberg (1989) finds that in the allocation of lobbying resources on the MX missile issue Common Cause did concentrate more on likely "fence straddlers." By extension, his analysis provides an excellent guide for modeling the effect of expected voting behavior on contributions. See Smith 1984 for an important formulation of this argument.

2. Kingdon found that there was no conflict in the member's "field of forces" in almost half of the important votes that members cast on the House floor. In an additional 33% of the votes all of the personal goals that were relevant to a vote pointed the member in the same direction (1981, 255). While his study was conducted before the precipitous rise of PAC contributions, Kingdon found little evidence of group influence on members' voting decisions (chap. 5).

3. In adapting our model from Hall 1987, we retained only the variables that were found to be consistently significant and collapsed the several specific leadership positions into a single dichotomous variable.

4. This assumption is especially valid for the dairy and natural gas cases, though somewhat problematic for the JPTA. Like so many of the issues that come before the House Agriculture Committee, the dairy program is a classic constituency issue. If anything, the administration's assault on the price levels intensified such interests in the minds of the legislators. Likewise, the Natural Gas Market Policy Act evoked strong sentiment among consumers, distributors, and pipelines in some states and producers in others, sentiments that were loudly communicated to their representatives in Washington (Murray 1983). The resulting regional split within the committee was noted at length in virtually every account of its deliberations (see e.g., Maraniss 1983; Murray 1983).

5. In attempting to capture the representation of constituency interests, however, we necessarily neglect constituents' preferences regarding the public goods dimensions of each of these bills. On the importance of public goods preferences to political representation, see J. Jackson and King (1989).

6. The principal grass roots campaigns in the natural gas case were conducted by the Citizen/Labor Energy Coalition (CLEC) (which conducted door-to-door efforts in a number of states) and the public utility companies (who used inserts in monthly utility bills to encourage their customers to write letters to their representatives). Both were also actively engaged in lobbying members of the Energy and Commerce Committee. (Indeed, the CLEC was one of the most vigorous in this respect; see Pressman 1983.) Neither of the two were major campaign contributors, however. The CLEC did not have an organized PAC, and of the various segments of the gas industry the utility companies contributed relatively little money. (The major gas producers, for instance, contributed more than the distributors by a factor greater than seven to one.) Similarly, there were dozens of groups active in lobbying on the Job Training Partnership Act that contributed little or nothing in the way of campaign money, including various public interest groups, state and local officials, education organizations, and the National Governors' Association (Baumer and Van Horn 1985). The correlation between contributions

and other interest group activities is probably higher for the dairy stabilization case, but even here it should be fairly modest. The various dairy organizations were in fact active in getting local dairy producers to write letters and meet with their representatives during visits to the district. But such a grass roots strategy was only feasible in districts that had a significant number of dairy producers, and the correlation between district dairy production and dairy industry PAC contributions was only .09 for the period 1979–80. Likewise, while the dairy industry gave a great deal of money to some House Agriculture members and none to others, the National Milk Producers by themselves contacted *every* committee member regarding the dairy stabilization bill, either through letters to the member's Washington office or meetings with the member or the member's staff.

7. On this point, we are especially indebted to conversations with Jack Wright.

8. Data on the first four activities were taken directly from the committee and subcommittee markup minutes and transcripts. Indexes of authorship role and behind-the-scenes participation were coded on four-point scales from semistructured interviews with both minority and majority staffers who had primary responsibility for staffing the bill under study. On the collection and coding of these data, see Hall 1987, though the data-reduction technique used here loses less information than the Guttman scale scores and the informal participation indexes that were used in that analysis. The factor analysis that generated the scores retained only one factor using conventional methods, the weights assigned were similar across the three cases, and (most importantly) the ordinal ranking of the weights for each activity were precisely those hypothesized in Hall 1987. In addition to the results reported here, however, we also estimated the model using both the Guttman scales and the informal participation index as well as a simple summary of the two. These several measures of participation are all highly correlated, and various estimates of the model using them generally confirmed the findings that we report here. Problems of measurement undoubtedly remain, however; and addressing them is an important matter for future work.

9. The measure of district natural gas production was constructed from county-level data acquired directly from state departments of natural resources. Where counties were not wholly contained within a single district, the proportion of natural gas production credited to particular districts was estimated by comparing congressional district maps with the geologic surveys showing the geographic location of natural gas production within counties. The production data are for the year 1983, the year in which the Energy and Commerce Committee began consideration of the Natural Gas Market Policy Act.

10. District-level data on natural gas price changes were not immediately available, but the intrastate variations should be sufficiently small as to make the state-level data reasonable approximations of the inflation in district natural gas prices. However, there are dramatic variations in the use of natural gas from one district to the next, so that the economic effect of a given price increase on residential energy consumers may vary dramatically across districts within a state (e.g., many rural districts that depended primarily on fuel oil for home heating were virtually unaffected by major increases in the price of natural gas). Fortunately, however, district-level information about household fuel use is available. In order to create a district-level indicator of consumer interest, then, we simply multiplied the state-level price increase for 1981–82 times the percentage of households in the district that used natural gas for their home heating. State data on the average price of natural gas delivered to consumers were taken from the *Natural Gas Annual 1982* (vol. 1, Table 17) and the *Natural Gas Annual 1983* (vol. 1, Table 18). District-level data on household energy sources were taken from the U.S. Bureau of the Census 1981.

11. District-level data on CETA expenditures were calculated from *The Employment and Training Reporter* (1980), which lists the 1981 allocations to counties, cities, or other "prime sponsors" located within members' districts. In cases where a prime sponsor was located in more than one congressional district, the expenditure for that sponsor was allocated equally among the several districts in which the sponsor administered its program.

12. It is important to note, however, that we are not assuming that NFU, ADA, or any other voting index measures members' personal

ideology (much less their true preferences); a number of factors combine to determine these voting patterns, ideology being only one. (See Jackson and Kingdon 1990; Carson and Oppenheimer 1984.) Rather, we simply assume that the rating summarizes members' past voting behavior, which in turn form the basis for particular groups' expectations about what positions members will take in the future. Indeed, one of the principal reasons that groups construct their own indexes is to help them distinguish between friend and foe, and raters themselves report that the ratings "have their greatest impact on the distribution of campaign funds, because they provide a simple test of support or opposition" (Fowler 1982). The NFU scores were taken from the National Farmers Union Newsletter (1982a, 1982b).

13. We measured dairy industry contributions for each member as the summary of contributions from the three main dairy PACs during the previous election cycle: Committee for Thorough Agricultural Political Education of Associated Milk Producers; Mid-America Dairymen; and Dairymen Special Political Agricultural Community Education.

14. The Moody's entry included a brief description of each business's activities that usually indicated whether it belonged primarily in one category or another. Where that description mentioned interests in more than one category, we went to the financial statements or audit summaries provided in the Moody's entry and classified businesses as producer, interstate pipeline, intrastate pipeline, or distributor according to the principal sources of their natural gas revenues. Such information permitted an unambiguous classification in almost every case. Natural gas peak associations were categorized according to the nature of the businesses they represented. In addition, some of the classifications were checked against similar classifications made by Eric Uslaner using both interview and archival data. In every case where our data overlapped, our classifications matched his (see Uslaner 1989).

15. Other groups interested in the legislation included the National Governors' Association, national education groups, city and county officials, and the various organizations that represented them, such as the National League of Cities (Baumer and Van Horn, 1985). Of these, however, only the education groups contributed money; and they tended to align with, and contribute to, the same members as organized labor. The education contributions were very small in any case, and the alternative strategy of adding them to the labor PAC total had no effect on the coefficients.

16. Included in this category were the American Business Association, the Business Industry Council, the Chamber of Commerce, the National Association of Manufacturers, and the National Federation of Independent Businesses.

17. We believe that there is far less reason a priori to believe that PAC contributions should be considered endogenous in modeling members' participation than in modeling their roll-call voting behavior. While it is likely that PACs will give disproportionately to members with important committee positions, there is little evidence to suggest that the anticipated participation of member i on some particular bill j (independent of what one would anticipate given the member's institutional position or positions, seniority, and interests—factors that are built into our model) figures prominently in PAC allocation decisions. Such calculations, at least, have been nowhere evident in the considerable political science or journalistic literature on this subject. Hence, we also estimated the equations for both cases using ordinary least squares. The parameter estimates from the ordinary least squares and two-stage least squares (2SLS) were very similar, with the exception that the magnitude of the 2SLS mobilization coefficients were somewhat smaller in the natural gas and job training cases. By presenting the 2SLS results, then, we address the potential endogeneity problem and, as it turns out, slightly bias our results against our main conclusions.

18. While the first-stage results are not relevant to our substantive interests here, they do bear on the confidence of the second-stage results and thus warrant some attention. In estimating the first stage, we adapted the contributions model from the substantial literature on the allocation strategies of

national PACs (e.g., Evans 1986; Grenzke 1989b; Gopoian 1984; Grier and Munger 1989), including three variables that qualified as instruments: party, the relevant voting index, and the marginality of the district. In all three cases the first-stage results were satisfactory. The adjusted R-squared was .34 for the model of dairy industry contributions to Agriculture Committee members, .58 for the model of net producer contributions to Commerce members, and .48 for the model of net labor contributions to Education and Labor members. More importantly, in every case the coefficient on at least one of the three instruments was large, correct in sign, and statistically significant at the .05 level. Checks for multicollinearity among the independent variables in the second stage equations likewise provided little cause for concern. Regarding the appropriateness and implementation of the two-stage least squares estimation procedure, see Hanushek and Jackson 1977, chap. 9; Pindyck and Rubinfeld 1981, 328–31.

19. As a check on the results reported here, we also estimated for the effects of contributions on participation without interacting them with anticipated support or opposition, and, as our theory would predict, the effects, were consistently weaker. Note, secondly, that we do not include the relevant group support score separately in the model, a variable that has proven important in estimating the effects of contributions on roll calls. Even if ideology is what the voting scores capture (see Jackson and Kingdon 1990), there is no theoretical reason to expect that liberals will be more active than conservatives (or vice versa) or for that matter that ideological moderates will be less active than either conservatives or liberals. In any case, we tested for the effect of past voting behavior on the participation of members in each case. For all three, the t-statistics for the voting score coefficients were less than .5.

REFERENCES

Arnold, R. Douglas. 1979. *Congress and the Bureaucracy: A Theory of Influence.* New Haven: Yale University Press.

Bauer, Raymond, Ithiel de Sola Pool, and Lewis A. Dexter. 1963. *American Business and Public Policy.* Chicago: Aldine & Atherton.

Baumer, Donald C., and Carl E. Van Horn. 1985. *The Politics of Unemployment.* Washington: Congressional Quarterly Press.

Berry, Jeffrey M. 1984. *The Interest Group Society.* Boston: Little, Brown.

Bureau of National Affairs, Inc. 1980. "FY 1981 CETA Allocations and Government's Grants." *The Employment and Training Reporter.* Oct. 29.

Carson, Richard A., and Joe Oppenheimer. 1984. "A Method of Estimating the Personal Ideology of Political Representatives." *American Political Science Review* 78:163–78.

Chamberlin, John R., and Paul N. Courant. 1983. "Representative Deliberations and Representative Decisions: Proportional Representation and the Borda Rule." *American Political Science Review* 77:718–33.

Chappell, Henry. 1982. "Campaign Contributions and Congressional Voting: A Simultaneous Probit-Tobit Model." *Review of Economics and Statistics* 62:77–83.

Davis, Joseph A. 1984. "House Energy Committee Approves Natural Gas Bill." *Congressional Quarterly Weekly Report* 14 April:888–89.

Denzau, Arthur, and Michael C. Munger. 1986. "Legislators and Interest Groups: How Unorganized Interests Get Represented." *American Political Science Review* 80:89–106.

Donnelly, Harrison. 1982. "Job Training Bills: No 'CETA' Revisited." *Congressional Quarterly Weekly Report* 8 May:1035.

Drew, Elizabeth. 1982. "Politics and Money." *The New Yorker* 6 December: 54–149.

Etzioni, Amitai. 1984. *Capital Corruption: The New Attack on American Democracy.* New York: Harcourt, Brace, Jovanovich.

Evans, C. Lawrence. N.d. "Participation in U.S. Senate Committees." *Political Science Quarterly.* Forthcoming.

Evans, Diana. 1986. "PAC Contributions and Roll-Call Voting: Conditional

Power." In *Interest Group Politics,* 2d ed., ed. Allan J. Cigler and Burdett A. Loomis. Washington, DC: Congressional Quarterly Press.

Evans, Diana. 1988. "Oil PACs and Aggressive Contribution Strategies." *Journal of Politics* 50:1047–56.

Fenno, Richard F. 1978. *Home Style: House Members in Their Districts.* Boston: Little, Brown.

Fiorina, Morris P. 1974. *Representatives, Roll Calls, and Constituencies.* Lexington, MA: D.C. Heath.

Fowler, Linda L. 1982. "How Interest Groups Select Issues for Rating Voting Records of Members of the U.S. Congress." *Legislative Studies Quarterly* 7:401–13.

Franklin, Grace A., and Randall B. Ripley. 1984. *CETA: Politics and Policy.* Knoxville: University of Tennessee Press.

Gais, Thomas, Mark Peterson, and Jack Walker. 1984. "Interest Groups, Iron Triangles, and Representative Institutions in American National Government." *British Journal of Political Science* 14:161–85.

Gopoian, J. David. 1984. "What Makes PACs Tick? An Analysis of the Allocation Patterns of Economic Interest Groups." *American Journal of Political Science* 28:259–81.

Grenzke, Janet M. 1989a. "Shopping in the Congressional Supermarket: The Currency Is Complex." *American Journal of Political Science* 33:1–24.

Grenzke, Janet M. 1989b. "Candidate Attributes and PAC Contributions." *Western Political Quarterly* 42:245–64.

Grier, Kevin B., and Michael C. Munger. 1986. "The Impact of Legislator Attributes on Interest-Group Campaign Contributions." *Journal of Labor Research* 7:349–61.

Grier, Kevin B., and Michael C. Munger. 1989. "Committee Assignments, Constituent Preferences, and Campaign Contributions to House Incumbents." Typescript.

Hall, Richard L. 1987. "Participation and Purpose in Committee Decision Making." *American Political Science Review* 81:105–27.

Hall, Richard L. 1989. "Committee Decision Making in the Postreform Congress." In *Congress Reconsidered,* 4th ed., ed. Lawrence C. Dodd and Bruce I. Oppenheimer. Washington, DC: Congressional Quarterly Press.

Hall, Richard L., and C. Lawrence Evans. 1990. "The Power of Subcommittees." *Journal of Politics* 52:335–55.

Hanushek, Erik A., and John E. Jackson. 1977. *Statistical Methods for Social Scientists.* Orlando: Academic.

Hayes, Michael T. 1981. *Lobbyists and Legislators.* New Brunswick: Rutgers University Press.

Herndon, James F. 1982. "Access, Record, and Competition as Influences on Interest Group Contributions to Congressional Campaigns." *Journal of Politics* 44:996–1019.

Jackson, Brooks. 1988. *Honest Graft.* New York: Knopf.

Jackson, John E. 1974. *Constituencies and Leaders in Congress: Their Effects on Senate Voting Behavior.* Cambridge: Harvard University Press.

Jackson, John E., and David C. King. 1989. "Public Goods, Private Interests, and Representation." *American Political Science Review* 83:1143–64.

Jackson, John E., and John W. Kingdon. 1990. "Ideology, Interest Group Scores, and Legislative Votes." University of Michigan. Typescript.

Jacobson, Gary C. 1980. *Money in Congressional Elections.* New Haven: Yale University Press.

Kau, James B., and Paul H. Rubin. 1982. *Congressmen, Constituents, and Contributors: Determinants of Roll Call Voting in the House of Representatives.* Boston: Martinus Nijhoff.

Kingdon, John W. 1981. *Congressmen's Voting Decisions,* 2d ed. New York: Harper & Row.

Maitland, Ian. 1985. "Interest Groups and Economic Growth Rates." *Journal of Politics* 47:44–58.

Maraniss, David. 1983. "Power Play: Chairman's Gavel Crushes Gas Decontrol

Vote." *Washington Post* 20 November:A1.

Matthews, Donald R. [1960] 1973. *U.S. Senators and Their World.* Reprint. New York: W. W. Norton.

Mayhew, David R. 1974. *Congress: The Electoral Connection.* New Haven: Yale University Press.

Milbrath, Lester M. 1963. *The Washington Lobbyists.* Chicago: Rand McNally.

Moody's Investor Service. 1983a. *Moody's Industrial Manual.* New York: Moody's Investor Service.

Moody's Investor Service. 1983b. *Moody's Public Utilities Manual.* New York: Moody's Investor Service.

Murray, Alan. 1983. "Pressure from Consumers Pushes Congress into Action on Pricing of Natural Gas." *Congressional Quarterly Weekly Report* 5 March:443–47.

National Farmers Union. 1982a. "1981 Voting Record—House." *National Farmers Union Washington Newsletter* 5 February:4–8.

National Farmers Union. 1982b. "1982 Voting Record—House." *National Farmers Union Washington Newsletter* 15 October:4–8.

Pindyck, Robert S., and Daniel L. Rubinfeld. 1981. *Econometric Models and Economic Forecasts.* 2d ed. New York: McGraw-Hill.

Pressman, Steven. 1983. "Lobbying Free-for-all Opens as Congress Begins Mark-up of National Gas Pricing Bills." *Congressional Quarterly Weekly Report.* April 23:793–97.

Ripley, Randall B., and Grace Franklin. 1980. *Congress, the Bureaucracy, and Public Policy.* Rev. ed. Homewood, IL: Dorsey.

Rothenberg, Lawrence S. 1989. "Do Interest Groups Make a Difference? Lobbying, Constituency Influence, and Public Policy." Presented at the annual meeting of the Midwest Political Science Association, Chicago.

Salisbury, Robert H. 1984. "Interest Representation: The Dominance of Institutions." *American Political Science Review* 78:64–76.

Salisbury, Robert H., and Kenneth A. Shepsle. 1981. "U.S. Congressmen As Enterprise." *Legislative Studies Quarterly* 6:559–76.

Schattschneider, E. E. 1960. *The Semisovereign People.* Hinsdale, IL: Dryden.

Schlozman, Kay L., and John T. Tierney. 1986. *Organized Interests and American Democracy.* New York: Harper & Row.

Shepsle, Kenneth A. 1978. *The Giant Jigsaw Puzzle.* Chicago: University of Chicago.

Silberman, Jonathan, and Garey C. Durden. 1976. "Determining Legislative Preferences on the Minimum Wage: An Economic Approach." *Journal of Political Economy* 84:317–29.

Smith, Richard A. 1984. "Advocacy, Interpretation, and Influence in the U.S. Congress." *American Political Science Review* 78:44–63.

Smith, Steven S., and Christopher J. Deering. 1984. *Committees in Congress.* Washington, DC: Congressional Quarterly Press.

Stern, Phillip M. 1988. *The Best Congress Money Can Buy.* New York: Pantheon.

Uslaner, Eric M. 1989. *Shale Barrel Politics.* Stanford: Stanford University Press.

U.S. Bureau of the Census. 1981. *Fuels and Financial Characteristics of Housing Units: 1980, Congressional Districts in the 98th Congress.* Washington: GPO.

Wayman, Frank W. 1985. "Arms Control and Strategic Arms Voting in the U.S. Senate: Patterns of Change, 1967–1983." *Journal of Conflict Resolution* 29:225–51.

Wayman, Frank W., and Edward Kutler. 1985. "The Changing Politics of Oil and Gas: Ideology, Campaign Contributions, and Interests." Presented at the annual meeting of the American Political Science Association, New Orleans.

Wehr, Elizabeth. 1982a. "Dairy, Grain Proposals Draw Administration Fire." *Congressional Quarterly Weekly Report* 24 July:1751.

Wehr, Elizabeth. 1982b. "New Farm Support Plans, Food Stamp Changes Push Savings Totals Over Top." *Congressional Quarterly Weekly Report* 21 August:2050–51.

Welch, William P. 1982. "Campaign Contributions and Legislative Voting: Milk Money and Dairy Price Supports." *Western Political Quarterly* 35:478–95.

Wilhite, Allen, and John Theilmann. 1987. "Labor PAC Contributions and Labor Legislation: A Simultaneous Logit Approach." *Public Choice* 53:267–76.

Wright, John R. 1985. "PACs, contributions, and Roll Calls: An Organizational Perspective." *American Political Science Review* 79:400–14.

Wright, John R. 1989. "Contributions, Lobbying, and Committee Voting in the U.S. House of Representatives." University of Iowa. Typescript.

PROJECT

Hall and Wayman suggest that the intensity of participation (especially at key stages) can be far more important than identifying participation through roll-call voting. What consequences does this insight hold for American democracy? In other words, how does the level of hyperparticipation by those who are engaged in the political process manifest itself in public policies?

23

Structure and Uncertainty in Private Interest Representation

JOHN P. HEINZ
EDWARD O. LAUMANN
ROBERT L. NELSON
ROBERT H. SALISBURY

One of the most comprehensive studies of interest group behavior, *The Hollow Core,* represents a significant advance in the knowledge of group power. Heinz, Laumann, Nelson, and Salisbury interviewed more than 300 interest groups, 300 government officials, and more than 800 lobbyists to gain a greater understanding of group politics in Washington, D.C. This excerpt from their concluding chapter questions the real influence groups possess. Like many of the other scholars in this text, Heinz, Laumann, Nelson, and Salisbury find pinpointing group power to be a difficult task. They bring a number of the concepts and authors addressed throughout this reader together in their analysis. In the end, the power of interest groups is hard to assess—yet we know that some groups wield power, other groups seek power, and some groups have little power.

QUESTIONS TO CONSIDER

1. What "classic" readings in this text are relevant to Heinz, Laumann, Nelson, and Salisbury's analysis of group power?

2. What do these authors say about group power?

3. How do they attempt to determine group power?

4. How has modern electoral politics changed group power?

5. In what ways do different policy domains affect group power?

6. Why are short-term gains frowned upon by interest groups?

IS INFLUENCE AN INDIVIDUAL ATTRIBUTE?

What, then, can we conclude about the nature of influence wielded by individual representatives? Is it possible to analyze influence as an individual trait? That is, can the capacity of lobbyists to shape policy be explained by their particular characteristics? . . . We [are] largely unable to explain self-reported success on policy events. But influence of a more general sort, which is not well expressed by success reports, may nonetheless exist in policy-making systems.

Students of community power (see, for example, Hunter 1953; Dahl 1961; Polsby 1980) have sharply disagreed about the methods appropriate to their task. Some have insisted that power can only be examined in its exercise, and have chosen to study discrete decision processes to determine who influenced whom. Others have relied on reputational measures of influence; the more votes an individual receives from the group polled, the greater his or her influence is assumed to be. Our data permit us to follow the latter strategy. Each of the respondents was asked to name three representatives who were regarded as "most effective" in shaping national policy in the relevant domain. In addition to these effectiveness votes, we can use the number of votes each representative received as a named ally or adversary. . . . We include the latter because these mentions also

reflect the prominence of the representatives. Nomination as an adversary might be thought to be negatively associated with the other two measures, but this was not the case. All three measures were strongly positively correlated. (Effectiveness correlates with allies, $r = .65$, and with adversaries, $r = .67$. The correlation between ally votes and adversary votes is .37.) Given the statistical advantages of having more votes to analyze, we pooled the three questions and examined the total number of mentions of each representative.

Many of the representatives who were mentioned are, of course, not present in our sample, but a significant portion of our sample received at least one vote. Some 263 respondents in the random and nonrandom samples, or one-third of the total representatives, received votes. Not surprisingly, the selected sample of notables garnered many more votes than did other respondents. Of the notables, 89% were mentioned, as compared to 28% of the remaining respondents. Almost two-thirds of the notables attracted 5 or more votes, but only 6% of the non-notables achieved a similar level of notice.[1]

We computed regression analyses seeking to account for the number of mentions by using independent variables concerning the work of representatives (percent of time spent contacting Congress, percent of time spent contacting executive agencies, percent of time spent in the domain), career attributes (years in government, law degree), characteristics of the employing organization (organization type, number of professionals in the organization), and

SOURCE: From John P. Heinz, Edward O. Laumann, Robert L. Nelson, and Robert H. Salisbury, "Structure and Uncertainty in Private Interest Representation," in *The Hollow Core: Private Interests in National Policy Making* (Cambridge, MA: Harvard University Press, 1993), 405–413. Copyright 1993 by the President and Fellows of Harvard College.

political activities and party affiliation (whether they were an active Democrat or an active Republican, whether they had helped distribute PAC money, whether they had engaged in political fund-raising in the past two years, and their score on the economic liberalism scale). We also included two other variables that arguably are alternative measures of influence rather than independent determinants of it: the number of notables known and the average level of self-reported success on events.

The regression model in which the four domains were combined explained 20% of the variance in the number of mentions. Only three variables had statistically significant effects (at the .10 level): self-reported success on events and the number of notables known had positive effects net of other variables, and being an active Democrat had a significant negative effect. The number of notables known had the greatest effect by far; the standardized coefficient for this variable was .34 versus coefficients of .10 and −.08 for the success and Democrat variables, respectively.

The explanatory power of the regression models and of the specific measures differs across domains. The same model explains 21% of the variance in agriculture, 31% in energy, 22% in health, and 34% in labor. Only one variable, number of notables known, has significant effects in all four domains. Self-reported success is significant ($p = .10$) only in the labor domain, although it comes close to achieving conventional significance levels in agriculture ($p = .13$) and energy ($p = .18$). Being an active Democrat has a significant negative effect only in energy, although it approaches significance in health ($p = .12$). Active Republicans receive significantly more mentions in the labor domain, but nowhere else. Economic liberalism is positively related to the number of mentions in agriculture and health, but negatively related in labor. Possessing a law degree significantly increases mentions in the energy domain, as does political fund-raising. These effects do not hold elsewhere. The percent of time spent contacting executive agencies is positively related to mentions in the energy and labor domains, but not in agriculture or health.

These findings suggest that a general reputation for influence, like success on particular events, is not well explained by individual characteristics of the broad sort measured here. Organization type, career variables, work characteristics, political ideology, and political activities do not provide consistent returns in notice or recognition. The two variables that had the strongest relationship with the number of mentions could themselves be construed as measures of influence. A track record of success on policy events in the four years preceding the interview might well have increased reputation, but we have no way of knowing whether the reputation preceded the success. It also is not possible to say whether connections to notables led to a reputation for effectiveness or vice versa.

If we could effectively explain event success, we might be better able to understand the bases for reputed influence in Washington. . . . We did even worse in accounting for the variance in success. Nor does our measure of reputed influence do much to improve the prediction of event success. Although the number of mentions has a statistically significant effect on average success, adding this variable to the regression models does not significantly increase the variance explained.

Researchers should be wary of celebrating null findings. The absence of striking effects may result from the failure to develop adequate measures. But we think that the absence of strong effects here is not a methodological failing so much as a reflection of the uncertain and situational nature of influence in national policy-making systems. We were able to select a list of notable representatives in each domain, and the notability of these people has been validated through both quantitative and qualitative means. But the standing of these individuals is apparently based on the unique characteristics of their careers in government and in interest representation. Even the elaborate data that we gathered about the characteristics of the representatives and their work do not explain much of the variance in reputed influence.

These findings suggest—in quantitative, systematic terms—much the same lesson that we saw in the story of the lawyer and the heavyweight, with which we began this book. It is possible to talk about "Washington heavyweights." One can construct a list of notable representatives who will be recognized as prominent players in the policy process. But the characteristics of these elites, and the occasions on which their influence is effective, vary by domain, by issue, and by historical period. The search for influential individuals will no doubt continue. It is fed by journalistic interest, and there is a market for reputed influence. Clients who are well heeled, if somewhat uninformed, will no doubt continue to seek out expensive talent in the hope of achieving a policy-making coup. But we doubt that the search for individual influence is likely to produce many theoretical insights into the nature of the national policy-making process.

IMPLICATIONS

Several theoretical issues . . . shaped the design of this research, but much of the ambition of the project has been avowedly empirical. Despite all that had been written about the nature of private influence in Washington, about the roles of lawyers and lobbyists in shaping national policy, and about the inner circles of American political elites, many prominent features of the interest representation system had not been subjected to systematic observation. While we had considerable experience with the methods employed, we could not accurately forecast our findings about the

nature of national policy systems in these particular contexts. . . . Thus, our project has been a kind of probe into the inner space of the American policy system. Many of the findings we have brought back are not radically divergent from those of preceding studies; others challenge important elements of previous conceptions of interest representation.

It is conventional to conclude enterprises of this sort with some assessment of the significance of the findings, and we are nothing if not conventional. We close, therefore, by considering whether these policy systems allow democratic participation and whether they have the capacity for rational planning.

Democracy

We can say little about two critical questions: What segments of the polity go unrepresented? And what is the universe of questions that is open for discussion and debate? Our sample can be taken, we think, as a reasonable approximation of the variety of interest groups that are active in the four domains. The composition of the represented interests varies by domain, but organized groups predominate. Many of these are traditional power holders: major corporations, trade and producer associations, professional associations, and unions. Also present, although in smaller numbers, are representatives of more recently and less fully organized groups: civil rights advocates, environmentalists, consumers, and special claimant populations such as veterans, the aged, and victims of various diseases. We have no way to catalogue the segments of society that lack a voice in discussions of policies affecting them or that are unable even to initiate discussion of their concerns. Thus, despite the great range and diversity in the political orientations of the interest groups in these domains, we cannot conclude that national policy systems have overcome the problems of exclusiveness and limited participation noted by so many scholars. Indeed, our individual-level data contain some evidence of exclusion. Women and minorities constitute only a small proportion of representatives. We have no measure of their availability among the pool of qualified individuals, and we are not sure that such a measure would be an appropriate yardstick in any event, but it is obvious that, despite the increased participation by women and minorities in politics and in the work force, most of the voices speaking on national policy are those of white men.

Nor can we offer original insights regarding the range of alternatives that are considered. Most of the policy proposals we analyzed dealt with incremental changes in current policies. This is consistent with the argument of many theorists that fundamental, systemic alternatives do not appear on the agenda, and that the most pervasive form of power in decision-making systems is largely invisible—the power not only to determine what issues enter the realm of discussion, but to define the features of society that will be recognized as issues (Lukes 1974; Bachrach and Baratz 1962; Alford and Friedland 1985). We acknowledge these critiques and recognize that broader comparisons of political systems across historical periods and societal contexts might reveal deeper conflicts (Higley and Burton 1989; Tilly 1984).

Yet it would be odd to dismiss the contests we have studied as trivial tinkering within otherwise well-settled policy-making systems. Certainly, the client organizations considered the issues important enough to require the expenditure of very substantial resources, and the representatives themselves were convinced that they were involved in substantively significant debates that were often highly conflictual. The careers of representatives, the social and political values they embrace, the networks in which they move, and the alliances and antagonisms they form make it clear that the system of interest representation reflects fundamental social and political divisions in our society. Debates about

the level of government price supports for agricultural commodities, about the extent to which national energy policy should be centrally planned or left to market mechanisms, about the financing and distribution of medical care for the poor and the aged, and about the legal empowerment of management and labor in collective bargaining disputes are, we would assert, matters of considerable systemic importance.

The policy domains vary in the degree to which they are divided by basic political ideologies. Labor policy, because it consistently pits unions against management, is the most ideologically conflictual domain. Agriculture, which retains the residual effects of compromises worked out by the farm bloc, is the least divided ideologically. We are not specialists in the substantive policy debates that take place in these domains and cannot address the political subtleties of how policy options are defined and debated, and how alternative perspectives are suppressed or advanced. Policy representation in these domains may not be completely inclusive, but the domains are not assembly lines of ideological uniformity.

Given the considerable diversity of participants in Washington policy making, how are the diverse interests brought together to produce policy? Some accounts argue that closed circles of elites perform this function. Critical scholars characterize these elites as coordinating the interests of the capitalist class; functionalist scholars view elite governance as an inherent, necessary tendency of group political life. Our data do not support either version. No cohesive private elite consistently occupies a central, mediating position in the networks among representatives. Some elites may be in the center on some issues, at some times, but this is not a stable equilibrium. Nor do any government institutions, such as the White House, the leading cabinet departments, or the congressional leadership, consistently occupy the center of the contact structure between representatives and government agencies. The visual metaphor we have offered to describe the structure of policy-making networks is the hollow core. In this conception, elite representatives are instructed by the clients that retain them. The composition of dominant coalitions changes from issue to issue, and coalitions thus form and re-form at various points around the circle of interests.

Some may be inclined to celebrate these findings as additional evidence that democracy is alive and well. But the absence of an inner circle of powerful elites is no guarantee that the constantly emerging and shifting coalitions produce desirable outcomes. According to some versions of democratic theory, a correct outcome is one that does not distort the aggregation of individual preferences (Olson 1982). Yet, as Kenneth Arrow has demonstrated, even straightforward systems of rule by majority vote often result in such distortions (Arrow 1951). Even if we ignore the problem of unequal participation, in the absence of data that somehow measure the true preferences of participants it is impossible to establish empirically that policy systems with hollow cores produce outcomes that are better likenesses than those produced by other structures.

Coherence

Many scholars have expressed concern about the capacity of our national government to develop and pursue long-range strategies (for example, Lowi 1969; Olson 1982). Some of our findings may reinforce these concerns; policy domains that are segmented by interest group sectors and that lack mediating elites may not have sufficient stability to permit planning and coordination. As we noted above, however, the system of interest representation may give government agencies a substantial degree of autonomy in policy making. If the government is relatively autonomous, it may have sufficient flexibility to be able

to produce coherent government policies. But changes in the procedures for nominating candidates for the presidency may have resulted in the executive branch becoming more ideologically extreme (Shafer 1988), and presidential appointees may therefore be more likely to pursue agendas that diverge significantly from those of preceding administrations.

While presidents can push their proposals onto the agenda, however, they often cannot control the final form that legislation will take, nor can they insure its adoption. The policy proposals that we analyzed were of three predominant types. Some were crises that demanded government reaction. This reactive component of the policy agenda enjoyed the highest level of legislative success. Incremental policy proposals that maintained existing programs also enjoyed high levels of adoption. Presidential initiatives were least likely to succeed and most conflictual.

Given the structure of policy making, both private and public organizations have little incentive to look beyond short-term interests. Private groups must constantly be aware of the uncertainty of the policy-making process. Their resources are expended in monitoring policy developments, reacting to events in the political and economic environment that are largely beyond their control, and responding to the political initiatives of Congress or the administration. Contrary to the image of the lobbyist as strategic planner, most of what interest representatives do is reactive. Government officials, both elected and appointed, also focus primarily on immediate political gains, such as the consolidation of an electoral base or the accommodation of political constituencies. Because national policy-making systems process an immense volume of proposals, contested by a large and diverse universe of interest groups that present and manipulate a daunting array of information about the options, it is not surprising that the actors have time for little more than the most immediate and urgent decisions.

One of the dangers of the hollow core, therefore, may be that the pursuit of immediate interests by individual representatives and officials will produce policies that go around in circles. Though the velocity and volume of policy-making activity may be great, the ultimate product may be a return to the place at which one started. Thus, the policy system may move very little despite escalating effort. The issues remain in much the same form over long periods of time. New proposals look much like the old. The participating groups and their representatives are, or soon become, old hands. Though changes do occur, innovation is generally meager and exceedingly gradual. It may seem a paradox, but the principal result of the vast amount of interest group activity may be stability in the systems of policy formation.

NOTES

1. Unfortunately for purposes of this analysis, the notables list was presented to respondents prior to the questions about the most effective representatives and about their allies and adversaries. The sequence of questions may thus have inflated the number of votes received by notables.

REFERENCES

Alford, Robert R., and Roger Friedland. 1985. *Powers of Theory: Capitalism, the State, and Democracy.* New York: Cambridge University Press.

Arrow, Kenneth 1951. "Alternative Theories of Decision-Making in Risk-Taking Situations," *Econometrica* 19: 404–437.

Bachrach, Peter, and M. S. Baratz. 1962. "The Two Faces of Power." *American Political Science Review* 56: 947–952.

Dahl, Robert A. 1961. Who *Governs? Democracy and Power in an American City.* New Haven: Yale University Press.

Higley, John, and Michael G. Burton. 1989. "The Elite Variable in Democratic Transitions and Breakdowns." *American Sociological Review* 54: 17–32.

Hunter, Floyd. 1953. *Community Power Structure.* Chapel Hill: University of North Carolina Press.

Laumann, Edward O., John P. Heinz, with Robert L. Nelson, and Robert H. Salisbury. 1985. "Washington Lawyers: The Structure of Washington Representation." *Stanford Law Review* 37: 465.

Lowi, Theodore. 1969. *The End of Liberalism.* New York: Norton.

Lukes, Steven. 1974. *Power.* New York: New York University Press.

Olson, Mancur. 1982. *The Rise and Decline of Nations.* New Haven, Conn.: Yale University Press.

Polsby, Nelson W. 1980. *Community Power and Political Theory: A Further Look at Problems of Evidence and Inference.* New Haven: Yale University Press.

Shafer, Byron. 1988. *Bifurcated Politics.* Cambridge: Harvard University Press.

Tilly, Charles. 1984. *Big Structures, Large Processes, Huge Comparisons.* New York: Russell Sage Foundation.

PROJECT

The authors of *The Hollow Core* discuss using a reputational measure of influence, which may be a means to track real influence. To find out which groups policy makers believe hold the most control, develop a survey to assess group power. Your survey should list a number of different interest groups that you believe to be powerful. Call, e-mail, or mail members of your city council, your state legislature, or the U.S. Congress and ask them to respond to your survey and rank which groups they believe to be most powerful.

Index

Page numbers in *italic* refer to tables and figures.